The Penguin Pocket Book of

FACTS

Edited by David Crystal

PENGUIN BOOKS

PENGUIN BOOKS

Published by the Penguin Group
Penguin Books Ltd, 80 Strand, London WC2R 0RL, England
Penguin Group (USA) Inc., 375 Hudson Street, New York, New York 10014, USA
Penguin Group (Canada), 90 Eglinton Avenue East, Suite 700, Toronto,
Ontario, Canada M4P 2Y3 (a division of Pearson Penguin Canada Inc.)
Penguin Ireland, 25 St Stephen's Green, Dublin 2, Ireland (a division of Penguin Books Ltd)
Penguin Group (Australia), 250 Camberwell Road,
Camberwell, Victoria 3124, Australia (a division of Pearson Australia Group Pty Ltd)
Penguin Books India Pvt Ltd, 11 Community Centre, Panchsheel Park, New Delhi – 110 017, India
Penguin Group (NZ), cnr Airborne and Rosedale Roads, Albany,
Auckland 1310, New Zealand (a division of Pearson New Zealand Ltd)
Penguin Books (South Africa) (Pty) Ltd, 24 Sturdee Avenue, Rosebank 2196, South Africa

Penguin Books Ltd, Registered Offices: 80 Strand, London WC2R 0RL, England

www.penguin.com

The New Penguin Factfinder first published 2003
Revised edition published as The Penguin Factfinder 2005
This concise edition published as The Penguin Pocket Book of Facts 2005
1

Copyright © Crystal Reference Systems Ltd, 2003, 2005
All rights reserved

The moral right of the author has been asserted

Set in 8/8.5pt Swift in QuarkXPress™
Typeset by Crystal Reference Systems Ltd, Holyhead
Printed in England by Clays Ltd, St Ives plc

Acknowledgements

Crystal Reference Systems Ltd

Editor
David Crystal

Associate Editor
Ann Rowlands

Assistant Editor
Hilary Crystal

Taxonomy Editor
Jan Thomas

Database Management
Tony McNicholl
Philip Johnstone
Dan Wade

Database Assistance
Peter Preston
Todd Warden-Owen

Administration
Ian Saunders
Rob Phillips
Dave Morris

Typesetting
Crystal Reference Systems Ltd, Holyhead

Penguin Books

Publisher
Nigel Wilcockson

Editorial Assistance
Ellie Smith

Production
Andrew Henty

TABLE OF CONTENTS

PART ONE

The Universe

THE COSMOS

Star distances

Star	Distance (l y)[a]
Proxima Centauri	4.24
Alpha Centauri A	4.34
Alpha Centauri B	4.34
Barnard's Star	5.97
Wolf 359 (CN Leonis)	7.80
Lalande 21185	8.19
UV Ceti A	8.55
UV Ceti B	8.55
Sirius A	8.67
Sirius B	8.67
Ross 154	9.52
Ross 248 (HH Andromedae)	10.37
Epsilon Eridani	10.63
Ross 128 (Fl Virginis)	10.79
L 789–6	11.12
GX Andromedae	11.22
GQ Andromedae	11.22
61 Cygnus A	11.22
61 Cygnus B	11.22
HD 173739	11.25
Epsilon Indi	11.25
Tau Ceti	11.41

[a] l y = light years.

Star magnitudes

Star	Common name	Magnitude	Distance (l y)[a]
Alpha Canis Majoris	Sirius	−1.47	8.7
Alpha Carinae	Canopus	−0.72	98
Alpha Centauri	Rigil Kentaurus	−0.29	4.3
Alpha Boötis	Arcturus	−0.04	36
Alpha Lyrae	Vega	0.03	26
Alpha Aurigae	Capella	0.08	45
Beta Orionis	Rigel	0.12	815
Alpha Canis Minoris	Procyon	0.34	11
Alpha Orionis	Betelgeuse	0.50 (v)	520
Alpha Eridani	Achernar	0.50	118
Beta Centauri	Hadar	0.60 (v)	490
Alpha Crucis	Acrux	0.76	370
Alpha Aquilae	Altair	0.77	16
Alpha Tauri	Aldebaran	0.85 (v)	68
Alpha Scorpii	Antares	0.96	520
Alpha Virginis	Spica	0.98	220
Beta Geminorum	Pollux	1.15	35
Alpha Piscis Austrini	Fomalhaut	1.16	23
Beta Crucis	Mimosa	1.20 (v)	490
Alpha Cygni	Deneb	1.25	1600
Alpha Leonis	Regulus	1.35	85

[a] l y = light years.
(v) = variable.

The constellations

Latin name	Astronomical name
Andromeda	Andromeda
Antlia	Air Pump
Apus	Bird of Paradise
Aquarius (Z)	Water Bearer
Aquila	Eagle
Ara	Altar
Aries (Z)	Ram
Auriga	Charioteer
Boötes	Herdsman
Caelum	Chisel
Camelopardalis	Giraffe
Cancer (Z)	Crab
Canes Venatici	Hunting Dogs
Canis Major	Great Dog
Canis Minor	Little Dog
Capricornus (Z)	Sea Goat
Carina	Keel
Cassiopeia	Cassiopeia
Centaurus	Centaur
Cepheus	Cepheus
Cetus	Whale
Chamaeleon	Chameleon
Circinus	Compasses
Columba	Dove
Coma Berenices	Berenice's Hair
Corona Australis	Southern Crown
Corona Borealis	Northern Crown
Corvus	Crow
Crater	Cup
Crux	Southern Cross

Latin name	Astronomical name
Cygnus	Swan
Delphinus	Dolphin
Dorado	Goldfish/Swordfish
Draco	Dragon
Equuleus	Little Horse
Eridanus	River Eridanus
Fornax	Furnace
Gemini (Z)	Twins
Grus	Crane
Hercules	Hercules
Horologium	Clock
Hydra	Sea Serpent
Hydrus	Water Snake
Indus	Indian
Lacerta	Lizard
Leo (Z)	Lion
Leo Minor	Little Lion
Lepus	Hare
Libra (Z)	Scales
Lupus	Wolf
Lynx	Lynx
Lyra	Harp
Mensa	Table
Microscopium	Microscope
Monoceros	Unicorn
Musca	Fly
Norma	Level
Octans	Octant
Ophiuchus	Serpent Bearer
Orion	Orion

Latin name	Astronomical name
Pavo	Peacock
Pegasus	Winged Horse
Perseus	Perseus
Phoenix	Phoenix
Pictor	Easel
Pisces (Z)	Fishes
Piscis Austrinus	Southern Fish
Puppis	Ship's Stern
Pyxis	Mariner's Compass
Reticulum	Net
Sagitta	Arrow
Sagittarius (Z)	Archer
Scorpius (Z)	Scorpion
Sculptor	Sculptor
Scutum	Shield
Serpens	Serpent
Sextans	Sextant
Taurus (Z)	Bull
Telescopium	Telescope
Triangulum	Triangle
Triangulum Australe	Southern Triangle
Tucana	Toucan
Ursa Major	Great Bear
Ursa Minor	Little Bear
Vela	Sails
Virgo (Z)	Virgin
Volans	Flying Fish
Vulpecula	Little Fox

Z = zodiac constellation.

The northern sky

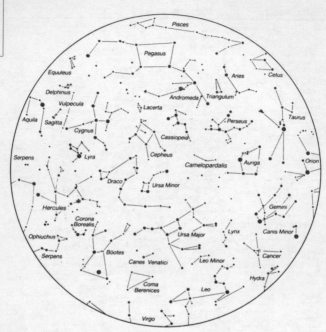

'Alpha' stars within constellations[a]

Name	Constellation	Name	Constellation	Name	Constellation
Achernar	Eridanus	Alnair	Grus	Atria	Triangulum Australe
Acrux	Crux	Alphard	Hydra	Betelgeuse	Orion
Acubens	Cancer	Alphekka	Corona Borealis	Canopus	Carina
Al Giedi	Capricornus	Alpheratz	Andromeda	Capella	Auriga
Al Rijil	Centaurus	Altair	Aquila	Castor	Gemini
Aldebaran	Taurus	Ankaa	Phoenix	Choo	Ara
Alderamin	Cepheus	Antares	Scorpius	Cor Caroli	Canes Venatici
Alkes	Crater	Arcturus	Boötes	Deneb	Cygnus
Alkhiba	Corvus	Arneb	Lepus	Diadem	Coma Berenices

[a]'Alpha' denotes the brightest star in a constellation.

The southern sky

Name	Constellation	Name	Constellation	Name	Constellation
Dubhe	Ursa Major	Phakt	Columba	Sadalmelik	Aquarius
Fomalhaut	Piscis Austrinus	Polaris	Ursa Minor	Shedir	Cassiopeia
Hamal	Aries	Praecipua	Leo Minor	Sirius	Canis Major
Kaïtain	Pisces	Procyon	Canis Minor	Spica	Virgo
Kitalpha	Equuleus	Rasalgethi	Hercules	Svalocin	Delphinus
Markab	Pegasus	Rasalhague	Ophiuchus	Thuban	Draco
Men	Lupus	Rasalmothallah	Triangulum	Unukalhai	Serpens
Menkar	Cetus	Regulus	Leo	Vega	Lyra
Mirphak	Perseus	Rukbat	Sagittarius	Zubenelgenubi	Libra

Meteor showers

Name	Dates of maximum	Hourly rate
Quadrantids	3–4 Jan	100
Lyrids	21–2 Apr	10
Eta Aquarids	5–6 May	35
Delta Aquarids	28–9 Jul	20
Perseids	12–13 Aug	75
Orionids	22 Oct	25
Taurids	4 Nov	10
Leonids	17–18 Nov	10
Geminids	13–14 Dec	75

Historic comets

Name	First seen	Period of orbit (years)	Date of last perihelion[a] passage
Arend-Roland	1957	not known	8 Apr 57
Mrkos	1957	not known	1 Aug 57
Humason	1962	3 000	14 May 62
Ikeya	1963	not known	21 Mar 63
Ikeya-Seki	1965	879.88	21 Oct 65
Tago-Sato-Kosaka	1969	420 000	21 Dec 69
Bennett	1970	1680	20 Mar 70
Kohoutek	1973	75 000	28 Dec 73
Kobayashi-Berger-Milon	1975	not known	5 Sep 75
West	1976	500 000	25 Feb 76
Halley	240 BC	76.1	9 Feb 86
Hale-Bopp	1995	6 580	1 Apr 97

[a] 'Perihelion' refers to the position of the closest approach to the Sun of an object in an elliptical orbit.

THE SOLAR SYSTEM

The Sun

Age 4 500 000 000 years
Diameter 1 392 000 km/864 950 mi
Mass 2×10^{30} kg
Mean density 1.4 g/cm^3
Luminosity 3.9×10^{27} kW
Effective surface temperature 5 770 K/ 5 496.8 °C
Average orbital velocity 107 210 kph/ 66 620 mph

Solar eclipses 2000–2015

Date	Extent of eclipse	Visible from parts of[a]
25 Dec 2000	Partial	N America, Caribbean
21 Jun 2001	Total	S America, S Atlantic, Africa
14 Dec 2001	Annular[b]	Hawaii, SW Canada, W & C America, Caribbean
4 Dec 2002	Total	S Africa, Australia
23 Nov 2003	Annular	Antarctica
8 Apr 2005	Annular/Total	S & C Pacific, C America
29 Mar 2006	Total	C Atlantic, W & N Africa, C Asia
1 Aug 2008	Total	Greenland, N & C Asia
22 Jul 2009	Total	S Asia, C Pacific
11 Jul 2010	Total	S Pacific
13 Nov 2013	Annular/Total	N Australia, S Pacific
20 Mar 2015	Total	N Atlantic, Arctic

[a] The eclipse begins in the first area named. [b] In an annular eclipse a ring-shaped part of the Sun remains visible.

Planetary data (1)

Planet	Distance from Sun				Sidereal period[a]	Axial rotation (equatorial)	Diameter (equatorial)	
	maximum		minimum					
	(million km)	(million mi)	(million km)	(million mi)			(km)	(mi)
Mercury	69.4	43.0	46.8	29.0	88 d	58 d 16 h	4878	3032
Venus	109.0	67.6	107.6	66.7	224.7 d	243 d	12104	7520
Earth	152.6	94.5	147.4	91.4	365.26 d[b]	23 h 56 m 4 s	12756	7926
Mars	249.2	154.5	207.3	128.5	687 d	24 h 37 m 22 s	6794	4222
Jupiter	817.4	506.8	741.6	459.8	11.86 y	9 h 55 m 41 s	142984	88846
Saturn	1512	937.6	1346	834.6	29.46 y	10 h 14 m	120536	74898
Uranus	3011	1867	2740	1699	84.01 y	17.2 h[c]	51118	31764
Neptune	4543	2817	4466	2769	164.79 y	16.11 h[c]	49532	30778
Pluto	7346	4566	4461	2766	247.7 y	6.387 d	2274	1412

[a] 'Sidereal period' refers here to the period of revolution around the Sun with respect to the stars.
[b] Precisely 365 d 5 h 48 m 46 s.
[c] Different latitudes rotate at different speeds.
y: years d: days h: hours m: minutes s: seconds
km: kilometres mi: miles.

Planetary data (2)

Mercury
Atmosphere hydrogen, helium, neon; *satellites* 0; *features* lunar-like crust, crustal faulting, small magnetic field.

Venus
Atmosphere carbon dioxide; *satellites* 0; *features* shrouded in clouds, 70% rolling plains, 10% highlands, 20% lowlands, craters.

Earth
Atmosphere nitrogen, oxygen; *satellites* 1; *features* liquid water oceans filling lowland regions between continents, permanent ice caps at each pole, unique in supporting life, magnetic field.

Mars
Atmosphere carbon dioxide; *satellites* 2; *features* cratered uplands, lowland plains, massive volcanic regions.

Jupiter
Atmosphere hydrogen, methane; *satellites* 63; *features* covered by clouds, craters, volcanic features, dark ring of dust, magnetic field.

Saturn
Atmosphere hydrogen, helium; *satellites* 33 (the exact number is not yet determined); *features* several cloud layers, magnetic field, thousands of rings.

Uranus
Atmosphere methane, helium, hydrogen; *satellites* 27; *features* clouds, layers of mist, magnetic field, c. 11 rings.

Neptune
Atmosphere methane, hydrogen; *satellites* 13; *features* unable to detect these telescopically from Earth.

Pluto
Atmosphere methane; *satellites* 1; *features* unable to detect these telescopically from Earth, thought to be partially covered with frozen methane.

The 'asteroid belt' is found mainly in a large series of orbits lying between Mars and Jupiter.

Main planetary satellites

	Year discovered	Distance from planet		Diameter	
		(km)	(mi)	(km)	(mi)
Earth					
Moon	–	384 000	238 000	3476	2155
Mars					
Phobos	1877	937 800	582 700	27	17
Deimos	1877	2 346 000	1458 000	15	9
Jupiter					
Metis	1979	128 000	79 000	40	25
Adrastea	1979	129 000	80 000	24	15
Amalthea	1892	181 000	112 000	270	168
Thebe	1979	222 000	138 000	100	60
Io	1610	422 000	262 000	3650	2260
Europa	1610	671 000	417 000	3140	1950
Ganymede	1610	1 070 000	665 000	5260	3270
Callisto	1610	1 883 000	1 170 000	4800	3000
Leda	1974	11 100 000	6 900 000	20	12
Himalia	1904	11 480 000	7 134 000	186	116
Lysithea	1938	11 720 000	7 283 000	36	22
Elara	1905	11 740 000	7 295 000	80	50
Ananke	1951	21 200 000	13 174 000	30	19
Carme	1938	22 600 000	14 044 000	40	25
Pasiphae	1908	23 500 000	14 603 000	50	30
Sinope	1914	23 700 000	14 727 000	36	22
Saturn					
Pan	1990	134 000	83 000	10	6
Atlas	1980	138 000	86 000	40	25
Prometheus	1980	139 000	86 000	100	60
Pandora	1980	142 000	88 000	100	60
Epimetheus	1980	151 000	94 000	140	90
Janus	1966	151 000	94 000	200	120
Mimas	1789	186 000	116 000	390	240
Enceladus	1789	238 000	148 000	500	310
Calypso	1980	295 000	183 000	30	19
Telesto	1980	295 000	183 000	30	19
Tethys	1684	295 000	183 000	1060	660
Dione	1684	377 000	234 000	1120	700
Helene	1980	377 000	234 000	15	9
Rhea	1672	527 000	327 000	1530	950
Titan	1655	1 222 000	759 000	5150	3200
Hyperion	1848	1 481 000	920 000	480	300
Iapetus	1671	3 560 000	2 212 000	1460	910
Phoebe	1898	12 950 000	8 047 000	220	137
Uranus					
Miranda	1948	130 000	81 000	480	300
Ariel	1851	191 000	119 000	1160	720
Umbriel	1851	266 000	165 000	1170	730
Titania	1787	436 000	271 000	1580	980
Oberon	1787	583 000	362 000	1524	947
Neptune					
Triton	1846	355 000	221 000	2705	1681
Nereid	1949	5 510 000	3 424 000	340	210
Pluto					
Charon	1978	19 600	12 200	1200	745

The near side of the Moon

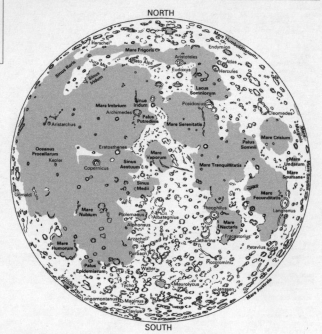

NORTH

SOUTH

The lunar 'maria'[a]

Latin name	English name	Latin name	English name
Lacus Somniorum	Lake of Dreams	Mare Serenitatis	Sea of Serenity
Mare Australe	Southern Sea	Mare Smythii	Smyth's Sea
Mare Crisium	Sea of Crises	Mare Spumans	Foaming Sea
Mare Fecunditatis	Sea of Fertility	Mare Tranquillitatis	Sea of Tranquillity
Mare Frigoris	Sea of Cold	Mare Undarum	Sea of Waves
Mare Humboldtianum	Humboldt's Sea	Mare Vaporum	Sea of Vapours
Mare Humorum	Sea of Humours	Oceanus Procellarum	Ocean of Storms
Mare Imbrium	Sea of Showers	Palus Epidemiarum	Marsh of Epidemics
Mare Ingenii	Sea of Geniuses	Palus Putredinis	Marsh of Decay
Mare Marginis	Marginal Sea	Palus Somnii	Marsh of Sleep
Mare Moscoviense	Moscow Sea	Sinus Aestuum	Bay of Heats
Mare Nectaris	Sea of Nectar	Sinus Iridum	Bay of Rainbows
Mare Nubium	Sea of Clouds	Sinus Medii	Central Bay
Mare Orientale	Eastern Sea	Sinus Roris	Bay of Dew

[a]'Maria' refers to the lowland areas of the moon flooded by lava 3.5 thousand million years ago.

The far side of the Moon

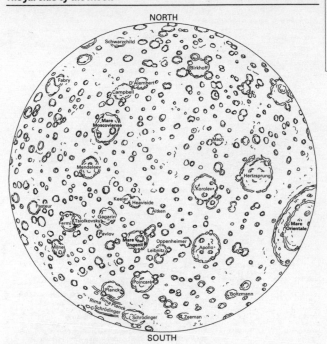

NORTH

SOUTH

Lunar eclipses 2000–2010

Date	Extent of eclipse	Time of mid-eclipse (universal)	Date	Extent of eclipse	Time of mid-eclipse (universal)
21 Jan 2000	Total	04.45	17 Oct 2005	Partial[u]	12.03
16 Jul 2000	Total	13.57	14 Mar 2006	Partial	23.47
9 Jan 2001	Total	20.22	7 Sep 2006	Partial[u]	18.51
5 Jul 2001	Partial[u]	14.55	3 Mar 2007	Total	23.21
30 Dec 2001	Partial	10.29	28 Aug 2007	Total	10.37
26 May 2002	Partial	12.03	21 Feb 2008	Total	03.26
24 Jun 2002	Partial	21.27	16 Aug 2008	Partial[u]	21.10
20 Nov 2002	Partial	01.46	9 Feb 2009	Partial	14.38
16 May 2003	Total	03.40	7 Jul 2009	Partial	09.38
9 Nov 2003	Total	01.18	6 Aug 2009	Partial	00.39
4 May 2004	Total	20.30	31 Dec 2009	Partial[u]	19.23
28 Oct 2004	Total	03.04	26 June 2010	Partial[u]	11.38
24 Apr 2005	Partial	09.55	21 Dec 2010	Total	08.17

[u]Umbral; all others are penumbral

SPACE EXPLORATION

Major space events/missions

Name of event/mission	Country/agency	Date of launch	Event description
Sputnik 1	USSR	4 Oct 1957	First Earth satellite
Sputnik 2	USSR	3 Nov 1957	Biosatellite
Explorer 1	USA	31 Jan 1958	Discovery of Earth's radiation belts
Luna 1	USSR	2 Jan 1959	Escaped Earth gravity; discovery of the solar wind
Vanguard 2	USA	17 Feb 1959	First Earth photo
Luna 2	USSR	12 Sep 1959	Lunar impact
Luna 3	USSR	4 Oct 1959	First lunar photo (hidden side)
TIROS 1	USA	1 Apr 1960	Weather satellite
Transit 1B	USA	13 Apr 1960	Navigation satellite
ECHO 1	USA	12 Aug 1960	Communications satellite
Sputnik 5	USSR	19 Aug 1960	Orbited animals
Vostok 1	USSR	12 Apr 1961	First manned orbital flight (Yuri Gagarin)
Mercury	USA	20 Feb 1962	First US manned orbital flight (John Glenn)
Mariner 2	USA	26 Aug 1962	Venus flyby
Mars 1	USSR	1 Nov 1962	Mars flyby
Vostok 6	USSR	16 June 1963	First woman in orbit (Valentina Tereshkova)
Ranger 7	USA	28 Jul 1964	First close-up TV pictures of lunar surface
Mariner 4	USA	28 Nov 1964	Mars flyby pictures
Voskhod 2	USSR	18 Mar 1965	First spacewalk (AA Leonov)
Venera 3	USSR	16 Nov 1965	Venus impact
Luna 9	USSR	31 Jan 1966	Lunar soft landing; first picture from the lunar surface
Gemini 8	USA	16 Mar 1966	Manned docking
Luna 10	USSR	31 Mar 1966	Lunar orbiter
Surveyor 3	USA	17 Apr 1967	Lunar surface sampler
Cosmos 186/188	USSR	22/28 Oct 1967	Automatic docking
OAO 2	USA	1968	First orbiting astronomical observatory
Zond 5	USSR	14 Sep 1968	Animals moon orbit
Apollo 8	USA	21 Dec 1968	Manned lunar orbit
Apollo 11	USA	16 Jul 1969	First person on the moon (Neil Armstrong)
Copernicus	USA	1970	First far ultra-violet observatory
Venera 7	USSR	17 Aug 1970	Venus soft landing
Mars 2	USSR	19 May 1971	Mars orbit
Mars 3	USSR	28 May 1971	Mars soft landing
Pioneer 10	USA	3 Mar 1972	Jupiter flyby; crossed Pluto orbit; escaped Solar System
Skylab	USA	1973	High-resolution images of solar corona in X-rays
Pioneer 11	USA	6 Apr 1973	Saturn flyby
Mariner 10	USA	3 Nov 1973	First detailed picture of Mercury
Venera 9	USSR	8 Jun 1975	Venus orbit; first picture of Venusian surface
Apollo/Soyuz	USA/USSR	15 Jul 1975	First manned international co-operative mission
Viking 1, 2	USA	Aug/Sep 1975	First pictures taken on the Martian surface
Voyager 1, 2	USA	Aug/Sep 1977	First images of Jupiter, Saturn, Uranus, and Neptune
IUE	USA/UK/ESA	1978	First international space observatory
ISEE C	USA	12 Aug 1978	Comet intercept
STS 1	USA	12 Apr 1981	First launch of *Columbia* space shuttle
STS 6	USA	4 Apr 1983	First launch of *Challenger*
Soyuz T 9	USSR	27 Jun 1983	Construction in space
STS 9	USA	28 Nov 1983	First flight of the ESA spacelab
STS 41 D	USA	30 Aug 1984	First launch of *Discovery*
STS 51 A	USA	8 Nov 1984	Recovery of satellites 'Westar 6' and 'Palapa B2'
Vega 1	USSR	15 Dec 1984	Halley flyby
STS 51 J	USA	3 Oct 1985	First launch of *Atlantis*
Giotto	ESA	1986	First high-resolution image of Halley's nucleus

Major space events/missions (continued)

STS 26	USA	29 Sep 1988	First launch after *Challenger* disaster
Magellan	USA	5 May 1989	Global radar map of Venus
STS 34	USA	18 Oct 1989	*Galileo* launch
Muses A	Japan	24 Jan 1990	Two satellites placed in orbit round the moon
STS 31	USA/ESA	24 Apr 1990	Launch of Hubble Space Telescope
STS 41	USA/ESA	6 Oct 1990	Launch of *Ulysses*; first flight above the solar poles
STS 37	USA	5 Apr 1991	Launch of Compton Gamma Ray Observatory
STS 47	USA	7 May 1992	First launch of *Endeavour*
STS 49	USA/ESA	31 Jul 1992	Launch of *Eureca* (European recoverable carrier)
STS 59	USA	2 Dec 1993	Hubble Space Telescope repaired in space
STS 69	USA/Russia	29 Jun 1995	*Atlantis* docked with *Mir* space station
Mars Pathfinder	USA	4 Dec 1996	Microrover's first exploration of Mars surface, Jul 1997
Cassini	NASA/ESA/ASI	15 Oct 1997	Cassini Orbiter to Saturn, with Huygens probe to Titan
DSI	USA	24 Oct 1998	Deep Space 1, first technology demonstration probe
STS 106	USA/NASA	8 Sep 2000	Crew aboard *Atlantis* prepare International Space Station for arrival of first resident crew
Mars Surveyor	USA/NASA	Apr 2001	*Odyssey* spacecraft launched to orbit Mars
STS 111	USA/NASA	Jun 2002	*Endeavour* is 14th shuttle mission to the ISS
Mars Express	ESA	Jun 2003	Mission to Mars: remote sensing orbiter and small lander named *Beagle 2* (lost during landing)
Mars Exploration Rover	NASA	Jun 2003	Rover probe (*Spirit*) landed on Mars, Jan 2004; sent back coloured images of surface
Smart 1	ESA	28 Aug 2003	Europe's first mission to the Moon: Lunar probe to map surface composition, entered Moon's orbit Nov 2004
Rosetta probe	ESA	Mar 2004	Probe to rendezvous with comet 67P/Churyumov-Gerasimoto in 2014; release lander *Philae* onto comet's surface
Cassini	NASA/ESA/ASI	Jul 2004	First space vehicle to go into orbit around Saturn
Mercury Messenger	NASA	Aug 2004	Probe launched to reach Mercury in 2011; to orbit for 1 year

(ESA = European Space Agency; ASI = Italian Space Agency)

Satellite launch centres

Country	Launch base	Organization responsible	First launch
USA	Cape Canaveral	US Air Force/NASA	31 Jan 1958 (Explorer 1)
	Kennedy Space Center	NASA	9 Nov 1967 (Apollo 4)
	Vandenberg AFB	US Air Force/SAMTO/NASA	28 Feb 1959 (Discoverer 1)
	Wallops Island	NASA Goddard Space Flight Center	16 Feb 1961 (Explorer 9)
USSR (now CIS)	Kapustin Yar, or Volgograd cosmodrome	Ministry of Defence/Academy of Sciences/Intercosmos	16 Mar 1962 (Cosmos 1)
	Plesetsk, or Northern cosmodrome	Ministry of Defence/Academy of Sciences	17 Mar 1966 (Cosmos 112)
	Tyuratam Leninsk, or Baikonur cosmodrome	Ministry of Defence/Academy of Sciences	4 Oct 1957 (Sputnik 1)
Australia	Woomera Range	WRE/British DTI/ELDO	29 Nov 1967 (Wresat)
Brazil	Alcantara Launch Centre	Ministry of Aeronautics/COBAE/CTA	2 Nov 1977 (VLS, unsuccessful)
China	Jiuquan SLC	Ministry of Defence/MOA	24 Apr 1970 (SKW1/Tungfanghung)
	Xichang SLC	MOA	29 Jan 1984 (STW1)
France	Guianan Space Centre at Kouru	CNES/ESA/Arianespace	10 Mar 1970 (Dial)
	Hammaguir/Colomba Bechar	CIEES/CNES	26 Nov 1965 (A1 'Asterix')
India	SHAR/Sriharikota Range	ISRO	18 Jul 1980 (Rohini RS1)
Italy	San Marco platform	CRA/University of Rome	26 Apr 1967 (San Marco 2)
Japan	Kagoshima Space Centre	ISAS/University of Tokyo	11 Feb 1970 (Ohsumi)
	Tanegashima Space Centre	Nasda	9 Sep 1975 (ETS1/Kiku)
Sweden	Esrange, Kiruna	Swedish Space Corporation	20 Nov 1966 (Centaure)

PART TWO

The Earth

HISTORY

The developing world

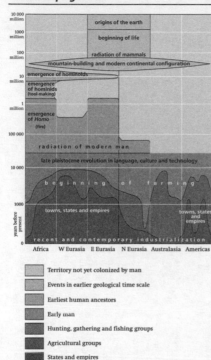

Territory not yet colonized by man

Events in earlier geological time scale

Earliest human ancestors

Early man

Hunting, gathering and fishing groups

Agricultural groups

States and empires

Major ice-age periods

A schematic presentation of the major glacial periods (dark grey) in the Earth's history. It is likely that a number of glaciations occurred within each epoch. Note the change in scale on the time axis at 1 000 million years ago.

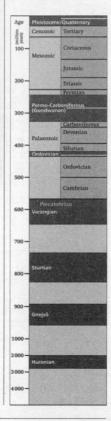

THE EARTH

Geological time scale

Eon	Era	Period	Epoch	Million years before present	Geological events	Sea life	Land life
Phanerozoic	Cenozoic	Quaternary	Holocene		Glaciers recede. Sea level rises. Climate becomes more equable.	As now.	Forests flourish again. Humans acquire agriculture and technology.
				0.01			
			Pleistocene		Widespread glaciers melt periodically, causing seas to rise and fall.	As now.	Many plant forms perish. Small plant forms abundant. Primitive humans established.
				2.0			
		Tertiary	Pliocene		Continents and oceans adopting their present form. Present climatic distribution established. Ice caps develop.	Giant sharks extinct. Many fish varieties.	Some plants and mammals die out. Primates flourish.
				5.1			
			Miocene		Seas recede further. European and Asian land masses join. Heavy rain causes massive erosion. Red Sea opens.	Bony fish common. Giant sharks.	Grasses widespread. Grazing mammals become common.
				24.6			
			Oligocene		Seas recede. Extensive movements of Earth's crust produce new mountains (eg Alpine-Himalayan chain).	Crabs, mussels, and snails evolve.	Forests diminish. Grasses appear. Pachyderms, canines, and felines develop.
				38.0			
			Eocene		Mountain formation continues. Glaciers common in high mountain ranges. Greenland separates. Australia separates.	Whales adapt to sea.	Large tropical jungles. Primitive forms of modern mammals established.
				54.9			
			Palaeocene		Widespread subsidence of land. Seas advance again. Considerable volcanic activity. Europe emerges.	Many reptiles become extinct.	Flowering plants widespread. First primates. Giant reptiles extinct.
				65			
	Mesozoic	Cretaceous	Late Early		Swamps widespread. Massive alluvial deposition. Continuing limestone formation. S America separates from Africa. India, Africa and Antarctica separate.	Turtles, rays, and now-common fish appear.	Flowering plants established. Dinosaurs become extinct.
				97.5			
				144			
		Jurassic	Malm Dogger Lias		Seas advance. Much river formation. High mountains eroded. Limestone formation. N America separates from Africa. Central Atlantic begins to open.	Reptiles dominant.	Early flowers. Dinosaurs dominant. Mammals still primitive. First birds.
				163			
				188			
				213			
		Triassic	Late Middle		Desert conditions widespread. Hot climate slowly becomes warm and wet.	Ichthyosaurs, flying fish, and crustaceans appear.	Ferns and conifers thrive. First mammals, dinosaurs, and flies.
				231			

Era	Period	Epoch	Million years	Geological events	Animal life	Plant / land life
		Early	243	Break up of Pangea into supercontinents Gondwana (S) and Laurasia (N).		Deciduous plants. Reptiles dominant. Many insect varieties.
Palaeozoic	Permian	Late	248	Some sea areas cut off to form lakes. Earth movements form mountains. Glaciation in southern hemisphere.	Some shelled fish become extinct.	
		Early	258			
	Carboniferous	Pennsylvanian	286	Sea-beds rise to form new land areas. Enormous swamps. Partly-rotted vegetation forms coal.	Amphibians and sharks abundant.	Extensive evergreen forests. Reptiles breed on land. Some insects develop wings.
		Mississippian	320			
	Devonian	Late	360	Collision of continents causing mountain formation (Appalachians, Caledonides, and Urals). Sea deeper but narrower. Climatic zones forming. Iapetus ocean closed.	Fish abundant. Primitive sharks. First amphibians.	Leafy plants. Some invertebrates adapt to land. First insects.
		Middle	374			
		Early	387			
	Silurian	Pridoli	408	New mountain ranges form. Sea level varies periodically. Extensive shallow sea over the Sahara.	Large vertebrates.	First leafless land plants.
		Ludlow	414			
		Wenlock	421			
		Llandovery	428			
	Ordovician	Ashgill	438	Shore lines still quite variable. Increasing sedimentation. Europe and N America moving together.	First vertebrates. Coral reefs develop.	None.
		Caradoc	448			
		Llandeilo	458			
		Llanvirn	468			
		Arenig	478			
		Tremadoc	488			
			505			
	Cambrian	Merioneth	525	Much volcanic activity, and long periods of marine sedimentation.	Shelled invertebrates. Trilobites.	None.
		St David's	540			
		Caerfai	590			
Proterozoic (Precambrian)	Vendian		650	Shallow seas advance and retreat over land areas. Atmosphere uniformly warm.	Seaweed. Algae and invertebrates.	None.
	Riphean	Late	900	Intense deformation and metamorphism.	Earliest marine life and fossils.	None.
		Middle	1300			
		Early	1600			
	Early Proterozoic		2500	Shallow shelf seas. Formation of carbonate sediments and 'red beds'.	First appearance of stromatolites.	None.
Archaean	Archaean (Azoic)		4600	Banded iron formations. Formation of the Earth's crust and oceans.	None.	None.

STRUCTURE

The Earth

Age 4 500 000 000 years
Area 509 600 000 km²/197 000 000 sq mi
Mass 6.0 × 10²⁴ kg
Land surface 148 000 000 km²/57 000 000 sq mi
(c.29% of total area)
Water surface 361 000 000 km²/140 000 000 sq mi
(c.71% of total area)
Circumference (equator) 40 076 km/24 902 mi
Circumference (meridian) 40 000 km/24 860 mi
Diameter (equator) 12 757 km/7 927 mi

Diameter (meridian) 12 714 km/7 900 mi
Period of axial rotation 23 h 56 m 4.0996 s
Lithosphere 80 km/50 mi thick
Thickness of upper mantle 700 km/430 mi
Thickness of lower mantle 2 200 km/1 370 mi
Thickness of outer core 2 250 km/1 400 mi
Radius of inner core 3 480 km/2 160 mi
Density of core 13.09 g/cm³
Temperature at core 4 500°C

The structure of the Earth

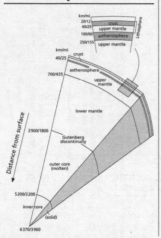

Earth's crust composition

This pie chart shows percentages of the most abundant elements in the Earth's crust.

a Oxygen 46.6%
b Silicon 27.72%
c Aluminium 8.13%
d Iron 5.0%
e Calcium 3.63%
f Sodium 2.83%
g Potassium 2.59%
h Magnesium 2.09%
i Other elements 1.41%

Chemical composition of rocks

	Type of rock						
Oxide component (%)	Granite	Basalt	Amphibolite	Schist	Shale	Sandstone	Limestone
SiO_2	70.8	49.0	49.3	63.3	62.4	94.4	5.2
TiO_2	0.4	1.0	1.2	1.4	1.1	0.1	0.1
Al_2O_3	14.5	18.2	16.9	17.9	16.6	1.1	0.8
Fe_2O_3	1.6	3.2	3.6	3.6	3.2	0.4	0.3
FeO	1.8	6.0	6.8	2.6	2.1	0.2	0.2
MgO	0.9	7.6	7.0	1.6	2.5	0.1	7.9
CaO	1.8	11.0	9.5	1.9	1.7	1.6	42.6
Na_2O	3.3	2.5	2.9	1.3	0.9	0.1	0.1
K_2O	4.0	0.9	1.1	3.1	3.0	0.2	0.3
H_2O	0.8	0.4	1.5	2.6	5.2	0.3	0.7
CO_2					1.0	1.1	41.6

Mineral composition of rocks

Mineral component (%)	Type of rock						
	Granite	Basalt	Amphibolite	Schist	Shale	Sandstone	Limestone
Quartz	30			32	17	97	3
Alkali feldspar	60	5				1	1
Plagioclase	5	45	42	18			
Pyroxene		40					
Amphibole			50				
Olivine		5					
Biotite	4		5	5			
Muscovite				38	1	1	
Magnetite	1	5	3	3	1	1	1
Staurolite				2			
Clay minerals					80		1
Calcite					1		94

Mohs scale of hardness

Friedrich Mohs (1773–1839) introduced a simple definition of hardness, according to which one mineral is said to be harder than another if the former scratches the latter. The Mohs scale is based on a series of common minerals, arranged in order of increasing hardness.

Mineral	Composition	Simple hardness test	Hardness
Talc	$Mg_3Si_4O_{10}(OH)_2$	Crushed by finger nail	1
Gypsum	$CaSO_4 \cdot 2H_2O$	Scratched by finger nail	2
Calcite	$CaCO_3$	Scratched by copper coin	3
Fluorite	CaF_2	Scratched by glass	4
Apatite	$Ca_5(PO_4)_3F$	Scratched by penknife	5
Orthoclase (feldspar)	$KAlSi_3O_8$	Scratched by quartz	6
Quartz	SiO_2	Scratched by steel file	7
Topaz	$Al_2SiO_4F_2$	Scratched by corundum	8
Corundum	Al_2O_3	Scratched by diamond	9
Diamond	C		10

Layers of the atmosphere

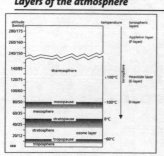

The composition of dry air at sea level

Gas	Volume (%)
Nitrogen (N_2)	78.08
Oxygen (O_2)	20.95
Argon (Ar)	0.93
Carbon dioxide (CO_2)	0.031
Neon (Ne)	0.0018
Helium (He)	0.00052
Krypton (Kr)	0.00011
Xenon (Xe)	0.0000087
Hydrogen (H_2)	0.00005
Methane (CH_4)	0.0002
Nitric oxide (NO)	0.00005
Ozone (O_3)	0.000002 (winter) 0.000007 (summer)

Continental drift

240 million years ago
The single supercontinent *Pangea* is formed, with a single superocean, *Panthalassa*.

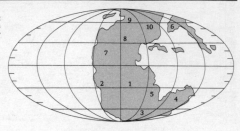

120 million years ago
Tethys, a broad gulf, divides Pangea into two huge landmasses: *Laurasia* in the north; *Gondwana* in the south.

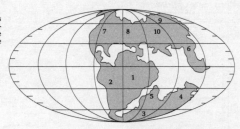

60 million years ago
Laurasia and Gondwana have split to begin to form the continents as we know them today.

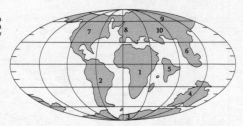

Major lithospheric plates

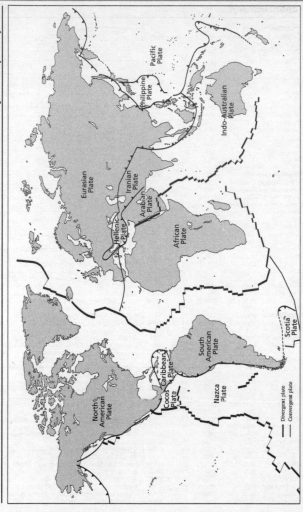

Pacific
Plate

Philippine
Plate

Indo-Australian
Plate

Eurasian
Plate

Iranian
Plate

Arabian
Plate

Hellenic
Plate

African
Plate

North
American
Plate

Cocos
Plate

Caribbean
Plate

South
American
Plate

Nazca
Plate

Scotia
Plate

Divergent plate
Convergent plate

THE EARTH

Major earthquakes

All magnitudes on the Richter scale[a]

Location	Country	Year	Magnitude	Deaths
Indian Ocean	Indonesia	2005	8·7	1000+
Zarand	SE Iran	2005	6.4	400+
Indian Ocean	Indonesia[b]	2004	9.3	300000
Niigata	Japan	2004	6.8	40
Yunnan Prov.	S W China	2004	5.6	4
Bam	S E Iran	2003	6·3	26000+
Xinjiang	China	2003	6·8	268
Quazvin	N W Iran	2002	6·3	230
Hindu Kush Mts	Afghanistan	2002	6·1	1800
Arequipa	Peru	2001	7·9	100+
Gujarat	India	2001	7·9	100000
El Salvador	El Salvador	2001	7·7	680+
Taiwan	Taiwan	1999	7·6	2000+
Izmit	Turkey	1999	7·4	15000+
Armenia	Colombia	1999	6·0	2000+
Rostaq	Afghanistan	1998	7·1	2000
NW Afghanistan	Afghanistan	1998	6·1	4000+
Khorasan	Iran	1997	7·1	4000
Lijiang, Yunan	China	1996	7·0	250
Neftegorsk	Russia	1995	7·6	1989
Kobe	Japan	1995	7·2	5477
Cauca	Colombia	1994	6·8	269
Sumatra	Indonesia	1994	7·0	215
Los Angeles	USA	1994	6·8	57
Maharashtra	India	1993	6·4	9748
Hokkaido	Japan	1993	7·7	200
Cairo	Egypt	1992	5·9	500
Erzincan	Turkey	1992	6·2	2000
Uttar Pradesh	India	1991	6·1	1000
Georgia	CIS	1991	7·2	100
Hindu Kush Mts	Afghanistan/Pakistan	1991	6·8	1300
Cabanatuan	Philippines	1990	7·7	1653
Caspian Sea	Iran	1990	7·7	40000
Luzon Island	Philippines	1990	7·7	1600
San Francisco	USA	1989	6·9	100
N Armenia	Armenia	1988	7·0	25000
Mexico City	Mexico	1985	8·1	7200
Naples	Italy	1980	7·2	4500
El Asnam	Algeria	1980	7·3	5000
Tabas	Iran	1978	7·7	25000
Tangshan	China	1976	8·2	242000
Guatemala City	Guatemala	1976	7·5	22778
Kashmir	Pakistan	1974	6·3	5200
Managua	Nicaragua	1972	6·2	5000
Tehran	Iran	1972	6·9	5000
Chimbote	Peru	1970	7·7	66000
Agadir	Morocco	1960	5·8	12000
Ashkhabad	Turkmenistan	1948	7·3	19800
Erzincan	Turkey	1939	7·9	23000
Chillan	Chile	1939	7·8	30000
Quetta	India	1935	7·5	60000
Gansu	China	1932	7·6	70000
Nan-Shan	China	1927	8·3	200000
Kanto	Japan	1923	8·3	143000
Gansu	China	1920	8·6	180000
Avezzano	Italy	1915	7·5	30000
Messina	Italy	1908	7·5	120000
Valparaiso	Chile	1906	8·6	20000
San Francisco	USA	1906	8·3	500
Calabria	Italy	1783		50000
Lisbon	Portugal	1755		70000
Calcutta	India	1737		300000
Hokkaido	Japan	1730		137000
Catania	Italy	1693		60000
Shemaka	Caucasia	1667		80000
Shensi	China	1556		830000
Chihli	China	1290		100000
Cilicia	Turkey	1268		60000
Corinth	Greece	856		45000
Antioch	Turkey	526		250000

[a] A logarithmic scale, devised in 1935 by Charles Richter, for representing the energy released by earthquakes. A figure of 2 or less is barely perceptible, while an earthquake measuring over 5 may be destructive.

[b] Epicentre off NW Sumatra caused a major tsunami which devastated territories in and around the Indian Ocean.

Earthquake severity

Modified Mercalli intensity scale (1956 revision)

I Not felt; marginal and long-period effects of large earthquakes.

II Felt by persons at rest, on upper floors or favourably placed.

III Felt indoors; hanging objects swing; vibration like passing of light trucks; duration estimated; may not be recognized as an earthquake.

IV Hanging objects swing; vibration like passing of heavy trucks, or sensation of a jolt like a heavy ball striking the walls; standing cars rock; windows, dishes, doors rattle; glasses clink; crockery clashes; in the upper range of IV, wooden walls and frames creak.

V Felt outdoors; direction estimated; sleepers wakened; liquids disturbed, some spilled; small unstable objects displaced or upset; doors swing, close, open; shutters, pictures move; pendulum clocks stop, start, change rate.

VI Felt by all; many frightened and run outdoors; persons walk unsteadily; windows, dishes, glassware break; knickknacks, books, etc, fall off shelves; pictures off walls; furniture moves or overturns; weak plaster and masonry D crack; small bells ring (church, school); trees, bushes shake visibly, or heard to rustle.

VII Difficult to stand; noticed by drivers; hanging objects quiver; furniture breaks; damage to masonry D, including cracks; weak chimneys broken at roof line; fall of plaster, loose bricks, stones, tiles, cornices, also unbraced parapets and architectural ornaments; some cracks in masonry C; waves on ponds, water turbid with mud; small slides and caving in along sand or gravel banks; large bells ring; concrete irrigation ditches damaged.

VIII Steering of cars affected; damage to masonry C and partial collapse; some damage to masonry B; none to masonry A; fall of stucco and some masonry walls; twisting, fall of chimneys, factory stacks, monuments, towers, elevated tanks; frame houses move on foundations if not bolted down; loose panel walls thrown out; decayed piling broken off; branches broken from trees; changes in flow or temperature of springs and wells; cracks in wet ground and on steep slopes.

IX General panic; masonry D destroyed; masonry C heavily damaged, sometimes with complete collapse; masonry B seriously damaged; general damage to foundations; frame structures, if not bolted, shift off foundations; frames racked; serious damage to reservoirs; underground pipes break; conspicuous cracks in ground; in alluviated areas sand and mud ejected, earthquake fountains, sand craters.

X Most masonry and frame structures destroyed with their foundations; some well-built wooden structures and bridges destroyed; serious damage to dams, dykes, embankments; large landslides; water thrown on banks of canals, rivers, lakes, etc; sand and mud shifted horizontally on beaches and flat land; rails bent slightly.
XI Rails bent greatly; underground pipelines completely out of service.
XII Damage nearly total; large rock masses displaced; lines of sight and level distorted; objects thrown into the air.

Note *Masonry A* Good workmanship, mortar and design; reinforced, especially laterally, and bound together using steel, concrete etc; designed to resist lateral forces. *Masonry B* Good workmanship and mortar; reinforced, but not designed in detail to resist lateral forces. *Masonry C* Ordinary workmanship and mortar; no extreme weakness like failing to tie in at corners, but neither reinforced nor designed against horizontal forces. *Masonry D* Weak materials, such as adobe; poor mortar; low standards of workmanship; weak horizontally.

THE EARTH

Major volcanoes and eruptions

Name	Location	Height (m)	(ft)	Major eruptions (year/s)	Last eruption (year)
Aconcagua	Argentina	6960	22831	extinct	
Ararat	Turkey	5198	18350	extinct	Holocene
Awu	Sangir Is	1327	4355	1711, 1856, 1892, 1968	1992
Bezymianny	Russia	2800	9186	1955–6, 1984	1997
Coseguina	Nicaragua	847	1598	1835	1859
El Chichón	Mexico	1349	4430	1982	1982
Erebus	Antarctica	4023	13200	1947, 1972, 1986	1991
Etna, Mt	Italy	3236	10625	122, 1169, 1329, 1536, 1669, 1928 1964, 1971, 1986, 1992, 1994, 2001	2002
Fuji	Japan	3776	12388	1707	1707
Galunggung	Java	2180	7155	1822, 1918, 1982	1984
Hekla	Iceland	1491	4920	1693, 1845, 1947–8, 1970, 1981, 1991	2000
Helgafell	Iceland	215	706	1973	1973
Hudson	Chile	1740	5742	1971, 1973	1991
Jurullo	Mexico	1330	4255	1759–74	1774
Katmai	Alaska	2298	7540	1912, 1920, 1921, 1931	1974
Kilauea	Hawaii	1247	4100	1823–1924, 1952, 1955, 1960, 1967–8, 1968–74, 1983–7, 1988, 1991, 1992	1994
Kilimanjaro	Tanzania	5895	19340	extinct	Pleistocene
Klyuchevskoy	Russia	4850	15910	1700–1966, 1984, 1985	1994
Krakatoa	Sumatra	818	2685	1680, 1883, 1927, 1952–3, 1969	1980
La Soufrière	St Vincent	1232	4048	1718, 1812, 1902, 1971–2	1979
Laki	Iceland	500	1642	1783, 1784, 1938	1996
Lamington	Papua New Guinea	1780	5844	1951	1956
Lassen Peak	USA	3186	10453	1914–15	1921
Mauna Loa	Hawaii	4172	13685	1859, 1880, 1887, 1919, 1950, 1984	1987
Mayon	Philippines	2462	8084	1616, 1766, 1814, 1897, 1968, 1978, 1993	2001
Nyamuragira	Democratic Republic of Congo	3056	10026	1921–38, 1971, 1980, 1984, 1988, 1991	2002
Paricutín	Mexico	3188	10460	1943–52	1952
Pelée, Mont	Martinique	1397	4584	1902, 1929–32	1932
Pinatubo	Philippines	1758	5770	1391, 1991, 1992	2001
Popocatépetl	Mexico	5483	17990	1920, 1943	1999
Rainier, Mt	USA	4392	14416	1st-c BC, 1820	1882
Ruapehu	New Zealand	2796	9175	1945, 1953, 1969, 1975, 1986, 1995	1996
St Helens, Mt	USA	2549	8364	1800, 1831, 1835, 1842–3, 1857, 1980, 1986, 1991	2005
Santorini/ Thera	Greece	556	1824	1470 BC, 197 BC, AD 46, 1570–3, 1707–11, 1866–70	1950
Stromboli	Italy	931	3055	1768, 1882, 1889, 1907, 1930, 1936, 1941, 1950, 1952, 1986, 1990	1994

Major volcanoes and eruptions (continued)

Surtsey	Iceland	174	570	1963–7	1967
Taal	Philippines	1448	4752	1911, 1965, 1969, 1977	1988
Tambora	Sumbawa	2868	9410	1815	1880
Tarawera	New Zealand	1 149	3 770	1886	1973
Unzen, Mt	Japan	1360	4462	1360, 1791, 1991, 1994	1996
Vesuvius	Italy	1289	4230	79, 472, 1036, 1631, 1779, 1906	1944
Vulcano	Italy	502	1650	antiquity, 1444, 1730–40, 1786, 1873, 1888–90	1890

Major tsunamis

Tsunamis are long-period ocean waves produced by movements of the sea floor associated with earthquakes, volcanic explosions, or landslides. They are also referred to as *seismic sea waves*, and in popular (but not technical) oceanographic use as *tidal waves*.

Location of source	Year	Height		Location of deaths/damage	Deaths
		(m)	(ft)		
Indian Ocean	2004	10	32	NW Indonesia, Sri Lanka, SE India, Thailand, Myanmar, Indian Ocean territories, E Africa	150 000+
Bismarck Sea	1998	10	32	NW Papua New Guinea	3000
Mindoro	1994	15	49	Philippine Is	60
Banyuwangi	1994	5	16	Indonesia	200
Sea of Japan	1983	15	49	Japan, Korea	107
Indonesia	1979	10	32	Indonesia	187
Celebes Sea	1976	30	98	Philippine Is	5000
Alaska	1964	32	105	Alaska, Aleutian Is, California	122
Chile	1960	25	82	Chile, Hawaii, Japan	1 260
Aleutian Is	1957	16	52	Hawaii, Japan	0
Kamchatka	1952	18.4	60	Kamchatka, Kuril Is, Hawaii	many
Aleutian Is	1946	32	105	Aleutian Is, Hawaii, California	165
Nankaido (Japan)	1946	6.1	20	Japan	1997
Kii (Japan)	1944	7.5	25	Japan	998
Sanriku (Japan)	1933	28.2	93	Japan, Hawaii	3000
E Kamchatka	1923	20	66	Kamchatka, Hawaii	3
S Kuril Is	1918	12	39	Kuril Is, Russia, Japan, Hawaii	23
Sanriku (Japan)	1896	30	98	Japan	27 122
Sunda Strait	1883	35	115	Java, Sumatra	36 000
Chile	1877	23	75	Chile, Hawaii	many
Chile	1868	21	69	Chile, Hawaii	25 000
Hawaii	1868	20	66	Hawaii	81
Japan	1854	6	20	Japan	3000
Flores Sea	1800	24	79	Indonesia	400–500
Ariake Sea	1792	9	30	Japan	9 745
Italy	1783	?	?	Italy	30 000
Ryukyu Is	1771	12	39	Ryukyu Is	11 941
Portugal	1775	16	52	W Europe, Morocco, W Indies	60 000
Peru	1746	24	79	Peru	5000
Japan	1741	9	30	Japan	1000
SE Kamchatka	1737	30	98	Kamchatka, Kuril Is	?
Peru	1724	24	79	Peru	?
Japan	1707	11.5	38	Japan	30 000
W Indies	1692	?	?	Jamaica	2000
Banda Is	1629	15	49	Indonesia	?
Sanriku (Japan)	1611	25	82	Japan	5000
Japan	1605	?	?	Japan	4000
Kii (Japan)	1498	?	?	Japan	5000

Recent hurricanes

A hurricane (H) is an intense, often devastating, tropical storm which occurs as a vortex spiralling around a low-pressure system. Wind speeds are high – above 120 kmh/75 mph. Hurricanes originate over tropical oceans and move in a W or NW direction in the northern hemisphere, and SW in the southern hemisphere, losing energy as they reach land. They are also known as *typhoons* in the western N Pacific and *cyclones* in the Bay of Bengal. Hurricane naming began in 1950, using the phonetic alphabet of the time (Able, Baker, etc.), changing to female first-names in 1953, and alternating male and female names for Atlantic Basin hurricanes in 1979, and introducing male names a year later.

Name	Location	Year	Deaths	Damage (US $bn)
Typhoon Nanmadol	Philippines	2004	1000+	n.a.
Typhoon Tokage	Japan	2004	82	n.a.
H Jeanne	Dominican Republic, Haiti, Florida	2004	1500+	n.a.
H Ivan	Florida, S USA, Grenada, SE Caribbean Is	2004	103	n.a.
H Frances	Florida	2004	2	4.4
H Charley	West Florida	2004	26	7.4
Typhoon Rananim	East China	2004	164	1.85
Typhoon Megi	S & N Japan, S Korea	2004	13	n.a.
Cyclone Heta	South Pacific, Niue	2004	1	n.a.
Typhoon Maemi	South Korea, Kyongsang	2003	117	4.1
Typhoon Dujuan	China	2003	23	n.a.
Cyclone Zoë	Pacific, Solomon Is	2002	none	n.a.
H Michelle	Cuba, Florida, C America	2001	20	n.a.
H Iris	Belize	2001	18	n.a.
Cyclone Orissa, India		1999	9000+	n.a.
H Floyd	Caribbean, E Coast America	1999	17	n.a.
H Mitch	C America	1998	8347	5.0
H Georges	Caribbean, US Gulf Coast	1998	581	2.0
Typhoon Linda	Vietnam, South Coast	1997	358	n.a.
H Pauline	Mexico	1997	240+	n.a.
H Opal	Florida, Gulf Coast	1995	19	n.a.
H Marilyn	Virgin Is, Puerto Rico	1995	9	n.a.
H Luis	Caribbean	1995	12	n.a.
Typhoon Angela	Philippine Is	1995	500+	n.a.
H Andrew	S Florida, Bahamas	1992	88	16.5
H Iniki	Kauai, Hawaii	1992	3	1.0
H Bob	NE USA	1991	17	1.5
Cyclone	Bangladesh	1991	200000	n.a.
H Hugo	South Carolina	1989	49	7.0
H Gilbert	Caribbean, Mexico	1988	318	5.0
H Joan	Caribbean	1988	216	
H Elena	Mississippi, Alabama, NW Florida	1985	2	1.25
H Gloria	E USA	1985	15	0.9
H Juan	Louisiana	1985	12	1.5
H Kate	Florida	1985	16	0.3
Cyclone	Bangladesh	1985	11000	
H Alicia	N Texas	1983	18	2.0
H Allen	S Texas	1980	235	0.3
H David	Florida	1979	2400	0.3
H Frederic	Alabama, Mississippi	1979	31	2.3
H Eloise	NW Florida	1975	100	0.49
H Carmen	Louisiana	1974	1	0.15
H Fifi	Honduras, C America	1974	10000	1.0
Cyclone Tracey	Darwin, Australia	1974	65	1.0

CLIMATE

Meteorological records

Hottest place	El Azizia, Libya	58°C / 136.4°F (hottest recorded temperature)
Coldest place	Vostok, Antarctica	−89°C / −128.20°F (coldest recorded temperature)
Driest place	Arica-Antofagasta, Pacific coast, Chile	0.1 mm / 0.004 in (annual mean rainfall)
Wettest place	Mawsynram, Meghalaya State, India	861 mm / 467 in (annual mean rainfall)
Windiest place	Honolulu, Hawaii	380 kmh/236 mph (highest recorded gust)

Source: UK Met Office (Hadley Centre)

Cloud types

Depressions

Plan view of the six idealized stages in the development and final occlusion of a depression along the polar front in the northern hemisphere. Stage 4 shows a well-developed depression system and stage 5 shows the occlusion. The cross-section is taken along the line AB in stage 4. The cloud types are:

Cb – cumulonimbus;
As – altostratus;
Ac – altocumulus;
Cs – cirrostratus;
Ns – nimbostratus;
Ci – cirrus.

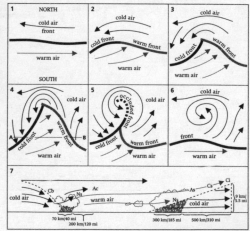

Meteorological sea areas around the British Isles

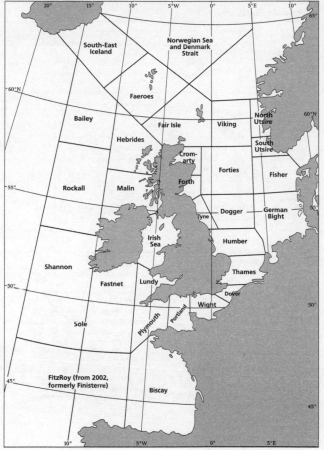

Wind force and sea disturbance

Beaufort number	Wind speed		Wind name	Observable wind characteristics
	(kmh)	*(mph)*		
0	<1	<1	Calm	Smoke rises vertically
1	1–5	1–3	Light air	Wind direction shown by smoke drift but not by wind vanes
2	6–11	4–7	Light breeze	Wind felt on face; leaves rustle; vanes moved by wind
3	12–19	8–12	Gentle breeze	Leaves and small twigs in constant motion; wind extends light flag
4	20–8	13–18	Moderate	Raises dust, loose paper; small branches moved
5	29–38	19–24	Fresh	Small trees begin to sway
6	39–49	25–31	Strong	Large branches in motion; difficult to use umbrellas
7	50–61	32–8	Near gale	Whole trees in motion; difficult to walk against wind
8	62–74	39–46	Gale	Breaks twigs off trees; impedes progress
9	75–88	47–54	Strong gale	Slight structural damage caused
10	89–102	55–63	Storm	Trees uprooted; considerable damage occurs
11	103–17	64–72	Violent storm	Widespread damage
12–17	>118	>73	Hurricane	

Sea disturbance number (Beaufort)	Average wave height		Observable sea characteristics
	(m)	*(ft)*	
0 (0)	0	0	Sea like a mirror
0 (1)	0	0	Ripples like scales
1 (2)	0.3	0–1	More definite wavelets
2 (3)	0.3–0.6	1–2	Large wavelets; crests beginning
3 (4)	0.6–1.2	2–4	Small waves becoming longer; fairly frequent white horses
4 (5)	1.2–2.4	4–8	Moderate waves with longer form; many white horses; some foam spray
5 (6)	2.4–4	8–13	Large waves forming; more white foam crests; spray
6 (7)	4–6	13–20	Sea heaps up; streaks of white foam blown along
6 (8)	4–6	13–20	Moderately high waves of greater length; well-marked streaks of foam
6 (9)	4–6	13–20	High waves; dense streaks of foam; sea begins to roll; spray affects visibility
7 (10)	6–9	20–30	Very high waves with overhanging crests; generally white appearance of surface; heavy rolling
8 (11)	9–14	30–45	Exceptionally high waves; long white patches of foam; poor visibility; ships lost to view behind waves
9 (12–17)	14	>45	Air filled with foam and spray; sea completely white; very poor visibility

SURFACE

World physical map

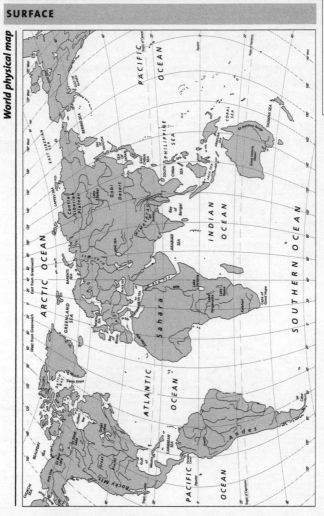

Continents

Name	Area		% of total	Lowest point below sea level			Highest elevation		
	(km²)	(sq mi)			(m)	(ft)		(m)	(ft)
Africa	30 970 000	11 690 000	20.2	Lake Assal, Djibouti	156	512	Kilimanjaro, Tanzania	5 895	19 340
Antarctica	15 500 000	6 000 000	9.3	Bently subglacial trench	2 538	8 327	Vinson Massif	5 140	16 864
Asia	44 493 000	17 179 000	29.6	Dead Sea, Israel/Jordan	400	1 312	Mt Everest, China/Nepal	8 848	29 028
Oceania	8 945 000	3 454 000	6	Lake Eyre, S Australia	15	49	Puncak Jaya, Indonesia	5 030	16 500
Europe	10 245 000	3 956 000	6.8	Caspian Sea, Russia	29	94	Elbrus, Russia	5 642	18 510
North America	24 454 000	9 442 000	16.3	Death Valley, California	86	282	Mt McKinley, Alaska	6 194	20 320
South America	17 838 000	6 887 000	11.9	Peninsular Valdez, Argentina	40	131	Aconcagua, Argentina	6 960	22 831

Oceans

Name	Area		% of total	Average depth		Greatest depth		
	(km²)	(sq mi)		(m)	(ft)		(m)	(ft)
Arctic	13 986 000	5 400 000	3	1 330	4 300	Eurasia Basin	5 122	16 804
Atlantic	82 217 000	31 700 000	24	3 700	12 100	Puerto Rico Trench	8 648	28 372
Indian	73 426 000	28 350 000	20	3 900	12 800	Java Trench	7 725	25 344
Pacific	181 300 000	70 000 000	46	4 300	14 100	Marianas Trench	11 040	36 220

Major island groups

Name	Country	Sea/Ocean	No. of islands	Main islands	Area		Inhabitants
					(km²)	(sq mi)	
Aeolian	Italy	Mediterranean	7	Stromboli, Lipari, Vulcanö, Salina	90	30	11 000 (2000e)
Åland	Finland	Gulf of Bothnia	6554	Eckerö, Lemland, Vardö, Lumparland	1 500	570	25 000 (2000e)
Aleutian	USA	Pacific	150	Andreanof, Adak	18 000	6 800	14 500 (2000e)
Alexander	Canada	Pacific	1100	Baranof, Prince of Wales	na	na	40 000 (2000e)
Andaman	India	Bay of Bengal	300+	N Andaman, S Andaman	8 300	3 200	288 000 (2000e)
Arctic Archipelago	Canada	Arctic	na	Baffin	1 300 000	500 000	largely uninhabited
Azores	Portugal	Atlantic	9	São Miguel, Flores	2 300	900	239 000 (2000e)
Bahamas	Bahamas	Atlantic	700	New Providence, Grand Bahama	13 900	5 400	287 500 (2000e)
Balearic	Spain	Mediterranean	5	Mallorca, Menorca, Ibiza	5 000	1 900	712 000 (2000e)
Bismarck	Papua New Guinea	Pacific	2 000	New Britain, New Ireland, Admiralty Island	49 700	19 200	473 000 (2000e)
Bijagos	Guinea-Bissau	Atlantic	88	Orango, Formoza, Caravela, Roxa	50	30	27 000 (2000e)
Canary	Spain	Atlantic	7	Tenerife, Gomera, Lanzarote, Las Palmas	7 300	2 800	1 475 000 (2000e)

Name	Country	Sea/Ocean	No. of islands	Main islands	Area		Inhabitants
					(km²)	(sq mi)	
Cape Verde	Cape Verde	Atlantic	10	Barlavento group, Sotavento group	4000	1500	411500 (2000e)
Caroline	USA	Pacific	680	Yop, Pohnpei, Truk	1300	500	153000 (2000e)
Channel	UK	English Channel	4	Guernsey, Jersey, Sark, Alderney	200	80	151600 (2000e)
Commander	Russia	Bering Sea	4	Bering, Medny	1800	700	750 (2000e)
Comoros	Republic of Comoros	Mozambique Channel	4	Grand Mohore, Anjouan, Moheli, Mayotte	1900	700	580500 (2000e)
Cook	New Zealand	Pacific	15	Palmerston, Rarotonga, Mangaia	240	90	20400 (2000e)
Cyclades	Greece	Aegean	c.220	Andros, Mikonos, Paros	2600	990	99300 (2000e)
Dodecanese	Greece	Aegean	12	Rhodes, Kos, Patmos	2700	1000	175000 (2000e)
Falkland	UK	Atlantic	200	W Falkland, E Falkland, S Georgia	12200	4700	2000 (2000e)
Faroe	Denmark	Atlantic	22	Strømø, Østerø	1400	540	40200 (2000e)
Fiji	Fiji	Pacific	844	Viti Levu, Vanua Levu	18330	7080	823000 (2000e)
Galapagos	Ecuador	Pacific	16	Santa Cruz, Santiago	7800	3010	12100 (2000e)
Gotland	Sweden	Baltic	2	Gotland, Fårö	3140	1210	60000 (2000e)
Greenland	Denmark	N Atlantic, Arctic	2	Greenland, Disko	2175600	840000	60000 (2000e)
Hawaiian	USA	Pacific	8	Hawaii, Oahu	16760	6470	1052000 (2000e)
Hebrides	UK	Atlantic	10+	Lewis, Skye, Mull		na	40000 (2000e)
Ionian	Greece	Aegean	7	Kerkira, Levkas	2300	890	200000 (2000e)
Japan	Japan	Pacific	1000+	Honshu, Hokkaido, Kyushu, Shikoku	370000	145000	126434000 (2000e)
Juan Fernandez	Chile	Pacific	3	Robinson Crusoe, Alejandro Selkirk, Santa Clara	180	70	500 (2000e)
Kuril	Russia/Japan	Pacific	56	Shumsu, Iturup	15600	6000	20000 (2000e)
Laccadive	India	Arabian Sea	27	Laccadive, Amaindivi	30	10	61000 (2000e)
Lofoten	Norway	Norwegian Sea	5	Hinnoy, Austvagoy	1420	550	24500 (2000e)
Madeira	Portugal	Atlantic	4	Madeira	790	310	259000 (2000e)
Malay Archipelego	Indonesia, Malaysia, Philippines	Pacific/ Indian	20000	Borneo, New Guinea, Sumatra, Jarva, Philippine Is (>> p.40)	329750	127280	322000000 (2000e)
Maldives	Republic of Maldives	Indian	1190	Male	300	120	310500 (2000e)
Malta	Republic of Malta	Mediterranean	5	Malta, Gozo	320	120	383000 (2000e)
Mariana	Mariana Is	Pacific	14	Saipan, Tinian, Rota	470	180	72000 (2000e)
Marquesas	France	Pacific	10	Nukultiva	1190	460	9300 (2000e)
Marshall	Marshall Islands	Pacific	1200+	Bikini	180	70	68000 (2000e)
Mascarene	France	Indian	3	Réunion, Mauritius, Rodrigues	na	na	1969000 (2000e)
Melanesia		Pacific	na	Solomon, Bismarck, Fiji, New Guinea	540000	210000	6578000 (2000e)
Micronesia		Pacific	na	Caroline, Gilbert, Marshall, Kiribati	3270	1260	390000 (2000e)

Major island groups (continued)

Name	Country	Sea/Ocean	No. of islands	Main islands	Area (km²)	(sq mi)	Inhabitants
New Hebrides	Republic of Vanuatu	Pacific	72	Espiritu Santo	14 760	5 700	193 000 (2000e)
New-foundland	Canada	Atlantic	na	Newfoundland	405 720	156 650	636 000 (2000e)
New Zealand	New Zealand	Pacific	4+	North, South	268 810	103 760	3 698 000 (2000e)
Nicobar	India	Bay of Bengal	19+	Great Nicobar	1 625	625	40 000 (2000e)
Novaya Zemlya	Russia	Arctic	5	North, South	81 300	31 400	no permanent population
Orkney	UK	North Sea	20	Mainland, Ronaldsay	980	380	20 400 (2000e)
Philippines	Republic of the Philippines	Pacific	7 100	Luzon, Mindanao, Samar	300 680	110 680	80 961 000 (2000e)
Polynesia		Pacific	na	Hawaii, Tonga, Kiribati, Easter, Samoa	17 200	10 700	1 900 000 (2000e)
Queen Charlotte	Canada	Pacific	150	Graham	6 361	2 455	5 900 (2000e)
São Tomé and Príncipe	Republic of São Tomé & Príncipe	Atlantic	2	São Tomé, Príncipe	970	370	160 000 (2000e)
Scilly	UK	English Channel	140	St Mary's, St Martin's	20	10	1 970 (2000e)
Seychelles	Republic of Seychelles	Indian	115	Mahé, La Digue	450	170	80 000 (2000e)
Shetland	UK	North Sea	500+	Mainland, Unst	1 400	550	23 100 (2000e)
Society	France	Pacific	2	Tahiti	1 500	590	193 000 (2000e)
Solomon	Solomon Islands	Pacific	6+	New Georgia, San Cristobal	27 560	10 640	470 000 (2000e)
South Orkney	UK	Atlantic	2	Coronation, Laurie	620	240	uninhabited
Sri Lanka	Republic of Sri Lanka	Indian	2	Sri Lanka, Mannar	65 610	25 200	19 355 000 (2000e)
Taiwan	Republic of China	China Sea/Pacific	na	Taiwan	36 000	13 900	22 319 000 (2000e)
Tasmania	Australia	Tasman Sea	5+	Tasmania, King Flinders, Bruny	67 800	26 200	501 000 (2000e)
Tierra del Fuego	Argentina/Chile	Pacific			73 700	28 500	78 200 (2000e)
Tristan da Cunha	UK	Atlantic	5	Gough, Inaccessible, Nightingale	100	40	370 (2000e)
Tuamotu	France	Pacific	80	Rangiroa, Hao, Fakarava	800	320	13 500 (2000e)
Tuvalu	Tuvalu	Pacific		Funafuti Atoll, Nanumea	30	10	10 700 (2000e)
Virgin	USA	Caribbean	50+	St Croix, St Thomas	340	130	121 000 (2000e)
Virgin	UK	Caribbean	36	Tortola, Virgin Gorda	150	60	19 600 (2000e)
Zanzibar	Tanzania	Indian	3	Zanzibar, Tumbatu	1 600	640	494 000 (2000e)

na – data not available.

Considerable variation will be found among sources giving area estimates for island groups, because of the difficulty in deciding where the group boundary line should lie.

All estimates above 100 km²/sq mi have been rounded to the nearest 10, and all above 1 000 km²/sq mi to the nearest 100.

Largest seas

Name	Area[a]	
	(km²)	(sq mi)
Coral Sea	4 791 000	1 850 200
Arabian Sea	3 863 000	1 492 000
S China (Nan) Sea	3 685 000	1 423 000
Mediterranean Sea	2 516 000	971 000
Caribbean Sea	2 516 000	971 000
Bering Sea	2 304 000	890 000
Bay of Bengal	2 172 000	839 000
Sea of Okhotsk	1 590 000	614 000
Gulf of Mexico	1 543 000	596 000
Gulf of Guinea	1 533 000	592 000
Barents Sea	1 405 000	542 000
Norwegian Sea	1 383 000	534 000
Gulf of Alaska	1 327 000	512 000
Hudson Bay	1 232 000	476 000
Greenland Sea	1 205 000	465 000
Arafura Sea	1 037 000	400 000
Philippine Sea	1 036 000	400 000
Sea of Japan	978 000	378 000
E Siberian Sea	901 000	348 000
Kara Sea	883 000	341 000
E China Sea	664 000	256 000
Andaman Sea	565 000	218 000
North Sea	520 000	201 000
Black Sea	508 900	196 000
Red Sea	453 000	175 000
Baltic Sea	414 000	160 000
Celebes Sea	280 000	110 000

Oceans are excluded.
[a]Areas are rounded to nearest 1000 km²/sq mi.

Largest islands

Name	Area[a]	
	(km²)	(sq mi)
Greenland	2 175 600	830 780
New Guinea	790 000	305 000
Borneo	737 000	285 000
Madagascar	587 000	227 600
Baffin	507 000	196 000
Sumatra	425 000	164 900
Honshu (Hondo)	228 000	88 000
Great Britain	219 000	84 400
Victoria, Canada	217 300	83 900
Ellesmere, Canada	196 000	75 800
Sulawesi (Celebes)	174 000	67 400
South I, New Zealand	151 000	58 200
Java	129 000	50 000
North I, New Zealand	114 000	44 200
Newfoundland	109 000	42 000
Cuba	110 860	42 790
Luzon	105 000	40 400
Iceland	103 000	40 000
Mindanao	94 600	36 500
Novaya Zemlya (two islands)	90 600	35 000
Ireland	70 280	27 100
Hokkaido	78 500	30 300
Hispaniola	77 200	29 800
Sakhalin	75 100	29 000
Tierra del Fuego	71 200	27 500

[a]Areas are rounded to the nearest three significant digits.

Largest lakes

Name/location	Area[a]	
	(km²)	(sq mi)
Caspian Sea, Iran	371 000	143 240[b]
Superior, USA/Canada	82 260	31 760[c]
Victoria, E Africa	62 940	24 300
Huron, USA/Canada	59 580	23 000[c]
Michigan, USA	58 020	22 400
Tanganyika, E Africa	32 000	12 350
Baikal, Russia	31 500	12 160
Great Bear, Canada	31 330	12 100
Aral Sea, Kazakhstan	30 000	11 580[b]
Great Slave, Canada	28 570	11 030
Erie, USA/Canada	25 710	9920[c]
Winnipeg, Canada	24 390	9420
Malawi/Nyasa, E Africa	22 490	8680
Balkhash, Kazakhstan	18 300	7000[b]
Ontario, Canada/USA	19 270	7440[c]
Ladoga, Russia	18 130	7000
Chad, W Africa	10 000–26 000	4000–10 000
Maracaibo, Venezuela	13 010	5020[d]
Patos, Brazil	10 140	3920[d]
Onega, Russia	9800	3800

[a]Areas given to the nearest 10 km²/sq mi. Caspian & Aral Seas, entirely surrounded by land, are classified as lakes. [b]Salt lakes. [c]Average of areas given by Canada & USA. [d]Salt lagoons.

Pollution is reducing the size of many lakes, notably the Aral Sea, which is now less than half its original size. Lake Chad has shrunk by 95% since 1960s; Lake Balkash shrank by 770 sq mi/1995 sq km in 2003.

Largest deserts

Name/location	Area[a]	
	(km²)	(sq mi)
Sahara, N Africa	8 600 000	3 320 000
Arabian, SW Asia	2 330 000	900 000
Gobi, Mongolia and NE China	1 166 000	450 000
Patagonian, Argentina	673 000	260 000
Great Basin, SW USA	492 000	190 000
Chihuahuan, Mexico	450 000	175 000
Great Sandy, NW Australia	450 000	175 000
Great Victoria, SW Australia	235 000	125 000
Sonoran, SW USA	310 000	120 000
Kyzyl-Kum, Kazakhstan/Uzbekistan	300 000	115 000
Takla Makan, N China	270 000	105 000
Kalahari, SW Africa	260 000	100 000
Kara-Kum, Turkmenistan	260 000	100 000
Kavir, Iran	260 000	100 000
Syrian, Saudi Arabia/Jordan/ Syria/Iraq	260 000	100 000
Nubian, Sudan	260 000	100 000
Thar, India/Pakistan	200 000	77 000
Ust'-Urt, Kazakhstan/Uzbekistan	160 000	62 000
Bet-Pak-Dala, Kazakhstan	155 000	60 000
Simpson, C Australia	145 000	56 000
Dzungaria, China	142 000	55 000
Atacama, Chile	140 000	54 000
Namib, SE Africa	134 000	52 000
Sturt, SE Australia	130 000	50 000
Bolson de Mapimi, Mexico	130 000	50 000
Ordos, China	130 000	50 000
Alashan, China	116 000	45 000

[a]Desert areas are very approximate, because clear physical boundaries may not occur.

Highest mountains

Name	Height[a]		Location
	(m)	(ft)	
Everest	8850	29030	China–Nepal
K2	8610	28250	Kashmir–Jammu
Kangchenjunga	8590	28170	India–Nepal
Lhotse	8500	27890	China–Nepal
Kangchenjunga S Peak	8470	27800	India–Nepal
Makalu I	8470	27800	China–Nepal
Kangchenjunga W Peak	8420	27620	India–Nepal
Llotse E Peak	8380	27500	China–Nepal
Dhaulagiri	8170	26810	Nepal
Cho Oyu	8150	26750	China–Nepal
Manaslu	8130	26660	Nepal
Nanga Parbat	8130	26660	Kashmir–Jammu
Annapurna I	8080	26500	Nepal
Gasherbrum I	8070	26470	Kashmir–Jammu
Broad-highest	8050	26400	Kashmir–Jammu
Gasherbrum II	8030	26360	Kashmir–Jammu
Gosainthan	8010	26290	China
Broad-middle	8000	26250	Kashmir–Jammu
Gasherbrum III	7950	26090	Kashmir–Jammu
Annapurna II	7940	26040	Nepal
Nanda Devi	7820	25660	India
Rakaposhi	7790	25560	Kashmir
Kamet	7760	25450	India
Ulugh Muztagh	7720	25340	Tibet
Tirich Mir	7690	25230	Pakistan
Muz Tag Ata	7550	24760	China
Communism Peak	7490	24590	Tajikistan
Pobedy Peak	7440	24410	China–Kyrgyzstan
Aconcagua	6960	22830	Argentina
Ojos del Salado	6910	22660	Argentina–Chile

[a]Heights are given to the nearest 10 m/ft.

Highest waterfalls

Name	Height[a]		Location
	(m)	(ft)	
Angel (upper fall)	807	2648	Venezuela
Itatinga	628	2060	Brazil
Cuquenan	610	2000	Guyana–Venezuela
Ormeli	563	1847	Norway
Tysse	533	1749	Norway
Pilao	524	1719	Brazil
Ribbon	491	1612	USA
Vestre Mardola	468	1535	Norway
Roraima	457?	1500?	Guyana
Cleve-Garth	450?	1476?	New Zealand

[a]Distances are given for individual leaps.

Deepest caves

Name/location	Depth	
	(m)	(ft)
Jean Bernard, France	1494	4900
Snezhnaya, Russia	1340	4397
Puertas de Illamina, Spain	1338	4390
Pierre-Saint-Martin, France	1321	4334
Sistema Huautla, Mexico	1240	4067
Berger, France	1198	3930
Vqerdi, Spain	1195	3921
Dachstein-Mammuthöhle, Austria	1174	3852
Zitu, Spain	1139	3737
Badalona, Spain	1130	3707
Batmanhöhle, Austria	1105	3626
Schneeloch, Austria	1101	3612
GES Malaga, Spain	1070	3510
Lamprechtsofen, Austria	1024	3360

Longest rivers

Name	Outflow	Length[a]	
		(km)	(mi)
Nile-Kagera-Ruvuvu-Ruvusu-Luvironza	Mediterranean Sea (Egypt)	6690	4160
Amazon-Ucayali-Tambo-Ene-Apurimac	Atlantic Ocean (Brazil)	6570	4080
Mississippi-Missouri-Jefferson-Beaverhead-Red Rock	Gulf of Mexico (USA)	6020	3740
Chang Jiang (Yangtze)	E China Sea (China)	5980	3720
Yenisey-Angara-Selenga-Ider	Kara Sea (Russia)	5870	3650
Amur-Argun-Kerulen	Tartar Strait (Russia)	5780	3590
Ob-Irtysh	Gulf of Ob, Kara Sea (Russia)	5410	3360
Plata-Parana-Grande	Atlantic Ocean (Argentina–Uruguay)	4880	3030
Huang He (Yellow)	Yellow Sea (China)	4840	3010
Congo (Zaire)-Lualaba	Atlantic Ocean (Angola–Democratic Republic of Congo)	4630	2880
Lena	Laptev Sea (Russia)	4400	2730
Mackenzie-Slave-Peace-Finlay	Beaufort Sea (Canada)	4240	2630
Mekong	S China Sea (Vietnam)	4180	2600
Niger	Gulf of Guinea (Nigeria)	4100	2550

[a]Lengths are given to the nearest 10 km/mi, and include the river plus tributaries comprising the longest watercourse.

National Parks in England and Wales

Name (Date of designation)	Location	Area	
		(km²)	(sq mi)
Brecon Beacons (1957)	Powys, Dyfed, Gwent, Mid Glamorgan	1351	522
Dartmoor (1951)	Devon	954	368
Exmoor (1954)	Somerset, Devon	693	268
Lake District (1951)	Cumbria	2292	885
New Forest (2005)	S Hampshire	571	220
Northumberland (1956)	Northumberland	1049	405
North York Moors (1952)	North Yorkshire, Cleveland	1436	554
Peak District (1951)	Derbyshire, Staffordshire, South Yorkshire, Cheshire, West Yorkshire, Greater Manchester	1438	555
Pembrokeshire Coast (1952)	Dyfed	584	225
Snowdonia (1951)	Gwynedd	2142	817
The Broads³ (1988)	Norfolk and Suffolk	303	117
Yorkshire Dales (1954)	N Yorkshire, Cumbria	1769	683

³Does not bear the title National Park but is part of the Association of National Park Authorities.

National Parks in Scotland

Name (Date of designation)	Location	Area	
		(km²)	(sq mi)
Loch Lomond and the Trossachs (2002)	W Central Scotland	1600	618
Cairngorms (2003)	NE Central Scotland	4000	1544

National Parks in the USA

Park (Date authorized)	Location	Area	
		(ha)	(ac)
Acadia (1916)	SE Maine	15 770	38 971
American Samoa (1988)	American Samoa	3 642	9 000
Arches (1929)	E Utah	29 695	73 379
Badlands (1929)	SW South Dakota	98 461	243 302
Big Bend (1935)	W Texas	286 565	708 118
Biscayne (1968)	SE Florida	72 900	180 128
Bryce Canyon (1923)	SW Utah	14 502	35 835
Canyonlands (1964)	SE Utah	136 610	337 570
Capitol Reef (1937)	S Utah	97 895	214 904
Carlsbad Caverns (1923)	SE New Mexico	18 921	46 755
Channel Islands (1938)	S California	100 910	249 354
Crater Lake (1902)	SW Oregon	64 869	160 290
Death Valley (1994)	California, Nevada	1 362 879	3 367 627
Denali (1917)	S Alaska	1 645 240	4 065 493
Dry Tortugas (1992)	Florida	26 184	64 700
Everglades (1934)	S Florida	566 075	1 398 800
Gates of the Arctic (1978)	N Alaska	2 854 000	7 052 000
Glacier (1910)	NW Montana	410 188	1 013 595
Glacier Bay (1925)	SE Alaska	1 569 481	3 878 269
Grand Canyon (1908)	NW Arizona	493 059	1 218 375
Grand Teton (1929)	NW Wyoming	125 661	310 516
Great Basin (1986)	E Nevada	31 206	77 109
Great Smoky Mountains (1926)	SW North Carolina, SE Tennessee	210 550	520 269
Guadalupe Mountains (1966)	W Texas	30 875	76 293
Haleakala (1916)	Maui Is, Hawaii	11 956	28 655
Hawaii Volcanoes (1916)	Hawaii Is, Hawaii	92 745	229 177
Hot Springs (1832)	C Arkansas	2 358	5 826
Isle Royale (1931)	NW Michigan	231 398	571 796
Joshua Tree (1994)	California	320 825	792 749
Katmai (1918)	SW Alaska	1 792 810	4 430 125
Kenai Fjords (1978)	S Alaska	229 457	567 000

National Parks in the USA (continued)

Park (Date authorized)	Location	Area	
		(ha)	(ac)
Kobuk Valley (1978)	N Alaska	692 000	1 710 000
Lake Clark (1978)	S Alaska	987 000	2 439 000
Lassen Volcanic (1907)	N California	43 047	106 372
Mammoth Cave (1926)	C Kentucky	21 230	52 452
Mesa Verde (1906)	SW Colorado	21 078	52 085
Mount Rainier (1899)	SW Washington	95 265	235 404
North Cascades (1968)	N Washington	204 277	504 781
Olympic (1909)	NW Washington	370 250	914 890
Petrified Forest (1906)	E Arizona	37 835	93 493
Redwood (1968)	NW California	44 280	109 415
Rocky Mountain (1915)	C Colorado	106 762	263 809
Saguaro (1994)	Arizona	36 875	91 116
Sequoia and Kings Canyon (1890, 1940)	E California	349 539	863 700
Shenandoah (1926)	N Virginia	78 845	194 826
Theodore Roosevelt (1947)	W North Dakota	28 497	70 416
Virgin Islands (1956)	St John, Virgin Islands	5 947	14 695
Voyageurs (1971)	N Minnesota	88 678	219 128
Wind Cave (1903)	SW South Dakota	11 449	28 292
Wrangell-St Elias (1978)	SE Alaska	3 297 000	8 147 000
Yellowstone (1872)	Idaho, Montana, Wyoming	898 350	2 219 823
Yosemite (1890)	E California	307 932	760 917
Zion (1909)	SW Utah	59 308	146 551

PART THREE

The Environment

CLIMATE

The climate system

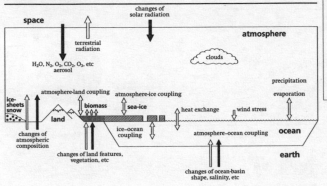

Schematic illustration of the climate system components and interactions (from Houghton, J.T. (ed), 1984, *The Global Climate*; Cambridge University Press).

Climate alterations produced by cities

Element	Compared to rural environs	Element	Compared to rural environs
Contaminants		**Snowfall: inner city**	5–10% less
Condensation nuclei	10 times more	Snowfall: lee of city	10% more
Particulates	10 times more	Thunderstorms	10–15% more
Gaseous admixtures	5–25 times more		
		Temperature	
Radiation		Annual mean	0.5–30°C/0.9–54°F more
Total on horizontal surface	0–20% less	Winter minimums (average)	1–2°C/1.8–3.6°F more
Ultraviolet: winter	30% less	Summer maximums	1–3°C/1.8–5.4°F more
Ultraviolet: summer	5% less	Heating degree days	10% less
Sunshine duration	5–15% less		
		Relative humidity	
Cloudiness		Annual mean	6% less
Clouds	5–10% more	Winter	2% less
Fog: winter	100% more	Summer	8% less
Fog: summer	30% more		
		Wind speed	
Precipitation		Annual mean	20–30% less
Amounts	5–15% more	Extreme gusts	10–20% less
Days with less than 5 mm/0.2 in	10% more	Calm	5–20% more

THE ENVIRONMENT

The greenhouse effect

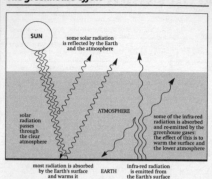

- SUN
- some solar radiation is reflected by the Earth and the atmosphere
- ATMOSPHERE
- solar radiation passes through the clear atmosphere
- some of the infra-red radiation is absorbed and re-emitted by the greenhouse gases: the effect of this is to warm the surface and the lower atmosphere
- most radiation is absorbed by the Earth's surface and warms it
- EARTH
- infra-red radiation is emitted from the Earth's surface

Greenhouse gases

The share of greenhouse warming due to different greenhouse gases. The contribution from ozone may also be significant, but cannot be quantified at present.

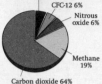

- Other halocarbons 5%
- CFC-12 6%
- Nitrous oxide 6%
- Methane 19%
- Carbon dioxide 64%

Source: World Resources Institute, 1998.

POLLUTION

Pollutants and the ecosystem

Pathways of pollutants and other substances in ecosystems.

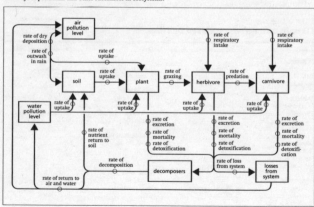

THE ENVIRONMENT

RECENT ENVIRONMENTAL DISASTERS

Date	Event	Location	Consequence
1970	Collision of the tanker *Othello*	Tralhavet Bay, Sweden	17 640 000–29 400 000 gallons of oil spilled.
1971	Overflow of water storage space at Northern States Power Company's reactor	Monticello, Minnesota, USA	50 000 gallons of radioactive waste dumped into Mississippi River. Contamination of St Paul water system.
1972	Collision of the tanker *Sea Star*	Gulf of Oman	33 810 000 gallons of oil spilled.
1974	Explosion of container of cyclohexane	Flixborough, UK	28 deaths.
1975	Fire at Brown's Ferry reactor	Decatur, Alabama, USA	$100 million damage. Cooling water level lowered significantly.
1976	Leak of toxic gas TCDD	Seveso, Italy	Topsoil had to be removed in worst contaminated areas.
1976	Grounding of the supertanker *Urquiola*	La Coruña, Spain	Spillage of 29 400 000 gallons of oil.
1977	Well blow-out at Ecofisk oil field	North Sea	Spillage of 8 200 000 gallons of oil.
1977	Fire on the *Hawaiian Patriot*	Northern Pacific	Spillage of 29 106 000 gallons of oil.
1978	Grounding of the Cyprus tanker *Amoco Cadiz*	Portsall, France	Spillage of 65 562 000 gallons of oil. Pollution of 160 km/99 mi of French coast.
1979	Uranium released from secret nuclear fuel plant	Erwin, Tennessee, USA	Approximately 1 000 people contaminated.
1979	Collision of *Burmah Agate*	Galveston Bay, Texas	Spillage of 10 700 000 gallons of oil.
1979	Release of radioactive steam after water pump breaks down	Three Mile Island, Pennsylvania, USA	Pollution by radioactive gases. Partial core meltdown in reactor.
1979	Blowout in Ixtoc oil well	Gulf of Mexico	176 400 000 gallons of oil spilled.
1979	Collision of the *Atlantic Empress* and *Aegean Captain*	Trinidad and Tobago	88 200 000 gallons of oil spilled.
1980	Chemical spill due to Sandoz factory fire	Basel, Switzerland	Rhine polluted for 200 km/124 mi.
1983	Blow-out in Nowruz oil field	Persian Gulf	Spillage of 176 400 000 gallons of oil.
1984	Union Carbide pesticide plant leaks toxic gas	Bhopal, India	Death of 2 352 people officially. Unofficially, an estimated 10 000 died.
1986	Explosion of nuclear reactor	Chernobyl, Ukraine	Official death toll 50. Radioactive cloud spread across Europe contaminating farmland. Long-term effects on inhabitants of surrounding areas.
1987	Abandoned radiotherapy unit containing radioactive material leaks	Goiana, Brazil	Radioactive contamination affected 249 people.
1988	Accident at water-treatment works resulting in aluminium sulphate being flushed into local rivers	Camelford, Cornwall, UK	Local people suffer from stomach and skin disorders. Thousands of fish killed.
1989	Grounding of the tanker *Exxon Valdez* on Bligh Reef	Prince William Sound, Alaska, USA	Spillage of 10 080 000 gallons of oil; 1 170 km/1 162 mi of Alaskan coastline polluted. More than 3 600 km²/1 390 sq mi contaminated. Thousands of birds and animals killed.
1991	Break-up of the Greek tanker *Kiriki*	Cervantes, W Australia	Spillage of 5 880 000 gallons of crude oil and pollution of conservation and fishing areas.
1991	Oil fields set alight by Iraqi forces during the Gulf War	Kuwait	Spillage estimated between 25 000 000–130 000 000 gallons. Air pollution and potential increase in acid rain.
1992	Grounding of the Greek oil tanker *Aegean Sea*, with subsequent fire	La Coruña, Spain	Spillage of an estimated 16 000 000 gallons of crude oil, creating a slick 19 km/12 mi long and 2 km/1 mi wide and causing contamination of 80 km/50 mi of Spanish coastline. Serious pollution of sealife and clam and oyster fisheries.
1993	Break-up of the tanker *Braer* on the rocks of Fitful Head	Shetland, Scotland, UK	Spillage of 26 000 000 gallons of oil. Slick contained to 180–270 m/200–300 yd, but serious pollution of fishing grounds and fish farms, as well as sea animals and birds.

THE ENVIRONMENT

Date	Event	Location	Consequence
1994	Rupture of oil pipeline	Usinsk, Russia	Spillage of 4 300 000 gallons of oil, causing extensive pollution of surrounding Arctic habitat.
1996	Cargo Freighter *North Cape* ran aground	Block Island Sound, off Rhode Island	Spillage of 820 000 gallons of home heating oil.
1996	Oil tanker *Sea Empress* grounded on rocks	Milford Haven, Wales, UK	Spillage of 73 450 tonnes of oil causing long-term environmental and socio-economic effects.
1997	Super-tanker *Diamond Grace* runs against reef	Tokyo Bay	Spillage of 13 400 tons of crude oil. Many people taken ill from fumes.
1998	Waste spill at Aznalcóllar mineral plant	Southern Spain	Toxic waste poisons thousands of hectares of farmland and threatens Doñana National Park.
2000	Waste spill at Baia-Mare mine	Romania	Spillage of 100 tonnes of cyanide into rivers in Romania and Hungary.
2002	Blazing bushfires	Arizona, USA	Wildlife devastated; 30 000 people forced from their homes.
2002	Sinking of tanker *Prestige*	NW Spain	Spillage of at least 3 million gallons of fuel oil, before the vessel split and sank, taking rest of its 20-million-gallon cargo to the sea-bed; over 400 km/250 mi of coastline polluted.
2002	Collision of freighter *Tricolor* with container ship	English Channel	Sank with cargo of 3000 cars; became hazard to shipping; oil spillage.
2003	Blazing forest fires	S and C Portugal	Crops and livestock lost, massive soil erosion; many homes lost.
2004	Blazing forest fires	S Portugal and S Spain	Thousands of hectares destroyed.
2004	Fire at Iraq chemical plant	Nr Mosul, Iraq	Largest recorded man-made release of sulphur dioxide (600 000 tonnes). US$40 million of damage to local crops; respiratory problems in local people.

PART FOUR

Natural History

CLASSIFICATION OF LIVING ORGANISMS

It has been estimated that between 3 million and 20 million different kinds of organism are alive in the world today. Large numbers of other organisms have become extinct, and some of these are preserved as fossils. Most modern schemes of classification of living organisms are based upon the pioneering work of the Swedish biologist Carl von Linné (in Latin, Carolus Linnaeus; 1707–78), who established the practice of *binomial nomenclature*, by which all organisms are given two names, traditionally printed in italics. The first name is that of the *genus*, and is common to a group of closely related organisms. The second is that of the *species* and is unique to a particular type of organism. Higher levels of classification show a hierarchy of relationships. These are illustrated here using the human species as an example.

Classification of the human species

Taxonomic level

Kingdom	Animalia	(animals)
Phylum (division)[a]	Chordata	(chordates)
Subphylum	Vertebrata	(vertebrates)
Class	Mammalia	(mammals)
Order	Primates	
Family	Hominida	(hominids)
Genus	*Homo*	
Species	*sapiens*	

[a] In classifying plants, fungi and bacteria, the term *division* is used rather than *phylum*.

The five kingdoms

While almost all modern systems of classification use the same basic taxonomic system, there are several different ways of grouping living organisms together. This book uses the popular Whittaker system, which divides the living world into five kingdoms.

Kingdom	Members of kingdom
Prokaryotae*	Monera, or bacteria
Protoctista	Algae, protozoans, slime moulds
Fungi	Mushrooms, moulds, lichens
Animalia	Animals
Plantae	Plants

* The kingdom Prokaryotae is sometimes given to include the viruses. Other systems describe viruses as being outside normal systems of classification.

ANIMALS

The animal kingdom is usually divided into about 30 phyla, which differ enormously in size and are listed here in order of primitive to advanced.

Classification of animals

Phylum	Common name/examples	No. of species	Comments
Placozoa	*Trichoplax adhaerens*	1	The only species in the phylum, this is the simplest animal known. No tissues, organs, or symmetry.
Porifera	Sponges	10 000	All aquatic; vast majority in sea-water, 150 in fresh water. No tissues, organs, or symmetry.
Cnidaria	Coelenterates; *Hydra*; true jellyfish; corals; sea anemones	9 500	Nearly all marine. Radially symmetrical with tissues and organs; have stinging cells (nematocysts) on tentacles.
Ctenophora	Comb jellies; sea gooseberries	90	Aquatic; transparent.
Mesozoa	Mesozoans	50	Small, worm-like organisms.
Platyhelminthes	Flatworms; flukes; tapeworms	15 000	Ribbon-shaped and soft-bodied; the least complex of the animals that have heads.
Nemertina	Ribbon worms or proboscis worms	900	Characteristic feature is long, sensitive anterior proboscis, used to explore the environment and capture prey.
Gnasthostomulida	Jaw worms or gnasthostomulids	80	Microscopic marine worms.
Gastrotricha	Gastrotrichs	400	Aquatic microscopic animals with cilia on their bodies.

Classification of animals (continued)

Phylum	Common name/examples	No. of species	Comments
Rotifera	Rotifers or wheel animals	2 000	Aquatic microscopic animals with their anterior end modified into a ciliary organ called a *corona*, the beating of which resembles a rotating wheel.
Kinorhyncha	Kinorhynchs	150	Small worm-like marine animals.
Loricifera	Loriciferans	10	Tiny marine animals whose abdomen is covered by a girdle of spiny plates called a *lorica*.
Acanthocephala	Spiny-headed worms	600	Gut parasites of vertebrates, usually of carnivores.
Entoprocta	Entoprocts	150	Small marine animals, mostly sedentary, living in colonies attached to rocks, shells, algae, or other animals.
Nematoda	Nematodes or roundworms	>80 000	Unsegmented, more or less cylindrical worms which occur free-living in all types of environment, and also as parasites of plants and animals. It has been estimated that there may be as many as 1 million species of nematode in the world (ie vast numbers of undiscovered species). In terms of numbers of individuals, nematodes are the most abundant group of multicellular animals.
Nematomorpha	Horsehair worms; hair-worms; Gordian worms	240	Very long, thin worms which are parasitic in insects and crustaceans as juveniles, and free-living in water as adults.
Ectoprocta	Ectoprocts	5 000	Small aquatic animals, mostly colonial.
Phoronida	Horseshoe worms; phoronids	10	Marine worms with as many as 1 500 hollow tentacles. Live in tubes which they secrete and strengthen with sand or shell fragments.
Brachiopoda	Lamp shells	335	Bottom-living marine animals with shells with two valves. They thrived during the Palaeozoic era – more than 30 000 extinct species have been described.
Mollusca	Molluscs, including snails, slugs (gastropods), clams, mussels, oysters (bivalves), octopus, squid (cephalopoda)	110 000	The second largest phylum of animals, molluscs live in aquatic or moist environments, are soft-bodied, and are usually protected by a calcareous shell which is secreted by a fold of the body wall called the *mantle*.
Priapulida	Priapulids	10	Small carnivorous marine worms.
Sipuncula	Peanut worms	>300	Unsegmented marine worms, which live in crevices or are burrowing.
Echiura	Spoon worms	140	Unsegmented marine worms, which burrow in marine deposits.
Annelida	Annelids, including earthworms, leeches, ragworms	8 900	Worms with a well-developed coelom, and with the body divided up into a number of more or less similar segments. Terrestrial, freshwater, or marine.
Tardigrada	Water bears; tardigrades	380	Minute animals which live in films of water around mosses and other low terrestrial features. Four pairs of stubby legs armed with terminal claws.

Phylum	Common name/examples	No. of species	Comments
Pentastoma	Tongue worms	70	Parasitic worms in the respiratory passages of air-breathing vertebrates. They have a chitinous cuticle which is periodically moulted to allow growth.
Onychophora	Velvet worms; onychophorans	80	Soft-bodied, segmented animals with many paired but unjointed legs. Confined to humid tropics.
Arthropoda	Arthropods, including crustaceans (shrimps, barnacles, woodlice, crabs), scorpions, mites, ticks, spiders, insects, centipedes, millipedes	>2 000 000	By far the largest animal phylum, with more species than all the other phyla combined (more than 800 000 species of insects alone have been described; some zoologists think there may be as many as 10 million). Arthropods are segmented animals with paired, jointed appendages on some or all of their body segments.
Pogonophora	Beard worms	100	Extremely slender, gutless, tube-living marine worms.
Echinodermata	Echinoderms, including starfish, sea urchins, sea cucumbers	6 000	Marine, mostly bottom-dwelling animals, usually displaying five-fold symmetry. The fluid-filled tube feet are used for locomotion and feeding.
Chaetognatha	Arrow worms	>100	Small, slender, torpedo-shaped marine planktonic animals which are voracious carnivores.
Hemichordata	Hemichordates	90	Small soft-bodied animals which inhabit shallow U-shaped burrows in sandy or muddy sea bottoms.
Chordata	Mammals; birds; amphibians; reptiles; fish; plus a small number of invertebrates	45 000	The best known phylum of Animalia, containing all the species which, in the minds of many, are considered 'animals'. Chordates are distinguished by having (i) the walls of their pharynx, at some stage in their life cycle, perforated by gill clefts; (ii) a hollow dorsal nerve cord; (iii) an axial cartilaginous rod – the *notochord* – lying immediately beneath the nerve cord. Most chordates have backbones and are called *vertebrates*, but two of the three subphyla are small *invertebrate* groups.

Animal records

Size

This table shows the largest species in the animal kingdom, plus some others of particular interest. Unless otherwise stated: (i) *largest* means bulkiest and heaviest; (ii) the size given is the largest size regularly attained by the species, not that of individual 'record-holders'.

	Species	Dimension	Size (m)	Size (ft)	Comments
Mammals					
Cetacea	Blue whale *(Balaenoptera musculis)*	Length	35.0	115	The largest and longest-living mammal, and the largest animal ever known.
	Sperm whale *(Physeter catadon)*	Length	25.0	82	The largest-toothed mammal and the largest marine carnivore[a].
Marine carnivores	Sperm whale (see above)				
	Southern elephant seal *(Mirounga leonina)*	Length	6.0	20	The largest seal.

Animal records (continued)

NATURAL HISTORY

	Species	Dimension	Size (m)	Size (ft)	Comments
Ungulates	African elephant (*Loxodonta africana*)	Height	3.2	10.5	The largest land mammal.
	Giraffe (*Giraffa camelopardalis*)	Height	5.5	18.0	The tallest land mammal.
Terrestrial carnivores	Kodiak bear (*Ursus arctos middendorffi*)	Length	2.4	7.8	The largest land carnivore.
	Indian tiger (*Panthera tigris tigris*)	Length	3.15	10.3	The largest member of the cat family.
Primates	Eastern lowland mountain gorilla (*Gorilla gorilla graueri*)	Height (standing)	1.88	6.2	The largest and tallest primate[b].
Rodents	Capybara (*Hydrochoerus hydrochoerus*)	Length	1.4	4.6	The largest rodent.
	Coypu (*Myocastor coypus*)	Length	0.9	2.9	
Marsupials	Red kangaroo (*Megaleia rufa*)	Height	2.15	7.1	The largest marsupial.
Birds	Ostrich (*Struthio camelus*)	Height	2.75	9.0	The largest and tallest bird.
Reptiles	Estuarine or saltwater crocodile (*Crocodylus porosus*)	Length	4.8	15.7	The largest reptile.
Snakes	Anaconda (*Eunectes murinus*)	Length	8.5	27.8	The largest snake.
	Reticulated python (*Python reticulatus*)	Length	10.0	32.8	The longest snake.
Lizards	Komodo monitor (*Varanus komodoensis*)	Length	2.25	7.4	The largest lizard.
	Salvadori monitor (*Varanus salvadori*)	Length	4.75	15.6	The longest lizard.
Amphibians	Giant salamander (*Andrias davidianus*)	Length	1.2	3.9	The largest amphibian.
Fishes					
Marine	Whale shark (*Rhincodon typus*)	Length	13.0	43.0	The largest marine fish.
Freshwater	Sturgeon (*Acipenseridae* spp.)	Length	5.0	16.4	The largest freshwater fish.
	European catfish (*Siluridae* spp.)	Length	4.0	13.1	
Molluscs	Atlantic giant squid (*Architeuthis dux*)	length	17.0	56.0	The largest mollusc and the largest invertebrate.
	Pacific giant octopus (*Octopus dofleini*)	length	10.0	32.8	
Crustaceans					
Marine	Giant spider crab (*Macrocheira kaempferi*)	Claw span	2.7	8.8	The largest crustacean.
	North Atlantic lobster (*Homarus americanus*)	Length	1.06	3.5	The heaviest crustacean.
Freshwater	Crayfish (*Astacopsis gouldi*)	Length	0.6	1.9	The largest freshwater crustacean.
Worms	Bootlace worm (*Lineus longissimus*)	Length	40.0	131.0	The longest worm.
Jellyfish	Arctic giant (*Cyanae capillata arctica*)	Diameter	2.2	7.2	The largest jellyfish.
		Length of tentacles	35.0	115.0	
Insects	Goliath beetle (*Scarabaeidae* spp.)	Length	0.11	0.4	The largest insect.
	Queen Alexandra's birdwing (*Ornithoptera alexandrae*)	Wing-span	0.28	0.9	The largest butterfly.
Spiders	Goliath bird-eating spider (*Theraphosa leblondi*)	Leg-span	0.25	0.8	The largest spider.

[a] Discounting the filter-feeding baleen whales (eg the blue whale) which feed on small crustaceans such as krill.

[b] Humans (*Homo sapiens*) regularly exceed this height. In fact, the tallest recorded human, Robert Pershing Wadlow (1918-40), who measured 2.72 m/8.9 ft at his death, is probably the tallest ever primate.

spp. = species

Weight

	tonnes
Blue whale	120
Sperm whale	50
Right whale	50
Whale shark	43
Basking shark	40
African elephant	6
White shark	5
Elephant seal	4
Hippopotamus	3
Manta ray	3
White rhinoceros	2
Moonfish	2
Saltwater crocodile	1.5
American bison	1.5
Leatherback turtle	0.8
Kodiak bear	0.74
Gorilla	0.35
Anaconda	0.23

Speed in the air

	km/h	mph
Mammals		
Bat	20–50	12–30
Birds		
Diving		
Peregrine falcon	350	217
Golden eagle	300	185

	km/h	mph
Horizontal flight		
Peregrine falcon	200	124
Teal	120	75
Oystercatcher	100	60
Swan	90	55
Duck	85	53
Partridge	84	52
Pheasant	60	35
Crane	50	30
Gull	40	25
Crow	40	25
Fish		
Flying fish	90	55
Insects		
Dragonfly	75	45
Hawkmoth	50	30
Hoverfly	14	9
Bumblebee	11	7

Speed in water

	km/h	mph
Mammals		
Dolphin	64	40
Killer whale	55	34
Sea lion	40	25
Birds		
Penguin	40	25
Reptiles		
Leatherback turtle	35	22

	km/h	mph
Fish		
Sailfish	110	68
Swordfish	90	55
Blue shark	70	44
Tuna	70	44
Salmon	40	25
Trout	37	23
Pike	33	20

Speed on the ground

	km/h	mph
Mammals		
Cheetah	110	68
Roe deer	98	61
Antelope	95	59
Lion	80	50
Red deer	78	48
Hare	70	44
Horse	69	43
Zebra	65	40
Greyhound	60	35
Giraffe	50	30
Wolf	45	28
Elephant	40	25
Birds		
Ostrich	50	30
Reptiles		
Crocodile	13	8
Mamba	11	7

Mammals

Order	Family	Common name/examples	No. of species	Distribution of order	General characteristics of order
Monotremes	Ornithorhynchidae	Platypus	1	Australia	Lay eggs from which young are hatched.
	Tachyglossidae	Echidna (spiny anteater)	2		
Marsupialia	Didelphidae	Opossums	65	Australia, S and C America	Premature birth of young and continued development outside the womb.
	Thylacinidae	Tasmanian wolf	1		
	Dasyuridae	Native cats; marsupial mice	48		
	Myrmecobiidae	Numbat	1		
	Notoryctidae	Marsupial moles	2		
	Peramelidae	Bandicoots	22		
	Thylacomyidae	Burrowing bandicoots	20		
	Caenolestidae	Rat opossums	7		
	Phalangeridae	Phalangers; cuscuses	15		
	Burramyidae	Pigmy possums; feathertail gliders	6		
	Petauridae	Gliding phalangers	25		
	Macropodidae	Kangaroos; wallabies	47		
	Phascolarctidae	Koala	1		
	Vombatidae	Wombats	4		
	Tarsipedidae	Honey possum	1		
Insectivora	Erinaceidae	Hedgehogs; gymnures	14	Europe, N and S America, Asia, Australia	Active mainly at night; do not need to rely on vision for orientation.
	Talpidae	Moles	22		
	Tenrecidae	Tenrecs	20		
	Potamogalidae	Otter shrews	3		
	Chrysochloridae	Golden moles	11		

NATURAL HISTORY

Mammals (continued)

Order	Family	Common name/examples	No. of species	Distribution of order	General characteristics of order
	Solenodontidae	Solenodon, almiqui	2		
	Soricidae	Shrews	291		
	Macroscelididae	Elephant shrews	28		
	Tupaiidae	Tree shrews	15		
Chiroptera	Pteropodidae	Old World fruit bats; flying foxes	154	Europe, N and S America, Asia, Africa, Australia	Insectivorous; nocturnal; migrate annually to and from summer roosts and winter migration sites; use echolocation for orientation; order defined by true flight.
	Rhinopomatidae	Mouse-tailed bats	3		
	Emballonuridae	Sheath-tailed or sac-winged bats	50		
	Nycteridae	Slit-faced or hollow-faced bats	13		
	Megadermatidae	False vampires	5		
	Hipposideridae	Old World leaf-nosed bats	60		
	Rhinolophidae	Horseshoe bats	70		
	Noctilionidae	Bulldog bats	2		
	Mormoopidae	Insectivorous bats	9		
	Phyllostomatidae	American leaf-nosed bats	120		
	Desmodontidae	Vampire bats	3		
	Natalidae	Funnel-eared bats	4		
	Furipteridae	Smoky bats	2		
	Thyropteridae	Disk-wing bats	2		
	Myzopodidae	Old World sucker-footed bats	1		
	Vespertilionidae	Common bats	290		
	Mystacinidae	New Zealand short-tailed bats	1		
	Molossidae	Free-tailed bats	90		
Rodentia	Aplodontidae	Mountain beaver or sewellel	1	Europe, Asia, N and S America, Africa, Australia	One pair of upper and lower incisors which grow throughout life; broadly herbivorous; gnawing mechanism; clawed digits.
	Sciuridae	Squirrels; chipmunks; marmots	250		
	Cricetidae	Field mice; deer mice; voles; lemmings; muskrats	560		
	Muridae	Old World rats and mice	450		
	Heteromyidae	Mice; pocket mice; kangaroo rats	75		
	Geomyidae	Pocket gophers	40		
	Zapodidae	Jumping and birch mice	10		
	Dipodidae	Jerboas	25		
	Spalacidae	Mole rats	3		
	Rhizomyidae	Bamboo rats; African mole rats	18		
	Octodontidae	Octodonts; degus	7		
	Echimyidae	Spiny rats; rock rats	40		
	Ctenomyidae	Tuco-tucos	26		
	Abrocomidae	Abrocomes or chinchilla rats	2		
	Chinchillidae	Chinchillas; viscachas	6		
	Capromyidae	Hutias; coypus	10		
	Dasyproctidae	Pacas; agoutis	13		
	Dinomyidae	Pacarana or Branick's paca	1		
	Caviidae	Cavies; guinea pigs; maras	12		
	Hydrochoeridae	Capybaras	2		
	Erethizontidae	New World porcupines	8		
	Petromuridae	Rock or dassie rat	1		
	Thryonomyidae	Cane rats	2		
	Bathyergidae	Blesmols or African mole rats	9		
	Hystricidae	Old World porcupines	15		
	Castoridae	Beavers	2		
	Anomaluridae	Scaly-tailed squirrels	7		
	Ctenodactylidae	Gundis	8		
	Pedetidae	Cape jumping hare or springhaas	1		
	Gliridae	Dormice	20		
	Seleveniidae	Jumping dormouse	1		

Order	Family	Common name/examples	No. of species	Distribution of order	General characteristics of order
Edentata	Myrmecophagidae	Anteaters	3	S and N America	Reduced dentition; long sticky tongue; powerful clawed forefeet.
	Bradypodidae	Tree sloths	5		
	Dasypodidae	Armadillos	20		
Lagomorpha	Ochotonidae	Pikas	14	Asia, N America, Europe, S Africa, S America, Australia	Herbivorous; well-developed incisors which grow continuously from roots; elongation of the limbs distally.
	Leporidae	Hares; rabbits	46		
Carnivora	Canidae	Dogs; foxes; wolves; jackals	35	Europe, Asia, N America, S America, Africa, Australia	High level of intelligence; highly developed sense of smell; varied dentition; well-developed carnassials.
	Ursidae	Bears; giant panda	7		
	Otariidae	Eared seals; walrus	15		
	Procyonidae	Raccoons; coatis; lesser panda	15		
	Mustelidae	Weasels; otters; skunks; badgers; mink	65		
	Phocidae	Earless seals	20		
	Felidae	Cats	35		
	Viverridae	Civets; mongooses; genet	70		
	Hyaenidae	Hyenas	4		
Cetacea	Balaenidae	Right whales	3	S America, Africa, N America, Europe, Asia, Antarctica, Australia	Breathe through blowholes; tapered body; develop young internally and give birth at sea; long breeding period; hearing is major sense; migrate seasonally.
	Eschrichtiidae	Grey whales	1		
	Balaenopteridae	Rorquals; humpbacks	8		
	Platanistidae	River dolphins	4		
	Delphinidae	Dolphins; killer whales	30		
	Phocoenidae	Porpoises	6		
	Monodontidae	Beluga; narwhal	2		
	Physeteridae	Sperm whales	3		
	Hyperoodontidae (formerly Ziphiidae)	Beaked whales	15		
	Stenidae	Long-snouted dolphins	4		
Proboscidea	Elephantidae	African elephant, Asian elephant	2	Africa, Asia	Bulky bodies and elongated snout; each toe has heavy hoof nail; no canine teeth; herbivorous.
Sirenia	Dugongidae	Dugong	1	Australia, S America, Africa	Herbivorous; totally aquatic; torpedo-shaped bodies; tough, almost hairless skin; body contains much fat.
	Trichechidae	Manatees	3		
Perissodactyla	Equidae	Horses; asses; zebras; donkeys	7	Africa, Europe, Asia	Herbivorous; high-crowned grinding teeth.
	Tapiridae	Tapirs	4		
	Rhinocerotidae	Rhinoceroses	5		
Artiodactyla	Tragulidae	Chevrotains	4	Asia, Africa, C and S America	Ruminants; herbivorous; cloven-hoofed; moderately large brain; migrate seasonally.
	Antilocapridae	Pronghorn	1		
	Giraffidae	Giraffe; okapi	2		
	Cervidae	Deer	35		
	Bovidae	Cattle; goats; sheep; antelopes; gazelles	110		
	Camelidae	Camels; llamas	4		
	Suidae	Pigs	8		
	Tayassuidae	Peccaries	3		
	Hippopotamidae	Hippopotamuses	2		
Tubulidentata	Orycteropodidae	Aardvark	1	S Africa	Long, tapering tail used for burrowing; tubular snout; sticky tongue; rootless teeth.

NATURAL HISTORY

Mammals (continued)

Order	Family	Common name/examples	No. of species	Distribution of order	General characteristics of order
Primates	Lemuridae	Lemurs	14	Africa, Asia, S America (man is distributed worldwide)	Omnivorous; multi-purpose dentition; large brain; body position upright; five-digit hands and feet; stereoscopic vision.
	Cheirogaleidae	Dwarf lemurs; mouse lemurs	4		
	Indriidae	Indris; sifaka; avahi	4		
	Daubentoniidae	Aye aye (lemur)	1		
	Lepilmuridae	Sportive lemurs	2		
	Galagidae	Galagos	7		
	Lorisidae	Lorises; pottos; bushbabies	12		
	Tupaiidae	Tree shrews	17		
	Tarsiidae	Tarsiers	3		
	Callitrichidae	Tamarins; marmosets	15		
	Cebidae	New World monkeys	30		
	Cercopithecidae	Old World monkeys	72		
	Hylobatidae	Gibbons; siamang	7		
	Pongidae	Great apes: gorilla, chimpanzee, orangutan	4		
	Hominidae	Man	1		

Length of pregnancy in some mammals

Animal	Gestation period[a]	Animal	Gestation period[a]	Animal	Gestation period[a]
Camel	406	Hamster	16	Pig	113
Cat	62	Hedgehog	35–40	Rabbit	32
Cow	280	Horse	337	Rat	21
Chimpanzee	237	Human	266	Reindeer	215–45
Dog	62	Hyena	110	Seal, northern fur	350
Dolphin	276	Kangaroo	40	Sheep	148
Elephant, African	640	Lion	108	Skunk	62
Ferret	42	Mink	50	Squirrel, grey	44
Fox	52	Monkey, rhesus	164	Tiger	105–9
Giraffe	395–425	Mouse	21	Whale	365
Goat	151	Opossum	13		
Guinea pig	68	Orangutan	245–75		

[a]Average number of days.

Classification of birds

This table uses the Voous taxonomic sequence running from what are supposed to be the most primitive families to the newest ones.

Order	Family	Common name/examples	No. of species	Distribution of family	General characteristics of order
Struthioniformes	Struthionidae	Ostrich	1	Africa	The ostrich is the world's largest living bird. Swift-running, flightless and gregarious; ground-nesting; feeds on vegetable matter.
Rheiformes	Rheidae	Rheas	2	S America	Swift-running, flightless ground-nesting birds which feed on vegetation and insects. Ostrich-like with short wings and no tailfeathers.
Casuariiformes	Casuariidae	Cassowaries	3	Australia and adjacent islands	Large, flightless, running birds with three toes and rough, hair-like plumage.
	Dromaiidae	Emu	1		

Order	Family	Common name/ examples	No. of species	Distribution of family	General characteristics of order
Apterygiformes	Apterygidae	Kiwis	3	New Zealand	Small-eyed, flightless, tailless birds with vestigial wings. They nest in burrows; are mainly nocturnal, insectivorous, and forest-dwelling.
Tinamiformes	Tinamidae	Tinamous	45	S and C America	Terrestrial, ground-nesting birds which can fly but do so rarely. They have patterned plumage; feed on vegetation; and live in grassland, brush, and forest.
Sphenisciformes	Spheniscidae	Penguins	16	Antarctica, Australia, Africa, S America	Black-and-white, flightless, aquatic birds. They nest in burrows or on the ground and are good swimmers, living off fish, squid, and crustacea. Walk upright or glide on their stomachs. Specially adapted feet feature a highly efficient heat-exchange mechanism to ensure survival in cold climates.
Gaviiformes	Gaviidae	Divers or loons	4	N America, Eurasia	Black and brown diving birds which breed on inland lakes and nest on the ground. They eat mostly fish, and winter on sea coasts. Clumsy on land, their legs are adapted for swimming and diving.
Podicipediformes	Podicipedidae	Grebes	20	Africa, Europe, Asia, Australia, N and S America	Large grey and brown short-winged diving birds with partly webbed feet. They eat fish, and nest on the water. They inhabit freshwater lakes in the summer and sea coasts in winter. Some are migratory.
Procellariiformes	Diomedeidae	Albatrosses	14	Seas worldwide	Generally long-winged, partly webbed-toed seabirds which feed on fish and nest on isolated islands and cliffs. Some species discharge oil in self-defence.
	Procellariidae	Petrels; fulmars; shearwaters	55		
	Hydrobatidae	Storm petrels	20		
	Pelecanoididae	Diving petrels	4		
Pelecaniformes	Pelecanidae	Pelicans	7	All continents	Diverse order of diving birds, found in marine and freshwater coastal habitats worldwide. They nest on cliffs or in trees; have a diet of mostly fish; and are generally web-toed.
	Sulidae	Gannets; boobies	9	N Atlantic, S Africa, Australasia, tropical oceans	
	Phaethontidae	Tropicbirds	3	Tropical oceans	
	Phalacrocoracidae	Cormorants	29	Worldwide	
	Fregatidae	Frigatebirds	5	Tropical oceans	
	Anhingidae	Darters	4	N and S America, Africa, Asia, Australasia	

NATURAL HISTORY

Classification of birds (continued)

Order	Family	Common name/ examples	No. of species	Distribution of family	General characteristics of order
Ciconiiformes	Ardeidae	Herons; bitterns	60	Worldwide except northernmost America and Eurasia	Upright, wading birds with specialized bills. Their toes are sometimes webbed and the middle claw is often serrated, or pectinate, for preening.
	Scopidae	Hammerhead	1	SW Arabia, Sub-Saharan Africa	
	Balaenicipitidae	Whale-headed stork	1	Africa	
	Ciconiidae	Storks	17	N America, Eurasia	
	Threskiornithidae	Spoonbills; ibises	31	Worldwide	
	Phoenicopteridae	Flamingos	5	Tropical zones	
Anseriformes	Anatidae	Ducks; geese; swans	147	Worldwide except Antarctica	Marsh-dwelling waterbirds which eat mostly vegetation and nest on the ground.
	Anhimidae	Screamers	3	S America	
Falconiformes	Cathartidae	Vultures (New World)	7	Americas	Birds of prey, or raptors. Expert fliers, they have hooked beaks and talons; and are generally large, heavily feathered birds with excellent eyesight and good hearing.
	Sagittariidae	Secretary-bird	1	Sub-Saharan Africa	
	Pandionidae	Osprey	1	Worldwide	
	Falconidae	Falcons; caracaras	60	Worldwide except Antarctica	
	Accipitridae	Kites; Old World vultures; harriers; hawks; eagles; buzzards	217	Worldwide except Antarctica	
Galliformes	Megapodidae	Megapodes	9	E Indies, Malaysia, New Guinea, Australia	The Galliformes, or gamebirds, have short, rounded wings, ill-adapted for sustained flight. They have large feet and claws, and are usually omnivorous in diet. The male plumage is often brilliant. Many are endangered owing to habitat destruction and over-hunting.
	Cracidae	Guans; curassows; chachalacas	42	Americas	
	Tetraonidae	Grouse	16	Eurasia, Americas	
	Phasianidae	Pheasants; quail; partridge	180	Worldwide, except N Eurasia and S America	
	Numididae	Guineafowl	7	Sub-Saharan Africa	
	Meleagrididae	Turkeys	2	N and S America	
Gruiformes	Mesitornithidae	Mesites	3	Madagascar	Diverse order of ground-feeding birds, generally with brown or grey plumage and long, rounded wings.
	Turnicidae	Buttonquails; hemipodes	16	Sub-Saharan Africa, China, Australia, Philippines, Mediterranean	
	Pedionomidae	Plains wanderer or collared hemipode	1	Australia	
	Gruidae	Cranes	15	All continents except S America and Antarctica	
	Aramidae	Limpkin	1	Americas	
	Psophiidae	Trumpeters	3	S America	
	Rallidae	Rails	130	Worldwide	
	Heliornithidae	Finfoots	3	Tropical America, tropical Africa and SE Asia	
	Rhynochetidae	Kagu	1	New Caledonia	
	Eurypygidae	Sunbittern	1	S America	
	Cariamidae	Seriemas	2	S America	
	Otididae	Bustards	22	Africa, Eurasia, Australia	

Order	Family	Common name/ examples	No. of species	Distribution of family	General characteristics of order
Charadriiformes (Sub-order Charadrii)	Jacanidae	Jacanas or lily-trotters	7	Americas, Africa, SE Asia, N Australia	Diverse order of mostly small to medium-sized shorebirds and seabirds. They generally have long, narrow wings, except for auks whose shorter wings can act as paddles underwater.
	Rostratulidae	Painted snipe	2	S America, SE Asia, Australia	
	Haematopodidae	Oystercatchers	6	All continents	
	Charadriidae	Plovers; lapwings	62	Worldwide	
	Scolopacidae	Sandpipers	81	All continents	
	Recurvirostridae	Avocets; stilts	7	All continents	
	Phalaropodidae	Phalaropes	3	N Eurasia, N America	
	Dromadidae	Crab plover	1	Indian ocean coastlines	
	Burhinidae	Stonecurlews or thick-knees	9	All continents except N America	
	Glareolidae	Pratincoles; coursers	17	Eurasia, Africa, Australia	
	Thinocoridae	Seed snipe	4	S America	
	Chionididae	Sheathbills	2	Antarctica and sub-Antarctic islands	
(Sub-order Lari)	Stercorariidae	Skuas; jaegers	6	Worldwide	
	Laridae	Gulls	45	Worldwide	
	Sternidae	Terns; noddies	42	Worldwide	
	Rynchopidae	Skimmers	3	Tropical Africa, SE Asia, eastern N America, C and S America	
(Sub-order Alcae)	Alcidae	Auks	22	Northern hemisphere seas	
Columbiformes	Pteroclididae	Sandgrouse	16	Africa, S Europe, Asia	Small to medium-sized arboreal and terrestrial birds with thick, heavy plumage.
	Columbidae	Pigeons; doves	300	Worldwide except Antarctica	
Psittaciformes	Psittacidae	Parrots; lories; cockatoos; lovebirds; macaws; budgerigars	330	All continents except Antarctica	The parrots have zygodactyl toes: two pointing forward, and two backward, enabling them to climb and hold objects. They have strong, hooked bills – (with mobile upper mandible) used for cracking nuts, holding things and climbing – as a 'third foot'. Often colourful, they nest in trees and on ledges and have a largely vegetarian diet.
Cuculiformes	Musophagidae	Turacos	22	Sub-Saharan Africa	Diverse order of arboreal and terrestrial birds. Many cuckoos are brood parasites, relying on other species to raise their young.
	Cuculidae	Cuckoos; anis; roadrunner; coucals	128	Worldwide	
	Opisthocomidae	Hoatzin	1	S America	
Strigiformes	Strigidae	Owls (typical)	124	Worldwide except Antarctica	The owls are nocturnal raptors found in grassland and woodland habitats,

NATURAL HISTORY

Classification of birds (continued)

Order	Family	Common name/ examples	No. of species	Distribution of family	General characteristics of order
	Tytonidae	Barn owls	10	Worldwide except C Asia, New Zealand and Antarctica	usually nesting in cavities. Their large, forward-facing eyes peer out of a facial disc and give them binocular vision. Owls can turn their heads in either direction more than 180°, and also have acute hearing.
Caprimulgiformes	Caprimulgidae	Nightjars or goatsuckers	70	Open habitats in temperate and tropical regions	These are generally insectivorous. Some hibernate and many are migratory. They have wide, gaping mouths with hooked beaks, large eyes and short legs with weak feet. Many species are two-coloured, featuring grey and red phases.
	Podargidae	Frogmouths	12	SE Asia, Australia	
	Aegothelidae	Owlet-nightjars	8	Australia, SE Asia	
	Nyctibiidae	Potoos	5	S America	
	Steatornithidae	Oilbird	1	S America	
Apodiformes	Apodidae	Swifts	80	Worldwide	Aerial birds that depend on their flying skills for food. Swifts are insectivorous and migratory. While on the wing they feed, mate, collect nest material, drink, and even, in some species, pass the night at high altitudes. Hummingbirds feed on nectar, supplemented with insects.
	Hemiprocnidae	Crested swifts	3	SE Asia	
	Trochilidae	Hummingbirds	320	Americas	
Coliiformes	Coliidae	Mousebirds or colies	6	Sub-Saharan Africa	These acrobatic, highly social birds live in scrub and bushes, feeding on fruit and vegetation – often becoming agricultural pests.
Trogoniformes	Trogonidae	Trogons	35	America, Asia, Sub-Saharan Africa	Colourful, sedentary, arboreal birds that feed on fruit and insects. They nest in tree cavities and termite mounds.
Coraciiformes	Alcedinidae	Kingfishers	87	Worldwide	The three anterior toes on these birds are united, an adaptation for perching and tree-climbing. Many are brightly coloured, some are social. All nest in cavities, digging holes in, for example, earth banks or rotten trees.
	Todidae	Todies	5	W Indies	
	Momotidae	Motmots	8	S America	
	Meropidae	Bee-eaters	24	Africa, Eurasia, Australia	
	Leptosomatidae	Cuckoo-roller	1	Madagascar, Comoros Islands	
	Coraciidae	Rollers	16	Africa, Eurasia, Australia	
	Upupidae	Hoopoe	1	Africa, Eurasia	
	Phoeniculidae	Woodhoopoes	6	Sub-Saharan Africa	
	Bucerotidae	Hornbills	45	Sub-Saharan Africa, SE Asia	

Order	Family	Common name/ examples	No. of species	Distribution of family	General characteristics of order
Piciformes	Galbulidae	Jacamars	15	S America	These birds are zygodactylous (see Psittaciformes). Colourful and arboreal, they feed on vegetation and insects, and nest in holes.
	Bucconidae	Puffbirds	30	S America	
	Capitonidae	Barbets	76	Americas, Sub-Saharan Africa, SE Asia	
	Indicatoridae	Honeyguides	15	Sub-Saharan Africa, Himalayas, SE Asia	
	Ramphastidae	Toucans	40	S America	
	Picidae	Woodpeckers; piculets; wrynecks	200	Worldwide	
Passeriformes (Sub-order Eurylaimi)	Eurylaimidae	Broadbills	14	Africa, Asia	Around 5 200 species, well over half of all birds, belong to the order Passeriformes, the perching birds or passerines. The order includes the most familiar garden birds – tits, chickadees, robins and sparrows – as well as other species found in virtually all land habitats. No passerine is a true water bird, though the dippers come close. Most are small or medium-sized birds (the largest species are the raven and the Australian lyrebird). The perching feet have four well-developed, separate toes. These are very vocal, singing birds. The male is often more brightly coloured than the female. Most are opportunistic feeders, being dependent on high-energy foods such as seeds and insects. Monogamy is the norm.
(Sub-order Menurae)	Menuridae	Lyrebirds	2	SE Australia	
	Atrichornithidae	Scrub-birds	2	W and E Australia	
(Sub-order Tyranni)	Furnariidae	Ovenbirds	220	C and S America	
	Dendrocolaptidae	Woodcreepers	48	S America	
	Formicariidae	Antbirds	230	S America	
	Tyrannidae	Tyrant flycatchers	375	Americas	
	Pittidae	Pittas	29	Africa, SE Asia, Australia	
	Pipridae	Manakins	53	S America	
	Cotingidae	Cotingas	65	S America	
	Conopophagidae	Gnateaters	9	S America	
	Rhinocryptidae	Tapaculos	29	S America	
	Oxyruncidae	Sharpbill	1	S America	
	Phytotomidae	Plantcutters	3	S America	
	Xenicidae	New Zealand wrens	4	New Zealand	
	Philepittidae	Sunbird asities	4	Madagascar	
(Sub-order Oscines)	Hirundinidae	Swallows; martins	74	Worldwide	
	Alaudidae	Larks	75	All continents	
	Motacillidae	Wagtails; pipits	54	Worldwide	
	Pycnonotidae	Bulbuls	120	S Asia, Africa	
	Laniidae	Shrikes	69	N America, Africa, Eurasia	
	Campephagidae	Cuckoo-shrikes	72	Africa, Australia, S and E Asia	
	Irenidae	Leafbirds	14	S and E Asia	
	Prionopidae	Helmet shrikes	9	Sub-Saharan Africa	
	Vangidae	Vanga shrikes	13	Madagascar, Comoros	
	Bombycillidae	Waxwings; silky flycatchers	8	N Eurasia, S America	
	Dulidae	Palmchat	1	S America	
	Cinclidae	Dippers	5	N Africa, Eurasia, W America	
	Troglodytidae	Wrens	60	NW Africa, Eurasia, N and S America	
	Mimidae	Mockingbirds	30	Americas	
	Prunellidae	Accentors	13	N Africa, Eurasia, S Asia	

NATURAL HISTORY

Classification of birds (continued)

Order	Family	Common name/examples	No. of species	Distribution of family	General characteristics of order
	Subfamilies of the family Muscicapidae				
	Turdidae	Thrushes	305	Worldwide	
	Timaliidae	Babblers	252	Africa, S Asia, Australasia, N America	
	Sylviidae	Warblers (Old World)	350	Worldwide	
	Muscicapinae	Flycatchers (Old World)	155	Australasia, Old World	
	Malurinae	Fairy-wrens	26	Australia, New Guinea	
	Paradox-ornithinae	Parrotbills	19	Asia, Europe	
	Monarchinae	Monarch flycatchers	133	Sub-Saharan Africa, S Asia, Australasia	
	Orthonychinae	Logrunners	20	SE Asia, Australia	
	Acanthizinae	Australian warblers	65	SE Asia, Australasia	
	Rhipidurinae	Fantail flycatchers	39	SE Asia, Australasia	
	Pachycephalinae	Thickheads	46	SE Asia, Australasia	
	Paridae	Tits	46	Africa, Eurasia, N America	
	Aegithalidae	Long-tailed tits	7	Eurasia, N America	
	Remizidae	Penduline tits	10	Africa, Eurasia, N America	
	Sittidae	Nuthatches	21	N America, Eurasia, N Africa, Australia	
	Climacteridae	Australasian treecreepers	8	Australia, New Guinea	
	Certhiidae	Holarctic treecreepers	5	Eurasia, Africa, N America	
	Rhabdornith-idae	Philippine treecreepers	2	Philippines	
	Zosteropidae	White-eyes	85	Sub-Saharan Africa, S and E Asia, Australasia	
	Dicaeidae	Flowerpeckers	50	SE Asia, Australasia	
	Pardalotidae	Pardalotes or diamond eyes	5	Australia	
	Nectariniidae	Sunbirds; spiderhunters	116	Old World tropics, Africa to Australia	
	Meliphagidae	Honeyeaters	169	Australasia, S Africa	
	Ephthianuridae	Australian chats	5	Australia	
	Subfamilies of the family Emberizidae				
	Emberizinae	Old World buntings; New World sparrows	281	Worldwide except SE Asia and Australasia	
	Catambly-rhynchinae	Plush-capped finch	1	S America	
	Thraupinae	Tanagers; honeycreepers	233	Americas	
	Cardinalinae	Cardinals and grosbeaks	37	S America	
	Tersininae	Swallow tanager	1	S America	
	Parulidae	Wood warblers	119	Americas	
	Vireonidae	Vireos; pepper shrikes	43	Americas	
	Icteridae	American blackbirds	94	Americas	
	Subfamilies of the family Fringillidae				
	Fringillinae	Fringilline finches	3	Eurasia, Canary Islands	
	Carduelinae	Cardueline finches	122	Worldwide except Australia	

NATURAL HISTORY

Order	Family	Common name/ examples	No. of species	Distribution of family	General characteristics of order
	Drepanidinae	Hawaiian honeycreepers	23	Hawaiian Islands	
	Estrildidae	Waxbills	124	Africa, S Asia, Australia	
	Subfamilies of the family Ploceidae				
	Ploceinae	True weavers	95	Africa, S Asia	
	Viduinae	Widow birds	10	Sub-Saharan Africa	
	Bubalornithinae	Buffalo weavers	3	Sub-Saharan Africa	
	Passerinae	Sparrow weavers; sparrows	37	Africa, Eurasia	
	Sturnidae	Starlings	106	Africa, Eurasia, Australia, New Zealand	
	Oriolidae	Orioles; figbirds	28	Africa, Eurasia, Australia	
	Dicruridae	Drongos	20	Sub-Saharan Africa, S Asia, N and E Australia	
	Callaeidae	New Zealand wattlebirds	3	New Zealand	
	Grallinidae	Magpie larks	2	Australia	
	Corcoracidae	Australian mudnesters	2	E Australia	
	Artamidae	Wood swallows	10	SE Asia, Australia	
	Cracticidae	Bell magpies	9	New Guinea, Australia	
	Ptilonorhynch-idae	Bowerbirds	18	New Guinea, Australia	
	Paradisaeidae	Birds of paradise	43	New Guinea, Australia	
	Corvidae	Crows; magpies; jays	113	Worldwide	

Incubation and fledgling periods

Bird family	Incubation period (days)	Fledgling period (days)
Hole nesters		
Bee-eaters	20	23
Hornbills	35	46
Kingfishers	22	29
Owls	30	30
Rollers	18	28
Swifts	20	44
Open nesters		
Anis	13	11
Cuckoos	12	22
Passerines	13	13
Pigeons	15	17
Turacos	17	28
Seabirds		
Wandering albatross	78	280
Fulmar	49	49
Gannet	44	90
King penguin	53	360
Adelie penguin	33	51
Giant petrel	59	108
Storm petrel	41	63
Shag	30	53
Common tern	23	30
Sandwich tern	23	35

Wingspans

Common name (Latin name)	Length (m)	(ft)
Wandering albatross (*Diomedea exulans*)	3.5	11.5
Marabou stork (*Leptoptilos dubius*)	3.3	11.0
Andean condor (*Vultur gryphus*)	3.2	10.5
White pelican (*Pelicanus onocrotalus*)	3.1	10.0
Lammergeier (*Gypaetus barbatus*)	2.7	9.0
Mute swan (*Cygnus olor*)	2.3	7.5
Crane (*Grus grus*)	2.3	7.5
Golden eagle (*Aquila chrysaetos*)	2.2	7.2
White stork (*Ciconia ciconia*)	2.1	7.0
Grey heron (*Ardea cinerea*)	1.9	6.0
Northern gannet (*Sulla bassana*)	1.8	5.9
Canada goose (*Branta canadensis*)	1.8	5.9
Greater flamingo (*Phoenicopterus ruber*)	1.65	5.4
Herring gull (*Larus argentatus*)	1.6	5.2
Osprey (*Pandion haliaetus*)	1.6	5.2
Barn owl (*Tyto alba*)	0.9	3.0

Life-history features

Species	Maximum recorded age (years)	Annual adult mortality (%)	Age of first breeding (years)	No. of eggs	Body weight (g)	Body weight (oz)
Blue tit	10	70	1	12–14	11	0.4
European robin	13	52	1	4–6	18	0.6
Song sparrow	8	44	1	4–6	30	1.0
House sparrow	12	50	1	3–6	30	1.0
European starling	20	50	1–2	4–6	80	3.0
American robin	10	48	1	4–6	100	3.5
European blackbird	20	42	1	3–5	80–110	3.0–4.0
Barn swallow	16	63	1	4–6	20	0.7
Common swift	21	15	2	2–3	36–50	1.0–2.0
Tawny owl	18	26	2	2–4	680–750	24.0–26.5
Mourning dove	17	55	1	2	140	5.0
Woodpigeon	16	36	1	2	450–550	16.0–19.0
Atlantic puffin	22	5	4	1	350–550	12.0–19.0
Black-legged kittiwake	21	14	4–5	2–3	300–500	10.5–17.5
Herring gull	36	6	3–5	3	750–1 250	26.5–44.0
Curlew	32	26	2	4	575–800	20.0–28.0
Redshank	17	31	1–2	4	110–155	4.0–5.5
Lapwing	23	32	1–2	4	200–300	7.0–10.5
Avocet	25	22	2–3	4	250–400	9.0–14.0
Pheasant	8	58	1–2	8–15	900–1 400	32.0–49.0
Kestrel	17	34	1–2	4–6	190–240	6.5–8.5
Buzzard	26	19	2–3	2–4	550–1 200	19.0–42.0
Osprey	32	18	2–3	2–3	1 200–2 000	42.0–71.0
Mallard	29	48	1–2	9–13	850–1 400	30.0–49.0
Tufted duck	15	46	1–2	8–11	550–900	19.0–32.0
Eider	18	20	2–3	4–6	1 200–2 800	42.0–99.0
Barnacle goose	23	9	3	3–5	1 400–1 600	49.0–56.5
Mute swan	22	10	3–4	5–8	10 000–12 000	353.0–424.0
Grey heron	25	30	2	4–5	1 600–2 000	56.5–71
White stork	26	21	3–5	3–5	3 000–3 500	106.0–123.5
Shag	21	16	3–4	3–4	1 750–2 250	62.0–79.0
Short-tailed shearwater	31	5	5–8	1	530	19.0
Royal albatross	36	3	8–10	1	8 300	293.0
Yellow-eyed penguin	18	10	2–4	2	5 200	183.5

Reptiles

Order	Family	Common name/ examples	No. of species	Distribution	General characteristics of order
Chelonia	Dermatemydidae	Central American river turtle	1	C America, Mexico	Aquatic and terrestrial reptiles – turtles, terrapins and tortoises. These have a rigid body shell comprising a dorsal carapace and a ventral plastron, into which most species draw their head and legs for protection. The jaws are beaked, without teeth.
	Chelydridae	Common and alligator snapping turtles	2	N and S America	
	Kinosternidae	Mud and musk turtles	21	Tropical regions	
	Testudinidae	Tortoises	40	All continents except Australia	
	Platysternidae	Big-headed turtle	1	SE Asia	
	Emydidae	Common turtle	76	Abundant in northern hemisphere	
	Cheloniidae	Sea turtles	5	Worldwide	
	Dermochelyidae	Leatherback turtle	1	Worldwide	
	Carettochelyidae	New Guinea plateless turtle	1	New Guinea	
	Trionychidae	Soft-shell turtles	20	All continents except S America and Australia	
	Pelomedusidae	Side-necked turtles	14	Africa, S America	

Order	Family	Common name/ examples	No. of species	Distribution	General characteristics of order
	Chelyidae	Snake-necked turtles	31	Australia, S America	
Rhynchocephalia	Sphenodontidae	Tuatara	1	New Zealand	Primitive nocturnal reptile, feeds on snails, worms, occasionally small lizards and birds.
Squamata (Sub-order Sauria)	Gekkonidae	Geckos	650	Worldwide	The Squamata are a large and very diverse order comprising three suborders, Sauria (lizards), Serpentes or Ophidia (snakes), and Amphisbaenia (worm lizards). This order contains the great majority of living reptiles. Lizards vary in size from a few centimetres (some geckos) to about 3 m/10 ft in length (the Komodo dragon). They feed as herbivores, insectivores or as predators of small vertebrates. The skull is made up of several separate mobile elements (a form of modification known as cranial kinesis). Limbs may be reduced in burrowing forms.
	Pygopodidae	Flap-footed lizards	15	Australia, New Guinea	
	Dibamidae	Burrowers	3	Philippines, Vietnam, New Guinea	
	Iguanidae	Iguanas	600	N and S America, W Indies, Galapagos, Fiji, Madagascar	
	Agamidae	Agamid lizard	300	Tropical regions worldwide	
	Chameleontidae	Old World chameleons	85	Africa, W Asia, India	
	Scincidae	Skinks	800	Worldwide except polar regions	
	Cordylidae	Girdle-tailed lizards	50	S Africa, Madagascar	
	Lacertidae	Old World terrestrial lizards	150	Europe, Asia, Africa	
	Teiidae	Whiptail lizards	200	Tropical regions	
	Anguidae	Glass lizards; alligator lizards; galliwasps	67	Americas	
	Anniellidae	California legless lizards	2	California	
	Xenosauridae		4	Mexico, China	
	Helodermatidae	Gila monster lizard; bearded lizard	2	N America, Mexico	
	Varanidae	Monitor lizards	30	Tropical regions	
	Lanthanotidae	Earless monitor lizard	1	Borneo	
	Xantusiidae	Night lizards	12	C America, Cuba	
(Sub-order Serpentes)	Typhlopidae	Blind snakes; worm snakes	200	Tropical regions	Snakes have no limbs, have long, cylindrical scaly bodies, lidless eyes and highly mobile jaws (cranial kinesis). They eat animals (or eggs), killing by suffocation, by biting, or by venom, and cannot chew. They moult their skin several times each year.
	Letotyphlopidae	Slender blind snakes	40	N and S America, SW Asia, Africa	
	Xenopeltidae	Sunbeam snake	1	India	
	Uropeltidae	Shieldtail snakes	50	S Asia	
	Boidae	Pythons; boas; woodsnakes	60	Tropical regions	
	Acrochordidae	Wart snakes	2	Australia, E Indies, SE Asia	
	Colubridae	Terrestrial, arboreal and aquatic snakes	>1500	Worldwide	
	Viperidae	Vipers; rattlesnakes; moccasins	180	Europe, Asia, Africa, not Australia	
	Elapidae	Cobras; mambas; coral snakes	170	Asia, Africa, N and S America	
	Hydrophiidae	Sea snakes	50	Indian and Pacific oceans	

NATURAL HISTORY

Reptiles (continued)

Order	Family	Common name/ examples	No. of species	Distribution	General characteristics of order
(Sub-order Amphisbaenia)	Amphisbaenidae	Worm lizards	100	Africa, C and S America, SE Asia and Seychelle Islands	Small, limbless burrowing lizards with concealed eyes and wedge-shaped skulls to aid with digging. They eat small animals.
Crocodilia	Alligatoridae	Alligators; caiman	7	S America, Africa, Asia, Australia	Small to very large (7 m/23 ft) carnivorous, amphibious reptiles. Heavy cylindrical body armoured with bony plates; elongated snout; webbed toes; powerful tail; mainly nocturnal.
	Crocodilidae	True crocodile	13	India	
	Gavialidae	Gavial or gharial	1		

Amphibians

Order	Family	Common name/ examples	No. of species	Distribution	General characteristics of order
Trachystomata		Sirens	3	N America	Aquatic, eel-like amphibians; no hindlimbs; forelimbs tiny; without external eyes or ears.
Gymnophiona		Caecilians	160	C and S America, Africa, SE Asia, Seychelle Islands	Caecilians are limbless, worm-like subterranean amphibians with annuli (rings) along length of body.
Urodela or Caudata	Hynobiidae	Asiatic salamanders	30	N Asia (from Ural Mountains to Japan and Taiwan)	The tailed amphibians salamanders and newts. Adults aquatic or terrestrial, occasionally arboreal; eggs and larvae primitively aquatic. Feed on slow-moving invertebrates (worms, slugs and snails).
	Cryptobranchidae	Giant salamanders; hellbenders	3	N America, China and Japan	
	Sirenidae	Sirens; dwarf sirens	3	SE United States, Mexico	
	Proteidae	Olm	1	Balkan peninsula	
	Necturidae	Mud puppies	5	N America	
	Amphiumidae	Congo eels	3	SE United States	
	Salamandridae	Salamanders and newts	42	Europe, N Africa, Middle East, S Asia, N America	
	Ambystomatidae	Mole salamanders; axolotl	33	N America	
	Plethodontidae	Lungless salamanders	210	Americas, S Europe	
Anura	Leiopelmatidae	Primitive frogs	4	New Zealand, N America	The frogs and toads. Tail absent; hindlimbs enlarged for jumping. Adults aquatic or terrestrial, occasionally arboreal or burrowing. Eggs
	Discoglossidae	Fire-bellied toads; midwife toads	8	Europe, Asia, N America, Philippines	
	Rhinophrynidae	Burrowing toad	1	C America	
	Pipidae	Tongueless frogs	14	Africa, S America	

Order	Family	Common name/ examples	No. of species	Distribution	General characteristics of order
	Pelobatidea	Spadefoots	59	Europe, Asia, N America, Australia	and larvae (tadpoles) typically aquatic, but reproductive strategies vary. Largely insectivorous. (Smooth wet-skinned species of Anura are usually known as frogs, rough dry-skinned species as toads, but there is no technical difference between the two.)
	Myobatrachidae	Terrestrial, arboreal and aquatic frogs	95	New Guinea, Australia, South Africa	
	Rhinodermatidae	Mouth-breeding frog	1	S America	
	Leptodactylidae	Terrestrial neotropical frogs	650	Americas, Caribbean	
	Bufonidae	True toads	235	Worldwide	
	Brachycephalidae	Terrestrial toads	2	Brazil	
	Dendrobatidae	Arrow-poison frogs	70	C and S America	
	Pseudidae	Fully aquatic frogs	5	S America	
	Centrolenidae	Leaf frogs	60	C and S America	
	Hylidae	Tree frogs	400	Worldwide	
	Ranidae	True frogs	850	Worldwide	
	Sooglossidae	Terrestrial frogs	3	Seychelle Islands	
	Microhylidae	Narrow-mouthed frogs	230	Africa, Asia, N and S America, Australia	

Fishes

There have been many different systems of fish classification, and today there is still much debate about taxonomy. Most systems divide the world of fishes into three: the jawless fishes, the cartilaginous fishes and the bony fishes. This table lists some of the best-known types of fish.

Order	Common name/ examples	No. of species	Distribution	General characteristics of order
Class Agnatha *(jawless fishes)*				
Cyclostomata	Lampreys	30	Cool, fresh, and coastal waters of all continents, except Africa	Eel-shaped body; well-developed dorsal and caudal fins; horny teeth; feed on the blood of other fishes; only breed in fresh water.
	Hagfishes	30	Cold, marine bottom waters; equatorial oceans	soft-skinned; nearly cylindrical; eyes vestigial, covered by skin; feed on dead or moribund fishes or invertebrates; locate food by scent; only breed in marine water.
Class Chondrichthyes *(fishes with a cartilage skeleton)*				
Selachii	Sharks	>200	Tropical and temperate zones; particularly New Zealand, S Africa	Large group of predatory fishes belonging to nineteen separate families; streamlined bodies; highly sensitive sense of smell; attacks on humans very rare, usually occur in water warmer than 21°C (70°F); an exception, however, is the white shark, which is also the most dangerous; others include hammerheads (very mobile using rudder effect of head), tiger and sand sharks; largest are the whale and basking sharks.

NATURAL HISTORY

Fishes (continued)

Order	Common name/ examples	No. of species	Distribution	General characteristics of order
Batoidei	Rays; skates; stingrays	>300	All oceans from tropical to temperate latitudes	Bottom dwellers, preying on other animals on sea floor; differ externally from sharks having gill openings confined to lower surface; eyes on dorsal surface; many armed with thorns, tubercles or prickles; stingrays live in shallow, coastal waters; if provoked, will lash back their tails; electric rays are sluggish, stun invertebrates and fishes by shocks produced from electric organs. Skates lie on bottom, often partially buried; rise in pursuit of prey, particularly herring; trap victims by swimming over them and settling upon them; their egg cases ('mermaid's purses') are often washed ashore.

Class Osteichthyes (fishes with a bony skeleton)

Order	Common name/ examples	No. of species	Distribution	General characteristics of order
Dipnoi	Lungfishes	6	Freshwater; Australia, Africa, N America	Voracious, eating aquatic animals, including own species; most grow to substantial size; sac-shaped, pneumatic organs that lie along alimentary tract, whose structure and function are like primitive lungs of amphibians.
Acipenseriformes	Sturgeons	25	Marine and freshwater; Europe, Asia, N America	Braincase mostly cartilaginous; ground feeding by dragging tactile, whisker-like barbels over bottom; toothless mouth with protractile lips surrounded by taste buds; food fish for humans, source of caviar.
	Paddlefishes	2	Marine and freshwater; China and N America	Braincase mostly cartilaginous; feed by straining plankton through gill system; elongated, paddle-shaped snout composed entirely of cartilage, measuring one-third of the total body length.
Polypteriformes	Bichirs or reedfishes	11	Tropical swamps and flood rivers in C Africa	Inhabit edges of streams and flood plains, concealed by day, forage for worms, insect larvae, small fishes by night.
Elopiformes	Bonefishes	4	Coastal and deep waters of warm oceans	Specialized bottom feeders; grubs with snout for worms and shellfish which they crush with rounded palatal teeth.
	Tarpons	2	Warm coastal waters Atlantic	Fast-swimming predator; swim bladder lung-like, partially compartmented, highly vascularized; obligate air breathers, can die from asphyxiation if prevented from reaching surface.
	Ladyfish	6	Warm coastal waters circumtropical	Fast-swimming predators; appear to 'roll' at sea surface apparently for intake of air; open duct to swim bladder when air is taken through mouth.

Order	Common name/ examples	No. of species	Distribution	General characteristics of order
Anguilliformes	Eels	>500	Marine and freshwater; of Europe and N America; some in shallow water or deep sea	Elongate, cylindrical body form; carnivorous until maturity; morays and congers inhabit rock crevices, others form vast colonies of individuals in tropical reef areas; return to sea to spawn.
Clupeiformes	Herrings	190	Virtually worldwide in marine waters, and in many bodies of freshwater	Teeth usually absent or weakly developed; single schools of herring estimated to include many millions.
	Anchovies	200	Widespread in surface coastal waters of tropical and temperate seas; a few anadromous (returning to fresh water to spawn)	Snout projects beyond very wide mouth; upper and lower jaws usually armed with rows of minute teeth; found in large schools, some spreading over 100 m/330 ft, contracting to writhing sphere of thousands of fishes only a few metres across at approach of a predator.
Osteoglossiformes	Bony tongues	6	Freshwater; rivers and lakes, turbid waters or regions with dense aquatic vegetation	Strongly-toothed jaws; large mouth; well-developed swim bladder; some species, upper portion of ear (for balance) completely separated from lower part (for hearing).
	Freshwater butterfly fish	1	Freshwater; Africa	Greatly expanded wing-like pectoral fins (behind gills) which are used for short flights to the air, either to escape predators or to catch insects.
Salmoniformes	Salmons; trouts; chars; smelts; graylings; whitefishes	150	Widespread, marine or freshwater. Salmon common in N Atlantic; return to freshwater to breed	Trim, fusiform body; powerful caudal (tail) muscles; commonly migrate upstream to spawn; very important food fishes.
	Pikes; mudminnows	10	Freshwater; northern hemisphere	Long bodies; dorsal and anal fins positioned posteriorly, adipose fin absent.
Ostariophysi	Carps; minnows; barbs; suckers; loaches	3 500	Fresh to brackish waters; Africa, S and C America, Eurasia	Small to medium-sized fishes; upper jaw protractile, jaw teeth usually absent. Body covered in scales.
	Catfishes	2 500	Low saline, brackish freshwater or marine	Order of small to very large freshwater fishes; oral incubation of eggs by some species; most active at night or under conditions of reduced light.
Characiformes	Tetras; darters; piranhas	>1 300	Freshwater; S and C America, Africa	Mostly small, colourful fishes; upper jaw projectile, jaws bearing teeth; of prime importance in aquarium trade.
Paracanthopterygii	Toadfishes	45	Primarily marine, mainly tropical and temperate shallow waters along continental coasts; occasionally freshwater	Generally have two dorsal fins; nine venomous species restricted to coast and rivers of C and S America.
	Trout-perches	8	All freshwater; N America	Live under conditions of dim light; can be found in clear water of the Great Lakes at depths of about 64 m/210 ft.
	Codfishes	800	Primarily marine, shallow-water, some deep-sea types, worldwide distribution; particularly N Atlantic	Largest of order, growing to about 2 m/6.5 ft in length and attain weights that may exceed 90 kg/ 200 lb; migrate over long distances, gathering in late winter and early spring to spawn, each species goes to particular area.

NATURAL HISTORY

Fishes (continued)

Order	Common name/ examples	No. of species	Distribution	General characteristics of order
Atheriniformes	Flying fishes	50	Surface marine waters, worldwide	Surface fishes of the open ocean where they breed; capable of leaping or skipping on surface to escape predators; tail (caudal) fin usually asymmetrical, lower lobes longer than body so while out of water lower lobe vibrates as a scull driving fish along.
	Needlefishes; garfishes	25	Mostly temperate and tropical marine; a few freshwater	Pelagic (inhabiting the open ocean); predatory habit highly developed; long, formidable toothed jaws elongated into strong-toothed beak; breed near shore.
	Cyprinodonts	500	Tropical and subtropical distribution, including hot springs of Africa and America	Diminutive; many important as experimental animals in biological research; among hardiest of fishes, some surviving in rigorous environments, including water temperatures in hot springs approaching coagulation point of protoplasm.
Gasterosteiformes	Sticklebacks	11	Fresh, brackish, and marine waters of northern hemisphere	Small, scaleless fishes; short jaws armed with sharp teeth; body more nearly fusiform (tapered at both ends).
	Tube snout	1	NE Pacific Ocean	Elongated, slender, cylindrical body, tipped by prolonged snout; small toothed mouth has hinged upper jaw; scale-less body armoured with series of embedded bony plates.
	Sea horses	24	Widely distributed; marine	Bony rings instead of scales; use coiled tail to grip seaweed and other plants/objects; propulsion by means of dorsal fin (midline of back); tiny pectoral fin used for steering; rise or settle to another depth by changing air volume within the bladder.
Scorpaeniformes	Scorpion fishes; rockfishes; redfishes; turkeyfishes; gunards	330	Tropical, temperate, and northern seas	Live on coral or rocky bottom; many possess remarkable degree of concealing coloration and shape; dorsal fin spines long and numerous; head spiny; body scaly; some with venom glands on fin spines.
Perciformes				The largest group of fishes, comprising about 7 000 species in 150 families.
	Perches	125	Freshwater temperate species	Possess numerous short, fine, pointed teeth; prefer quiet waters; pike-perches semi-migratory, prefer quiet, running waters.

Order	Common name/ examples	No. of species	Distribution	General characteristics of order
	Tunas	40	Open waters of tropics and warm seas of world	May travel across entire Pacific Ocean from California coast to Japan, or reverse, to spawn; one of the larger predatory perciforms; carnivorous; well-developed vascular system under skin, associated with sustained high-speed swimming and a body temperature a few degrees higher than surrounding water.
	Marlins	7	Worldwide in warm seas	Greatest game fishes of the ocean; black marlin is the largest at 900 kg/2 000 lb.
Pleuronectiformes	Flatfishes	2	Indo-Pacific and Africa	Asymmetrical; found in depths up to 1 000 m/3 300 feet, most occur on continental shelf in less than 200 m/650 ft of water; swim by undulating movement of body and fins; lie on bottom, generally covered by sand or mud, with only eyes protruding; eyes can be raised, lowered and moved independently.
	Flounders	300+	Marine and freshwater, tropic and temperate seas	Either right-eyed (dextral) or left-eyed (sinistral); asymmetrical; feed primarily on crustaceans, other bottom invertebrates and small fish; when feeding lie motionless and then pounce on close prey.
	Soles	100+	Tropic and temperate seas, some freshwater	Asymmetrical; strongly compressed; eyes, usually small, on one side (dextral); mouth curved downward; caudal fin with numerous rays.
Tetraodontiformes	Box fishes	25	Prominent around coral reefs, open sand and grassy flats; worldwide	Carapace closed behind anal and usually behind dorsal fin; no ventral keel; blow jet of water out of mouth onto sand bottom to expose burrowing invertebrates.
	Puffer fishes	7	Prominent around coral reefs, open sand and grassy flats; worldwide	Poisonous flesh, at least during certain seasons of year; most of highly poisonous substance contained in viscera; flesh can be eaten if professionally cleaned.
	Ocean sunfishes	3	Prominent around coral reefs, open sand and grassy flats; tropical and subtropical oceans worldwide	Massive, crushing jaws and teeth; feed extensively on soft-bodied invertebrates, such as jellyfishes.

Insects

Order	Common name/ examples	No. of species	Distribution	General characteristics of order
Collembola	Springtails	2 000	Worldwide	Blind, primitively wingless insects with entognathous mouthparts (ie contained within an invagination of the head). They leap by means of a forked springing organ on the underside of the abdomen.
Diplura	Diplurans	660	Worldwide	Small, slender, blind, whitish insects, with entognathous mouthparts; found in damp soil, under logs and stones.

NATURAL HISTORY

Insects (continued)

Order	Common name/ examples	No. of species	Distribution	General characteristics of order
Protura	Proturans	120	Worldwide	Primitively wingless; white; blind; no antennae; reduced mouthparts; found under bark, stones or rotting vegetation.
Thysanura	Bristletails; silverfish	600	Worldwide	Primitive wingless insects found amongst decaying wood etc, in human habitations, and in association with ants and termites; feed on fungi, lichens, algae, pollen, or decaying vegetable matter.
Ephemeroptera	Mayflies	2000	Worldwide, except Antarctica	Some species carnivorous, but majority are herbivorous. Life cycle consists of four stages. Nymph can live for 2 weeks to 2 years; the adults are winged and non-feeding, living from 2 to 72 hours, during which time they mate.
Odonata	Dragonflies; damselflies	5000	Worldwide	Carnivorous, often brightly coloured; aquatic larvae; adults have powerful predatory mouthparts and two pairs of richly veined wings. Larvae feed on aquatic larvae, tadpoles, worms, and small fishes; adults on flying insects.
Orthoptera	Grasshoppers; locusts; crickets	24000	Worldwide	Wings, when present, number four; chewing mouthparts; mostly plant feeders. Hindlimbs usually specialized for jumping; many species produce sounds by rubbing together forewings. Of immense economic importance.
Phasmida (Phasmoptera)	Stick insects; leaf insects	2500	Tropical areas	Arboreal; nocturnal; feed on plant juices; camouflage and mimicry highly developed.
Blattaria	Cockroaches	3700	Worldwide	Depressed body; long legs; forewings hard or leathery; hindwings membranous, but may be reduced or absent. Typically live on the ground, under stones, or in litter and wood debris. Some are household pests.
Embioptera	Webspinners	200	Tropical regions	Inhabit extensive galleries or labyrinths of silk on bark, litter, moss, lichens, or within the soil. Body slender; legs short; females and some males wingless.
Zoraptera	Zorapterans	20	Tropical regions	Tiny insects resembling slender termites.
Dermaptera	Earwigs	1500	Worldwide	Feed as scavengers or predators with large pincers variously used for predation, defence, courtship, and grooming. Wings frequently reduced or absent.
Mantodea	Mantids; mantises	1800	Tropical and subtropical areas	Predatory insects in which body shape is highly adapted for camouflage; head very mobile, eyes large; in some species female eats male headfirst during copulation.
Isoptera	Termites or white ants	2000	Europe, Australia, Asia, N America	Cellulose-eating, social insects that construct nests which vary in size from a few centimetres to several metres. Caste system includes morphologically distinct soldiers and workers.
Phthiraptera	Sucking lice (Anoplura); biting lice (Mallophaga); booklice and barklice (Psocoptera)	3400	Worldwide	Parasites of birds or mammals; eyes reduced or absent; reduced antennae; mouthparts mandibulate or piercing.

Order	Common name	No. of species	Distribution	General characteristics of order
Thysanoptera	Thrips	5000	Tropical regions	Fringed wings, bristles on body wall; mouthparts specialized for piercing and sucking. Feed on plant juices, fungi, spores, pollen, or body fluids of other arthropods. Some species hibernate in winter in cold climates.
Homoptera	Cicadas; hoppers; whiteflies; aphids; scale insects	45000	Worldwide	Plant feeders with mouth parts adapted for sucking plant sap; wings number two or four when present. Many are crop pests.
Hemiptera	True bugs	35000	Worldwide	Sucking mouthparts adapted to pierce plant or animal tissue; most species terrestrial, a few aquatic; well-developed compound eyes; scent glands usually present. Many are crop pests.
Neuroptera	Alderflies; dobsonflies (Megaloptera); lacewings (Plannipennia); snakeflies (Raphidiodea)	4500	Worldwide	Biting mouthparts; two pairs of wings. Alderflies and dobsonflies have aquatic larvae. Snakeflies arboreal, characterized by elongate and highly mobile thorax.
Trichoptera	Caddisflies	7000	Worldwide	Moth-like; wings covered with hairs; long antennae; large compound eyes; larvae almost exclusively aquatic.
Lepidoptera	Butterflies; moths; skippers	138000	Worldwide	Two pairs of wings, covered by dustlike scales; four stages of life; day-flying; herbivorous; complete metamorphosis occurs (larvae are caterpillars). Adults typically with slender, coiled, sucking proboscis.
Coleoptera	Beetles; weevils	250000	Worldwide	Two pairs of wings, front pair modified into horny covers; antennae variable; large compound eyes; mouthparts adapted for chewing; hard outer skeleton; complete metamorphosis.
Hymenoptera	Ants; bees; sawflies; wasps	130000	Worldwide except polar regions	Pollinators of wild and cultivated flowering plants; some species have complex social organization; complete metamorphosis; four membranous wings; mouthparts adapted for chewing and sucking; larvae usually maggot-like.
Strepsiptera	Stylopids	400	Worldwide	Parasites of other insects; male winged, female wingless and larvae-like.
Mecoptera	Scorpion flies	450	Mostly tropical, subtropical areas	Inhabit moist forests feeding on nectar or preying on other insects.
Diptera	True flies	150000	Worldwide	Forewings membranous, hindwings modified as minute club-like balancing organs (halteres). Feed on plant and animal juices or other insects; two wings; sucking mouthparts; some pupae aquatic. Many are disease vectors, though many are also beneficial as pollinators.
Siphonaptera	Fleas	1750	Worldwide	Wingless; parasitic; mouthparts adapted to piercing and sucking; larvae elongated and often enclosed in cocoons. Feed mainly on mammals, but also some birds. Disease vectors.

PLANTS

Classification of plants

Phylum	Common name/examples	No. of species	Comments
Bryophyta	Liverworts (*Hepaticae*); hornworts (*Anthocerotae*); mosses (*Musci*)	24 000	Small plants living in moist habitats (their sperm must swim through water to reach their eggs). Reproduce by spores.
Psilophyta	Whiskferns	12	Simple vascular plants lacking true roots and, in some species, leaves. Reproduce by spores.
Lycopodophyta	Club mosses	1 000	Small, terrestrial or epiphytic (ie grow on other plants); needle or scale-like leaves arranged spirally on stem. Reproduce by spores.
Sphenophyta or Equisetophyta	Horsetails; scouring rushes	20	Primarily found in moist, muddy habitats; stems creeping underground and producing erect annual or perennial stems with tiny leaves whorled into sheaves around stem. Jointed hollow stems and rough, ribbed texture caused by the mineral silica. Reproduce by spores.
Filicinophyta or Pteridophyta	Ferns	12 000	Vascular plants which reproduce by spores; stems mostly creeping, large leaves (megaphylls) with branching veins. The most complex, diverse and abundant of the plant phyla that do not form seeds.
Cycadophyta	Cycads	100	Evergreen perennial shrubs or trees with stems that are usually unbranched but thickened by some secondary growth. Palm-like or fern-like compound leaves; they contain symbiotic cyanobacteria in special roots.
Ginkgophyta	Ginkgo; maidenhair tree	1	Native to China but cultivated worldwide, the ginkgo is a tall tree with deciduous fan-shaped leaves; the only living descendant of a once-large group.
Coniferophyta or Pinatae	Conifers	550	By far the most familiar of the gymnosperms (plants having naked seeds); usually evergreen shrubs or trees with simple needle-like leaves, spirally arranged. Commercially important for timber, pulp, turpentine, and resin products.
Gnetophyta	Gnetophytes (cone-bearing desert plants)	70	Cone-bearing desert plants. Resemble flowering plants in many ways; were once thought to be a link between conifers and angiosperms.
Angiospermophyta or Magnoliophyta	Angiosperms; flowering plants	>230 000	The dominant land vegetation of the Earth, including nearly every familiar tree, shrub, or garden plant that produces flowers and seeds. Characterized by the aggregation of sexual reproductive structures with specialized shoots (flowers), which typically comprise four kinds of modified leaves: sepals, petals, stamens (male organs), and carpels (female organs).

Flowering plants

Common name	Latin name	Height		Colour
		(cm)	(in)	
Annuals and biennials				
Baby's breath	Gypsophila	30–45	12–18	White, pink
Begonia	Begonia	15–45	6–18	Pink, white, red
Black-eyed Susan	Thunbergia	120–300	47–118	Yellow
Busy Lizzie	Impatiens	15–30	6–12	White, pink, red, orange, mauve
Canterbury bell	Campanula	45–75	18–30	Purple, white
Chrysanthemum	Chrysanthemum	45–60	18–24	Yellow, red, white
Corn cockle	Agrostemma	75	30	Pale lilac
Cornflower	Centaurea	30–75	12–30	Blue, pink
Dahlia	Dahlia	30–60	12–24	White, red, yellow
Daisy	Bellis	8–15	3–6	White, pink, red
Flower of an hour	Hibiscus	60	24	Cream
Forget-me-not	Myosotis	15–30	6–12	Blue
Foxglove	Digitalis	90–150	35–59	Purple
Godetia	Godetia	20–60	8–24	Pink, orange
Heliotrope	Heliotropium	45	18	White, dark blue, purple
Hollyhock	Althea	90–150	35–59	Pink
Larkspur	Delphinium	30–120	12–47	White, pink, red, blue
Morning glory	Ipomoea	180–360	71–142	Blue, purple, red
Nasturtium	Tropaeolum	30–180	12–71	Yellow, orange
Pansy	Viola	15–25	6–10	Violet, yellow
Petunia	Petunia	15–45	6–18	Pink, red ,blue, white
Phlox	Phlox	15–45	6–18	Pink, red, white, yellow
Poppy	Papaver	15–90	6–35	Red, pink, white
Pot marigold	Calendula	15–30	6–12	Yellow, orange
Snapdragon	Antirrhinum	90–120	35–47	Crimson, scarlet
Sunflower	Helianthus	60–300	24–118	Yellow
Sweet alyssum	Alyssum	8–15	3–6	White, purple, lilac, pink
Sweet pea	Lathyrus	30–240	12–94	Orange, crimson
Sweet William	Dianthus	30–60	12–24	White, red
Wallflower	Cheiranthus	20–60	8–24	Crimson, white, purple, orange, cream
Bulbs				
Begonia	Begonia	30–45	12–18	Pink, yellow, white, cream
Bluebell	Scilla	8	3	Blue, purple
Crocus	Crocus	8–10	3–4	White, purple, yellow
Cyclamen	Cyclamen	8–15	3–6	Red, pink, white
Daffodil	Narcissus	15–30	6–12	Yellow, white
Freesia	Freesia	15	6	White, red, yellow, pale blue
Hyacinth	Hyacinthus	8–15	3–6	Yellow, white, blue, pink, violet, red
Iris	Iris	15–30	6–12	Blue, yellow, white, purple
Lily of the valley	Convallaria	20	8	White
Snowdrop	Galanthus	13	5	White
Star of Bethlehem	Ornithogalum	15–30	6–12	White
Sword lily	Gladiolus	90–150	35–49	Yellow, red, pink, peach, orange
Tulip	Tulipa	20–80	8–31	Red, yellow, white, purple, peach
Border perennials				
Campion	Lychnis	90	35	Red, pink
Chinese bellflower	Platycodon	15–30	6–12	White, pink, pale blue
Clematis	Clematis	90–125	35–49	Blue, white
Columbine	Aquilegia	60–90	24–35	Yellow, red, blue
Crane's-bill	Geranium	45	18	Violet, pink
Lady's mantle	Alchemilla	45	18	Yellow
Lamb's ear	Stachys	45	18	Lilac, pink
Lupin	Lupinus	90–125	35–49	Pink, lilac, white, blue
Michaelmas daisy	Aster	60–125	24–49	Pink, white, crimson, blue
Peony	Paeonia	60	24	White, pink, red
Primrose	Primula	15–60	6–24	Yellow, red, lilac
Red hot poker	Kniphofia	75–155	30–61	Orange-red
Solomon's seal	Polygonatum	60–90	24–35	Cream
Speedwell	Veronica	45–155	18–61	Blue, pink, white
Violet	Viola	10–15	4–6	Violet, white, lilac, pink

Shrubs

Common name	Latin name	Height		Colour
		(cm)	(in)	
Azalea	Rhododendron	180	71	Pink, red, white, yellow
Bay laurel	Laurus	610	240	Yellow
Broom	Genista	210	83	Yellow
Butterfly bush	Buddleia	250	98	Purple, white, mauve
Camellia	Camellia	180–250	71–98	Red, pale pink, white, bright pink
Fatsia	Fatsia	300	118	White
Firethorn	Pyracantha	370	145	Red, yellow
Fuchsia	Fuchsia	180	71	Red
Gorse	Ulex	180	71	Yellow
Heather	Erica	20–60	8–24	White, purple, yellow
Holly	Ilex	1 500	590	Red
Honeysuckle	Lonicera	210–300	83–118	Pink, cream
Hydrangea	Hydrangea	90–150	35–59	Pale blue, white, pink, purple
Japonica	Chaenomeles	120–90	47–75	Red, white
Jasmine	Jasminum	300	118	Yellow
Lavender	Lavandula	90	35	Blue
Lilac	Syringa	370	145	Purple, white, lavender, lilac
Magnolia	Magnolia	150–610	59–240	White, red
Myrtle	Myrtus	300	118	White
Oleaster	Elaeagnus	230–300	90–118	White
Periwinkle	Vinca	20–5	8–10	White, blue
Rhododendron	Rhododendron	180	71	Red, purple, pink, white
Silk tassel bush	Garrya	275	108	White
Veronica	Hebe	30–300	12–118	Blue, white
Viburnum	Viburnum	180–300	71–118	White, pink, red, blue
Winter sweet	Chimonanthus	275	108	Yellow

Trees

Common name	Latin name	Varieties	Height	
			(m)	(ft)
Alder	Alnus	Common; Italian; golden leaf	20	65
Antarctic beech	Nothofagus	False beech	12	39
Ash	Fraxinus	Common; raywood; manna	18	59
Avocado	Persia	americana; drymifolia	18	59
Bamboo	Bambusoidae	Dendrocalamus strictus; Bambusa arundinacea	36	118
Baobab	Andansonia	digitata; gregorii	9–12	29–39
Beech	Fagus	Dawyck; fern-leaved; weeping; copper; golden	30	98
Birch	Betula	Silver; Swedish	10	33
Coconut palm	Cocus nucifera	Coconut palm	30	98
Cypress	Chamaecyparis	Lawson cypress	30–6	98–118
Elm	Ulmus	Wych; Dutch; English; weeping; Chinese	27–36	88–118
False acacia	Robinia	frisia; pseudoacacia	18	59
Flame tree	Delonix regia	Flame tree	15	49
Flowering cherries	Prunus	Ornamental almond; ornamental plum; ornamental peach; ornamental cherry	6–12	20–39
Flowering crab	Malus	John Downie; golden hornet; Japanese; Montreal beauty; profusion; Van Eseltine; lemoinei	6–15	20–49
Golden rain	Laburnum	Common; scotch; vosii	4	13
Gum	Eucalyptus	Gum; snow gum	15	49
Handkerchief	Davidia	involucrata	15	49
Hawthorn	Crataegus	monogyna; Paul's scarlet; crusgalli; orientalis; prunifolia	4	13
Hazel	Corylus	Common; aurea, corkscrew; filbert; giant; purpurea	3–9	10–29
Honey locust	Gleditsia	Sunburst; elegantissima	7	23
Hornbeam	Carpinus	Common	12	39
Horse chestnut	Aesculus	Red; common	18	59
Indian bean	Catalpa	Indian bean; aurea	6	20
Judas	Cercis	Judas; white Judas	4	13

Trees (continued)

Common name	Latin name	Varieties	Height	
			(m)	(ft)
Juniper	*Juniperus*	*communis; virginiana; sabina; chinensis; phoenicea; horizontales; thuinfera*	3-6	10-20
Larch	*Larix*	European; golden	24-30	79-98
Lime	*Tilia*	Common; large-leaved; American	24-7	79-88
Mango	*Mangifera indica*	Mango	18	59
Maple	*Acer*	Field; Norway; purple Norway; sycamore	6-9	20-9
Mountain ash	*Sorbus*	Rowan; Joseph rock; Swedish whitebeam	15	49
Mulberry	*Morus*	Black mulberry	6	20
Oak	*Quercus*	English; sessile; Turkey; red; holm; willow	24	78
Ornamental pear	*Pyrus*	*pendula*	6	20
Palm	*Palmae*	Sugar; cohune; *palmyra*; silver; coconut; *carnaulsa*; doum; coco de mer; date; royal; cabbage	20	65
Paulownia	*Paulownia*	*tomentosa*	7	23
Pea	*Caragana*	*pendula*; dwarf	4	13
Pine	*Pinus*	Scots; Corsican; Austrian; Monterey	18-36	59-118
Plane	*Platanus*	London plane	24	79
Poplar	*Populus*	White; grey; *aurora*; *Italica*; aspen	24	79
Pride of India	*Koelreuteria*	*paniculata*	6	20
Sweet chestnut	*Castanea*		30	98
Sweet gum	*Liquidambar*	*styraciflua*	45	148
Tree of heaven	*Ailanthus*	*altissima*	20	65
Tulip	*Liriodendron*	*tulipifera*	35	115
Tupelo	*Nyssa*	*sylvatica*	9	29
Walnut	*Juglans*		30	98
Willow	*Salix*	Golden; weeping; American; Kilmarnock; purple; corkscrew	3-9	10-29
Yew	*Taxus baccata*	Common; Irish	4-15	13-49

Plants as foodstuffs

Temperate fruits

Common name	Latin name	Family
Apple	*Malus pumila*	Rosaceae
Pear	*Pyrus communis*	Rosaceae
Quince	*Cydonia vulgaris*	Rosaceae
Peach; nectarine	*Prunus persica*	Rosaceae
Sweet cherry	*P. avium*	Rosaceae
Sour cherry; cooking cherry; morello	*P. cerasus*	Rosaceae
Plum	*P. domestica*	Rosaceae
Bullace; damson	*P. insititia*	Rosaceae
Gage; greengage; mirabelle	*P. insititia var italica, var syriaca*	Rosaceae
Cherry plum	*P. cerasifera*	Rosaceae
Japanese plum	*P. salicina*	Rosaceae
American plum	*P. americana*	Rosaceae
Apricot	*P. armeniaca*	Rosaceae
Medlar	*Mespilus germanica*	Rosaceae
Raspberry	*Rubus idaeus*	Rosaceae
American red raspberry	*R. ideaus var strigosus*	Rosaceae
Black raspberry	*R. occidentalis*	Rosaceae
Blackberry; bramble	*R. fruticosus*	Rosaceae
Evergreen blackberry	*R. laciniatus*	Rosaceae
Cloudberry	*R. chamaemorus*	Rosaceae
Pacific dewberry	*R. ursinus*	Rosaceae

Common name	Latin name	Family
Loganberry; boysenberry; veitchberry	*R.* × *loganbaccus*	Rosaceae
Wineberry	*R. phoenicolasius*	Rosaceae
Strawberry	*Fragaria* × *ananassa* (= *F. virginiana* × *F. chiloensis*)	Rosaceae
Gooseberry	*Ribes uva-crispa* (= *R. grossularia*)	Rosaceae
Blackcurrant	*R. nigrum*	Rosaceae
Redcurrant	*R. rubrum*	Rosaceae
Fig	*Ficus carica*	Moraceae
Olive	*Olea europaea*	Oleaceae
Mulberry; black mulberry	*Morus nigra*	Moraceae
Red mulberry	*M. rubra*	Moraceae
Grape	*Vitis vinifera*	Vitaceae
Frost grape	*V. riparia; V. vulpina*	Vitaceae
Bush or sand grape	*V. rupestris*	Vitaceae
Fox or skunk grape	*V. labrusca*	Vitaceae
Muscadine; bullace grape	*V. rotundifolia*	Vitaceae
Bilberry	*Vaccinium myrtillus*	Ericaceae
Cranberry	*V. oxycoccus; V. macrocarpon*	Ericaceae
Cowberry	*V. vitis-idaea*	Ericaceae
Lowbush blueberry	*V. angustifolium*	Ericaceae
Highbush blueberry	*V. corymbosum*	Ericaceae
Strawberry tree	*Arbutus unedo*	Ericaceae
Chinese gooseberry; kiwiberry	*Actinidia chinensis*	Actinidiaceae

Plants as foodstuffs (continued)

Tropical and subtropical fruits

Common Name	Latin name	Family
Sweet orange	Citrus sinensis	Rutaceae
Sour, Seville or bitter orange	C. aurantium	Rutaceae
Lime	C. aurantiifolia	Rutaceae
Lemon	C. limon	Rutaceae
Rangpur lime; mandarin lime	C. × limonia	Rutaceae
Shaddock; pummelo	C. maxima	Rutaceae
Citron	C. medica	Rutaceae
King orange	C. × nobilis	Rutaceae
Grapefruit	C. × paradisi	Rutaceae
Mandarin; satsuma; tangerine; clementine	C. reticulata	Rutaceae
Kumquat	Fortunella japonica	Rutaceae
Loquat; Japanese medlar	Eriobotrya japonica	Rosaceae
Breadfruit	Artocarpus altilis	Moraceae
Jackfruit	A. heterophyllus	Moraceae
Cherimoya	Annona cherimolia	Annonaceae
Custard apple; bullock's heart	A. reticulata	Annonaceae
Soursop; guanabana	A. muricata	Annonaceae
Sugarapple; sweetsop	A. squamosa	Annonaceae
Banana; edible plantain	Musa acuminata; M. × paradisiaca	Musaceae
Fehi banana	M. fehi	Musaceae
Avocado; aguacate; alligator pear	Persaea americana (= P. gratissima)	Lauraceae
Coconut	Cocos nucifera	Palmae
Date	Phoenix dactylifera	Palmae
Pineapple	Ananas comosus	Bromeliaceae
Mango	Mangifera indica	Anacardiaceae
Cashew apple	Anacardium occidentale	Anacardiaceae
Granadilla; passion fruit	Passiflora edulis	Passifloraceae
Sweet granadilla	P. ligularis	Passifloraceae
Yellow granadilla	P. laurifolia	Passifloraceae
Sweet calabash	P. maliformis	Passifloraceae
Curuba	P. mollissima	Passifloraceae
Giant granadilla	P. quadrangularis	Passifloraceae
Papaw; pawpaw	Carica papaya	Caricaceae
Durian	Durio zibethinus	Bombacaceae
Mangosteen	Garcinia mangostana	Guttiferae
Rambutan	Nephelium lappaceum	Sapindaceae
Longan	Euphoria longan	Sapindaceae
Akee	Blighia sapida	Sapindaceae
Guava	Psidium guajava	Myrtaceae
Cape gooseberry	Physalis peruviana	Solanaceae
Tomatillo; jamberry	P. ixocarpa	Solanaceae
Mammey apple; mammee	Mammea americana	Guttiferae
Sapodilla	Manilkara sapota	Sapotaceae
Sapote	Pouteria sapota (= Calocarpoum sapota)	Sapotaceae

Common name	Latin name	Family
Tamarind	Tamarindus indica	Leguminosae
Carambola; caramba; blimbing; bilimbi	Averrhoa carambola	Oxalidaceae
Persimmon	Diospyros kaki	Ebenaceae
Pomegranate	Punica granatum	Punicaceae
Litchi; lychee	Litchi chinensis	Sapindaceae

Vegetables

Common name	Latin name	Family
BRASSICAS		
Cabbage, spring		Cruciferae
Cabbage, savoy		Cruciferae
Cauliflower		Cruciferae
Broccoli; calabrese	Brassica oleracea	Cruciferae
Kale		Cruciferae
Brussel sprouts		Cruciferae
Turnip; swede	B. campestris	Cruciferae
Pak-choi	B. campestris, subspecies chinensis	Cruciferae
Pe-tsai	B. campestris, subspecies pekinensis	Cruciferae
LEAF AND STEM VEGETABLES		
Asparagus	Asparagus officinalis	Liliaceae
Wild asparagus	A. acutifolius	Liliaceae
Chives	Allium schoenoprasum	Liliaceae
Celery	Apium graveolens	Umbelliferae
Fennel	Foeniculum vulgare var vulgare	Umbelliferae
Florence fennel; finocchio	F. vulgare var azoricum	Umbelliferae
Chicory; asparagus chicory; witloof; belgian endive	Cichorium intybus	Compositae
Radicchio; red verona chicory; treviso chicory; castelfranco chicory	C. intybus	Compositae
Grumolo; broad-leaved chicory	C. intybus	Compositae
Endive; escarolle; batavian endive	C. endivia	Compositae
Lettuce; cabbage lettuce; cos lettuce	Lactuca sativa	Compositae
Wild lettuce	L. taraxaciflora	Compositae
Spinach; summer or round-seeded, winter or prickly-seeded	Spinacia oleracea	Chenopodiaceae
Spinach beet	Beta vulgaris var cicla	Chenopodiaceae
Seakale beet; Swiss chard	B. vulgaris var cicla	Chenopodiaceae
Orache	Atriplex hortensis	Chenopodiaceae

Common name	Latin name	Family
New Zealand spinach	Tetragonia expansa	Aizoaceae
Amaranth spinach	Amaranthus caudatus; A. hybridus; A. tricolor	Amaranthaceae
Sea kale	Crambe maritima	Cruciferae
Bamboo shoots	Bambusa arundinacea B. beecheyana; B. vulgaris; Phyllostachys dulcis; P. pubescens etc	Gramineae
Globe artichoke	Cynara scolymus	Compositae
Cardoon	C. cardunculus	Compositae
Okra; gumbo; lady's fingers	Hibiscus esculentus (= Abelmoschus esculentus)	Malvaceae
Jew's mallow	Corchorus olitorius	Tiliaceae
Jute	C. capsularis	Tiliaceae
Water spinach	Ipomoea aquatica	Convolvulaceae
Rhubarb, garden	Rheum rhabarbarum	Polygonaceae

ROOT VEGETABLES

Common name	Latin name	Family
Radish	Raphanus sativus	Cruciferae
Winter radish	R. sativus cv 'Longipinnatus'	Cruciferae
Black salsify	Scorzonera hispanica	Compositae
Salsify; oyster plant	Tragopogon porrifolius	Compositae
Carrot	Daucus carota subspecies sativus	Umbelliferae
Parsnip	Pastinaca sativa	Umbelliferae
Celeriac; turnip-rooted celery	Apium graveolens var rapaceum	Umbelliferae
Arracacha	Arracacia xanthorrhiza	Umbelliferae
Turnip-rooted parsley; hamburg parsley	Petroselinum crispum var tuberosum	Umbelliferae
Chervil, turnip-rooted	Chaerophyllum bulbosum	Umbelliferae
Jerusalem artichoke	Helianthus tuberosus	Compositae
Chinese artichoke	Stachys tuberifera	Labiatae
Oca	Oxalis tuberosa	Oxalidaceae
Ulluco; ullucu	Ullucus tuberosus	Basellaceae
Anu; anyu	Tropaeolum tuberosum	Tropaeolaceae
Yam bean	Pachyrhizus erosus	Leguminosae
Yam bean; potato bean	P. tuberosus	Leguminosae
Sacred or East Indian lotus	Nelumbo nucifera	Nymphaeaceae
Kaffir potato; Hausa potato	Plectranthus (Coleus) esculentus	Labiatae
Onion	Allium cepa	Liliaceae
Shallot	A. cepa var aggregatum (= A. ascalonicum)	Liliaceae
Welsh onion; Japanese onion	A. fistulosum	Liliaceae
Garlic	A. sativum	Liliaceae
Leek	A. porrum	Liliaceae

Fruit vegetables

Common name	Latin name	Family
Tomato	Lycopersicum esculentum	Solanaceae
Aubergine	Solanum melongena	Solanaceae
Cucumber	Cucumis sativa	Cucurbitaceae
Gherkin	C. anguria	Cucurbitaceae
Bitter gourd; bitter cucumber	Momordica charantia	Cucurbitaceae
Bottle gourd; calabash gourd; white gourd	Lagenaria siceraria	Cucurbitaceae
Snake gourd	Trichosanthes cucumerina	Cucurbitaceae
Wax, ash gourd	Benincasa hispida	Cucurbitaceae
Chayote; christophine pumpkins; marrows; squashes	Sechium edule	Cucurbitaceae
Breadfruit	Artocarpus altilis	Moraceae
Jackfruit	A. heterophyllus	Moraceae
Pepper; sweet pepper	Capsicum annuum	Solanaceae
Avocado; alligator pear	Persea americana	Lauraceae

Root crops

Common name	Latin name	Family
TEMPERATE		
Turnip	Brassica campestris ssp rapifera	Cruciferae
Swede; rutabaga	B. napus var napobrassica	Cruciferae
Mangel; mangel-wurzel; mangold	Beta vulgaris ssp vulgaris	Chenopodiaceae
Beet; sugarbeet; beetroot	B. vulgaris ssp vulgaris	Chenopodiaceae
Potato	Solanum tuberosum	Solanaceae
TROPICAL		
Sweet potato	Ipomoea batatas	Convolvulaceae
Topee-tambu	Calathea alloula	Marantaceae
Cassava; manihot	Manihot esculenta	Euphorbiaceae
Taro; tanier cocoyams, arrowroots		
Yam, white Guinea	Dioscorea rotundata	Dioscoreaceae
Yam, yellow Guinea	D. cayenensis	Dioscoreaceae
Yam, greater	D. alata	Dioscoreaceae
Yam, bitter	D. dumetorum	Dioscoreaceae
Yam, Asiatic	D. esculenta	Dioscoreaceae
Yam, American	D. trifida	Dioscoreaceae

Plants as foodstuffs (continued)
Legumes and pulses

Common name	Latin name	Part consumed
COOL TEMPERATE AND WARM TEMPERATE		
Garden pea	Pisum sativum	Seeds; young pods
Field pea	P. arvense	Seeds
Asparagus pea; winged pea	Tetragonolobus purpureus	
French, kidney, haricot, green, runner, string, salad, wax bean	Phaseolus vulgaris	Young pods; seeds
Runner; scarlet runner	P. coccineus	Young pods
Butter, sieva, civet, Madagascar, Carolina sewee bean	P. lunatus	Seeds
Lima bean	P. limensis	Seeds
Soybean	Glycine max (G. soja)	Seeds; sprouts; oil
Lentil	Lens culinaris	Seeds
Broad bean	Vicia faba	Seeds
Lupin	Lupinus albus; L. pilosus; L. luteus; L. mutabilis	Seeds
Carob bean; locust bean; St John's bread	Ceratonia siliqua	Pods
TROPICAL		
Tepary bean	Phaseolus acutifolius var latifolius	Seeds
Cluster bean; guar	Cyamopsis tetragonolobus	Young pods; seeds
Goa bean; asparagus pea; winged pea	Psophocarpus tetragonolobus	Young pods
Yam bean; chopsui potato	Pachyrhizus erosus; P. tuberosus	Young pods; roots
Lablab; hyacinth	Dolichos lablab	Pods; seeds
Madras gram; horse gram	D. biflorus	Seeds
Chick pea	Cicer arietinum	Seeds
Bambara; groundnut; kaffir pea	Voandzeia subterranea	Seeds
Kersting's groundnut	Kerstingiella geocarpa	Seeds
Tamarind	Tamarindus indica	Pulp from pods; seeds
Moth bean	Vigna aconitifolia	Seeds
Adzuki bean	V. angularis	Seeds
Cowpea	V. unguiculata	Seeds
Black-eyed pea	V. unguiculata subspecies unguiculata	Seeds
Yard long bean	V. unguiculata subspecies sesquipedalis	Pods
Black gram	Vigna mungo (Phaseolus mungo)	Seeds; young pods
Green gram; mung bean	V. radiata (Phaseolus aureus)	Seeds; pods; sprouts

Common name	Latin name	Part consumed
Rice bean	V. umbellata	Seeds
Jack bean	Canavalia ensiformis	Young pods; seeds
Sword bean	C. gladiata	Young pods; seeds
Groundnut	Arachis hypogaea	Seeds; oil
Pigeon pea; Cajan congo pea; red gram	Cajanus cajan	Seeds
African locust bean	Parkia filicoidea; P. biglobosa	Seeds; pulp of pod
Yam bean	Sphenostylis stenocarpa	seeds

Main cereal crops

Common name	Latin name
Wheat	Triticum
wild emmer	T. diococcoides
cultivated emmer	T. diococcum
einkorns	T. monococcum var monococcum; var boeoticum
hard (durum)	T. durum
turgidum	T. turgidum
bread	T. aestivum var aestivum
spelt	T. spelta
club	T. compactum
Barley	Hordeum vulgare
two-rowed	H. distichum
six-rowed	H. hexastichum
Rye	Secale cereale
Maize (US corn)	Zea mays
Rice	Oryza sativa
African rice	O. glaberrima
Oats	Avena
hexaploid	A. sativa; A. byzantina; A. nuda
tetraploid	A. abyssinica
diploid	A. strigosa; A. brevis
Sorghum	Sorghum bicolor
Millets	
finger or African	Eleusine coracana;
bulrush; pearl	Pennisetum americanum;
bajra; common;	Panicum miliaceum
proso	
Japanese barnyard; sanwa	Echinachloa frumentacea
Foxtail, German and Italian	Setaria italica
Teff	Eragrostis tef
Fonio; fundi	Digitaria spp
Koda; kodo	Paspalum scrobiculatum

Sugar and starch crops

Common name	Latin name	Family
SUGAR PLANTS		
Sugar cane	Saccharum officinarum	Gramineae
Sugar beet	Beta vulgaris	Chenopodiaceae
Sugar maple	Acer saccharum	Aceraceae

Common name	Latin name	Family
Black maple	A. nigrum	Aceraceae
Barley (germinating)	Hordeum vulgare	Gramineae
Sweet sorghum; sorgo	Sorghum bicolor	Gramineae
Wild date palm	Phoenix sylvestris	Palmae
Palmyra palm	Borassus flabellifer	Palmae
Toddy palm; sago palm; jaggery palm	Caryota urens	Palmae
Coconut palm	Cocos nucifera	Palmae
Gomuti palm; sugar palm	Arenga pinnata	Palmae
Honey palm; syrup palm	Jubaea chilensis	Oleaceae
Nypa palm	Nypa fruticans	Oleaceae
Manna ash	Fraxinus ornus	Oleaceae

STARCH PLANTS

Common name	Latin name	Family
Potato	Salanum tuberosum	Solanaceae
Cassava; manioc	Manihot esculenta	Euphorbiaceae
Arrowroot	Maranta arundinacea	Marantaceae
Queensland arrowroot	Canna edulis	Cannaceae
Taro	Colocasia esculenta	Araceae
Giant taro	Alocasia macrorrhiza	Araceae
Dasheen	Colocasia esculenta var globifera	Araceae
Giant swamp taro	Cyrtosperma chamissonis (C. edule)	Araceae
Tanier; cocoyam	Xanthosma atrovirens; X. sagittifolium; X. violaceum	Araceae
East Indian arrowroot	Curcuma angustifolia	Zingiberaceae
Fijian arrowroot; Tahitian arrowroot	Tacca leontopetaloides (T. pinnatifida)	Taccaceae
Greater Asiatic yam	Dioscorea alata	Dioscoreaceae
White Guinea yam	D. rotundata	Dioscoreaceae
Yellow Guinea yam	D. cayenensis	Dioscoreaceae
Air potato	D. bulbifera	Dioscoreaceae
Cush-cush; yampee	D. trifida	Dioscoreaceae
Sago palm	Metroxylon rumphii; M. sagu	Palmae
Sago palm; gomuti palm	Arenga pinnata	Palmae
American cabbage palm; caribee palm	Oreodoxa oleracea; Roystonea oleracea	Palmae / Palmae

Common name	Latin name	Family
Kaffir bread	Encephalartos caffer	Zamiaceae
Bread tree	E. altensteinii	Zamiaceae
Sago palm; queen sago	Cycas circinalis	Cycadaceae
Japanese sago palm	C. revoluta	Cycadaceae
Maize	Zea mays	Gramineae
Wheat	Triticum spp	Gramineae
Rice	Oryza sativa	Gramineae

Edible nuts

Common name	Latin name	Main areas of cultivation
Hazelnut; cob; European filbert	Corylus avellana	Turkey; Italy; Spain; France; England; Oregon
Giant filbert	C. maxima (C. americana)	(As above)
Turkish cobnut	C. colurna	Turkey
Sweet chestnut	Castanea sativa	S Europe; N America
American chestnut	C. dentata	N America
Japanese chestnut	C. crenata	Japan; N America
Chinese chestnut	C. mollissima	China; Korea; N America
Almond	Prunus amygdalus (= P. dulcis)	Mediterranean; SW Asia; N America
Sweet almond	P. amygdalus var amygdalus	Americas
Bitter almond	P. amygdalus var amara	
Walnut	Juglans regia	Europe; Asia; N America
Black walnut; eastern walnut	J. nigra	N America
Butternut	J. cinerea	N America
Japanese walnut	J. ailanthifolia	Japan; N America
Chinese walnut	J. cathayensis	China; N America
Pecan	Carya illinoinensis	N America
Shagbark hickory	C. ovata	N America
Shellbark hickory	C. laciniosa	N America
Brazil nut; paranut	Bertholletia excelsa	Amazon region (wild)
Sapucaia; sapucaya	Lecythis sabucayo	S America (wild)
Monkey nut	L. usitata	S America (wild)
Cashew nut	Anacardium occidentale	Tropical S America; India; E Africa
Coconut	Cocos nucifera	India; Sri Lanka; Malaysia; Indonesia; Philippines

NATURAL HISTORY

Plants as foodstuffs (continued)

Common name	Latin name	Main areas of cultivation	Common name	Latin name	Main areas of cultivation
Macadamia; Australia, or Queensland nut (smooth shell)	Macadamia integrifolia	Australia; California	Pistachio	Pistacia vera	E Mediterranean; India; S USA
Macadamia nut (rough shell)	M. tetraphylla	Australia; California	Betel nut	Areca catechu	Old World tropics
Moreton bay chestnut	Castanospermum australe	Australia (wild)	Kola	Cola nitida	W Africa; Caribbean
Oysternut	Telfairia pedata	E Africa		C. acuminata	W Africa; Brazil
Peanut; ground nut	Arachis hypogaea	India; tropical Africa; China	Water chestnut	Trapa natans; T. bicornis; T. maximowiczii	E Asia; Malaysia; India
Pilt nut	Canarium luzonicum; C. ovatum	Philippines	Pine nut; pine kernel	Pinus pinea; P. pinaster	Mediterranean Mediterranean
			Swiss stone pine	P. cembra	Europe
Java almond	C. commune	Java	Mexican stone pine	P. cembroides	Mexico

Herbs and spices

Common name	Latin name	Forms	Area of origin
Anise	Pimpinella anisum	Seeds; leaves	Middle East, now Southern Russia; Turkey; India; parts of Europe
Basil	Ocimum basilicum	Leaves	Europe
Bay	Laurus nobilis	Leaves	Mediterranean
Bergamot	Monarda didyma	Flowers; leaves	N America
Caraway	Carum carvi	Seeds (ground); leaves; tap roots	Temperate Asia; Europe; N America
Cardamom	Elettaria cardomomum	Pods; seeds (dried)	India; Middle East
Chervil	Anthriscus cerfolium	Leaves	S Russia, now Europe
Chilli	Capsicum annuum	Whole (fresh or dried)	N America; Europe
Chives	Allium schoenoprasum	Stems; flowers	Europe
Cinnamon	Cinnamomum zeylanicum	Bark (dried or ground)	Sri Lanka
Cloves	Eugenia aromatica	Buds (whole and ground)	SE Asia; Indonesia; Madagascar; Tanzania; Sri Lanka; Malaysia; Grenada
Coriander	Coriandrum sativum	Leaves; seeds (ground)	S Europe; Middle East
Cumin	Cuminum cyminum	Seeds (whole and ground)	The East; India; Egypt; Arabia
Dill	Anethum graveolens	Leaves; seeds	Scandinavia; Germany; C and E Europe
Fennel	Foeniculum vulgare	Leaves; stalks; seeds	S Europe
Ginger	Zingiber officinale	Root	Tropical Asia; Middle East; S Europe
Juniper	Juniperus communis	Berries	S Europe
Lovage	Levisticum officinale	Leaves; seeds; stems	Europe
Marjoram	Origanum majorana	Leaves	Mediterranean regions
Mint	Mentha	Leaves	Europe; Middle East
Mustard	Brassica nigra; B. juncea; B. alba	Seeds	Europe (white mustard – Mediterranean region)
Nutmeg	Myristica fragrans	Whole; ground	SE Asia
Oregano	Oregano vulgare	Leaves	Mediterranean regions
Paprika	Capsicum tetragonum	Fresh (whole); dried (ground)	Mexico; Spain; Morocco; Hungary
Parsley	Petroselinum crispum	Leaves	S Europe, now all the world's temperate regions
Poppy seeds	Papaver somniferum	Seeds	Middle East; India, N America; Europe
Rosemary	Rosmarinus officinalis	Leaves; flowers	Mediterranean region
Saffron	Crocus sativus	Flowers (dried and ground)	Mediterranean countries, particularly Spain

Herbs and spices (continued)

Common name	Latin name	Forms	Area of origin
Sage	*Salvia officinalis*	Leaves	N Mediterranean coast
Sassafras	*Sassafrass albidum, S. officinalis*	Leaves; bark (dried)	N America
Sesame seeds	*Sesamum indicum*	Seeds	Africa; India; China
Sorrel	*Rumex acetosa, R. scutatus*	Leaves	Europe; particularly France
Tamarind	*Tamarindus indica*	Pulp	E Africa; S Asia
Tansy	*Chrysanthemum vulgare*	Leaves	Europe
Tarragon	*Artemisia dracunculus*	Leaves	Siberia; now Europe
Thyme	*Thymus vulgaris*	Leaves	Mediterranean regions
Turmeric	*Curcuma longa*	Root (whole or ground)	India; China; Middle East
Vanilla	*Vanilla plainfolia*	Pods	S Mexico; Madagascar; C America; Puerto Rico; Réunion

FUNGI

Phylum	No. of species	Class	Examples	Characteristics of class
Zygomycota	600	Mucorales	Black bread mould *(Rhizopus stolonifer)*; Mucor	Many saprozoic on dung or organic debris. Others parasites of invertebrates, other fungi, and plants.
		Entomophthorales	*Basidiobolus*	Most parasites of animals, mainly insects.
		Zoopagales	*Cochlonema; Endocochlus*	Parasites of amoebas, nematodes, and other small animals.
Ascomycota	15 000	Hemiascomycetae	Yeasts, eg baker's yeast *(Saccharomyces cerevisiae)*	Morphologically simple. Short mycelia or none at all.
		Euascomycetae	Morels; truffles *(Tuber)*; most fungal partners in lichens; *Neurospora*	Largest and best known class of Ascomycota.
		Loculoascomycetae	*Mycosphaerella; Elsinoe*	Many are parasites of economically important food plants.
		Laboulbeniomycetae	*Rhizomyces; Amorphomyces*	Parasites of insects.
Basidiomycota	25 000	Heterobasidiomycetae	Jelly fungi; rusts; smuts	
		Homobasidiomycetae	Common mushrooms; shelf fungi; coral fungi; puffballs; earthstars; stinkhorns; bird's nest fungi	Contains most of the fungi known as mushrooms and toadstools.
Deuteromycota (Fungi Imperfecti)	25 000	Sphaeropsida	*Clypeoseptoria aparothospermi*	
		Melanconia	*Cryptosporium lunasporum*	
		Monilia	*Penicillium; Candida albicans*	Pathogenic yeasts; other yeasts that do not form asci or basidia.
		Mycelia Sterilia	*Rhizoctonia*	

PART FIVE

Human Beings

EARLY HUMANS

Evolution of early humans

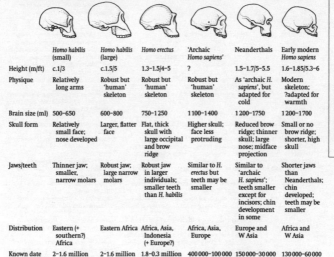

	Homo habilis (small)	Homo habilis (large)	Homo erectus	'Archaic Homo sapiens'	Neanderthals	Early modern Homo sapiens
Height (m/ft)	c.1/3	c.1.5/5	1.3–1.5/4–5	?	1.5–1.7/5–5.5	1.6–1.85/5.3–6
Physique	Relatively long arms	Robust but 'human' skeleton	Robust but 'human' skeleton	Robust but 'human' skeleton	As 'archaic H. sapiens', but adapted for cold	Modern skeleton; ?adapted for warmth
Brain size (ml)	500–650	600–800	750–1250	1100–1400	1200–1750	1200–1700
Skull form	Relatively small face; nose developed	Larger, flatter face	Flat, thick skull with large occipital and brow ridge	Higher skull; face less protruding	Reduced brow ridge; thinner skull; large nose; midface projection	Small or no brow ridge; shorter, high skull
Jaws/teeth	Thinner jaw; smaller, narrow molars	Robust jaw; large narrow molars	Robust jaw in larger individuals; smaller teeth than H. habilis	Similar to H. erectus but teeth may be smaller	Similar to 'archaic H. sapiens'; teeth smaller except for incisors; chin development in some	Shorter jaws than Neanderthals; chin developed; teeth may be smaller
Distribution	Eastern (+ southern?) Africa	Eastern Africa	Africa, Asia, Indonesia (+ Europe?)	Africa, Asia, Europe	Europe and W Asia	Africa and W Asia
Known date (years ago)	2–1.6 million	2–1.6 million	1.8–0.3 million	400 000–100 000	150 000–30 000	130 000–60 000

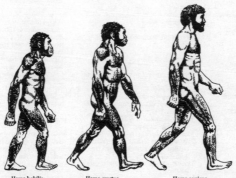

Homo habilis   *Homo erectus*   *Homo sapiens*

HUMAN BEINGS

Early human behaviour/ecology

Hominids and time periods (years ago)	Inference	Nature of the evidence
A Hominid ancestors ?8–5 million	Equatorial African origin.	Humans are genetically closest to African apes, which today are distributed across equatorial Africa; earliest hominid fossils are in eastern Africa.
B Earliest hominids 5–3 million	Habitually bipedal on the ground; occasionally arboreal.	Postcranial anatomy of fossils from Hadar in Ethiopia (but disagreements about similarity to modern human bipedalism and degree of arboreality).
	Inhabited a mosaic of grassland, woodland and thick shrub.	Faunas from Laetoli in Tanzania, Hadar and Makapansgat in South Africa.
3–2 million	Occupation of open savannas.	Fossil pollen and fauna.
	Emphasis on a fibrous plant diet in robust australopithecines.	Microwear on teeth; large teeth and jaws.
	First known manufacture of stone tools.	Tools from Ethiopia, Kenya, Malawi, and Democratic Republic of Congo dated between 2.5 and 2.0 million years.
C Plio-Pleistocene hominids 2.0–1.5 million (Stone technology and changes in diet, brain size, etc. are usually associated with *Homo*)	Increased commitment to bipedalism on the ground.	Postcranial anatomy associated with archaic *Homo* established.
	Increased dexterity related to tool use and toolmaking, and possibly foraging.	Anatomy of hand bones and characteristics of stone tools and cores.
	Stones and animal bones carried repeatedly to specific sites.	Earliest known complex sites with many stone artifacts and fossils.
	Use of tools to procure and process food.	Bone and stone tools with distinctive traces of use.
	Dietary increase in protein and fat from large animals.	Cut marks made by stone tools on animal bones.
	Scavenging and possible hunting of large animals; processing of animals at specific spots.	Limb bones of animals concentrated at undisturbed archaeological sites.
	Increased cognitive capacities associated with making tools, foraging, social arrangements, and/or developing linguistic skills.	Increase in brain size from about a third to a half that of modern humans.
	Changes in maturation rate.	Implied by brain size increase and possible changes in tooth development.
	Increased mobility and predator defence.	Large stature evident in skeletal remains of early *Homo erectus* from West Turkana in Kenya.
D Early Pleistocene hominids 1.5–0.1 million	Occupation of new habitats and geographic zones.	Sites occur in previously unoccupied areas of eastern Africa; first appearance of hominids outside Africa.
	Definite preconception of tool form.	Biface handaxes of consistent shape made from rocks of varying original shape.
	Manipulation of fire.	Indications of fire differentially associated with archaeological sites.
	Increased levels of activity and stress on skeletons.	Massive development of postcranial and cranial bones.
E Late Pleistocene hominids 100 000–35 000 (Neanderthals)	Increased sophistication of toolkit and technology; still slow rate of change to tool assemblage.	Larger number of stone-tool types than before; complex preparation of cores.
	Intentional burial of dead and suggestions of ritual.	Preservation of skeletons, some with objects.
	Maintenance of high activity levels (locomotor endurance; powerful arms) and high levels of skeletal stress (eg teeth used as tools).	Robust skeletons, especially thick leg bones and large areas for muscle attachment on arm bones; prominent wear patterns on incisor teeth.
35 000–10 000 (fully modern *Homo sapiens*)	Decreased levels of activity and stress on skeleton.	Decrease in skeletal robusticity (also seen in early modern humans before 35 000 years ago).

Hominids and time periods (years ago)	Inference	Nature of the evidence
	Enhanced technological efficiency.	Innovations in stone- and bone-tool production (eg blades and bone points).
	Innovations in hunting and other foraging activities, including systematic exploitation of particular animal species.	Evidence of spearthrower and harpoon, and trapping and netting of animals; animal remains in archaeological middens.
	Colonization of previously uninhabited zones.	For example, sites in tundra in Europe and Asia; colonization of the Americas (Australasia was probably first inhabited around 50 000 years ago).
	Elaboration of artistic symbolic expression and notation.	Engraving, sculpting and painting of walls and figurines; repetitive marks on bones; jewellery.
	Surge of technological and cultural differentiation and change.	Variation in toolkits over space and time.
	Harvesting and first cultivation of grains; first domestication of animals.	Evidence of seeds and fauna from sites dating to the end of the Pleistocene.

THE BODY

DNA

DNA or *deoxyribonucleic acid* contains the genetic information for most living organisms. Each human cell contains about 2 m/6.6 ft of DNA supercoiled on itself such that it fits within the cell nucleus (less than 10 μm (micrometres) in diameter).

DNA consists of four *bases* (adenine [A], guanine [G], thymine [T], and cytosine [C]), a sugar (2-deoxy-D-ribose), and phosphoric acid, arranged in the famous *double helical* structure discovered by geneticists James Watson and Francis Crick in 1953. In the helical structure, A pairs only with T, and G only with C.

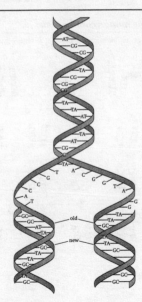

DNA structure and replication, following Watson and Crick. The two strands of the double helix separate, and a new strand is assembled alongside each, the base sequence being determined by complementary pairing with the base sequence of the existing strand.

The genetic code

The four DNA bases A, G, T, and C, like the letters of the alphabet, can be used to store information. This genetic information is passed on via RNA or *ribonucleic acid* (consisting of the four bases adenine, guanine, cytosine, and uracil [U]), which provides a template for the assembly of amino acids in a particular sequence, thereby building a protein.

A group of three DNA or RNA bases is known as a *triplet* or *codon*, and codes for a particular amino acid. Information is passed from DNA to RNA by *complementary pairing*: A pairs only with U, and G only with C.

Genetic code in RNA triplets

1st base	2nd base				3rd base
	U	C	A	G	
U	Phenylalanine	Serine	Tyrosine	Cysteine	U
	Phenylalanine	Serine	Tyrosine	Cysteine	C
	Leucine	Serine	—[a]	—[a]	A
	Leucine	Serine	—[a]	Tryptophan	G
C	Leucine	Proline	Histidine	Arginine	U
	Leucine	Proline	Histidine	Arginine	C
	Leucine	Proline	Glutamine	Arginine	A
	Leucine	Proline	Glutamine	Arginine	G
A	Isoleucine	Threonine	Asparagine	Serine	U
	Isoleucine	Threonine	Asparagine	Serine	C
	Isoleucine	Threonine	Lysine	Arginine	A
	Methionine	Threonine	Lysine	Arginine	G
G	Valine	Alanine	Aspartic acid	Glycine	U
	Valine	Alanine	Aspartic acid	Glycine	C
	Valine	Alanine	Glutamic acid	Glycine	A
	Valine	Alanine	Glutamic acid	Glycine	G

[a] Chain termination.

The human chromosomes

The 46 human chromosomes, showing the banding patterns characteristic of each, grouped according to convention.

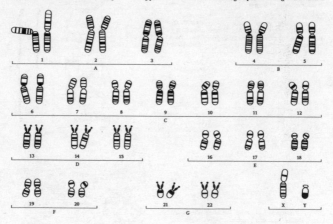

The human skeleton

The bones of the skeleton are often divided into two groups: the *axial skeleton* comprises the bones of the vertebral column, skull, ribs, and sternum; and the *appendicular skeleton* comprises the remainder.

1 Skull, displaying the frontal bone, and the front parts of the parietal and temporal bones. **2** Maxilla. **3** Mandible. **4** Clavicle. **5** Humerus. **6** Radius. **7** Ulna. **8** Sternum. **9** Scapula (obscured in this view by the upper ribs). **10** Ribs. **11** Vertebral column, displaying (from above to below) cervical, thoracic, lumbar, sacral, and coccygeal vertebrae. **12** Ilium. **13** Sacrum. **14** Coccyx. **15** Femur. **16** Kneebone. **17** Fibula. **18** Tibia. **19** Bones of the hand, comprising the eight carpals, the five metacarpals, the three phalanges in each finger, and the two phalanges in the thumb. **20** Bones of the foot, comprising the seven tarsals, the five metatarsals, the two phalanges in the big toe, and the three phalanges in the other toes.

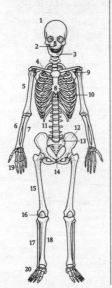

Bones of the human body

Skull

1	Occipital
2	Parietal – 1 pair
1	Sphenoid
1	Ethmoid
2	Inferior nasal conchae
1	Frontal – 1 pair, fused
2	Nasal – 1 pair
2	Lacrimal – 1 pair
2	Temporal – 1 pair
2	Maxilla – 1 pair
2	Zygomatic – 1 pair
1	Vomer
2	Palatine – 1 pair
1	Mandible – 1 pair, fused (jawbone)
22	

The ears

2	Malleus (hammer)	
2	Incus (anvil)	ossicles
2	Stapes (stirrups)	
6		

Vertebrae

7	Cervical
12	Thoracic
5	Lumbar
1	Sacral – 5, fused to form the sacrum
1	Coccyx – between 3 and 5, fused
26	

Vertebral ribs

14	Ribs, 'true' – 7 pairs
10	Ribs, 'false' – 5 pairs of which 2 pairs are floating
24	

Sternum (breastbone)

1	Manubrium
1	'The body' (sternebrae)
1	Xiphisternum
3	

1	Hyoid (in the throat)

Pectoral girdle

2	Clavicle – 1 pair (collar bone)
2	Scapula (including coracoid) – 1 pair (shoulder blade)
4	

Upper extremity (each arm)

1	Humerus	
1	Radius	forearm
1	Ulna	
	Carpus:	
1	Scaphoid	
1	Lunate	
1	Triquetral	
1	Pisiform	wrist
1	Trapezium	
1	Trapezoid	
1	Capitate	
1	Hamate	hand
5	Metacarpals	
	Phalanges:	
2	First digit	
3	Second digit	
3	Third digit	fingers
3	Fourth digit	
3	Fifth digit	
30		

Pelvic girdle

Ilium, ischium and pubis (combined) – 1 pair of hip
2 bones, innominate

Lower extremity (each leg)

1	Femur (thighbone)	
1	Tibia	
1	Fibula	
1	Patella (kneebone)	
	Tarsus:	
1	Talus	
1	Calcaneus	
1	Navicular	
1	Cuneiform medial	ankle
1	Cuneiform, intermediate	
1	Cuneiform, lateral	foot
1	Cuboid	
5	Metatarsals	
	Phalanges:	
2	First digit	
3	Second digit	
3	Third digit	toes
3	Fourth digit	
3	Fifth digit	
30		

Total

22	Skull
6	The ears
26	Vertebrae
24	Vertebral ribs
3	Sternum
1	Throat
4	Pectoral girdle
60	Upper extremity (arms) – 2 × 30
2	Hip bones
60	Lower extremity (legs) – 2 × 30
208	

HUMAN BEINGS

Muscles and internal organs

In human beings the musculature normally accounts for some 40% of the total body weight. There are 639 named muscles in the human anatomy.

1 Trapezius muscle
2 Deltoid muscles
3 Triceps muscles (the biceps, at the front of the arm, cannot be seen from this view)
4 Latissimus dorsi muscle
5 Gluteus maximus muscle (largest muscle in the body)
6 Kidney
7 Trachea
8 Lungs
9 Heart
10 Liver (only a small part of the liver can be seen in this illustration)
11 Stomach
12 Spleen
13 Colon
14 Small intestine
15 Appendix
16 Bladder

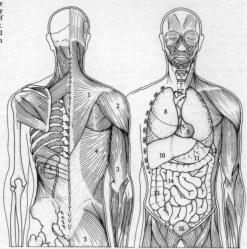

The heart

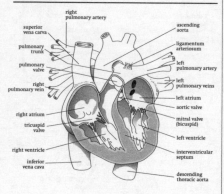

Human pulse rates

Normal resting pulse rates in healthy persons.

	Beats per minute
Foetus *in utero*	150
New born (full term)	140
First year	120
Second year	110
5 years	100
10 years	90
20 years	71
50 years	72
70 years	75
>80	78

Human temperature

Normal human body temperature is about 37°C (98.6°F); some people have a norm slightly higher or lower – especially young children. Norms change during the day – usually rising a little by mid-afternoon and falling a little during sleep.

The composition of blood

In an average human being blood accounts for 7–8% of body weight. Blood consists of:

Plasma: Water (90%), proteins (7%), nutrients, salts, nitrogen waste, carbon dioxide, hormones

Red blood cells (erythrocytes), 54% of which is haemoglobin. Normal count = 4–6 million per mm^3

White blood cells (leukocytes). Normal count = 4500–11000 per mm^3

Platelets (thrombocytes). Normal count = 150000–300000 per mm^3

The brain in section

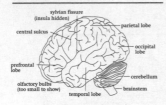

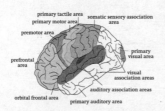

The ear

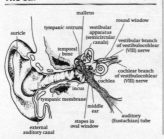

The eye

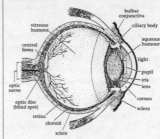

Normal eye

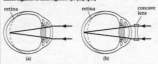

The image is in focus on the retina without a correcting lens in front.

Short-sighted or near-sighted eye (myopia)

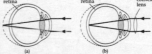

(a) The eye is too long and the image is not in focus on the retina.
(b) The use of a concave lens brings the image into focus.

Long-sighted or far-sighted eye (hypermetropia)

(a) The eye is too short and the image is not in focus on the retina.
(b) The use of a convex lens brings the image into focus.

The teeth

The approximate times of eruption and shedding of teeth.

Milk	Eruption	Shed	Permanent	Eruption
Incisor 1	6–10 months	6–7 years	Incisor 1	7–8 years
Incisor 2	8–12 months	7–8 years	Incisor 2	8–9 years
Canine	16–22 months	10–12 years	Canine	10–12 years
Molar 1	13–19 months	9–11 years	Premolar 1	10–11 years
Molar 2	25–33 months	10–12 years	Premolar 2	11–12 years
			Molar 1	6–7 years
			Molar 2	12 years
			Molar 3	17–21 years

Note: The lower teeth usually appear before the equivalent upper teeth.

The reproductive organs

Females
Main female organs of reproduction and surrounding structures

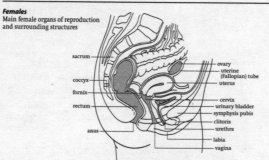

Males
Main male organs of reproduction and surrounding structures

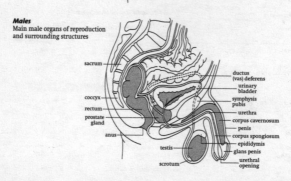

MEDICAL MATTERS

Communicable diseases

Name	Cause	Transmission	Incubation period
AIDS (Acquired Immune Deficiency Syndrome)	Human Immuno-deficiency Virus (HIV)	Sexual relations; sharing of syringes; blood transfusion	several years
Brucellosis	*Brucellus abortus* or *B meliteusis* bacteria	Cattle or goats	3–6 years
Chickenpox (varicella)	Varicella zoster virus (US) Herpes zoster virus (UK)	Infected persons; articles contaminated by discharge from mucous membranes	10–21 days
Cholera	*Vibrio cholerae* bacterium	Contaminated water and seafood	a few hours – 5 days
Common cold	Numerous viruses	Respiratory droplets of infected person	1–4 days
Diphtheria	*Corynebacterium diphtheriae* bacterium	Respiratory secretions and saliva of infected persons or carriers	2–6 days
Encephalitis	Viruses	Bite from infected mosquito	4–21 days
Gas gangrene	*Clostridium welchii* bacterium	Soil or soil-contaminated articles	1–4 days
Gonorrhoea	*Neisseria gonorrhoeae* bacterium	Urethral or vaginal secretions of infected persons	3–8 days
Hepatitis A (infectious)	Hepatitis A virus	Contaminated food and water	15–50 days
Hepatitis B (serum type B)	Hepatitis B virus	Infected blood; parenteral injection	6 weeks – 6 months
Infectious mononucleosis (US) Glandular fever (UK)	Epstein-Barr virus	Saliva; direct oral contact with infected person	2–6 weeks
Influenza	Numerous viruses (types A, B, C)	Direct contact; respiratory droplets, possibly airborne	1–4 days
Legionnaires' disease	*Legionella pneumophila* bacterium	Water droplets in contaminated hot-water systems, cooling towers, etc.	1–3 days
Leprosy	*Mycobacterium leprae* bacillus	Droplet infection (minimally contagious)	variable
Malaria	*Plasmodium* protozoa	Bite from infected mosquito	6–37 days
Measles (rubeola)	Rubeola virus	Droplet infection	10–15 days
Meningitis	Various bacteria (bacterial meningitis) and viruses (viral meningitis)	Respiratory droplets	varies with causative agent
Mumps	Virus	Direct contact with infected persons; respiratory droplets and oral secretions	14–21 days
Paratyphoid fevers	*Salmonella* bacteria	Ingestion of contaminated food and water	1–14 days
Pneumonia	*Streptococcus pneumoniae* bacterium	Droplet infection	1–3 weeks
Poliomyelitis	Polio viruses	Direct contact with nasopharyngeal secretions of infected persons; vomit	7–21 days
Rabies	Virus	Bite from rabid animal	10 days – 6 months
Rubella (German measles)	Rubella virus	Direct contact or droplet spread of nasopharyugeal secretion	14–21 days
SARS (severe acute respiratory syndrome)	SARS-associated coronavirus	Direct contact with infected persons, or respiratory droplets	2–7 days
Scarlet fever	Group A haemolytic *Streptococcus* bacteria	Direct or indirect contact with infected persons, or droplet infection	1–5 days
Shingles	*see* chickenpox	*see* chickenpox	
Smallpox (variola)	Poxvirus variola	Direct contact; droplet	7–14 days
Syphilis	*Treponema pallidum* bacterium	Sexual relations; contact with open lesions; blood transfusion	10–90 days
Tetanus (lockjaw)	*Clostridium tetani* bacillus	Animal faeces and soil	3–21 days
Tuberculosis	*Mycobacterium tuberculosis* bacillus	Droplet spread; ingestion from contaminated milk	variable
Typhoid fever	*Salmonella typhi* bacillus	Contaminated food and water	7–21 days
Whooping cough (pertussis)	*Bordetella pertussis* bacterium	Droplet spread	10–21 days
Yellow fever	Arbovirus	Bite from infected mosquito	3–6 days

HUMAN BEINGS

Phobias

An A to Z of phobias arranged by everyday name

HUMAN BEINGS

Everyday name	Technical term
Air	Aero-
Animals	Zoo-
Astral	Astra-
Birds	Orthino-
Blood	Hemato-
Blushing	Erythro-
Carriages	Amaka-
Cats	Ailouro-
Closed spaces	Claustro-
Clouds	Nepho- (nephelo-)
Cold	Cheima-
Colour	Chromo-
Comets	Cometo-
Contamination	Miso- (myso-)
Corpses	Necro-
Crowds	Demo-
Crystals	Chrystallo-
Darkness	Achluo-
Dawn	Eoso-
Death	Thanato-
Demons	Demono-
Disease	Noso- (patho-)
Dogs	Cyno-
Dreams	Oneiro-
Drinks	Poto-
Duration	Chrono-
Dust	Amatho-
Electricity	Elektro-
Everything	Pan- (panto-)
Eyes	Ommato-
Failure	Kakorraphia-
Fatigue	Kopo-
Fears	Phobo-
Feathers	Pterono-
Fire	Pyro-
Flashes	Sela-
Flogging	Mastigo-
Flood	Antlo-
Flute	Aulo-
Fog	Homichlo-
Food	Sito-
Fur	Dora-
Germs	Sperma- (spermato-)
Ghosts	Phasmo-
Girls	Partheno-

Everyday name	Technical term
Glass	Nelo-
God	Theo-
Gravity	Baro-
Heat	Thermo-
Heaven	Ourano-
Heights	Acro-
Hell	Stygio- (hade-)
Heredity	Patroio-
Home	Oiko-
Ice	Kristallo-
Ideas	Ideo-
Infinity	Apeiro-
Insanity	Lysso- (mania-)
Insects	Entomo-
Jealousy	Zelo-
Justice	Dike-
Light	Photo-
Machinery	Mechano-
Man	Anthropo-
Many things	Poly-
Men	Andro-
Metals	Metallo-
Meteors	Meteoro-
Mice	Muso-
Microbes	Bacillo-
Mirrors	Eisoptro-
Money	Chrometo-
Motion	Kineso-
Music	Musico-
Narrowness	Angino-
Needles	Belone-
Newness	Neo-
Northern Lights	Aurora-
Nudity	Gymno- (gymnoto-)
One thing	Mono-
Open spaces	Agora-
Pain	Algo-
Pins	Enete-
Pleasure	Hedono-
Points	Aichuro-
Poison	Toxi-
Poverty	Penia-
Punishment	Poine-
Reptiles	Batracho-
Responsibility	Hypegia-

Everyday name	Technical term
Ridicule	Katagelo-
Robberies	Harpaxo-
Ruin	Ate-
Satan	Satano-
Sea	Thalasso-
Sex	Geno-
Shock	Horme-
Sin	Hamartio-
Sitting	Thasso-
Skin	Dermato-
Sleep	Hypno-
Smell	Olfacto-
Smothering	Pnigero-
Snakes	Ophidio-
Snow	Chiono-
Soiling	Rypo-
Solitude	Eremo-
Sound	Akoustico-
Sourness	Acero-
Spiders	Arachno-
Standing	Stasi-
Stars	Sidero-
Stealing	Klepto-
Stings	Cnido-
Strangers	Xeno-
String	Linono-
Stuttering	Lalo-
Syphilis	Syphilo-
Taste	Geuma- (geumato-)
Teeth	Odonto-
Thirteen	Triskaideka-
Thunder	Bronto- (tonitro-)
Touch	Hapto-
Travel	Hodo-
Trembling	Tremo-
Vehicles	Ocho-
Void	Keno-
Walking	Baso-
Water	Hydro-
Weakness	Astheno-
Wind	Anemo-
Women	Gyno-
Words	Logo-
Work	Ergo-
Worms	Helmintho-
Writing	Grapho-

Commonly used drugs

Common name	Drug type	Use	Comments
Adrenaline	Bronchodilator	Counteracts cardiac arrest; relieves severe allergic reactions; and controls symptoms of asthma.	Constricts blood vessels and is used to control bleeding in surgery.
Anabolic steroids	Male sex hormones	Increase muscle bulk and body growth. Help increase production of blood cells in some forms of anaemia.	Risk of serious side-effects. Abused by some athletes to improve performance.
Aspirin	Analgesic; anti-inflammatory; anti-platelet	Relieves pain; reduces fever; helps prevent blood clots from forming.	Introduced by Hermann Dresser, 1893. Can cause irritation to the stomach and even bleeding.
AZT (azidothymidine)	Anti-viral drug	Suppresses activity of the virus that causes Aids, and can alleviate symptoms.	Effective only in certain cases, and not a cure.
Beta blockers	Beta blockers	Treat angina, hypertension, and irregular heart rhythms. Can also prevent migraines.	Minor side-effects of reduced circulation and reduced capacity for strenuous exercise.
Chloral hydrate	Sleeping drug	Short-term treatment of insomnia.	Suitable for use by children.
Cimetidine	Anti-ulcer drug	Reduces level of acid and pepsin, and promotes healing of stomach and duodenal ulcers.	Also affects actions of certain enzymes in the liver. Prescribed only when possibility of stomach cancer has been ruled out.
Codeine	Narcotic analgesic	Relieves mild pain. Also effective as a cough suppressant.	Introduced at turn of century. Can be habit-forming, but addiction seldom occurs if drug used for limited period.
Cortisone	Corticosteroid	Treats rheumatoid arthritis. Anti-inflammatory drug.	Discovered by Edward Calvin Kendall, 1934, as adrenal cortisone extracts.
Co-trimoxazole	Antibacterial	Treats respiratory, constipating, and urinary tract infections.	Can have side-effects of nausea and vomiting.
Diazepam	Benzodiazepine anti-anxiety drug	Treats anxiety, insomnia. Also prescribed as muscle relaxant.	Can be habit-forming if taken over a long period.
Digoxin	Digitalis drug	Slows down rate of heart. Controls tiredness, breathlessness, and fluid retention.	Treatment must be monitored carefully.
Ethambutol	Antituberculosis	Used with other antituberculosis drugs it helps boost their effects.	Side-effect can be eye damage.
Frusemide	Loop diuretic	Treats fluid retention caused by heart failure and some liver and kidney disorders.	Discovered 1960.
Ibuprofen	Analgesic; anti-inflammatory	Treats symptoms of rheumatoid arthritis as well as headaches and menstrual pain.	Few-side effects and does not cause bleeding in the stomach.
Insulin	For diabetes	Supplements or replaces natural insulin in diabetes mellitus.	Isolated by Frederick Banting, C H Best, 1921. Only effective treatment for juvenile diabetes.
Magnesium hydroxide	Antacid	Neutralizes stomach acid. Also acts as laxative.	
Morphine	Narcotic analgesic	Relieves severe pain.	Discovered by Friedrich Serturner, 1805. Derives from opium and can be addictive.
Paracetamol/ acetaminophen	Analgesic	Relieves bouts of mild pain and fever. Does not cause damage to stomach.	First used by Joseph von Mering, 1893. Large doses can be toxic and an overdose can cause serious damage to liver and kidneys.
Penicillin	Antibiotic	Treats many common infections.	Discovered by Alexander Fleming, 1928. Can cause allergic reactions.
Pethidine	Narcotic analgesic	Used particularly to relieve pain in childbirth. Effect short-lasting.	Introduced by Hoechst, 1939. Habit-forming if taken over long period of time.
Phenylpropan-olamine	Decongestant	Relieves nasal congestion in colds and hay fever.	Can raise the heart rate and cause palpitations.
Quinidine	Anti-arrhythmic drug	Treats abnormal heart rhythms.	Can cause allergic reactions.

Commonly used drugs (continued)

Common name	Drug type	Use	Comments
Quinine	Antimalarial drug	Treats malaria and leg cramps.	Discovered by P J Pelletier, J B Caventou, 1818. Now rarely prescribed due to side-effects of headaches, nausea, hearing loss and blurred vision.
Ranitidine	Anti-ulcer drug	Prevents gastric and duodenal ulcers. Reduces amount of acid produced by stomach.	Prescribed only when possibility of stomach cancer has been ruled out.
Salbutamol/ albuterol	Bronchodilator	Treats asthma, bronchitis, and emphysema.	Little stimulant effect on heart rate and blood pressure. Gives rapid relief and is more effective if inhaled rather than taken by mouth.
Sodium bicarbonate	Antacid	Relieves indigestion and discomfort caused by peptic ulcers. Relieves pain from urinary tract infections.	If given by injection, can also be effective in treatment of acidity of the blood.
Temazepam	Benzodiazepine sleeping drug	Short-term treatment of insomnia.	Can be habit-forming.
Terfenadine	Antihistamine	Treats allergic rhinitis, particularly hay fever.	Little or no sedative effect on the nervous system.
Testosterone	Male sex hormone	Increases fertility in men with testicular disorders. Also used to induce puberty in cases of hormone deficiency.	Can interfere with growth or cause over-rapid sexual development.
Tetracycline	Antibiotic	Treats pneumonia, bronchitis, and chest infections.	Common side-effects are nausea and vomiting.

Commonly abused drugs

Name	Common name	Effects	Comments
Alcohol	Booze, drink	Acts as central-nervous-system depressant, so reduces anxiety, impairs concentration, slows reactions.	Long-term effects include liver disease (cirrhosis, liver cancer, hepatitis), heart disease, and inflammation of stomach. Alcoholics have above-average chance of developing dementia.
Amphetamines	Uppers, speed, bennies	Promote feelings of alertness; increases speech and physical activity.	Can produce toxic effects, mood swings, circulatory and cardiac disturbances, feelings of paranoia, hallucinations, and convulsions.
Barbiturates (Nembutal, Seconal, Amytal)	Barbs, reds, downers	Calm the nerves; induce sleep; have hypnotic effect.	Highly addictive; overdose is lethal; can induce state of coma. Often fatal if taken with alcohol.
Benzodiazepines	Tranquillizers	Reduce mental activity and anxiety; slow body's reactions; reduce alertness.	Can cause dependency. Withdrawal symptoms occur on stopping the drug – anxiety, insomnia, panic attacks, headaches, and palpitations.
Cocaine	Coke, crack, ice, snow (crack is a blend of cocaine, baking powder, and water)	Increases blood pressure, heart rate, breathing, and body temperature; gives feelings of euphoria, illusions of increased sensory awareness and mental and physical strength, decreased hunger, pain, and need for sleep.	Regular use can cause anxiety, insomnia, weight loss, increased paranoia, and psychosis. Crack is highly addictive and has more intense effects than cocaine. Increased risk of abnormal heart rhythms, high blood pressure, stroke, and death. Long-term consequences include mental deterioration, personality changes, paranoia, or violent behaviour.
Heroin	Junk, smack	Induces euphoria; relieves pain; often induces sleep.	Highly addictive; overdose can result in death; serum hepatitis is common; as are skin abscesses, inflammation of the veins, constipation, and respiratory depression.
Lysergic acid diethylamide	LSD, acid	Causes hallucinations, alters vision, raises temperature and heart-beat; evokes flashbacks.	Long-term use causes anxiety and depression, impaired memory and attention span, difficulty with abstract thinking.

HUMAN BEINGS

Name	Common name	Effects	Comments
Marijuana	Grass, pot, weed, dope	Increases heartbeat; heightens senses; gives feelings of euphoria and relaxation.	Reduces the ability to perform tasks requiring concentration; slows reactions; and impairs coordination.
MDMA	Ecstasy, E	Promotes mental relaxation, increased sensitivity to stimuli, and sometimes hallucinations.	High doses have amphetamine-like effects. Can produce severe or fatal reactions, sometimes after only one dose.
Mescaline	Peyote, cactus buttons	Induces hallucinations; affects sensations and perceptions.	Loss of control of normal thought processes; long-term depression and anxiety; can induce 'breaks from reality'.
Methadone		Induces sleep and feeling of relaxation.	Addictive; overdose can result in death.
Nicotine		Stimulates the nervous system; increases concentration; relieves tension and fatigue; increases heart rate and blood pressure.	Taken regularly, can cause increase in fatty acids in bloodstream, increased risk of heart disease, and circulatory problems; can also increase risk of peptic ulcers. Increased risk of lung, throat, and mouth cancers from tobacco smoke.
Nitrites	Poppers	Give the user a rapid high, felt as rush of energy. Heart rate increases; there are feelings of dizziness and nausea. High doses can cause fainting.	Lasting physical damage, in the form of cardiac problems, can occur.
Phencyclidine	PCP, angel dust	Gives feeling of euphoria; floating sensation; numbness; change in user's perception of the body; visual disturbances.	Can produce violent behaviour against the user or others; and schizophrenic-like psychosis which can last for days or weeks.
Solvents		Cause lightheadedness, dizziness, and drowsiness. Large doses can lead to loss of consciousness.	Some products can seriously disrupt heart rhythm or cause heart failure and sometimes death. Aerosols can cause suffocation by coating the lungs. Risk of death also from depression of the breathing mechanism. Long-term misuse leads to kidney and liver damage.

HUMAN BEINGS

NUTRITION

Ideal weights for men and women over 25 years of age

Women				Men			
Height		Ideal weight		Height		Ideal weight	
(cm)	(in)	(kg)	(lb)	(cm)	(in)	(kg)	(lb)
153	60	46.3–53.9	102.0–118.8	155	61	53.5–63.9	117.9–140.9
155	61	47.6–55.3	104.9–121.9	157	62	54.8–65.3	120.8–143.9
157	62	48.9–57.1	107.8–125.9	160	63	56.2–67.1	143.7–147.9
160	63	50.3–58.9	110.9–129.8	162	64	57.6–68.9	127.0–151.9
162	64	51.7–61.2	114.0–134.9	165	65	58.9–70.8	129.9–156.1
165	65	53.5–63.0	117.9–138.9	168	66	60.8–73.0	134.0–160.9
168	66	55.3–64.8	121.9–142.8	170	67	62.6–75.3	138.0–166.0
170	67	57.1–66.7	125.9–147.0	173	68	65.4–77.1	144.2–170.0
173	68	58.9–68.5	129.9–151.0	175	69	66.2–78.9	145.9–173.9
175	69	60.8–70.3	134.0–155.0	178	70	68.0–81.2	149.9–179.0
178	70	62.6–72.1	138.0–158.9	180	71	69.8–83.5	153.9–184.1
180	71	64.4–73.9	142.0–162.9	183	72	71.6–86.7	157.8–191.1
183	72	66.2–75.7	145.9–166.9	185	73	73.5–87.9	162.0–193.8
185	73	68.0–77.6	149.9–171.0	188	74	75.7–90.2	166.9–198.8
188	74	69.8–79.3	153.9–174.8	190	75	78.0–92.5	171.9–203.9
				193	76	80.3–94.8	177.0–209.0

Composition of foods

Figures (approximate) per 100 g of food.

Food	Protein (g)	Carbohydrates (g)	Fat (g)	Fibre (g)	Energy value (calories[a])
Meat, poultry, fish					
Bacon, back, grilled	15	2	24	0	271
Bacon, streaky, grilled	16	2	27	0	308
Beef, minced	31	0	16	0	221
Beef, rump steak, grilled	30	0	12	0	218
Chicken, meat only, roast	19	0	4	0	142
Cod, cooked	19	0	1	0	94
Crab, cooked	18	1	5	0	129
Haddock, cooked	19	0	1	0	96
Ham, lean	22	0	5	0	168
Lamb chop, boned, grilled	24	0	29	0	353
Liver, cooked	20	6	13	0	254
Lobster, cooked	20	trace	3	0	119
Mackerel, cooked	25	0	11	0	188
Mussels, cooked	17	0	1	0	86
Pork chop, boned, grilled	28	0	24	0	328
Prawns, cooked	18	0	1	0	107
Salmon, cooked	20	0	13	0	196
Tuna, canned in brine	28	0	1	0	118
Turkey, meat only, roast	36	0	3	0	140
Vegetables					
Asparagus, cooked	2	4	trace	1	18
Aubergine/egg-plant, cooked	1	4	trace	2	14
Beans, broad, cooked	4	66	1	4	46
Beans, dried white, cooked	8	21	7	25	118
Beans, green, cooked	2	5	trace	4	25
Beetroot, cooked	1	7	trace	2	43
Broccoli, cooked	3	5	trace	4	26
Brussel sprouts, cooked	4	6	trace	3	18
Cabbage, cooked	2	trace	trace	2	11
Cabbage, raw	2	5	trace	3	25
Carrots, cooked	1	5	trace	3	20
Carrots, raw	1	6	trace	3	25
Cauliflower, cooked	2	4	trace	2	22
Celery, raw	1	2	trace	2	36
Chick peas, dry	20	50	6	15	320
Corn (on the cob)	3	21	1	5	91
Courgettes/zucchini, cooked	1	3	trace	1	14
Cucumber, raw	1	3	trace	trace	15
Leeks, cooked	1	7	0	4	25
Lentils, cooked	8	19	trace	4	106
Lettuce, raw	1	3	trace	1	12
Mushrooms, raw	3	4	trace	2	14
Onions, raw	2	9	trace	1	38
Parsnip, cooked	1	17	trace	4	50
Peas, fresh, cooked	5	4	trace	5	54
Pepper, green, raw	1	5	trace	1	14
Pepper, red, raw	1	7	trace	1	20
Potatoes, baked in skin	3	21	trace	2	86
Potatoes, boiled in skin	2	17	trace	2	75
Spinach, cooked	3	4	trace	6	23
Swede, cooked	1	4	trace	3	18
Turnip, cooked	1	5	trace	2	14
Fruit					
Apples	trace	15	trace	2	38
Apricots, dried	5	67	1	24	182
Apricots, raw	1	13	trace	2	25
Avocados	2	6	16	2	221
Bananas	1	22	trace	2	85

[a]Multiply calories by 4·187 to convert to kilojoules.

HUMAN BEINGS

Food	Protein (g)	Carbohydrates (g)	Fat (g)	Fibre (g)	Energy value (calories[a])
Blackberries	1	13	1	7	29
Blackcurrants	2	14	trace	9	29
Cherries	1	17	trace	1	70
Dates	2	73	1	7	214
Figs, dried	4	69	1	19	214
Grapefruit	1	11	trace	trace	41
Grapes	1	16	1	1	69
Melon, honeydew	1	5	trace	1	21
Melon, water	trace	5	trace	1	21
Nectarines	1	17	trace	2	64
Oranges, peeled	1	12	trace	2	49
Peaches	1	8	trace	1	38
Pears	1	15	trace	2	61
Pineapple	trace	14	trace	1	46
Prunes	1	77	trace	14	136
Raisins	3	77	trace	7	246
Raspberries	1	14	1	7	25
Strawberries	1	8	1	2	37
Tomatoes	1	5	trace	1	14
Dairy products					
Butter, salted	1	trace	82	0	740
Cheese, Brie	19	2	23	0	314
Cheese, Cheddar	25	2	32	0	414
Cheese, cottage	17	2	4	0	96
Cheese, Edam	30	trace	23	0	314
Cream, double	2	3	48	0	446
Milk, cow's, skimmed	4	5	trace	0	36
Milk, cow's, whole	4	5	4	0	65
Yogurt, skimmed milk	3	5	2	0	50
Yogurt, whole milk	3	5	3	0	62
Grain products					
Flour, white	9	80	1	4	350
Flour, wholemeal	13	56	2	10	318
Oatmeal, cooked	2	10	1	7	399
Oats, porridge	10	70	7	7	377
Pasta, dry	12	71	2	4	353
Rice, brown, cooked	3	26	1	1	129
Rice, white, cooked	3	33	trace	1	121
Legumes, nuts, and seeds					
Almonds	19	20	54	15	564
Brazil nuts	14	11	67	9	618
Peanuts, fresh	26	19	48	8	571
Walnuts	15	16	64	5	525
Miscellaneous					
Biscuit, chocolate digestive	6	64	25	4	506
Biscuit, digestive	7	62	23	5	486
Chocolate bar, plain	4	63	29	0	510
Crisps	6	40	37	11	517
Egg, boiled	13	1	12	0	163
Honey	trace	82	0	0	289
Jam	1	79	trace	1	261
Margarine	trace	1	80	0	730
Oil, vegetable	0	0	100	0	900
Orange juice	1	10	trace	0	45
Sugar	0	100	0	0	394

[a]Multiply calories by 4.187 to convert to kilojoules.

HUMAN BEINGS

Main types of vitamin

Fat-soluble vitamins

Vitamin	Chemical name	Precursor	Main symptom of deficiency	Dietary source
A	Retinol	Beta-carotene	Xerophthalmia (eye disease)	Retinol: milk, butter, cheese; egg yolk; liver; fatty fish Carotene: green vegetables; yellow and red fruits and vegetables, especially carrots
D	Cholecalciferol	UV-activated 7-dehydro-cholesterol	Rickets; osteomalacia	Fatty fish; margarine; some fortified milks
K	Phytomenadione		Haemorrhagic problems	Green leafy vegetables; liver
E	Tocopherols		Multiple effects	Vegetable oils

Water-soluble vitamins

Vitamin	Chemical name		Main symptom of deficiency	Dietary source
C	Ascorbic acid		Scurvy	Citrus fruits; potatoes; green leafy vegetables
B-vitamins				
B_1	Thiamine		Beri-beri	Seeds and grains: widely distributed
B_2	Riboflavin		Failure to thrive	Liver; milk; cheese; yeast
–	Nicotinic acid		Pellagra	Meat; fish; cereals; pulses
B_6	Pyridoxine		Dermatitis; neurological disorders	Cereals; liver; meat; fruits; leafy vegetables
B_{12}	Cyanocobalamin		Anaemia	Meat; milk; liver
–	Folic acid		Anaemia	Liver; green vegetables
–	Pantothenic acid		Dermatitis	Widespread
–	Biotin		Dermatitis	Liver; kidney; yeast extracts

Main trace minerals

Mineral	Main symptom of deficiency	Dietary source	Proportion of total body weight (%)
Calcium	Rickets in children; osteoporosis in adults	Milk; butter; cheese; sardines; green leafy vegetables; citrus fruits	2.5
Chromium	Adult-onset diabetes	Brewer's yeast; black pepper; liver; wholemeal bread; beer	<0.01
Copper	Anaemia; Menkes' syndrome	Green vegetables; fish; oysters; liver	<0.01
Fluorine	Tooth decay; possibly osteoporosis	Fluoridated drinking water; seafood; tea	<0.01
Iodine	Goitre; cretinism in new-born children	Seafood; salt-water fish; seaweed; iodized salt; table salt	<0.01
Iron	Anaemia	Liver; kidney; green leafy vegetables; egg yolk; dried fruit; potatoes; molasses	0.01
Magnesium	Irregular heartbeat; muscular weakness; insomnia	Green leafy vegetables (eaten raw); nuts; whole grains	0.07
Manganese	Not known in humans	Legumes; cereals; green leafy vegetables; tea	<0.01
Molybdenum	Not known in humans	Legumes; cereals; liver; kidney; some dark-green vegetables	<0.01
Phosphorus	Muscular weakness; bone pain; loss of appetite	Meat; poultry; fish; eggs; dried beans and peas; milk products	1.1
Potassium	Irregular heartbeat; muscular weakness; fatigue; kidney and lung failure	Fresh vegetables; meat; orange juice; bananas; bran	0.10
Selenium	Not known in humans	Seafood; cereals; meat; egg yolk; garlic	<0.01
Sodium	Impaired acid-base balance in body fluids (very rare)	Table salt; other naturally occurring salts	0.10
Zinc	Impaired wound healing; loss of appetite; impaired sexual development	Meat; whole grains; legumes; oysters; milk	<0.01

PART SIX

History

THE CALENDAR

Perpetual calendar 1821–2020

The calendar for each year is given under the corresponding letter below.

1821 C	1841 K	1861 E	1881 M	1901 E	1921 M	1941 G	1961 A	1981 I	2001 C
1822 E	1842 M	1862 G	1882 A	1902 G	1922 A	1942 I	1962 C	1982 K	2002 E
1823 G	1843 A	1863 I	1883 C	1903 I	1923 C	1943 K	1963 E	1983 M	2003 G
1824 J	1844 D	1864 L	1884 F	1904 L	1924 F	1944 N	1964 H	1984 B	2004 J
1825 M	1845 G	1865 A	1885 I	1905 A	1925 I	1945 C	1965 K	1985 E	2005 M
1826 A	1846 I	1866 C	1886 K	1906 C	1926 K	1946 E	1966 M	1986 G	2006 A
1827 C	1847 K	1867 E	1887 M	1907 E	1927 M	1947 G	1967 A	1987 I	2007 C
1828 F	1848 N	1868 H	1888 B	1908 H	1928 B	1948 J	1968 D	1988 G	2008 F
1829 I	1849 C	1869 K	1889 E	1909 K	1929 E	1949 M	1969 G	1989 A	2009 I
1830 K	1850 E	1870 M	1890 G	1910 M	1930 G	1950 A	1970 I	1990 C	2010 K
1831 M	1851 G	1871 A	1891 I	1911 A	1931 I	1951 C	1971 K	1991 E	2011 M
1832 B	1852 J	1872 D	1892 L	1912 D	1932 L	1952 F	1972 N	1992 H	2012 B
1833 E	1853 M	1873 G	1893 A	1913 G	1933 A	1953 I	1973 C	1993 K	2013 E
1834 G	1854 A	1874 I	1894 C	1914 I	1934 C	1954 K	1974 E	1994 M	2014 G
1835 I	1855 C	1875 K	1895 E	1915 K	1935 E	1955 M	1975 G	1995 A	2015 I
1836 L	1856 F	1876 N	1896 H	1916 N	1936 H	1956 B	1976 J	1996 D	2016 L
1837 A	1857 I	1877 C	1897 K	1917 C	1937 K	1957 E	1977 M	1997 G	2017 A
1838 C	1858 K	1878 E	1898 M	1918 E	1938 M	1958 G	1978 A	1998 I	2018 C
1839 E	1859 M	1879 G	1899 A	1919 G	1939 A	1959 I	1979 C	1999 K	2019 E
1840 H	1860 B	1880 J	1900 C	1920 J	1940 D	1960 L	1980 F	2000 N	2020 H

A

January
S M T W T F S
1 2 3 4 5 6 7
8 9 10 11 12 13 14
15 16 17 18 19 20 21
22 23 24 25 26 27 28
29 30 31

February
S M T W T F S
1 2 3 4
5 6 7 8 9 10 11
12 13 14 15 16 17 18
19 20 21 22 23 24 25
26 27 28

March
S M T W T F S
1 2 3 4
5 6 7 8 9 10 11
12 13 14 15 16 17 18
19 20 21 22 23 24 25
26 27 28 29 30 31

April
1
2 3 4 5 6 7 8
9 10 11 12 13 14 15
16 17 18 19 20 21 22
23 24 25 26 27 28 29
30

May
1 2 3 4 5 6
7 8 9 10 11 12 13
14 15 16 17 18 19 20
21 22 23 24 25 26 27
28 29 30 31

June
1 2 3
4 5 6 7 8 9 10
11 12 13 14 15 16 17
18 19 20 21 22 23 24
25 26 27 28 29 30

July
1
2 3 4 5 6 7 8
9 10 11 12 13 14 15
16 17 18 19 20 21 22
23 24 25 26 27 28 29
30 31

August
1 2 3 4 5
6 7 8 9 10 11 12
13 14 15 16 17 18 19
20 21 22 23 24 25 26
27 28 29 30 31

September
1 2
3 4 5 6 7 8 9
10 11 12 13 14 15 16
17 18 19 20 21 22 23
24 25 26 27 28 29 30

October
1 2 3 4 5 6 7
8 9 10 11 12 13 14
15 16 17 18 19 20 21
22 23 24 25 26 27 28
29 30 31

November
1 2 3 4
5 6 7 8 9 10 11
12 13 14 15 16 17 18
19 20 21 22 23 24 25
26 27 28 29 30

December
1 2
3 4 5 6 7 8 9
10 11 12 13 14 15 16
17 18 19 20 21 22 23
24 25 26 27 28 29 30
31

B (leap year)

January
S M T W T F S
1 2 3 4 5 6 7
8 9 10 11 12 13 14
15 16 17 18 19 20 21
22 23 24 25 26 27 28
29 30 31

February
S M T W T F S
1 2 3 4
5 6 7 8 9 10 11
12 13 14 15 16 17 18
19 20 21 22 23 24 25
26 27 28 29

March
S M T W T F S
1 2 3
4 5 6 7 8 9 10
11 12 13 14 15 16 17
18 19 20 21 22 23 24
25 26 27 28 29 30 31

April
1 2 3 4 5 6 7
8 9 10 11 12 13 14
15 16 17 18 19 20 21
22 23 24 25 26 27 28
29 30

May
1 2 3 4 5
6 7 8 9 10 11 12
13 14 15 16 17 18 19
20 21 22 23 24 25 26
27 28 29 30 31

June
1 2
3 4 5 6 7 8 9
10 11 12 13 14 15 16
17 18 19 20 21 22 23
24 25 26 27 28 29 30

July
1 2 3 4 5 6 7
8 9 10 11 12 13 14
15 16 17 18 19 20 21
22 23 24 25 26 27 28
29 30 31

August
1 2 3 4
5 6 7 8 9 10 11
12 13 14 15 16 17 18
19 20 21 22 23 24 25
26 27 28 29 30 31

September
1
2 3 4 5 6 7 8
9 10 11 12 13 14 15
16 17 18 19 20 21 22
23 24 25 26 27 28 29
30

October
1 2 3 4 5 6
7 8 9 10 11 12 13
14 15 16 17 18 19 20
21 22 23 24 25 26 27
28 29 30 31

November
1 2 3
4 5 6 7 8 9 10
11 12 13 14 15 16 17
18 19 20 21 22 23 24
25 26 27 28 29 30

December
1
2 3 4 5 6 7 8
9 10 11 12 13 14 15
16 17 18 19 20 21 22
23 24 25 26 27 28 29
30 31

Perpetual calendar 1821–2020 (continued)

C

January

S	M	T	W	T	F	S
	1	2	3	4	5	6
7	8	9	10	11	12	13
14	15	16	17	18	19	20
21	22	23	24	25	26	27
28	29	30	31			

February

S	M	T	W	T	F	S
				1	2	3
4	5	6	7	8	9	10
11	12	13	14	15	16	17
18	19	20	21	22	23	24
25	26	27	28			

March

S	M	T	W	T	F	S
				1	2	3
4	5	6	7	8	9	10
11	12	13	14	15	16	17
18	19	20	21	22	23	24
25	26	27	28	29	30	31

April

S	M	T	W	T	F	S
1	2	3	4	5	6	7
8	9	10	11	12	13	14
15	16	17	18	19	20	21
22	23	24	25	26	27	28
29	30					

May

S	M	T	W	T	F	S
		1	2	3	4	5
6	7	8	9	10	11	12
13	14	15	16	17	18	19
20	21	22	23	24	25	26
27	28	29	30	31		

June

S	M	T	W	T	F	S
					1	2
3	4	5	6	7	8	9
10	11	12	13	14	15	16
17	18	19	20	21	22	23
24	25	26	27	28	29	30

July

S	M	T	W	T	F	S
1	2	3	4	5	6	7
8	9	10	11	12	13	14
15	16	17	18	19	20	21
22	23	24	25	26	27	28
29	30	31				

August

S	M	T	W	T	F	S
			1	2	3	4
5	6	7	8	9	10	11
12	13	14	15	16	17	18
19	20	21	22	23	24	25
26	27	28	29	30	31	

September

S	M	T	W	T	F	S
						1
2	3	4	5	6	7	8
9	10	11	12	13	14	15
16	17	18	19	20	21	22
23	24	25	26	27	28	29
30						

October

S	M	T	W	T	F	S
	1	2	3	4	5	6
7	8	9	10	11	12	13
14	15	16	17	18	19	20
21	22	23	24	25	26	27
28	29	30	31			

November

S	M	T	W	T	F	S
				1	2	3
4	5	6	7	8	9	10
11	12	13	14	15	16	17
18	19	20	21	22	23	24
25	26	27	28	29	30	

December

S	M	T	W	T	F	S
						1
2	3	4	5	6	7	8
9	10	11	12	13	14	15
16	17	18	19	20	21	22
23	24	25	26	27	28	29
30	31					

D (leap year)

January

S	M	T	W	T	F	S
	1	2	3	4	5	6
7	8	9	10	11	12	13
14	15	16	17	18	19	20
21	22	23	24	25	26	27
28	29	30	31			

February

S	M	T	W	T	F	S
				1	2	3
4	5	6	7	8	9	10
11	12	13	14	15	16	17
18	19	20	21	22	23	24
25	26	27	28	29		

March

S	M	T	W	T	F	S
					1	2
3	4	5	6	7	8	9
10	11	12	13	14	15	16
17	18	19	20	21	22	23
24	25	26	27	28	29	30
31						

April

S	M	T	W	T	F	S
	1	2	3	4	5	6
7	8	9	10	11	12	13
14	15	16	17	18	19	20
21	22	23	24	25	26	27
28	29	30				

May

S	M	T	W	T	F	S
			1	2	3	4
5	6	7	8	9	10	11
12	13	14	15	16	17	18
19	20	21	22	23	24	25
26	27	28	29	30	31	

June

S	M	T	W	T	F	S
						1
2	3	4	5	6	7	8
9	10	11	12	13	14	15
16	17	18	19	20	21	22
23	24	25	26	27	28	29
30						

July

S	M	T	W	T	F	S
	1	2	3	4	5	6
7	8	9	10	11	12	13
14	15	16	17	18	19	20
21	22	23	24	25	26	27
28	29	30	31			

August

S	M	T	W	T	F	S
				1	2	3
4	5	6	7	8	9	10
11	12	13	14	15	16	17
18	19	20	21	22	23	24
25	26	27	28	29	30	31

September

S	M	T	W	T	F	S
1	2	3	4	5	6	7
8	9	10	11	12	13	14
15	16	17	18	19	20	21
22	23	24	25	26	27	28
29	30					

October

S	M	T	W	T	F	S
		1	2	3	4	5
6	7	8	9	10	11	12
13	14	15	16	17	18	19
20	21	22	23	24	25	26
27	28	29	30	31		

November

S	M	T	W	T	F	S
					1	2
3	4	5	6	7	8	9
10	11	12	13	14	15	16
17	18	19	20	21	22	23
24	25	26	27	28	29	30

December

S	M	T	W	T	F	S
1	2	3	4	5	6	7
8	9	10	11	12	13	14
15	16	17	18	19	20	21
22	23	24	25	26	27	28
29	30	31				

E

January

S	M	T	W	T	F	S
		1	2	3	4	5
6	7	8	9	10	11	12
13	14	15	16	17	18	19
20	21	22	23	24	25	26
27	28	29	30	31		

February

S	M	T	W	T	F	S
					1	2
3	4	5	6	7	8	9
10	11	12	13	14	15	16
17	18	19	20	21	22	23
24	25	26	27	28		

March

S	M	T	W	T	F	S
					1	2
3	4	5	6	7	8	9
10	11	12	13	14	15	16
17	18	19	20	21	22	23
24	25	26	27	28	29	30
31						

April

S	M	T	W	T	F	S
	1	2	3	4	5	6
7	8	9	10	11	12	13
14	15	16	17	18	19	20
21	22	23	24	25	26	27
28	29	30				

May

S	M	T	W	T	F	S
			1	2	3	4
5	6	7	8	9	10	11
12	13	14	15	16	17	18
19	20	21	22	23	24	25
26	27	28	29	30	31	

June

S	M	T	W	T	F	S
						1
2	3	4	5	6	7	8
9	10	11	12	13	14	15
16	17	18	19	20	21	22
23	24	25	26	27	28	29
30						

July

S	M	T	W	T	F	S
	1	2	3	4	5	6
7	8	9	10	11	12	13
14	15	16	17	18	19	20
21	22	23	24	25	26	27
28	29	30	31			

August

S	M	T	W	T	F	S
				1	2	3
4	5	6	7	8	9	10
11	12	13	14	15	16	17
18	19	20	21	22	23	24
25	26	27	28	29	30	31

September

S	M	T	W	T	F	S
1	2	3	4	5	6	7
8	9	10	11	12	13	14
15	16	17	18	19	20	21
22	23	24	25	26	27	28
29	30					

October

S	M	T	W	T	F	S
		1	2	3	4	5
6	7	8	9	10	11	12
13	14	15	16	17	18	19
20	21	22	23	24	25	26
27	28	29	30	31		

November

S	M	T	W	T	F	S
					1	2
3	4	5	6	7	8	9
10	11	12	13	14	15	16
17	18	19	20	21	22	23
24	25	26	27	28	29	30

December

S	M	T	W	T	F	S
1	2	3	4	5	6	7
8	9	10	11	12	13	14
15	16	17	18	19	20	21
22	23	24	25	26	27	28
29	30	31				

F (leap year)

January

S	M	T	W	T	F	S
		1	2	3	4	5
6	7	8	9	10	11	12
13	14	15	16	17	18	19
20	21	22	23	24	25	26
27	28	29	30	31		

February

S	M	T	W	T	F	S
					1	2
3	4	5	6	7	8	9
10	11	12	13	14	15	16
17	18	19	20	21	22	23
24	25	26	27	28	29	

March

S	M	T	W	T	F	S
						1
2	3	4	5	6	7	8
9	10	11	12	13	14	15
16	17	18	19	20	21	22
23	24	25	26	27	28	29
30	31					

April

S	M	T	W	T	F	S
		1	2	3	4	5
6	7	8	9	10	11	12
13	14	15	16	17	18	19
20	21	22	23	24	25	26
27	28	29	30			

May

S	M	T	W	T	F	S
				1	2	3
4	5	6	7	8	9	10
11	12	13	14	15	16	17
18	19	20	21	22	23	24
25	26	27	28	29	30	31

June

S	M	T	W	T	F	S
1	2	3	4	5	6	7
8	9	10	11	12	13	14
15	16	17	18	19	20	21
22	23	24	25	26	27	28
29	30					

July

S	M	T	W	T	F	S
		1	2	3	4	5
6	7	8	9	10	11	12
13	14	15	16	17	18	19
20	21	22	23	24	25	26
27	28	29	30	31		

August

S	M	T	W	T	F	S
					1	2
3	4	5	6	7	8	9
10	11	12	13	14	15	16
17	18	19	20	21	22	23
24	25	26	27	28	29	30
31						

September

S	M	T	W	T	F	S
	1	2	3	4	5	6
7	8	9	10	11	12	13
14	15	16	17	18	19	20
21	22	23	24	25	26	27
28	29	30				

October

S	M	T	W	T	F	S
			1	2	3	4
5	6	7	8	9	10	11
12	13	14	15	16	17	18
19	20	21	22	23	24	25
26	27	28	29	30	31	

November

S	M	T	W	T	F	S
						1
2	3	4	5	6	7	8
9	10	11	12	13	14	15
16	17	18	19	20	21	22
23	24	25	26	27	28	29
30						

December

S	M	T	W	T	F	S
	1	2	3	4	5	6
7	8	9	10	11	12	13
14	15	16	17	18	19	20
21	22	23	24	25	26	27
28	29	30	31			

G

```
January                 February                March
S  M  T  W  T  F  S     S  M  T  W  T  F  S     S  M  T  W  T  F  S
         1  2  3  4                     1                       1
5  6  7  8  9 10 11      2  3  4  5  6  7  8      2  3  4  5  6  7  8
12 13 14 15 16 17 18     9 10 11 12 13 14 15      9 10 11 12 13 14 15
19 20 21 22 23 24 25    16 17 18 19 20 21 22     16 17 18 19 20 21 22
26 27 28 29 30 31       23 24 25 26 27 28        23 24 25 26 27 28 29
                                                 30 31

April                   May                     June
      1  2  3  4  5                  1  2  3     1  2  3  4  5  6  7
6  7  8  9 10 11 12      4  5  6  7  8  9 10      8  9 10 11 12 13 14
13 14 15 16 17 18 19    11 12 13 14 15 16 17     15 16 17 18 19 20 21
20 21 22 23 24 25 26    18 19 20 21 22 23 24     22 23 24 25 26 27 28
27 28 29 30             25 26 27 28 29 30 31     29 30

July                    August                  September
      1  2  3  4  5                     1  2           1  2  3  4  5  6
6  7  8  9 10 11 12      3  4  5  6  7  8  9      7  8  9 10 11 12 13
13 14 15 16 17 18 19    10 11 12 13 14 15 16     14 15 16 17 18 19 20
20 21 22 23 24 25 26    17 18 19 20 21 22 23     21 22 23 24 25 26 27
27 28 29 30 31          24 25 26 27 28 29 30     28 29 30
                        31

October                 November                December
         1  2  3  4                        1           1  2  3  4  5  6
5  6  7  8  9 10 11      2  3  4  5  6  7  8      7  8  9 10 11 12 13
12 13 14 15 16 17 18     9 10 11 12 13 14 15     14 15 16 17 18 19 20
19 20 21 22 23 24 25    16 17 18 19 20 21 22     21 22 23 24 25 26 27
26 27 28 29 30 31       23 24 25 26 27 28 29     28 29 30 31
                        30
```

H (leap year)

```
January                 February                March
S  M  T  W  T  F  S     S  M  T  W  T  F  S     S  M  T  W  T  F  S
         1  2  3  4                     1       1  2  3  4  5  6  7
5  6  7  8  9 10 11      2  3  4  5  6  7  8      8  9 10 11 12 13 14
12 13 14 15 16 17 18     9 10 11 12 13 14 15     15 16 17 18 19 20 21
19 20 21 22 23 24 25    16 17 18 19 20 21 22     22 23 24 25 26 27 28
26 27 28 29 30 31       23 24 25 26 27 28 29     29 30 31

April                   May                     June
      1  2  3  4                     1  2     1  2  3  4  5  6
5  6  7  8  9 10 11      3  4  5  6  7  8  9      7  8  9 10 11 12 13
12 13 14 15 16 17 18    10 11 12 13 14 15 16     14 15 16 17 18 19 20
19 20 21 22 23 24 25    17 18 19 20 21 22 23     21 22 23 24 25 26 27
26 27 28 29 30          24 25 26 27 28 29 30     28 29 30
                        31

July                    August                  September
      1  2  3  4                        1              1  2  3  4  5
5  6  7  8  9 10 11      2  3  4  5  6  7  8      6  7  8  9 10 11 12
12 13 14 15 16 17 18     9 10 11 12 13 14 15     13 14 15 16 17 18 19
19 20 21 22 23 24 25    16 17 18 19 20 21 22     20 21 22 23 24 25 26
26 27 28 29 30 31       23 24 25 26 27 28 29     27 28 29 30
                        30 31

October                 November                December
         1  2  3       1  2  3  4  5  6  7           1  2  3  4  5
4  5  6  7  8  9 10      8  9 10 11 12 13 14      6  7  8  9 10 11 12
11 12 13 14 15 16 17    15 16 17 18 19 20 21     13 14 15 16 17 18 19
18 19 20 21 22 23 24    22 23 24 25 26 27 28     20 21 22 23 24 25 26
25 26 27 28 29 30 31    29 30                    27 28 29 30 31
```

I

```
January                 February                March
S  M  T  W  T  F  S     S  M  T  W  T  F  S     S  M  T  W  T  F  S
         1  2  3       1  2  3  4  5  6  7       1  2  3  4  5  6  7
4  5  6  7  8  9 10      8  9 10 11 12 13 14      8  9 10 11 12 13 14
11 12 13 14 15 16 17    15 16 17 18 19 20 21     15 16 17 18 19 20 21
18 19 20 21 22 23 24    22 23 24 25 26 27 28     22 23 24 25 26 27 28
25 26 27 28 29 30 31                             29 30 31

April                   May                     June
      1  2  3  4                     1  2     1  2  3  4  5  6
5  6  7  8  9 10 11      3  4  5  6  7  8  9      7  8  9 10 11 12 13
12 13 14 15 16 17 18    10 11 12 13 14 15 16     14 15 16 17 18 19 20
19 20 21 22 23 24 25    17 18 19 20 21 22 23     21 22 23 24 25 26 27
26 27 28 29 30          24 25 26 27 28 29 30     28 29 30
                        31

July                    August                  September
      1  2  3  4                        1              1  2  3  4  5
5  6  7  8  9 10 11      2  3  4  5  6  7  8      6  7  8  9 10 11 12
12 13 14 15 16 17 18     9 10 11 12 13 14 15     13 14 15 16 17 18 19
19 20 21 22 23 24 25    16 17 18 19 20 21 22     20 21 22 23 24 25 26
26 27 28 29 30 31       23 24 25 26 27 28 29     27 28 29 30
                        30 31

October                 November                December
         1  2  3       1  2  3  4  5  6  7           1  2  3  4  5
4  5  6  7  8  9 10      8  9 10 11 12 13 14      6  7  8  9 10 11 12
11 12 13 14 15 16 17    15 16 17 18 19 20 21     13 14 15 16 17 18 19
18 19 20 21 22 23 24    22 23 24 25 26 27 28     20 21 22 23 24 25 26
25 26 27 28 29 30 31    29 30                    27 28 29 30 31
```

J (leap year)

```
January                 February                March
S  M  T  W  T  F  S     S  M  T  W  T  F  S     S  M  T  W  T  F  S
         1  2                1  2  3  4  5  6             1  2  3  4  5
3  4  5  6  7  8  9      7  8  9 10 11 12 13      6  7  8  9 10 11 12
10 11 12 13 14 15 16    14 15 16 17 18 19 20     13 14 15 16 17 18 19
17 18 19 20 21 22 23    21 22 23 24 25 26 27     20 21 22 23 24 25 26
24 25 26 27 28 29 30    28 29                    27 28 29 30 31
31

April                   May                     June
      1  2                            1           1  2  3  4
3  4  5  6  7  8  9      2  3  4  5  6  7  8      5  6  7  8  9 10 11
10 11 12 13 14 15 16     9 10 11 12 13 14 15     12 13 14 15 16 17 18
17 18 19 20 21 22 23    16 17 18 19 20 21 22     19 20 21 22 23 24 25
24 25 26 27 28 29 30    23 24 25 26 27 28 29     26 27 28 29 30
                        30 31

July                    August                  September
      1  2             1  2  3  4  5  6                1  2  3
3  4  5  6  7  8  9      7  8  9 10 11 12 13      4  5  6  7  8  9 10
10 11 12 13 14 15 16    14 15 16 17 18 19 20     11 12 13 14 15 16 17
17 18 19 20 21 22 23    21 22 23 24 25 26 27     18 19 20 21 22 23 24
24 25 26 27 28 29 30    28 29 30 31              25 26 27 28 29 30
31

October                 November                December
               1       1  2  3  4  5  6                 1  2  3
2  3  4  5  6  7  8      7  8  9 10 11 12 13      4  5  6  7  8  9 10
9 10 11 12 13 14 15     14 15 16 17 18 19 20     11 12 13 14 15 16 17
16 17 18 19 20 21 22    21 22 23 24 25 26 27     18 19 20 21 22 23 24
23 24 25 26 27 28 29    28 29 30                 25 26 27 28 29 30 31
30 31
```

Perpetual calendar 1821–2020 (continued)

HISTORY

K

January

S	M	T	W	T	F	S
					1	2
3	4	5	6	7	8	9
10	11	12	13	14	15	16
17	18	19	20	21	22	23
24	25	26	27	28	29	30
31						

February

S	M	T	W	T	F	S
	1	2	3	4	5	6
7	8	9	10	11	12	13
14	15	16	17	18	19	20
21	22	23	24	25	26	27
28						

March

S	M	T	W	T	F	S
	1	2	3	4	5	6
7	8	9	10	11	12	13
14	15	16	17	18	19	20
21	22	23	24	25	26	27
28	29	30	31			

April

S	M	T	W	T	F	S
				1	2	3
4	5	6	7	8	9	10
11	12	13	14	15	16	17
18	19	20	21	22	23	24
25	26	27	28	29	30	

May

S	M	T	W	T	F	S
						1
2	3	4	5	6	7	8
9	10	11	12	13	14	15
16	17	18	19	20	21	22
23	24	25	26	27	28	29
30	31					

June

S	M	T	W	T	F	S
		1	2	3	4	5
6	7	8	9	10	11	12
13	14	15	16	17	18	19
20	21	22	23	24	25	26
27	28	29	30			

July

S	M	T	W	T	F	S
				1	2	3
4	5	6	7	8	9	10
11	12	13	14	15	16	17
18	19	20	21	22	23	24
25	26	27	28	29	30	31

August

S	M	T	W	T	F	S
1	2	3	4	5	6	7
8	9	10	11	12	13	14
15	16	17	18	19	20	21
22	23	24	25	26	27	28
29	30	31				

September

S	M	T	W	T	F	S
			1	2	3	4
5	6	7	8	9	10	11
12	13	14	15	16	17	18
19	20	21	22	23	24	25
26	27	28	29	30		

October

S	M	T	W	T	F	S
					1	2
3	4	5	6	7	8	9
10	11	12	13	14	15	16
17	18	19	20	21	22	23
24	25	26	27	28	29	30
31						

November

S	M	T	W	T	F	S
	1	2	3	4	5	6
7	8	9	10	11	12	13
14	15	16	17	18	19	20
21	22	23	24	25	26	27
28	29	30				

December

S	M	T	W	T	F	S
			1	2	3	4
5	6	7	8	9	10	11
12	13	14	15	16	17	18
19	20	21	22	23	24	25
26	27	28	29	30	31	

L (leap year)

January

S	M	T	W	T	F	S
					1	2
3	4	5	6	7	8	9
10	11	12	13	14	15	16
17	18	19	20	21	22	23
24	25	26	27	28	29	30
31						

February

S	M	T	W	T	F	S
	1	2	3	4	5	6
7	8	9	10	11	12	13
14	15	16	17	18	19	20
21	22	23	24	25	26	27
28	29					

March

S	M	T	W	T	F	S
		1	2	3	4	5
6	7	8	9	10	11	12
13	14	15	16	17	18	19
20	21	22	23	24	25	26
27	28	29	30	31		

April

S	M	T	W	T	F	S
					1	2
3	4	5	6	7	8	9
10	11	12	13	14	15	16
17	18	19	20	21	22	23
24	25	26	27	28	29	30

May

S	M	T	W	T	F	S
1	2	3	4	5	6	7
8	9	10	11	12	13	14
15	16	17	18	19	20	21
22	23	24	25	26	27	28
29	30	31				

June

S	M	T	W	T	F	S
			1	2	3	4
5	6	7	8	9	10	11
12	13	14	15	16	17	18
19	20	21	22	23	24	25
26	27	28	29	30		

July

S	M	T	W	T	F	S
					1	2
3	4	5	6	7	8	9
10	11	12	13	14	15	16
17	18	19	20	21	22	23
24	25	26	27	28	29	30
31						

August

S	M	T	W	T	F	S
	1	2	3	4	5	6
7	8	9	10	11	12	13
14	15	16	17	18	19	20
21	22	23	24	25	26	27
28	29	30	31			

September

S	M	T	W	T	F	S
				1	2	3
4	5	6	7	8	9	10
11	12	13	14	15	16	17
18	19	20	21	22	23	24
25	26	27	28	29	30	

October

S	M	T	W	T	F	S
						1
2	3	4	5	6	7	8
9	10	11	12	13	14	15
16	17	18	19	20	21	22
23	24	25	26	27	28	29
30	31					

November

S	M	T	W	T	F	S
		1	2	3	4	5
6	7	8	9	10	11	12
13	14	15	16	17	18	19
20	21	22	23	24	25	26
27	28	29	30			

December

S	M	T	W	T	F	S
				1	2	3
4	5	6	7	8	9	10
11	12	13	14	15	16	17
18	19	20	21	22	23	24
25	26	27	28	29	30	31

M

January

S	M	T	W	T	F	S
						1
2	3	4	5	6	7	8
9	10	11	12	13	14	15
16	17	18	19	20	21	22
23	24	25	26	27	28	29
30	31					

February

S	M	T	W	T	F	S
		1	2	3	4	5
6	7	8	9	10	11	12
13	14	15	16	17	18	19
20	21	22	23	24	25	26
27	28					

March

S	M	T	W	T	F	S
		1	2	3	4	5
6	7	8	9	10	11	12
13	14	15	16	17	18	19
20	21	22	23	24	25	26
27	28	29	30	31		

April

S	M	T	W	T	F	S
					1	2
3	4	5	6	7	8	9
10	11	12	13	14	15	16
17	18	19	20	21	22	23
24	25	26	27	28	29	30

May

S	M	T	W	T	F	S
1	2	3	4	5	6	7
8	9	10	11	12	13	14
15	16	17	18	19	20	21
22	23	24	25	26	27	28
29	30	31				

June

S	M	T	W	T	F	S
			1	2	3	4
5	6	7	8	9	10	11
12	13	14	15	16	17	18
19	20	21	22	23	24	25
26	27	28	29	30		

July

S	M	T	W	T	F	S
					1	2
3	4	5	6	7	8	9
10	11	12	13	14	15	16
17	18	19	20	21	22	23
24	25	26	27	28	29	30
31						

August

S	M	T	W	T	F	S
	1	2	3	4	5	6
7	8	9	10	11	12	13
14	15	16	17	18	19	20
21	22	23	24	25	26	27
28	29	30	31			

September

S	M	T	W	T	F	S
				1	2	3
4	5	6	7	8	9	10
11	12	13	14	15	16	17
18	19	20	21	22	23	24
25	26	27	28	29	30	

October

S	M	T	W	T	F	S
						1
2	3	4	5	6	7	8
9	10	11	12	13	14	15
16	17	18	19	20	21	22
23	24	25	26	27	28	29
30	31					

November

S	M	T	W	T	F	S
		1	2	3	4	5
6	7	8	9	10	11	12
13	14	15	16	17	18	19
20	21	22	23	24	25	26
27	28	29	30			

December

S	M	T	W	T	F	S
				1	2	3
4	5	6	7	8	9	10
11	12	13	14	15	16	17
18	19	20	21	22	23	24
25	26	27	28	29	30	31

N (leap year)

January

S	M	T	W	T	F	S
						1
2	3	4	5	6	7	8
9	10	11	12	13	14	15
16	17	18	19	20	21	22
23	24	25	26	27	28	29
30	31					

February

S	M	T	W	T	F	S
		1	2	3	4	5
6	7	8	9	10	11	12
13	14	15	16	17	18	19
20	21	22	23	24	25	26
27	28	29				

March

S	M	T	W	T	F	S
			1	2	3	4
5	6	7	8	9	10	11
12	13	14	15	16	17	18
19	20	21	22	23	24	25
26	27	28	29	30	31	

April

S	M	T	W	T	F	S
						1
2	3	4	5	6	7	8
9	10	11	12	13	14	15
16	17	18	19	20	21	22
23	24	25	26	27	28	29
30						

May

S	M	T	W	T	F	S
	1	2	3	4	5	6
7	8	9	10	11	12	13
14	15	16	17	18	19	20
21	22	23	24	25	26	27
28	29	30	31			

June

S	M	T	W	T	F	S
				1	2	3
4	5	6	7	8	9	10
11	12	13	14	15	16	17
18	19	20	21	22	23	24
25	26	27	28	29	30	

July

S	M	T	W	T	F	S
						1
2	3	4	5	6	7	8
9	10	11	12	13	14	15
16	17	18	19	20	21	22
23	24	25	26	27	28	29
30	31					

August

S	M	T	W	T	F	S
		1	2	3	4	5
6	7	8	9	10	11	12
13	14	15	16	17	18	19
20	21	22	23	24	25	26
27	28	29	30	31		

September

S	M	T	W	T	F	S
					1	2
3	4	5	6	7	8	9
10	11	12	13	14	15	16
17	18	19	20	21	22	23
24	25	26	27	28	29	30

October

S	M	T	W	T	F	S
1	2	3	4	5	6	7
8	9	10	11	12	13	14
15	16	17	18	19	20	21
22	23	24	25	26	27	28
29	30	31				

November

S	M	T	W	T	F	S
			1	2	3	4
5	6	7	8	9	10	11
12	13	14	15	16	17	18
19	20	21	22	23	24	25
26	27	28	29	30		

December

S	M	T	W	T	F	S
					1	2
3	4	5	6	7	8	9
10	11	12	13	14	15	16
17	18	19	20	21	22	23
24	25	26	27	28	29	30
31						

The seasons

N hemisphere	S hemisphere	Duration
Spring	Autumn	From vernal/autumnal equinox (c. 21 Mar) to summer/winter solstice (c. 21 Jun)
Summer	Winter	From summer/winter solstice (c. 21 Jun) to autumnal/spring equinox (c. 23 Sept)
Autumn	Spring	From autumnal/spring equinox (c. 23 Sept) to winter/summer solstice (c. 21 Dec)
Winter	Summer	From winter/summer solstice (c. 21 Dec) to vernal/autumnal equinox (c. 21 Mar)

Wedding anniversaries

In many Western countries, different wedding anniversaries have become associated with gifts of different materials. There is some variation between countries.

1st	Cotton	14th	Ivory
2nd	Paper	15th	Crystal
3rd	Leather	20th	China
4th	Fruit; flowers	25th	Silver
5th	Wood	30th	Pearl
6th	Sugar	35th	Coral
7th	Copper; wool	40th	Ruby
8th	Bronze; pottery	45th	Sapphire
9th	Pottery; willow	50th	Gold
10th	Tin	55th	Emerald
11th	Steel	60th	Diamond
12th	Silk; linen	70th	Platinum
13th	Lace		

Year equivalents

Jewish[a] (AM)		Islamic[b] (H)		Hindu[c] (SE)	
5756	(25 Sep 1995–13 Sep 1996)	1416	(31 May 1995–18 May 1996)	1917	(22 Mar 1995–20 Mar 1996)
5757	(14 Sep 1996–1 Oct 1997)	1417	(19 May 1996–8 May 1997)	1918	(22 Mar 1996–21 Mar 1997)
5758	(2 Oct 1997–20 Sep 1998)	1418	(9 May 1997–27 Apr 1998)	1919	(22 Mar 1997–21 Mar 1998)
5759	(21 Sep 1998–10 Sep 1999)	1419	(28 Apr 1998–16 Apr 1999)	1920	(22 Mar 1998–21 Mar 1999)
5760	(11 Sep 1999–29 Sep 2000)	1420	(17 Apr 1999–5 Apr 2000)	1921	(22 Mar 1999–21 Mar 2000)
5761	(30 Sep 2000–17 Sep 2001)	1421	(6 Apr 2000–25 Mar 2001)	1922	(21 Mar 2000–21 Mar 2001)
5762	(18 Sep 2001–6 Sep 2002)	1422	(26 Mar 2001–14 Mar 2002)	1923	(22 Mar 2001–21 Mar 2002)
5763	(7 Sep 2002–26 Sep 2003)	1423	(15 Mar 2002–4 Mar 2003)	1924	(22 Mar 2002–21 Mar 2003)
5764	(27 Sep 2003–15 Sep 2004)	1424	(5 Mar 2003–21 Feb 2004)	1925	(22 Mar 2003– 20 Mar 2004)
5765	(16 Sep 2004–3 Oct 2005)	1425	(22 Feb 2004–9 Feb 2005)	1926	(21 Mar 2004–21 Mar 2005)
5766	(4 Oct 2005–22 Sep 2006)	1426	(10 Feb 2005–30 Jan 2006)	1927	(22 Mar 2005–21 Mar 2006)

Gregorian equivalents are given in parentheses and are AD (= Anno Domini).

[a] Calculated from 3761 BC, said to be the year of the creation of the world. AM = Anno Mundi.
[b] Calculated from AD 622, the year in which the Prophet went from Mecca to Medina. H = Hegira.
[c] Calculated from AD 78, the beginning of the Saka era (SE), used alongside Gregorian dates in Government of India publications since 22 Mar 1957. Other important Hindu eras include: Vikrama era (58 BC), Kalacuri era (AD 248), Gupta era (AD 320), and Harsa era (AD 606).

Month equivalents

Gregorian equivalents to other calendars are given in parentheses; the figures refer to the number of solar days in each month. The Islamic calendar, being purely lunar, is shorter than the Gregorian by 11 days; its months therefore regress through the seasons, and the same Gregorian equivalents recur only every 33 years.

Gregorian	Jewish	Islamic	Hindu
(Basis: Sun)	(Basis: Moon)	(Basis: Moon)	(Basis: Moon)
January (31)	Tishri (Sep–Oct) (30)	Muharram (30)	Caitra (Mar–Apr) (29 or 30)
February (28 or 29)	Heshvan (Oct–Nov) (29 or 30)	Safar (29)	Vaisakha (Apr–May) (29 or 30)
March (31)	Kislev (Nov–Dec) (29 or 30)	Rabi I (30)	Jyaistha (May–Jun) (29 or 30)
April (30)	Tevet (Dec–Jan) (29)	Rabi II (29)	Asadha (Jun–Jul) (29 or 30)
May (31)	Shevat (Jan–Feb) (30)	Jumada I (30)	Dvitiya Asadha *certain leap years*
June (30)	Adar (Feb–Mar) (29 or 30)	Jumada II (29)	Svrana (Jul–Aug) (29 or 30)
July (31)	Adar Sheni *leap years only*	Rajab (30)	Dvitiya Sravana *certain leap years*
August (31)	Nisan (Mar–Apr) (30)	Shaban (29)	Bhadrapada (Aug–Sep) (29 or 30)
September (30)	Iyar (Apr–May) (29)	Ramadan (30)	Asvina (Sep–Oct) (29 or 30)
October (31)	Sivan (May–Jun) (30)	Shawwal (29)	Karttika (Oct–Nov) (29 or 30)
November (30)	Tammuz (Jun–Jul) (29)	Dhu al-Qadah (30)	Margasirsa (Nov–Dec) (29 or 30)
December (31)	Av (Jul–Aug) (30)	Dhu al-Hijjah (29 or 30)	Pausa (Dec–Jan) (29 or 30)
	Elul (Aug–Sep) (29)		Magha (Jan–Feb) (29 or 30)
			Phalguna (Feb–Mar) (29 or 30)

HISTORY

Names of the months

Month	Name origin
January	Janus, the two-faced god of gates
February	Februa, day of purification (February 15)
March	Mars, god of War
April	Apru, Etruscan goddess of love
May	Maia, eldest daughter of Atlas
June	Juno, wife of Jupiter
July	Julius Caesar
August	Augustus, adopted son of Julius Caesar
September	The seventh month of the earlier Roman calendar
October	The eighth month of the earlier Roman calendar
November	The ninth month of the earlier Roman calendar
December	The tenth month of the earlier Roman calendar

Months: associations

In many Western countries, the months are traditionally associated with gemstones and flowers. There is considerable variation between countries. The following combinations are widely recognized in North America and the UK.

Month	Gemstone	Flower
January	Garnet	Carnation, snowdrop
February	Amethyst	Primrose, violet
March	Aquamarine, bloodstone	Jonquil, violet
April	Diamond	Daisy, sweet pea
May	Emerald	Hawthorn, lily of the valley
June	Alexandrite, moonstone, pearl	Honeysuckle, rose
July	Ruby	Larkspur, water lily
August	Peridot, sardonyx	Gladiolus, poppy
September	Sapphire	Aster, morning glory
October	Opal, tourmaline	Calendula, cosmos
November	Topaz	Chrysanthemum
December	Turquoise, zircon	Holly, narcissus, poinsettia

Names of the days

Day	Name origin
Sunday	Sun day
Monday	Moon day
Tuesday	Tiw's day (God of battle)
Wednesday	Woden's or Odin's day (God of poetry and the dead)
Thursday	Thor's day (God of thunder)
Friday	Frigg's day (Goddess of married love)
Saturday	Saturn's day (God of fertility and agriculture)

Chinese animal years and times 1984–2007

Chinese	English	Years		Time of day (hours)
Shu	Rat	1984	1996	2300–0100
Niu	Ox	1985	1997	0100–0300
Hu	Tiger	1986	1998	0300–0500
T'u	Hare	1987	1999	0500–0700
Lung	Dragon	1988	2000	0700–0900
She	Serpent	1989	2001	0900–1100
Ma	Horse	1990	2002	1100–1300
Yang	Sheep	1991	2003	1300–1500
Hou	Monkey	1992	2004	1500–1700
Chi	Cock	1993	2005	1700–1900
Kou	Dog	1994	2006	1900–2100
Chu	Boar	1995	2007	2100–2300

Chinese agricultural calendar

(Basis: Sun and Moon)

Fortnight

Li Chun ('Spring Begins')
Yu Shui ('Rain Water')
Jing Zhe ('Excited Insects')
Chun Fen ('Vernal Equinox')
Qing Ming ('Clear and Bright')
Gu Yu ('Grain Rains')
Li Xia ('Summer Begins')
Xiao Man ('Grain Fills')
Mang Zhong ('Grain in Ear')
Xia Zhi ('Summer Solstice')
Xiao Shu ('Slight Heat')
Da Shu ('Great Heat')
Li Qiu ('Autumn Begins')
Chu Shu ('Limit of Heat')
Bai Lu ('White Dew')
Qui Fen ('Autumn Equinox')
Han Lu ('Cold Dew')
Shuang Jiang ('Frost Descends')
Li Dong ('Winter Begins')
Xiao Xue ('Little Snow')
Da Xue ('Heavy Snow')
Dong Zhi ('Winter Solstice')
Xiao Han ('Little Cold')
Da Han ('Severe Cold')

HISTORY

Zodiac

Spring signs

Aries, the Ram
(Mar 21–Apr 19)

Taurus, the Bull
(Apr 20–May 20)

Gemini, the Twins
(May 21–Jun 20)

Summer signs

Cancer, the Crab
(Jun 21–Jul 22)

Leo, the Lion
(Jul 23–Aug 22)

Virgo, the Virgin
(Aug 23–Sep 22)

Autumn signs

Libra, the Balance
(Sep 23–Oct 22)

Scorpio, the Scorpion
(Oct 23–Nov21)

Sagittarius, the Archer
(Nov 22–Dec 21)

Winter signs

Capricorn, the Goat
(Dec 22–Jan 29)

Aquarius, the
Water Bearer
(Jan 20–Feb 18)

Pisces, the Fishes
(Feb19–Mar 20)

ANCIENT AND MODERN

Seven wonders of the Ancient World

Name	Date built	History
Egyptian Pyramids	more than 4000 years ago	Oldest of the ancient wonders and the only one surviving today. Served as tombs for Egyptian pharoahs.
Colossus of Rhodes	c.305–292 BC	32 m (105 ft) high bronze statue of the sun god Helius. Destroyed by an earthquake in 224 BC.
Hanging Gardens of Babylon	6th century BC	Series of terraces of trees and flowers along the banks of the Euphrates. Built by Nebuchadnezzar II (also known in the Book of Daniel as Nebuchadrezzar).
Mausoleum at Halicarnassus	4th century BC	Tomb of Mausolus built by his widow. Destroyed by an earthquake before the 15th century.
Pharos of Alexandria	c.270 BC	The world's first known lighthouse, at the entrance of Alexandria harbour in Egypt. 122 m/400 ft high. In ruins by 15th century.
Statue of Zeus at Olympia	5th century BC	9 m/30 ft high wooden statue covered with gold and ivory. Designed by Athens sculptor Phidias. Destroyed by fire AD 475.
Temple of Artemis at Ephesus, Asia Minor	6th century BC	Marble temple in honour of goddess of hunting and the moon. Rebuilt in 4th century BC but destroyed by Goths in 3rd century AD.

Rulers of the Roman Empire

HISTORY

Name	Dates	History	Name	Dates	History
Augustus	27 BC–AD 14	Grandnephew of Julius Caesar	Gordian III	238–44	Son of Gordian II
Tiberius	AD 14–37	Stepson of Augustus	Philip	244–9	Assassin of Gordian III
Gaius Caesar (Caligula)	37–41	Grandnephew of Tiberius	Decius	249–51	Proclaimed by soldiers
			Hostilianus	251	Son of Decius
Claudius I	41–54	Uncle of Caligula	Gallus	251–3	Military commander
Nero	54–68	Stepson of Claudius	Aemilianus	253	Military commander
Galba	68–9	Proclaimed by soldiers	Valerian	253–60	Military commander
Otho	69	Military commander	Gallienus	253–68	Son of Valerian; co-emperor with his father, then emperor
Vespasian	69–79	Military commander			
Titus	79–81	Son of Vespasian			
Domitian	81–96	Son of Vespasian	Claudius II	268–70	Military commander
Nerva	96–8	Elected interim ruler	Aurelian	270–5	Chosen by Claudius as successor
Trajan	98–117	Adopted son of Nerva			
Hadrian	117–38	Ward of Trajan	Tacitus	275–6	Chosen by senate
Antoninus Pius	138–61	Adopted by Hadrian	Florianus	276	Half-brother of Tacitus
Marcus Aurelius	161–80	Adopted by Antoninus Pius	Probus	276–82	Military commander
			Carus	282–3	Proclaimed by the Praetorian guard
Lucius Verus	161–9	Adopted by Antoninus Pius and ruled together with Marcus Aurelius	Carinus	283–5	Son of Carus
			Numerianus	283–4	Son of Carus and ruled together with Carinus
Commodus	180–92	Son of Marcus Aurelius	Diocletian	284–305	Military commander; ruled with Maximian and Constantius; Empire divided
Pertinax	193	Proclaimed emperor by the Praetorian guard			
Didius Julianus	193	Bought office from the Praetorian guard	Maximian	286–305	Appointed by Diocletian
Septimius Severus	193–211	Proclaimed emperor	Constantius I	305–6	Successor of Diocletian
Caracalla	211–17	Son of Severus	Galerius	305–10	Ruled with Constantius
Geta	211–12	Son of Severus and ruled together with Caracalla	Maximin	308–13	Nephew of Galerius
			Licinius	308–24	Appointed emperor in West by Galerius
Macrinus	217–18	Proclaimed by soldiers			
Heliogabalus	218–22	Cousin of Caracalla	Maxentius	306–12	Son of Maximin
Alexander Severus	222–35	Cousin of Heliogabalus	Constantine I	306–37	Son of Constantius
			Constantine II	337–40	Son of Constantine I
Maximin	235–8	Proclaimed by soldiers	Constans	337–50	Son of Constantine I
Gordian I and Gordian II, Balbinus, Pupienus	238	Proclaimed by senate and all ruled together	Constantius II	337–61	Son of Constantine I
			Magnentius	350–3	Usurped Constans
			Julian	361–3	Nephew of Constantine I
			Jovian	363–4	Elected by the army

Name	Dates	History
Valentinian I	364–75	Proclaimed by the army; ruled in the West
Valens	364–78	Brother of Valentinian I; ruled in the East
Grantian	375–83	Son of Valentinian I; co-ruler in West with Valentinian II
Maximus	383–8	Usurper in the West
Valentinian II	375–92	Son of Valentinian I
Eugenius	392–4	Usurper in West
Theodosius I (the Great)	375–95	Appointed ruler in the East by Gratian; last ruler of united empire
Arcadius	395–408[a]	Son of Theodosius I
Theodosius II	408–50[a]	Son of Arcadius
Marcian	450–7[a]	Brother-in-law of Theodosius II
Leo I	457–74[a]	Chosen by senate
Leo II	474[a]	Grandson of Leo I
Honorius	395–423[b]	Son of Theodosius I
Maximus	409–11[b]	Usurper in Spain

Name	Dates	History
Constantius III	421[b]	Named joint emperor by Honorius
Valentinian III	425–55[b]	Nephew of Honorius and son of Constantius III
Petronius Maximus	455[b]	Bribed his way into office
Avitus	455–6[b]	Placed in office by Goths
Majorian	457–61[b]	Puppet emperor of Ricimer
Libius Severus	461–5[b]	Puppet emperor of Ricimer
Anthemius	467–72[b]	Appointed by Ricimer and Leo I
Olybrius	472[b]	Appointed by Ricimer
Glycerius	473–4[b]	Appointed by Leo I
Julius Nepos	474–5[b]	Appointed by Leo I
Romulus Augustus	475–6[b]	Placed in office by his father Orestes

[a]Emperor in the East
[b]Emperor in the West

The Roman Empire in the 1st century AD

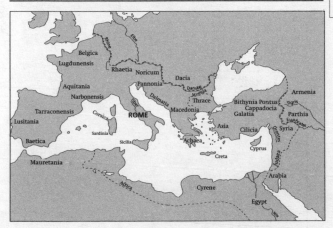

HISTORY

British royal family tree

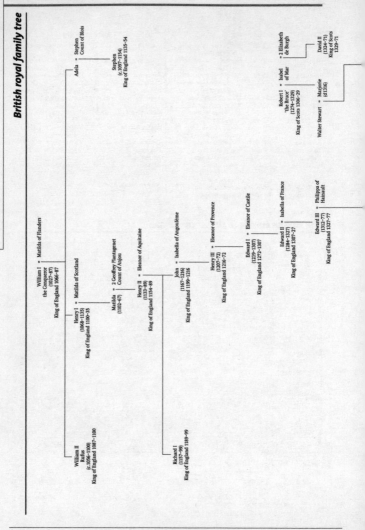

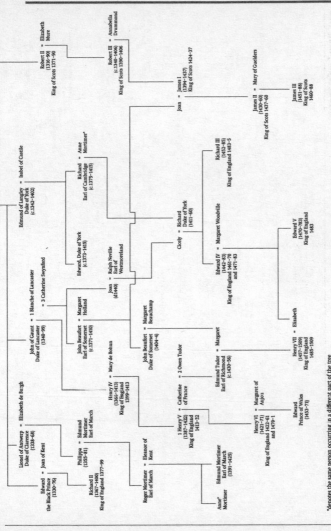

HISTORY

*denotes the same person occurring in a different part of the tree
1 denotes first marriage; 2, second marriage; 3, third marriage

HISTORY

British royal family tree (continued)

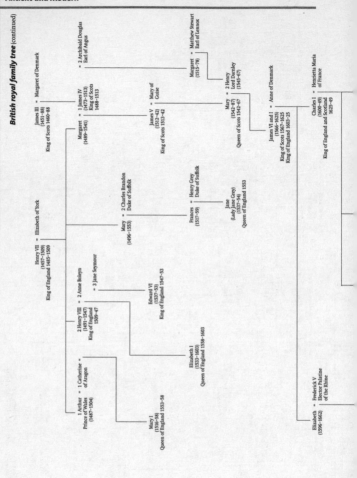

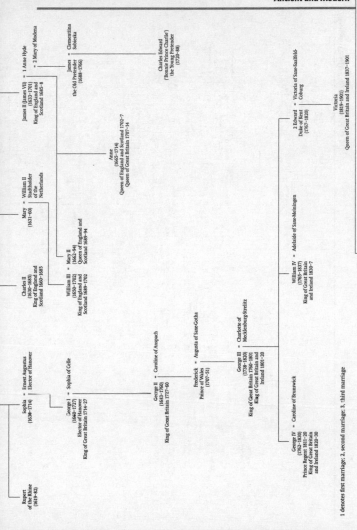

Rupert
of the Rhine
(1619–82)

Sophia = Ernest Augustus
(1630–1714)   Elector of Hanover

James II (James VII) = 1 Anne Hyde
(1633–1701)
King of England and   = 2 Mary of Modena
Scotland 1685–8

Clementina
Sobieska

James
the Old Pretender
(1688–1766)

Charles Edward
('Bonnie Prince Charlie')
the Young Pretender
(1720–88)

Mary = William II
(1631–60)   Stadtholder
of the
Netherlands

Charles II
(1630–1685)
King of England and
Scotland 1660–1685

William III = Mary II
(1650–1702)   (1662–94)
King of England and   Queen of England and
Scotland 1689–1702   Scotland 1689–94

Anne
(1665–1714)
Queen of England and Scotland 1702–7
Queen of Great Britain 1707–14

George I
(1660–1727)
Elector of Hanover
King of Great Britain 1714–27

George II = Caroline of Anspach
(1683–1760)
King of Great Britain 1727–60

Frederick = Augusta of Saxe-Gotha
Prince of Wales
(1707–51)

George III = Charlotte of
(1738–1820)   Mecklenburg-Strelitz
King of Great Britain 1760–1801
King of Great Britain and
Ireland 1801–20

George IV = Caroline of Brunswick
(1762–1830)
Prince Regent 1811–20
King of Great Britain
and Ireland 1820–30

William IV = Adelaide of Saxe-Meiningen
(1765–1837)
King of Great Britain
and Ireland 1830–7

2 Edward = Victoria of Saxe-Saalfeld-
Duke of Kent   Coburg
(1767–1820)

Victoria
(1819–1901)
Queen of Great Britain and Ireland 1837–1901

1 denotes first marriage; 2, second marriage; 3, third marriage

HISTORY

The British Royal Family today

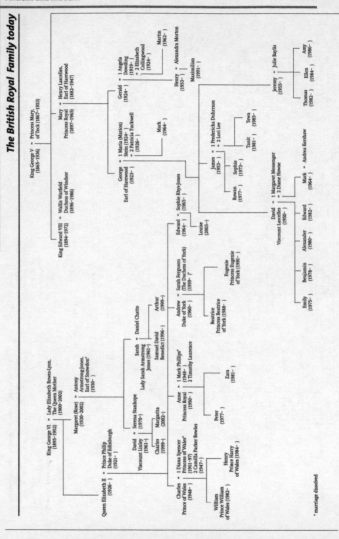

* marriage dissolved

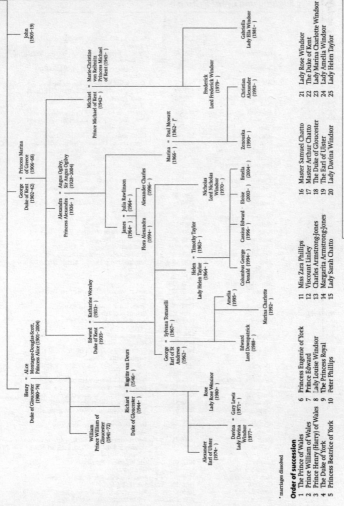

John
(1905–19)

Henry = Alice
Duke of Gloucester   Montague-Douglas-Scott,
(1900–74)   Princess Alice (1901–2004)

George = Princess Marina
Duke of Kent   of Greece
(1902–42)   (1906–68)

Alexandra = Angus Ogilvy,
Princess Alexandra   Sir Angus Ogilvy
(1936–)   (1928–2004)

Michael = Marie-Christine
Prince Michael of Kent   von Reibnitz
(1942–)   Princess Michael
   of Kent (1945–)

William
Prince William of
Gloucester
(1941–72)

Richard = Birgitte van Deurs
Duke of Gloucester   (1946–)
(1944–)

Edward = Katharine Worsley
Duke of Kent   (1933–)
(1935–)

Frederick
Lord Frederick Windsor
(1979–)

Gabriella
Lady Ella Windsor
(1981–)

Christian
Alexander
(1993–)

Rose
Lady Rose Windsor
(1980–)

George = Sylvana Tomaselli
Earl of St   (1967–)
Andrews
(1962–)

Helen = Timothy Taylor
Lady Helen Taylor   (1963–)
(1964–)

James = Julia Rawlinson
(1964–)   (1964–)

Marina = Paul Mowatt
(1966–)   (1962–) *

Alexander
Earl of Ulster
(1974–)

Davina
Lady Davina
Windsor
(1977–)

Rose = Gary Lewis
Lady Rose Windsor   (1971–)
(1980–)

Edward
Lord Downpatrick
(1988–)

Martina Charlotte
(1992–)

Amelia
(1995–)

Columbus George
Donald (1994–)

Cassius Edward
(1996–)

Flora Alexandra
(1994–)

Alexander Charles
(1996–)

Nicholas
Lord Nicholas
Windsor
(1970–)

Eloise
(2003–)

Estella
(2004–)

Zenouska
(1990–)

* marriages dissolved

Order of succession

1 The Prince of Wales
2 Prince William of Wales
3 Prince Henry (Harry) of Wales
4 The Duke of York
5 Princess Beatrice of York
6 Princess Eugenie of York
7 Prince Edward
8 Lady Louise Windsor
9 The Princess Royal
10 Peter Phillips
11 Miss Zara Phillips
12 Viscount Linley
13 Charles Armstrong-Jones
14 Margarita Armstrong-Jones
15 Lady Sarah Chatto
16 Master Samuel Chatto
17 Master Arthur Chatto
18 The Duke of Gloucester
19 The Earl of Ulster
20 Lady Davina Windsor
21 Lady Rose Windsor
22 The Duke of Kent
23 Lady Marina Charlotte Windsor
24 Lady Amelia Windsor
25 Lady Helen Taylor

Rulers of England and Great Britain

Period	Name of ruler	Dates of rule	History
Saxons and Danes	Egbert	802–39	King of Essex.
	Ethelwulf	839–58	Son of Egbert. King of Wessex, Sussex, Kent, Essex.
	Ethelbald	858–60	Son of Ethelwulf. Displaced his father as King of Wessex.
	Ethelbert	860–5	Second son of Ethelwulf. United Kent and Wessex.
	Ethelred	865–71	Third son of Ethelwulf. King of Wessex.
	Alfred (the Great)	871–99	Fourth son of Ethelwulf. Defeated the Danes.
	Edward (the Elder)	899–924	Son of Alfred. United England and claimed Scotland.
	Athelstan (the Glorious)	924–39	Son of Edward. King of Mercia, Wessex.
	Edmund	939–46	Third son of Edward. King of Wessex, Mercia.
	Edred	946–55	Fourth son of Edward.
	Edwy (the Fair)	955–9	Eldest son of Edmund. King of Wessex.
	Edgar (the Peaceful)	959–75	Younger son of Edmund. Ruled all England.
	Edward (the Martyr)	975–8	Son of Edgar. Murdered by stepmother.
	Ethelred II (the Unready)	978–1016	Second son of Edgar.
	Edmund (Ironside)	1016	Son of Ethelred II. King of London.
	Canute	1016–35	The Dane. Became ruler by conquest.
	Harold I (Harefoot)	1037–40	Illegitimate son of Canute.
	Hardecanute	1040–2	Son of Canute by Emma. King of Denmark.
	Edward (the Confessor)	1042–66	Younger son of Ethelred II.
	Harold II	1066	Brother-in-law of Edward the Confessor. Last Saxon King.
House of Normandy	William I (the Conqueror)	1066–87	Became ruler by conquest.
	William II (Rufus)	1087–1100	Third son of William I.
	Henry I	1100–35	Youngest son of William I.
House of Blois	Stephen	1135–54	Grandson of William I.
House of Plantagenet	Henry II	1154–89	Grandson of Henry I.
	Richard I (Coeur de Lion)	1189–99	Third son of Henry II. Crusader.
	John	1199–1216	Youngest son of Henry II. Signed Magna Carta 1215.
	Henry III	1216–72	Son of John.
	Edward I (Longshanks)	1272–1307	Son of Henry III.
	Edward II	1307–27	Son of Edward I. Deposed by parliament.
	Edward III	1327–77	Son of Edward II.
	Richard II	1377–99	Grandson of Edward III. Deposed.
House of Lancaster	Henry IV	1399–1413	Grandson of Edward III.
	Henry V	1413–22	Son of Henry IV. Victor of Battle of Agincourt 1415.
	Henry VI	1422–61	Son of Henry V.
		1470–71	Second period of rule.
House of York	Edward IV	1461–70	Great-grandson of Edward III.
		1471–83	Second period of rule.
	Edward V	1483	Son of Edward IV. Murdered in Tower of London.
	Richard III (Crookback)	1483–5	Brother of Edward IV. Fell at Bosworth Field.
House of Tudor	Henry VII	1485–1509	Descendant of Edward III.
	Henry VIII	1509–47	Son of Henry VII. Created Church of England.
	Edward VI	1547–53	Son of Henry VIII (by Jane Seymour).
	Mary I	1553–8	Daughter of Henry VIII (by Catherine of Aragon).
	Elizabeth I	1558–1603	Younger daughter of Henry VIII (by Anne Boleyn).
House of Stuart	James I/James VI of Scotland	1603–25	Descendant of Henry VII. First King of Great Britain (official in 1607 with the Act of the Union).
	Charles I	1625–49	Son of James I. Beheaded.
Commonwealth	Oliver Cromwell	1653–8	Lord Protector.
	Richard Cromwell	1658–9	Lord Protector. Son of Oliver Cromwell.
House of Stuart	Charles II	1660–85	Son of Charles I.
	James II	1685–8	Younger son of Charles I. Deposed.
	William III	1689–1702	Son of Mary, daughter of Charles 1.

Period	Name of ruler	Dates of rule	History
	Mary II	1689–94	Daughter of James II. Ruled together with William III.
	Anne	1702–14	Younger daughter of James II.
House of Hanover	George I	1714–27	Great-grandson of James I.
	George II	1727–60	Only son of George I.
	George III	1760–1820	Grandson of George II.
	George IV	1820–30	Eldest son of George III.
	William IV	1830–7	Third son of George III.
	Victoria	1837–1901	Granddaughter of George III.
House of Saxe-Coburg	Edward VII	1901–10	Son of Victoria.
House of Windsor	George V	1910–36	Son of Edward VII.
	Edward VIII	1936	Eldest son of George V. Abdicated.
	George VI	1936–52	Second son of George V.
	Elizabeth II	1952–	Daughter of George VI.

MILITARY WARS AND CAMPAIGNS

Major wars of mediaeval and modern times

War	Dates	History
Norman Conquest of England	1066	France (William the Conqueror)–England (Harold II). Battle of Hastings (14 Oct 1066). Most decisive battle on English soil which led to the successful conquest by the Normans. Harold II died in battle. Began rule of a dynasty of Norman Kings and almost complete replacement of English nobility by Normans, Bretons, and Flemings.
The Crusades	1095–1272	Christians–Turks. Holy Wars authorized by the Pope; fought against infidels in the East, heretics who threatened Catholic unity, and against Christian lay powers who opposed the Papacy.
Conquests of Genghis Khan	1190–1227	Mongols–N China, Kara–Chitai Empire. Subjugation of hostile tribes – Naimans, Tanguts, and Turkish Uigurs.
War of the Sicilian Vespers	1282–1302	Sicily–France. Massacre of the French in Sicily marked the beginning of revolt of Sicilians against Charles of Anjou. War of Sicilian Vespers ensued. Angevins supported by papacy, Italian Guelphs, and Philip II of France, while Aragonese helped by Italian Ghibellines. James II ascended to throne, made peace with papacy, France, and Angevins (to whom he renounced Sicily) by Treaty of Anagni.
Hundred Years War	1337–1453	England–France. Edward III claimed French throne in 1340 and styled himself 'King of England and France'. Traditional rivalries exploded into a dynastic struggle. 1415 Battle of Agincourt – Henry V led overwhelming victory over French. 1417 English then began systematic conquest of Normandy, a task beyond their resources. Evicted from Guyenne (1453) which reduced England's French territories to Calais (lost in 1558) and the Channel Islands. However, the title of King of France was not relinquished until 1801.
Fall of Constantinople	1453	Turks–Byzantine Empire. Collapse of the Byzantine Empire. Since 1261, when Constantinople had been retaken from Latin rule by Michael VII Paleologus, the Byzantine Empire had been threatened by growing power of Ottoman Turks in Asia Minor. 1422 Ottoman Sultan of Turkey Murad II laid siege to the city. This failed but attempt thirty years later by Mehmed II succeeded. Constantinople fell 1453. Last Byzantine emperor Constantine XI Paleologus died in battle.
Wars of the Roses	1455–85	Civil wars in England. Between two rival factions of the House of Plantagenet – York (white rose) and Lancaster (red rose). Began when Richard, Duke of York, claimed protectorship of crown after King Henry VI's mental breakdown and ended with Henry Tudor's defeat of Richard III in Battle of Bosworth. Wars escalated by gentry and by aristocratic feuds.

Major wars of mediaeval and modern times (continued)

War	Dates	History
French Wars of Religion	1562–98	Catholics–Huguenots. Caused by growth of Calvinism, noble factionalism, and weak royal government. From 1550s Calvinist or Huguenot numbers increased, fostered by missionary activities of Geneva. Noble factions of Bourbons, Guise, and Montmorency were split by religion as well as by family interests. Civil wars were encouraged by Philip II's support of Catholic Guise faction and by Elizabeth I's aid to Huguenots. They ended when Henry of Navarre returned to Catholicism and crushed the Guise Catholic League.
Thirty Years' War	1618–48	France–Habsburg rulers. Power struggle between Kings of France and Habsburg rulers of Holy Roman Empire and Spain. War fuelled by conflict between Calvinism and Catholicism, and also by the underlying constitutional conflict between Holy Roman Emperor and the German Princes. With Frederick V's defeat (1620) and intervention by other powers (such as Sweden, Denmark, and France), the conflict intensified and spread. Spain collapsed and left the emperor isolated. Peace negotiations opened and ended German war at the Peace of Westphalia.
Bishops' Wars	1639–40	Scotland–England. Two wars between Charles I and Scotland caused by Charles I's unpopular policies towards the Scottish kirk. Resulted in English defeats and bankruptcy for Charles who was then forced to call the Short and Long Parliaments in 1640, bringing to an end his personal rule.
English Civil Wars	1642–51	Charles I–Parliamentarians. Parliamentary opposition to Royal policies. First battle at Edgehill (Oct 1642), but neither side victorious. Royalists then threatened London, the Parliamentarians' stronghold. By autumn the North and West were in their hands. Crucial event was 1643 alliance of Parliament with the Scots. This increased military strength helped the parliamentarians, led by Oliver Cromwell, defeat the Royalists at Marston Moor. 1646 saw end of first civil war with Charles' surrender to the Scots at Newark in May. 1646–8 negotiations between parliament and King began. Aug 1647 army presented King with Head of Proposals asking for religious tolerance and parliamentary control of the armed forces. Charles made secret pact with the Scots, promising to establish Presbyterianism in England. Scots invaded England and were only repulsed in Battle of Preston. Around 100 000 men died in the two wars (1 in 10 of the adult male population). Charles brought to trial by Cromwell (who was also signatory of his death warrant) and executed Jan 1649.
War of League of Augsburg	1688–97	Louis XIV–European Alliance. The third major war of Louis XIV of France in which his expansionist plans were blocked by the alliance led by England, United Provinces (of the Netherlands), and Austrian Habsburgs. The issue underlying the war was the balance of power between Bourbon and Habsburg dynasties. War began when French marched into the Palatinate while Austria was defeating Turks in the East. Grand alliance of United Provinces, England, Saxony, Bavaria, and Spain, all fearful of French annexations, joined together against France. The war was costly and lengthy. Louis XIV opened negotiations for peace 1696 and in 1697 Treaty of Rijswijk drawn up. This did not resolve conflict between Habsburgs and Bourbons, nor English and French, both of which erupted again only four years later in the War of Spanish Succession.
War of Spanish Succession	1701–14	Alliance–Louis XIV. Alliance of British, Dutch, and Habsburg Emperor against French, supported by Spanish. War arose out of conflict as to succession to throne of Spain following death of childless Charles II. Claimants were England, United Provinces, and France. When alliance collapsed the war was concluded by Treaties of Utrecht which divided inheritance among the powers. Britain's imperial power grew at the expense of France and Spain.
War of Jenkin's Ear	1739–43	Britain–Spain. Began in 1739 but then merged into the War of Austrian Succession. Anti-Spanish feeling in Britain provoked war as Captain Robert Jenkins claimed Spanish coastguards in the Caribbean cut off his ear.

HISTORY

War	Dates	History
War of Austrian Succession	1740-8	Prussia–Austria. Struggle for mastery of German states. Hostilities prompted by Frederick II of Prussia's seizure of Habsburg province of Silesia. French allied with Bavaria and Spain and later Saxony and Prussia. Austria was supported by Britain who feared France's hegemony in Europe which would threaten Britain's colonial and commercial empire. After 1744 this developed into a colonial conflict between Britain and the Franco-Spanish bloc. Peace concluded only by Treaty of Aix-la-Chapelle (1748) which preserved Austrian inheritance but also confirmed Prussian inheritance of Silesia.
Seven Years' War	1756-63	A major European conflict rooted in the rivalry between Austria and Prussia and the imminent colonial struggle between Britain and France in the New World and the Far East. Hostilities in N America (1754) pre-dated the Diplomatic Revolution in Europe (1756), which created two opposing power blocs: Austria, France, Russia, Sweden, and Saxony against Prussia, Britain, and Portugal. British maritime superiority countered Franco-Spanish naval power and prevented an invasion by the French. The European war, precipitated by Prussia's seizure of Saxony, was marked by many notable pitched land battles. Saved from total defeat when Russia switched sides, Frederick II of Prussia retained Silesia in 1763.
US War of Independence	1775-83	American settlers–Britain. Insurrection of thirteen of Britain's N American colonies. Began as civil war but America was later joined by France (1778), Spain (1779), and Netherlands (1780). America rejected Britain's offer of peace in the civil war conflicts and declared independence. Britain ultimately defeated.
French Revolutionary Wars	1792-1802	A series of campaigns between France and neighbouring European states hostile to the Revolution and to French hegemony, merging ultimately with the Napoleonic Wars.
Napoleonic Wars	1800-15	Fought to preserve French hegemony in Europe. Initially a guarantee for political, social, and economic changes of the Revolution, but increasingly became manifestation of Napoleon's territorial ambitions. War began with Napoleon's destruction of the Second Coalition (1800). Britain resumed hostilities (1803), prompting Napoleon to prepare for invasion and encouraging the formation of a Third Coalition. Britain retained naval superiority but Napoleon established territorial domination with the invasions of Spain (1808) and Russia (1812). French finally overwhelmed by the Fourth Coalition and war ended with the Battle of Waterloo (1815).
Peninsular War	1808-14	France–Britain. Struggle for the Iberian peninsula which began as Spanish revolt against imposition of Napoleon's brother, Joseph, as King of Spain, but developed into bitter conflict, with British forces under Wellington liberating Spain (1811). Following Napoleon's Moscow campaign (1812), French resources were overextended, enabling Wellington's army to invade SW France (1813-14).
Greek War of Independence	1821-8	Greece–Turkey. Greece fought alone until 1825 when her cause was seconded by Britain, Russia, and later France. Turks defeated and Greece's independence guaranteed by her allies.
Crimean War	1853-6	Britain and France – Russia. Fought in Crimean Peninsula by Britain and France against Russia. Origins lay in the Russian successes against the Turks in the Black Sea area, and the British and French desire to prevent further Russian expansion westward which threatened the Mediterranean and overland routes to India. Major battles were fought at the River Alma (Sep 1854), Balaclava (1854), and Inkermann (Nov 1854). Fall of Russian fortress at Sebastopol (Sep 1855) led to negotiations for peace. Finally agreed in Paris 1856 that Russia would cede South Bessarabia to Moldavia.
American Civil War	1861-5	Unionists – Confederates. Conflict between Unionists and Confederates. Dealt with two great issues: the nature of the Federal Union and the relative power of the states and central government; and the existence of Black slavery. When Lincoln and the Republican Party's election demonstrated that the South could no longer expect to control the high offices of state, eleven Southern states withdrew from the Union and established the Confederate States

Major wars of mediaeval and modern times (continued)

War	Dates	History

of America. War broke out (12 Apr 1861) when the Southern batteries opened fire on a Union emplacement in the harbour of Charleston, SC. Lincoln at first defined the issue as preservation of the Union, without any reference to slavery, but he broadened the war aims (Jan 1861), proclaiming the emancipation of all slaves in areas then under arms against the government. The winning strategy began in 1863 when the Unionist General Grant won control of the whole Mississippi valley, isolating the western Confederate states from the rest. After several fierce battles (Gettysburg, Fredericksburg, and the Chattanooga campaign), the South's position became untenable and General Lee, leader of the Confederate forces, abandoned the Confederate capital in Apr 1865 and finally capitulated at Appomattox Court House. The last surrender took place on 26 May.

Franco-Prussian War   1870   France – Prussia.

Marked the end of French hegemony in Europe and the foundation of a German empire. In Napoleon III's ambition to conquer Prussia, Bismarck saw an opportunity to bring the S German states into unity with the Prussian-led N German states and build a strong German empire. Conflict was sparked off by disputed candidature for the Spanish throne. The Ems Telegram, sent by Wilhelm I of Prussia refusing the French conditions, succeeded in provoking the French to declare war five days later. After only four weeks the French found themselves trapped at Metz. Main French army tried to relieve them but were surrounded and trapped by Germans at Sedan. French army, with Napoleon III and Macmahon, surrendered. French resistance continued with the new government, and the Germans then began to besiege Paris. Paris surrendered Jan 1871. Treaty of Frankfurt drawn up. Germany annexed Alsace and Lorraine, imposed a high war indemnity on France, and occupied northern territory until indemnity paid.

Boer Wars   1880–1,   Britain – Boers.
                      1899–1902

Wars fought by Britain for the mastery of South Africa. British had made several attempts to re-incorporate the Boers into a South African confederation. First war ended with defeat of British at Majuba Hill and the signing of the Pretoria and London conventions in 1881 and 1884. Second Boer War (1899–1902) can be divided into three phrases – series of Boer successes; counter-offensives by British which captured Pretoria; period of guerilla warfare. Boers effectively won the peace. Retained control of 'native affairs', won back representative government in 1907, and federated South Africa on their own terms (1910). Nevertheless, British interests in South Africa remained protected.

World War 1   1914–18   Allies (Britain, France, Russia, Japan, and Italy) – Central Powers (Germany, Austria-Hungary, Turkey, and Bulgaria).

Origins lay in reaction of other great powers to ambitions of German Empire. The political tensions divided Europe into two camps – the Triple Alliance (Britain, France, and Russia) and the Triple Entente (Germany, Austria-Hungary, and Italy).

Catalyst to war was the assassination of heir to Habsburg throne, Franz Ferdinand, in Bosnia. Austria declared war on Serbia. Germany then declared war on Russia and France and invaded neutral Belgium. This brought the British into the war on the side of the French. Japan joined Britain, as did Italy in 1915. Germany was joined by Turkey (1914) and Bulgaria (1915). Military campaigns centre on France and Belgium in W Europe. First battle of Ypres prevented the Germans from reaching the ports. By end 1914 static line of defence had been established from Belgian coast to Switzerland. Position of stalemate reached. 1916 allies launched offensive for the W front but stopped by Germans who attacked French at Verdun. To relieve situation Battle of the Somme was launched but proved indecisive. Spring 1918 Germany launched major offensive on West but was driven back by the allies with help from USA. By November armistice was signed with allies having recaptured Belgium and nearly all French territory. Treaty of Versailles drawn up 1919 assigning responsibility for causing the war to Germany and establishing her liability for reparations payments. Germany lost all overseas territories and considerable territory in Poland. Rhineland demilitarized and occupied by allied forces. Germany called treaty a

War	Dates	History
		'Diktat' and its harshness was bitterly resented throughout the interwar years.
Spanish Civil War	1936–9	Republicans–Nationalists (led by General Franco).
		Both sides attracted foreign assistance; Republic from the USSR and the International Brigades and the Nationalists from Fascist Italy and Nazi Germany. Nationalist victory due to balance of foreign aid, to nonintervention on part of the Western democracies and to greater internal unity in the Nationalist army under Franco.
World War 2	1939–45	Allies (Britain and British Commonwealth, China, France, USA, USSR)–Axis Powers (Germany, Italy, Japan).
		Origins lay in three different conflicts which merged after 1941: Germany's desire for expansion, Japan's struggle against China, conflict between Japanese and US interests in the Pacific. War in Europe caused by German unwillingness to accept Treaty of Versailles, which was systematically dismantled aided by the allied policy of appeasement. Increased German aggression finally resulted in the invasion of Czechoslovakia, after which Britain and France abandoned policy of appeasement and pledged support to Poland which was now threatened. Germany signed alliance with Russia and invaded Poland. Britain and France then declared war on Germany. Little fighting took place but Germany proceeded to occupy Norway and Denmark. German Blitzkrieg tactics (a combination of tank warfare and airpower) brought about the surrender of Holland in four days, Belgium in three weeks, and France in seven weeks. After failed attempt to gain air supremacy over Britain (Battle of Britain) the invasion of Britain was postponed. Germany then moved east into Greece and Yugoslavia. British military efforts were concentrated against Italy in Mediterranean and N Africa. Allied forces finally ejected German and Italian forces in mid-1943, invaded Sicily and Italy itself, and forced Italy to make a separate peace. June 1941 Germany invaded her ally Russia and advanced towards Moscow, Leningrad, and the Volga. After two years of occupation and the Battle of Stalingrad in winter 1942–3 (a major turning point in the allied campaign), they were driven out. Allies launched a second front through invasion of Normandy and Paris was liberated in August. Allies advanced into Germany and linked with the Russians on the River Elbe. Germans surrendered unconditionally at Rheims 7 May 1945. Japan's desire for expansion led to her attack on Pearl Harbor, Hawaii, and US declared war on Japan next day (8 Dec 1941). In reply, Germany and Italy declared war on US. Not until June 1942 did naval victories halt Japanese advance. Fighting continued until 1945 when US dropped two atomic bombs on Hiroshima and Nagasaki (6 and 9 Aug). Japan then surrendered.
First Indochinese War	1946–54	Vietnam–France.
		Vietnam controlled by France as colony 1883–1939 and then as a possession 1940–45. Ho Chi Minh proclaimed its independence on 2 Sep 1945 and French opposed the move. Ho Chi Minh led guerrilla warfare against French which ended in Vietnamese victory at Dien Bien Phu in May 1954. Agreement signed in Geneva providing temporary division of the country at the 17th parallel of latitude between the communist-dominated North and the US-supported South. Activities of procommunist rebels would lead to the second Vietnam War.
Korean War	1950–3	Communists and non-Communists.
		Communist North invaded South after series of border clashes. UN forces intervened driving the invaders back to Chinese frontier. China entered conflict and with N Koreans occupied Seoul. UN forces counterattacked and retook territory south of 38th parallel.
Suez War	1956	Britain, France, Israel–Egypt.
		In July 1956 Egyptian President Abdel Nasser nationalized the Suez Canal following American and British decision not to finance construction of the Aswan Dam. When diplomacy failed France and Britain planned military action to regain control of the canal, allied with Israel. In Oct Israel invaded Egypt. Britain and France ordered Israel to leave and also landed at Port Said, apparently to enforce the UN ceasefire. Growing opposition at home, hostile position of USA, and the threatened intervention of the Soviets forced them to withdraw. The outcome of the incident was Israel regaining shipping rights to the canal, though

HISTORY

Major wars of mediaeval and modern times (continued)

War	Dates	History
		France and Britain lost influence in the area.
Vietnam War	1956–75	The war between communist North Vietnam and non-communist South Vietnam, also known as the Second Indochinese War. The Geneva settlement had left North Vietnam under communist rule, and the South ruled first by the emperor Bao Dai (until 1955) and then by Ngo Dinh Diem's dictatorial regime. From 1961, US aid and numbers of 'military advisers' increased considerably. From 1964, US aircraft bombarded the North, and by 1968 over 500 000 troops were involved. These troops were withdrawn in 1973, and hostilities ceased in 1975 when the North's victory was completed with the capture of Saigon (renamed Ho Chi Minh City).
Six Day War	1967	Syrian bombings of Israeli villages intensified early 1967. Israeli air force shot down six Syrian planes. In retaliation Abdel Nasser mobilized Egyptian forces near Sinai border. Israel defeated Egyptian forces and established air superiority. War cost Arabs Old City of Jerusalem, Sinai and Gaza Strip, West Bank, and the Golan Heights.
Cambodian War	1970–5	Cambodia, S Vietnam, US–N Vietnam, Viet Cong, Khmer Rouge. Cambodia had achieved independence in 1953, under Prince Norodom Sihanouk. He assumed position of neutrality in Vietnam war and allowed Vietnamese communists sanctuary in Cambodia. In 1970 he was deposed by coup and US and S Vietnam forces invaded Cambodia to destroy communist sanctuaries. New Cambodian government faced growing threat from Cambodian communists (Khmer Rouge). US launched series of raids by which it hoped to halt Khmer activity but, after five years of civil war, Phnom Penh fell to Khmer Rouge. In 1979 Vietnamese forces invaded and installed a puppet government.
Iran–Iraq War	1980–8	Iran–Iraq. After the Islamic Revolution in Iran, the Iranians accused Baghdad of encouraging the Arabs of Iran's Khuzestan province to demand autonomy. Iraq also feared Iranian provocation of its own large Shi'ite population. Border fighting followed and Iraqi forces advanced into Iran (Sep 1980). Peace finally agreed in 1988 after deaths of around half a million on each side. Iraq accepted Iran's terms in 1990.
Falklands War	1982	Britain–Argentina. Argentinian invasion of the islands ruled by Britain since 1833. War ended after three months in Argentinian surrender.
Gulf War	1991	Iraq–US led allies (29 member coalition). War caused by Iraqi invasion of Kuwait and failure to comply with UN resolution calling for withdrawal. Hostilities suspended after 43 days of fighting when Iraq accepted the UN resolution.
Yugoslavian Civil War	1991–5	Declaration of independence by Slovenia, Macedonia, and Croatia considered illegal by central Yugoslav government. Confrontation between Croatia and Serb-dominated national army developed into civil war. Croatian independence was internationally recognized in 1991, but fighting continued throughout 1992–3, despite several rounds of negotiations, and peace proposal. Serb attacks on Sarajevo, 1994–5, resulted in NATO air strikes and hostage-taking. Serbs captured Muslim safe-area enclave of Srebrenica, which brought reports of major atrocities. Successful Croatian offensive in NW Bosnia restored territorial balance in the area. Serb attack on Sarajevo led to NATO/UN attacks on Bosnian Serb targets, and Serb withdrawal. A peace agreement was signed in Dayton, Ohio (Nov). Bosnia was to stay a single state, made up of the Bosnian-Croat Federation and the Bosnian Serb Republic, with a united Sarajevo, and the establishment of a NATO peace implementation force.
Iraq War	2003	A war (Mar–Apr) between Iraq and US-led coalition forces, brought about by Iraq's apparent continued failure to comply with UN Security Council Resolution 1441 to disarm itself of weapons of mass destruction. US President George Bush and UK Prime Minister Tony Blair set a deadline for Iraqi cooperation. No positive response was received from Iraqi leader Saddam Hussein, and the conflict began with air missile strikes on the capital, Baghdad, launched from warships in The Gulf in a "shock and awe" campaign. The port of Umm Qasr was surrounded and US troops marched towards Baghdad, took control of the

War	Dates	History
		international airport and entered the city. British troops advanced towards Basra and surrounded the city. A large US force advanced through Kurdish N Iraq to secure the oilfields around Kirkuk and Mosul. The campaign was notable for its live global television coverage, which included the historic moment (9 Apr) when Saddam's giant statue in Baghdad was toppled. In December he was captured by US forces near Tikrit and held as a prisoner-of-war. Fighting continued into 2004 between local militias and occupying forces. US Coalition Provisional Authority established. Handover of power to interim Iraqi government.

The main crusades to the East

	Background	Leader(s)	Outcome
First Crusade (1096–9)	Proclaimed by Urban II to aid the Greeks against the Seljuk Turks in Asia Minor, liberate Jerusalem and the Holy Land from Seljuk domination, and safeguard pilgrim routes to the Holy Sepulchre.	Bohemond I Godfrey of Bouillon Raymond, Count of Toulouse Robert, Count of Flanders Robert Curthose, Duke of Normandy Stephen, Count of Blois	Capture of Nicaea in Anatolia (Jun 1097); Turks vanquished at Battle of Dorylaeum (Jul 1097); capture of Antioch in Syria (Jun 1098), Jerusalem (Jul 1099). Godfrey of Bouillon became ruler of the new Latin kingdom of Jerusalem, and defeated the Fatimids of Egypt near Ascalon in Palestine (Aug 1099). Three other crusader states were founded: Antioch, Edessa, Tripoli.
Second Crusade (1147–8)	Proclaimed by Eugenius III to aid the crusader states after the Muslim reconquest of Edessa (1144).	Conrad III of Germany Louis VII of France	German army heavily defeated by Turks near Dorylaeum (Oct 1147), and the French at Laodicea (Jan 1148); Damascus in Syria invested, but siege abandoned after four days (Jul 1148). The crusaders' military reputation was destroyed, and the Syrian Muslims united against the Latins.
Third Crusade (1189–92)	Proclaimed by Gregory VIII after Saladin's defeat of the Latins at the Battle of Hattin (Jul 1187) and his conquest of Jerusalem (Oct 1187). (By 1189 all that remained of the kingdom of Jerusalem was the port of Tyre.)	Frederick I Barbarossa Philip II Augustus of France Richard I of England	Cyprus conquered from Greeks (May 1191), and established as new crusader kingdom (survived until 1489); capture of Acre in Palestine (Jul 1191); Saladin defeated near Arsuf (Sep 1191); three-year truce guaranteeing safe conduct of Christian pilgrims to Jerusalem. Most cities and castles of the Holy Land remained in Muslim hands.
Fourth Crusade (1202–4)	Proclaimed by Innocent III to recover the Holy Places	Boniface of Montferrat	Despite papal objections, crusade diverted from Egypt or Palestine: (1) to Zara, a Christian town in Dalmatia, conquered for Venetians (Nov 1202); (2) to Byzantium, where embroilment in dynastic struggles led to sack of Constantinople (Apr 1204) and foundation of Latin Empire of Constantinople (survived until 1261). The crusading movement was discredited; the Latins in Palestine and Syria were hardly helped at all; the Byzantine empire never fully recovered; and the opportunity was lost of a united front between the Latins and Greeks against the Muslims.

The main crusades to the East (continued)

	Background	Leader(s)	Outcome
Fifth Crusade (1217–21)	Proclaimed by Innocent III when a six-year truce between the kingdom of Jerusalem and Egypt expired.	Andrew II of Hungary John of Brienne, King of Jerusalem Leopold, Duke of Austria	Three indecisive expeditions against Muslims in Palestine (1217); capture of Damietta in Egypt after protracted siege (May 1218–Nov 1219), further conquests attempted, but crusaders forced to relinquish Damietta (Aug 1221) and withdrew.
Sixth Crusade (1228–9)	Emperor Frederick II, who first took the Cross in 1215, married the heiress to the kingdom of Jerusalem in 1225. Excommunicated by Gregory IX for delaying his departure, he finally arrived at Acre in Sep 1228.	Frederick II	Negotiations with Egyptians secured Jerusalem and other places, including Bethlehem and Nazareth (Feb 1229); Frederick crowned King of Jerusalem in church of Holy Sepulchre (Mar 1229). Jerusalem was held until recaptured by the Khorezmian Turks in 1244.
Seventh Crusade (1248–54)	Proclaimed by Innocent IV after the fall of Jerusalem and defeat of the Latin army near Gaza by the Egyptians and Khorezmians (1244).	Louis IX of France	Capture of Damietta (June 1249); defeat at Mansurah (Feb 1250); surrender of crusaders during attempted withdrawal. Damietta relinquished and large ransoms paid (May 1250). Louis spent four years in Palestine, refortifying Acre, Caesarea, Joppa, and Sidon, and fruitlessly attempting to regain Jerusalem by alliances with the Mameluks and Mongols.
Eighth Crusade (1270–2)	Proclaimed after the Mameluk conquest of Arsuf, Caesarea, Haifa (1265). Antioch and Joppa (1268).	Charles of Anjou, King of Naples-Sicily Edward of England (later Edward I) Louis IX of France	Attacked Tunisia in N Africa (Jul 1270); Louis died in Aug; Charles concluded treaty with Tunis and withdrew; Edward negotiated 11 years' truce with Mameluks in Palestine. By 1291 the Latins had been driven from the Holy Land.

The American Civil War

1859

16 Oct	John Brown's raid on Harper's Ferry

1860

6 Nov	Abraham Lincoln elected President
20 Dec	Secession of first Southern states

1861

4 Feb	Announcement of the Confederate States of America – Jefferson Davis named as President
4 Mar	Inauguration of Lincoln as President
12 Apr	Southern Bombardment of Fort Sumter
21 Jul	First Battle of Bull Run

1862

6 Apr	Battle of Shiloh
29–30 Aug	Second Battle of Bull Run
17 Sep	Battle of Antietam
22 Sep	Preliminary Emancipation Proclamation
13 Dec	Battle of Fredericksburg

1863

1 Jan	Emancipation Proclamation
2 May	Battle of Chancellorsville – death of Stonewall Jackson
3 Jul	Battle of Gettysburg
4 Jul	Fall of Vicksburg
19–20 Sep	Battle of Chickamauga
24–25 Nov	Battle of Chattanooga

1864

1 Sep	Fall of Atlanta
15–16 Dec	Battle of Nashville

1865

9 Apr	Surrender of Confederate forces at Appomattox
14 Apr	Assassination of Lincoln

EXPLORATION AND DISCOVERY

Great explorers

Name	Dates	Nationality	Major voyages of exploration
Amundsen, Roald	1872–1928	Norwegian	1911: Voyage to the South Pole.
Baffin, William	1584–1622	English	1616: Explores Baffin Bay.
Balboa, Vasco Núñez de	1475–1519	Spanish	1513: Reaches the Pacific Ocean.
Bougainville, Louis de	1729–1811	French	1766: Begins circumnavigation of the globe.
Burke, Robert O'Hara	1820–61	Irish	1860: Leads Burke and Wills expedition across Australia.
Byrd, Richard	1888–1957	American	1926: First flight over North Pole.
Cabot, John	1425–c.1500	Genoese	1497: Discovers mainland of North America.
Cabral, Pedro Álvarez	c.1467–1520	Portuguese	1500: Reaches Brazil.
Cartier, Jacques	1491–1557	French	1534: Explores the coast of N America.
Columbus, Christopher	1451–1506	Genoese	1492: Discovers the Bahamas.
			1498: Discovers mainland of South America.
Cook, James	1728–79	British	1769: Maps coast of New Zealand and Australia.
			1770: Lands at Botany Bay.
			1775: Reaches S Georgia and the Sandwich Is.
			1778: Explores islands now known as Hawaii.
Cousteau, Jacques	1910–97	French	1950: Commands underwater ship *Calypso*.
Dampier, William	1652–1715	English	1683: Crosses Pacific.
			1699: Explores NW coast of Australia.
Davis, John	c.1550–1605	English	1585: Discovers Davis Strait, Greenland.
Diaz, Bartolomeu	c.1450–1500	Portuguese	1488: Sails round Cape of Good Hope.
Diaz, Dinís	c.15th century	Portuguese	1446: Reaches Cape Verde and Senegal.
Drake, Francis	c.1540–96	English	1580: Completes circumnavigation of the globe.
Eriksson, Leif	10th–c.	Norwegian	1000: Discovers Vinland (possibly America).
Erik the Red	10th–c.	Norwegian	985: Explores Greenland coast.
Fiennes, Ranulph	1944–	British	1993: First unsupported crossing on foot of Antarctica.
Flinders, Matthew	1774–1814	British	1801–3: Circumnavigates Australia.
Fuchs, Vivian	1908–99	British	1958: First land crossing of Antarctica.
Gama, Vasco da	c.1469–1525	Portuguese	1497: Sails round Cape of Good Hope.
			1498: Explores coast of Madagascar and discovers sea route to India.
Gomes, Diogo	c.1440–84	Portuguese	1469: Crosses the equator.
Heyerdahl, Thor	1914–	Norwegian	1947: Crosses Atlantic in balsa raft *Kon-Tiki*.
Hillary, Edmund	1919–	New Zealander	1953: First ascent of Mount Everest, with Norgay Tenzing.
Hudson, Henry	c.1565–1611	English	1610: Discovers Hudson's Bay.
Livingstone, David	1813–73	British	1849: Reaches Lake Ngami.
			1855: Reaches the Victoria Falls.
López de Cárdenas, García		Spanish	1540: Reaches the Grand Canyon.
Magellan, Ferdinand	c.1480–1521	Portuguese	1520: Discovers the Strait of Magellan.
			1521: Explores the Philippines.
Mendoza, Pedro de	1487–1537	Spanish	1536: Founds Buenos Aires.
Nansen, Fridtjof	1861–1930	Norwegian	1888: Crosses Greenland.
Nobile, Umberto	1885–1978	Italian	1926: First airship crossing of North Pole.
Park, Mungo	1771–1806	British	1795–6: Explores Niger River.
Peary, Robert	1856–1920	American	1909: Successful voyage to reach North Pole.
Polo, Marco	1254–1324	Italian	1275–92: Explores China.
Raleigh, Walter	1552–1618	English	1595: Explores Orinoco River.
			1617: Explores Guiana.
Scott, Robert Falcon	1868–1912	British	1912: Reaches South Pole.
Shackleton, Ernest	1874–1922	British	1914: Leads expedition to Antarctica.
Speke, John	1827–64	British	1858: Discovers Lakes Tanganyika and Victoria.
Stanley, Henry Morton	1841–1904	British	1874: Traces Congo to the Atlantic.
Tasman, Abel Janszoon	1603–c.1659	Dutch	1642: Reaches Tasmania and New Zealand.
Tenzing Norgay	1914–86	Nepalese	1953: First ascent of Mount Everest, with Edmund Hillary.
Verrazano, Giovanni da	1485–1528	Italian	1524: Reaches New York Bay, Hudson River.
Vespucci, Amerigo	1454–1512	Italian	1499: Discovers mouth of River Amazon.
			1501: Explores coast of S America.

HISTORY

POLITICAL LEADERS AND RULERS

Australia

Head of State: British monarch, represented by Governor-General.

Prime Minister

1901–3	Edmund Barton *Prot*
1903–4	Alfred Deakin *Prot*
1904	John Christian Watson *Lab*
1904–5	George Houstoun Reid *Free*
1905–8	Alfred Deakin *Prot*
1908–9	Andrew Fisher *Lab*
1909–10	Alfred Deakin *Fusion*
1910–13	Andrew Fisher *Lab*
1913–14	Joseph Cook *Lib*
1914–15	Andrew Fisher *Lab*
1915–17	William Morris Hughes *Nat Lab*
1917–23	William Morris Hughes *Nat*
1923–9	Stanley Melbourne Bruce *Nat*
1929–32	James Henry Scullin *Lab*
1932–9	Joseph Aloyslus Lyons *Un*
1939	Earle Christmas Grafton Page *Co*
1939–40	Robert Gordon Menzies *Un*
1941	Arthur William Fadden *Co*
1941–5	John Joseph Curtin *Lab*
1945	Francis Michael Forde *Lab*
1945–9	Joseph Benedict Chifley *Lab*
1949–66	Robert Gordon Menzies *Lib*
1966–7	Harold Edward Holt *Lib*
1967–8	John McEwen *Co*
1968–71	John Grey Gorton *Lib*
1971–2	William McMahon *Lib*
1972–5	(Edward) Gough Whitlam *Lab*
1975–83	John Malcolm Fraser *Lib*
1983–91	Robert James Lee Hawke *Lab*
1991–6	Paul Keating *Lab*
1996–	John Howard *Lib*

Co Country; *Free* Free Trade; *Lab* Labor; *Lib* Liberal; *Nat* Nationalist; *Nat Lab* National Labor; *Prot* Protectionist; *Un* United.

Canada

Head of State: British monarch, represented by Governor-General.

Prime Minister

1867–73	John Alexander MacDonald *Con*
1873–8	Alexander Mackenzie *Lib*
1878–91	John Alexander MacDonald *Con*
1891–2	John J C Abbot *Con*
1892–4	John Sparrow David Thompson *Con*
1894–6	Mackenzie Bowell *Con*
1896	Charles Tupper *Con*
1896–1911	Wilfrid Laurier *Lib*
1911–20	Robert Laird Borden *Con*
1920–1	Arthur Meighen *Con*
1921–6	William Lyon Mackenzie King *Lib*
1926	Arthur Meighen *Con*
1926–30	William Lyon Mackenzie King *Lib*
1930–5	Richard Bedford Bennett *Con*
1935–48	William Lyon Mackenzie King *Lib*
1948–57	Louis Stephen St Laurent *Lib*
1957–63	John George Diefenbaker *Con*
1963–8	Lester Bowles Pearson *Lib*
1968–79	Pierre Elliott Trudeau *Lib*
1979–80	Joseph Clark *Con*
1980–4	Pierre Elliott Trudeau *Lib*
1984	John Napier Turner *Lib*
1984–93	(Martin) Brian Mulroney *Con*
1993	Kim Campbell *Con*
1993–2003	Jean Chrétien *Lib*
2003–	Paul Martin *Lib*

Con Conservative; *Lib* Liberal.

France

Prime Minister

1815	Charles-Maurice, Prince de Talleyrand-Perigord
1815–18	Armand-Emmanuel Vignerot-Duplessis, Duc de Richelieu
1818–19	Jean Joseph, Marquis Dessolle
1819–20	Duc Élie Decazes
1820–1	Armand-Emmanuel Vignerot-Duplessis, Duc de Richelieu
1821–9	Guillaume-Aubin, Comte de Villèle
1829–30	Auguste, Prince de Polignac
1830–1	Jacques Lafitte
1831–2	Casimir Périer
1832–4	Nicolas Soult
1834	Etienne, Comte Gérard
1834	Napoléon Joseph Maret, Duc de Bassano
1834–5	Étienne Mortier, Duc de Trévise
1835–6	Achille, Duc de Broglie
1836	Adolphe Thiers
1836–9	Louis, Comte Molé
1839–40	Nicolas Soult
1840	Adolphe Thiers
1840–7	Nicolas Soult
1847–8	François Guyzot
1848	Jacques Charles Dupont de L'Eure
1848	Louis-Eugène Cavaignac
1848–9	Odilon Barrot
1849–70	*No Prime Minister*

Third Republic

1870–1	Jules Favre
1871–3	Jules Dufaure
1873–4	Albert, Duc de Broglie
1874–5	Ernest Louis Courtot de Cissey
1875–6	Louis Buffet
1876	Jules Dufaure
1876–7	Jules Simon
1877	Albert, Duc de Broglie
1877	Gaetan de Grimaudet de Rochebouët
1877–9	Jules Dufaure
1879	William H Waddington
1879–80	Louis de Freycinet
1880–1	Jules Ferry
1881–2	Léon Gambetta
1882	Louis de Freycinet
1882–3	Eugène Duclerc
1883	Armand Fallières
1883–5	Jules Ferry
1885–6	Henri Brisson
1886	Louis de Freycinet
1886–7	René Goblet
1887	Maurice Rouvier
1887–8	Pierre Tirard
1888–9	Charles Floquet
1889–90	Pierre Tirard
1890–2	Louis de Freycinet
1892	Émile Loubet
1892–3	Alexandre Ribot
1893	Charles Dupuy
1893–4	Jean Casimir-Périer
1894–5	Charles Dupuy
1895	Alexandre Ribot
1895–6	Léon Bourgeois
1896–8	Jules Méline
1898	Henri Brisson
1898–9	Charles Dupuy
1899–1902	Pierre Waldeck-Rousseau
1902–5	Emile Combes
1905–6	Maurice Rouvier
1906	Jean Sarrien
1906–9	Georges Clemenceau
1909–11	Aristide Briand
1911	Ernest Monis
1911–12	Joseph Caillaux
1912–13	Raymond Poincaré
1913	Aristide Briand
1913	Jean Louis Barthou
1913–14	Gaston Doumergue
1914	Alexandre Ribot
1914–15	René Viviani
1915–17	Aristide Briand

Political leaders and rulers (continued)

1917	Alexandre Ribot
1917	Paul Painlevé
1917–20	Georges Clemenceau
1920	Alexandre Millerand
1920–1	Georges Leygues
1921–2	Aristide Briand
1922–4	Raymond Poincaré
1924	Frédéric François-Marsal
1924–5	Édouard Herriot
1925	Paul Painlevé
1925–6	Aristide Briand
1926	Édouard Herriot
1926–9	Raymond Poincaré
1929	Aristide Briand
1929–30	André Tardieu
1930	Camille Chautemps
1930	André Tardieu
1930–1	Théodore Steeg
1931–2	Pierre Laval
1932	André Tardieu
1932	Édouard Herriot
1932–3	Joseph Paul-Boncour
1933	Édouard Daladier
1933	Albert Sarrault
1933–4	Camille Chautemps
1934	Édouard Daladier
1934	Gaston Doumergue
1934–5	Pierre Étienne Flandin
1935	Fernand Bouisson
1935–6	Pierre Laval
1936	Albert Sarrault
1936–7	Léon Blum
1937–8	Camille Chautemps
1938	Léon Blum
1938–40	Édouard Daladier
1940	Paul Reynaud
1940	Philippe Pétain

Vichy Government

1940–4	Philippe Pétain

Provisional Government of the French Republic

1944–6	Charles de Gaulle
1946	Félix Gouin
1946	Georges Bidault

Fourth Republic

1946–7	Léon Blum
1947	Paul Ramadier
1947–8	Robert Schuman
1948	André Marie
1948	Robert Schuman
1948–9	Henri Queuille
1949–50	Georges Bidault
1950	Henri Queuille
1950–1	René Pleven
1951	Henri Queuille
1951–2	René Pleven
1952	Edgar Faure
1952–3	Antoine Pinay
1953	René Mayer
1953–4	Joseph Laniel
1954–5	Pierre Mendès France
1955–6	Edgar Faure
1956–7	Guy Mollet
1957	Maurice Bourgès-Maunoury

1957–8	Félix Gaillard
1958	Pierre Pflimlin
1958–9	Charles de Gaulle

Fifth Republic

1959–62	Michel Debré
1962–8	Georges Pompidou
1968–9	Maurice Couve de Murville
1969–72	Jacques Chaban Delmas
1972–4	Pierre Messmer
1974–6	Jacques Chirac
1976–81	Raymond Barre
1981–4	Pierre Mauroy
1984–6	Laurent Fabius
1986–8	Jacques Chirac
1988–91	Michel Rocard
1991–2	Edith Cresson
1992–3	Pierre Bérégovoy
1993–5	Édouard Balladur
1995–7	Alain Juppé
1997–2002	Lionel Jospin
2002–	Jean-Pierre Raffarin

President

Third Republic

1870–1	Commune
1871–3	Louis Adolphe Thiers
1873–9	Marie Edmé de Mac-Mahon
1879–87	Jules Grévy
1887–94	Sadi Carnot
1894–5	Jean Paul Pierre Casimir-Périer
1895–9	François Félix Faure
1899–1906	Émile Loubet
1906–13	Armand Fallières
1913–20	Raymond Poincaré
1920	Paul Deschanel
1920–4	Alexandre Millerand
1924–31	Gaston Doumergue
1931–2	Paul Doumer
1932–40	Albert Lebrun
1940–5	German occupation
1945–7	No President

Fourth Republic

1947–54	Vincent Auriol
1954–8	René Coty

Fifth Republic

1958–69	Charles de Gaulle
1969–74	Georges Pompidou
1974–81	Valéry Giscard d'Estaing
1981–5	François Mitterrand
1995–	Jacques Chirac

Germany

Chancellor

1871–90	Otto von Bismarck
1890–4	Georg Leo, Graf von Caprivi
1894–1900	Chlodwic, Fürst zu Hohenlohe-Schillingfürst
1900–9	Bernard Heinrich, Prince

	von Bülow
1909–17	Theobald von Bethmann Hollweg
1917–18	Georg von Herfling
1918	Prince Max of Baden
1918	Friedrich Ebert
1919–20	Philipp Scheidemann
1920	Hermann Müller
1920–1	Konstantin Fehrenbach
1921–2	Karl Joseph Wirth
1922–3	Wilhelm Cuno
1923	Gustav Stresemann
1923–5	Wilhelm Marx
1925–6	Hans Luther
1926–8	Wilhelm Marx
1928–9	Hermann Müller
1929–32	Heinrich Brüning
1932	Franz von Papen
1932–3	Kurt von Schleicher
1933–45	Adolf Hitler (from 1934 Führer)

German Democratic Republic (East Germany)

President

1949–60	Wilhelm Pieck

Chairman of the Council of State

1960–73	Walter Ulbricht
1973–6	Willi Stoph
1976–89	Erich Honecker
1989	Egon Krenz
1989–90	Gregor Gysi

Premier

1949–64	Otto Grotewohl
1964–73	Willi Stoph
1973–6	Horst Sindermann
1976–89	Willi Stoph
1989–90	Hans Modrow
1990	Lothar de Maizière

The German Democratic Republic ceased to exist as a separate state and East Germany became part of the German Federal Republic in 1990.

German Federal Republic (until 1990 West Germany)

President

1949–59	Theodor Heuss
1959–69	Heinrich Lübke
1969–74	Gustav Heinemann
1974–9	Walter Scheel
1979–84	Karl Carstens
1984–94	Richard, Baron von Weizsäcker
1994–9	Roman Hertzog
1999–	Johannes Rau

Chancellor

1949–63	Konrad Adenauer
1963–6	Ludwig Erhard
1966–9	Kurt Georg Kiesinger
1969–74	Willy Brandt
1974–82	Helmut Schmidt
1982–98	Helmut Kohl
1998–	Gerhard Schröder

HISTORY

Russia and the Union of Soviet Socialist Republics

RUSSIA

Grand Duke of Moscow

House of Riurik

1283– 1303	Daniel
1303–25	Yuri
1325–41	Ivan I Kalita
1341–53	Semeon
1353–9	Ivan II
1359–89	Dmitri I Donskoy
1389– 1425	Vasily I
1425–62	Vasily II
1462–72	Ivan II 'the Great'

Ruler of all Russia

House of Riurik

1472– 1505	Ivan III 'the Great'
1505–33	Vasily III
1533–47	Ivan IV 'the Terrible'

Tsar of Russia

House of Riurik

1547–84	Ivan IV 'the Terrible'
1584–98	Fedor I
1598– 1605	Boris Godunov
1605	Fedor II
1605–6	Dmitri II (the 'false Dmitri')
1606–10	Vasily IV Shuisky
1610–13	*Civil war*

House of Romanov

1613–45	Mikhail (Michael Romanov)
1645–76	Alexey I Mihailovitch
1676–82	Fedor III
1682– 1725	Peter I 'the Great' *Joint ruler to 1696*
1682–96	Ivan V *Joint ruler*
1725–7	Catherine I
1727–30	Peter II
1730–40	Anna Ivanovna
1740–1	Ivan VI
1741–62	Elizabeth Petrovna
1762	Peter III
1762–96	Catherine II 'the Great'
1796– 1801	Paul
1801–25	Alexander I
1825–55	Nicholas I
1855–81	Alexander II 'the Liberator'
1881–94	Alexander III
1894– 1917	Nicholas II

SOVIET UNION

President

1917	Lev Borisovich Kamenev
1917–19	Yakov Mikhailovich Sverlov
1919–46	Mikhail Ivanovich Kalinin
1946–53	Nikolai Mikhailovich Shvernik
1953–60	Kliment Yefremovich Voroshilov
1960–4	Leonid Ilyich Brezhnev
1964–5	Anastas Ivanovich Mikoyan
1965–77	Nikolai Viktorovich Podgorny
1977–82	Leonid Ilyich Brezhnev
1982–3	Vasily Vasiliyevich Kuznetsov *Acting*
1983–4	Yuri Vladimirovich Andropov
1984	Vasily Vasiliyevich Kuznetsov *Acting*
1984–5	Konstantin Ustinovich Chernenko
1985	Vasily Vasiliyevich Kuznetsov *Acting*
1985–8	Andrei Andreevich Gromyko
1988–90	Mikhail Sergeyevich Gorbachev

Executive President

1990–1	Mikhail Sergeyevich Gorbachev

RUSSIAN FEDERATION

President

1991–9	Boris Nikolayevich Yeltsin
1999–	Vladimir Putin

Prime Minister

1991–2	Yegor Gaidar
1992–8	Viktor Chernomyrdin
1998	Sergey Kiriyenko
1998–9	Yevgeny Primakov
1999	Sergey Stepashin
1999– 2000	Vladimir Putin
2000–	Mikhail Kasyanov

United Kingdom

Prime Minister

1721–42	Robert Walpole, Earl of Orford *Whig*
1742–3	Spencer Compton, Earl of Wilmington *Whig*
1743–54	Henry Pelham *Whig*
1754–6	Thomas Pelham (Pelham-Hollies), Duke of Newcastle *Whig*
1756–7	William Cavendish, 1st Duke of Devonshire *Whig*
1757–62	Thomas Pelham (Pelham-Hollies), Duke of Newcastle *Whig*
1762–3	John Stuart, 3rd Earl of Bute *Tory*
1763–5	George Grenville *Whig*
1765–6	Charles Watson Wentworth, 2nd Marquis of Rockingham *Whig*
1766–8	William Pitt, 1st Earl of Chatham *Whig*
1768–70	Augustus Henry Fitzroy, 3rd Duke of Grafton *Whig*
1770–82	Frederick, 8th Lord North *Tory*
1782	Charles Watson Wentworth, 2nd Marquis of Rockingham *Whig*
1782–3	William Petty, 2nd Earl of Shelburne *Whig*
1783	William Henry Cavendish, Duke of Portland *Coal*
1783– 1801	William Pitt *Tory*
1801–4	Henry Addington *Tory*
1804–6	William Pitt *Tory*
1806–7	William Wyndham Grenville, 1st Baron Grenville *Whig*
1807–9	William Henry Cavendish, Duke of Portland *Coal*
1809–12	Spencer Perceval *Tory*
1812–27	Robert Banks Jenkinson, 2nd Earl of Liverpool *Tory*
1827	George Canning *Tory*
1827–8	Frederick John Robinson, 1st Earl of Ripon *Tory*
1828–30	Arthur Wellesley, 1st Duke of Wellington *Tory*
1830–4	Charles Grey, 2nd Earl Grey *Whig*
1834	William Lamb, 2nd Viscount Melbourne *Whig*
1834–5	Robert Peel *Con*
1835–41	William Lamb, 2nd Viscount Melbourne *Whig*
1841–6	Robert Peel *Con*
1846–52	Lord John Russell, 1st Earl Russell *Lib*
1852	Edward Geoffrey Smith Stanley, 14th Earl of Derby *Con*
1852–5	George Hamilton-Gordon, 4th Earl of Aberdeen *Peelite*
1855–8	Henry John Temple, 3rd Viscount Palmerston *Lib*
1858–9	Edward Geoffrey Smith Stanley, 14th Earl of Derby *Con*
1859–65	Henry John Temple, 3rd Viscount Palmerston *Lib*
1865–6	Lord John Russell, 1st Earl Russell *Lib*
1866–8	Edward Geoffrey Smith Stanley, 14th Earl of Derby *Con*
1868	Benjamin Disraeli *Con*
1868–74	William Ewart Gladstone *Lib*
1874–80	Benjamin Disraeli *Con*
1880–5	William Ewart Gladstone *Lib*
1885–6	Robert Arthur Talbot Gascoyne-Cecil, 3rd Marquis of Salisbury *Con*
1886	William Ewart Gladstone *Lib*
1886–92	Robert Arthur Talbot

Political leaders and rulers (continued)

	Gascoyne-Cecil, 3rd Marquis of Salisbury *Con*
1892–4	William Ewart Gladstone *Lib*
1894–5	Archibald Philip Primrose, 5th Earl of Rosebery *Lib*
1895– 1902	Robert Arthur Talbot Gascoyne-Cecil, 3rd Marquis of Salisbury *Con*
1902–5	Arthur James Balfour *Con*
1905–8	Henry Campbell-Bannerman *Lib*
1908–15	Herbert Henry Asquith *Lib*
1915–16	Herbert Henry Asquith *Coal*
1916–22	David Lloyd-George *Coal*
1922–3	Andrew Bonar Law *Con*
1923–4	Stanley Baldwin *Con*
1924	James Ramsay MacDonald *Lab*
1924–9	Stanley Baldwin *Con*
1929–31	James Ramsay MacDonald *Lab*
1931–5	James Ramsay MacDonald *Nat*
1935–7	Stanley Baldwin *Nat*
1937–40	(Arthur) Neville Chamberlain *Nat*
1940–5	Winston Leonard Spencer Churchill *Coal*
1945–51	Clement Richard Attlee *Lab*
1951–5	Winston Leonard Spencer Churchill *Con*
1955–7	(Robert) Anthony Eden, 1st Earl of Avon *Con*
1957–63	(Maurice) Harold Macmillan *Con*
1963–4	Alexander Frederick (Alec) Douglas-Home *Con*
1964–70	(James) Harold Wilson *Lab*
1970–4	Edward Richard George Heath *Con*
1974–6	(James) Harold Wilson *Lab*
1976–9	(Leonard) James Callaghan *Lab*
1979–90	Margaret Hilda Thatcher *Con*
1990–7	John Major *Con*
1997–	Tony Blair *Lab*

Coal Coalition; *Con* Conservative; *Lab* Labour; *Lib* Liberal; *Nat* Nationalist.

United States of America

President

Vice President in parentheses

1789–97	George Washington (1st)
	(John Adams)
1797– 1801	John Adams (2nd) *Fed*
	(Thomas Jefferson)
1801–9	Thomas Jefferson (3rd) *Dem-Rep*
	(Aaron Burr, 1801–5)
	(George Clinton, 1805–9)

1809–17	James Madison (4th) *Dem-Rep*
	(George Clinton, 1809–12)
	No Vice President 1812–13
	(Elbridge Gerry, 1813–14)
	No Vice President 1814–17
1817–25	James Monroe (5th) *Dem-Rep*
	(Daniel D Tompkins)
1825–9	John Quincy Adams (6th) *Dem-Rep*
	(John Caldwell Calhoun)
1829–37	Andrew Jackson (7th) *Dem*
	(John Caldwell Calhoun, 1829–32)
	No Vice President 1832–3
	(Martin Van Buren, 1833–7)
1837–41	Martin Van Buren (8th) *Dem*
	(Richard Mentor Johnson)
1841	William Henry Harrison (9th) *Whig*
	(John Tyler)
1841–5	John Tyler (10th) *Whig*
	No Vice President
1845–9	James Knox Polk (11th) *Dem*
	(George Mifflin Dallas)
1849–50	Zachary Taylor (12th) *Whig*
	(Millard Fillmore)
1850–3	Millard Fillmore (13th) *Whig*
	No Vice President
1853–7	Franklin Pierce (14th) *Dem*
	(William Rufus King, 1853)
	No Vice President 1853–7
1857–61	James Buchanan (15th) *Dem*
	(John C Breckinridge)
1861–5	Abraham Lincoln (16th) *Rep*
	(Hannibal Hamlin, 1861–5)
	(Andrew Johnson, 1865)
1865–9	Andrew Johnson (17th) *Dem-Nat*
	No Vice President
1869–77	Ulysses Simpson Grant (18th) *Rep*
	(Schuyler Colfax, 1869–73)
	(Henry Wilson, 1873–5)
	No Vice President 1875
1877–81	Rutherford Birchard Hayes (19th) *Rep*
	(William A Wheeler)
1881	James Abram Garfield (20th) *Rep*
	(Chester Alan Arthur)
1881–5	Chester Alan Arthur (21st) *Rep*
	No Vice President
1885–9	Stephen Grover Cleveland (22nd) *Dem*
	(Thomas A Hendricks, 1885)

	No Vice President 1885–9
1889–93	Benjamin Harrison (23rd) *Rep*
	(Levi Parsons Morton)
1893–7	Stephen Grover Cleveland (24th) *Dem*
	(Adlai Ewing Stevenson)
1897– 1901	William McKinley (25th) *Rep*
	(Garret A Hobart, 1897–9)
	No Vice President 1899–1901
	(Theodore Roosevelt, 1901)
1901–9	Theodore Roosevelt (26th) *Rep*
	No Vice President 1901–5
	(Charles W Fairbanks, 1905–9)
1909–13	William Howard Taft (27th) *Rep*
	(James S Sherman, 1909–12)
	No Vice President 1912–13
1913–21	Thomas Woodrow Wilson (28th) *Dem*
	(Thomas R Marshall)
1921–3	Warren G Harding (29th) *Rep*
	(Calvin Coolidge)
1923–9	Calvin Coolidge (30th) *Rep*
	No Vice President 1923–5
	(Charles Gates Dawes, 1925–9)
1929–33	Herbert Clark Hoover (31st) *Rep*
	(Charles Curtis)
1933–45	Franklin Delano Roosevelt (32nd) *Dem*
	(John N Garner, 1933–41)
	(Henry Agard Wallace, 1941–5)
	(Harry S Truman, 1945)
1945–53	Harry S Truman (33rd) *Dem*
	No Vice President 1945–9
	(Alben W Barkley, 1949–53)
1953–61	Dwight David Eisenhower (34th) *Rep*
	(Richard Milhous Nixon)
1961–3	John Fitzgerald Kennedy (35th) *Dem*
	(Lyndon Baines Johnson)
1963–9	Lyndon Baines Johnson (36th) *Dem*
	No Vice President 1963–5
	(Hubert Horatio Humphrey, 1965–9)
1969–74	Richard Milhous Nixon (37th) *Rep*
	(Spiro Theodore Agnew, 1969–73)
	No Vice President Oct–Dec 1973
	(Gerald Rudolph Ford, 1973–4)

Political leaders and rulers (continued)

1974–7	Gerald Rudolph Ford (38th) *Rep* *No Vice President* Aug–Dec 1974 (Nelson Aldrich Rockefeller 1974–7)	1981–9	Ronald Wilson Reagan (40th) *Rep* (George Herbert Walker Bush)		(Albert Arnold Gore, Jr)
1977–81	James Earl (Jimmy) Carter (39th) *Dem* (Walter Frederick Mondale)	1989–92	George Herbert Walker Bush (41st) *Rep* (J Danforth (Dan) Quayle)	2001–	George W(alker) Bush (43rd) *Rep* (Dick Cheney)
		1992– 2001	William Jefferson (Bill) Clinton (42nd) *Dem*		

Dem Democrat; *Dem-Rep* Democratic Republican; *Fed* Federalist; *Nat* National Union; *Rep* Republican.

PART SEVEN

Human Geography

The world's largest nations by area

	Nation	Area km²	sq mi		Nation	Area km²	sq mi
1	Russian Federation	17 075 400	6 591 100	76	United Kingdom	244 755	94 500
2	Canada	9 971 500	3 848 900	77	Uganda	241 038	93 040
3	China	9 597 000	3 704 000	78	Ghana	238 537	92 100
4	United States	9 160 454	3 535 935	79	Romania	237 500	91 675
5	Brazil	8 511 965	3 285 618	80	Laos	236 800	91 405
6	Australia	7 692 300	2 969 228	81	Philippines	229 679	115 676
7	India	3 166 829	1 222 396	82	Guyana	214 969	82 978
8	Argentina	2 780 092	1 073 115	83	Belarus	207 600	80 134
9	Kazakhstan	2 717 300	1 048 878	84	Kyrgyzstan	198 500	76 621
10	Sudan, The	2 505 870	967 243	85	Senegal	196 790	75 729
11	Algeria	2 460 500	949 753	86	Syria	185 180	71 479
12	Saudi Arabia	2 331 000	899 766	87	Cambodia	181 035	68 879
13	Congo, Democratic Republic of	2 234 585	905 365	88	Uruguay	176 215	68 018
14	Mexico	1 978 800	763 817	89	Tunisia	164 150	63 362
15	Indonesia	1 906 200	735 800	90	Suriname	163 265	63 020
16	Libya	1 758 610	678 823	91	Nicaragua	148 000	57 128
17	Iran	1 648 000	636 128	92	Nepal	145 391	56 121
18	Mongolia	1 566 500	604 800	93	Bangladesh	143 998	55 583
19	Peru	1 284 640	495 871	94	Tajikistan	143 100	55 200
20	Chad	1 284 000	495 871	95	Greece	131 957	50 935
21	Niger	1 267 000	489 191	96	Korea, North	122 098	47 130
22	Ethiopia	1 251 282	483 123	97	Malawi	118 484	45 735
23	Angola	1 246 700	480 354	98	Liberia	113 370	43 760
24	Mali	1 240 192	478 841	99	Benin	112 622	43 484
25	South Africa	1 233 404	476 094	100	Honduras	112 088	43 266
26	Colombia	1 140 105	440 080	101	Bulgaria	110 912	42 812
27	Bolivia	1 098 580	424 052	102	Cuba	110 860	42 792
28	Mauritania	1 029 920	397 549	103	Guatemala	108 889	42 031
29	Egypt	1 001 449	386 559	104	Iceland	103 000	40 000
30	Tanzania	945 087	364 900	105	Serbia-Montenegro	102 173	39 438
31	Nigeria	923 768	356 669	106	Korea, South	98 913	38 180
32	Venezuela	912 050	352 051	107	Hungary	93 033	35 912
33	Namibia	824 292	318 261	108	Portugal	91 630	35 370
34	Pakistan	803 943	310 322	109	Jordan	89 544	34 564
35	Mozambique	799 380	308 641	110	Azerbaijan	86 600	33 428
36	Turkey	779 452	300 868	111	Austria	83 854	32 368
37	Chile	756 626	292 058	112	United Arab Emirates	83 600	32 300
38	Zambia	752 613	290 586	113	Czech Republic	78 864	30 441
39	Myanmar (Burma)	678 776	261 930	114	Panama	77 082	29 753
40	Afghanistan	647 497	249 934	115	Sierra Leone	71 740	27 692
41	Somalia	637 357	246 201	116	Ireland	70 282	27 129
42	Central African Republic	622 984	240 535	117	Georgia	69 700	26 900
43	Ukraine	603 700	233 028	118	Sri Lanka	65 610	25 325
44	Madagascar	587 041	226 658	119	Lithuania	65 200	25 167
45	Botswana	581 730	224 711	120	Latvia	64 600	24 900
46	Kenya	580 367	224 081	121	Togo	56 790	21 921
47	France	551 000	212 686	122	Croatia	56 538	21 824
48	Yemen	531 570	205 186	123	Bosnia-Herzegovina	51 129	19 736
49	Thailand	513 115	198 062	124	Costa Rica	51 022	19 694
50	Spain	504 750	194 833	125	Slovak Republic	49 035	18 927
51	Turkmenistan	488 100	188 400	126	Dominican Republic	48 442	18 699
52	Cameroon	475 442	183 569	127	Bhutan	46 600	18 000
53	Papua New Guinea	462 840	178 656	128	Estonia	45 100	17 409
54	Uzbekistan	447 400	172 696	129	Denmark	43 076	16 627
55	Iraq	434 925	167 881	130	Switzerland	41 228	15 914
56	Sweden	411 479	158 830	131	Guinea-Bissau	36 125	13 948
57	Morocco	409 200	157 951	132	Taiwan	36 000	13 896
58	Paraguay	406 750	157 000	133	Netherlands, The	33 929	13 097
59	Zimbabwe	390 759	150 873	134	Moldova	33 700	13 008
60	Japan	377 728	145 803	135	Belgium	30 518	11 780
61	Germany	357 868	138 136	136	Lesotho	30 355	11 720
62	Congo	341 945	132 047	137	Armenia	29 800	11 500
63	Finland	338 145	130 524	138	Albania	28 748	11 097
64	Malaysia	329 749	127 283	139	Equatorial Guinea	28 051	10 828
65	Vietnam	329 566	127 212	140	Burundi	27 834	10 747
66	Norway	323 895	125 023	141	Haiti	27 750	10 712
67	Côte d'Ivoire	322 462	124 503	142	Solomon Islands	27 556	10 637
68	Poland	312 683	120 695	143	Rwanda	26 338	10 169
69	Italy	301 255	116 314	144	Macedonia, former Yugoslav Republic of	25 713	9 925
70	Oman	300 000	115 800	145	Djibouti	23 200	8 958
71	Burkina Faso	274 200	105 870	146	Belize	22 963	8 864
72	Ecuador	270 699	104 490	147	El Salvador	21 476	8 290
73	New Zealand	268 812	103 761	148	Israel	20 770	8 017
74	Gabon	267 667	103 347	149	Slovenia	20 251	7 817
75	Guinea	245 857	94 926	150	Fiji	18 333	7 076

The world's largest nations by area (continued)

Nation	Area km²	sq mi		Nation	Area km²	sq mi
151 Kuwait	17 818	6 878		171 Bahrain	678	262
152 Swaziland	17 363	6 702		172 Tonga	646	249
153 East Timor	14 874	5 743		173 Singapore	618	238
154 Vanuatu	14 763	5 698		174 St Lucia	616	238
155 Bahamas, The	13 934	5 378		175 Andorra	453	175
156 Qatar	11 437	4 415		176 Antigua and Barbuda	442	171
157 Gambia, The	11 295	4 361		177 Barbados	430	166
158 Jamaica	10 957	4 229		178 St Vincent and the Grenadines	390	150
159 Lebanon	10 452	4 034		179 Grenada	344	133
160 Cyprus	9 251	3 571		180 Malta	316	122
161 Brunei	5 765	2 225		181 Maldives	300	116
162 Trinidad and Tobago	5 128	1 979		182 St Kitts and Nevis	269	104
163 Cape Verde	4 033	1 557		183 Liechtenstein	160	62
164 Samoa	2 842	1 097		184 San Marino	61	23
165 Luxembourg	2 586	998		185 Tuvalu	26	10
166 Mauritius	1 865	720		186 Nauru	21.3	8.2
167 Comoros	1 862	719		187 Monaco	1.95	0.75
168 São Tomé and Principe	1 001	387				
169 Dominica	751	290		This list is not exhaustive, particularly among the smaller		
170 Kiribati	717	277		nations. Differences of status of many of the 'nations' listed		

This list is not exhaustive, particularly among the smaller nations. Differences of status of many of the 'nations' listed also make direct comparisons difficult.

World population estimates

Date (AD)	Millions		Date (AD)	Millions		Date (AD)	Millions
1	200		1960	3 050		1997	5 880
1000	275		1970	3 700		1998	5 950
1250	375		1980	4 450		1999	6 030
1500	420		1985	4 845		2000	6 100
1700	615		1990	5 246		2050	11000
1800	900		1991	5 385			
1900	1 625		1992	5 480		Estimates for 2000 and 2050 are United
1920	1 860		1993	5 544		Nations 'medium' estimates. They
1930	2 070		1994	5 607		should be compared with the 'low'
1940	2 295		1995	5 734		estimates for these years of 5 400 and
1950	2 500		1996	5 800		8 500 and 'high' estimates of 7 000 and

Estimates for 2000 and 2050 are United Nations 'medium' estimates. They should be compared with the 'low' estimates for these years of 5 400 and 8 500 and 'high' estimates of 7 000 and 13 000, respectively.

World population (billions) 1950–2050 [a]

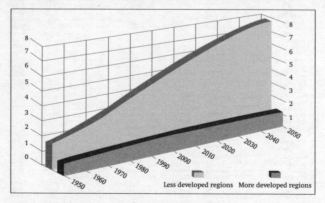

Less developed regions   More developed regions

Source: United Nations publication, ST/ESA/SER.A/176.
Copyright (C) United Nations 1999.

[a] 1 billion = 1000 million

The world's largest nations by population

	Nation	Population total (2000) estimates		Nation	Population total (2000) estimates		Nation	Population total (2000) estimates
1	China	1 275 133 000	65	Zimbabwe	12 627 000	128	Lebanon	3 496 000
2	India	1 008 937 000	66	Burkina Faso	11 535 000	129	Uruguay	3 337 000
3	United States	283 230 000	67	Guatemala	11 385 000	130	Albania	3 134 000
4	Indonesia	212 092 000	68	Mali	11 351 000	131	Congo	3 018 000
5	Brazil	170 406 000	69	Malawi	11 308 000	132	Liberia	2 913 000
6	Russian Federation	145 491 000	70	Cuba	11 199 000	133	Panama	2 856 000
7	Pakistan	141 256 000	71	Niger	10 832 000	134	Mauritania	2 665 000
8	Bangladesh	137 439 000	72	Greece	10 610 000	135	United Arab Emirates	2 606 000
9	Japan	127 096 000	73	Serbia-Montenegro	10 552 000	136	Jamaica	2 576 000
10	Nigeria	113 862 000	74	Zambia	10 421 000	137	Oman	2 538 000
11	Mexico	98 872 000	75	Czech Republic	10 272 000	138	Mongolia	2 533 000
12	Germany	82 017 000	76	Belgium	10 249 000	139	Latvia	2 421 000
13	Vietnam	78 137 000	77	Belarus	10 187 000	140	Bhutan	2 085 000
14	Philippines	75 653 000	78	Portugal	10 016 000	141	Lesotho	2 035 000
15	Iran	70 330 000	79	Tunisia	9 459 000	142	Macedonia, former Yugoslav Republic of	2 034 000
16	Egypt	67 884 000	80	Tunisia	9 459 000			
17	Turkey	66 668 000	81	Senegal	9 421 000			
18	Ethiopia	62 908 000	82	Sweden	8 842 000	143	Slovenia	1 988 000
19	Thailand	62 806 000	83	Somalia	8 778 000	144	Kuwait	1 914 000
20	United Kingdom	59 415 000	84	Dominican Republic	8 373 000	145	Namibia	1 757 000
21	France	59 238 000	85	Bolivia	8 329 000	146	Botswana	1 541 000
22	Italy	57 530 000	86	Guinea	8 154 000	147	Estonia	1 393 000
23	Congo, Democratic Republic of	50 948 000	87	Haiti	8 142 000	148	Gambia, The	1 303 000
24	Ukraine	49 568 000	88	Austria	8 080 000	149	Trinidad and Tobago	1 294 000
25	Myanmar	47 749 000	89	Azerbaijan	8 041 000			
26	Korea, South	46 740 000	90	Bulgaria	7 949 000	150	Gabon	1 230 000
27	South Africa	43 309 000	91	Chad	7 885 000	151	Guinea-Bissau	1 199 000
28	Colombia	42 105 000	92	Rwanda	7 609 000	152	Mauritius	1 161 000
29	Spain	39 910 000	93	Switzerland	7 170 000	153	Swaziland	925 000
30	Poland	38 605 000	94	China, Hong Kong (SAR)[1]	6 860 000	154	Fiji	814 000
31	Argentina	37 032 000				155	Cyprus	784 000
32	Tanzania	35 119 000	95	Honduras	6 417 000	156	Guyana	761 000
33	Sudan, The	31 095 000	96	Burundi	6 356 000	157	East Timor	737 000
34	Canada	30 757 000	97	El Salvador	6 278 000	158	Reunion	721 000
35	Kenya	30 669 000	98	Benin	6 272 000	159	Comoros	706 000
36	Algeria	30 291 000	99	Tajikistan	6 087 000	160	Bahrain	640 000
37	Morocco	29 878 000	100	Israel	6 040 000	161	Djibouti	632 000
38	Peru	25 662 000	101	Paraguay	5 496 000	162	Qatar	565 000
39	Uzbekistan	24 881 000	102	Slovak Republic	5 399 000	163	Equatorial Guinea	457 000
40	Venezuela	24 170 000	103	Denmark	5 320 000	164	Solomon Islands	447 000
41	Uganda	23 300 000	104	Libya	5 290 000	165	China, Macao (SAR)[2]	444 000
42	Nepal	23 043 000	105	Laos	5 279 000	166	Luxembourg	437 000
43	Iraq	22 946 000	106	Georgia	5 262 000	167	Guadeloupe	428 000
44	Romania	22 438 000	107	Finland	5 172 000	168	Cape Verde	427 000
45	Taiwan	22 319 000	108	Nicaragua	5 071 000	169	Suriname	417 000
46	Korea, North	22 268 000	109	Kyrgyzstan	4 921 000	170	Malta	390 000
47	Malaysia	22 218 000	110	Jordan	4 913 000	171	Martinique	383 000
48	Afghanistan	21 765 000	111	Papua New Guinea	4 809 000	172	Brunei	328 000
49	Saudi Arabia	20 346 000	112	Turkmenistan	4 737 000	173	Bahamas, The	304 000
50	Ghana	19 306 000	113	Croatia	4 654 000	174	Maldives	291 000
51	Australia	19 138 000	114	Togo	4 527 000	175	Iceland	279 000
52	Sri Lanka	18 924 000	115	Norway	4 469 000	176	Barbados	267 000
53	Yemen	18 349 000	116	Sierra Leone	4 405 000	177	Western Sahara	252 000
54	Mozambique	18 292 000	117	Moldova	4 295 000	178	French Polynesia	233 000
55	Syria	16 189 000	118	Costa Rica	4 024 000	179	Belize	226 000
56	Kazakhstan	16 172 000	119	Singapore	4 018 000	180	Netherlands Antilles	215 000
57	Côte D'Ivoire	16 013 000	120	Bosnia-Herzegovina	3 977 000	181	New Caledonia	215 000
58	Madagascar	15 970 000	121	Puerto Rico	3 915 000	182	Vanuatu	197 000
59	Netherlands, The	15 864 000	122	Ireland	3 803 000	183	French Guiana	165 000
60	Chile	15 211 000	123	Armenia	3 787 000	184	Samoa	159 000
61	Cameroon	14 876 000	124	New Zealand	3 778 000	185	São Tomé and Principe	159 000
62	Angola	13 134 000	125	Central African Republic	3 717 000	186	Guam	155 000
63	Cambodia	13 104 000	126	Lithuania	3 696 000	187	St Lucia	148 000
64	Ecuador	12 646 000	127	Eritrea	3 659 000	188	Channel Islands	144 000

1 As of 1 July 1997, Hong Kong became a Special Administrative Region (SAR) of China.
2 As of 20 July 1999, Macao became a Special Administrative Region (SAR) of China.
Source: United Nations Population Division, World Prospects: The 2001 Revision

HUMAN GEOGRAPHY

The world's largest cities by population

Population estimates for cities vary greatly, depending on how the notion of 'city' is defined. The following list gives 2000 estimates for agglomerations. An *agglomeration* consists of a central city (sometimes more than one central city) and neighbouring communities linked to it by continuous built-up areas or by many commuters. The figures in this list are on the high side compared with some other listings: a comparable list from the UN Population Division, gives agglomeration estimates which are usually considerably lower, and a different set of rankings emerges.

Population (millions)	City	Population (millions)	City	Population (millions)	City
34.9	Tokyo, Japan	4.2	Berlin, Germany	2.6	San Juan, Puerto Rico
21.6	New York, USA	4.2	Algiers, Algeria	2.5	Budapest, Hungary
21.2	Seoul, South Korea	4.1	Guadalajara, Mexico	2.5	Cali, Colombia
20.7	Mexico City, Mexico	4.1	Pune, India	2.5	Dar es Salaam, Tanzania
20.2	São Paulo, Brazil	4.0	Miami, USA	2.5	Faisalabad, Pakistan
18.1	Mumbai, India	4.0	Pusan, South Korea	2.5	Izmir, Turkey
18.0	Osaka, Japan	3.9	Abidjan, Cote d'Ivoire	2.5	Brussels, Belgium
17.1	Delhi, India	3.8	Barcelona, Spain	2.5	Aleppo, Syria
16.8	Los Angeles, USA	3.8	Kuala Lumpur, Malaysia	2.5	Lucknow, India
15.8	Jakarta, Indonesia	3.8	Milan, Italy	2.5	Manchester, UK
15.1	Cairo, Egypt	3.8	Porto Alegre, Brazil	2.5	Tampa, USA
14.1	Calcutta, India	3.7	Casablanca, Morocco	2.4	Colombo, Sri Lanka
13.7	Buenos Aires, Argentina	3.7	Recife, Brazil	2.4	Havana, Cuba
13.4	Manila, Philippines	3.7	Monterrey, Mexico	2.4	Rawalpindi, Pakistan
13.2	Moscow, Russia	3.7	Seattle, USA	2.4	Accra, Ghana
12.3	Karachi, Pakistan	3.6	Chengdu, China	2.4	Hangzhou, China
12.2	Rio de Janeiro	3.6	Pyongyang, North Korea	2.4	Pittsburgh, USA
12.2	Shanghai, China	3.5	Montreal, Canada	2.4	Portland, USA
11.8	London, UK	3.5	Phoenix, USA	2.4	Tashkent, Uzbekistan
11.1	Tehran, Iran	3.5	Ankara, Turkey	2.4	Warsaw, Poland
11.0	Istanbul, Turkey	3.5	Athens, Greece	2.3	Brasília, Brazil
10.3	Dhaka, Bangladesh	3.5	Melbourne, Australia	2.3	Guayaquil, Ecuador
9.8	Paris, France	3.4	Medellin, Colombia	2.3	Jinan, China
9.4	Chicago, USA	3.4	Salvador, Brazil	2.3	Mashhad, Iran
9.3	Lagos, Nigeria	3.4	Chittagong, Bangladesh	2.3	Bucharest, Romania
9.2	Beijing, China	3.3	Kiev, Ukraine	2.3	Dakar, Senegal
7.9	Lima, Peru	3.3	Jedda, Saudi Arabia	2.3	Nagpur, India
7.8	Washington, DC, USA	3.3	Rome, Italy	2.3	Sapporo, Japan
7.7	Bogota, Colombia	3.3	Singapore, Singapore	2.3	Zhengzhou, China
7.5	Bangkok, Thailand	3.3	Fortaleza, Brazil	2.2	Shijiazhuang, China
7.5	Johannesburg, South Africa	3.1	Surat, India	2.1	Donetsk, Ukraine
7.4	Taipei, Taiwan	3.1	Kano, Nigeria	2.1	Irbil, Iraq
7.3	San Francisco, USA	3.1	Minneapolis, USA	2.1	Amsterdam, Netherlands
7.2	Chongqing, China	3.1	Nanjing, China	2.1	Beirut, Lebanon
7.1	Madras, India	3.0	Cape Town, South Africa	2.1	Medan, Indonesia
6.9	Hong Kong, China	3.0	Cleveland, USA	2.1	San Salvador, El Salvador
6.6	Kinshasa, Dem. Rep. of the Congo	3.0	Naples, Italy	2.1	Tunis, Tunisia
6.5	Lahore, Pakistan	2.9	Addis Ababa, Ethiopia	2.1	Vancouver, Canada
6.3	Bangalore, India	2.9	Amman, Jordan	2.0	Belém, Brazil
6.3	Philadelphia, USA	2.9	Bandung, Indonesia	2.0	Cincinnati, USA
6.1	Hyderabad, India	2.9	Changchun, China	2.0	Fukuoka, Japan
6.0	Ruhr, Germany	2.9	Curitiba, Brazil	2.0	Leeds, UK
5.9	Khartoum, Sudan	2.9	Kanpur, India	2.0	Taiyuan, China
5.9	Boston, USA	2.9	Luanda, Angola	2.0	Kharkov, Ukraine
5.8	Detroit, USA	2.9	Surabaya, Indonesia	2.0	Maracaibo, Venezuela
5.7	Tianjin, China	2.9	Lisbon, Portugal	2.0	Frankfurt, Germany
5.5	St Petersburg, Russia	2.9	San Diego, USA	1.9	Conakry, Guinea
5.5	Dallas, USA	2.9	Xi'an, China	1.9	Kunming, China
5.4	Santiago, Chile	2.8	Dalian, China	1.9	Port-au-Prince, Haiti
5.1	Madrid, Spain	2.8	Katowice, Poland	1.9	Dammam, Saudi Arabia
5.1	Nagoya, Japan	2.8	Santo Domingo, Dominican Republic	1.9	Changsha, China
5.0	Ahmadabad, India	2.8	Taegu, South Korea	1.9	Munich, Germany
5.0	Baghdad, Iraq	2.7	Tel Aviv-Yafo, Israel	1.9	Nizhni Novgorod, Russia
4.9	Alexandria, Egypt	2.7	Denver, USA	1.9	Puebla, Mexico
4.9	Houston, USA	2.7	Ibadan, Nigeria	1.9	Baku, Azerbaijan
4.9	Toronto, Canada	2.7	Qingdao, China	1.9	Campinas, Brazil
4.7	Belo Horizonte, Brazil	2.7	Durban, South Africa	1.9	Patna, India
4.7	Wuhan, China	2.7	Harare, Zimbabwe	1.9	Cologne, Germany
4.7	Guangzhou, China	2.7	Nairobi, Kenya	1.9	Rabat, Morocco
4.7	Yangon, Myanmar	2.7	Stuttgart, Germany	1.9	Sacramento, USA
4.5	Riyadh, Saudi Arabia	2.6	Kabul, Afghanistan	1.9	Vienna, Austria
4.5	Harbin, China	2.6	Kaohsiung, Taiwan	1.8	Minsk, Belarus
4.4	Atlanta, USA	2.6	St Louis, USA	1.8	Kansas City, USA
4.4	Caracas, Venezuela	2.6	Birmingham, UK	1.8	Lusaka, Zambia
4.4	Shenyang, China	2.6	Damascus, Syria	1.8	Belgrade, Serbia and Montenegro
4.2	Sydney, Australia	2.6	Hamburg, Germany	1.8	Guatemala City, Guatemala
4.2	Saigon, Vietnam	2.6	Jaipur, India		

Source: United Nations, Department of Economic and Social Affairs.

Country summaries

All population figures provided are the latest available authoritative figures. Estimates are indicated using the suffix 'e'. Gross Domestic Product (GDP) and Gross National Product (GNP) figures are provided in US $ in millions (mn) or billions (bn = 1 000 mn). In the majority of cases, the Heads of State/Heads of Government given are those most recently in office. Unless stated, 'Head of State' refers to the president and 'Head of Government' to the prime minister. The UN Human Development Index (HDI) measures average achievements in basic human development (such as life expectancy, literacy, and standard of living) in a single composite index.

AFGHANISTAN

Local name Afghânestân

Timezone GMT +4.5

Area 647 497 km²/249 934 sq mi

Population total (2002e) 27 756 000, plus an estimated 2.5 million members of nomadic tribes, and c.5 million living in Pakistan and Iran as refugees

Status Democratic republic

Date of independence 1919

Capital Kabul

Languages Pushtu, Dari

Ethnic groups Pathans (50%), Tajik (20%), Uzbek (9%), Hazara (9%), Chahar Aimak (3%), Turkmen (2%), Baluchi (1%)

Religions Muslim (Sunni 84%, Shi'ite 15%)

Physical features Mountainous, landlocked country centred on and divided E–W by the Hindu Kush mountain range which reaches heights of over 7 000 m/24 000 ft. Three distinctive regions: fertile valley of Herat in NW; arid uplands to the S; and 129 495 km²/50 000 sq mi of desert in the SW plateau (including the Rigestan Desert). Amu Darya (Oxus) R forms N border.

Climate Continental climate; summers warm everywhere except on highest peaks; rain mostly during spring and autumn; average annual rainfall 338 mm/13.25 in; winters generally cold, with much snow at higher altitudes (central highlands have a sub-polar climate); at lower levels desert or semi-arid climate.

Currency 1 Afghani (Af) = 100 puls

Economy Traditionally based on agriculture, especially wheat, fruit, vegetables, maize, barley, cotton, sugar-beet, sugar cane, sheep, cattle, goats, natural-gas production in the N, largely for export; most sectors have been affected by civil war, especially sugar, carpets, textiles; natural resources also include oil, coal, copper, sulphur, lead, zinc, iron, salt, precious and semi-precious stones; many of these resources remain untapped owing to inaccessibility. Main trading partners: Eastern European and CIS countries, Japan, China.

GDP (2002e) $19 bn, per capita $700

History Nation first formed in 1747, under Ahmed Shah Durrani; seen as a bridge between India and the Middle East; Britain tried but failed to gain control during a series of Afghan Wars (the last in 1919); independence declared in 1919 after World War 1; feudal monarchy survived until after World War 2, when the constitution became more liberal under several Soviet-influenced five-

☐ International Airport

year economic plans; king deposed in 1973, and a republic formed; new constitution, 1977; coup (1979) brought to power Hafizullah Amin, which led to invasion by USSR forces and establishment of Babrak Karmal as Head of State; new constitution in 1987 provided for an executive President, bicameral National Assembly, and council of ministers; Soviet withdrawal 1988–9; new regime met with heavy guerrilla resistance from the Mujahadeen (Islamic fighters); resignation of President Najibullah in April 1992; Islamic State of Afghanistan declared, 1992; continuing unrest among Mujahadeen groups, hindering progress of UN-backed peace plans; new conflict, 1994–5, with the *taliban* (army of students), a Muslim force whose military organization emerged in late 1994; Taliban seize Kabul and drive out government forces, imposition of strict Islamic regime, and execution of Najibullah, 1996; government of Burhanuddin Rabbani continued to control part of the country in rebellion against the Taliban government under Mohammad Omar Akhondzada; called Islamic Emirate of Afghanistan, 1997; following the attack on the World Trade Center in New York (11 Sep 2001), US-led coalition forces launch aerial bombardment of Taliban-controlled military installations linked to Osama bin Laden, Oct 2001; Afghan delegations set up interim administration under the auspices of the UN, Dec 2001; International Security Assistance Force (ISAF) established; US-led ongoing operations against remaining Taliban resistance, 2002; ISAF taken over by NATO, Aug 2003; interim president Hamid Karzai elected, Nov 2004.

Head of State

2002–   Hamid Karzai

Afghanistan (continued)

Head of Government
1996   Gulbardin Hekmatyar

Interim Council
1996–2001 Mohammad Rabbani (Chairman)

Interim government
2001–2   Hamid Karzai

ALBANIA

Local name Shqipëri

Timezone GMT +1

Area 28 748 km²/11 097 sq mi

Population total (2002e) 3 108 000

Status Republic

Date of independence 1912

Capital Tiranë

Languages Albanian (official) (Gheg and Tosk, the main dialects), Greek

Ethnic groups Albanian (96%), Greek (2%), Macedonian, Vlach, Gypsy, Bulgarian

Religions Muslim (Sunni 70%), Roman Catholic (5%), Greek Orthodox (2%) (before April 1991, Albania was constitutionally atheist)

Physical features Mountainous country, relatively inaccessible and untravelled; geologically active – earthquakes severe and relatively frequent; N Albanian Alps rise to 2692 m/8832 ft; mountainous highlands (N, S, and E) account for c.70% of the land; coastal lowland in the W is agricultural; rivers include the Drin i zi, Shkumbin, Seman, Vijosë; 45% of land is forested; 25% is arable, mostly grain-producing; c.20% is permanent pasture land.

Climate Mediterranean climate, hot and dry on the plains in summer; average annual temperatures, 8–9°C (Jan), 24–5°C (Jul); thunderstorms frequent; mild, damp, cyclonic winters.

Currency 1 Lek (L) = 100 qintars

Economy Seventh five-year plan (1981–5) focused on industrial expansion, especially in oil (new sources were located), mining, chemicals, natural gas; hydroelectric power plans for several rivers (eg the Koman hydroelectric complex on the Drin i zi R); agricultural product processing, textiles, oil products, cement; main crops are wheat, sugar-beet, maize, potatoes, fruit, grapes, oats; all industry is nationalized; progressive transformation of farm cooperatives into state farms; chromate, low-grade iron ore, and soft coal are exported; other natural resources: crude petroleum, asphalt, lignite (brown coal), phosphorus, bauxite, precious metals.

GDP (2002e) $15.69 bn, per capita $440

HDI (2002) 0.733

History Albanians descended from Illyrians, who occupied W Balkan peninsula c.1000 BC; King Argon and, after him, his wife Teuta conquered many territories, provoking the military might of Rome; despite Roman occupation and invasions by Visigoths, Slavs, and Huns, the Albanians were one of the few peoples to retain their Illyrian language and customs; Turkish invasions, 14th-

□ International Airport   ∴ World heritage site

c; independence after the end of Turkish rule, 1912; occupied by Italian forces, 1914–20; became a republic in 1925, and a monarchy in 1928, under King Zog I; occupied by Germany and Italy during World War 2; new republic instigated in 1946, headed by Enver Hoxha (until 1985); dispute with the Soviet Union in 1961 led to withdrawal from Warsaw Pact in 1968, but close links with China maintained; People's Socialist Republic instituted, 1976; renamed Republic of Albania, 1991; first free elections, 1991, giving a decisive majority to the communists; however general strike and demonstrations forced government to resign; Communist Party renamed itself the Socialist Party; Democratic Party elected in 1992 elections; collapse of fraudulent pyramid finance schemes, 1997, leading to rebellion in the S, arrival of UN protection force, and early elections, with unrest continuing in 1998; new constitution, 1998; People's Assembly (supreme legislative body) elects the President and Council of Ministers.

Head of State
1997–2002 Rexhep Mejdani
2002–   Alfred Moisiu

Head of Government
1999–2002 Ilir Meta
2002   Pandeli Majko
2002–   Fatos Nano

ALGERIA

Local name(s) Al-Jazā'ir (Arabic), Algérie (French)

Timezone GMT +1

Area 2 460 500 km²/949 753 sq mi

Population total (2002e) 31 261 000

Status Democratic republic

Date of independence 1962

Capital Algiers (Alger)

Languages Arabic (official), Berber, French

Ethnic groups Arab (75%), Berber (25%)

Religions Muslim (Sunni 99%), Roman Catholic (0.5%)

Physical features Mountainous area in N Africa: mountains rise in a series of ridges and plateaux to the Atlas Saharien; Ahaggar Mts in the far S, rising to 2918 m/9573 ft at Mt Tahat; 85% of land is Saharan desert.

Climate Mediterranean in N, with cool, rainy winters and hot dry summers; average annual temperatures 12°C (Jan), 25°C (Jul); average annual rainfall 400–800 mm/15.8–31.5 in (mostly Nov–Mar); essentially rainless Saharan climate in S.

Currency 1 Algerian Dinar (AD, DA) = 100 centimes

Economy Petroleum products account for about 30% of national income; natural-gas liquification; jointly built with Italy first trans-Mediterranean gas pipeline; agriculture mainly on N coast: wheat, barley, oats, grapes, citrus fruits, vegetables; also food processing, textiles, clothing.

GDP (2002e) $173.8 bn, per capita $5400

HDI (2002) 0.697

History Islamic Berber empires followed collapse of Numidian, Roman, Vandal, and Byzantine rule; Turkish invasion; 16th-c; French colonial campaign in 19th-c led to French control from 1902; guerrilla war (1954–62) with French forces by the National Liberation Front (FLN) led to independence, 1962; first President of the republic, Ahmed Ben Bella, replaced after coup, 1965; new con-

stitution, 1976; military took control of government in 1992, and a state of emergency declared; continuing violence involving Islamic fundamentalists, including attacks on foreigners, from 1993; legislative power shared by the President and National Assembly.

Head of State
1999–   Abdelaziz Bouteflika

Head of Government
2003–   Ahmed Ouyahia

AMERICAN SAMOA >> UNITED STATES OF AMERICA

ANDORRA

Local name Vallée d'Andorre (French), Valls d'Andorra (Spanish)

Timezone GMT +1

Area 453 km²/175 sq mi

Population total (2002e) 66 500

Status Independent State

Capital Andorra la Vella

Languages Catalan (official), French, Spanish

Ethnic groups Catalan (50%), Andorran (29%), French (8%), Portuguese (7%)

Religion Roman Catholic (94%)

Physical features Mountainous country, located on the S slopes of the C Pyrénées between France and Spain, peaks reaching 2946 m/9665 ft at Coma Pedrosa; two valleys (del Norte and del Orient) of the R Valira.

Climate Alpine climate: heavy snow in winter, warm summers; average annual temperature 2°C (Jan), 19°C (Jul); lowest average monthly rainfall, 34 mm/1.34 in (Jan).

Currency 1 euro = 100 cents (previous to February 2002, 1 French Franc (Fr) = 100 centimes, 1 peseta (Pta, Pa) = 100 céntimos)

Andorra (continued)

Economy No restriction on currency exchange, and no direct value-added taxes, therefore a marketing centre for goods imported from Europe and Asia; commerce, agriculture; skiing at five mountain resorts; in recent years, textiles, publishing, leather, mineral water, tourism.

GDP (2000e) $1.3 bn, per capita $19 000

History One of the oldest states in Europe, under the joint protection of France and Spain since 1278; Co-Princes of Principality are the President of France and the Bishop of Urgel; General Council of the Valley appoints the head of the government; independent state since 1993.

Heads of State (Co-Princes)
President of France
Bishop of Urgel, Spain

Head of Government (chief executive)
1994–   Marc Forné Molné

□ International Airport

ANGOLA

Local name Angola

Timezone GMT +1

Area 1 245 790 km²/480 875 sq mi

Population total (2002e) 10 593 000

Status Republic

Date of independence 1975

Capital Luanda

Languages Portuguese (official), Bantu languages, including: Ovimbundu, Kimbundu, Bakongo, Chokwe

Ethnic groups Ovimbundu (37%), Mbundu (22%), Bakongo (13%), Lunda-Tchokwe (5%); also Nganguela, Nyaneka-Humbe, Herero, Ambo, Portuguese

Religions Traditional religions (12%), Roman Catholic (68%), Protestant (20%)

Physical features Located in SW Africa; narrow coastal plain; in S and E the planalto central (central plateau, continuation of great SW African plateau), covers c.60% of the country; in N, highland plateau, mean elevation 1200 m/4000 ft; highest point, Serro Môco 2619 m/8592 ft; coastal desert in W; in E, upland escarpments; c.40% of land forested.

Climate tropical plateau climate; at Huambo, on the plateau, average annual rainfall 1450 mm/57 in; rainfall varies greatly from SW to NE (negligible rainfall on SW coastal desert caused by Benguela current); average daily temperatures 24–9°C; temperature much reduced on the coast, which is semi-desert as far N as Luanda.

Currency 1 New Kwanza (kw, kz) = 100 lweis

Economy Reserves of several minerals; extraction and refining of oil (mainly off the coast of Cabinda Province)

□ International Airport

provides over 90% of current export earnings; diamond exporter; large producer of honey; principal livestock are cattle, goats, pigs, sheep; agriculture and fishing (mackerel and sardines) industries small; several airfields and railways.

GDP (2002e) $18.36 bn, per capita $1700

HDI (2002) 0.403

History Angola became a Portuguese colony in 1482 after exploration; slave trade flourished, causing friction and war (in early 17th-c, c.10 000 slaves were exported from Luanda annually); boundaries formally defined during the Berlin West Africa Congress (1884–5); became an overseas province of Portugal, 1951; Portuguese finally withdrew in 1975, and the People's Republic of Angola achieved full independence; civil war followed independence, involving three internal factions – the Marxist MPLA (Popular Movement for the Liberation of Angola), UNITA (the National Union for the Total Independence of Angola), and the FNLA (National Front for the Liberation of Angola); Cuban combat troops arrived in 1976, at request of MPLA; at the end of 1988, Geneva agreement linked arrangements for independence of Namibia with withdrawal of Cuban troops, and the cessation of South African attacks and support for UNITA; peace agreement in 1991 established a one-party state, governed by a President, Council of Ministers, and National People's Assembly; adopted the name Republic of Angola; first multi-party legislative elections held in 1992; MPLA victory rejected by UNITA led to resumption of conflict in 1993; Lusaka peace protocol, October 1994; withdrawal of UN peace-keeping force (Jan 1999) as fighting resumed between government and UNITA forces; peace agreement signed, 2002; lifting of UN economic sanctions against UNITA (Dec 2002).

Head of State
1979– José Eduardo dos Santos

Head of Government
1999–2002 José Eduardo dos Santos
2002– Fernando da Piedade Dias dos Santos

ANGUILLA >> UNITED KINGDOM

ANTIGUA AND BARBUDA

Local name Antigua and Barbuda

Timezone GMT –4

Area 442 km²/171 sq mi; (Antigua: 280 km²/108 sq mi; Barbuda: 161 km²/62 sq mi; Redonda: 1 km²/0.4 sq mi)

Population total (2002e) 76 400

Status Independent republic within the Commonwealth

Date of independence 1981

Capital St John's (on Antigua)

Language English (official)

Ethnic groups African descent (92%), Portuguese, Lebanese, British (4%)

Religions Anglican (80%), Roman Catholic (10%)

Physical features Group of three islands in the Leeward group of the Lesser Antilles, E Caribbean; W part of Antigua rises to 470 m/1542 ft at Boggy Peak; Barbuda is a flat coral island reaching only 44 m/144 ft at its highest point, with a large lagoon on its W side; Redonda is an uninhabited, volcanic island, rising to 305 m/1000 ft at its highest point.

Climate Tropical; temperatures range from 24°C (Jan) to 27°C (Aug–Sep); mean annual rainfall 1000 mm/40 in.

Currency 1 East Caribbean Dollar (EC$) = 100 cents

Economy Tourism; sugar (40% of national income, marked decline in 1960s, now recovering); cotton.

GDP (2002e) $750 mn, per capita $11 000

HDI (2002) 0.800

History Antigua claimed for Spain by Columbus, 1493; colonized by British, 1632; ceded to Britain, 1667; Barbuda colonized from Antigua, 1661; administered as part of the Leeward Is Federation, 1871–1956; associated state of the

□ International Airport

UK, 1967; independence achieved, 1981; legislative power is vested in a bicameral parliament; Governor-General appoints the Prime Minister and Cabinet.

Head of State
(British monarch represented by Governor-General)
1993– Sir James Carlisle

Head of Government
1994–2004 Lester Bird
2004– Baldwin Spencer

ANTILLES, NETHERLANDS >> NETHERLANDS

ARGENTINA

Local name Argentina

Timezone GMT –3

Area American continent: 2780092 km²/1073115 sq mi on Antarctic continent: 964250 km²/372200 sq mi

Population total (2002e) 36446000

Status Republic

Date of independence 1816

Capital Buenos Aires

Language Spanish (official)

Ethnic groups European origin (c.85%), mestizo European/Indian origin (15%)

Religions Roman Catholic (90%), Protestant and Jewish minorities

Physical features Divided into four regions: subtropical NE plains, the Pampa, Patagonia, and the Andes; Andes stretch the entire length of Argentina (N–S), forming the boundary with Chile; highest peak, Aconcagua 6960 m/22 831 ft; uneven, semi-desert, arid steppes in the S (Patagonia); grassy, treeless Pampa to E; N drained by the Paraguay, Paraná, and Uruguay rivers, which join in the R Plate estuary; island of Tierra del Fuego off the S tip.

Climate Moderately humid sub-tropical climate in the NE; average annual temperature 16°C; average annual rainfall 500–1000 mm/20–40 in; semi-arid in interior S lowlands; Pampa temperate, dry in W and humid in E, with temperatures ranging from tropical to moderately cool; S directly influenced by strong prevailing westerlies; serious flooding in NE (May 2003).

Currency 1 Peso = 100 centavos (formerly the austral)

Economy Major contribution to economy from agricultural produce and meat processing; deposits of oil and natural gas, chiefly off the coast of Patagonia; important reserves of iron ore, coal, copper, lead, zinc, gold, silver, uranium, manganese.

GDP (2002) $403.8 bn, per capita $10 500

HDI (2002) 0.844

History Pre-colonially, nomadic Indian hunters lived in S and Inca farmers in NW; after a long battle, settled in the 16th-c by the Spanish; declared independence as the federal Republic of Argentina in 1816, and United

□ International Airport   ∴ World heritage site

Provinces of the Río de la Plata established; dictatorship of Juan Manuel de Rosas during 1829–52; federal constitution in 1853; ranchers' oligarchy of 1916 ended by military coup in 1930; acquisition of the Gran Chaco after war with Paraguay, 1865–70; considerable European settlement since the opening up of the Pampas in the 19th-c; Juan Perón elected president (1946 and 1973); eventually succeeded by his wife Isabel (Martínez de Perón) who was deposed in 1976; attempt to control the Falkland Is (1982) failed following war with the UK; successive military governments, until federal constitution re-established in 1983; governed by a President and a bicameral National Congress, with a Chamber of Deputies and a Senate; four presidents resigned amid riots and lootings in protests over stringent economic sanctions (2001–2).

Head of State /Government
2002–3   Eduardo Duhalde
2003–   Néstor Kirchner

ARMENIA

Local name Hayastan

Timezone GMT +3

Area 29800 km²/11 500 sq mi

Population total (2002e) 3800000

Status Republic

Date of independence 1991

Capital Yerevan

Language Armenian (official)

Ethnic groups (1991) Armenian (90%), Azer (3%), Kurd (2%), Russian (2%) (ethnic conflict since 1990 makes accurate statistical analysis impossible)

Religions Christian (Armenian Church), Russian Orthodox

Physical features Mountainous region in S Transcaucasia, rising to 4090 m/13 418 ft at Mt Aragats (W); rivers include Razdan and Vorotan; largest mountain lake is the Sevan, 1401 km²/541 sq mi – the main source of irrigation system and hydroelectric power.

Climate Varies with elevation; chiefly dry and continental with considerable regional variation.

Currency 1 Dram (Drm) = 100 loumas

Economy Large mineral resources, chiefly copper; also molybdenum, gold, silver; electrical equipment and machinery, chemicals, textiles, cognac; agriculture based on fruits, wheat, wine grapes, cotton, tobacco.

GDP (2002e) $12.13 bn, per capita $3600

HDI (2002) 0.754

History Proclaimed a Soviet Socialist Republic in 1920; constituent republic of the USSR from 1936; civil war over Nagorno-Karabakh began in 1989; declaration of independence, 1990; independence recognized and joined CIS, 1991; ongoing conflict with Azerbaijan over disputed enclave of Nagorno-Karabakh.

Head of State
1998–   Robert Kocharyan

Head of Government
2000–   Andranik Margarian

ARUBA >> NETHERLANDS, THE

□ International Airport

AUSTRALIA

Local name Australia

Timezone GMT +8 (Western Australia); GMT +10 (New South Wales, Queensland, Tasmania, Victoria, Australian Capital Territory); GMT +9.5 (South Australia, Northern Territory)

Area 7 692 300 km²/2 969 228 sq mi

Population total (2002e) 19 702 000

Status Independent state within the Commonwealth

Date of independence 1901

Capital Canberra

Language English (official)

Ethnic groups European descent (95%), Asian and Pacific (2%), Aboriginal (1%)

Religions Christian (74%, including Roman Catholic 27%, Anglican 24%)

Physical features Smallest continent, consists largely of plains and plateaux, most of which average 600 m/ 2000 ft above sea level; four main regions: Western Craton (or Western Shield), the Great Artesian Basin, the Great Dividing Range (or Eastern Uplands), the Flinders-Mt Lofty ranges; W Australian Plateau occupies nearly half of the country; MacDonnell Ranges lie in the centre, highest point Mt Liebig, 1525 m/5000 ft; most of the plateau is dry, barren desert; Nullarbor Plain in the S is crossed by the Trans-Australian Railway; Great Dividing Range parallel to the Great Barrier Reef, rising to 2 228 m/7310 ft at Mt Kosciusko, Australia's highest point; Great Barrier Reef off NE coast stretches for over 1900 km/ 1200 mi; island of Tasmania rises to 1617 m/5305 ft at Mt Ossa; separated from the mainland by the Bass Strait; longest river is the Darling, a tributary of the Murray;

other chief tributaries, the Murrumbidgee, Lachlan; Lake Eyre occupies 8800 km²/3400 sq mi; c.18% of area forested; c.6% arable.

Climate More than a third of Australia receives under 260 mm/10 in mean annual rainfall; less than a third receives over 500 mm/20 in; prolonged drought and frequent heatwaves in many areas; average daily temperature 26–34°C (Nov) and 19–31°C (Jul) in N; rainfall varies from 286 mm/15.2 in (Jan) to zero (Jul); fertile land with a temperate climate and reliable rainfall only in the lowlands and valleys near the E and SE coast, and a small part of the SW corner; Tasmania and Mt Kosciusko have snowfields in winter.

Currency 1 Australian Dollar ($A) = 100 cents

Economy Free-enterprise economy; world's largest wool producer, and a top exporter of veal and beef; most important crop is wheat; major mineral producer; petroleum reserves, coal, bauxite, nickel, lead, zinc, copper, tin, uranium, iron ore, and other minerals in early 1960s; manufacturing industry expanded rapidly since 1945, especially engineering, shipbuilding, car manufacture, metals, textiles, clothing, chemicals, food processing, wine; self-sufficient in lumber; marine fishing (especially tuna) important, as are tourism and winter sports.

GDP (2002e) $525.5 bn, per capita $26 900

HDI (2002) 0.939

History Aboriginal people thought to have arrived in Australia from SE Asia c.40 000 years ago; first European visitors were the Dutch, who explored the Gulf of Carpentaria in 1606 and settled in 1616; became known as New Holland in 1644; Captain James Cook arrived in Botany Bay in 1770, and claimed the E coast for Britain; New South Wales established as a penal colony in 1788; gold discov-

Australia (continued)

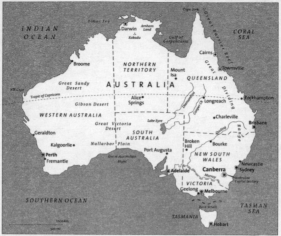

□ International Airport   ∴ World heritage site

ered in New South Wales and Victoria in 1851, and in Western Australia in 1892; transportation of convicts to E Australia ended in 1840, but continued until 1853 in Tasmania and 1868 in Western Australia; during this period the colonies drafted their own constitutions and set up governments: New South Wales (1855), Tasmania and Victoria (1856), South Australia (1857), Queensland (1860), and Western Australia (1890); Commonwealth of Australia established in 1901, with Canberra subsequently chosen as capital (1901); policy of preventing immigration by non-whites remained in force from the end of the 19th-c until 1974; issue of Aboriginal civil rights a major issue since the 1960s; Northern Territory self-governing since 1978; divided into six states and two territories: each state has its own legislature, government, and constitution; legislature comprises a bicameral Federal Parliament with a Prime Minister and Cabinet; British monarch is Head of State, represented by a Governor-General; republican movement growing since the late 1980s; proposal on the issue rejected by referendum, late 1999.

Head of State
(British monarch represented by Governor-General)
2003–   Michael Jeffery

Head of Government
1991–6   Paul Keating
1996–   John Howard

>> Political leaders and rulers, p.126

Australian States

Name	Area		State capital
	km²	sq mi	
Australian Capital Territory	2 400	930	Canberra
New South Wales	801 400	309 400	Sydney
Northern Territory	1 346 200	519 800	Darwin
Queensland	1 727 200	666 900	Brisbane
South Australia	984 000	379 900	Adelaide
Tasmania	67 800	26 200	Hobart
Victoria	227 600	87 900	Melbourne
Western Australia	2 525 500	975 000	Perth

External territories

Name	Area		Population total	Date under Australian administration
	km²	sq mi		
The Ashmore and Cartier Islands	3.0	2.0	Uninhabited	1931
Australian Antarctic Territory	6 043 852.0	2 332 927.0	Uninhabited	1936
Christmas Island	155.0	60.0	(2000e) 2700	1958
Cocos (Keeling) Islands	14.2	5.5	(2000e) 780	1955
Coral Sea Island	2.0*	0.8*	Uninhabited	1969
Heard Island and McDonald Islands	412.0	159.0	Uninhabited	1947
Norfolk Island	35.0	13.0	(2000e) 2200	1913

* Land figure only. Islands cover 1 000 000 km²/286 000 sq mi of ocean.

HUMAN GEOGRAPHY

AUSTRIA

Local name Österreich

Timezone GMT +1

Area 83 854 km²/32 368 sq mi

Population total (2002e) 8 077 000

Status Republic

Date of independence 1955

Capital Vienna (Wien)

Languages German (official), Croatian, Slovene

Ethnic groups Austrian (99%), Croatian, Slovakian, Turkish, German

Religions Roman Catholic (85%), Protestant (12%), Muslim (1%), Jewish (1%)

Physical features One of the most mountainous countries in Europe; lies at E end of the Alps; highest point, Grossglockner, 3797 m/12 457 ft; largest lake, Neusiedler See; divided into three regions: Alpine; the highland Bohemian Massif; and the hilly lowland region, including the Vienna basin; R Danube drains whole country; most densely forested country in central Europe (40% of land is forested).

Climate Three climatic regions: the Alps (often sunny in winter, but cloudy in summer); the Danube valley and Vienna basin (driest region); and the SE, a region of often severe winters but warmer summers; average annual temperature: 2°C (Jan), 20°C (Jul) in Vienna; most rain in summer months; average annual rainfall 868 mm/34 in; winters cold, especially with winds from the E or NE; humid, continental climate in NE.

Currency 1 euro = 100 cents (previous to February 2002, 1 Schilling (S, Sch) = 100 Groschen)

Economy Mixed free market; principal agricultural areas to the N of the Alps, and along both sides of the Danube; principal crops: cereals; dairy cattle and pigs; wine industry; wide range of metal and mineral resources; tourism (summer and winter); well-developed transportation networks; river ports at Linz and Vienna; airports at Vienna, Graz, Linz, Klagenfurt, Salzburg, Innsbruck; much power produced hydroelectrically.

GDP (2002e) $227.7 bn, per capita $27 900

☐ International Airport

HDI (2002) 0.926

History Early Iron-Age settlement at Hallstatt; later Illyrian settlers driven out by the Celts; part of Roman Empire until 5th-c, then occupied by Germanic tribes, most significantly Bavarians; Charlemagne drove out the Slavic Avars who also settled in the region; area became a duchy and passed to the Habsburg family in 1282, who made it the foundation of their Empire; Hungarian nationalism and Habsburg defeats in 19th-c led to the dual monarchy of Austria–Hungary from 1867; Nationalist protest resulted in assassination of Archduke Ferdinand in 1914 and World War 1, which ended the Austrian Empire; republic established, 1918; annexed by the German Reich in 1938 (the Anschluss) and named Ostmark; occupied by British, American, French, and Russian troops from 1945; obtained independence, 1955; neutrality declared, since when Austria has been a haven for many refugees; governed by a Federal Assembly; Federal President appoints a Federal Chancellor.

Head of State (Federal President)
1992–2004 Thomas Klestil
2004– Heinz Fischer

Head of Government (Federal Chancellor)
2000– Wolfgang Schüssel

HUMAN GEOGRAPHY

AZERBAIJAN

Local name Azerbaijan

Timezone GMT +3

Area 86 600 km²/33 428 sq mi

Population total (2002e) 8 176 000

Status Republic

Date of independence 1991

Capital Baku

Languages Azeri (official), Russian

Ethnic groups Azeri (83%), Russian (6%), Armenian

(6%) (ethnic conflict since 1990 makes accurate statistical analysis impossible)

Religion Shi'ite Muslim

Physical features Mountainous country in E Transcaucasia: 10% of country is above 1494 m/4900 ft; 40% of land is lowland, 396–1494 m/1300–4900 ft; Bazar-Dyuzi rises to 4480 m/14 698 ft; rivers include the Kara and Araks.

Climate Central and eastern Azerbaijan dry and subtropical with mild winters and long, hot summers (often as hot as 43°C); SE is humid with annual rainfall 1193–1396 mm/47–55 in.

Azerbaijan (continued)

Currency 1 Manat = 100 gopik

Economy Once the former Soviet Union's most important oil-producing region, but now in decline; manufacturing industries include building materials, chemicals, textiles; mineral resources include natural gas, iron, copper, lead, zinc; exports include cotton, wheat, tobacco.

GDP (2002e) $28.61 bn, per capita $3700

HDI (2002) 0.741

History Proclaimed a Soviet Socialist Republic, 1920; constituent republic of the USSR, 1936; declaration of independence; 1991; became a member of UN, 1992; ongoing conflict with Armenia over disputed enclave of Nagorno-Karabakh; governed by a President, Prime Minister, and National Council.

Head of State
2003– Ilham Aliyev

Head of Government
2003– Artur Rasizade *Acting*

AZORES >> PORTUGAL

□ International Airport ⌒⌒ Nagorno-Karabakh

BAHAMAS

Local name Bahamas

Timezone GMT −5

Area 13 934 km²/5378 sq mi

Population total (2002e) 309 000

Status Independent state within the Commonwealth

Date of independence 1973

Capital Nassau

Language English (official)

Ethnic groups African (85%), European/N American descent (15%)

Religions Baptist (29%), Anglican (29%), Roman Catholic (23%)

Physical features Coral archipelago of 700 islands and 2400 uninhabited cays, forming a chain extending c.800 km/500 mi SE from the coast of Florida; population centres on the two oceanic banks of Little and Great Bahama; highest point, Mt Alvernia, 120 m/394 ft.

Climate Sub-tropical; average temperatures 21°C (Jan) and 27°C (Jul); mean annual rainfall 750–1500 mm/30–60 in; hurricanes frequent (Jun–Nov).

Currency 1 Bahamian Dollar (BA$, B$) = 100 cents

Economy Market economy based on tourism; important financial centre (no income tax); oil refining, fishing, rum and liqueur distilling; cement; pharmaceuticals.

GDP (2002e) $4.59 bn, per capita $15 300

HDI (2002) 0.826

History Visited by Columbus in 1492, but first perma-

□ International Airport

nent European settlement not until 1647 by British and Bermudan religious refugees; British Crown Colony from 1717; independence, 1973; governed by a bicameral Parliament.

Head of State
(British monarch represented by Governor-General)
1995–2001 Orville Turnquest
2001– Dame Ivy Dumont

Head of Government
1992–2002 Hubert Alexander Ingraham
2002– Perry Christie

BAHRAIN

Local name al-Bahrayn

Timezone GMT +3

Area 678 km²/262 sq mi

Population total (2002e) 672000

Status Independent state

Date of independence 1971

Capital Manama

Languages Arabic (official), Farsi, Urdu, and English

Ethnic groups Bahraini Arab (63%), Asian (13%), Arab (10%), Iranian (9%)

Religions Muslim (Shi'ite 65%), Sunni 35%)

Physical features Island of Bahrain c.48 km/30 mi long, 13–16 km/8–10 mi wide, area 562 km²/217 sq mi; highest point Jabal Dukhan, 135 m/443 ft; largely bare and infertile.

Climate Temperate (Dec–Mar); hot and humid (particularly Jun–Sep); cool N/NE winds with a little rain (Dec–Mar); average annual rainfall 35 mm/1.4 in; average annual temperature 19°C (Jan), 36°C (Jul).

Currency 1 Bahrain Dinar (BD) = 1000 fils

Economy Major centre for oil trading, banking, commerce.

GDP (2002e) $9.91 bn, per capita $15 100

HDI (2002) 0.831

History Flourishing centre of trade during 2000–1800 BC; treaty of protection with the UK, 1861; independence in 1971, with a constitutional monarchy governed by an Emir; National Assembly dissolved in 1975 and not yet revived; historic territorial dispute with Qatar over

☐ International Airport

Hawar Is began with brief occupation of Fasht al-Dibal by Qatari troops, 1986; joined UN coalition during the Iraqi invasion of Kuwait, 1990; became monarchy, 2002.

Head of State (Emir, title changed to King when country officially changed its status from an emirate to a monarchy, 2002)

1999–   Shaikh Hamad II bin Isa al-Khalifa

Head of Government

1971–   Shaikh Khalifa bin Sulman al-Khalifa

BALEARIC ISLANDS >> SPAIN

BANGLADESH

Local name Bangladesh

Timezone GMT +6

Area 143 998 km²/55 583 sq mi

Population total (2002e) 133 377 000

Status Republic

Date of independence 1971

Capital Dhaka

Languages Bengali (official), also local dialects and English widely spoken

Ethnic groups Bengali (98%), Bihari (1%), tribal: Garo, Khasi, Santal (1%)

Religions Muslim (86%), Hindu (12%), Buddhist (1%), small Christian majority

Physical features Mainly a vast, low-lying alluvial plain, cut by a network of rivers, canals, swamps, marshes; main rivers the Ganges (Padma), Brahmaputra

(Jamuna), Meghna; joining in the S to form the largest delta in the world, subject to frequent flooding (notably in 1998 and 2004); Chittagong Hill Tracts in the E rise to 1200 m/3900 ft.

Climate Tropical climate; monsoon season (Jun–Oct).

Currency 1 Taka (TK) = 100 paisa

Economy Agriculture, especially rice (employs 86% of population); and supplies 80% of the world's jute; also paper, aluminium, textiles, glass, shipbuilding, fishing, natural gas.

GDP (2002e) $238.2 bn, per capita $1800

HDI (2002) 0.478

History Part of the State of Bengal until Muslim East Bengal created in 1905, separate from Hindu West Bengal; reunited, 1911; partitioned again in 1947, with West Bengal remaining in India and East Bengal forming East Pakistan; rebellion in 1971 led to independence as the People's Republic of Bangladesh; political unrest led to

Bangladesh (continued)

suspension of constitution, and assassination of first President, Sheikh Mujib, 1975; further coups in 1975, 1977, and 1982; constitution restored, 1986; last military dictator, Hossain Mohammad Ershad, overthrown, 1990; constitutional amendments in 1991 restricted powers of President to ceremonial and restored full powers to uni-cameral legislature, *Jatiya Sangsad*; further amendment in 2004 reserved 45 seats for women in the 300-member legislature.

Head of State
1996–2001 Shehabuddin Ahmed
2001–2 A.Q.M. Badruddoza Chowdhury
2002– Iajuddin Ahmed

Head of Government
2001– Khaleda Zia

□ International Airport ∴ World heritage site

BARBADOS

Local name Barbados

Timezone GMT −4

Area 430 km²/166 sq mi

Population total (2002e) 270 000

Status Independent state within the Commonwealth

Date of independence 1966

Capital Bridgetown

Language English (official)

Ethnic groups African (80%), mixed race (16%)

Religions Anglican (40%), Protestant (15%), Roman Catholic (4%)

Physical features Small, triangular island in the Atlantic Ocean; length 32 km/20 mi (NW–SE); rising to 340 m/1115 ft at Mt Hillaby; ringed by a coral reef.

Climate Tropical climate, with average annual temperature 27°C; mean annual rainfall 1420 mm/56 in.

Currency 1 Barbados Dollar (Bds$) = 100 cents

Economy Market economy based on tourism and sugar cane; cotton, bananas; natural gas; textiles.

GDP (2002e) $4.153 bn, per capita $1500

□ International Airport

HDI (2002) 0.871

History Colonized by the British, 1627; self-government, 1961; independent within the Commonwealth, 1966; executive power rests with the Prime Minister, appointed by a Governor-General, the Senate, and the House of Assembly.

Head of State
(British monarch represented by Governor-General)
1996– Sir Clifford Husbands

Head of Government
1994– Owen Seymour Arthur

BELARUS

Local name Belarus

Timezone GMT +3

Area 207 600 km²/80 134 sq mi

Population total (2002e) 9 933 000

Status Republic

Date of independence 1991

Capital Minsk (Mensk)

Languages Belorussian (official), Russian

Ethnic groups (1989) Belorussian (78%), Russian (13%), Polish (4%), Ukrainian (3%), Jewish (1%)

Religions Roman Catholic, Orthodox

Physical features Hilly lowlands with marshes, swamps; Dzyarzhynskaya Mt rises to 346 m/1135 ft; largest lake, Narach; Belaruskaya Hrada, largest glacial ridge, runs NW into Minsk Upland; rivers include the Pripyat and Dnepr; Pripyat marshes in E.

Climate Varies from maritime, near Baltic, to continental and humid; average annual temperatures, 18°C (Jul), –6°C (Jan); average annual rainfall 550–700 mm/22–8 in.

Currency Belorussian Rouble = 100 kopec

Economy Main exports include textiles, timber, chemical products, fertilizers, electrical goods; valuable resource: peat marshes.

GDP (2002e) $90.19 bn, per capita $8700

HDI (2002) 0.788

History Neolithic remains widespread; colonized by E Slavic tribes, 5th-c; Mongols conquered Slavs, 13th-c; Catherine the Great of Russia acquired E Belorussia (White Russia) in the first Polish partition in 1772; gained Minsk in 1793 and the remainder in 1795; W Belorussia ceded to Poland in 1921 as part of the Treaty of Riga which ended Soviet–Polish War; regained by Soviet Union as part of Nazi–Soviet Non-aggression Pact of 1939,

□ International Airport

and Belorussia became Belorussian Soviet Socialist Republic; admitted to UN, 1945; declared independence, 1991; co-founder of Commonwealth of Independent States (CIS), 1991.

Head of State
1994– Alexander Lukashenko

Head of Government
2003– Sergey Sidorski

BELAU

Local names Belau, also Pelau, Palau

Timezone GMT +10

Area 494 km²/191 sq mi

Population total (2002e) 19 900

Status Republic

Date of independence 1994

Capital Koror

Languages Palauan, English

Ethnic groups Palauan (83%)

Religions Christianity (66%), traditional beliefs (25%)

Physical features A group of c. 350 small islands and islets, c. 960 km/600 mi E of the Philippines; most W

HUMAN GEOGRAPHY

Belau (continued)

group of the Caroline Is; largest island, Babeldoab (367 km²/142 sq mi).

Climate Warm all year, with high humidity; average annual temperature, 27°C; average annual rainfall, 3810 mm/150 in; typhoons common.

Currency US dollar = 100 cents

Economy Tourism, taro, pineapple, breadfruit, bananas, yams, citrus fruit, coconuts, pepper, fishing.

GDP (2001e) $174.8 mn, per capita $9000

History The smallest of the four political units to emerge out of the US Trust Territory of the Pacific Islands; organized into 16 states; held by Germany, 1899–1914; mandated to Japan by League of Nations, 1920; invaded by USA, 1944; compact of free association with the USA, signed in 1982, but not confirmed until 1993; independence, 1994; governed by a President and a bicameral National Congress; constitution also provides for an advisory body of chiefs.

Head of State
2001–   Tommy Remengesau

□ International Airport

BELGIUM

Local names Belgique (French), België (Flemish)

Timezone GMT +1

Area 30 540 km²/11 788 sq mi

Population total (2002e) 10 280 000

Status Kingdom

Date of independence 1830

Capital Brussels

Languages Flemish/Dutch (56%), French (32%), German (1%); (Brussels officially bilingual Flemish/French)

Ethnic groups Flemish (Teutonic origin) (55%), Walloon (French Latin) (33%)

Religions Roman Catholic (90%), Muslim (1%), Protestant (0.4%)

Physical features Mostly low-lying, with some hills in the SE region (Ardennes), average elevation 300–500 m/1000–1600 ft; large areas of fertile soil, intensively cultivated for many centuries; main river systems linked by complex network of canals; low-lying, dune-fringed coastline.

Climate Cool and temperate with strong maritime influences; average annual temperatures 2°C (Jan), 18°C (Jul) in Brussels; average annual rainfall 825 mm/35 in.

Currency 1 euro = 100 cents (previous to February 2002, 1 Belgian Franc (BFr) = 100 centimes)

Economy One of the earliest countries in Europe to industrialize, using rich coalfields of the Ardennes;

□ International Airport

Flanders textile industry; long-standing centre for European trade; major iron and steel industry, with wide range of metallurgical and engineering products; agriculture mainly livestock; full economic union (Benelux Economic Union) between Belgium, Netherlands, and Luxembourg, 1948; Brussels is the headquarters of several major international organizations, including the Commission of the EU.

GDP (2002e) $299.7 bn, per capita $29 200

HDI (2002) 0.939

History Part of the Roman Empire until 2nd-c; then

became part of the Frankish Empire following Celt and Germanic invasions; ruled by the Habsburgs from 1477 until the Peace of Utrecht in 1713, when sovereignty passed to Austria; conquered by the French, 1794; part of the French Republic and Empire until 1815, then united with the Netherlands; Belgian rebellion against Dutch rule in 1830, led to recognition as an independent kingdom under Leopold of Saxe-Coburg; occupied by Germany in both World Wars; became a constitutional monarchy with bicameral Parliament; political tension between Walloons in S and Flemings in N, 1980; federal constitution divided Belgium into the autonomous regions of Flanders, Wallonia, and Brussels, 1989; constitutional Monarch has limited powers; a Chamber of Deputies and a Senate.

Head of State (Monarch)
1950–93   Baudouin I
1993–   Albert II

Head of Government
1992–9   Jean Luc Dehaene
1999–   Guy Verhofstadt

BELIZE

Local name Belice (Spanish)

Timezone GMT –6

Area 22963 km²/8864 sq mi

Population total (2002e) 251 000

Status Independent state within the Commonwealth

Date of independence 1981

Capital Belmopan

Languages English (official), Spanish, Garifuna, Maya

Ethnic groups Creole (40%), mestizo (33%), Mayan (9.5%), Carib (8%), Garifuna (8%)

Religions Roman Catholic (62%), Protestant (30%)

Physical features Located in Central America; extensive coastal plain; swampy in the N, fertile in the S; Maya Mts extend almost to the E coast, rising to 1120 m/ 3674 ft at Victoria Peak; Belize R flows W–E; inner coastal waters protected by world's second longest barrier reef.

Climate Generally sub-tropical, but tempered by trade winds; average annual temperature 24°C (Jan), 27°C (Jul); variable rainfall; average annual rainfall 1295 mm/51 in (N), 4445 mm/175 in (S); hurricanes frequent.

Currency 1 Belize Dollar (Bz$) = 100 cents

Economy Developing free-market economy based on timber and forest products, more recently on agriculture.

GDP (2002e) $1.28 bn, per capita $4900

HDI (2002) 0.784

History Evidence of early Mayan settlement; colonized in the 17th-c by shipwrecked British sailors and disbanded soldiers from Jamaica; created a British colony, 1862; administered from Jamaica until 1884; internal

□ International Airport   ∴ World heritage site

self-government, 1964; changed name from British Honduras to Belize, 1973; full independence, 1981; Guatemalan claims over Belize territory have led to a continuing British military presence; Guatemala accord, respecting Belize self-determination, 1991; bicameral National Assembly.

Head of State
(British Monarch represented by Governor-General)
1993–   Colville Norbert Young

Head of Government
1993–8   Manuel Esquivel
1998–   Said Musa

BENIN

Local name Bénin

Timezone GMT +1

Area 112622 km²/43472 sq mi

Population total (2002e) 6 788 000

Status Republic

Date of independence 1960

Capital Porto Novo (nominal), Cotonou (political and economic)

Languages French (official), Fon (47%), Adja (12%), Bariba (10%), Yoruba (9%), Fulani (6%), Somba (5%), Aizo (5%)

Ethnic groups Fon (40%), Yoruba (10%), Bariba (20%), minority of Fulani nomads

Religions Traditional beliefs (c.70%), Christian (15%), Muslim (13%)

Physical features Located in N Africa; rises from a 100 km/62 mi-long, sandy coast with lagoons to low-lying plains; savannah plateau, c. 400 m/1300 ft, in N; descend

Benin (continued)

to forested lowlands in S fringing the Bight of Benin; Atakora Mts rise to over 500 m/1600 ft in NW; rivers include Ouémé, Alibori, Mekrou; Pendjari National Park in NW.

Climate Tropical climate divided into three zones: in the S, rain throughout the year, especially during the Guinea Monsoon (May–Oct); in C, two rainy seasons (peaks in May–Jun and Oct); in the N, one rainy season (Jul–Sep); dry season in N (Oct–Apr): hot, with low humidity, subject to the dry harmattan wind from the NE.

Currency 1 CFA Franc (CFAFr) = 100 centimes

Economy Agriculture, especially palm-oil products, cashew nuts, maize, cassava, rice, cotton, coffee; no known natural resources in commercial quantity; small offshore oilfield.

GDP (2002e) $7.38 bn, per capita $1100

HDI (2002) 0.420

History Pre-colonially a collection of small, warring principalities, including the Fon Kingdom of Dahomey (founded 17th-c); Portuguese colonial activities centred on slave trade; subjugated by French, becoming the French Protectorate of Dahomey, 1892; territory within French West Africa from 1904; independent from 1960; Marxist-Leninist regime gained power, 1972; name changed from Dahomey to the People's Republic of Benin, 1975; Marxism-Leninism abandoned, 1989, and a new multi-party constitution approved, 1990; changed name to Republic of Benin, 1990; multi-party elections held, 1991; President elected for five-year term, and a National Assembly.

Head of State
1991–6   Nicéphore Soglo
1996–   Mathieu Kerekou

Head of Government
1996–8   Adrien Houngbedji

BERMUDA >> UNITED KINGDOM

BERMUDA >> UNITED KINGDOM

BHUTAN

Local name Druk-yul

Timezone GMT +5.5

Area 46 600 km²/18 000 sq mi

Population total (2002e) 1 996 000

Status Kingdom

Capital Thimphu

Languages Dzongkha (official) (60%), Nepalese (25%), English

Ethnic groups Bhote (60%), Nepalese (25%), indigenous or migrant tribes (15%)

Religions Lamaistic Buddhist (75%), Hindu (20%), Muslim (5%)

Physical features High peaks of E Himalayas in the N, over 7000m/23 000 ft; forested mountain ridges with fertile valleys descend to low foothills in the S; rivers include Wong Chu, Manas; permanent snowfields in the mountains; sub-tropical forest in S.

Climate Affected by altitude; snowcapped in glaciated N; average monthly temperatures 4°C (Jan), 17°C (Jul); torrential rain common, average 1000 mm/40 in (C valleys) and 5000 mm/200 in (S).

☐ International Airport

Currency 1 Ngultrum (Nu) = 100 chetrum

Economy Largely based on agriculture, mainly rice, wheat, maize, mountain barley, potatoes, vegetables, fruit (especially oranges); also timber (large area of plantation forest); sales of tobacco products banned, 2004.

GDP (2002e) $2.7 bn, per capita $1300

HDI (2002) 0.494

History British involvement since treaty of 1774 with the East India Company; S part of the country annexed, 1865; Anglo-Bhutanese Treaty signed, in which Britain agreed not to interfere in internal affairs of Bhutan, 1910; similar treaty (Indo-Bhutan Treaty of Friendship) signed with India, 1949; governed by a maharajah from 1907, now addressed as King of Bhutan; National Assembly (Tsogdu) established, 1953; constitutional monarchy with power shared between the King, the Council of Ministers, the National Assembly, and the monastic head of the kingdom's Buddhist priesthood; King devolved executive powers to the Council of Ministers, 1998; separatist movements associated with Assam and Bodoland located in the S.

Head of State (Monarch)
1972– Jigme Singye Wangchuk

Chairman of the Council of Ministers
2004– Lyonpo Yeshey Zimba

BOLIVIA

Local name Bolivia

Timezone GMT –4

Area 1 098 580 km²/424 052 sq mi

Population total (2002e) 8 401 000

Status Republic

Date of independence 1825

Capital La Paz (administrative), Sucre (legal)

Languages Spanish, Quechua, Aymará (all used officially)

Ethnic groups Mestizo (31%), Quechua (25%), Aymará (25%), white (14%)

Religions Roman Catholic (95%), Baha'i (3%)

Physical features Landlocked country, bounded W by the Cordillera Occidental of the Andes, rising to 6542 m/21 463 ft at Sajama; separated from the Cordillera Real to the E by the flat, 400 km/250 mi-long Altiplano plateau, 3600 m/11 800 ft; major lakes, Titicaca and Poopó.

Climate Varies with altitude, ranging from consistently warm (26°C) and damp conditions (1800 mm/71 in of rainfall per year) in NE rainforests of Amazon Basin, to drought conditions in S; over 500 m/16 000 ft, conditions become sub-polar.

Currency 1 Boliviano (Bs) = 100 centavos

Economy Dependent on minerals for foreign exchange; silver largely exhausted, but replaced by tin (a fifth of world supply); oil and natural-gas pipelines to Argentina and Chile; illegally-produced cocaine.

GDP (2002e) $21.15 bn, per capita $2500

HDI (2002) 0.653

☐ International Airport

History Part of Inca Empire, conquered by Spanish in 16th-c; independence after war of liberation, 1825; much territory lost after wars with neighbouring countries; several changes of government and military coups during 1964–82; returned to civilian rule, 1982; governed by a bicameral Congress and an elected President and Cabinet.

Head of State/Government
2002–3 Gonzalo Sánchez de Lozada
2003– Carlos Mesa

BOSNIA–HERZEGOVINA

Local name Bosna-Hercegovina

Timezone GMT +2

Area 51 129 km²/19 736 sq mi

Population total (2002e) 3 964 000

Status Republic

Date of independence 1992

Capital Sarajevo

Language Serbian, Croatian, Bosnian

Ethnic groups (pre-civil war) Slav (44%), Serbian (31%), Croatian (17%)

Religions Muslim (Sunni), Serbian Orthodox, Roman Catholic

Physical features Mountainous region in the Balkan peninsula, noted for its stone gorges, lakes, rivers, mineral springs; reaches heights of 1800 m/6000 ft above

Bosnia-Herzegovina (continued)

sea level; principal rivers are Bosna, Una, Drina, Neretva, Sava; in the SW lies the dry, limestone plateau (karst).

Climate Ranges from Mediterranean to mildly continental; sirocco wind brings rain from SW; strong NE wind (bora) affects coastal area in winter.

Currency 1 Convertible Mark (KM) = 100 convertible pfennigs

Economy Highly industrialized, particularly iron and steel; large cellulose factory at Banja Luka; forestry strong in Bosnia; inflation rate high; war (1992–3) disrupted all economic activity.

GDP (2002e) $7.3 bn, per capita $1900

History Annexed by Austria in 1908; Serbian opposition to the annexation led to the murder of Archduke Francis Ferdinand and World War 1; ceded to Yugoslavia, 1918; declaration of sovereignty, 1991; Bosnian Serbs proclaimed three autonomous regions (Bosanska Krajina, Romanija, and Northern Bosnia), 1991; declaration of independence in 1992 led to ongoing military conflict between formerly integrated communities of Bosnians, Croats, and Serbs; UN peace-keeping forces deployed, and air-exclusion ('no-fly') zone imposed, 1992; conflict continued until ceasefire in Oct 1995; peace accord leaves Bosnia-Herzegovina a single state, comprising the Bosnian-Croat Federation (in the west) and the Bosnian Serb Republic (in the east), with Sarajevo a united city; centrally governed by a national parliament and president, and people allowed freedom of movement; Nato peace implementation force established.

☐ International Airport

Head of State[a]

2003–	Borislav Paravac (*Serb*)
2002–5	Dragan Covic (*Croat*)
2002–	Sulejman Tihic (*Bosniak*)

Head of Government

2002–	Adnan Terzic

[a]A collective presidency with an 8-month rotating leadership.

HUMAN GEOGRAPHY

BOTSWANA

Local name Botswana

Timezone GMT +2

Area 581 730 km²/224 711 sq mi

Population total (2002e) 1 679 000

Status Independent republic within the Commonwealth

Date of independence 1966

Capital Gaborone

Languages English (official), Tswana

Ethnic groups Tswana (75%), Shona (12%), San (Bushmen) (3%), Khoikhoin (Hottentot) (3%), Ndebele (1%)

Religions Mainly local beliefs; Christian (20%)

Physical features Landlocked S African republic; undulating, sand-filled plateau, part of the S African Plateau; mean elevation c.1000 m/3300 ft; N–S plateau divides country into two regions: hilly grasslands (velt) to E, and Okavango Swamps to W; most of the population lives in fertile, hilly E; SE terrain hilly, 1402 m/4600 ft; dry scrubland, savannah, and the Kalahari Desert in W; salt lakes in N.

☐ International Airport

Climate Largely sub-tropical; rainfall in N and E almost totally in summer (Oct–Apr); average annual temperature 26°C (Jan), 13°C (Jul) in Gaborone; average annual rainfall 450 mm/17.7 in.

Currency 1 Pula (P, Pu) = 100 thebes

Economy Mainly subsistence farming, especially livestock; continual problems of drought and disease; some crops, especially sorghum; main minerals, nickel, diamonds (jointly mined by the government and De Beers Consolidated Mines of South Africa), cobalt; tourism, especially wildlife observation; Central Kalahari Game Reserve (54388 km²/21000 sq mi) attracts tourists; Trans-Kalahari Highway completed, 1998; principal trading partners, members of South African Customs Union.

GDP (2002e) $13.48 bn, per capita $8500

BRAZIL

Local name Brasil

Timezone GMT −2 (Atlantic Islands); GMT −3 (E); GMT −4 (mid-W); GMT −5 (extreme W)

Area 8 511 965 km²/3 285 618 sq mi

Population total (2002e) 174 619 000

Status Republic

Date of independence 1822

Capital Brasília

Language Portuguese (official)

Ethnic groups White (53%), mixed (34%), black (6%)

Religions Roman Catholic (80%), Protestant, Spiritualist

Physical features Located in E and C South America; low-lying Amazon basin in the N; where forest canopy cleared, soils susceptible to erosion; Brazilian plateau in the C and S, average height 600–900 m/2000–3000 ft; Guiana Highlands (S) contain Brazil's highest peak, Pico da Neblina, 3014 m/9888 ft; eight river systems, notably Amazon (N), São Francisco (C), Paraguay, Paraná, and Uruguay (S); 30% of population concentrated on a thin coastal strip on the Atlantic, c.100 km/325 mi wide.

Climate Almost entirely tropical, equator passing through the N region, and Tropic of Capricorn through the SE; Amazon basin, annual rainfall 1500–2000 mm/60–80 in; no dry season, average midday temperatures 27–32°C; dry region in the NE, susceptible to long droughts; hot, tropical climate on narrow coastal strip, with rainfall varying greatly N–S; S states have a seasonal temperate climate.

Currency 1 Cruzeiro Real (Cr$) = 100 centavos

Economy One of the world's largest farming countries, agriculture employing 35% of population; world's largest exporter of coffee, second largest exporter of cocoa and soya beans; iron-ore reserves (possibly world's largest); timber reserves, third largest in the world, but continuing destruction of Amazon rainforest is causing much concern; road network being extended through Amazon rainforest.

GDP (2002e) $1.376 tn, per capita $7600

HDI (2002) 0.757

HDI (2002) 0.572

History San (Bushmen) were the earliest inhabitants, followed by Sotho peoples who migrated to Botswana c.1600; explored by Europeans, 1801; visited by missionaries during 19th-c; London Missionary Society established a mission on the Kuruman R, 1813; Ndebele raided Botswana; Boers arrived, 1835; gold discovered, 1867; under British protection from 1885; S became a Crown Colony, then part of Cape Colony, 1895; N became the Bechuanaland Protectorate; self-government from 1964; independence and change of name to Botswana, 1966; governed by a legislative National Assembly, President, and Cabinet; House of Chiefs considers chieftaincy matters but has no right of veto.

Head of State/Government
1998–   Festus Mogae

□ International Airport   ∴ World heritage site

History Claimed for the Portuguese by Pedro Alvares Cabral in 1500, first settlement at Salvador da Bahia; King of Portugal moved seat of government to Brazil, 1808; his son, Dom Pedro, declared himself emperor, 1818; independence established, 1822; Dom Pedro forced to abdicate in 1831 and succeeded by his 14-year-old son, Dom Pedro II, 1840; abolition of slavery in 1888, persuaded former slave-owners in declining sugar-plantation areas to join Republican opposition to the king, who was overthrown in the coup of 1889; ruled by dictator, Getúlio Vargas, 1930–45; Vargas deposed by military, and liberal republic restored, 1946; returned to office, 1950, but committed suicide, 1954; capital moved from Rio de Janeiro to Brasília, 1960; another coup in 1964 led to a military-backed presidential regime; President da Costa e Silva resigned and military junta took control, 1969; new elections, 1985; new constitution approved, transferring power from the President to the Congress, 1988; bicameral National Congress.

Head of State/Government
1992–5   Itamar Franco
1995–2002 Fernando Henrique Cardosa
2002–   Luiz Inacio Lula da Silva

BRITISH ANTARCTIC TERRITORY >> UNITED KINGDOM
BRITISH INDIAN OCEAN TERRITORY >> UNITED KINGDOM
BRITISH VIRGIN ISLANDS >> UNITED KINGDOM

BRUNEI

Local name Negara Brunei Darussalam

Timezone GMT +8

Area 5765 km²/2225 sq mi

Population total (2002e) 351 000

Status Independent state

Date of independece 1984

Capital Bandar Seri Begawan

Languages Malay (official), English

Ethnic groups Malay (65%), Chinese (20%)

Religions Muslim (Sunni 65%), Buddhist (12%), Christian (9%)

Physical features Swampy coastal plain; equatorial rainforest covers 75% of land area; rivers include Belait, Tutong Brunei; mountainous tract on Sarawak border, average height 500 m/1640 ft.

Climate Tropical; high temperatures and humidity and no marked seasons; average daily temperature 24–30°C; average annual rainfall 2540 mm/100 in on coast, doubling in the interior.

Currency 1 Brunei Dollar (Br$) = 100 cents

Economy Largely dependent on oil (discovered 1929) and gas resources.

GDP (2002e) $6.5 bn, per capita $18 600

HDI (2002) 0.856

History Formerly a powerful Muslim sultanate, with dominion over all of Borneo, its neighbouring islands, and parts of the Philippines by early 16th-c; under British

☐ International Airport

protection from 1888; occupied by Japanese, 1941; liberated and reverted to former status as a British residency, 1945; internal self-government, 1971, and full independence, 1984; a constitutional monarchy with the Sultan as Head of State, who presides over a Council of Cabinet Ministers, a Religious Council, and a Privy Council.

Head of State/Government (Sultan)
1967–   Muda Hassan al Bolkiah Mu'izz-Din-Waddaulah

BULGARIA

Local name Bălgarija

Timezone GMT +2

Area 110 912 km²/42 812 sq mi

Population total (2002e) 7 890 000

Status Republic

Date of independence 1908

Capital Sofia

Languages Bulgarian (official), Turkish

Ethnic groups Bulgarian (85%), Turkish (9%)

Religions Bulgarian Orthodox (85%), Muslim (13%)

Physical features Traversed W–E by the Balkan Mts, averaging 2000 m/6500 ft; in the SW, Rhodope Mts, rising to 3000 m/9600 ft; rivers include Maritsa, Iskur, Danube.

Climate Continental climate, with hot summers, cold winters; average annual temperatures –2°C (Jan), 21°C (Jul); average annual rainfall 635 mm/25 in.

Currency 1 Lev (Lv) = 100 stotinki

Economy Mainly agricultural produce; coal, iron ore;

☐ International Airport

offshore oil (Black Sea), natural gas; tourism; tobacco, wine exports.

GDP (2002e) $49.23 bn, per capita $6500

HDI (2002) 0.779

History Bulgars crossed the Danube, 7th-c; their empire continually at war with Byzantines until destroyed by Turks, 14th-c; remained under Turkish rule, 1396–1878; full independence, 1908; became a kingdom, 1908–46; aligned with Germany in both World Wars; occupied by USSR, 1944; Socialist People's Republic founded, 1946; unicameral National Assembly established, 1971; proclaimed Republic of Bulgaria, 1990; new constitution, 1991, with a directly elected President, and a 250-member National Assembly.

Head of State
2001–   Georgi Parvanov

Head of Government
2001–   Simeon Borisov Sakskoburggotski

BURKINA FASO

Local name Burkina Faso

Timezone GMT

Area 274 200 km²/105 870 sq mi

Population total (2002e) 12 603 000

Status Republic

Date of independence 1960

Capital Ouagadougou

Languages French (official), with Moré, Mossi, Mande, Fulani, Lobi, and Bobo also spoken

Ethnic groups Mossi (48%), over 50 other groups

Religions Traditional beliefs (45%), Muslim (43%), Christian (12%)

Physical features Landlocked republic in W Africa; low-lying plateau, falling away to the S; tributaries of the Volta and Niger unnavigable in dry season; wooded savannahs in S; semi-desert in N.

Climate Tropical; average annual rainfall 894 mm/35 in; dry season (Dec–May), rainy season (Jun–Oct); average annual temperature 24°C (Jan), 28°C (Jul) in Ouagadougou; violent storms (Aug); subject to drought conditions.

Currency 1 CFA Franc (CFAFr) = 100 centimes

Economy Based on agriculture, largely at subsistence level; millet, corn, rice, livestock, peanuts, sugar cane, cotton.

GDP (2002e) $14.51 bn, per capita $1100

HDI (2002) 0.325

History Mossi empire in 18th–19th-c; Upper Volta created by French, 1919; abolished in 1932, with most land joined to Ivory Coast; original borders reconstituted,

BURMA >> MYANMAR

□ International Airport

1947; autonomy within French community, 1958; independence, 1960, with several military coups since; changed name from Upper Volta to Burkina Faso ('land of upright men'), 1984; end of military rule, 1991; governed by a president and an appointed Council of Ministers; new constitution, 1991, which promulgated an Assembly of People's Deputies (from 1997, with 111 members).

Head of State
1987–   Blaise Compaoré

Head of Government
2000–   Paramanga Ernest Yonli

BURUNDI

Local name Burundi

Timezone GMT +2

Area 27 834 km²/10 744 sq mi

Population total (2002e) 6 373 000

Status Republic

Date of independence 1962

Capital Bujumbura

Languages French and Kirundi (official), Swahili

Ethnic groups Hutu (82%), Tutsi (14%), Twa Pygmy (1%)

Religions Roman Catholic (62%), traditional beliefs (32%)

Physical features Located in C Africa; lies across Nile–Congo watershed; interior plateau, c.1500 m/5000

HUMAN GEOGRAPHY

Burundi (continued)

ft; highest point, Mt Karonje 2685 m/8809 ft; R Ruzizi forms part of NW frontier with Zaïre and links Lake Kiki in Rwanda, with Lake Tanganyika in S and E; river Malagarasi valley in E.

Climate Equatorial; moderately wet; dry season (Jun–Sep); average annual temperature 23°C; average annual rainfall at Bujumbura, 850 mm/33.5 in.

Currency 1 Burundi Franc (BuFr, FBu) = 100 centimes

Economy Mainly agriculture; cash crops include coffee, cotton, tea; light consumer goods, shoes, blankets; reserves of rare-earth metals.

GDP (2002e) $3.146 bn, per capita $500

HDI (2002) 0.313

History Ruled by the Tutsi kingdom, 16th-c; occupied by Germany in 1890, and included in German East Africa, 1890; League of Nations mandated territory, administered by Belgians, 1919; joined with Rwanda to become the UN Trust Territory of Ruanda-Urundi, 1946; independent, 1962; full republic following the overthrow of the monarchy, 1966; civil war, 1972; military coup, 1976; new constitution provided a National Assembly, 1981; Assembly dissolved after 1987 coup; Military Council for National Salvation disbanded, 1990; new constitution, 1992; political instability following assassination of president, 1993; major inter-ethnic (Hutu/l'utsi) conflict, 1993–4, followed by periods of transitional governance and ongoing conflict to 2002; peace agreement with Hutu rebels, 2003, and demobilization planned for 2004.

Head of State
1996–2003 Pierre Buyoya
2003–   Domitien Ndayizeye

☐ International Airport

Head of Government
1996–8   Pascal-Firmin Ndimira

CAMBODIA

Local name Cambodia

Timezone GMT +7

Area 181 035 km²/69 879 sq mi

Population total (2002e) 13 414 000

Status Kingdom

Date of independence 1953

Capital Phnom Penh

Languages Khmer (official), French

Ethnic groups Khmer (93%), Chinese (3%), Cham (2%)

Religions Theravada Buddhist (88%), Muslim (2%)

Physical features Kingdom in SE Asia; crossed E by floodplain of Mekong R; Cardamom mountain range 160 km/100 mi across Thailand border, rising to 1813 m/5948 ft at Phnom Aural; Tonlé Sap (Greek Lake) in NW.

Climate Tropical monsoon climate, with a wet season (May–Sep); high temperatures in lowland region throughout the year; average annual temperature 21°C (Jan), 29°C (Jul); average annual rainfall 5000 mm/71 in (SW), 1300 mm/51 in (interior lowlands).

Currency 1 Riel (CRl) = 100 sen

☐ International Airport   ∴ World heritage site

Economy Subsistence agriculture, rice and corn; industrial development disrupted by the civil war.

GNP (2002e) $20.42 bn, per capita $1600

HDI (2002) 0.543

History Originally part of Funan Kingdom, then part of the Khmer Empire, 6th-c; in dispute with Vietnamese and Thais from 15th-c; French Protectorate, 1863; part of Indo-China, 1887; independence, 1953; Prince Sihanouk deposed and Khmer Republic formed, 1970; fighting involved troops from N and S Vietnam and USA; surrender of Phnom Penh to Khmer Rouge, country renamed Kampuchea, 1975; attempt to reform economy by Pol Pot (1975–8) caused deaths of c.3 million people; Phnom Penh captured by Vietnamese, causing Khmer Rouge to flee, 1979; 1981 constitution established Council of State and Council of Ministers; name of Cambodia restored, 1989; Vietnamese troops completed withdrawal, 1989; UN peace plan agreed, with ceasefire and return of Sihanouk as Head of State, 1991; Sihanouk crowned king, 1993; further conflict following Khmer Rouge refusal to take part in 1993 elections; two main parties agreed to form coalition government, 2004; abdication of Sihanouk, Oct 2004.

Head of State (Monarch)
2004   Prince Norodom Ranariddh *Interim*
2004–   Norodom Sihamoni

Head of Government
1998–   Hun Sen

CAMEROON

Local name Cameroun

Timezone GMT +1

Area 475 439 km²/183 519 sq mi

Population total (2002e) 16 185 000

Status Republic

Date of independence 1960

Capital Yaoundé

Languages French and English (official); 24 major African languages including Fang, Bamileke, Luanda, Fulani, Tika, Maka

Ethnic groups Highlanders (31%), Equatorial Bantu (19%), Kirdi (11%), Fulani (10%)

Religions Christian (40%), traditional beliefs (39%), Muslim (21%)

Physical features Located in W Africa; equatorial forest, with low coastal plain. C plateau 1300 m/4200 ft; W forested and mountainous; Mt Cameroon, 4070 m/ 13 353 ft (active volcano and the highest peak in W Africa); low savannah, semi-desert towards L Chad; rivers include Sanaga and Dja.

Climate Rain all year in equatorial S; daily temperature in Yaoundé 27–30°C; average annual rainfall 4030 mm/159 in.

Currency 1 CFA Franc (CFAFr) = 100 centimes

Economy Agriculture (employs c.80% of workforce); world's fifth largest producer of cocoa; tourism, especially to national parks.

GNP (2002e) $26.84 bn, per capita $1700

HDI (2002) 0.512

History First explored by Portuguese navigator Fernando Po; later by traders from Spain, Netherlands, Britain; German protectorate of Kamerun, 1884; divided into French and British Cameroon, 1919; confirmed by League of Nations mandate, 1922; UN trusteeships, 1946; French Cameroon independent as Republic of Cameroon, 1960; N sector of British Cameroon voted to become part of Nigeria, S sector part of Cameroon; became Federal Republic of Cameroon, with separate parliaments, 1961; federal system abolished, 1972, and name changed to United Republic of Cameroon; changed name to the Republic of Cameroon, 1984; multiparty legislative and presidential elections, 1992; governed by a President, executive Prime Minister, Cabinet, and National Assembly.

Head of State
1982–   Paul Biya

Head of Government
1996–   Peter Mafany Musonge

□ International Airport   ∴ World heritage site

HUMAN GEOGRAPHY

CANADA

Local name Canada

Timezone GMT W −9, to E −3

Area 9 971 500 km²/3 848 900 sq mi

Population total (2002e) 31 244 000

Status Independent nation within the Commonwealth

Date of independence 1867 (Dominion of Canada)

Capital Ottawa

Languages English and French (official)

Ethnic groups British origin (45%), French origin (29%), other European, Indian, and Inuit (23%)

Religions Roman Catholic (49%), United Church (18%), Anglican (12%)

Physical features Dominated in the NE by the Canadian Shield; flat prairie country S and W of the Shield, stretching to the Western Cordillera, which includes the Rocky, Cassiar, and Mackenzie Mts; Coast Mts flank a rugged, heavily indented coastline; Mt Logan in the Yukon, 5950 m/19 521 ft, the highest peak in Canada; major rivers; the Mackenzie (W), and St Lawrence (E); Great Bear, 31 330 km²/11 030 sq mi, and Great Slave, 28 570 km²/11 030 sq mi, are lakes in NW Territories.

Climate N coast permanently ice-bound or obstructed by ice floes, but for Hudson Bay (frozen c.9 months each year); mild winters and warm summers on Pacific coast and around Vancouver Island; average annual rainfall 145 mm/57 in.

Currency 1 Canadian Dollar (C$, Can$) = 100 cents

Economy Traditionally based on natural resources and agriculture: world's second largest exporter of wheat; world's largest producer of asbestos, zinc, silver, nickel; second largest producer of potash, gypsum, molybdenum, sulphur; hydroelectricity, oil (especially Alberta), natural gas; major industrial development in recent decades.

GDP (2002e) $934.1 bn, per capita $29 300

HDI (2002) 0.940

History Evidence of Viking settlement c.1000; Newfoundland claimed for England, 1583; Champlain founded Quebec, 1608; Hudson's Bay Company founded, 1670; conflict between British and French in late 17th-c; Britain gained large areas from Treaty of Utrecht, 1713; after Seven Years' War, during which British General James Wolfe captured Quebec from Louis Montcalm's forces in 1759, Treaty of Paris gave Britain almost all France's possessions in North America; province of Quebec created, 1774; migration of loyalists from USA after War of Independence led to division of Quebec into

☐ International Airport

Upper and Lower Canada; reunited as Canada, 1841; Dominion of Canada created (1867) by confederation of Quebec, Ontario, Nova Scotia, and New Brunswick; Rupert's Land and Northwest Territories bought from Hudson's Bay Company, 1869–70; joined by Manitoba (1870), British Columbia (1871), Prince Edward I (1873), Alberta and Saskatchewan (1905), and Newfoundland (1949); recurring political tension in recent decades arising from French-Canadian separatist movement in Quebec; Canada Act, 1982, gave Canada full responsibility for constitution; bicameral Federal Parliament includes Senate and a House of Commons; British monarch is Head of State, represented by a Governor-General; referendum on Quebec separation narrowly defeated in 1995.

Head of State
(British monarch represented by Governor-General)
1999–   Adrienne Clarkson

Head of Government
1993   Kim Campbell
1993–2003 Jean Chrétien
2003–   Paul Martin

CANARY ISLANDS >> SPAIN

CAPE VERDE

Local name Cabo Verde

Timezone GMT –1

Area 4033 km²/1557 sq mi

Population total (2002e) 453 000

Status Island group

Date of independence 1975

Capital Praia (on São Tiago Island)

Languages Portuguese (official), Crioulo (Portuguese-based creole)

Ethnic groups Creole (mulatto) (60%), African (28%), European (2%)

Religion Roman Catholic (80%), others (20%)

Physical features Island group in the Atlantic Ocean off W Coast of Africa, c.500 km/310 mi W of Dakar, Senegal; Barlavento (windward) group in N, Sotavento (leeward) group in S; mostly mountainous islands of volcanic origin; highest peak, Pico do Cano, 2829 m/9281 ft; active volcano on Fogo I; fine sandy beaches on most islands.

Climate Arid climate; located at N limit of tropical rain belt; low and unreliable rainfall (Aug–Sep); small temperature range throughout year; average annual temperature 23°C; average annual rainfall 250 mm/10 in.

Currency 1 Escudo (CVEsc) = 100 centavos

Economy Suffering because of drought; substantial emigration in early 1970s; c.70% of workforce are farmers occupying irrigated inland valleys; increase in fishing since 1975.

GDP (2002e) $600 mn, per capita $1400

HDI (2002) 0.715

CAYMAN ISLANDS >> UNITED KINGDOM

>> *Political leaders and rulers, p.126*

Canadian provinces and territories

Name	Area		Capital
	km²	sq mi	
Alberta	661 190	255 285	Edmonton
British Columbia	947 800	365 945	Victoria
Manitoba	649 950	250 945	Winnipeg
New Brunswick	73 440	28 355	Fredericton
Newfoundland	405 720	156 648	St John's
Northwest Territories	1 346 106	519 597	Yellowknife
Nova Scotia	55 490	21 424	Halifax
Nunavut	2 093 190	807 971	Iqaluit
Ontario	1 068 580	412 578	Toronto
Prince Edward Island	5 660	2 185	Charlottetown
Quebec	1 540 680	594 856	Quebec City
Saskatchewan	652 380	251 883	Regina
Yukon Territory	483 450	186 660	Whitehorse

HUMAN GEOGRAPHY

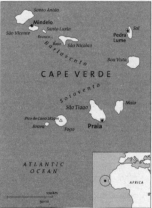

□ International Airport

History Colonized by Portuguese in 15th-c, also used as a penal colony; administered with Portuguese Guinea until 1879; overseas province of Portugal, 1951; independence, 1975; governed by a President, Council of Ministers, and People's National Assembly; multi-party elections held, 1991.

Head of State
2001–   Pedro Verona Rodrigues Pires

Head of Government
2001–   José Maria Pereira Neves

CENTRAL AFRICAN REPUBLIC

Local name République Centrafricaine

Timezone GMT +1

Area 622 984 km²/240 535 sq mi

Population total (2002e) 3 643 000

Status Republic

Date of independence 1960

Capital Bangui

Languages French (official), Sangho

Ethnic groups Baya (34%), Banda (28%), Sara (10%), over 80 other groups

Religions Christian (50%), (Protestant 25%, Roman Catholic 25%), also Muslim and traditional beliefs

Physical features Located in C Africa; plateau forming a watershed between Chad and Congo river basins; Massif des Bongos rises 1400 m/4593 ft in NW; granite ranges of Mont Karre, 1220 m/4003 ft in W.

Climate Tropical; single rainy season in N (May–Sep); average annual rainfall 875–1000 mm/34–9 in; more equatorial climate in S; rainfall 1500–2000 mm/60–80 in.

Currency 1 CFA Franc (CFAFr) = 100 centimes

Economy Agriculture employs c.85% of working population; also sawmilling, brewing, diamond splitting, leather and tobacco processing.

GDP (2002e) $4.296 bn, per capita $1200

HDI (2002) 0.375

History Part of French Equatorial Africa (Ubangi Shari); autonomous republic within the French community, 1958; independence, 1960; coup deposed country's first President, David Dacko, 1965; Jean-Bédel Bokassa declared himself emperor for life, and country's name changed to the Central African Empire, 1976; Bokassa deposed and country reverted to a republic, 1979; mili-

☐ International Airport

tary coup established Committee for National Recovery, 1981–5; Committee dissolved and National Assembly established, 1987; movement towards multiparty democracy, 1991; legislative and presidential elections, 1993; President Patasse overthrown in coup by General Bozize, 2003; governed by a president, prime minister, and 85-member National Assembly.

Head of State
2003– General François Bozize

Head of Government
2003– Célestin Gaombalet

CHAD

Local name Tchad

Timezone GMT +1

Area 1 284 640 km²/495 871 sq mi

Population total (2002e) 8 997 000

Status Republic

Date of independence 1960

Capital N'djamena

Languages Arabic and French (official), many local languages spoken

Ethnic groups Sara, Bagirmi, and Kreish (30%); Sudanic Arab (26%), Teda (17%), Masalit, Maba, Mimi (6%), over 200 groups

Religions Muslim (50%), Christian (Roman Catholic 21%, Protestant 12%), and local religions

Physical features Landlocked in C Africa; mostly arid, semi-desert plateau at edge of Sahara Desert; average altitude of 200–500 m/650–1650 ft; Tibesti Mts (N) rise to 3415 m/11 204 ft at Emi Koussi; rivers in S (Chari and Logne) flow NW to Lake Chad.

Climate Tropical, moderately wet in S (May–Oct); hot, arid N, almost rainless; C plain hot, dry, with brief rainy season (Jun–Sep).

Currency 1 CFA Franc (CFAFr) = 100 centimes

Economy Severely damaged in recent years by drought, locusts, and civil war; export of cotton, kaolin, animal products; salt mined around L Chad.

GDP (2002e) $9.297 bn, per capita $1000

HDI (2002) 0.365

History Part of French Equatorial Africa, 1908; colonial status, 1920; independence, 1960; Libyan troops occupied the Aozou Strip in extreme N, 1973; fighting between Libyan-supported rebels and French-supported government until cease-fire agreed, 1987; new constitution established a National Assembly, 1989; replaced by a Provisional Council of the Republics, 1991; Chad and Libya presented their individual territorial claims to Aozou Strip, 1990; President Habré ousted by coup and new constitution adopted, 1991; transitional charter, 1993, with elections planned for 1995; Aouzou strip returned to Chad by Libya, 1994; peace agreement, 2001; draft peace agreement signed with the National Resistance Army (ANR), 2003; constitution amended to lift limit on number of presidential terms, May 2004; governed by a president, prime minister, Council of Ministers, and a 57-member Higher Transitional Council.

Head of State
1990–   Idriss Déby

Head of Government
2002–3   Haroun Kabadi
2003–5   Moussa Faki Mahamat
2005–   Pascal Yoadimnadji

□ International Airport

CHANNEL ISLANDS >> UNITED KINGDOM

CHILE

Local name Chile

Timezone GMT −4

Area 756 626 km²/292 058 sq mi (excluding territory claimed in Antarctica)

Population total (2002e) 15 082 000

Status Republic

Date of independence 1818

Capital Santiago

Language Spanish (official)

Ethnic groups Mestizo (92%), Indian (6%), European (2%)

Religions Roman Catholic (89%), Protestant (10%), small Jewish and Muslim minority

Physical features Coastal Cordillera, Pampa Central, and the Chilean Andes are parallel regions running almost the entire length of the country; narrow coastal belt, backed by Andean mountain ridges rising in the NW to 6910 m/22 660 ft at Ojos del Salado; Atacama Desert in far NW, rich in minerals; arable land and forest in the S; S Andes still experiences volcanic activity; main river, the Bío-Bío; Punta Arenas located on southern tip of Chile's mainland; Chilean possessions include a rock measuring 424 m/1390 ft on Horn Island in the Wollaston group, and 1 250 000 km²/ 482 628 sq mi of Antarctic territory.

Climate Varied climate (spans 37° of latitude, with altitudes from Andean peaks to coastal plain); extreme

□ International Airport

Chile (continued)

aridity in N Atacama Desert, temperatures averaging 20°C; cold, wet, and windy in far S; Mediterranean climate in C Chile, with warm wet winters and dry summers; average temperature at Santiago 19°C (Jan), 8°C (Jul); average annual rainfall 375 mm/14.8 in.

Currency 1 Chilean Peso (Ch$) = 100 centavos

Economy Based on agriculture and mining; wheat, corn, potatoes, sugar beet, fruit, livestock; fishing in N, timber in S; copper, iron ore, nitrates, silver, gold, coal, molybdenum; oil and gas discovered in far S (1945); steel, wood pulp, cellulose, mineral processing.

GDP (2002e) $156.1 bn, per capita $10 100

HDI (2002) 0.831

History Originally occupied by South American Indians; arrival of Spanish in 16th-c; part of Viceroyalty of Peru; independence from Spain declared in 1810, with a provisional government set up in Santiago; Spain reasserted its authority, 1814; patriot leader, Bernardo O'Higgins, escaped and returned, with military help of José de San Martín, to defeat the Spanish at Chacabuco,

1817; O'Higgins became first president and independence was declared, 1818; border disputes with Bolivia, Peru, and Argentina brought Chilean victory in War of the Pacific, 1879–84; economic unrest in late 1920s led to military dictatorship under Carlos Ibáñez until 1931; Marxist coalition government of Salvador Allende Gossens ousted in 1973, and replaced by military junta under Augusto Pinochet Ugarte, which banned all political activity; constitution providing for eventual return to democracy came into effect, 1981; plebiscite held in 1988 resulted in a defeat for Pinochet's candidacy as President beyond 1990, and limited political reforms; National Congress restored, comprising a Senate and a Chamber of Deputies in 1990; 6-year term for president agreed in 1994.

Head of State/Government

1990–4	Patricio Aylwin Azócar
1994–9	Eduardo Frei Ruíz-Tagle
1999–	Ricardo Lagos Escobar

CHINA

Local name Zhongguo

Timezone GMT +8

Area 9 597 000 km²/3 705 000 sq mi (also claims island of Taiwan)

Population total (2002e) 1 284 211 000

Status People's republic

Capital Beijing (Peking)

Languages Standard Chinese (Putonghua) or Mandarin, also Yue (Cantonese), Wu, Minbei, Minnan, Xiang, Gan and Hakka

Ethnic groups Han Chinese (92%), over 50 minorities, including Chuang, Manchu, Hui, Miao, Uighur, Hani, Kazakh, Tai and Yao

Religions Officially atheist; widespread Confucianism and Taoism (20%), Buddhism (6%)

Physical features Over two-thirds of country are upland hills, mountains, and plateaus; highest mountains in the W, where the Tibetan plateau rises to average altitude of 4000 m/13 000 ft; Mt Everest rises to 8848m/29 028 ft on the Nepal–Tibet border; land descends to desert/semi-desert of Xinjiang and Inner Mongolia (NE); broad and fertile plains of Manchuria (NE); further E and S, Sichuan basin, drained by Yangtze R (5980 km/ 3720 mi in length); Huang He (Yellow) R runs for 4840 km/3010 mi; heavily populated S plains and E coast, with rich, fertile soils.

Climate Varied, with seven zones: (1) NE China: cold winters, with strong N winds, warm and humid summers, unreliable rainfall; (2) C China: warm and humid summers, sometimes typhoons or tropical cyclones on coast; (3) S China: partly within tropics; wettest area in summer, frequent typhoons; (4) SW China: summer temperatures moderated by altitude, winters mild with little rain; (5) Xizang autonomous region: high plateau

surrounded by mountains; winters severe with frequent light snow and hard frost; (6) Xinjiang and W interior: arid desert climate, cold winters; rainfall well distributed throughout year; (7) Inner Mongolia: extreme continental climate; cold winters, warm summers.

Currency 1 Renminbi Yuan (RMBY, $, Y) = 10 jiao = 100 fen

Economy Since 1949, economy largely based on heavy industry; more recently, light industries; special economic zones set up to attract foreign investment; rich mineral deposits; largest oil-producing country in Far East; major subsistence crops include rice, grain, beans, potatoes, tea, sugar, cotton; economy hit by SARS, 2003.

GDP (2002e) $5.989 tn, per capita $4700

HDI (2002) 0.726

History Chinese civilization believed to date from the Xia dynasty (2200–1799 BC); Qin dynasty (221–207 BC) unified warring states and provided system of centralized control; expansion W during Western and Eastern Han dynasties (206 BC–AD 220), and Buddhism introduced from India; split into Three Kingdoms (Wei, Shu, Wu, 220–65); from 4th-c, series of N dynasties set up by invaders, with several dynasties in S; gradually reunited during the Sui (590–618) and Tang (618–906) dynasties; partition into the Five Dynasties (907–60); Song (Sung) dynasty (960–1279), remembered for literature, philosophy, inventions; Kublai Khan established Mongol Yuan dynasty which ruled China 1279–1368; visits by Europeans, such as Marco Polo, 13th–14th-c; Ming dynasty (1368–1644) overthrown by Manchus, who ruled China during 1644–1911 under the Qing dynasty, and enlarged empire to include Manchuria, Mongolia, Tibet, Taiwan; opposition to foreign imports led to Opium Wars 1839–42, 1858–60; Sino-Japanese War, 1895; Boxer Rising, 1900; Republic of China founded by Sun Yatsen, 1912; unification under

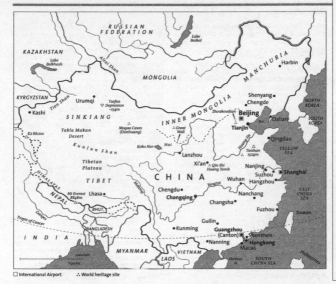

□ International Airport   ∴ World heritage site

Jiang Jieshi (Chiang Kai-shek), who made Nanjing capital in 1928; conflict between Nationalists and Communists led to the Long March, 1934–5, with Communists moving to NW China under Mao Zedong (Mao Tse-tung); Nationalist defeat by Mao and withdrawal to Taiwan, 1949; People's Republic of China proclaimed, 1949, with capital at Beijing; first Five-Year Plan (1953–7) period of nationalization and collectivization; Great Leap Forward, 1958–9, emphasized local authority and establishment of rural communes; Cultural Revolution initiated by Mao Zedong, 1966; many policies reversed after Mao's death in 1976, and drive towards rapid industrialization and wider trade relations with West; after 1980, Deng Xiaoping became the dominant figure within the ruling

Chinese Communist Party, retiring from his last official post in 1990, but remained influential until his death in 1997; governed by elected National People's Congress who elect a State Council; Hong Kong returned to China, 1997; Hu Jintao elected Communist Party chief, 2002.

Head of State
1993–2003 Jiang Zemin
2003–   Hu Jintao

Head of Government
1998–2003 Zhu Rongji
2003–   Wen Jibao

Hong Kong *(Became part of China on 1 July 1997. Because of its special historical interest, details are given below)*

Timezone GMT +8

Area 1066 km²/412 sq mi

Population total (2002e) 7 049 000

Capital Hong Kong

Languages English and Cantonese (official), with Mandarin widely spoken

Ethnic groups Chinese (98%), including many illegal immigrants from China and refugees from Vietnam; 59% of population born in Hong Kong, 37% in China

Religions Buddhist, Taoist and Confucianist majorities, Christian, Muslim, Hindu, Sikh, and Jewish minorities

Physical features Located off the coast of SE China, on the South China Sea; divided into Hong Kong Island, Kowloon, and New Territories (includes most of the colony's 235 islands); highest point, Tai Mo Shan, 957 m/3140 ft; hilly terrain, sharply indented coastline; natural harbour between Kowloon and Hong Kong Island; built-up areas on artificially levelled or reclaimed land.

Climate Subtropical climate, with hot, humid sum-

China (continued)

mers and cool, dry winters; average annual temperatures 16°C (Jan), 29°C (Jul); average annual rainfall 2225 mm/ 88 in.

Currency 1 Hong Kong Dollar (HK$) = 100 cents

Economy Based on banking, import-export trade, tourism, shipbuilding, and a diverse range of light industry; an important freeport acting as a gateway to China for the West.

GDP (2002e) $198.5 bn, per capita $27 200

HDI (2002) 0.888

History Ceded to Britain, 1842, New Territories leased to Britain, 1898; occupied by the Japanese in World War 2; British Crown Colony, Governor represented the British Crown, advised by an Executive Council; in 1997, Britain's 99-year lease of New Territories expired, and Hong Kong was restored to China, 1 July; China has designated Hong Kong a special administrative region; it will remain a freeport, foreign markets will be retained, and the Hong Kong dollar will remain as official currency; new chief executive appointed (first incumbent, Tung Chee-hwa), with new membership of advisory councils; however, anxiety over the colony's political future remains.

Chief Executive
2005–   Donald Tsang

□ International Airport

Macao (Became part of China on 20 December 1999)

Local name Macáu (Port.), Aomen (Chin.)

Timezone GMT +8

Area 16 km²/6 sq mi

Population total (2002e) 464 000

Status Special administrative region of China

Capital Macáu

Languages Portuguese and Cantonese (official), with English generally spoken

Ethnic group Chinese (99%)

Religions Roman Catholic, Buddhist

Physical features Flat, maritime tropical peninsula in SE China; also includes the nearby islands of Taipa and Colôane; on the Pearl R delta, 64 km/40 mi W of Hong Kong; ferry links with Hong Kong.

Climate Subtropical; cool winters, warm summers.

Currency 1 Pataca = 100 avos

Economy Textiles, electronics, toys, tourism, fishing.

History Portuguese trade with China began in 16th-c; became Portuguese colony, 1557; right of permanent occupation granted to Portugal by the Sino-Portuguese treaty, 1887; Portugal changed Macao's status from overseas province to a 'territory under Portuguese administration', 1979; Portugal and China agreed that Macao would revert to China in 1999 as a 'special administrative region' governed by a 23-member Legislative Assembly.

Chief Executive
1999–   Edmund Ho

COLOMBIA

Local name Colombia

Timezone GMT −5

Area 1 140 105 km²/440 080 sq mi

Population total (2002e) 41 008 000

Status Republic

Date of independence 1819

Capital Bogotá

Language Spanish (official)

Ethnic groups Mestizo (58%), European descent (20%), mulatto (14%)

Religion Roman Catholic (95%), other (5%)

Physical features Located in NW South America, includes several island possessions (Providencia, San Andrés and Mapelo); Andes run N–S, dividing narrow coastal plains from forested lowlands of Amazon basin; Cordillera Central rises 5000 m/16 000 ft to the high peak of Huila, 5750 m/18 865 ft; rivers include Vaupés, Magdalena, Cauca, and Guaviare.

Climate Hot, humid coastal plains (NW and W); annual rainfall over 2500 mm/100 in; drier period on Caribbean coast (Dec–Apr); hot, humid tropical lowlands in E.

Currency 1 Colombian Peso (Col$) = 100 centavos

Economy Virtually self-sufficient in food; major crops include coffee, bananas, cotton; leather; gold, silver, emeralds, coal, oil; widespread illegal cocaine trafficking.

GDP (2002e) $251.6 bn, per capita $6100

HDI (2002) 0.772

History Spanish occupation from early 16th-c, displacing Amerindian peoples; governed by Spain within Viceroyalty of Peru, later Viceroyalty of New Granada; independence in 1819, after the campaigns of Simón Bolívar; union with Ecuador, Venezuela, and Panama as Gran Colombia, 1821–30; civil war in 1950s; considerable political unrest in 1980s; new constitution, 1991; ongoing conflict with FARC (Colombian Revolutionary Armed Forces) led to establishment of a FARC-controlled zone in S Colombia, 1998, as part of peace negotiations, but con-

☐ International Airport

flict continuing into 2004; governed by a President, bicameral Congress and Cabinet.

Head of State/Government

1998–2002 Andrés Pastrana Arango
2002– Alvaro Uribe

HUMAN GEOGRAPHY

COMMONWEALTH OF INDEPENDENT STATES, THE (CIS)

A multilateral group of independent states which were once members of the USSR; formed in December 1991; membership included all the states that once comprised the USSR, with the exceptions of the Baltic States (Latvia, Lithuania and Estonia) and Georgia; Georgia joined in December 1993.

>> See map on p.168.

CIS >> ARMENIA, AZERBAIJAN, BELARUS, GEORGIA, KAZAKHSTAN, KYRGYZSTAN, MOLDOVA, RUSSIA, TAJIKISTAN, TURKMENISTAN, UKRAINE, UZBEKISTAN

Commonwealth of Independent States, The (CIS) (continued)

☐ International Airport

COMOROS

Local name Comores

Timezone GMT +3

Area 1862 km²/719 sq mi

Population total (2002e) 583 000

Status Federal republic

Date of independence 1975

Capital Moroni (on Njazidja Island)

Languages Arabic, French (official), Kiswahili

Ethnic groups Comorian (97%), Makua (2%)

Religions Sunni Muslim (86%), Roman Catholic (14%)

Physical features Located in the Mozambique Channel between mainland Africa and Madagascar; group of three volcanic islands: Njazidja (Grande Comore), Nzwani (Anjouan), and Mwali (Mohéli); largest island, Njazidja, with an active volcano, Mt Kartala, 2361 m/7746 ft.

Climate Tropical; dry season (May–Oct), hot, humid season (Nov–Apr); average temperatures, 20°C (Jul), 28°C (Nov).

Currency 1 Comorian Franc (CFr) = 100 centimes

Economy Largely agricultural economy: vanilla, copra, cacao, sisal, coffee, cloves, vegetable oils; perfume.

GDP (2002e) $441 mn, per capita $700

HDI (2002) 0.511

History Under French control, 1843–1912; French overseas territory, 1947; internal political autonomy, 1961; unilateral independence declared, 1975; Mayotte, island in the archipelago, has remained under French rule; established as a Federal Islamic Republic in 1978; a one-party state, governed by a President, Council of Ministers, and unicameral Federal Assembly; new constitu-

☐ International Airport

tion, 2001, provided for the creation of a new federation, the Comoros Union, with greater autonomy for each of the three islands, a president, elected for a 4-year term, heads a central government, and a 33-member legislature.

Head of State/Government
2002	Hamada Madi *Interim*
2002–	Azali Assoumani

Prime Minister
1999–2000	Tarmidi Bianrifi
2000–	Hamada Madi

CONGO

Local name Congo

Timezone GMT +1

Area 341 945 km²/132 047 sq mi

Population total (2002e) 2 899 000

Status Republic

Date of independence 1960

Capital Brazzaville

Language French (official), with local languages, including Kongo and Téké

Ethnic groups Kongo (45%), Sangha (15%), Téké (20%)

Religions Roman Catholic (40.5%), Protestant (9.5%), local traditional beliefs

Physical features Niari valley rises to 1040 m/3412 ft at Mont de la Lékéti; mainly covered by dense grassland, mangrove, and tropical rainforest; rivers include Sangha and Alima in N.

Climate Hot, humid equatorial climate; annual rainfall 1250–1750 mm/50–70 in, annual daily temperature 28–33°C in Brazzaville; dry season (Jun–Sep).

Currency 1 CFA Franc (CFAFr) = 100 centimes

Economy Mainly agriculture and forestry; sugar cane, coffee, cocoa, palm oil, tobacco; oil, timber, diamonds; sugar-refining.

GDP (2002e) $2.5 bn, per capita $512

HDI (2002) 0.512

History Visited by Portuguese, 14th-c; part of French Equatorial Africa, known as 'Middle Congo', 1908–58; independence as Republic of Congo, 1960; military coup created first Marxist state in Africa, renamed People's Republic of the Congo, 1968; Congolese Labour Party (PCT), the single ruling party in Congo, renounced Marxism, 1990; transitional government formed, 1991, and country renamed the Republic of Congo; new

□ International Airport

constitution, 1992, recognized a multi-party system; violence following disputes over the election process, 1993; new constitution, 2001; executive authority vested in the President, elected for a 7-year term, and a bicameral legislature.

Head of State
1997–   Denis Sassou-Nguesso

Head of Government
1997–2002 Bernard Kolelas

COOK ISLANDS >> NEW ZEALAND

CORSICA >> FRANCE

CONGO, THE DEMOCRATIC REPUBLIC OF (from 1997; formerly, ZAIRE)

Local name République Démocratique du Congo

Timezone GMT +1 (W) to +2 (E)

Area 2 234 585 km²/905 365 sq mi

Population total (2002e) 52 557 000

Status Republic

Date of independence 1960

Capital Kinshasa

Languages French (official), English, with various Bantu dialects (including Swahili, Lingala, Ishiluba, and Kikongo) spoken

Ethnic groups Bantu, with Sudanese, Nilotes, Pygmies, Hamite and Angolan minorities

Religions Christian (70%) (Roman Catholic 50%, Protestant 20%), Kimbanguist (10%), Muslim (10%), traditional beliefs (10%)

Physical features Located in C Africa, land rises E from a low-lying basin to a densely forested plateau; Ruwenzori Mts (NE) rise to 5110 m/16 765 ft in the Mt Stanley massif; Mitumba Mts further S; Rift Valley chain of lakes, Albert, Edward, Kivu, and Tanganyika; Congo R.

Climate Equatorial, hot and humid; average annual temperature, 26°C (Jan), 23°C (Jul) in Kinshasa; average

Congo, The Democratic Republic of (continued)

annual rainfall 1125 mm/44 in; dry coastal region; dry season (May–Sep) S of the Equator, (Dec–Feb) N of the Equator.

Currency 1 Congolese Franc (CDF) = 100 centimes

Economy Subsistence farming employs c.80% of population; palm oil, rubber, quinine, fruit, vegetables, tea, cocoa; extensive mineral reserves; world's biggest producer of cobalt; industrial diamonds, copper; coffee, petroleum, cotton, tobacco processing, chemicals, cement.

GDP (2002) $34 bn, per capita $600

HDI (2002) 0.431

History Visited by the Portuguese, 1482; expeditions of Henry Morton Stanley, 1874–7; claimed by King Leopold of Belgium, recognized, 1885; Congo Free State ceded to the state, 1907, and renamed Belgian Congo; independence as the Democratic Republic of the Congo, 1960; shortly after, mineral-rich Katanga (later, Shaba) province claimed independence, leading to civil war; UN peace-keeping force present until 1964; renamed the Republic of Zaire, 1971; further conflict, 1977–8, as Katangese rebels invaded Shaba province from Angola; ongoing conflict during 1980s; new constitution and period of transition established, 1994; further conflict, 1996; Alliance of Democratic Forces for the Liberation of Congo-Zaire, led by Laurent Kabila, take control; new transitional government, 1997; further fighting with rebel movements, 1998, with troops from Uganda and Rwanda supporting rebels, and troops from Zimbabwe, Angola, and Namibia supporting government; assassination of Kabila, 2001; peace negotiations disrupted by ongoing fighting, 2002; power-sharing agreements between government and key rebel groups, 2002; emer-

☐ International Airport   ∴ World heritage site
1 Lake Albert 2 Lake Edward 3 Lake Kivu 4 Lake Tanganyika

gency UN peace-keeping force deployed, 2003; interim government established, with leaders of main rebel groups as vice-presidents, 2003; tensions with Rwanda mount after renegade soldiers seized E town of Bukavu, Jun 2004.

Head of State and Goverment

2001–   Joseph Kabila

COSTA RICA

Local name Costa Rica

Timezone GMT −6

Area 51 022 km²/19 694 sq mi

Population total (2002e) 3 960 000

Status Republic

Date of independence 1821

Capital San José

Language Spanish (official)

Ethnic groups European (87%), mestizo (7%), black/mulatto (3%), E Asian (mostly Chinese) (2%), Amerindian (1%)

Religions Roman Catholic (85%), Protestant (15%)

Physical features Second smallest republic in Central America; formed by series of volcanic ridges: Cordillera de Guanacaste (NW), Cordillera Central, and Cordillera de Talamanca; highest peak, Chirripó Grande, 3819 m/12 529 ft. C plateau; swampy land near coast, rising to tropical forest.

Climate Tropical; small temperature range; abundant rainfall; dry season (Dec–May); average annual temperature 26–8°C.

☐ International Airport

Currency 1 Costa Rican Colón (CR¢) = 100 céntimos

Economy Primarily agriculture, mainly coffee (especially in Meseta Central), bananas, sugar, cattle; silver, bauxite; exploration for oil in collaboration with Mexico.

GDP (2002e) $32 bn, per capita $8300

HDI (2002) 0.820

History Visited by Columbus, 1502; named Costa Rica ('rich coast') in the belief that vast gold treasures existed;

independence from Spain, 1821; member of Federation of Central America, 1824–39; new constitution, 1949, established Costa Rica as a democratic state; governed by an executive President, Legislative Assembly, and Cabinet.

Head of State/Government
1998–2002 Miguel Angel Rodríguez Echeverría
2002– Abel Pacheco

CÔTE D'IVOIRE

Local name Côte d'Ivoire

Timezone GMT

Area 322 462 km²/124 503 sq mi

Population total (2002e) 16 805 000

Status Republic

Date of independence 1960

Capital Yamoussoukro (formerly Abidjan)

Languages French (official), Akan, Kru

Ethnic groups Akan (41%), Kru (17%), Voltaic (16%), Malinke (15%), Southern Mande (10%)

Religions Traditional beliefs (63%), Muslim (25%), Christian (12%)

Physical features Sandy beaches and lagoons backed by broad forest-covered coastal plain; Mt Nimba massif in NW, 1752 m /5748 ft; rivers include Comoé, Sassandra, Bandama

Climate Tropical, varying with distance from coast; average annual rainfall at Yamoussoukro 2100 mm/ 83 in; average annual temperatures 25–7°C.

Currency 1 CFA Franc (CFAFr) = 100 centimes

Economy Largely based on agriculture (employs c.82% of the population): palm oil, rice, maize, ground nuts, bananas; world's largest cocoa producer, third largest coffee producer.

GDP (2002e) $24.03 bn, per capita $1400

HDI (2002) 0.428

History Explored by Portuguese, 15th-c; declared a French protectorate, 1889; colony, 1893; territory within French West Africa, 1904; independence, 1960; constitution provides for multi-party system, but opposition parties only allowed since 1990; post of Prime

☐ International Airport ∴ World heritage site

Minister created, 1990; governed by a National Assembly, executive President, and Council of Ministers; fighting between rebel groups, 2002; French intervention to support ceasefire, 2002; UN mission to support peace plan, 2003; ceasefire (Nov 2003), broken (Nov 2004).

Head of State
2000– Laurent Gbagbo

Head of Government
2003– Seydou Diarra

CROATIA

Local name Hrvatska

Timezone GMT +1

Area 56 540 km²/21 825 sq mi

Population total (2002e) 4 405 000

Status Republic

Date of independence 1991

Capital Zagreb

Language Croatian

Ethnic groups (1990) Croat (75%), Serb (12%), Slovenes (1%)

Religions Roman Catholic, Eastern Orthodox

Physical features Fertile Pannonian Plain in C and E; mountainous, barren coastal region near Dinaric Alps; Adriatic coast to W; one third of country forested; main rivers: Drava, Danube, Sava; coastal Velebit and Velika

HUMAN GEOGRAPHY

Croatia (continued)

Kapela ranges reach heights of 2200 m/7200 ft; islands include Korčula, Lošinj, Dugi Otok, Cres, Krk.

Climate Continental in Pannonian Basin: average temperatures 19°C (Jul), –1°C (Jan); average annual rainfall 750 mm/30 in; Mediterranean climate on Adriatic coast: average temperatures 24°C (Jul), 6°C (Jan).

Currency 1 kuna = 100 lipa

Economy Agriculture; corn, oats, sugar-beet, potatoes, meat and dairy products; tourism on Adriatic coast; electrical engineering; metal-working; machinery manufacture; lumber; aluminium, textiles, petroleum refining, chemicals, rubber; natural resources include bauxite, coal, copper, iron; all economic activity adversely affected by war of independence.

GDP (2002e) $43.12 bn, per capita $9800

HDI (2002) 0.809

History Slavic Croat tribes (Chrobati, Hrvati) migrated to White Russia (now Ukraine) during 6th-c; converted to Christianity between 7th and 9th-c and adopted Roman alphabet; Frankish and Byzantine invaders repelled, and Croat kingdom reached its peak during 11th-c; Turkish defeat of Hungary in 1526 placed Pannonian Croatia under Ottoman rule; rest of Croatia elected Ferdinand of Austria as king and fought Turkey; Croatia and Slovenia became part of Hungary until collapse of Austria-Hungary in 1918; formed the Kingdom of Serbs, Croats and Slovenes with Montenegro and Serbia, 1918; became part of Yugoslavia, 1929; proclaimed an independent state during occupation by the Axis Powers, 1941–5; became a republic of Yugoslavia again, 1945; nationalist upsurges during 1950s against Communist rule, culminating in a bloody war with Serbian-dominated Yugoslav army, 1991; declaration of independence, 1991; autonomy claimed by Serb-dominated Krajina area; UN peacekeeping forces deployed, 1992; continued fighting between Croatian forces and Bosnian Serbs in the civil war in

☐ International Airport

Bosnia-Herzegovina; 1995 offensive restored territorial balance in Bosnia; ceasefire followed by peace treaty (Nov) recognized Bosnian-Croat Federation in W Bosnia; governed by an Assembly consisting of a Chamber of Deputies and a Chamber of Districts.

Head of State
2000– Stjepan Mesic

Head of Government
2003– Ivo Sanader

CUBA

Local name Cuba

Timezone GMT –5

Area 110 860 km²/42 792 sq mi

Population total (2002e) 11 267 000

Status Republic

Date of independence 1902

Capital Havana

Language Spanish (official)

Ethnic groups Mulatto (50%), Spanish (37%), African origin (11%)

Religions Roman Catholic (40%), Protestant (3%), Afro-Cuban syncretist (2%), non-religious (55%): Castro regime discourages religious practice

Physical features Archipelago in the Caribbean Sea, comprising the island of Cuba, Isla de la Juventud, and c.1600 islets and cays; main island of Cuba, 1250 km/

☐ International Airport

777 mi; three mountainous regions range E–W, the Oriental, including Cuba's highest peak, Pico Turquino, 2005 m/6578 ft, Central, and Occidental ranges; longest river is Rio Cauto in E.

Climate Subtropical climate, warm and humid; average annual temperature 25°C; dry season (Nov– Apr); mean annual rainfall, 1375 mm/54 in; hurricanes (Jun–Nov).

Currency 1 Cuban Peso (Cub$) = 100 centavos

Economy World's second largest sugar producer (accounting for 75% of export earnings); world's fifth largest producer of nickel; fish, coffee, tobacco, citrus fruits, rice.

GDP (2002e) $30.69 bn, per capita $2700

HDI (2002) 0.795

History Visited by Columbus, 1492; Spanish colony until 1898, following revolution under José Martí with support of USA: independence, 1902; struggle against dictatorship of General Batista led by Fidel Castro Ruz, finally successful in 1959, and a Communist state established; invasion of Cuban exiles with US support defeated at Bay of Pigs, 1961; US naval blockade, after Soviet installation of missile bases discovered in Cuba (Cuban Missile Crisis), 1962; Communist Party of Cuba established as the sole legal party, 1965; President of the State Council is Head of State; State Council, appointed by National Assembly of People's Power.

Head of State/Government
1976–   Fidel Castro Ruz

CYPRUS

Local names Kipros (Greek), Kibris (Turkish)

Timezone GMT +2

Area 9251 km²/3571 sq mi

Population total (2002e) 802 000

Status Republic

Date of independence 1960

Capital Nicosia (proposed new name Lefkosia, 1995–)

Languages Greek and Turkish (official), English

Ethnic groups Greek (78%), Turkish (18%), other (4%)

Religions Greek Orthodox (78%), Sunni Muslim (18%), other Christian (4%)

Physical features Third largest island in Mediterranean; Kyrenia Mts extend 150 km/90 mi along N coast, Mt Kyparissovouno, 1024 m/3360 ft; forest-covered Troödos Mts in SW, rising to 1951 m/6401 ft at Mt Olympus; fertile alluvial Mesaoria plain extends across island centre; SE plateau region slopes towards indented coastline, with several long, sandy beaches; major rivers include the Pedios, Karyota, Kouris.

Climate Mediterranean, with hot, dry summers and warm, wet winters; average annual rainfall ranges from 300–400 mm/12–16 in on the Mesaoria Plain to 1200 mm/47 in in the Troödos Mts; mean daily temperatures in Nicosia 10°C (Jan), 28°C (Jul); temperatures range from 22°C on Troödos Mts, to 29°C on Central plain (Jul–Aug); snow on higher land in winter.

Currency 1 Cyprus Pound (£C) = 100 cents

Economy Main exports include cement, clothing, footwear, citrus, potatoes, grapes, wine; tourism also recovering (now accounting for c.15% of national income); Famagusta (chief port prior to 1974 Turkish invasion) now under Turkish occupation, and declared closed by Cyprus government; Turkish Cypriot economy heavily dependent on agriculture.

GNP (1996) $8.9 bn, per capita $1370

HDI (1998) 0.886

History Recorded history of 4000 years; rulers included Greeks, Ptolemies, Persians, Romans, Byzantines, Arabs,

□ International Airport

Franks, Venetians, Turks (1571–1878). and British; British Crown Colony from 1925; Greek Cypriot demands for union with Greece (*enosis*) led to guerrilla warfare, under Grivas and Makarios, and four-year state of emergency, 1955–9; independence, 1960, with Britain retaining sovereignty over bases at Akrotiri and Dhekelia; Greek–Turkish fighting throughout 1960s, with UN peacekeeping force sent in 1964; Greek junta engineered coup d'état, 1974; Turkish invasion in 1974 led to occupation of over a third of the island; island divided into two parts by the Attila Line, cutting through Nicosia where it is called the Green Line; almost all Turks now live in N sector (37% of island); governed by a President (head of state), elected by the Greek community, and House of Representatives; Turkish members ceased to attend in 1983, when the Turkish community declared itself independent (as 'Turkish Republic of Northern Cyprus' (TRNC), with Rauf Denktas as president, recognized only by Turkey); UN peace proposals rejected, 1984; summit meeting between Kyprianou (Greek president of Cyprus) and Denktas failed, 1985; UN-sponsored peace negotiations, 1997; further talks, 2002; Green Line opened for daytime crossings, 2003; UN plan to reunite the island rejected by Greek Cypriots, 2004; inter-island trade between TRNC and Greek Cyprus resumed, Aug 2004.

Head of State/Government
2003–   Tassos Papadopoulos

CZECHOSLOVAKIA >> CZECH REPUBLIC; SLOVAK REPUBLIC

CZECH REPUBLIC

Local name Česká republika

Timezone GMT +1

Area 78 864 km²/30 441 sq mi

Population total (2002e) 10 210 000

Status Republic

Date of independence 1993

Capital Prague

Languages Czech (official), with several minorities

Ethnic groups Czech (94%), Slovak (4%), Hungarian, Polish, German, and Ukrainian minorities

Religions Roman Catholic (39%), Protestant (2%)

Physical features Landlocked in C Europe; Bohemian Massif, average height, 900 m/2953 ft, surrounds the Bohemian basin in W; Elbe-Moldau river system flows N into Germany; fertile plains of the Morava River divide Czech from Slovak Republic; c.40% land is arable.

Climate Continental, with warm, humid summers and cold, dry winters; average annual temperatures 2°C (Jan), 19°C (Jul) in Prague; average annual rainfall, 483 mm/19 in.

Currency 1 Koruna (Kcs) = 100 haléř

Economy Steel production around Ostrava coalfields; machinery, iron, glass, chemicals, motor vehicles, cement; wheat, sugar beet, potatoes, rye, corn, barley.

GDP (2002e) $157.1 bn, per capita $15 300

HDI (2002) 0.849

History From 880 ruled by the Premyslid dynasty; rise of Bohemian royal power, 14th-c; ruled by Austrian Habsburgs, early 17th-c; Czech lands united with Slovakia to form separate state of Czechoslovakia, 1918; occupied by

☐ International Airport

Germany, 1938; government in exile in London during World War 2; Czechoslovakian independence, with loss of some territory to USSR, 1946; communist rule imposed by Russia following 1948 coup; attempt at liberalization by Dubček terminated by intervention of Warsaw Pact troops, 1968; fall from power of the Communist Party, 1989; 1992 agreement to divide Czechoslovakia into its constituent republics, Czech and Slovak, by Jan 1993; Czech Republic now comprises former provinces of Bohemia, Silesia, Moravia; governed by a Chamber of Deputies and (1996) 81-member Senate.

Head of State
2003–   Václav Klaus

Head of Government
2005–   Jiri Paroubek

DENMARK

Local name Danmark

Timezone GMT +1

Area 43 076 km²/16 627 sq mi (excluding Greenland and Faroe Islands)

Population total (2002e) 5 364 000

Status Kingdom

Capital Copenhagen

Language Danish (official)

Ethnic groups Danish (97%), Turkish (0.5%), other Scandinavian (0.4%)

Religions Evangelical Lutheran (97%), Roman Catholic (0.5%), Jewish (0.1%)

Physical features Consists of most of the Jutland peninsula, several islands in the Baltic Sea, and some of the N Frisian Is in the North Sea; coastline 3400 km/ 2100 mi; uniformly low-lying; no large rivers and few lakes; shoreline indented by many lagoons and fjords, largest is Lim Fjord.

☐ International Airport

Climate Modified by Gulf Stream; cold and cloudy winters, warm and sunny summers; average annual temperatures range from 0.5°C (Jan) to 17°C (Jul); average annual rainfall 800 mm/32 in.

Currency 1 Danish Krone (Dkr) = 100 øre

Economy Lack of raw materials has resulted in development of processing industries; intensive agriculture; wide range of food processing; machinery, textiles, furniture, electronics; dairy products.

GDP (2002e) $155.3 bn, per capita $28 900

HDI (2002) 0.926

History Part of Viking kingdoms, 8th–10th-c; Danish Empire under Canute, 11th-c; joined with Sweden and Norway under Queen Margrethe of Denmark, 1389; Sweden separated from union in 16th-c, followed by Norway, 1814; Schleswig-Holstein lost to Germany, 1864; N Schleswig returned after plebiscite, 1920; occupied by Germany during World War 2; Iceland independent, 1944; Greenland and Faroe Is remain dependencies; constitutional monarchy since 1849; unicameral system adopted, 1953; legislative power lies with the Monarch and the Diet jointly.

Head of State (Monarch)
1972– Margrethe II

Head of Government
1993–2001 Poul Nyrop Rasmussen
2001– Anders Fogh Rasmussen

Faroe Islands (Faeroe)

Local name Faerøerne (Danish)

Timezone GMT

Area 1400 km²/540 sq mi

Population total (2002e) 47 000

Status Self-governing region of Denmark

Capital Tórshavn

Languages Faroese (official, derived from Old Norse), Danish

Religion Evangelical Lutheran

Physical features Group of 22 sparsely vegetated volcanic islands in the N Atlantic between Iceland and the Shetland Is; 17 inhabited; largest islands: Strømø, Østerø, Vagø, Suderø, Sandø, Borðø.

Climate Mild winters, overcast cool summers.

Currency 1 Danish Krone (Dkr) = 100 øre

Economy Main produce: fish, crafts, potatoes; denmark provides an annual economic subsidy.

History Settled by Norse, 8th-c; part of Norway, 11th-c; passed to Denmark, 1380; parliament restored, 1852; self-governing region of Denmark since 1948; unicameral Parliament (*Lagting*) consists of 34 members.

Head of State (Monarch)
1972– Margrethe II

Head of Government
2004– Joannes Eidesgaard

Greenland (Kalaalit Nunaat)

Local names Kalaalit Nunaat (Greenlandic), Grønland (Danish), Kalâtdlit-Nunât (Inuit)

Timezone GMT 0, -1, -4

Area 2 175 600 km²/839 800 sq mi

Population total (2002e) 57 000

Status Self-governing province of Denmark

Capital Nuuk (Godthåb)

Languages Danish (official), Inuit

Ethnic groups Largely Inuit (Eskimo), with Danish admixtures

Religions Lutheran, Shamanist

Physical features Located in N Atlantic and Arctic Oceans; largely covered by an ice-cap (up to 4300 m/14 000 ft thick); coastal mountains rise to 3702 m/12 145 ft at Gunnbjørn Fjeld (SE); less than 5% of island habitable.

Climate Arctic to subarctic.

Currency 1 Danish Krone (Dkr) = 100 Yre

Economy Largely dependent on fishing from ice-free SW ports; hunting for seal and fox furs in N and E; reserves of lead, zinc, molybdenum, uranium, coal, cryolite.

History Settled by seal-hunting Eskimos from North America, c.2500 BC; Norse settlers in SW, 12th–15th-c AD;

□ International Airport

Denmark (continued)

explored by Frobisher and Davis, 16th-c; Danish colony from 1721; self-governing province of Denmark, 1979; elected Provincial Council sends two members to the Danish Parliament.

Head of State (Monarch)
1972–   Margrethe II

Head of Government
2002–   Hans Enoksen

DJIBOUTI

Local name Jumhouriyya Djibouti

Timezone GMT +3

Area 23 200 km²/8958 sq mi

Population total (2002e) 473 000

Status Republic

Date of independence 1977

Capital Djibouti

Language Arabic (official)

Ethnic groups Somali (47%), Afar (20%), Arab (mostly Yemeni) (6%), European (4%), other refugees (10%)

Religions Muslim (94%), Christian (Roman Catholic 4%, Protestant 1%, Orthodox 1%)

Physical features Located in NE Africa; series of plateaux dropping down from mountains to flat, low-lying, rocky desert; fertile coastal strip around the Gulf of Tadjoura; highest point, Moussa Ali, rising to 2020 m/6627 ft in the N.

Climate Semi-arid climate, with hot season (May–Sep); very high temperatures on coastal plain all year round; average temperatures 26°C (Jan), 36°C (Jul); slightly lower humidity and temperatures in interior highlands; low rainfall; average annual rainfall 130 mm/5 in.

Currency 1 Djibouti Franc (DF, DjFr) = 100 centimes

Economy Crop-based agriculture possible only with irrigation; livestock-raising among nomadic population; some fishing on coast; port of Djibouti provides an important transit point for Red Sea trade, particularly for Ethiopia; small industrial sector.

GDP (2002e) $619 mn, per capita $1300

HDI (2002) 0.445

History French colonial interest in mid-19th-c; annexed by France as French Somaliland, 1896; French Overseas Territory, following World War 2; French Terri-

☐ International Airport

tory of the Afars and the Issas, 1967; independence, 1977. Political parties combined in 1979 to form People's Progress Assembly (RPP) as single ruling party; overwhelming majority voted in favour of a multi-party constitution, 1992; governed by a President, a Legislative Chamber, an executive Prime Minister, and a Council.

Head of State
1999–   Ismail Omar Guelleh

Head of Government
2001–   Dileila Mohamed Dileila

DOMINICA

Local name Dominica

Timezone GMT –4

Area 751 km²/290 sq mi

Population total (2002e) 71 700

Status Independent republic within the Commonwealth

Date of independence 1978

Capital Roseau

Languages English (official), with French widely spoken

Ethnic groups African or mixed African-European descent (97%), Amerindian (2%)

Religions Christian (Roman Catholic 77%, Protestant 16%)

Physical features Island in the Windward group of the West Indies; c.50 km/30 mi long and 26 km/16 mi wide; rises to 1447 m/4747 ft at Morne Diablotin; volcanic origin; central ridge, with several rivers; 67% of land area forested.

Climate Warm and humid tropical climate; temperatures ranging 25.6–32.2°C; rainy season (Jun–Oct); heavy rainfall, varies from 1750 mm/70 in average on the coast, to 6250 mm/246 in inland.

Currency 1 East Caribbean Dollar (EC$) = 100 cents

Economy Agriculture; tourism; coconut-based products, cigars, citrus fruits (notably limes), bananas, coconuts, bay oil.

GDP (2002e) $380 mn, per capita $5400

HDI (2002) 0.779

History Visited by Columbus, 1493; colonization attempts by French and British in 18th-c; British Crown Colony from 1805; part of Federation of the West Indies, 1958–62; independent republic within the Commonwealth, 1978; governed by a House of Assembly, President, Prime Minister, and Cabinet.

Head of State
1998–2003   Vernon Shaw
2003–   Dr Nicholas Liverpool

Head of Government
2001–4   Pierre Charles
2004–   Roosevelt Skerrit

□ International Airport

DOMINICAN REPUBLIC

Local name República Dominicana

Timezone GMT –4

Area 48 442 km²/18 699 sq mi

Population total (2002e) 8 833 000

Status Republic

Date of independence 1844

Capital Santo Domingo

Language Spanish (official)

Ethnic groups Spanish, or mixed Spanish and African descent

Religions Roman Catholic (92%), other (mostly Evangelical Protestant and followers of voodoo) (8%)

Physical features Crossed NW–SE by Cordillera Central, with many peaks over 3000 m/10 000 ft; Pico Duarte, 3175 m/10 416 ft is highest peak in the Caribbean; wide coastal plain in E; main rivers include Yaque del Sur, Yaque del Norte, Yuna (E).

Climate Tropical maritime climate with rainy season (May–Nov); Santo Domingo, average temperature 23.9°C (Jan), 27.2°C (Jul); annual rainfall 1400 mm/55 in; hurricanes (Jun–Nov).

Currency 1 Dominican Peso (RD$, DR$) = 100 centavos

Economy Mainly agriculture, especially sugar, cocoa; tourism expanding with new resort complexes on N coast.

GNP (2002e) $53.78 bn, per capita $6300

HDI (2002) 0.727

□ International Airport

History Visited by Columbus, 1492; Spanish colony, 16th–17th-c; E province of Santo Domingo remained Spanish after partition of Hispaniola, 1697; taken over by Haiti on several occasions; independence from Haiti, 1844, as Dominican Republic; occupied by USA, 1916–24, 1965; comprises 26 provinces and a National District which contains the capital; governed by a President and National Congress (Senate and Chamber of Deputies).

Head of State/Government
2000–4   Hipólito Mejía
2004–   Leonel Fernandez

EAST TIMOR

Local name (Port.) Timor Leste, (Tetum) Timor Loro Sae

Timezone GMT +8

Area 14 874 km²/5743 sq mi

Population total (2002e) 738 000

Status Republic

Date of independence 2002

Capital Dili

Language Tetum and Portuguese (official), Indonesian and English widely spoken

Ethnic groups Tetum

Religions Roman Catholic (91.4%), traditional animist beliefs

Physical features Occupies E half of the mountainous island of Timor and the enclave of Oecussi (Ambeno) in West Timor, SE Asia, in the Sunda Group, NW of Australia; W half of the island belongs to Indonesia (part of East Nusa Tengarra province); highest peak, Tata Mailau (2950 m/9679 ft); many rivers flowing from the mountains through the coastal plains.

Climate Hot with monsoon rains falling between December and March; average daily temperature 32°C (Oct–Dec), 21°C (Jan–Sep).

Currency 1 US dollar = 100 cents

Economy 90% of the population live off the land, with one in three households living below the poverty line; coffee is the main export crop, also coconuts, cloves, cacao, and marble; offshore gas and oil to be exploited from 2004.

GDP (2002e) $440 mn, per capita $500

History Former Portuguese colony of East Timor declared itself independent as the Democratic Republic of East Timor, 1975; invaded by Indonesian forces and annexed, the claim not recognized by the UN; administered by Indonesia as the province of Timor Timur; considerable local unrest (1989–90), and mounting international concern over civilian deaths; independence movement (Fretilin) largely supressed by 1993; UN-sponsored talks, 1993; ongoing conflict, mid-1990s; President Habibie grants referendum, 1999, resulting in 78.5% vote in favour of independence, immediately followed by widespread violence and destruction of property by pro-Jakarta militia groups and major refugee movements; growing threat to the UN presence in Dili led to arrival of UN-sponsored, Australian-led intervention force; administered by the UN since 1999, with a transitional administration, 2000; elections for a 38-member Constituent Assembly, 2001; Council of Ministers of the Second Transitional Government, 2001; presidential elections (Apr), followed by full independence, May 2002; UN Mission of Support in East Timor (Unmiset) to remain in place until 2003; parliamentary system of government with a largely ceremonial president.

BANDA SEA

INDONESIA

Pulau Atauro

Baucau

Liquica • Dili • Manatuto

Ermera △ *Tata Mailau* 2950m • Viqueque *Pulau Jaco*

Pante Makasar Suai

INDONESIA

EAST TIMOR

CHINA

TIMOR SEA

500km

500mi

AUSTRALIA

□ International Airport   1 AMBENO (OECUSSI)

Head of State
2002–   Xanana Gusmao

Head of Government
2001–   Mari Alkatiri

ECUADOR

Local name Ecuador

Timezone GMT –5

Area 270 699 km²/104 490 sq mi (including the Galápagos Islands, 7812 km²/3015 sq mi)

Population total (2002e) 13 095 000

Status Republic

Date of independence 1830

Capital Quito

Languages Spanish (official), with Quechua also spoken

Ethnic groups Quechua (50%), mestizo (40%), white (8.5%), other Amerindian (5%)

Religions Roman Catholic (94%), other (6%)

Physical features Located in NW South America; includes the Galápagos Is, Ecuadorian island group on the equator 970 km/600 mi W of South American mainland; coastal plain in the W, descending from rolling hills (N) to broad lowland basin; Andean uplands in C rising to snow-capped peaks which include Cotopaxi, 5896 m/19343 ft; forested alluvial plains in the E, dissected by rivers flowing from the Andes towards the Amazon (source of the Amazon located in Peru).

Climate Hot and humid, wet equatorial climate on coast; rain throughout year (especially Dec–Apr); average annual rainfall 1115 mm/44 in; average annual temperatures in Quito, 15°C (Jan), 14°C (Jul).

Currency 1 Sucre (Su, S/.) = 100 centavos

Economy Agriculture (employs c.35% of population); beans, cereals, livestock; bananas, coffee, fishing (especially shrimps); petrochemicals, steel, cement, pharmaceuticals; oil piped from the Oriente basin in E to refineries at Esmeraldas.

GDP (2002e) $42.65 bn, per capita $3200

□ International Airport

HDI (2002) 0.732

History Formerly part of Inca Empire; taken by Spanish, 1534; within Viceroyalty of New Granada; independent, 1822; joined with Panama, Colombia, and Venezuela to form Gran Colombia; left union, to become independent republic, 1830; highly unstable political history; constitution, 1978; comprises 21 provinces, including the Galápagos Is, each administered by a governor; governed by a President and a unicameral National Congress.

Head of State/Government

1998–2000	Jamil Mahuad Witt
2000–2	Gustavo Noboa Bejarano
2002–	Lucio Gutierrez

EGYPT

Local name Misr

Timezone GMT +2

Area 1 001 449 km²/386 559 sq mi

Population total (2002e) 66 341 000

Status Republic

Date of independence 1922

Capital Cairo

Language Arabic (official)

Ethnic group Population mainly of E Hamitic origin (90%)

Religions Sunni Muslim (c.90%), minority largely Coptic Christian (c.10%)

Physical features R Nile flows N from Sudan, dammed S of Aswan, creating L Nasser; huge delta N of Cairo, 250 km/150 mi across and 160 km/100 mi N–S; narrow Eastern Desert, sparsely inhabited, between Nile and Red Sea; broad Western Desert, covering over two-thirds of the country; Sinai Peninsula (S), desert region in E with mountains rising to 2637 m/8651 ft at Gebel Katherina, Egypt's highest point; 90% of population lives on Nile floodplain (c.3% of country's area).

Climate Mainly desert climate, except for 80 km/50 mi wide Mediterranean coastal fringe; very hot on coast where dust-laden khamsin wind blows N from Sahara (Mar–Jun); Alexandria, average maximum daily temperatures 18–30°C; elsewhere rainfall less than 50 mm/2 in.

Currency 1 Egyptian Pound (E£, LE) = 100 piastres

Economy Agriculture on floodplain of R Nile accounts for about a third of national income; building of Aswan High Dam extended irrigated cultivation; a major tourist area.

Egypt (continued)

GDP (2002e) $289.8 bn, per capita $4000

HDI (2002) 0.642

History Neolithic cultures on R Nile from c.6000 BC; Pharaoh dynasties from c.3100 BC; Egyptian power greatest during the New Empire period, 1576–1085 BC; became Persian province, 6th-c BC; conquered by Alexander the Great, 4th-c BC; Ptolemaic Pharaohs ruled Egypt until 30 BC; conquered by Arabs, AD 672; Suez Canal constructed, 1869; revolt in 1879 put down by British, 1882; British protectorate from 1914; declared independence, 1922; King Farouk deposed by Nasser, 1952; Egypt declared a republic, 1953; attack on Israel followed by Israeli invasion, 1967; Suez Canal remained blocked, 1967–75; changed name to Arab Republic of Egypt, 1971; Yom Kippur War against Israel, 1973; Israel returned disputed Taba Strip, 1989; participated in Gulf War with US-led coalition, 1991; governed by a People's National Assembly, President, Prime Minister, and Council of Ministers.

Head of State
1981–   Mohammed Hosni Mubarak

Head of Government
2004–   Ahmed Nazif

□ International Airport   ∴ World heritage site   – – Border in dispute

EL SALVADOR

Local name El Salvador

Timezone GMT –6

Area 21 476 km²/8290 sq mi

Population total (2002e) 6 354 000

Status Republic

Date of independence 1841

Capital San Salvador

Language Spanish (official)

Ethnic groups Spanish-Indian (89%), Indian (mostly Pipil) (5%)

Religions Roman Catholic (93%), other (mostly Evangelical Protestant) (7%)

Physical features Smallest of Central America republics; two volcanic ranges run E–W; narrow coastal belt in S, rises to mountains in N; highest point, Santa Ana, 2381 m/7812 ft; many volcanic lakes; earthquakes common.

Climate Varies greatly with altitude; hot tropical on coastal lowlands; single rainy season (May–Oct); temperate uplands; average annual temperature at San Salvador 23°C (Jul), 22°C (Jan); average annual rainfall 1775 mm/70 in.

Currency 1 Colón (ES¢) = 100 centavos

Economy Largely based on agriculture; main crops coffee and cotton; sugar, maize, balsam (world's main source); chemicals, rubber, rubber goods, oil products.

□ International Airport

GDP (2002e) $29.41 bn, per capita $4600

HDI (2002) 0.706

History Originally part of the Aztec kingdom; conquest by Spanish, 1526; independence from Spain, 1821; member of the Central American Federation until its dissolution in 1839; independent republic, 1841; war with Honduras, 1965, 1969; considerable political unrest in 1970s and 80s, with guerrilla activity directed against the US-supported government; civil war, 1979–91; peace plan agreed, 1991; governed by a President and Council of Ministers; unicameral Legislative Assembly.

Head of State/Government
1999–2004 Francisco Flores
2004–   Tony Saca

ENGLAND >> UNITED KINGDOM

EQUATORIAL GUINEA

Local name Guinea Ecuatorial

Timezone GMT +1

Area 26 016 km²/10 042 sq mi (mainland area)

28 051 km²/10 828 sq mi (total area)

Population total (2002e) 498 000

Status Republic

Date of independence 1968

Capital Malabo

Language Spanish (official)

Ethnic groups Mainland population, mainly Fang (83%), Bubi (10%), Ndowe (4%), Annobonés (2%), Bujeba (1%)

Religions Roman Catholic (80%), traditional beliefs (5%)

Physical features Located in WC Africa; comprises the mainland area (Rio Muni) and several islands in the Gulf of Guinea; mainland rises sharply from a narrow coast of mangrove swamps towards the heavily forested African plateau; Bioko, fertile volcanic island in NW, contains Guinea's highest point, Pico de Basilé, 3007 m/ 9865 ft.

Climate Hot and humid equatorial climate; average maximum daily temperature, 29–32°C; average annual rainfall c.2000 mm/80 in.

Currency 1 CFA Franc (CFA Fr) = 100 centimes

Economy Largely based on agriculture; cocoa, coffee, timber, bananas, cassava, palm oil, sweet potatoes.

GDP (2002e) $1.27 bn, per capita $2700

HDI (2002) 0.679

☐ International Airport

History First visited by Europeans in 15th-c; island of Fernando Póo claimed by Portugal, 1494–1788; occupied by Britain, 1781–1843; rights to the area acquired by Spain, 1844; independence, 1968; military coup, 1975; governed by Supreme Military Council headed by a President; new constitution, 1991; first multi-party elections, 1993.

Head of State
1968–79   Francisco Macias Nguema
1979–   Teodoro Obiang Nguema Mbasogo

Head of Government
2004–   Miguel Abia Biteo Borico

ERITREA

Local name Ertra

Timezone GMT +3

Area 93 700 km²/36 200 sq mi

Population total (2002e) 3 981 000

Status Republic

Date of Independence 1993

Capital Asmara

Language Tigrinya, Tigray, Amharic

Ethnic groups Tigray, Amhara

Religions Islam (50%), Coptic Christianity (50%)

Pysical features Ethiopian plateau drops to low plains; E plain includes the Danakil Depression, descending to 116 m/381 ft below sea level.

Climate Tropical climate varied by altitude; annual average temperature at Asmara, 16°C, at Mitsiwa (on coast) 30°C; hot, semi-arid NE and SE lowlands receive

☐ International Airport

less than 500 mm/20 in rainfall annually; severe droughts have caused widespread famine.

Currency Ethiopian birr replaced (1997) by the nakfa

Eritrea (continued)

Economy Largely devoted to agriculture, but badly affected by drought, and heavily dependent on irrigation and foreign aid; textiles, leather, salt, food production.

GDP (2002e) $3.3 bn, per capita $700

HDI (2002) 0.421

History Federated as part of Ethiopia, 1952; province of Ethiopia, 1962, led to political unrest; civil war in 1970s, with major gains for separatists; Soviet- and Cuban-backed government forces regained most areas, 1978; fall of President Mengistu (1991) led to new status as autonomous region, with provisional government established by Eritrean People's Liberation Front; referendum followed by declaration of independence, 1993; transitional government for 4 years, consisting of a National Assembly, which elects the president, and a State Council; escalating conflict with Ethiopia over disputed border territory, 1999–2000; Permanent Court of Arbitration at The Hague issued border ruling, 2002; government accepted ruling 'in principle', Nov 2004.

Head of State
1993– Isaias Afwerki

ESTONIA

Local name Eesti

Timezone GMT +2

Area 45 100 km²/17 409 sq mi

Population total (2002e) 1 359 000

Status Republic

Date of independence 1991

Capital Tallinn

Languages Estonian (official), also Russian

Ethnic groups Estonian (65%), Russian (28%), Ukrainian (3%), Belorussian (2%)

Religions Evangelical Lutheran, with Orthodox minority

Physical features Consists of mainland area and c.800 islands (including the Baltic island of Saaremaa); S covered with morainal hills, C with elongated glacial hills usually arrayed in the direction of glacial movement; most lakes and rivers drain either E into Lake Peipus, N into the Gulf of Finland; a few W into Gulf of Riga.

Climate Mild climate. Average annual temperatures –6°C (Jan) and 17°C (Jul); average annual rainfall 650 mm/26 in.

Currency 1 Kroon = 100 cents

Economy Major industries: agricultural machinery, electric motors; agricultural produce of grain, vegetables; livestock.

GDP (2002e) $15.52 bn, per capita $11 000

HDI (2002) 0.826

History Ceded to Russia, 1721; independence, 1918; proclaimed a Soviet Socialist Republic, 1940; occupied by

□ International Airport

Germany in World War 2; resurgence of nationalist movement in the 1980s; declared independence, 1991; 105-member Parliament; 495-member Congress of Estonia.

Head of State
1992–2001 Lennart Meri
2001– Arnold Rüütel

Head of Government
2003– Juhan Parts

ETHIOPIA

Local name Ityopiya

Timezone GMT +3

Area 1 251 282 km²/483 123 sq mi

Population total (2002e) 67 673 000

Status Republic

Capital Addis Ababa

Language Amharic (official)

Ethnic groups Oromo (40%), Amhara and Tigray (32%)

Religions Muslim (45%), Ethiopian Orthodox (37%), traditional beliefs (11%)

Physical features Located in NE Africa; dominated by mountainous C plateau, mean elevation 1800–2400 m/ 6–8000 ft; split diagonally by the Great Rift Valley; highest point, Ras Dashan Mt, 4620 m/15 157 ft; crossed E–W by Blue Nile; Danakil Depression (NE) dips to 116 m/ 381 ft below sea level.

Climate Tropical climate, moderated by higher altitudes; distinct wet season (Apr–Sep); hot, semi-arid NE and SE lowlands receive less than 500 mm/20 in of rainfall annually; droughts in 1980s caused widespread famine, deaths, and resettlement; major famine, 2003.

Currency 1 Ethiopian Birr (Br) = 100 cents

Economy One of the world's poorest countries; over 80% of population employed in agriculture, especially subsistence farming; production severely affected by drought; distribution of foreign aid hindered by internal civil war and poor local organization.

GDP (2002e) $48.53 bn, per capita $700

HDI (2002) 0.327

History Oldest independent country in sub-Saharan Africa; first Christian country in Africa; Eritrea occupied by Italy, 1882; independence of Abyssinia (former name of Ethiopia) recognized by League of Nations, 1923; Haile Selassie became Emperor in 1930, and began programme of modernization and reform; Italian invasion, 1935; annexation as Italian East Africa, 1936–41; Italians forced from Ethiopia by the Allies, and Haile Selassie returned to power, 1941; military coup, 1974; ongoing conflict with Somalia over Ogaden region; internal conflict with regional separatist Eritrean and Tigrean forces; transfer of power to People's Democratic Republic, 1987; government overthrown by separatist forces, 1991; Council of Representatives formed; Eritrea formally recognized as an independent state, 1993; multi-party elections, 1994; new constitution, 1994, recognizing a

☐ International Airport

federal government of nine states, and providing for regional autonomy (allowing the right of secession); new Council of People's Representatives formed, 1995; escalating conflict with Eritrea over disputed border territory, 1999–2000; Permanent Court of Arbitration at The Hague issued a border ruling, 2002.

Head of State
2001– Woldegiorgis Girma

Head of Government
1995– Meles Zenawi

FAROE ISLANDS >> DENMARK

FALKLAND ISLANDS >> UNITED KINGDOM

FIJI

Local name Viti

Timezone GMT +12

Area 18 333 km²/7076 sq mi

Population total (2002e) 824 000

Status Republic

Date of independence 1970

Capital Suva (on Viti Levu Island)

Language English (official)

Ethnic groups Indigenous Fijians (44%), Indian (51%)

Religions Native Fijians, mainly Christian (Methodist c.85%, Roman Catholic 12%); Indo-Fijians, mainly Hindu (c.70%) and Muslim (25%)

Physical features Melanesian group of 844 islands and islets in the SW Pacific Ocean; highest peak, Tomaniivi (Mt Victoria) on Viti Levu, 1324 m/4344 ft; most smaller islands consist of limestone, little vegetation; Great Sea Reef stretches 500 km/300 mi along W

☐ International Airport

fringe; dense tropical forest on wet, windward side (SE); mainly treeless on dry, leeward side.

Fiji (continued)

Climate Tropical oceanic climate, high humidity; average annual temperature 27°C, ranging from 35°C(Dec–Apr) to 16°C (Jun–Sep); heavy rainfall; occasional hurricanes.

Currency 1 Fijian Dollar (F$) = 100 cents

Economy Agriculture; sugar cane (accounts for over two-thirds of export earnings); bananas, ginger; gold, silver, limestone, timber; major tourist area.

GDP (2002e) $4.822 bn, per capita $5600

HDI (2002) 0.758

History Visited by Tasman, 1643, and by Cook, 1774; British colony from 1874; independence within the Commonwealth, 1970; 1987 election brought to power an Indian-dominated coalition, which led to military coups (May and Sep), and proclamation of a republic out-

side the Commonwealth; civilian government restored, Dec 1987; constitution, 1990 and 1997; readmitted to the Commonwealth, 1997; coup, with prime minister and others held as hostages, May–July 2000; suspended from Commonwealth, June 2000; parliamentary elections, 2001; Commonwealth suspension lifted, December 2001; bicameral Parliament of a nominated Senate and an elected House of Representatives.

Head of State
1993–2000 Kamisese Mara
2000–   Ratu Josefa Iloilo

Head of Government
2001–   Laisenia Qarase

FINLAND

Local name Suomi (Finnish)

Timezone GMT +2

Area 338 145 km²/130 524 sq mi

Population total (2002e) 5 201 000

Status Republic

Date of independence 1917

Capital Helsinki

Languages Finnish and Swedish (official), also Saame (Lappish)

Ethnic groups Finnish (92%), Swedish (6%), Lappish, Russian minorities

Religions Lutheran (90%), Finnish/Greek Orthodox

Physical features Low-lying, glaciated plateau, average height 150 m/500 ft; highest peak Haltiatunturi, 1328 m/ 4357 ft, on NW border; over 60 000 shallow lakes in SE, providing a system of inland navigation; over a third of the country located N of the Arctic Circle; Archipelago of Saaristomeri (SW), with over 17 000 islands; including Åland Is (Ahvenanmaa) (SW); forest covers 65% of the country, water covers 10%.

Climate Extreme, N of the Arctic Circle: lowest winter temperatures –45–50°C; half annual precipitation falls as snow; polar night lasts 51 days; sun does not go down beyond the horizon for 73 days during summer; average temperatures –9°C (Jan), 20°C (Jul) at Helsinki; average annual rainfall 618 mm/24 in.

Currency 1 euro = 100 cents (previous to February 2002, 1 Markka (FMk) = 100 penni)

Economy Traditional focus on forestry, farming; rapid economic growth since 1950s; metals, clothing, chemicals, electronics, electrical equipment, telecommunications (Nokia); hydroelectric and nuclear power.

GDP (2002e) $133.8 bn, per capita $25 800

HDI (2002) 0.930

History Ruled by Sweden from 1157 until ceded to Russia in 1809; Grand Duchy of the Russian Czar, 19th-c; independent republic, 1917; parliamentary system

☐ International Airport

created, 1928; invaded by Soviets, 1939–40 (Winter War); lost territory to USSR, including Petsamo and Porkkala peninsula, 1944; signed a friendship treaty with Soviet Union in 1948 (renewed 1955, 1970, 1983), undertaking to resist any attack made on the Soviet Union launched through Finnish territory; Harri Holkeri became Finland's first post-war conservative Prime Minister, 1987; governed by a single-chamber House of Representatives and President assisted by a Council of State; joined the European Union, 1995.

Head of State
1994–2000 Martti Ahtisaarsi
2000–   Tarja Halonen

Head of Government
2003   Anneli Jaatteenmaki
2003–   Matti Vanhanen

FRANCE

Local name France

Timezone GMT +1

Area 551 000 km²/212 686 sq mi

Population total (2002e) 59 440 000

Status Republic

Capital Paris

Languages French (official), Breton, Occitan and Alsatian are also spoken

Ethnic groups Celtic and Latin origin (91%), Breton, Catalan, and large immigrant population (including Portuguese, Algerian, Moroccan, and Arab minorities)

Religions Roman Catholic (90%), Protestant (4%), Muslim (3%), Jewish (1%)

Physical features Bounded S and E by large mountain ranges, notably (interior) the Massif Central, Jura, and Alps (E), rising to 4807 m/15 771 ft at Mont Blanc, and the Pyrénées (S); chief rivers include Loire (longest at 1020 km/633 mi), Rhône, Seine, Garonne; 60% of land arable.

Climate Mediterranean climate in S, with warm, moist winters and hot, dry summers; average temperatures, 3°C (Jan), 18°C (Jul); continental climate in E; average annual rainfall 786 mm/31 in; heatwave in August 2003 caused deaths of many elderly people.

Currency 1 euro = 100 cents (previous to February, 2002, 1 French Franc (Fr) = 100 centimes)

Economy Main industries include wine, fruit, cheese; perfume, textiles, clothing; steel, chemicals, machinery, cars, aircraft; natural resources of coal, iron ore, bauxite, timber; tourism important.

GDP (2002e) $1.558 tn, per capita $26 000

HDI (2002) 0.928

History Celtic-speaking Gauls dominant by 5th-c BC; part of Roman Empire, 125 BC to 5th-c AD; feudal monarchy founded by Hugh Capet, 987; Plantagenets of England acquired several territories, 12th-c; lands gradually recovered in Hundred Years' War, 1337–1453, apart from Calais (regained in 1558); Capetian dynasty followed by the Valois, from 1328, and the Bourbons, from 1589; Wars of Religion, 1562–95; monarchy overthrown by the French Revolution, 1789; First Republic declared, 1792; First Empire, ruled by Napoleon, 1804–14; monarchy restored, 1814–48; Second Republic, 1848–52, and Second Empire, 1852–70, ruled by Louis Napoleon. Third Republic, 1870–1940; great political instability between World Wars, with several governments holding office for short periods; occupied by Germany 1940–4, with pro-German government at Vichy, and Free French in London under de Gaulle; Fourth Republic, 1946; war with Indo-China, 1946–54; conflict in Algeria, 1954–62. Fifth Republic, 1958; governed by a President, an appointed Prime Minster, a Council of Ministers, bicameral National Assembly, and Senate.

Head of State

Fifth Republic

1974–81	Valéry Giscard d'Estaing
1981–95	François Mitterrand
1995–	Jacques Chirac

□ International Airport

Head of Government

Fifth Republic

1997–2002	Lionel Jospin
2002–	Jean-Pierre Raffarin

>> Political leaders and rulers, pp.126–7

Internal Collective Territory

Island of Corsica in the Mediterranean Sea: area 8680 km²/3350 sq mi; capital, Ajaccio; GMT +1

1 BASSE-NORMANDIE
2 HAUTE-NORMANDIE
3 NORD-PAS-DE-CALAIS
4 ÎLE-DE-FRANCE
5 CHAMPAGNE-ARDENNE

□ International Airport

France (continued)

Overseas departments

Name	Area km²	sq mi	Capital	GMT
Guadeloupe	1779	687	Basse-Terre	-4
Guiana	90909	35091	Cayenne	-3
Martinique	1079	416	Fort-de-France	-4
Mayotte	374	144	Dzaoudzi	+3
Réunion	2512	970	St Denis	+4
St Pierre et Miquelon	240	93	St Pierre	-3

Overseas territories

Name	Area km²	sq mi	Capital/ chief centre	GMT
French Polynesia	3941	1521	Papeete	-6
New Caledonia	18575	7170	Nouméa	+11
Southern and Antarctic Territories	10100	3900	Port-aux-Français	
Wallis and Futuna	274	106	Matu Utu	+12

GABON

Local name Gabon

Timezone GMT +1

Area 267667 km2/103347 sq mi

Population total (2002e) 1300000

Status Republic

Date of independence 1960

Capital Libreville

Languages French (official), Fang, Myene, Bateke, and other Bantu dialects spoken

Ethnic groups c.40 Bantu tribes (Fang 30%, Eshira 25%, Bateke and Bapounou 10%) and c.10% expatriate Africans and Europeans

Religions Christian (96%) (Roman Catholic 65%, Protestant 19%, other 12%), traditional beliefs

Physical features Located in W Africa; lies on the equator for 880 km/550 mi W–E; land rises towards the African central plateau, cut by several rivers, notably the Ogooué and N'Gounié; highest point, Mont Ibounoji, 980 m/3215 ft.

Climate Typical equatorial climate: hot, wet, and humid; mean annual temperature 27°C; annual average rainfall 1250–2000 mm/50–80 in inland.

Currency 1 CFA Franc (CFAFr) = 100 centimes

Economy Small area of land under cultivation, but employing 65% of population; coffee, cocoa, palm oil, rubber; timber extraction; rapid economic growth since independence, largely because of offshore oil, natural gas, and minerals; manganese, uranium, iron ore.

GDP (2002e) $8.354 bn, per capita $6500

HDI (2002) 0.637

History Visited by Portuguese, 15th-c; under French control from mid-19th-c; slave ship captured by the French in 1849, the liberated slaves forming the settle-

☐ International Airport

ment of Libreville; occupied by France, 1885; one of four territories of French West Africa, 1910; independence, 1960; multi-party elections held, 1990; new constitution, 1991; governed by a President, an appointed Council of Ministers, and a legislative National Assembly.

Head of State
1967– Omar (Albert-Bernard, to 1973) Bongo

Head of Government
1999– Jean-François Ntoutoume-Emane

GAMBIA, THE

Local name Gambia

Timezone GMT

Area 11 295 km²/4361 sq mi

Population total (2002e) 1 418 000

Status Independent republic within the Commonwealth

Date of independence 1965

Capital Banjul

Languages English (official), also Madinka, Wolof and Fula

Ethnic groups Madinka (40%), Fula (19%), Wolof (15%), Dyola (10%), Sonike (8%)

Religions Muslim (85%), Christian (14%), traditional local beliefs (1%)

Physical features Located in W Africa; surrounded, except for coastline, by Senegal; strip of land 322 km/ 200 mi E–W along R Gambia; flat country, not rising above 90 m/295 ft; c.25% of land arable.

Climate Tropical climate; average temperatures 23°C (Jan), 27°C (Jul), rising upland to over 40°C; rainy season (Jun–Sep) with high humidity and high night temperatures; rainfall decreasing inland.

Currency 1 Dalasi (D, Di) = 100 butut

Economy Agriculture, especially groundnuts; cotton, rice, millet, sorghum, fruit, vegetables, livestock; groundnut processing, brewing, soft drinks, agricultural machinery assembly, metal working, clothing, tourism.

□ International Airport

GDP (2002e) $2.582 bn, per capita $1800

HDI (2002) 0.405

History Visited by Portuguese, 1455; settled by English in 17th-c; independent British Crown Colony from 1843; independent member of Commonwealth, 1965; republic, 1970; joined Confederation of Senegambia, 1982–9; signed treaty of friendship with Senegal, 1991; military coup, 1994; governed by a House of Representatives, President and Cabinet.

Head of State/Government
1996–   Yayeh Jameh

GEORGIA

Local name Georgia

Timezone GMT +4

Area 69 700 km²/26 900 sq mi

Population total (2002e) 4 961 000

Status Republic

Date of independence 1991

Capital Tbilisi

Languages Georgian (official), also Russian

Ethnic groups Georgian (69%), Armenian (9%), Russian (7%), Azerbaijani (5%), Ossetian (3%), Abkhazian (2%)

Religion Georgian Church, independent of the Russian Orthodox Church since 1917

Physical features Mountainous country in C and W Transcaucasia; contains the Greater Caucasus (N) and Lesser Caucasus (S); highest point in the republic, Mt Shkhara, 5203 m/17 070 ft; chief rivers, Kura and Rioni; c.39% of land forested.

Climate Greater Caucasus in N borders temperate and subtropical climatic zones; average temperatures 1–3°C (Jan), 25°C (Jul) in E Transcaucasia; humid, sub-

□ International Airport

tropical climate with mild winters in W; Mediterranean climate with humid winters, dry summers in N Black Sea region.

Currency (1995) Lari

Georgia (continued)

Economy Kakhetia region famed for its orchards and wines; holiday resorts, spas on the Black Sea; manganese, coal, iron and steel, oil refining; tea, fruits, tung oil, tobacco, vines, silk, textiles, food processing.

GDP (2002e) $16.5 bn, per capita $3200

HDI (2002) 0.748

History Proclaimed a Soviet Socialist Republic, 1921; linked with Armenia and Azerbaijan as Transcaucasian Republic, 1922–36; made a constituent republic within the Soviet Union, 1936; declaration of independence, 1991; quest for regional autonomy led to declaration of secession by S Ossetia, 1991, and declaration of independence by Abkhazia, 1992; did not join Commonwealth of Independent States (CIS), 1991; President Gamsakhurdia overthrown in civil war, 1992, bringing military council to power; Parliament dismissed and powers transferred to a State Council headed by Shevardnadze, 1992; joined CIS, 1993; head of State holds executive power, advised by Cabinet of Ministers; new constitution, 1995; Shevardnadze resigned following people's revolution, replaced by leader of the opposition Mikhail Saakashvili (Jan 2004); post of prime minister reintroduced, 2004.

Head of State

1992–2003	Eduard Shevardnadze
2003–4	Nino Burjanadze *Acting*
2004–	Mikhail Saakashvili

Head of Government

2004–5	Zurab Zhvania
2005–	Zurab Noghaideli

Minister of State

2000–3	Gia Arsenishvili
2003–4	Zurab Zhvania

GERMANY

Local name Bundesrepublik Deutschland

Timezone GMT +1

Area 357 868 km²/138 136 sq mi

Population total (2002e) 82 506 000

Status Federal republic

Capital Berlin

Languages German (official)

Ethnic groups German (93%), Turkish (2%), Yugoslav (1%), Italian (1%), other European Community (3%)

Religions Lutheran (55%), Roman Catholic (38%), Muslim (3%)

Physical features Lowland plains rise SW through C uplands and Alpine foothills to the Bavarian Alps; highest peak, the Zugspitze, 2962 m/9718 ft; C uplands include the Rhenish Slate Mts, Black Forest, and Harz Mts; Rhine crosses the country S–N; complex canal system links chief rivers, Elbe, Weser, Danube, Rhine, Main.

Climate Oceanic climatic influences strongest in NW, where winters are mild, stormy; elsewhere continental climate; lower winter temperatures in E and S, with considerable snowfall; average annual temperatures –0.5°C (Jan) to 19°C (Jul); average annual rainfall 600–700 mm/23–7 in.

Currency 1 euro = 100 cents (previous to February 2002, 1 Deutsche Mark (DM) = 100 Pfennige)

Economy Economically powerful member of EC (accounts for 30% of European Community output): substantial heavy industry in NW, wine in Rhine and Moselle valleys; increasing tourism, especially in the S; leading manufacturer of vehicles, electrical and electronic goods; much less development in the E, after the period of socialist economy; following unification, a major socio-economic division emerged between W and E, leading to demonstrations in the E provinces, 1991.

GDP (2002e) $2.16 tn, per capita $26 200

HDI (2002) 0.925

□ International Airport

History Ancient Germanic tribes united in 8th-c within the Frankish Empire of Charlemagne; elective monarchy after 918 under Otto 1, with Holy Roman Empire divided into several hundred states; after Congress of Vienna, 1814–15, a confederation of 39 states under Austria; under Bismarck, Prussia succeeded

Austria as the leading German power; union of Germany and foundation of Second Reich, 1871, with King of Prussia as hereditary German Emperor; aggressive foreign policy, eventually leading to World War 1; after German defeat, second Reich replaced by democratic Weimar Republic; world economic crisis led to collapse of Weimar Republic and rise of National Socialist movement, 1929; Adolph Hitler became dictator of the totalitarian Third Reich, 1933; acts of aggression led to World War 2 and a second defeat for Germany, with collapse of the German political regime; partition of Germany in 1945, with occupation zones given to UK, USA, France, and USSR, who formed a Control Council; USSR withdrew from the Control Council in 1948, dividing Germany into W and E: W Germany controlled by the three remaining powers, UK, USA and France; E administered by USSR.

West Germany (former Federal Republic of Germany) Area 249 535 km²/96 320 sq mi; population total (1990) 62 679 035; including West Berlin; established, 1949; gained full sovereignty, 1954; entered NATO, 1955; founder member of the European Economic Community, 1957; federal system of government, built around 10 provinces (*Länder*) with considerable powers; two-chamber legislature, consisting of Federal Diet (*Bundestag*) and Federal Council (*Bundesrat*).

East Germany (former German Democratic Republic) Area 108 333 km²/41 816 sq mi; population total (1990) 16 433 796; administered by USSR after 1945 partition, andSoviet model of government established, 1949; anti-Soviet demonstrations put down, 1953; recognized by USSR as an independent republic, 1954; flow of refugees to West Germany continued until 1961, largely stopped by the Berlin Wall built along zonal lines, dividing-western sectors of Berlin from eastern; governed by the People's Chamber, a single-chamber parliament (*Volkskammer*) which elected a Council of State, a Council of Ministers, and a National Defence Council; movement for democratic reform culminated in Nov 1989 in the opening and removal of the Wall and other border crossings to the West, and a more open government policy; first free all-German elections since 1932, held in Mar 1990, paving the way for a currency union with West Germany, Jul 1990, and full political unification, Oct 1990.

United Germany The 10 provinces of West Germany joined by the 5 former East German provinces abolished after World War 2 (Brandenburg, Mecklenburg-West, Pomerania, Saxony, Saxony-Anhalt, Thuringia), along with unified Berlin; West German electoral system adopted in East Germany; first national elections, Dec 1990.

□ International Airport

Länder of Germany

Head of State
2004– Horst Koehler

Head of Government (Federal Chancellor)
1998– Gerhard Schröder

>> Political leaders and rulers, p.127

GHANA

Local name Ghana

Timezone GMT

Area 238 537 km²/92 100 sq mi

Population total (2002e) 20 244 000

Status Republic

Date of independence 1960

Capital Accra

Languages English (official), Akan, Ewe, Ga, several minority languages

Ethnic groups c.75 tribal groups, including Akan (44%), Mole-Dagbani (16%), Ewe (13%), and Ga (8%)

Religions Christian (43%), traditional local beliefs (38%), Muslim (12%)

Physical features Located in W Africa; low-lying plains inland, leading to the Ashanti plateau (W) and R Volta basin (E), dammed to form L Volta; mountains (E) rise to 885 m/2903 ft at Mt Afadjado; Ashanti plateau in Wand Akwapin Toto Mts in E.

Climate Tropical climate, including a warm dry coastal belt (SE); a hot, humid SW corner; and a hot, dry savannah (N); average temperatures 27°C (Jan), 25°C (Jul) in Accra.

Currency 1 Cedi (¢) = 100 pesewas

Ghana (continued)

Economy Agriculture; cocoa (world's leading producer) provides two-thirds of export revenue; tourism; commercial reserves of oil, diamonds, gold, manganese, bauxite, timber.

GDP (2002e) $41.25 bn, per capita $2000

HDI (2002) 0.548

History Visited by Europeans in 15th-c; centre of slave trade, 18th-c; modern state created by union of two former British territories, British Gold Coast (Crown Colony, 1874) and British Togoland, merging to form Ghana and declaring independence, 1957; independent republic within the Commonwealth, 1960; constitution provides for a Parliament, executive President, Cabinet, and Council of State; series of military coups (1966, 1972, 1979, 1982) led to the creation of a Provisional National Defence Council, which rules by decree; new multi-party constitution, 1992, allowing for a directly elected executive President and legislature.

Head of State/Government
(Chairman of the Provisional National Defence Council)
1981–92   Jerry John Rawlings

President
1992–2001   Jerry John Rawlings
2001–   John Kufuor

☐ International Airport

GIBRALTAR >> UNITED KINGDOM

HUMAN GEOGRAPHY

GREECE

Local name Ellás

Timezone GMT +2

Area 131 957 km²/50 935 sq mi

Population total (2002e) 10 994 000

Status Republic

Date of independence 1830

Capital Athens (Athínai)

Languages Greek (official), English and French widely spoken

Ethnic groups Greek (98%), Albanian, Slav, Turkish minorities, and others (2%)

Religions Christian (98%) (Greek Orthodox 97.5%, Roman Catholic 0.4%, Protestant 0.1%), Muslim, Judaism, and others (2%)

Physical features Located in SE Europe, occupying the S part of the Balkan peninsula and numerous islands in the Aegean and Ionian seas: mainland includes the Peloponnese (S), connected via the narrow Isthmus of Corinth; over 1400 islands (only 169 inhabited), including Crete, the largest, 8336 km²/3218 sq mi, Rhodes, Milos, Corfu, Lesbos, Kos: nearly 80% of Greece mountainous or hilly; Pindus Mts run N to S; highest point, Mt Olympus, 2917 m/9570 ft; principal rivers include the Néstos, Strimon, Arakhthos: c.30% of land arable or under permanent cultivation; c.20% forested.

Climate Mediterranean climate for coast and islands, with mild, rainy winters and hot, dry summers; rainfall almost entirely in winter; island of Corfu receives maximum rainfall 1320 mm/52 in; severe winters in mountains; average annual temperatures 9°C (Jan), 28°C (Jul) in Athens.

Currency 1 euro = 100 cents (previous to February 2002, 1 Drachma (Dr) = 100 lepta)

Economy Strong service sector accounts for c.60% of national income; agriculture based on cereals, cotton, tobacco, fruit, figs, raisins, wine, olive oil, vegetables; major tourist area, especially on islands; world's largest shipping fleet (under own and other flags); member of the EC from 1981.

GDP (2002e) $203.3 bn, per capita $19 100

HDI (2002) 0.885

History Prehistoric civilization culminated in Minoan-Mycenean culture of Crete; Dorians invaded from N, 12th-c BC; Greek colonies established along N and S Mediterranean and on Black Sea; many city-states on mainland, notably Sparta and Athens; Persian invasions, 5th-c BC, repelled at Marathon, Salamis, Plataea, Mycale; Greek literature and art flourished, 5th-c BC; conflict between Sparta and Athens (Peloponnesian War) weakened both, and hegemony passed to Thebes, and then Macedon under Philip II, 4th-c BC; his son, Alexander the Great, conquered Persian Empire; Macedonian power broken by Romans, 197 BC; part of Eastern Roman and Byzantine empires; ruled by Ottoman Turks from 15th-c until 19th-c; national reawakening led to independence as kingdom, 1830; territorial gains after Balkan War and World War 1; absorbed over 100 000 refugees after defeat in Asia Minor, 1922; republic established, 1924–35; German occupation, 1941–4; civil war, 1944–9; military coup, 1967; abolition of monarchy, 1969; democracy restored, 1974; Athens hosted 2004 Olympic Games; governed by a Prime Minister; Cabinet, unicameral Parliament, and President.

Head of State

1990–5	Konstantinos Karamanlis
1995–	Konstantinos Stephanopoulos

Head of Government

1996–2004	Kostas Simitis
2004–	Kostas Karamanlis

GREENLAND >> DENMARK

☐ International Airport

GRENADA

Local name Grenada

Timezone GMT −4

Area 344 km²/133 sq mi

Population total (2002e) 101 900

Status Independent state within the Commonwealth

Date of independence 1974

Capital St George's

Languages English (official), French patois

Ethnic groups African descent (84%), mixed (12%), E Indian (3%) European (1%)

Religions Roman Catholic (64%), Protestant (21%)

Physical features Most southerly of the Windward Is, E Caribbean; comprises the main island of Grenada, 34 km/21 mi long, 19 km/12 mi wide, and the S Grenadines; Grenada volcanic in origin, with a ridge of mountains along its entire length, the highest point, Mt St Catherine, rising to 843 m/2766 ft; many rivers and lakes, including Grand Étang.

Climate Sub-tropical climate; average annual temperature 23°C; wet season (Jun–Dec); annual rainfall varies from 1270 mm/150 in (coast) to 5000 mm/200 in (interior); lies within Caribbean hurricane zone.

☐ International Airport

Grenada (continued)

Currency 1 East Caribbean Dollar (EC$) = 100 cents
Economy Economy based on agriculture, notably fruit, vegetables, cocoa, nutmegs, bananas, mace; processing of agricultural products and their derivatives; cocoa and nutmeg crops destroyed by H Ivan, Sep 2004.

GDP (2002e) $440 mn, per capita $5000

HDI (2002) 0.747

History Visited by Columbus and named Concepción, 1498; settled by French, mid-17th-c; ceded to Britain, 1763; retaken by France, 1779; ceded to Britain, 1783; British Crown Colony, 1877; independence, 1974; peo-ple's revolution, 1979; Prime Minister Maurice Bishop killed in uprising, 1983; group of Caribbean countries requested US involvement, and troops restored stable government, Oct 1983; governed by a Senate, House of Representatives, Prime Minister, and Cabinet.

Head of State
(British monarch represented by Governor-General)
1996–   Daniel Charles Williams

Head of Government
1995–   Keith Mitchell

GUADELOUPE >> FRANCE

GUAM >> UNITED STATES OF AMERICA

HUMAN GEOGRAPHY

GUATEMALA

Local name Guatemala

Timezone GMT –6

Area 108 889 km²/42 031 sq mi

Population total (2002e) 11 987 000

Status Republic

Date of independence 1838

Capital Guatemala City

Languages Spanish (official), c.40% speak Indian dialects, including Quiche, Cakchiquel, Kekchi

Ethnic groups Indian (41%) and mestizo

Religions Roman Catholic (75%), Protestant (25%)

Physical features Northernmost of the Central American republics; over two-thirds mountainous, with large forested areas; narrow Pacific coastal plain, rising steeply to highlands of 2500–3000 m/8000–10 000 ft; many volcanoes on S edge of highlands; low undulating tableland of El Petén to the N.

Climate Humid tropical climate on lowlands and coast; average annual temperatures 17°C (Jan), 21°C (Jul) in Guatemala City; rainy season (May–Oct); average annual rainfall 1316 mm l51.8 in; area subject to hurricanes and earthquakes.

Currency 1 Quetzal (Q) = 100 centavos

Economy Agricultural products account for c.65% of exports, chiefly coffee, bananas, cotton, sugar; on higher ground, wheat, maize, beans; on the Pacific coastal plain, cotton, sugar cane, rice, beans.

GDP (2002e) $53.2 bn, per capita $3900

HDI (2002) 0.631

History Mayan and Aztec civilizations before Spanish conquest, 1523–4; independence as part of the Federation of Central America, 1821; independence as the Republic of Guatemala, 1838; 1985 constitution provides for the election of a President (who appoints a Cabinet), and a National Assembly; long-standing claim over Belize resolved in 1991.

Head of State/Government
1999–2003 Alfonso Portillo Cabrera
2003–   Oscar Berger

□ International Airport   ∴ World heritage site

GUIANA >> FRANCE

GUINEA

Local name Guinée

Timezone GMT

Area 246 048 km²/94 974 sq mi

Population total (2002e) 7 775 000

Status Republic

Date of independence 1958

Capital Conakry

Languages French (official), Fulani, Malinké, Susu, Kissi, Kpelle

Ethnic groups Fulani (40%), Malinké (25%), Susu (11%), Kissi (6%), Kpelle (5%)

Religions Muslim (75%), traditional beliefs (24%)

Physical features Located in W Africa; coast characterized by mangrove forests, rising to a forested and widely cultivated narrow coastal plain; Fouta Djallon massif beyond, c.900 m/3000 ft; higher peaks near Senegal frontier include Mt Tangue, 1537 m/5043 ft. savannah plains in E; forested Guinea Highlands in S.

Climate Tropical climate; wet season (May–Oct); annual rainfall 4923 mm/194 in at Conakry; average temperature 32°C (dry season) on coast, 23°C (wet season).

Currency 1 Guinean Franc (GFr) = 100 cauris

Economy Agriculture (employs 75% of population); rich in minerals, with a third of the world's bauxite reserves; gold, diamonds; independence brought fall in production as a result of withdrawal of French expertise and investment.

GDP (2002e) $18.69 bn, per capita $2100

HDI (2002) 0.414

History Part of Mali empire, 16th-c; French protec-

□ International Airport

torate, 1849; governed with Senegal as Rivières du Sud; separate colony, 1893; constituent territory within French West Africa, 1904; overseas territory, 1946; independent republic, 1958; death of Sékou Touré, Guinea's first President (1961–84); coup in 1984 established a Military Committee for National Recovery (CMRN); CMRN replaced by a mixed military and civilian Transitional Committee of National Recovery (CTRN), 1991; governed by a President and Council of Ministers; new constitution, 1990.

Head of State
1984–   Lansana Conté

Head of Government
2004   François Fall

GUINEA-BISSAU

Local name Guiné-Bissau

Timezone GMT

Area 36 125 km²/13 948 sq mi

Population total (2002e) 1 345 000

Status Republic

Date of independence 1973

Capital Bissau

Languages Portuguese (official), Criolo, Balante

Ethnic groups Balanta (32%), Fula (22%), Mandyako (14%), Mandingo (13%), Pepel (10%)

Religions Traditional beliefs (54%), Muslim (38%), Christian (5%)

Physical features Located in W Africa. indented coast backed by forested coastal plains; main rivers, Geba and Cacheu; low-lying, with savannah-covered plateaux (S, E), rising to 310 m/1017 ft on the Guinea border; includes the heavily-forested Bijagós archipelago in the

□ International Airport

Guinea-Bissau (continued)

Atlantic Ocean off the shores of the mainland.

Climate Tropical climate, hot and humid; wet season (Jun–Oct); average annual rainfall at Bissau, 1950 mm/76.8 in; average annual temperature 24°C (Jan), 27°C (Jul) in Bissau.

Currency 1CFA Franc (CFAFr) = 100 centimes

Economy Based on agriculture, especially rice, maize, beans, peanuts, coconuts, palm oil, groundnuts, shrimps, fish, timber; reserves of petroleum, bauxite, phosphate.

GDP (2002e) $901.4 mn, per capita $700

HDI (2002) 0.349

History Visited by the Portuguese, 1446; Portuguese colony, 1879; overseas territory of Portugal, 1952; independence, 1973; military coup, 1980; new constitution, 1984; National Assembly elects Council of State; President of the Council of State also the Head of Government; introduction of a multi-party system, 1991; governed by a president, prime minister, and a 100-seat National People's Assembly; President Yala deposed in military coup after repeatedly cancelling elections, 2003; transitional government formed; fresh elections planned, Mar 2005.

Head of State
2003–   Henrique Rosa *Interim*

Head of Government
2004–   Carlos Gomes Junior

GUYANA

Local name Guyana

Timezone GMT –3

Area 214 969 km²/82 978 sq mi

Population total (2002e) 775 000

Status Co-operative republic

Date of independence 1966

Capital Georgetown

Languages English (official), Hindi, Urdu, Amerindian dialects

Ethnic groups E Indian (51%), black (30.5%), Amerindian (5%) (Carib 4%, Arawak 1%)

Religions Christian (42%), Hindu (37%), Muslim (9%)

Physical features Located on N coast of South America; inland forest covers c.83% of land area; highest peak; Mt Roraima, rising to 2875 m/9432 ft in the Pakaraima Mts (W); main rivers, Essequibo, Rupununi, and Corantijn, with many rapids and waterfalls in upper courses.

Climate Equatorial climate in the lowlands; hot, wet, with constant high humidity; average annual temperature 26°C (Jan), 27°C (Jul) in Georgetown; two seasons of high rainfall (May–Jul, Nov–Jan); average annual rainfall 2175 mm/87 in.

Currency 1 Guyana Dollar (G$) = 100 cents

Economy High unemployment, influenced by labour unrest, low productivity, and high foreign debt; economy largely based on sugar, rice, bauxite, shrimps, livestock, cotton, molasses, timber.

GDP (2002e) $2.628 bn, per capita $3800

HDI (2002) 0.708

History Sighted by Columbus, 1498; settled by the Dutch, late 16th-c; several areas ceded to Britain, 1814; consolidated as British Guiana, 1831; independence, 1966; cooperative republic within the Commonwealth, 1970; governed by a President who holds executive

☐ International Airport

power, and appoints a Prime Minister and National Assembly, elected every five years.

Head of State/Government
1997–9   Janet Jagan
1999–   Bharrat Jagdeo

Prime Minister
1999–   Samuel Hinds

HAITI

Local name Haïti

Timezone GMT –5

Area 27 750 km²/10 712 sq mi

Population total (2002e) 7 064 000

Status Republic

Date of independence 1804

Capital Port-au-Prince

Languages French (official), with Creole French widely spoken

Ethnic groups African descent (95%), European (mulatto) (5%)

Religions Roman Catholic (80%), Voodoo

Physical features Consists of two mountainous peninsulas, Massif du Nord (N) and Massif de la Hotte (S), separated by a deep structural depression, the Plaine du Cul-de-Sac; highest peak, La Selle, 2680 m/8793 ft; includes islands of Gonâve (W) and Tortue (N).

Climate Tropical climate; average annual temperatures 25°C (Jan) 29°C (Jul) in Port-au-Prince; wet season (May–Sep); average annual rainfall for N coast and mountains 1475–1950 mm/58–77 in, but only 500 mm/20 in on W side; hurricanes common; 2000+ deaths from Hurricane Jeanne, Sep 2004.

Currency 1 Gourde (G, Gde) = 100 centimes

Economy Based on agriculture; large plantations grow coffee, sugar, sisal, rice, bananas, corn, sorghum, cocoa; sugar refining, textiles, flour milling; cement, bauxite; tourism; light assembly industries.

GDP (2002e) $10.6 bn, per capita $1400

HDI (2002) 0.471

History Visited by Columbus, 1492; created when W third of island ceded to France as Saint-Domingue, 1697; slave rebellion followed by independence as Haiti, 1804; united with Santo Domingo (Dominican Rep.), 1822–44; US occupation, 1915–34; Duvalier family had absolute power, 1957–86; after 1986 coup, new constitution pro-

☐ International Airport

vided for a bicameral National Congress consisting of a Senate and National Assembly; military coup, 1992, forced Jean-Bertrand Aristide to flee the country, provisional government created; Marc Bazin resigned as head of army-backed coalition government, 1993; talks deadlock between deposed President Aristide and coup leader Cedras, 1993; peaceful US invasion restored democratic government, 1994; Aristide re-elected, 2000, amid claims of fraudulent practice; conflict escalated early 2004 with failure of Aristide's political opposition to agree to US-backed power-sharing plan; rebel uprising forced Aristide into exile, Mar 2004 .

Head of State
2004– Boniface Alexandre *Interim*

Head of Government
2004– Gerard Latortue *Interim*

HONDURAS

Local name Honduras

Timezone GMT –6

Area 112 088 km²/43 266 sq mi

Population total (2002e) 6 561 000

Status Republic

Date of independence 1821

Capital Tegucigalpa

Languages Spanish (official), a number of Indian dialects also spoken by aboriginal population

Ethnic groups Spanish-Indian origin (90%), Indian (7%), black (2%)

Religions Roman Catholic (85%), Protestant (mainly Fundamentalist, Moravian, and Methodist) (10%)

Physical features Coastal lands (S) separated from Caribbean coastlands by mountains running NW–SE; S plateau rises to 2849 m/9347 ft at Cerro de las Minas; also includes Bay Is in the Caribbean Sea and nearly 300 islands in the Gulf of Fonseca.

Climate Tropical climate in coastal areas, temperate in C and W; average annual temperatures 19°C (Jan), 23°C (Jul) in Tegucigalpa; two wet seasons in upland areas (May–Jul, Sep–Oct); country devastated by Hurricane Mitch, 1998.

Currency 1 Lempira (L, La) = 100 centavos

Honduras (continued)

Economy Agriculture (provides a third of national income), forestry, mining, cattle raising; bananas, coffee, beef, cotton, tobacco, sugar; exports of silver, lead and zinc; offshore oil exploration in the Caribbean.

GDP (2002e) $16.29 bn, per capita $2500

HDI (2002) 0.638

History Centre of Mayan culture, 4th–9th-c; settled by the Spanish in early 16th-c, and became province of Guatemala; independence from Spain, 1821; joined Federation of Central America; independence, 1838; several military coups in 1970s; since 1980, a democratic constitutional republic, governed by a President and National Assembly.

Head of State/Government
1997–2001 Carlos Roberto Flores Facussé
2001– Ricardo Maduro

HONG KONG >> CHINA

☐ International Airport   ∴ World heritage site

HUNGARY

Local name Magyarország

Timezone GMT +1

Area 93 033 km²/35 912 sq mi

Population total (2002e) 10 162 000

Status Republic

Date of independence 1918

Capital Budapest

Language Hungarian (Magyar) (official)

Ethnic groups Magyar (92%), German (2%), Slovak (1%), Romanian and Yugoslav minorities

Religions Roman Catholic (67%), Calvinist (20%), Lutheran (5%)

Physical features Drained by the R Danube (flows N–S) and its tributaries; crossed (W) by a low spur of the Alps; highest peak, Kékestetö, 1014 m/3327 ft; frequent flooding, especially in the Great Plains (E). 54% of land is arable; 18% forested.

Climate Fairly extreme continental climate, due to landlocked position; average annual temperature 0°C (Jan), 21 °C (Jul) in Budapest; wettest in spring and early summer; average annual rainfall 600 mm/23.6 in; cold winters; R Danube sometimes frozen over for long periods; frequent fogs.

Currency 1 Forint (Ft) = 100 fillér

Economy Large-scale nationalization as part of centralized planning strategy of the new republic, 1946–9; greater independence to individual factories and farms, from 1968; grain, potatoes, sugar beet, fruit, wine; coal, bauxite, lignite; metallurgy, engineering, chemicals, textiles, food processing.

GDP (2002e) $134 bn, per capita $13 300

HDI (2002) 0.835

☐ International Airport

History Kingdom formed under St Stephen 1, 11th-c; conquered by Turks, 1526; part of Habsburg Empire, 17th-c; Austria and Hungary reconstituted as a dual monarchy, 1867; republic, 1918; communist revolt led by Béla Kun, 1919; monarchical constitution restored, 1920; new republic with communist government, 1949; uprising crushed by Soviet forces, 1956; during 1989, pressure for political change towards a multi-party system; multi-party elections in 1990 saw an end to communist rule; governed by a National Assembly which elects a Presidential Council and Council of Ministers.

Head of State
2000– Ferenc Madl

Head of Government
2004– Ferenc Gyurcsany

ICELAND

Local name Ísland

Timezone GMT

Area 103 000 km²/40 000 sq mi

Population total (2002e) 288 000

Status Republic

Date of independence 1944

Capital Reykjavik

Language Icelandic (official)

Ethnic groups Homogeneous (96%), with European minorities

Religions Protestant (95%) (Evangelical Lutheran 93%, other Lutheran 2%), Roman Catholic (1%), non-religious (1%)

Physical features Several active volcanoes, including Hekla, 1491 m/4920 ft; Helgafell, 215 m/706 ft; and Surtsey, 174 m/570 ft; famous for its geysers; many towns heated by subterranean hot water; heavily indented coastline with many long fjords; high ridges rise to 2119 m/6952 ft at Hvannadalshnjukur (SE); several large snowfields and glaciers.

Climate Changeable; summers cool and cloudy, mild winters; average annual temperature 1°C (Jan), 11°C (Jul); Reykjavik generally ice-free throughout year; average monthly rainfall reaches 94 mm/3.7 in (Oct).

Currency 1 Krónur (1Kr, 1SK) = 100 aurar

Economy Based on inshore and deep-water fishing (75% of national income); stock and dairy farming, potatoes, greenhouse vegetables; aluminium, diatomite; tourism.

GDP (2002e) $8.444 bn, per capita $30 200

HDI (2002) 0.936

History Settled by the Norse, 9th-c; world's oldest

□ International Airport

Parliament (*Althing*), 10th-c; union with Norway, 1262; union with Denmark, 1380; independent kingdom in personal union with Denmark, 1918; independent republic, 1944; extension of the fishing limit around Iceland in 1958 and 1975 precipitated the 'Cod War' disputes with the UK; governed by a bicameral Parliament (*Althing*), President, Prime Minister, and Cabinet.

Head of State
1996– Olafur Ragnar Grimsson

Head of Government
1991–2004 David Oddsson
2004– Halldor Asgrimsson

INDIA

Local name Bharat (Hindi)

Timezone CMT +5.5

Area 3 166 829 km²/1 222 396 sq mi

Population total (2002e) 1 047 671 000

Status Republic

Date of independence 1947

Capital New Delhi

Languages Hindi and English (official); others include Urdu, Panjabi, Gujarati, Marathi, Bengali, Oriya, Kashmiri, Assamese, Kannada, Malayalam, Sindhi, Tamil and Telugu

Ethnic groups Indo-Aryan (72%), Dravidian (25%), with Mongoloid and other minorities

Religions Hindu (83%), Muslim (11%), Christian (2%), Sikh (2%), Buddhist (1%)

Physical features Seventh largest country in the world, located in S Asia; includes Andaman and Nicobar

Is in the Bay of Bengal, and Laccadive Is in the Indian Ocean; folded mountain ridges and valleys in N, highest peaks over 7000 m/23 000 ft; C river plains of the Ganges, Yamuna, Ghaghari, and Brahmaputra to the S, with control measures needed to prevent flooding; Thar Desert in NW bordered by semi-desert areas; Deccan Plateau in the S peninsula, with hills and wide valleys, bounded by the Western and Eastern Ghats; the coastal plains are important areas of rice cultivation.

Climate Dominated by the Asiatic monsoon; rains come from the SW (Jun–Oct); rainfall decreases E–W on the N plains, with desert conditions in extreme W; tropical in S even in cool season; average annual temperature 14°C (Jan), 31°C (Jul) in New Delhi; average annual rainfall 640 mm/25.2 in; cyclones and storms on SE coast (especially Oct–Dec).

Currency 1 Indian Rupee (Re, Rs) = 100 paisa

Economy Agriculture employs over two-thirds of the labour force, tea, rice, wheat, coffee, sugar cane, cotton

HUMAN GEOGRAPHY

India (continued)

jute, oil seed, maize, pulses, milk; floods and drought cause major problems; considerable increase in industrial production since independence; iron, steel, oil products, chemicals, fertilizers, chromite, barytes, oil, natural gas; tourism.

GDP (2002e) $2.644 tn, per capita $2600

HDI (2002) 0.577

History Indus civilization emerged c.2500 BC, destroyed in 1500 BC by the Aryans, who developed the Brahmanic caste system; Mauryan Emperor Asoka unified most of India, and established Buddhism as the state religion, 3rd-c BC; spread of Hinduism, 2nd-c BC; Muslim influences during 7th-8th-c AD, with sultanate established at Delhi; Mughal Empire established by Babur in 1526 and extended by Akbar and Aurangzeb; Portuguese, French, Dutch, and British footholds in India, 18th-c; conflict between France and Britain, 1746–63; development of British interests represented by the East India Company; British power established after the Indian Mutiny crushed, 1857; movement for independence from the late 19th-c; Government of India Act of 1919 allowed election of Indian ministers to share power with appointed British governors; a further Act in 1935 allowed election of independent provincial governments; passive-resistance campaigns of Mahatma Gandhi from 1920s (assassinated, 1948); independence granted in 1947, on condition that a Muslim state be established (Pakistan); Indian states later reorganized on a linguistic basis; Pakistan–India war over disputed territory in Kashmir and Jammu, 1948; federal democratic republic within the Commonwealth, 1950; Hindu-Muslim hostility, notably in 1978, and further India-Pakistan conflict in 1965 and 1971; separatist movements continue, especially relating to Sikh interests in the Punjab; suppression of militant Sikh movement in 1984 led to assassination of Indira Gandhi; Rajiv Gandhi assassinated, 1991; ongoing tension with Pakistan over Kashmir, 2002; each of the 27 states administered by a governor through an Assembly; the President, advised by a Coun-

☐ International Airport ···Disputed boundary J&K Jammu & Kashmir
--- India/Pakistan line of control

cil of Ministers, appoints a Prime Minister; Parliament comprises the President, an Upper House, and a House of the People; SE coast devastated by tsunami, 2004.

Head of State
1997–2002 K(ocheril) R(aman) Narayanan
2002– Avul Pakir Jainulabdeen Abdul Kalam

Head of Government
2004– Manmohan Singh

INDONESIA

Local name Indonesia

Timezone GMT +7 to +9

Area 1 906 200 km²/735 800 sq mi

Population total (2002e) 211 023 000

Status Republic

Date of independence 1945

Capital Jakarta

Languages Bahasa Indonesia (official), English, Dutch, and Javanese widely spoken

Ethnic groups Maderuse (40%), Javanese (33%), Sundanese (15%), Bahasa Indonesian (12%)

Religions Muslim (88%), Christian (9%) (Roman Catholic 6%, Protestant 2%), Hindu (2%), Buddhist (1%)

Physical features World's largest island group of 13 677 islands and islets, c.6000 inhabited; five main islands: Sumatra, Java, Kalimantan (two-thirds of Borneo

I), Sulawesi, Irian Jaya (W half of New Guinea I); mountainous volcanic landscape and equatorial rainforest; many volcanic peaks – over 100 on Java, 15 active.

Climate Hot and humid equatorial climate; dry season (Jun–Sep), rainy season (Dec–Mar); average annual temperature 26°C (Jan), 27°C (Jul) in Jakarta; average annual rainfall 1775 mm/69 in.

Currency 1 Indonesian Rupiah (Rp) = 100 sen

Economy Mainly agrarian, notably rice; oil, natural gas, and petroleum products from Borneo and Sumatra account for nearly 60% of national income; small manufacturing industry.

GDP (2002e) $714.2 bn, per capita $3100

HDI (2002) 0.684

History Settled by Hindus and Buddhists; Islam introduced, 14th–15th-c; Portuguese settlers, early 16th-c; Dutch East India Company established, 1602; Japanese occupation in World War 2; independence proclaimed with

□ International Airport

Sukarno as President, 1945; changed name from Netherlands East Indies to the Republic of the United States of Indonesia, 1949: federal system replaced by unified control, 1950, and unitary Republic of Indonesia proclaimed (W New Guinea remained under Dutch control until 1963, now called Irian Jaya): military coup, 1966; governed by a President elected by a 700-member People's Consultative Assembly, and advised by a Cabinet and several advisory agencies; separatist movements in Irian Jaya, East Timor,

and Aceh; East Timor achieved independence, 2002 (>>East Timor); terrorist bomb in Kuta, Bali, 180 killed, 2002; military offensive launched in Aceh after failed peace talks with rebel Free Aceh Movement, 2003; NW devastated by tsunami after earthquake off coast of Sumatra, 2004.

Head of State/Government

2001–4   Megawati Sukarnoputri
2004–   Susilo Bambang Yudhoyono

IRAN

Local name Īrān

Timezone GMT +3.5

Area 1 648 000 km²/636 128 sq mi

Population total (2002e) 65 457 000

Status Islamic Republic

Date of independence 1925

Capital Teheran

Languages Farsi (Persian) (official), several minority languages including Kurdish, Baluchi, Luri, and Turkic (including Afshari, Shahsavani, and Turkish)

Ethnic groups Persian (63%), Turkic (18%), other Iranian (13%), Kurdish (3%), Arab, and other Semitic (3%)

Religions Muslim (Shi'ite 93%, Sunni 5%), Zoroastrian (2%), Jewish, Baha'i, and Christian (1%)

Physical features Largely composed of a vast arid C plateau, average elevation 1200 m/4000 ft bounded N by the Elburz Mts, rising to 5670 m/18 602 ft at Mt Damavand Zagros Mts in W and S.

Climate Mainly a desert climate, hot and humid on Persian Gulf: average annual temperatures 2.2°C (Jan), 29.4°C (Jul) in Teheran; average annual rainfall 246 mm/ 9.7 in; frequent earthquakes.

Currency 1 Iranian Rial (Rls, RI) = 100 dinars

Economy World's fourth largest oil producer, but production severely disrupted by 1978 revolution, and Gulf War, 1991: agriculture and forestry (employs a third of population); natural gas, iron ore, copper, coal, salt; textiles, sugar refining, petrochemicals; traditional handicrafts (especially carpets).

□ International Airport   ∴ World heritage site

GDP (2002e) $458.3 bn, per capita $6800

HDI (2002) 0.721

History Early centre of civilization, dynasties including the Achaemenids and Sassanids; ruled by Arabs, Turks, and Mongols until the Sasavid dynasty in the 16th-18th-c, and the Qajar dynasty in the 19th-20th-c; military coup, 1921,

Iran (continued)

with independence under Reza Shah Pahlavi, 1925; changed name from Persia to Iran, 1935; protests against Shah's regime in 1970s led to revolution, 1978; exile of Shah, and proclamation of Islamic Republic under Ayatollah Khomeini, 1979; Islamic Cultural Revolution under Khomeini saw a return to strict observance of Muslim principles and traditions; occupation of US Embassy in Teheran, 1979–81; Gulf War following invasion of Iraq, 1980–8; overall authority exercised by appointed spiritual leader: post of Prime Minister abolished, 1989; governed by a President and a Consultative Assembly (*Majlis*).

Leader of the Islamic Revolution

1979–89	Ayatollah Khomeini
1989–	Ayatollah Sayed Ali Khamenei

Head of State/Government

1989–97	Ali Akbar Hashemi Rafsanjani
1997–	Sayed Mohammad Khatami

IRAQ

Local name Al'Îrâq

Timezone GMT +3

Area 434 925 km²/167 881 sq mi

Population total (2002e) 24 002 000

Status Republic

Date of independence 1932

Capital Baghdad

Languages Arabic (official), also English, Kurdish, Persian, Turkish, and Assyrian spoken

Ethnic groups Arab (79%), Kurd (largely in NE) (16%), Persian (3%), Turkish (2%)

Religions Muslim (95%) (Shi'ite 63%, Sunni 32%), Christian (3%)

Physical features Comprises the vast alluvial tract of the Tigris–Euphrates lowland (ancient Mesopotamia); Tharthar and Euphrates rivers, divided by al-Jazirah plain, flow over dense swampland and join to form the navigable Shatt al-Arab; mountains (NE) rise to over 3000 m/9800 ft; desert in other areas.

Climate Mainly arid climate; summers very hot and dry; winters often cold; average annual temperature 10°C (Jan), 35°C (Jul) in Baghdad; average annual rainfall 140 mm/5.5 in.

Currency 1 Iraqi Dinar (ID) = 1000 fils

Economy World's second largest producer of oil, but production severely disrupted during both Gulf Wars; natural gas, oil refining, petrochemicals, cement, textiles; dates, cotton, winter wheat, rice, sheep, cattle.

GDP (2002e) $58 bn, per capita $2400

HDI (1998) 0.583

History Part of Ottoman Empire from 16th-c until World War I; captured by British forces, 1916; British-mandated territory, 1921; independence under Hashemite dynasty, 1932; monarchy replaced by military rule, and Iraq declared republic, 1958; since 1960s, Kurdish nationalists in NE fighting to establish separate state; invasion of Iran led to Iran-Iraq War (1980–88); invasion and annexation of Kuwait led to Gulf War 1991; UN imposed no-fly zone over S Iraq to protect Shi'ites, and security zone in N Iraq to protect Kurdish refugees, 1992; Iraq War, 2003 (>> p.188); interim constitution, March 2004; handover of power to interim Iraqi government, Jun 2004.

□ International Airport ∴ World heritage site

Head of State/Government

1979–2003	Saddam Hussein at-Takriti
2003–5	Coalition Provisional Authority (CPA)

President

2005–	Jalal Talabani

Prime Minister

2005–	Ibrahim Jaafari

IRELAND, REPUBLIC OF

Local name Éire (Gaelic)

Timezone GMT

Area 70 282 km²/27 129 sq mi

Population total (2002e) 3 926 000

Status Republic (occupying S, C, and NW Ireland; bounded NE by Northern Ireland, part of the UK)

Capital Dublin

Languages Irish Gaelic and English (official)

Ethnic groups Celtic (94%), small English minority

Religions Roman Catholic (95%), Anglican (Church of Ireland) (3%), Presbyterian (1%)

Physical features Mountainous landscapes in W, part of Caledonian system of Scandinavia and Scotland with quartzite peaks weathered into conical mountains such as Croagh Patrick, 765 m/2510 ft: landscape of ridges and valleys in SW, rising towards Macgillycuddy's Reek Mts; lowlands in E drained by slow-moving rivers such as the Shannon (S), Liffey (E), and Slaney (SE).

Climate Mild and equable climate. Average annual temperature 5°C (Jan), 15°C (Jul); rainfall heaviest in W, often over 3000 mm/10 in.

Currency 1 euro = 100 cents (previous to February 2002, 1 Irish Pound/Punt (1£, IRE) = 100 new pence)

Economy Primarily agriculture (two-thirds of country covered by improved agricultural land); forestry developed since 1950s; fishing; food, drink, tobacco, textiles; recent growth in light engineering; synthetic fibres, electronics, pharmaceuticals; major tourist area; member of the EC, 1973.

GDP (2002e) $113.7 bn, per capita $29 300

HDI (2002) 0.925

History Occupied by Goidelic-speaking Celts during the Iron Age; conversion to Christianity by St Patrick, 5th-c; SE attacked by Vikings, c.800; Henry II of England declared himself lord of Ireland, 1171; Catholic rebellion during English Civil War suppressed by Oliver Cromwell, 1649–50; supporters of deposed Catholic King James II defeated by William III at Battle of the Boyne, 1690; struggle for Irish freedom developed in 18th-19th-c; Act of Union, 1801; population reduced by half during famine, 1846; Land Acts, 1870–1903; Home Rule Bills introduced by Gladstone, 1886,1893; third Home Rule Bill passed in 1914, but never came into effect because of World War I; armed rebellion, 1916; republic proclaimed by Sinn Fein, 1919; partition proposed by Britain, 1920; treaty signed, giving dominion status, 1921; right of Northern Ireland to opt out exercised, 1925; renamed Éire, 1937; left Commonwealth, 1949; Anglo-Irish Agreement, 1985; governed by a President (*Uachtarán na h'Éireann*), elected for seven years, and a Prime Minister (*Taoiseach*); National Parliament (*Oireachtas*) includes a House of Representatives (*Dáil Éireann*) and a Senate (*Seanad Éireann*).

Head of State
1997–   Mary McAleese

Head of Government
1997–   (Patrick) Bertie Ahern

□ International Airport

Counties of Ireland

County	Area		Population	Admin. centre
	sq km	sq mi	(2000e)	
Carlow	896	346	41 000	Carlow
Cavan	1891	730	53 000	Cavan
Clare	3188	1231	92 000	Ennis
Cork	7459	2880	415 000	Cork
Donegal	4830	1865	130 000	Lifford
Dublin	922	356	1 038 000	Dublin
Galway	5939	2293	183 000	Galway
Kerry	4701	1815	123 000	Tralee
Kildare	1694	654	124 000	Naas
Kilkenny	2062	796	75 000	Kilkenny
Laoighis (Leix)	1720	664	53 000	Portlaoise
Leitrim	1526	589	24 000	Carrick
Limerick	2686	1037	164 000	Limerick
Longford	1044	403	31 000	Longford
Louth	821	317	92 000	Dundalk
Mayo	5398	2084	112 000	Castlebar
Meath	2339	903	107 000	Trim
Monaghan	1290	498	52 000	Monaghan
Offaly	1997	771	59 000	Tullamore
Roscommon	2463	951	53 000	Roscommon
Sligo	1795	693	55 000	Sligo
Tipperary	4254	1642	134 500	Clonmel
Waterford	1869	710	92 000	Waterford
Westmeath	1764	681	63 000	Mullingar
Wexford	2352	908	103 000	Wexford
Wicklow	2025	782	98 000	Wicklow

HUMAN GEOGRAPHY

HUMAN GEOGRAPHY

ISRAEL

Local names Yisra'el (Hebrew), Isrā'il (Arabic)

Timezone GMT +2

Area 20 770 km²/8017 sq mi (within boundaries defined by 1949 armistice agreements)

Population total (2002e) 6 394 000 (excluding E Jerusalem and Israeli settlers in occupied territories)

Status Republic

Date of independence 1948

Capital Jerusalem

Languages Hebrew and Arabic (official), also European languages spoken

Ethnic groups Jewish (83%), Arab (11%)

Religions Jewish (85%), Muslim (11%), Christian and others (4%)

Physical features Extends 420 km/261 mi N–S; width varies from 20 km/12 mi to 116 km/72 mi; mountainous interior, rising to 1208 m/3963 ft at Mt Meron; mountains near Galilee (Lake Tiberias) and Samaria in the West Bank, dropping E to below sea-level in the Jordan–Red Sea rift valley: R Jordan forms part of E border; Dead Sea, between Israel and Jordan, 400 m/1286 ft below sea level, is the largest lake and has no outlet; Negev desert (S) occupies c.60% of the country's area.

Climate Mediterranean climate in N and C, with hot, dry summers and warm, wet winters; average annual temperature 9°C (Jan), 23°C (Jul) in Jerusalem; rainfall 528 mm/21 in.

Currency 1 New Israeli Shekel (NIS) = 100 agorot

Economy Over 90% of exports are industrial products; major tourist area, primarily to the religious centres; copper, potash, phosphates, citrus fruits, cotton, sugar beet, bananas, beef and dairy products; a world leader in agrotechnology, with areas of intensive cultivation; the kibbutz system produces c.40% of food output, but in recent years has turned increasingly towards industry.

GDP (2002e) $117.4 bn, per capita $19 500

HDI (2002) 0.896

History Zionist movement founded by Theodor Herzl, end of 19th-c; thousands of Jews returned to Palestine, then part of the Ottoman Empire: Britain given League of Nations mandate to govern Palestine and establish Jewish national home there, 1922; British evacuated Palestine, and Israel proclaimed independence, 1948; invasion by Arab nations, resulting in armistice, 1949. Israel gained control of the Gaza Strip, Sinai Peninsula (as far as the Suez Canal), West Bank of the R Jordan (including E sector of Jerusalem), and the Golan Heights in Syria, during the Six-Day War, 1967; Camp David conference between Egypt and Israel, 1978; Israeli withdrawal from Sinai, 1979; invasion of Lebanon, forcing the PLO to leave Beirut, 1982–5; renewed tension with uprising of Arabs in occupied territories (the *intifada*), 1988; peace agreement with PLO, and planned recognition of Palestine, 1993; withdrawal from Gaza and Jeri-

☐ International Airport · · · · Palestinian National Authority

cho, 1994: conflict with Jordan formally ended, 1994: assassination of Yitzhak Rabin, 1995; Arafat elected president in first Palestine general election, 1996; withdrawal from S Lebanon, 2000; escalating reprisal attacks on Palestinian targets, 2001; siege of Bethlehem, 2002; US-initiated 'road map' and Geneva Accord peace plan proposed, 2003; ongoing conflict, 2003–4; a parliamentary democracy, with a Prime Minister, a Cabinet, and a unicameral Parliament (Knesset); President elected for a maximum of two five-year terms.

Head of State
2000   Avraham Burg *Interim*
2000–   Mosha Katzav

Head of Government
1999–2001 Ehud Barak
2001–   Ariel Sharon

ITALY

Local name Italia

Timezone GMT +1

Area 301 255 km²/116 314 sq mi

Population total (2002e) 57 988 000

Status Republic

Capital Rome

Languages Italian (official), with German spoken in the Trentino-Alto Adige, French in Valle d'Aosta, and Slovene in Trieste-Gorizia

Ethnic groups Homogeneous (98%), with German–Italian, French–Italian, and Slovene–Italian minorities

Religions Roman Catholic (83%), non-religious (14%)

Physical features Comprises the boot-shaped peninsula extending south into the Mediterranean Sea, as well as Sicily, Sardinia, and some smaller islands; Italian peninsula extends c.960 km/600 mi SE from the Lombardy plains; Apennines rise to peaks above 2900 m/9000 ft; Alps form a border in N; broad, fertile Lombardo-Venetian plain in basin of R Po; several lakes at foot of the Alps, including Maggiore, Como, Garda; flat and marshy on Adriatic coast (N); coastal mountains descend steeply to the Ligurian Sea on the Riviera (W); Mt Vesuvius, 1289 m/4230 ft, and Vulcano, 502 m/1650 ft, are active volcanoes; island of Sicily separated from the mainland by the 4 km/2.5 mi wide Strait of Messina; the island includes the volcanic cone of Mt Etna, 3390 m/11 122 ft.

Climate Warm and temperate in S; hot and sunny summers, short cold winters; average annual temperatures 7°C (Jan), 25°C (Jul); average annual rainfall 657 mm/26 in; cold, wet, often snowy in higher peninsular areas; Mediterranean climate in coastal regions; Adriatic coast colder than the W coast, and receives less rainfall.

Currency 1 euro = 100 cents (previous to February 2002, 1 Italian Lira (L, Lit) = 100 centesimi)

Economy Industry largely concentrated in N; machinery, iron and steel; tourism; poorer agricultural region in S; Po valley a major agricultural region, with wheat, maize, sugar, potatoes, rice, beef, dairy farming; foothills of the Alps produce apples, peaches, walnuts, wine; further S, citrus fruits, vines, olives, tobacco.

GDP (2002e) $1.455 tn, per capita $25 100

HDI (2002) 0.913

History Inhabited by the Etruscans (N), Latins (C), and Greeks (S) in pre-Roman times; most regions part of the Roman Empire by 3rd-c BC; invaded by barbarian tribes, 4th-c AD; last Roman emperor deposed, 476; ruled by the Lombards and by the Franks under Charlemagne, crowned Emperor of the Romans, 800; part of the Holy Roman Empire under Otto, 962; conflict between popes and emperors throughout Middle Ages; dispute between Guelphs and Ghibellines, 12th-c; divided among five powers, 14th–15th-c (Kingdom of Naples, Duchy of Milan, republics of Florence and Venice, the papacy); major contribution to European culture through the Renaissance; numerous republics set up after the French Revolution; Napoleon crowned King of Italy, 1804; upsurge of liberalism and nationalism (*Risorgimento*) in 19th-c; unification achieved under Victor Emmanuel II of Sardinia, aided by Cavour and Garibaldi, by 1870; fought alongside Allies in World War I; Fascist movement brought Mussolini to power, 1922; conquest of Abyssinia, 1935–6, and

□ International Airport ∴ World heritage site

Regions of Italy

HUMAN GEOGRAPHY

Italy (continued)

Albania, 1939; alliance with Hitler in World War 2 led to the end of the Italian Empire; monarchy abolished and institution of a democratic republic, 1946; Parliament consists of a Chamber of Deputies and a Senate; the President of the Republic is Head of State and appoints a Prime Minister; continued political instability, with some 50 governments in power since the formation of the republic.

Head of State
1992–9   Oscar Luigi Scalfaro
1999–   Carlo Ciampi

Head of Government
2000–1   Giuliano Amato
2001–   Silvio Berlusconi

JAMAICA

Local name Jamaica

Timezone GMT –5

Area 10 957 km²/4229 sq mi

Population total (2002e) 2 630 000

Status Independent state within the Commonwealth

Date of independence 1962

Capital Kingston

Languages English (official), with Jamaican Creole widely spoken

Ethnic groups African (76%), Afro-European (15%), East Indian and Afro-Indian (3%), white (3%), Chinese and Afro-Chinese (1%)

Religions Christian (Protestant 56%, Roman Catholic 5%), non-religious (17%)

Physical features Third largest island in the Caribbean; maximum length, 234 km/145 mi; width, 35–82 km/22–51 mi; mountainous and rugged, particularly in the E, where the Blue Mt Peak rises to 2256 m/7401 ft; over 100 small rivers, several used for hydroelectric power.

Climate Humid, tropical climate at sea-level; more temperate at higher altitudes; average annual temperature 24°C (Jan), 27°C (Jul); mean annual rainfall 1980 mm/ 70 in; virtually no rainfall on S and SW plain; lies within the hurricane belt.

Currency 1 Jamaican Dollar (J$) = 100 cents

Economy Plantation agriculture (still employs about a third of workforce); sugar, bananas, citrus fruits, coffee, cocoa, ginger, coconuts; bauxite (world's second largest producer); cement, fertilizer, textiles, rum, chemical products; tourism.

GNP (2002e) $10.08 bn, per capita $3800

☐ International Airport

HDI (2002) 0.742

History Visited by Columbus, 1494; settled by Spanish, 1509; West African slave labour imported for work on sugar plantations from 1640; British occupation, 1655; self-government, 1944; independence, 1962; Governor-General appoints Prime Minister and Cabinet; bicameral Parliament consists of a House of Representatives and a Senate.

Head of State
(British monarch represented by Governor-General)
1991–   Sir Howard Cooke

Head of Government
1989–1992   Michael Norman Manley
1992–   Percival Patterson

JAPAN

Local name Nihon (Nippon)

Timezone GMT +9

Area 377 728 km²/145 803 sq mi

Population total (2002e) 127 347 000

Status Monarchy

Capital Tokyo

Language Japanese (official)

Ethnic groups Japanese (99%), with Korean minorities

Religions Shintoist (40%), Buddhist (39%), Christian (4%)

Physical features Island state comprising four large islands (Hokkaido, Honshu, Kyushu, Shikoku) and several small islands; consists mainly of steep mountains with many volcanoes; Hokkaido (N) central range runs N–S, rising to over 2000 m/6500 ft, falling to coastal uplands and plains; Honshu, the largest island, comprises parallel arcs of mountains bounded by narrow coastal plains, and includes Mt Fuji, 3776 m/12388 ft; heavily populated Kanto plain in E; Shikoku and Kyushu (SW) consist of clusters of low cones and rolling hills, mostly 1000–2000 m/3000–6000 ft; Ryukyu chain of volcanic islands to the S, largest Okinawa; frequent earthquakes, notably in Kanto (1993), Kobe (1995).

Climate Oceanic climate, influenced by the Asian monsoon; heavy winter rainfall on W coasts of Honshu and in Hokkaido; short, warm summers in N, and severe winters, with heavy snow; variable winter weather throughout Japan, especially in N and W; typhoons in summer and early autumn; mild and almost subtropical winters in S Honshu, Shikoku, and Kyushu; average annual temperatures 5°C (Jan), 25°C (Jul) in Tokyo.

Currency 1 Yen (¥, Y) = 100 sen

Economy Limited natural resources (less than 20% of land under cultivation); intensive crop production (principally of rice); timber, fishing, engineering, ship-building, textiles, chemicals; major industrial developments since 1960s, especially in computing, electronics, and vehicles.

GDP (2002e) $3.651 tn, per capita $28700

HDI (2002) 0.933

History Originally occupied by the Ainu; developed into small states, 4th-c; culture strongly influenced by China, 7th–9th-c; ruled by feudal shoguns until power passed to the emperor, 1867; limited contact with the West until the Meiji Restoration, 1868; successful war with China, 1894–5; gained Formosa (Taiwan) and S Manchuria; formed alliance with Britain, 1902; war with Russia, 1904–5; Russia ceded southern half of Sakhalin; Korea annexed, 1910; joined allies in World War 1, 1914; received German Pacific islands as mandates, 1919; war with China; occupied Manchuria, 1931–2; renewed fighting, 1937; entered World War 2 with surprise attack on the US fleet at Pearl Harbor, Hawaii, 1941; occupied British and Dutch possessions in SE Asia, 1941–2; pushed back during 1943–5; atomic bombs dropped on Hiroshima and Nagasaki by allied forces in 1945, ending World War 2 with Japanese surrender; allied control commission took

Key
1. Yokohama
2. Nagoya
3. Kyoto
4. Kobe
5. Osaka
6. Hiroshima
7. Kitakyushu
8. Fukuoka
9. Takamatsu
10. Nagasaki

☐ International Airport

power, and Formosa and Manchuria returned to China; Emperor Hirohito became figurehead ruler, 1946; full sovereignty regained, 1952; joined United Nations, 1958; strong economic growth in 1960s; regained Bonin, Marcus, and Volcano Islands, 1972; a constitutional monarchy with Emperor as Head of State; government consists of a Prime Minister, Cabinet, and bicameral Diet (*Kokkai*), with a House of Representatives and a House of Councillors; co-location (with South Korea) of the 2002 FIFA World Cup.

Head of State (Emperor)
1989–   Akihito (Heisei)

Head of Government (Prime Minister)
2001–   Junichiro Koizumi

HUMAN GEOGRAPHY

JORDAN

Local name al'Urdun

Timezone GMT +2

Area 89544 km²/34564 sq mi

Population total (2002e) 5260000

Status Hashemite kingdom

Date of independence 1946

Capital Amman

Language Arabic (official)

Ethnic groups Arab (99%), Circassian, Armenian, Turkish, Kurd minorities

Religions Muslim (Sunni 95%), Christian (including Roman Catholic, Anglican, Coptic, Greek Orthodox, and Evangelical Lutheran) (5%)

Physical features Located in Middle East; divided N–S by Red Sea–Jordan rift valley, much lying below sea level; lowest point, –400 m/–1312 ft at the Dead Sea; highest point, Jebel Ram, 1754 m/5754 ft; land levels out to the Syrian desert (E); c.90% of Jordan is desert.

Climate Mediterranean; hot, dry summers, cool, wet winters; desert area uniformly hot, sunny; rainfall below 200 mm/8 in; average annual temperatures 7.5°C (Jan), 24.9°C (Jul) in Amman.

Currency 1 Jordan Dinar = 1000 fils

Economy Oil, cement, potash, phosphate (world's third largest exporter), light manufacturing; cereals, vegetables, citrus fruits, olives.

GDP (2002e) $22.63 bn, per capita $4300

HDI (2002) 0.717

HUMAN GEOGRAPHY

Jordan (continued)

History Part of Roman Empire; Arab control, 7th-c; part of Turkish Empire, 16th-c until World War 1; area divided into Palestine (W of R Jordan) and Transjordan (E of R Jordan), administered by Britain; independence as Transjordan, 1946; British mandate over Palestine ended, 1948; renamed Jordan, 1949; Israeli control of West Bank after Six-Day War, 1967; civil war, following attempts by Jordanian army to expel Palestinian guerrillas from West Bank, 1970–1; claims to the West Bank ceded to the Palestine Liberation Organization, 1974; links with the West Bank cut, and PLO established a government in exile, 1988; martial law formally abolished by King Hussein in 1992, and ban on political parties lifted; conflict with Israel formally ended, 1994; Monarch is Head of State and appoints a Prime Minister, who selects a Council of Ministers; Parliament consists of a Senate and a House of Representatives.

Head of State (Monarch)
1952–99   Hussein II
1999–   Abdullah II

Head of Government
2000–3   Ali Abu al-Ragheb
2003–5   Faisal al-Fayez
2005–   Adnan Badran

☐ International Airport   ∴ World heritage site

KAZAKHSTAN

☐ International Airport

Local name Kazakstan

Timezone GMT +5/6

Area 2717300 km²/1 048 878 sq mi

Population total (2002e) 14 888 000

Status Republic

Date of independence 1991

Capital Astana (from 1998), formerly Akmola (1997–8) and previously located at Almaty (Alma-Ata)

Languages Kazakh (official), Russian, German

Ethnic groups Kazakh (40%), Russian (37%), German (6%), Ukrainian (5%)

Religions Muslim (Sunni), Christian (Russian Orthodox, Protestant)

Physical features Bounded E by China and W by Caspian Sea; second largest republic in former USSR; mountain ranges in E and SE; steppeland (N) gives way to desert (S); lowest elevation near E shore of the Caspian Sea, 132 m/433 ft below sea-level; main rivers, Irtysh, Syr Darya, Ural, Ili; largest lake, L Balkhash; space launch centre at Tyuratam, near Baikonur.

Climate Continental; hot summers, extreme winters; wide range of temperatures, from −17°C in N and E ranges, to −3°C in S (Jan), 20°C in N, 29°C in S (Jul); strong, dry winds common in NW.

Currency 1 tenge = 100 kopecks

Economy Coal, iron ore, bauxite, copper, nickel, oil; oil refining, metallurgy, heavy engineering, chemicals, leatherwork, footwear, food processing; cotton, fruit, grain, sheep.

GDP (2002e) $120 bn, per capita $7200

HDI (2002) 0.750

History Under the control of the Mongols, 13th-c; gradually under Russian rule, 1730–1853; became constituent republic of USSR, 1936; independence movement, 1990–1; independence declared in 1991, and joined Commonwealth of Independent States; governed by a President, Prime Minister, and Supreme Soviet.

Head of State
1991–   Nursultan A Nazarbayev

Head of Government
2003–   Daniyal Akhmetov

KENYA

Local name Kenya

Timezone GMT +3

Area 580 367 km²/224 081 sq mi

Population total (2002e) 31 139 000

Status Republic

Date of independence 1963

Capital Nairobi

Languages English and Swahili (official), with many local languages spoken

Ethnic groups Kikuyu (21%), Luhya (13%), Luo (11%), Kamba (11%), Kalejin (6%), Kisii (6%), Meru (6%)

Religions Christian (66%) (Roman Catholic 28%, Protestant 38%), local beliefs (26%), Muslim (6%)

Physical features Crossed by the Equator; SW plateau rises to 600–3000 m/2000–10 000 ft, includes Mt Kenya, 5200 m/17 058 ft; Great Rift Valley (W) runs N–S; dry, arid semi-desert in N, generally under 600 m/2000 ft; rivers include Tana and Athi; L Turkana in NW.

Climate Tropical climate on coast, with high temperatures and humidity; average annual temperature 18°C (Jan), 16°C (Jul) in Nairobi; average annual rainfall 958 mm/38 in.

Currency 1 Kenyan shilling (KSh) = 100 cents

Economy Agriculture (accounts for c.35% of national income): coffee, tea, cashew nuts, rice, wheat, maize, sugar cane; textiles, chemicals, cement, oil refining, tobacco, rubber; reserves of soda ash, salt, limestone, lead, gemstones, silver, gold; 14 national parks attract large numbers of tourists.

GDP (2002e) $32.89 bn, per capita $1100

HDI (2002) 0.513

History Very early fossil hominids found in the region by anthropologists; coast settled by Arabs, 7th-c; Portuguese control, 16th–17th-c; British control as East African Protectorate, 1895; British colony, 1920; independence movement led to Mau Mau rebellion, 1952–60; inde-

□ International Airport − − Border dispute

pendence within the Commonwealth, 1963; declared Republic of Kenya, 1964; first leader, Jomo Kenyatta; multi-party elections, 1992, gave Arap Moi a fourth term of office; result condemned by opposition parties; Moi defeated (Dec 2002) after 24 years' rule; governed by a President elected for a 5-year term, with a unicameral National Assembly of 224 members; coast hit by Indian Ocean tsunami, 2004.

Head of State/Government
1978–2002   Daniel Arap Moi
2002–   Mwai Kibaki

KIRIBATI

Local name Kiribati

Timezone GMT −12

Area 717 km²/277 sq mi

Population total (2002e) 90 600

Status Republic

Date of independence 1979

Capital Bairiki (on Tarawa Atoll)

Languages English (official) and Gilbertese

Ethnic groups Micronesian, small Polynesian and non-Pacific minorities

Religions Roman Catholic (54%), Kiribati Protestant (39%), Baha'i (2%), Seventh-day Adventist (2%), Mormon (2%)

Physical features Group of 33 low-lying islands scattered over c.3 000 000 km²/1 200 000 sq mi of the C Pacific Ocean; comprises the Gilbert Is Group, Phoenix Is, and 8 of the 11 Line Islands, including Christmas I; islands seldom rise to more than 4 m/13 ft and usually consist of a reef enclosing a lagoon.

Climate Maritime equatorial climate in central islands, tropical further N and S; periodic drought in some islands; wet season (Nov–Apr); subject to typhoons; average annual temperatures 28°C (Jan), 27°C (July) in Tarawa; average annual rainfall 1977 mm/78 in.

Currency 1 Australian Dollar ($A) = 100 cents

Economy 50% of land under permanent cultivation; main exports include fish, particularly tuna; phosphates; copra, coconuts, bananas, pandanus, breadfruit, papaya; sea fishing.

GDP (2001e) $79 mn, per capita $800

History Gilbert and Ellice Is proclaimed a British protectorate, 1892; became a Crown Colony, 1916; occupied by Japan during World War 2, but driven out by US forces; Ellice Is severed links with Gilbert Is to form separate dependency of Tuvalu, 1975; Gilbert Is independence as Kiribati, 1979; a sovereign and democratic republic, with a President and an elected House of Assembly.

Head of State/Government
1994–2003   Teburoro Tito
2003–   Anote Tong

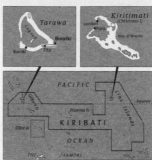

□ International Airport

KOREA, NORTH

Local name Chôsón Minjujuüi In'min Konghwaguk

Timezone GMT +9

Area 122 098 km²/47 130 sq mi

Population total (2002e) 22 224 000

Status Democratic people's republic

Date of independence 1948

Capital Pyongyang

Language Korean (official)

Ethnic groups Korean (99.8%), Chinese (0.2%)

Religions Atheist or non-religious (68%), Buddhist (2%), Christian (1%)

Physical features Located in E Asia, in the N half of the Korean peninsula; separated from South Korea to the S by a demilitarized zone of 1262 km²/487 sq mi; volcanic peak of Mount Paek-tu rises 2744 m/9003 ft in NE; Yalu river valley marks Korean–Chinese border in NW; fertile Chaeryong and Pyongyang plains in SW; 74% of land forested, 18% arable.

Climate Temperate; warm summers, severely cold winters; often rivers freeze for up to 3–4 months in winter; average annual temperatures −8°C (Jan), 24°C (Jul); average annual rainfall 916 mm/26 in.

Currency 1 Won (NKW) = 100 chon

Economy Agriculture (employs c.48% of workforce, generally on large-scale collective farms); rice, maize, vegetables, livestock, wheat, barley, beans, tobacco; timber, fishing; severely affected during the Korean War, but rapid recovery with Soviet and Chinese aid; machine building, mining, chemicals, textiles.

GDP (2002e) $22.26 bn, per capita $1000

History (>> KOREA, SOUTH history); formally annexed by Japan, 1910; N area occupied by Soviet troops following invasion by US and Russian troops and the dividing of the country into N and S, 1945; Democratic People's Republic of Korea declared, 1948; Korean War, 1950–3; demilitarized zone established, 1953; friendship and mutual-assistance treaty signed with China, 1961; unsuccessful reunification talks, 1980; member of UN, 1991; non-aggression agreement signed with S Korea, 1991; death of Kim Il-sung, 1994; withdrawal from 1970 Non-Proliferation treaty (2003); governed by a President and a Supreme People's Assembly; first road link between North and South Korea since Korean War, 2003.

Head of State
1972–4   Kim Il-sung
1994–   Kim Jong-il

Head of Government
1997–2003   Hong Song-nam
2003–   Pak Pong-ju

☐ International Airport

KOREA, SOUTH

Local name Taehan-Min'guk

Timezone GMT +9

Area 98 913 km²/38 180 sq mi

Population total (2002e) 47 640 000

Status Republic

Date of independence 1948

Capital Seoul

Language Korean (official)

Ethnic groups Korean (99.9%), Chinese (0.1%)

Religions Buddhist (18%), Christian (Protestant 41%, Roman Catholic 3%), Confucianist (1%)

Physical features Occupies the S half of the Korean peninsula; bordered N by North Korea, from which it is separated by a demilitarized zone at 38°N; Taebaek Sanmaek Mt range runs N–S along the E coast; descends to broad, undulating coastal lowlands; rivers include Naktong and Han; c.3000 islands off the W and S coasts; largest island is Cheju do, which contains Korea's highest peak, Hallasan, 1950 m/6398 ft.

Climate Extreme continental climate, cold winters, hot summers; average annual temperatures –5°C (Jan), 25°C (Jul); average annual rainfall 1250 mm/49 in.

Currency 1 Won (W) = 100 chon

Economy Light consumer goods, with a shift towards heavy industries; petrochemicals, textiles, electrical machinery, steel, ships, fish; one of the world's largest deposits of tungsten; only a fifth of land suitable for cultivation; rice, wheat, barley, grain, pulses, tobacco.

GDP (2002e) $941.5 bn, per capita $19 600

☐ International Airport

HDI (2002) 0.882

History Originally split into three rival kingdoms, united in 668 by the Silla dynasty; succeeded by the Koryo dynasty, 935; Yi dynasty, 1392–1910; independence recognized by China, 1895; annexation by Japan, 1910;

Korea, South (continued)

entered by Russia (from N) and USA (from S) to enforce the Japanese surrender, dividing the country in N and S at the 38th parallel, 1945; declared Republic of Korea, 1948; North Korean forces invaded, 1950; UN forces assisted South Korea in stopping the advance, 1950–3; military coup, 1961; assassination of Park Chung Hee, 1979; non-aggression pact signed with N Korea, 1991; President Roh Moo-hyun impeached (Mar 2004) but reinstated; governed by a President, a State Council, and a National Assembly; co-location (with Japan) of the 2002 FIFA World Cup; first road link between North and South Korea since Korean War, 2003.

Head of State
2003–   Roh Moo-hyun

Head of Government
2003–4   Goh Kun
2004–   Lee Hae-chan

KUWAIT

Local name Dowlat al-Kuwait (Arabic)

Timezone GMT +3

Area 17 818 km²/6878 sq mi

Population total (2002e) 2 253 000

Status Independent state

Date of independence 1961

Capital Kuwait City

Language Arabic (official)

Ethnic groups Kuwaiti (52%), non-Kuwaiti Arab (45%), Asian (3%)

Religions Muslim (90%), Christian (8%), Hindu (2%)

Physical features Consists of mainland and nine offshore islands; terrain flat or gently undulating, rising SW to 271 m/889 ft; Wadi al Batin on W border with Iraq; low ridges in NE generally stony with sparse vegetation.

Climate Hot and dry climate; summer temperatures very high, often above 45°C (Jul–Aug); humidity often over 90%; sandstorms common all year; average annual temperature 14°C (Jan) to 37°C (Jul) in Kuwait City; average annual rainfall 111 mm/4 in.

Currency 1 Kuwaiti Dinar (KD) = 1000 fils

Economy Oil discovered, 1938, providing 95% of government revenue; active programme of economic diversification; petrochemicals, fertilizers, construction materials, asbestos, batteries; agriculture gradually expanding; dates, citrus fruits, timber, livestock.

GDP (2002e) $36.85 bn, per capita $17 500

HDI (2002) 0.813

History Port founded in 18th-c; British protectorate, 1914; full independence from Britain, 1961; invasion and annexation by Iraq (Aug 1990), leading to Gulf War (Jan–Feb 1991), with severe damage to Kuwait City; Kuwait liberated with the aid of UN forces in 1991, and government returned from exile; large refugee emigration; major post-war problems, including burning of Kuwaiti oil wells by Iraq and pollution of Gulf waters by oil; Emir is Head of State, governing through an appointed Prime Minister and a Council of Ministers.

☐ International Airport

Head of State (Emir)
1978–   Jabir al-Ahmad al-Jabir

Head of Government (Prime Minister)
2003–   Sabah al-Ahmad al-Jabir al-Sabah

KYRGYZSTAN

Local name Kyrgyzstan

Timezone GMT +5

Area 198 500 km²/76 621 sq mi

Population total (2002e) 5 002 000

Status Republic

Date of independence 1991

Capital Bishkek (formerly Frunze)

Language Russian (official), Kyrgyz

Ethnic groups Kyrgyz (52%), Russian (21%), other (27%)

Religion Sunni Muslim (chief religion)

Physical features Located in C Asia, bounded SE and E by China; largely occupied by the Tien Shan Mts; highest point within the republic at Pik Pobedy, 7439 m/24 406 ft; chief river, the Naryn; largest lake, L Issyk-Kul.

Climate Typical desert climate in N, W, and SE; hot, dry summers in valleys; mean annual temperature –18°C (Jan), 28°C (Jul).

Currency 1 Kyrgyzstani som = 100 tyiyn

Economy Metallurgy; machines; coal; natural gas; textiles, food processing, gold; wheat, cotton, tobacco, animal husbandry.

GDP (2002e) $13.88 bn, per capita $2900

HDI (2002) 0.712

History Part of Turkestan republic, 1917–24; constituent republic of USSR, 1936; independence, and joined Commonwealth of Independent States, 1991; governed by a President, Prime Minister, and Supreme Soviet; President Akayev deposed in coup, Mar 2005.

☐ International Airport

Head of State
2005–   Kurmanbek Bakiev *Interim*

Head of Government
2002–   Nikolai Tanayev

LAOS

Local name Lao

Timezone GMT +7

Area 236 800 km²/91 405 sq mi

Population total (2002e) 5 777 000

Status Republic

Date of independence 1949

Capital Vientiane

Languages Lao (official), French, and tribal languages

Ethnic groups Laotian (60%), hill tribes (35%)

Religions Buddhist (58%), animist (largely the Lao-Theung) (34%), Christian (2%)

Physical features Landlocked country on the Indo-Chinese peninsula; dense jungle and rugged mountains (E), rising to 2751 m/9025 ft on Vietnamese border, and 2820 m/9252 ft at Phou Bia on the Xieng Khouang plateau; Mekong R flows NW–SE, fertile Mekong floodplains in W; 4% of land arable, 58% forested.

Climate Monsoonal climate, average annual rainfall 1715 mm/67.5 in; (heaviest, May–Sep); average annual temperature 14°C (Jan), 34°C (Jul) in Vientiane.

Currency (1992) 1 Kip (Kp) = 100 at

Economy Agricultural economy suffered severely in the civil war; rice, coffee, tobacco, cotton, spices, opium; tin, iron ore, potash; forestry (1991 logging ban to halt deforestation), rubber, cigarettes, matches; textiles.

GDP (2002e) $10.4 bn, per capita $1800

HDI (2002) 0.485

History Visited by Europeans, 17th-c; French protectorate, 1893; occupied by Japanese in World War 2; independence from France, 1949; civil war, 1953–75,

☐ International Airport

between the Lao government, supported by the USA, and the communist-led Patriotic Front *(Pathet Lao)*, supported by North Vietnam; monarchy abolished and communist republic established, 1975 draft constitution approved, 1991, provides for a directly elected National Assembly and executive President.

Head of State
1998–   Khamtay Siphandone

Head of Government
2001–   Boungnang Vorachith

LATVIA

Local name Latvija (Latvian)

Timezone GMT +2

Area 64 600 km²/24 900 sq mi

Population total (2002e) 2 331 000

Status Republic

Date of independence 1991

Capital Riga

Language Latvian (official)

Ethnic groups Latvian (52%), Russian (34%), Beloruss-ian (5%), Ukrainian (4%), Polish (2%), Lithuanian (1%)

Religions Predominantly Evangelical Lutheran, with Orthodox and Roman Catholic minorities

Physical features Flat, glaciated region; highest point, central Vidzeme (Livonia) elevation, 312 m/1024 ft; over 40% forested; coastline ranges over 472 km/293 mi; wooded lowland, marshes, lakes; NW coast indented by the Gulf of Riga; chief river, Daugava.

Climate Mild climate, with high humidity; only c.30–40 days of sunshine annually; summers cool and rainy; average mean temperature −2°C (Jan), 17°C (Jul); average annual rainfall 700–800 mm/28–31 in.

Currency (1991) 1 Lat (Ls) = 100 santims

Economy Machine-building, metalworking, electrical engineering, electronics, chemicals, furniture, food processing, fishing, timber, paper and woollen goods, meat and dairy products.

GDP (2002e) $20.99 bn, per capita $8900

HDI (2002) 0.800

History Incorporated into Russia, 1721; independent

□ International Airport

state, 1918–40; proclaimed a Soviet Socialist Republic, 1940; occupied by Germany in World War 2; USSR regained control, 1944; coalition government elected, 1989; declared independence, 1991; governed by a President, Prime Minister, and Congress of Latvia.

Head of State
1999–   Vaira Vike-Freiberga

Head of Government
2004   Indulis Emsis
2004–   Aigars Kalvitis

LEBANON

Local names al-Lubnān (Arab), Liban (French)

Timezone GMT +2

Area 10 452 km²/4034 sq mi

Population total (2002e) 3 678 000

Status Republic

Date of independence 1943

Capital Beirut

Languages Arabic (official), French, English, and Armenian also spoken

Ethnic groups Arab (93%), with several minorities

Religions Muslim (c.75%), Christian (c.25%), also many religious sects including Armenian, Greek, Roman Catholic, Alawite, Druze, and Jewish

Physical features Narrow coastal plain rises gradu-ally E to the Lebanon Mts (Jebel Liban), reaching 3087 m/10 128 ft at Qornet es Saouda; arid E slopes fall abruptly to the fertile Beqaa plateau, average elevation 1000 m/

3 300 ft; Anti-Lebanon range (Jebel esh Sharqi) in the E; R Litani flows S between the two ranges.

Climate Mediterranean climate, varying with alti-tude; hot, dry summers, warm, moist winters; average annual temperatures 13°C (Jan), 27°C (Jul); average annual rainfall 920 mm/36 in; much drier and cooler in the Bekaa valley.

Currency 1 Lebanese Pound/Livre (LL, £L) = 100 piastres

Economy Commercial and financial centre of the Middle East until the civil war, which severely damaged economic infrastructure and reduced industrial and agricultural production; oil refining, textiles, chemicals, food processing; citrus fruits, apples, grapes, bananas, sugar beet, olives, wheat; tourism has virtually collapsed, but signs of revival in 1993.

GDP (2002e) $17.61 bn, per capita $4800

HDI (2002) 0.755

History Part of the Ottoman Empire from 16th-c; after the massacre of (Catholic) Maronites by (Muslim) Druzes in 1860, Maronite area around Jabal Lubnan granted special autonomous status; Greater Lebanon, based on this area, created in 1920 under French mandate; Muslim coastal regions incorporated, despite great opposition; constitutional republic, 1926; independence, 1943; Palestinian resistance units established in Lebanon by late 1960s despite government opposition, including the Palestine Liberation Organization (PLO); several militia groups developed in the mid-1970s; following terrorist attacks, Israel invaded S Lebanon, 1978 and 1982; heavy Israeli bombardment of Beirut forced the withdrawal of Palestinian forces, 1982; unilateral withdrawal of Israeli and Syrian forces from Lebanon brought clashes between the Druze (backed by Syria) and Christian Lebanese militia; ceasefire announced in late 1982, broken many times; Syrian troops entered Beirut in 1988 in an attempt to restore order; release of Western hostages taken by militant groups began in 1990; timetable for militia disarmament introduced, 1991; Israeli withdrawal from South Lebanon border area, May 2000; constitution provides for a Council of Ministers, a President (a Maronite Christian), Prime Minister (a Sunni Muslim), a Cabinet, and a Parliament, equally divided between Christians and Muslims.

Head of State
1998–   Emile Lahoud

Head of Government
2000–4   Rafiq al-Hariri
2004–   Omar Karameh

□ International Airport

LESOTHO

Local name Lesotho

Timezone GMT +2

Area 30 355 km²/11 720 sq mi

Population total (2002e) 2 208 000

Status Independent kingdom within the Commonwealth

Date of independence 1960

Capital Maseru

Languages Lesotho (Sesotho) and English (official), Zulu, Afrikaans, French, Xhosa also spoken

Ethnic groups Basotho (99%), Zulu, Tembu, and Fingo tribes, European and Asian minorities

Religions Roman Catholic (44%), Protestant (mostly Lesotho Evangelical) (30%), Anglican (12%), other Christian (8%), traditional beliefs (6%)

Physical features S African kingdom completely bounded by South Africa; Drakensberg Mts in NE and E, highest peak Thabana-Ntlenyana, 3482 m/11 424 ft; serious soil erosion, especially in W; main rivers, the Orange and the Caledon; mountainous land, particularly in SW with the Maloti Mountain range.

Climate Mild, dry winters; warm summer season (Oct–Apr); average annual temperatures 15°C (Jan), 25°C (Jul); average annual rainfall 725 mm/28.5 in (Oct–Apr).

Currency 1 Loti (*plural* Maloti) (M, LSM) = 100 lisente

□ International Airport

Economy Economy based on intensive agriculture and contract labour working in South Africa; wheat, peas, beans, barley, cattle; diamonds, textiles, pharmaceuticals; jewellery, crafts, wool, mohair.

GDP (2002e) $5.106 bn, per capita $2700

HDI (2002) 0.535

Lesotho (continued)

History Originally inhabited by hunting and gathering bushmen; Bantu arrived 16th-c, and Basotho nation established; incorporated in Orange Free State, 1854; under British protection as Basutoland, 1869; independence, 1960; declared Kingdom of Lesotho in 1966, as a hereditary monarchy within the Commonwealth; constitution suspended and country ruled by Council of Ministers, 1970–86; Prime Minister deposed by coup and political activity banned, 1986, with Military Council as effective ruling body; King Moshoeshoe dethroned by military council in 1990, and replaced by eldest son; elections (first since 1970) to restore civilian rule, 1993;

Moshoeshoe returned to the throne, 1994, but died in a car accident, 1996; status of the monarchy a continuing issue; new electoral system introduced, 2002.

Head of State (Monarch)
1966–90	Moshoeshoe II
1990–4	Letsie III *Abdicated*
1994–6	Moshoeshoe II
1996–	Letsie III

Head of Government
1998–	Bethuel Pakalitha Mosisili

LIBERIA

Local name Liberia

Timezone GMT

Area 111 370 km²/42 989 sq mi

Population total (2002e) 3 288 000

Status Republic

Date of independence 1847

Capital Monrovia

Languages English (official) with many dialects/languages of Niger-Congo spoken

Ethnic groups Indigenous tribes (including Kpelle, Bassa, Gio, Kru, Gola, Kissi, Vai, and Bella) (95%), Americo-Liberians (repatriated slaves from the USA) (5%)

Religions Traditional animist beliefs (70%), Muslim (20%), Christian (10%)

Physical features Low coastal belt with lagoons, beaches, and mangrove marshes; land rises inland to mountains, reaching 1752 m/5748 ft at Mt Nimba; rivers include Mano, Moro, St Paul, St John, Cess, Duoubé, Cavalla.

Climate Equatorial climate; high temperatures, abundant rainfall; high humidity during rainy season (Apr–Sep), especially on coast; average annual temperatures 26°C (Jan), 24°C (Jul); average annual rainfall 5138 mm/202 in.

Currency 1 Liberian Dollar (L$) = 100 cents

Economy Based on minerals, especially iron ore; two-thirds of the population rely on subsistence agriculture; rubber, timber, palm oil, rice, cassava, coffee, cocoa, coconuts; large merchant fleet, including the registration of many foreign ships.

GDP (2002e) $3.116 bn, per capita $1000

History Mapped by the Portuguese in 15th-c; created as a result of the activities of several US philanthropic societies, wishing to establish a homeland for former

SIERRA LEONE · GUINEA · AFRICA
Voinjama
Mano · Wologisi Mts · Mt Nimba 1752m
Sanniquellie
Gbarnga · Ganta
Robertsport · St Paul
CÔTE D'IVOIRE
LIBERIA
Monrovia · Buchanan · Cess · Zwedru · Duobé
ATLANTIC OCEAN · Grain Coast · Greenville · Niete Mts · Kru Coast · Harper
300km
100mi

□ International Airport

slaves; founded in 1822; constituted as the Free and Independent Republic of Liberia 1847; military coup and assassination of President, 1980; new constitution, 1986, with an elected Senate and a House of Representatives; civil war, followed by arrival of West African peace-keeping force, 1990; transitional governments in early 1990s; peace accord signed, 1995; elections held, 1997; new rebel offensive, leading to exile of President Taylor, 2003; power-sharing government established, 2003; UN peace-keeping mission, 2003–4.

Head of State/Government
2003–	Gyude Bryant

LIBYA

Local name Lībiyā

Timezone GMT +1

Area 1 758 610 km²/678 823 sq mi

Population total (2002e) 5 369 000

Status Republic

Date of independence 1951

Capital Tripoli

Languages Arabic (official), with English and French widely spoken

Ethnic groups Berber and Arab (97%), Greek, Maltese, Italian, Egyptian, Pakistani, Turk, Indian, and Tunisian minorities (3%)

Religions Sunni Muslim (96%), Christian (Roman Catholic, Anglican, Coptic Orthodox) (3%), Jewish (1%)

Physical features Mainly low-lying Saharan desert or semi-desert; 93% of land is contained in the arid Saharan plateau; land rises (S) to over 2000 m/6500 ft in the Tibesti massif; highest point, Pic Bette, 2286 m/7500 ft; comparatively fertile region in Gefara plain and Jabal Nafusah plateau in Tripolitania region.

Climate Mediterranean climate on coast; rainy season (Oct–Mar) in NW and NE upland regions; average annual temperature 11°C (Jan), 27°C (Jul) in Tripoli; average annual rainfall 385 mm/15 in.

Currency 1 Libyan Dinar (LD) = 1000 dirhams

Economy Former agricultural economy; barley, olives, fruit, dates, almonds, tobacco; relatively poor until economy transformed by discovery of oil and natural gas, 1959; petroleum processing; iron, steel, aluminium; textiles; nomadic farming in S.

GDP (2002e) $33.36 bn, per capita $6200

HDI (2002) 0.773

History Controlled by Phoenicians, Carthaginians, Greeks, Vandals, and Byzantines; Arab domination during 7th-c; Turkish rule from 16th-c; Italians gained control, 1911; named Libya by the Italians, 1934; heavy fighting during World War 2, followed by British and French control; independent Kingdom of Libya, 1951; military coup established a republic under Muammar al-Gaddafi, 1969; Libyan troops occupied Aozou Strip, 1973 (returned to Chad, 1994); strained relations with other countries over alleged organization of international terrorism; diplomatic relations cut by UK after the murder of a policewoman in London, 1984; Tripoli and Benghazi bombed by US Air Force in response to alleged terrorist

□ International Airport   ∴ World heritage site

activity, 1986; alleged base of terrorist operation which caused the Lockerbie air disaster (1988), suspects extradited to stand trial in The Netherlands (1999), followed by suspension of international sanctions; responsibility for the disaster accepted, 2003; allowed international inspection of nuclear sites, 2003; US resumed diplomatic relations, Jun 2004; a socialist state, governed by a chief-of-state, a General People's Committee, and a 750-member General People's Congress.

Head of State/Government

1969–   Muammar al-Gaddafi

LIECHTENSTEIN

Local name Liechtenstein

Timezone GMT +1

Area 160 km²/62 sq mi

Population total (2002e) 33 300

Status Independent principality

Date of independence 1719

Capital Vaduz

Language German (official)

Ethnic groups Liechtensteiner (64%), Swiss (16%), Austrian (8%), German (4%)

Religions Roman Catholic (87%), Protestant (9%)

Physical features Alpine principality, located in C Europe; fourth smallest country in the world; land

□ International Airport

Liechtenstein (continued)

boundary 76 km/47 mi; bounded W by the R Rhine; mean altitude, 450 m/1 475 ft; forested mountains rise to 2 599 m/8 527 ft in the Grauspitz; Samina River flows N.

Climate Mild, equable climate; temperatures range from −15°C (Jan), 20−8°C (Jul); average annual rainfall 1050−1200 mm/41−47 in.

Currency 1 Swiss Franc (SFr, SwF) = 100 centimes

Economy Industrial sector developing since 1950s; export-based, centred on specialized and high-tech production; metal-working, engineering, chemicals, pharmaceuticals; international banking and finance; tourism.

GDP (1999e) $825 mn, per capita $25 000

History Became a sovereign state in 1342; independent principality within Holy Roman Empire, 1719; part of Holy Roman Empire until 1806; adopted Swiss currency, 1921; united with Switzerland in a customs union, 1923; became a member of UN, 1990; constitutional referendum approved, 2003; constitutional monarchy ruled by hereditary princes of the House of Liechtenstein; governed by a Prime Minister, four Councillors, and a unicameral Parliament.

Head of State (Monarch)
1989–   Hans Adam II

Head of Government
2001–   Otmar Hasler

LITHUANIA

Local name Lietuva

Timezone GMT +2

Area 65 200 km²/25 167 sq mi

Population total (2002e) 3 473 000

Status Republic

Date of independence 1991

Capital Vilnius

Language Lithuanian (official)

Ethnic groups Lithuanian (80%), Russian (9%), Polish (7%), Belorussian (2%)

Religions Roman Catholic, small minority of Evangelical Lutherans and Evangelical Reformists

Physical features Glaciated plains cover much of the area; central lowlands with gentle hills in W and higher terrain in SE; highest point, Jouzapine in the Asmenos Hills, 294 m/964 ft; 25% forested; some 3000 small lakes mostly in E and SE; complex sandy dunes on Kursiu Marios lagoon; chief river, the Nemunas.

Climate Continental climate, affected by maritime weather of W Europe and continental E; Baltic Sea influences a narrow coastal zone; average annual temperatures −5°C (Jan), 16°C (Jul); average annual rainfall 630 mm/25 in.

Currency 1 Litas (LT) = 100 centai

Economy Electrical engineering, computer hardware, instruments, machine tools, ship building; synthetic fibres, fertilizers, plastics, food processing, oil refining; cattle, pigs, poultry, grain, potatoes, vegetables.

GDP (2002e) $30.08 bn, per capita $8400

□ International Airport

HDI (2002) 0.808

History United with Poland, 1385–1795; intensive russification led to revolts in 1905 and 1917; occupied by Germany in both World Wars; proclaimed republic, 1918; annexed by USSR, 1940; growth of nationalist movement in late 1980s; declared independence in 1990, not recognized until 1991; President Paskas impeached for violating constitution (Apr 2004, later reinstated); governed by a President, Prime Minister, and Supreme Council.

Head of State
2004–   Valdas Adamkus

Head of Government
2001–   Algirdas-Mykolas Brazauskas

LUXEMBOURG

Local names Lëtzebuerg (Letz), Luxembourg (French), Luxemburg (German)

Timezone GMT +1

Area 2 586 km²/998 sq mi

Population total (2002e) 447 000

Status Grand Duchy

Date of independence 1867

Capital Luxembourg

Languages French, German, Letzeburgish

Ethnic groups Luxemburger (73%), Portuguese (9%), Italian (5%), French (3%), Belgian (3%), German (2%)

Religions Roman Catholic (97%), Protestant (2%), Jewish (1%)

Physical features Divided into the two natural regions of Ardennes (Ösling) (N); forest in N, and Gutland in S, flatter, average height 250 m/820 ft; principal rivers include the Sûre, Our, Moselle.

Climate Mild climate, influenced by warm S wind (*Fröhn*); average annual temperatures 0.7°C (Jan), 18°C (Jul) in Luxembourg; average annual rainfall, 1050–1200 mm/41–7 in.

Currency 1 Luxembourgish Franc (LFr) = 100 centimes

Economy Important international centre based in city of Luxembourg; iron and steel, food processing; chemicals, tyres, metal products; mixed farming, dairy farming; wine; forestry; tourism.

GDP (2002e) $21.94 bn, per capita $48 900

HDI (2002) 0.925

History Made a Grand Duchy by the Congress of Vienna, 1815; granted political autonomy, 1838; recognized as a neutral independent state, 1867; occupied by Germany in both World Wars; joined Benelux economic union, 1948; neutrality abandoned on joining NATO, 1949; a hereditary monarchy with the Grand Duke as Head of State; Parliament consists of Chamber of Deputies and State Council; Head of Government is the Minister of State.

☐ International Airport

Head of State (Grand Dukes and Duchesses)		**Head of Government**	
1964–2000	Jean	1984–95	Jacques Santer
2000–	Henri	1995–	Jean-Claude Juncker

MACAO >> CHINA

MACEDONIA, FORMER YUGOSLAV REPUBLIC OF

Local name Makedonija

Timezone GMT +2

Area 25 713 km²/9925 sq mi

Population total (2002e) 2 036 000

Status Republic

Date of independence 1991

Capital Skopje

Language Macedonian (status as language or dialect is a political issue with Greece) and Albanian

Ethnic groups Macedonian Slav (66%), Albanian (23%), with Turk (4%), Serb (3%), and other minorities (but minority totals disputed as underestimates by Albanians and Serbs)

Religions Macedonian Orthodox Christian (autocephalous), Muslim

Physical features Landlocked, mountainous region, bordered by Serbia, Bulgaria, Greece, Albania; divided from Greek Macedonia by the Kožuf and Nidže ranges, highest point, Korab, 2764 m/9068 ft; main rivers, Struma and Vardar.

☐ International Airport

Macedonia (continued)

Climate Continental; average annual temperatures 0°C (Jan), 24°C (Jul); often heavy winter snowfalls; average annual rainfall 500 mm/20 in.

Currency (1994) 1 Denar = 100 paras

Economy Agriculture; wheat, barley, corn, rice, tobacco; sheep, cattle; mining of minerals, iron ore, lead, zinc, nickel; steel, chemicals, textiles.

GDP (2002e) $10.57 bn, per capita $5100

HDI (2002) 0.772

History Part of Macedonian, Roman, and Byzantine Empires; settled by Slavs, 6th-c; conquered by Bulgars, 7th-c, and by Serbia, 14th-c; incorporated into Serbia after the Balkan Wars; united in 1918, in what later became Yugoslavia, but continuous demands for autonomy per-

sisted; occupied by Bulgaria during World War 2, 1941–44; declaration of independence, 1991; international discussions continue over the name under which the country will be accorded international recognition (the adjacent province of Greece bears the name Macedonia); received large numbers of refugees during the Kosovo crisis, 1999; peace agreement signed and NATO task force deployed, 2001; EU took over operations, 2003; governed by a President, Prime Minister, and Assembly.

Head of State
2004–   Branko Crvenkovski

Head of Government
2002–4   Branko Crvenkovski
2004   Hari Kostov
2004–   Vlado Buckovski

MADAGASCAR

Local name Madagasikara

Timezone GMT +3

Area 587 041 km²/228 658 sq mi

Population total (2002e) 16 473 000

Status Republic

Date of independence 1960

Capital Antananarivo

Languages Malagasy (official), with French widely spoken

Ethnic groups Malagasy (99%) (including Merina 26%, Betsimisaraka 15%, Betsileo 12%)

Religions Traditional animist beliefs (47%), Christian (48%) (Roman Catholic 26%, Protestant 23%), Muslim (5%)

Physical features World's fourth largest island, length (N–S) 1580 km/982 mi; dissected by a ridge of mountains (Tsaratanana Range), rising to 2876 m/9436 ft at Maromokotra; cliffs (E) drop down to a coastal plain through tropical forest; terraced descent (W) through savannah to coast, heavily indented in N.

Climate Tropical, variable rainfall; average annual rainfall 1000–1500 mm/40–60 in, higher in tropical coastal region; average annual temperatures 21°C (Jan), 15°C (Jul).

Currency 1 Malagasy Franc (FMG, MgFr) = 100 centimes

Economy Chiefly agricultural economy; rice, manioc, coffee, sugar, vanilla, cotton, peanuts, tobacco, livestock; food processing, tanning, cement, soap, paper, textiles, oil products; graphite, chrome, coal, ilmenite.

GDP (2002e) $12.59 bn, per capita $800

HDI (2002) 0.469

History Settled by Indonesians in 1st-c AD and by African traders in 8th-c; visited by Portuguese, 16th-c; French established trading posts in late 18th-c; claimed as a protectorate by the French, 1895; autonomous overseas French territory (Malagasy Republic), 1958; inde-

□ International Airport

pendence, 1960; became Madagascar, 1977; new multiparty constitution, 1992; new constitution, 1998; governed by a President, who appoints a Council of Ministers and is guided by a Supreme Revolutionary Council; National People's Assembly is elected every five years; ongoing crisis following elections, 2001, with Didier Ratsiraka refusing to yield power to opposition leader Marc Ravalomanana, eventually appointed president (2002); legislative elections (Dec) followed by new cabinet, 2003.

Head of State
1997–2002   Didier Ratsiraka
2002–   Marc Ravalomanana

Head of Government
1998–2002   Tantely Andrianarivo
2002–   Jacques Sylla

MADEIRA (ISLANDS) >> PORTUGAL

MALAWI

Local name Malawi (Malaêi)

Timezone GMT +2

Area 118 484 km²/47 747 sq mi

Population total (2002e) 10 520 000

Status Republic

Date of independence 1964

Capital Lilongwe

Languages English and Chichewa (official)

Ethnic groups Maravi (including Nyanja, Chewa, Tonga, Tumbuka) (60%), Lomwe (18%), Yao (13%), Ngoni (7%), also Asian and European minorities

Religions Protestant (55%), Roman Catholic (20%), Muslim (20%), traditional animist beliefs (3%)

Physical features Crossed N–S by the Great Rift Valley; contains Africa's third largest lake, L Malawi; main river, Shire; Shire highlands (S) rise to nearly 3000 m/10 000 ft at Mt Mulanje.

Climate Tropical climate in S; high year-round temperatures, 28–37°C; average annual temperatures 23°C (Jan), 16°C (Jul) in Lilongwe; average annual rainfall, 740 mm/30 in; more moderate temperatures in central areas.

Currency 1 Kwacha (MK) = 100 tambala

Economy Based on agriculture (employs 90% of population); tobacco, sugar, tea, cotton, groundnuts, maize; textiles, matches, cigarettes, beer, spirits, shoes, cement.

GDP (2002e) $6.811 bn, per capita $600

HDI (2002) 0.400

History Visited by the Portuguese, 17th-c; European contact established by David Livingstone, 1859; Scottish church missions in the area; claimed as the British Protectorate of Nyasaland, 1891; British colony, 1907; in

□ International Airport

the 1950s joined with N and S Rhodesia to form the Federation of Rhodesia and Nyasaland; independence, 1964; republic, 1966; governed by a President, Cabinet, and National Assembly.

Head of State/Government
1966–94   Hastings Kamuzu Banda
1994–2004 Bakili Muluzi
2004–   Bingu wa Mutharika

MALAYSIA

Local name Malaysia

Timezone GMT +8

Area 329 749 km²/127 283 sq mi

Population total (2002e) 24 437 000

Status Republic

Date of independence 1957

Capital Kuala Lumpur

Languages Bahasa Malaysia (Malay) (official), also Chinese, English, and Tamil widely spoken

Ethnic groups Malay (59%), Chinese (32%), Indian (9%)

Religions Muslim (53%), Buddhist (17%), Chinese folk-religionist (12%), Hindu (7%), Christian (6%)

Physical features Independent federation of states located in SE Asia, comprising 11 states and a federal territory in Peninsular Malaysia, and the E States of Sabah and Sarawak on the island of Borneo; mountain chain of granite and limestone running N–S, rising to Mt Tahan, 2189 m/7182 ft; peninsula length 700 km/435 mi, width up to 320 km/200 mi; mostly tropical rainforest and mangrove swamp; Mt Kinabalu on Sabah, Malaysia's highest peak, 4094 m/13 432 ft.

Climate Tropical climate strongly influenced by monsoon winds; high humidity; average annual rainfall in the peninsula, 260 mm/10 in (S), 800 mm/32 in (N); average daily temperatures, 21–32°C in coastal areas, 12–25°C in mountains.

Currency 1 Malaysian Dollar/Ringgit (M$) = 100 cents

Economy Discovery of tin in the late 19th-c brought

HUMAN GEOGRAPHY

Malaysia (continued)

European investment; rubber trees introduced from Brazil; minerals including iron ore, bauxite; oil, natural gas; electronic components, electrical goods; tourism.

GNP (2002e) $198.4 bn, per capita $8800

HDI (2002) 0.772

History Part of Srivijaya Empire, 9th–13th-c; Hindu and Muslim influences, 14th–15th-c; Portugal, the Netherlands, and Britain vied for control from 16th-c; Singapore, Malacca, and Penang formally incorporated into British Colony of the Straits Settlements, 1826; British protection extended over Perak, Selangor, Negeri Sembilan, and Pahang, constituted into the Federated Malay States, 1895; protection treaties with several other states (Unfederated Malay States), 1885–1930; Japanese occupation, World War 2; Federation of Malaya, 1948; independence, 1957; constitutional monarchy of Malaysia, 1963; Singapore withdrew from Federation, 1965; governed by a bicameral Federal Parliament; Head of State is a Monarch elected for five years by his fellow sultans; advised by a Prime Minister and a Cabinet; coast hit by tsunami, 2004.

Head of State (Sultan)
2001–   Syed Sirajuddin

☐ International Airport

Head of Government
2003–   Abdullah Ahmad Badawi

MALDIVES

Local name Dhivehi Jumhuriya

Timezone GMT +5

Area 300 km²/116 sq mi

Population total (2002e) 281 500

Status Independent republic within the Commonwealth

Date of independence 1968

Capital Malé

Languages Dhivehi (official), Arabic, Hindi, and English widely spoken

Ethnic groups Sinhalese (Dravidian extraction mainly), also Arab, Negrito, African influences

Religion Almost 100% Sunni Muslim

Physical features Island archipelago in the Indian Ocean; comprises c.1 190 islands (202 inhabited) in chain of 20 coral atolls; none of the islands rising above 1.8 m/5 ft; 10% of land arable, 3% forested.

Climate Generally warm and humid; wet season created by SW monsoons (Apr–Oct), dry season by NE monsoon (Dec–Mar); average annual rainfall, 2100 mm/83 in; average daily temperature 22°C.

Currency 1 Rufiyaa (MRf, Rf) = 100 laaris

Economy Agriculture; breadfruit, banana, mango, cassava, sweet potato, millet; fishing, shipping, tourism.

GDP (2002e) $1.25 bn, per capita $3900

HDI (2002) 0.743

History Former dependency of Ceylon (Sri Lanka); British protectorate, 1887–1965; became Republic within the Commonwealth, 1953; Sultan restored, 1954; inde-

☐ International Airport

pendence, 1965; rejoined Commonwealth, 1982; state of emergency following pro-democracy protests, 2004; governed by a president, a ministers' *Majlis* (cabinet), and a citizens' *Majlis* of 48 members elected for five years; several areas destroyed by tsunami, 2004.

Head of State/Government
1978–   Maumoon Abdul Gayoom

MALI

Local name Mali

Timezone GMT

Area 1 240 192 km²/478 714 sq mi

Population total (2002e) 11 340 000

Status Republic

Date of independence 1960

Capital Bamako

Languages French (official), local languages (including Bambara) widely spoken

Ethnic groups Mande (Bambara, Malinke, Sarakole) (50%), Peul (Fulani nomads) (17%), Voltaic (including Senufo, Bura, Senouto, Minianka) (12%), Songhai (6%), Tuareg and Moor (5%)

Religions Muslim (90%), traditional animist beliefs (9%), Christian (1%) (Roman Catholic 0.5%, Protestant 0.5%)

Physical features Landlocked country on the fringe of the Sahara; lower part of the Hoggar massif (N); arid plains 300–500 m/1000–1600 ft; mainly savannah land in the S; main rivers, Niger, Bani Sénégal; featureless desert land (N).

Climate Subtropical in S and SW, with rainy season (Jun–Oct). Average rainfall c.1 000 mm/40 in; average annual temperatures 24°C (Jan), 27°C (Jul) in Bamako.

Currency 1 CFA Franc (CFAFr) = 100 centimes

Economy Mainly subsistence agriculture; crops severely affected by drought conditions; fishing, livestock, food processing, textiles, leather, cement; some tourism.

GDP (2002e) $9.775 bn, per capita $900

HDI (2002) 0.386

□ International Airport

History Mediaeval state controlling the trade routes between savannah and Sahara, reaching its peak in the 14th-c; governed by France, 1881–95; territory of French Sudan (part of French West Africa) until 1959; partnership with Senegal as the Federation of Mali, 1959; separate independence, 1960; under 1979 constitution (suspended, 1991) governed by a President elected every six years, and a National Assembly.

Head of State
1992–2002 Alpha Oumar Konaré
2002– Amadou Toumani Touré

Head of Government
2002–4 Mohammed Ag Amani
2004– Ousmane Issoufi Maïga

MALTA

Local name Malta

Timezone GMT +1

Area 316 km²/122 sq mi

Population total (2002e) 386 000

Status Independent republic within the Commonwealth

Date of independence 1964

Capital Valletta

Languages English and Maltese (official)

Ethnic groups Maltese (mixed Arabic, Sicilian, Norman, Spanish, English, Italian racial origin) (95%), English (2%)

Religions Roman Catholic Apostolic (97%), Anglican Communion (2%)

Physical features Archipelago, comprising the islands of Malta (246 km²/95 sq mi), Gozo (67 km²/26 sq mi), and Comino (2.7 km²/1 sq mi), with the uninhabited islets of Cominotto, Filfla, and St Paul; highest point, 252

□ International Airport

HUMAN GEOGRAPHY

Malta (continued)

m/830 ft, on island of Malta; well-indented coastline with natural harbours, rocky coves; no rivers.

Climate Mediterranean, hot, dry summers, cool, rainy winters; rainy season (Oct–Mar); average annual rainfall 400 mm/16 in; average annual temperatures 13°C (Jan), 26°C (Jul) in Valletta.

Currency 1 Maltese pound (LM) = 100 cents

Economy Tourism; ship repair (naval dockyards now converted to commercial use); developing as a trans-shipment centre for the Mediterranean; tobacco, plastic and steel goods, paints, detergents; potatoes, tomatoes, oranges, grapes.

GDP (2002e) $6.818 bn, per capita $17 200

HDI (2002) 0.875

History Controlled at various times by Phoenicia, Greece, Carthage, and Rome; conquered by Arabs, 9th-c; given to the Knights Hospitallers, 1530; British Crown Colony, 1815; important strategic base in both World Wars; for its resistance to heavy air attacks, the island was awarded the George Cross, 1942; achieved independence, 1964; republic, 1974; British military base closed, 1979; governed by a President, Prime Minister, Cabinet and House of Representatives.

Head of State
2004–   Edward Fenech-Adami

Head of Government
2004–   Lawrence Gonzi

MARIANA ISLANDS, NORTHERN >> UNITED STATES OF AMERICA

MARSHALL ISLANDS

Timezone GMT +12

Area c.180 km²/70 sq mi

Population total (2002e) 56 600

Status Republic

Date of independence 1986

Capital Dalap-Uliga-Darrit (municipality on Majuro Atoll)

Languages Marshallese (Kajin-Majol) (official), English and Japanese also spoken

Ethnic group Micronesian (99%)

Religions Christian (Protestant 90%, Roman Catholic 8%)

Physical features Archipelago in C Pacific Ocean; comprising 34 islands, including Kwajalein and Jaluit, and 870 reefs; two parallel chains of coral atolls, Ratik (E) and Ralik (W), extending c.925 km/800 mi in length; volcanic islands, rise no more than a few metres above sea level.

Climate Hot and humid; wet season (May–Nov); typhoon season (Dec–Mar); average annual temperature 27°C.

Currency 1 US Dollar (US$) = 100 cents

Economy Farming; fishing; tropical agriculture; coconuts, tomatoes, melons, breadfruit.

GDP (2001e) $115 mn, per capita $1600

History Explored by the Spanish, 1529; part of UN Trust Territory of the Pacific, 1949–78, administered by the USA; US nuclear weapon tests held on Bikini and Eniwetak atolls, 1946–62; self-governing republic, 1979; compact of free association with the USA in 1986 with US recognizing independence; trusteeship ended, 1990; governed by a President elected by a Parliament.

☐ International Airport

Head of State/Government
1996–7   Kunio Lemari *Acting*
1997–2000   Imata Kabua
2000–   Kessia Note

MARTINIQUE >> FRANCE

MAURITANIA

Local names Mūritāniyā (Arabic), Mauritanie (French)

Timezone GMT

Area 1029920 km²/397549 sq mi

Population total (2002e) 2656000

Status Islamic republic

Date of independence 1960

Capital Nouakchott

Languages Arabic (official), French and local languages also spoken

Ethnic groups Moor (30%), black (30%), mixed (40%)

Religions Sunni Muslim (99%), Roman Catholic (1%)

Physical features Saharan zone in N comprises two-thirds of the country; coastal zone has minimal rainfall; Sahelian zone, with savannah grasslands; Sénégal R zone, the chief agricultural region; highest point, Kediet Ijill, 915 m/3002 ft in the NW.

Climate Dry, tropical climate, with sparse rainfall; average annual temperatures 22°C (Jan), 28°C (Jul) in Nouakchott; rainy season (May–Sep) in S, with occasional tornadoes; average annual rainfall 158 mm/6.2 in.

Currency 1 Ouguija (U, UM) = 5 khoums

Economy Subsistence agriculture (employs 80% of population); crops under constant threat from drought; crops ravaged by locusts, 2004; livestock, cereals, vegetables, dates; mining of iron ore, copper, gypsum.

GDP (2002e) $4.891 bn, per capita $1700

HDI (2002) 0.438

History Visited by Portuguese, 15th-c. French protectorate within French West Africa, 1903; French colony, 1920; independence, 1960; military coup, 1979; new constitution, 1991; became a republic, 1992; governed by

□ International Airport

an executive President (6-year term), Prime Minister, National Assembly, and Senate.

Head of State
1984–   Moaouia Ould Sidi Mohammed Taya

Head of Government
1998–2003 Cheikh el Avia Ould Mohamed Khouna
2003–   Sghair Ould M'barek

MAURITIUS

Local name Mauritius

Timeone GMT +4

Area 1865 km²/720 sq mi

Population total (2002e) 1211000

Status Republic within the Commonwealth

Date of independence 1968

Capital Port Louis

Languages English (creole-English) (official), French, Hindi, Urdu, Bojpoori, and Hakka also spoken

Ethnic groups Indo-Mauritian (68%), Creole (27%), Sino-Mauritian (3%), Franco-Mauritian (2%)

Religions Hindu (53%), Roman Catholic (26%), Muslim (13%), Protestant (4%)

Physical features Comprises the main island, 20 adjacent islets and the dependencies of Rodrigues I, Agalega I, and Cargados Carajos Is (St Brandon Is); volcanic main island; highest peak, 826 m/2710 ft, Piton de la Petite Rivière Noire; dry, lowland coast with wooded savannah,

□ International Airport

Mauritius (continued)

mangrove swamp, and (E) bamboo; surrounded by coral reefs enclosing lagoons and sandy beaches.

Climate Humid tropical-maritime climate; average annual temperatures 23°C (Jan), 27°C (Jul) in Port Louis; average annual rainfall 1000 mm/39 in; lies within Indian cyclone belt.

Currency 1 Mauritian Rupee (MR, MauRe) = 100 cents

Economy Sugar-cane (employs over 25% of the workforce); clothing; diamond-cutting, watches, rum, fertilizer; tea, tobacco, vegetables; fishing; tourism.

GDP (2002e) $12.15 bn, per capita $10 100

HDI (2002) 0.772

MAYOTTE >> FRANCE

MEXICO

Local name México

Timezone GMT −8 to −6

Area 1 978 800 km²/763 817 sq mi

Population total (2002e) 100 977 000

Status Republic

Date of independence 1821

Capital Mexico City

Languages Spanish (official), indigenous languages

Ethnic groups Indian-Spanish (mestizo) (60%), Amerindian (30%), white (9%)

Religions Roman Catholic (80%), Protestant (3%)

Physical features Narrow coastal plains; land rises steeply to C plateau, c.2400 m/7800 ft; volcanic peaks to S, notably Citlaltépetl, 5699 m/18 697 ft; limestone lowlands of the Yucatán peninsula stretch into the Gulf of Mexico (SE); region subject to earthquakes.

Climate Tropical climate in S; severe, arid conditions N and W; average annual temperatures 13°C (Jan), 16°C (Jul) in Mexico City; average annual rainfall 747 mm /29.4 in.

Currency 1 Mexican Peso (Mex$) = 100 centavos

Economy Wide range of mineral exports; major discoveries of oil and natural gas in the 1970s (now world's fourth largest producer); fluorite and graphite (world's leading producer); large petrochemical industry.

GDP (2002e) $924.4 bn, per capita $8900

HDI (2002) 0.796

History Centre of Indian civilizations for over 2500 years; Gulf Coast Olmecs based at La Venta, Zapotecs at Monte Albán near Oaxaca, Mixtecs at Mitla, Toltecs at Tula, Maya in the Yucatán, Aztecs at Tenochtitlán;

History Visited by the Portuguese and Dutch, 16th-c; settled by the French, 1715; ceded to Britain, 1814; governed jointly with Seychelles as a single colony until 1903; independent sovereign state within the Commonwealth, 1968; links with British monarchy broken, 1992, became a republic, remaining within the Commonwealth; President (ceremonial post) is elected by the National Assembly; Prime Minister appoints the Council of Ministers; a unicameral National Assembly.

Head of State
2003–   Aneerood Jugnauth

Head of Government
2003–   Paul Berenger

□ International Airport

Spanish arrival in 1516; Vice-royalty of New Spain established; struggle for independence from 1810; federal republic, 1824; lost territory to the USA, 1836, and after the Mexican War, 1846–8; civil war, 1858–61; occupation of Mexico City by French forces, 1863–7; revolution, 1910–17; major earthquake in Mexico City, 1985; revolt in S state of Chiapas by Zapatista National Liberation Army, 1994; negotiations over Indian rights in late 1990s, ongoing in 2002; major economic crises, 1994, followed by a package of loan guarantees from USA, 1995; governed by a President, Cabinet, and bicameral Congress with a Senate and a Chamber of Deputies.

Head of State/Government
1994–2000   Ernesto Zedillo
2000–   Vincente Fox

MICRONESIA, FEDERATED STATES OF

Timezone GMT +11

Area 700 km²/270 sq mi

Population total (2002e) 109 000

Status Republic

Date of independence 1991

Capital Palikir (on Pohnpei Island)

Languages English (official), with several indigenous languages also spoken

Pohnpei

Ethnic groups Trukese (41%), Pohnpeian (26%)

Religions Roman Catholic, Protestant

Physical features Group of four states in the W Pacific Ocean (Yap, Truk, Pohnpei, Kosrae); comprises all the Caroline I except Belau; islands vary from high mountainous terrain to low coral atolls.

Climate Tropical climate, with occasional typhoons; heavy rainfall all year.

Currency 1 US Dollar (US$) = 100 cents

Economy Agriculture; farming and fishing; tropical fruits, coconuts, vegetables; few mineral resources.

GDP (2002e) $277 mn, per capita $2000

History Settled by Spanish seafarers, 1565; formally annexed by Spain, 1874; sold to Germany, 1899; control mandated to Japan by League of Nations, 1920; American Navy took control following Japan's defeat in World War 2, 1945; part of UN Trust Territory of the Pacific, 1947; compact of free association with the US, 1982; trusteeship ended, 1990; independent state, 1991; under Compact of Free Association, the US continues to control its defence and foreign relations; governed by a President and a National Congress.

Head of State/Government
2003–   Joseph Urusemal

MOLDOVA

Local name Moldova

Timezone GMT +2

Area 33 700 km²/13 008 sq mi

Population total (2002e) 4 231 000

Status Republic

Date of independence 1991

Capital Chisinau (formerly Kishinev)

Languages Moldovan (official), Ukrainian also spoken

Ethnic groups Moldovan (64%), Ukrainian (14%), Russian (13%), Gagauzi (4%), Jewish (2%)

Religions Christian (mainly Russian Orthodox, also Baptist and Roman Catholic)

Physical features Landlocked area consisting of hilly plains, average elevation of 147 m/482 ft, cut by river valleys, ravines, and gullies; uplands in C, Kodry Hills, reach highest point, Mt Balaneshty, 429 m/1409 ft; chief rivers, the Dnestr and Prut; level plain of Bel'tsy Steppe and uplands (N); eroded Medobory-Toltry limestone ridges border R Prut (N).

Climate Warm, moderately continental; long dry periods in S; average annual temperatures –5°C (N), –3°C

□ International Airport

Moldova (continued)

(S) (Jan), 20°C (N), 23°C (S) (Jul); average annual rainfall 450–550 mm/18–22 in.

Currency Leu

Economy Main exports include wine, tobacco, food-canning, machinery, electrical engineering, knitwear, textiles, fruit.

GDP (2002e) $11.51 bn, per capita $2600

HDI (2002) 0.701

History Formerly part of Romania (the region known as Bessarabia); W part remained in Romania, Bessarabia in E became the Moldavian Soviet Socialist Republic in 1940;

occupied by Romania, who allied with Germany in World War 2; recaptured by USSR, 1944; Moldavian language granted official status, 1989, leading to tension between ethnic Russians and Moldovans; declaration of independence, 1991, joined Commonwealth of Independent States; tension due to separatist pressure from Gagauz and Dnestr Russian minorities, 1990–1; new constitution, 1994; governed by a President, Prime Minister and Supreme Soviet.

Head of State
2001–   Vladimir Voronin

Head of Government
2001–   Vasile Tarlev

MONACO

Local name Monaco

Timezone GMT +1

Area 1.95 km²/0.75 sq mi

Population total (2002e) 32 000

Status Principality

Capital Monaco

Languages French (official), English, Italian, and Monegasque also spoken

Ethnic groups French (58%), Italian (16%), Monegasque (16%)

Religion Roman Catholic (95%)

Physical features Located on Mediterranean Riviera, close to Italian frontier with France; surrounded landward by the French department of Alpes-Maritimes; steep and rugged landscape; area available for commercial development has been extended by land reclaimed from sea.

Climate Mediterranean; warm, dry summers, mild, wet winters; average annual temperatures 10°C (Jan), 23°C (Jul); average annual rainfall 758 mm/30 in.

Currency 1 euro = 100 cents (previous to February 2002, 1 French Franc (Fr) = 100 centimes)

Economy Tourism; chemicals, printing, textiles, plastics.

GDP (1999e) $870 mn, per capita $27 000

History Under protection of France since 17th-c, except period under Sardinia, 1815–61; 1911 constitution ended power of Prince as absolute ruler; constitution of 1911 suspended, 1959; new constitution adopted, 1962; governed by Prince as Head of State, a Minister of State, heading a Council of Government, and a National Council.

Head of State (Prince)
1949–2005 Rainier III
2005–   Albert

Head of Government (Minister of State)
2000–   Patrick Leclercq

MAP >> FRANCE

MONGOLIA

Local name Mongol Ard Uls

Timezone GMT +7 (W), +8 (C), +9 (E)

Area 1 566 500 km²/604 800 sq mi

Population total (2002e) 2 457 000

Status State

Date of independence 1911

Capital Ulaanbaatar

Languages Khalka (official), Russian and Chinese spoken by respective minorities

Ethnic groups Mongol (Khalka, Dorbed, Buryat, Dariganga) (90%), Kazakh (4%), Russian (2%), other (4%)

Religions Formerly Tibetan Buddhist (now only a single monastery remains in Ulaanbaatar); unreliable data on current situation as a result of religious suppression in 20th-c.

☐ International Airport

Physical features Landlocked mountainous country; highest point, Tavan-Bogdo-Uli, 4373 m/14 347 ft; high ground mainly in W, with mountains lying NW–SE to form Mongolian Altai chain; lower SE area runs into the Gobi Desert; lowland plains; mainly arid grasslands.

Climate Extreme continental climate, with hard and long-lasting frosts in winter; arid desert conditions prevail in the S; average annual temperatures −26°C (Jan), 16°C (Jul); average annual rainfall 208 mm/18.2 in.

Currency 1 Tugrik (Tug) = 100 möngö

Economy Traditionally a pastoral nomadic economy; series of 5-year plans aiming for an agricultural-industrial economy; 70% of agricultural production derived from cattle raising; foodstuffs, animal products; coal, gold, uranium, lead.

GDP (2002e) $5.06 bn, per capita $1900

HDI (2002) 0.655

History Originally the homeland of nomadic tribes, which united under Genghis Khan in the 13th-c to become part of the great Mongol Empire; assimilated into China, and divided into Inner and Outer Mongolia. Outer Mongolia declared itself an independent monarchy, 1911; changed name to Mongolian People's Republic, 1924, not recognized by China until 1946; governed by a Great People's Khural (parliament), a Council of Ministers, and a Presidium; chairman of Presidium is Head of State; changed name to State of Mongolia, 1992, and new constitution established.

Head of State
1997– Natsagiyn Bagabandi

Head of Government
2000–4 Nambariin Enkhbayar
2004– Tsakhiagiin Elbegdorj

MONTSERRAT >> UNITED KINGDOM

MOROCCO

Local name al-Magrib

Timezone GMT

Area 409 200 km²/157 951 sq mi

Population total (2002e) 29 632 000

Status Kingdom

Date of independence 1956

Capital Rabat

Languages Arabic (official), Berber, Spanish, and French also widely spoken

Ethnic groups Arab-Berber (99%), non-Moroccan (0.7%), Jewish (0.2%)

Religions Sunni Muslim (98%), Christian (1%), Jewish (0.2%)

Physical features Dominated by a series of mountain ranges, rising in the Atlas Mts (S) to 4165 m/13 664 ft at Jebel Toubkal; broad coastal plain; main rivers, Drâ'ar (S and SW) and Moulouya (N) draining into the Mediterranean.

Climate Mediterranean climate on N coast; semi-arid in S; Sahara virtually rainless; average annual temperatures 13°C (Jan), 22°C (Jul) in Rabat; average annual rainfall 564 mm/22.2 in.

Currency 1 Moroccan Dirham (DH) = 100 Moroccan francs

Economy Agriculture (employs over 50% of population); largest known reserves of phosphate in world; fishing, textiles, cement, soap, tobacco, chemicals, paper, timber products; tourism centred on the four imperial cities and the warm Atlantic resorts.

GDP (2002e) $121.8 bn, per capita $3900

HDI (2002) 0.602

History N coast occupied by Phoenicians, Carthaginians, and Romans since 12th-c BC; invasion by Arabs in 7th-c AD; conflicting French and Spanish interest in the region in 19th-c; Treaty of Fez in 1912, established Spanish

□ International Airport

Morocco (capital, Tétouan) and French Morocco (capital, Rabat); Tangier became an international zone, 1923–56; protectorates gained independence, 1956; became Kingdom of Morocco, 1957; Spanish withdrew from former Spanish Sahara (Western Sahara), 1975; Morocco laid claim to this area using the 'Green March' as a gesture of peaceful occupation; Mauritania withdrew from southern third of territory in 1979, leaving Morocco fighting with the Polisario for the whole of Western Sahara; ceasefire agreement signed, 1990; a 'constitutional' monarchy, but the King presides over his appointed Cabinet, which is led by a Prime Minister; a unicameral Chamber of Representatives. >> WESTERN SAHARA

Head of State (Monarch)
1999– Mohammed VI

Head of Government
2002– Driss Jettou

MOZAMBIQUE

Local name Moçambique

Timezone GMT +2

Area 799 380 km²/308 641 sq mi

Population total (2002e) 18 083 000

Status Republic

Date of independence 1975

Capital Maputo

Languages Portuguese (official), Swahili and Bantu dialects widely spoken

Ethnic groups Makua/Lomwe (52%), Thonga (24%), Malawi (12%), Shona (6%), Yao (3%)

Religions Local animist beliefs (60%), Christian (majority Roman Catholic) (30%), Muslim (10%)

Physical features Located in SE Africa; main rivers, the Zambezi and Limpopo, provide irrigation and hydro-electricity; savannah plateau inland, mean elevation 800–1000 m/2700–4000 ft; highest peak, Mt Binga, 2436 m/7992 ft. S of Zambezi is low-lying coast with sandy beaches and mangroves; low hills of volcanic origin inland, Zimbabwe plateau further N.

Climate Tropical with high humidity; rainy season (Dec–Mar); drought conditions in S; average annual temperatures 26°C (Jan), 18°C (Jul) in Maputo; average annual rainfall 560 mm/30 in; major flood disaster in S, Feb 2000.

Currency 1 Metical (Mt, MZM) = 100 centavos

Economy Badly affected by drought (1981–4), internal strife, and lack of foreign exchange; agriculture (employs 85% of population); cashew nuts, tea, cotton, sugar cane, copra, sisal, groundnuts, fruit, rice, cereals, tobacco; forestry; livestock; reserves of gemstones and minerals.

GDP (2002e) $19.52 bn, per capita $1100

HDI (2002) 0.322

History Originally inhabited by Bantu peoples from the N, 1st–4th-c AD; coast settled by Arab traders; visited by Portuguese explorers by late 15th-c; part of Portuguese Africa since 1751; Mozambique Portuguese East Africa in

□ International Airport

late 19th-c; overseas province of Portugal, 1951; independence movement, 1962, the Frente de Libertação de Moçambique (FRELIMO), with armed resistance to colonial rule; independence as the People's Republic of Mozambique, 1975; continuing civil war, with first peace talks in 1990; socialist one-party state, 1975–90; new constitution and change of name to Republic of Mozambique, 1990; peace accord signed between Chissanó (President of Mozambique) and Dhlakama (leader of the Renamo-Mozambique National Resistance), 1992; President (term of 5 years) rules with an Assembly of the Republic; new constitution adopted (Nov 2004).

Head of State
2005–   Armando Emilio Guebuza

Head of Government
2004   Luisa Diogo

MYANMAR (BURMA)

Local name Pyidaungsu Myanma Naingngandaw

Timezone GMT +6.5

Area 678 576 km²/261 930 sq mi

Population total (2002e) 42 238 000

Status Union

Date of independence 1948

Capital Yangon (Rangoon)

Languages Burmese (official), also tribal languages spoken

Ethnic groups Burman (Tibeto-Chinese) (72%), Shan (9%), Karen (7%), Chinese (3%), Indian (2%)

Religions Theravada Buddhist (85%), animist, Muslim, Hindu, Christian minorities (15%)

Physical features Bordered in the N, E, and W by mountains rising (N) to Hkakabo Razi, 5881 m/19 294 ft; located on Chinese frontier, forming part of Kumon Range; Chin Hills (W) descend into upland forests of the Arakan-Yoma range (S); principal rivers, Ayeyarwady (Irrawaddy), Thanlwin (Salween), and Sittang.

Climate Tropical monsoon climate; equatorial on coast; humid temperate in extreme N; SW monsoon season (Jun–Sep); cool, dry season (Nov–Apr); hot, dry season (May–Sep); average annual temperatures 23°C (Jan), 27°C (Jul) in Yangon; average annual rainfall 2616 mm/103 in.

Currency 1 Kyat (K) = 100 pyas

Economy Largely agriculture; rice, pulses, sugar cane; forestry (hardwoods); textiles, pharmaceuticals, petroleum refining, and mining of minerals.

GDP (2002e) $73.69 bn, per capita $1700

HDI (2002) 0.552

History First unified in the 11th-c by King Anawrahta; invasion by Kubla Khan, 1287; second dynasty under King Tabinshweti, 1486, but internal disunity and wars with Siam from 16th-c; new dynasty under King Alaungpaya, 1752; annexed to British India following Anglo-Burmese wars (1824–86); separated from India, 1937; occupied by Japanese in World War 2; independence as Union of Burma under Prime Minister U Nu, 1948; military coup under U Ne Win, 1962; single-party socialist republic, 1974; army coup in 1988, State Law and Order Restoration Council formed, headed by a Chairman; name changed to Union of Myanmar in 1989 and renamed capital Yangon; Aung San Sun Kyi (Nobel Peace Prize, 1991), main opposition leader, placed under house arrest 1989–95, 2000–2, 2003–; constitutional conference ongoing since 1992; rebel separatist groups causing unrest but peace talks held Jan 2004; coast severely hit by tsunami, 2004.

Head of State
1992–   Than Shwe

Head of Government
2004–   Soe Win

☐ International Airport

NAMIBIA

Local name Namibia

Timezone GMT +2

Area 824 292 km²/318 261 sq mi

Population total (2002e) 1 837 000

Status Republic

Date of independence 1990

Capital Windhoek

Languages English (official), Afrikaans, German, local languages

Ethnic groups African (chiefly Ovambo) (85%), white (7%), mixed (8%)

Religions Christian (Lutheran, Roman Catholic, Dutch Reformed, and Anglican) (90%), traditional animist beliefs (10%)

Physical features Located in SW Africa; Namib Desert runs parallel along the Atlantic Ocean coast; inland plateau, mean elevation 1500 m/5000 ft; highest point, Brandberg, 2606 m/8550 ft; Kalahari Desert to the E and S; Orange R forms S frontier with South Africa.

Climate Arid, continental tropical climate; average maximum daily temperature, 20–30°C; 49°C (Nov–Apr) in coastal desert (Namib); average annual rainfall 360 mm/14 in at Windhoek.

Currency 1 Namibian Dollar = 100 cents

Economy Agriculture (employs c.60% of population); indigenous subsistence farming in N; major world

☐ International Airport

producer of diamonds and uranium; fishing; brewing; textiles; plastics.

GDP (2002e) $13.15 bn, per capita $6900

HDI (2002) 0.610

History Visited by British and Dutch missionaries from late 18th-c; German protectorate, 1884; mandated to South Africa by the League of Nations, 1920; UN assumed direct

Namibia (continued)

responsibility in 1966, changing name to Namibia, 1968, and recognizing the Southwest Africa People's Organization (SWAPO) as representative of the Namibian people, 1973; South Africa continued to administer the area as Southwest Africa; SWAPO commenced guerrilla activities, 1966; bases established in S Angola, involving Cuban troops in 1970s; interim administration installed by South Africa, 1985; full independence, 1990; governed by a President, Prime Minister and Cabinet, and an elected National Assembly.

Head of State

2004–   Hifikepunye Pohamba

Head of Government

2002–   Theo-Ben Gurirab

NAURU

Local name Naeoro (Nauruan)

Timezone GMT +12

Area 21.3 km²/8.2 sq mi

Population total (2002e) 12 300

Status Republic

Date of independence 1968

Capital Yaren District (No official capital)

Languages Nauruan (official), English

Ethnic groups Nauruans (62%), Pacific islanders (26%), Asian (9%), Caucasian (3%)

Religions Christian (Nauruan Protestant, Roman Catholic)

Physical features Small isolated island in WC Pacific Ocean, 4000 km/2500 mi NE of Sydney, Australia; ground rises from sandy beaches to give fertile coastal belt, c.100–300 m/300–1000 ft wide, the only cultivable soil; central plateau inland, highest point 65 m/213 ft; mainly phosphate-bearing rocks.

Climate Tropical, hot, and humid; average annual temperatures 27°C (Jan), 28°C (Jul); average annual rainfall 1520 mm/60 in; monsoon season (Nov–Feb).

Currency 1 Australian Dollar ($A) = 100 cents

Economy Based on phosphate mining, now limited reserves; coconuts, some vegetables; tourism; tax haven.

GDP (2001e) $60 mn, per capita $5000

History Under German administration from 1880s to 1914; after 1919, League of Nations mandate, administered by Australia; occupied by Japan, 1942–5; independence movement, 1960s; self-government, 1966; full independence, 1968; unicameral Parliament elects a President, who appoints a Cabinet.

Head of State/Government

2001–4   René Harris

2004–   Ludwig Scotty

NEPAL

Local name Nepāl

Timezone GMT +5³/₄

Area 145 391 km²/56 121 sq mi

Population total (2002e) 23 692 000

Status Kingdom

Capital Kathmandu

Languages Nepali (official), Maithir, Bhojpuri

Ethnic groups Nepalese (58%), Bihari (19%), Tamang (4%), Tharu (3%), Newar (3%)

Religions Only official Hindu state in the world: Hindu (90%), Buddhist (5%), Muslim (3%), Christian (0.2%)

Physical features Landlocked, rises steeply from the Ganges basin in India; high fertile valleys in the 'hill country' at 1300 m/4300 ft, notably the Vale of Kathmandu (a world heritage site); dominated by the

☐ International Airport

Himalayas (glaciated), highest peak, Mt Everest, 8848 m/29 028 ft.

Climate Varies from subtropical lowland with hot, humid summers and mild winters, to an alpine climate over 3300 m/10 800 ft, with permanently snow-covered peaks; average annual temperatures 0°C (Jan), 24°C (Jul) in Kathmandu; monsoon season (Jun–Sep); average annual rainfall 1428 mm/56 in.

Currency 1 Nepalese Rupee (NRp, NRs) = 100 paise/pice

Economy Agriculture (employs 90% of population); rice, jute, cereals, sugar cane; agricultural and forest-based goods; carpets; garments; handicrafts; hydroelectric power developing; tourism increasingly important.

GDP (2002e) $37.32 bn, per capita $1400

HDI (2002) 0.490

History Originally a group of independent hill states, united in 18th-c; parliamentary system introduced, 1959; replaced by village councils (*panchayats*), 1960; a constitutional monarchy ruled by hereditary King; unrest, 1990, followed by reduction of King's powers, a new constitution and fresh elections, 1991; King now rules with a Council of Ministers, a bicameral Parliament consisting of an elected House of Representatives and a National Council; Crown Prince Dipendra allegedly murdered 10 members of his family, including his father and his mother, before killing himself, 2001; state of emergency following new conflict with Communist rebels, 2001–2; peace talks, followed by breakdown, 2003; over 2000 killed in clashes (by Mar 2004); King Gyanendra sacked cabinet and assumed direct power (Jan 2005).

Head of State (Monarch)
2001–   Gyanendra Bir Bikram Shah

Head of Government
2004–5   Sher Bahadur Deuba

NETHERLANDS, THE

Local name Nederland

Timezone GMT +1

Area 33 929 km²/13 097 sq mi

Population total (2002e) 16 142 000

Status Kingdom

Date of independence 1830

Capital Amsterdam

Language Dutch (official)

Ethnic groups Dutch (Germanic/Gallo-Celtic descent) (99%), Indonesian/Surinamese (1%)

Religions Roman Catholic (38%), Protestant (Dutch Reformed Church and other Protestant churches) (30%)

Physical features Generally low and flat, except SE where hills rise to 321 m/1053 ft. Much of coastal area below sea-level, reaching lowest point -6.7 m/-19.7 ft N of Rotterdam; protected by coastal dunes and artificial dykes; highest point, Vaalserberg, in SE; 27% of land area is below sea-level, an area inhabited by c.60% of population.

Climate Cool, temperate maritime climate, with continental influences. Average annual temperatures 1.7°C (Jan), 17°C (Jul); average annual rainfall exceeds 700 mm/27 in, evenly distributed throughout the year.

Currency 1 euro = 100 cents (previous to February, 2002, 1 Guilder (Gld)/ Florin (f) = 100 cents)

Economy Rotterdam and newly-constructed Europort are the major European ports of transshipment, handling goods for EC member countries; Amsterdam a world diamond centre; world's largest exporter of dairy produce; highly intensive agriculture; horticulture; engineering, chemicals, oil products, natural gas, high technology and electrical goods; fishing; tourism.

GDP (2002e) $437.8 bn, per capita $27 200

HDI (2002) 0.935

History Part of Roman Empire to 4th-c AD; part of Frankish Empire by 8th-c; incorporated into the Holy Roman Empire; lands passed to Philip II, who succeeded to

□ International Airport

Spain and the Netherlands, 1555; attempts to stamp out Protestantism led to rebellion, 1572; seven N provinces united against Spain, 1579; United Provinces independence, 1581; overrun by the French, 1795–1813, who established the Batavian Republic; united with Belgium as the Kingdom of the United Netherlands until 1830, when Belgium withdrew; neutral in World War 1; occupied by Germany, World War 2, with strong Dutch resistance; joined with Belgium and Luxembourg to form the Benelux economic union, 1948; conflict over independence of Dutch colonies in SE Asia in late 1940s; joined NATO, 1949; inde-

Netherlands, The (continued)

pendence granted to former colonies, Indonesia, 1949, with the addition of W New Guinea, 1963, and Suriname, 1975; a parliamentary democracy under a constitutional monarchy; government led by a Prime Minister; States General (*Staten-Generaal*) consists of a 75-member First Chamber, and a 150-member Second Chamber; resignation of entire cabinet, 2002, following critical report on Dutch peace-keeping role in Bosnia in 1995.

Head of State (Monarch)
1980–   Beatrix

Head of Government
1994–2002 Wim Kok
2002–   Jan-Peter Balkenende

Aruba

Timezone GMT

Area 193 km²/74.5 sq mi

Population total (2002e) 100 000

Status Self-governing region of The Netherlands

Date of independence 1996

Capital Oranjestad

Languages Dutch (official) with Papiamento, English, and Spanish widely spoken

Ethnic groups Large majority of mixed European/Caribbean Indian descent

Religions Christian (Roman Catholic and Protestant), small Hindu, Muslim, Confucian, and Jewish minorities

Physical features Island in the Caribbean, the westernmost of the Lesser Antilles, N of Venezuela; flat, rocky terrain, dry, with little vegetation.

Climate Dry, tropical, with little seasonal temperature variation; average annual temperature 27°C; annual rainfall often falls to below 488 mm/19 in; lies just outside the Caribbean hurricane belt.

Currency 1 Aruban Guilder/Florin = 100 cents

Economy Lack of natural resources limits agriculture and manufacturing; depends heavily on thriving tourist industry.

GDP (2002e) $1.94 bn, per capita $28 000

History Claimed by Dutch in 1634, but remained undeveloped; construction of an oil refinery brought employment and prosperity, 1929; acquired full internal self-government within kingdom of the Netherlands, 1954, as part of the Netherlands Antilles; growing resentment led to a campaign for Aruba's independence; closure of oil refinery, 1985; obtained separate status from the Netherlands Antilles with full internal autonomy in 1986; full independence in 1996; Sovereign of the Netherlands is Head of State, represented by a

CARIBBEAN

SOUTH AMERICA

Arasji •
△ 70m

Druif •   Santa Cruz •

Oranjestad   A R U B A
                        △ 188m

Pos Chiquino •

                Savaneta •   St Nicolas •

SEA   Seroe
                        Colorado *Punta Basora*

40 km / 20 mi

□ International Airport

Governor-General, a prime minister, Council of Ministers and a unicameral legislature.

Head of State
(Dutch monarch represented by Governor-General)
1992–2004 Olindo Koolman
2004–   Fredis Refunjol

Head of Government
1994–2001 Henry Eman
2001–   Nelson Oduber

Netherlands Antilles

Local name Nederlandse Antillen

Timezone GMT –4

Area 993 km²/383 sq mi

Population total (2002e) 221 000

Status Self-governing region of the Netherlands

Capital Willemstad (on Curaçao Island)

Languages Dutch (official), Papiamento, English, and Spanish widely spoken

Ethnic groups Large majority of mixed European/Caribbean Indian descent

Religions Christian (mainly Roman Catholic)

Physical features Islands in the Caribbean Sea, comprising the Southern group (Leeward Is) of Curaçao and Bonaire, 60–110 km/37–68 mi N of the Venezuelan coast, and the Northern group (Windward Is) of St Maarten, St Eustatius, and Saba; terrain generally hilly, with volcanic interiors.

Climate Tropical maritime climate; average annual temperature 27.5°C. Average annual rainfall varies from 500 mm/20 in (S) to 1000 mm/40 in (N); Northern group subject to hurricanes (Jul–Oct).

Currency 1 Netherland Antilles Guilder/Florin = 100 cents

Economy Based on refining of crude oil imported from Venezuela; aim of industrial diversification; ship repairing; tourism.

GDP (2002e) $2.4 bn, per capita $11 400

History Visited by Columbus, initially claimed for Spain; small-scale Spanish colonization in Curaçao, 1511; occupied by Dutch settlers, 17th-c; acquired full internal self-government within Kingdom of the Netherlands, 1954; Aruba separated from the other islands, 1986; Sovereign of the Netherlands is Head of State, represented by a Governor, a Council of Ministers and a unicameral legislature.

Head of State
(Dutch monarch represented by Governor-General)
1990–2002 Jaime Saleh
2002– Fritz Goedgedrag

Head of Government
2003–4 Mirna Louise-Godett
2004 Etienne Ys

NEW CALEDONIA >> FRANCE

NEW ZEALAND

Local name Aotearoa (Maori)

Timezone GMT +12

Area 268 812 km²/103 761 sq mi

Population total (2002e) 3 893 000

Status Independent member of the Commonwealth

Date of independence 1947

Capital Wellington

Languages English and Maori (official)

Ethnic groups European (mainly British, Australian and Dutch) (87%), Maori (9%)

Religions Christian (59%) (Anglican 25%, Presbyterian 18%, Roman Catholic 16%)

Physical features Consists of two principal islands (North and South) separated by the Cook Strait, and several minor islands; North Island mountainous in the centre with many hot springs; peaks rise to 2797 m/9176 ft at Mt Ruapehu; South Island mountainous for its whole length, rising in the Southern Alps to 3753 m/12 313 ft at Mt Cook, New Zealand's highest point; many glaciers and mountain lakes; largest area of level lowland is the Canterbury Plain, E side of South Island; L Taupo, largest natural lake, occupies an ancient volcanic crater; major lakes include Te Anau and Wakatipu.

Climate Cool, temperate climate, almost subtropical in extreme N; mean temperature range, 18°C in N, 9°C in S; lower temperatures in South Island; highly changeable weather, all months moderately wet; average daily temperature 16–23°C (Jan), 8–13°C (Jul) in Auckland; average annual rainfall 1053 mm/41 in; subject to periodic subtropical cyclones.

Currency 1 New Zealand Dollar ($NZ) = 100 cents

Economy Farming, especially sheep and cattle; one of the world's major exporters of dairy produce; third largest exporter of wool; Kiwi fruit, venison; textiles; timber, food processing; substantial coal and natural gas reserves; hydroelectric power; tourism.

GDP (2002e) $78.4 bn, per capita $20 100

HDI (2002) 0.917

HUMAN GEOGRAPHY

New Zealand (continued)

History Settled by Maoris from E Polynesia by c.1000 AD; first European sighting by Abel Tasman in 1642, named Staten Landt; later known as Nieuw Zeeland, after the Dutch Province; visited by Captain Cook, 1769; first European settlement, 1792; dependency of New South Wales until 1840; outbreaks of war between immigrants and Maoris, 1860–70; Dominion of New Zealand, 1907; independent within the Commonwealth, 1947; governed by a Prime Minister, a Cabinet and a unicameral, 97-member House of Representatives; elections every 3 years.

Head of State
(British monarch represented by Governor-General)
2001–   Dame Silvia Cartwright

Head of Government
1990–7   James Brendan Bolger
1997–9   Jenny Shipley
1999–   Helen Clark

Overseas territories

Name	Area		Capital	Population total
	km²	sq mi		
Cook Islands	238	92	Avarua	(2002e) 18 000
Niue	263	101	Alofi	(2002e) 2000
Ross Dependency	413 550	159 600	–	uninhabited
Tokelau	10	4	Nukunonu	(2002e) 2000

☐ International Airport

NICARAGUA

Local name Nicaragua

Timezone GMT –6

Area 148 000 km²/57 128 sq mi

Population total (2002e) 5 024 000

Status Republic

Date of independence 1821

Capital Managua

Languages Spanish (official), indigenous Indian languages and English (creole-English)

Ethnic groups Mestizo (69%), white (17%), black (9%), Indian (Sumu, Mikito, Ramaguie peoples) (5%)

Religions Roman Catholic (95%), Protestant (5%)

Physical features Mountainous W half, with volcanic ranges rising to over 2000 m/6500 ft (NW); two large lakes, L Nicaragua and L Managua, behind the coastal mountain range; rolling uplands and forested plains to the E; many short rivers flow into the Pacific Ocean and the lakes.

Climate Tropical climate; average annual temperatures, 26°C (Jan), 30°C (Jul) at Managua; rainy season (May–Nov), high humidity; average annual rainfall 1140 mm/45 in; country devastated by hurricane Mitch in 1998.

Currency 1 Córdoba (C$) = 100 centavos

Economy Agriculture (accounts for over two-thirds of total exports); cotton, coffee, sugar cane, rice, corn, tobacco; oil, natural gas; gold, silver, chemicals, textiles.

GDP (2002e) $11.16 bn, per capita $2200

☐ International Airport

HDI (2002) 0.635

History Colonized by Spaniards, early 16th-c; independence from Spain, 1821; left the Federation of Central America, 1838; dictatorship under Anastasio Somoza, 1938; Sandinista National Liberation Front seized power in 1979, and established a socialist junta of national reconstruction; under the 1987 constitution, a

President and Constituent Assembly are elected for 6-year terms; former supporters of the Somoza government (the Contras), based in Honduras and supported by the USA, carried out guerrilla activities against the junta from 1979; ceasefire and disarmament agreed in 1990.

Head of State/Government
1996–2001 Arnoldo Aleman Lacayo
2001– Enrique Bolaños Geyer

NIGER

Local name Niger

Timezone GMT +1

Area 1 267 000 km²/489 191 sq mi

Population total (2002e) 10 640 000

Status Republic

Date of independence 1960

Capital Niamey

Languages French (official) with Hausa, Songhai, Fulfulde, Tamashek, and Arabic widely spoken

Ethnic groups Hausa (54%), Djerma and Songhai (22%), Fulani (9%), Tuareg (8%), Beriberi (4%), Arab (2%)

Religions Muslim (80%), traditional beliefs and small Christian minority (primarily Roman Catholic) (20%)

Physical features Occupies S fringe of Sahara Desert, on a high plateau; Hamada Mangueni plateau (far N); Aïr Massif (C); Ténéré du Tafassasset desert (E); W Talk desert (C and N); water in quantity found only in the SW (R Niger) and SE (L Chad).

Climate One of the hottest countries in the world; average annual temperature 16°C (Jun–Oct), 41°C (Feb–May); rainy season in S (Jun–Oct); rainfall decreases N to almost negligible levels in desert areas; average annual rainfall at Niamey, 554 mm/22 in.

Currency 1 CFA Franc (CFAFr) = 100 cents

Economy Dominated by agriculture and mining; production badly affected by severe drought conditions in 1970s; uranium, tin, phosphates, coal, salt, natron; building materials, textiles, food processing.

GDP (2002e) $8.713 bn, per capita $800

HDI (2002) 0.277

History Occupied by the French, 1883–99; territory within French West Africa, 1904; independence, 1960; military coup, 1974; governed by a Higher Council for National Orientation led by a President who appoints a Council of Ministers; elected National Assembly, 1989; constitution suspended, 1991; multi-party constitution adopted, 1992.

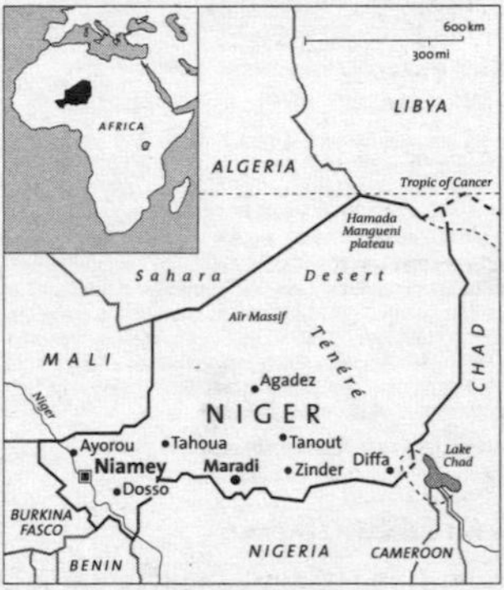

☐ International Airport ---- Disputed border

Head of State
1999 Daouda Malam Wanke
1999– Mamadou Tandjo

Head of Government
1997–2000 Ibrahim Assane Mayaki
2000– Hama Amadou

NIGERIA

Local name Nigeria

Timezone GMT +1

Area 923 768 km²/356 574 sq mi

Population total (2002e) 129 935 000

Status Republic

Date of independence 1960

Capital Abuja

Languages English (official), Hausa, Yoruba, Ibo, and other Niger-Congo dialects widely used

Ethnic groups Over 250 tribal groups, notably Hausa and Fulani, Yoruba and Ibo (65%); Kanuri, Tiv, Edo, Nupe, and Ibidio (25%)

Religions Muslim (50%), Christian (34%), indigenous animist beliefs (10%)

Physical features Long, sandy shoreline with mangrove swamp, dominated by R Niger delta; undulating area of tropical rainforest and oil palm bush behind a coastal strip; open woodland and savannah further N; numerous rivers, notably the Niger and the Benue; Gotel Mts on SE frontier, highest point, Mt Vogel, 2024 m/6640 ft.

Climate Tropical; uniformly high temperatures; average annual temperatures 21–7°C (Jan), 25–6°C (Jul); dry season in the N (Oct–Apr); average annual rainfall

HUMAN GEOGRAPHY

Nigeria (continued)

1836–2497 mm/54–98 in; subject to influence of the Saharan Harmattan in N.

Currency 1 Naira (N) = 100 kobos

Economy Oil (provides c.90% of exports); agriculture (employs 50% of population); palm oil, groundnuts, cotton, cassava, rice, sugar cane, tobacco; fishing, livestock, forestry; natural gas, tin, iron ore, columbite, tantalite, limestone; pulp, paper, textiles, rubber; crops in N devasted by locusts swarms, Aug 2004.

GDP (2002e) $112.5 bn, per capita $900

HDI (2002) 0.462

History Centre of the Nok culture, 500 BC–AD 200; Muslim immigrants, 15th–16th-c; British colony at Lagos, 1861; protectorates of N and S Nigeria, 1900; amalgamated as the Colony and Protectorate of Nigeria, 1914; federation, 1954; independence, 1960; federal republic, 1963; military coup, 1966; E area formed Republic of Biafra, 1967; civil war, and surrender of Biafra, 1970; military coups, 1983 and 1985; major civil and religious unrest, 1992; presidential elections held then annulled, 1993; military coup, 1993; restoration of civilian rule, 1999; governed by a president, a 360-seat House of Representatives, and a 109-seat senate.

Head of State/Government
1999– Olusegun Obasanjo

□ International Airport · ---- Disputed border

NIUE >> NEW ZEALAND

NORTHERN IRELAND >> UNITED KINGDOM

NORTH KOREA >> KOREA, NORTH

NORTHERN MARIANA ISLANDS >> UNITED STATES OF AMERICA

NORWAY

Local name Norge

Timezone GMT +1

Area 323 895 km²/125 023 sq mi

Population total (2002e) 4 537 000

Status Kingdom

Date of independence 1905

Capital Oslo

Languages Norwegian (official) (in the varieties of Bokmål and Nynorsk), Lappish- and Finnish-speaking minorities

Ethnic groups Germanic (Nordic, Alpine, Baltic descent) (97%), Sami/Lapp minority in far N

Religions Evangelical Lutheran (95%), Baptist, Pentecostalist, Methodist, and Roman Catholic

Physical features Mountainous country; Kjölen Mts form the N part of the boundary with Sweden; Jotunheimen range in SC Norway; much of the interior over 1500 m/5000 ft; numerous lakes, the largest being L Mjøsa, 368 km²/142 sq mi; irregular coastline with many small islands and long deep fjords.

□ International Airport

Climate Arctic winter climate in interior highlands, snow, strong winds and severe frosts; comparatively mild conditions on coast; average annual temperatures –4°C (Jan), 17°C (Jul) in Oslo; average annual rainfall 683 mm /27 in; rainfall heavy on W coast.

Currency 1 Norwegian Krone (NKr) = 100 øre

Economy Based on extraction and processing of raw materials, using plentiful hydroelectric power; oil and natural gas from North Sea fields; land under cultivation, less than 3%; productive forests covered 21% of land area in 1985.

GDP (2002e) $149.1 bn, per capita $33 000

HDI (2002) 0.942

History A united kingdom achieved by St Olaf in the 11th-c, whose successor, Cnut, brought Norway under Danish rule; united with Sweden and Denmark, 1389;

annexed by Sweden as a reward for assistance against Napoleon, 1814; growing nationalism resulted in independence, 1905; declared neutrality in both World Wars, but occupied by Germany, 1940–5, after heavy resistance; Free Norwegian government based in London; joined NATO, 1949; joined European Free Trade Association, 1960; a limited, hereditary monarchy; government led by a Prime Minister; Parliament (*Storting*) comprises upper (*Lagting*) and lower (*Odelsting*) chambers.

Head of State (Monarch)
1957–91 Olav V
1991–   Harald V

Head of Government
2000–1   Jens Stoltenberg
2001–   Kjell Magne Bondevik

OMAN

Local name 'Umān

Timezone GMT +4

Area 300 000 km²/115 800 sq mi

Population total (2002e) 2 522 000

Status Sultanate

Date of independence 1951

Capital Muscat

Languages Arabic (official), English, Baluchi (and other Mahri languages), Urdu and Indian dialects also spoken

Ethnic groups Arab, with small Baluchi, Iranian, Indian, Pakistani, and W European minorities

Religions Ibadhi Muslim (75%), Sunni Muslim, Shi'a Muslim and Hindu (25%)

Physical features Located on the SE corner of the Arabian peninsula; the tip of the Musandam peninsula in the Strait of Hormuz is separated from the rest of the country by an 80 km/50 mi strip belonging to the United Arab Emirates; several peaks in the Hajjar Mt range; Jabal Akhdar ridge rises to 3000 m/10 000 ft; vast sand desert in NE; Dhofar uplands in SW.

Climate Desert climate, hot and arid; hot, humid on coast (Apr–Oct); average annual temperature 22°C (Jan), 33°C (Jul); light monsoon rains in S (Jun–Sep); average annual rainfall 99 mm/3.9 in.

Currency 1 Rial Omani (RO) = 1000 baizas

Economy Oil discovered, 1964, now provides over 90% of government revenue; natural gas an important source of industrial power; c.70% of the population relies on agriculture; alfalfa, wheat, tobacco, fruit, vegetables, fishing.

GDP (2002e) $22.4 bn, per capita $8300

HDI (2002) 0.751

History Dominant maritime power of the W Indian Ocean in 16th-c; independent from UK, 1951; separatist tribal revolt, 1964, led to a palace coup that installed the

☐ International Airport   •••• Border awaiting demarcation

present Sultan in 1970; opened airbases to Western forces, following Iraqi invasion of Kuwait, 1990; independent state ruled by a Sultan who is both Head of State and Premier, and who appoints a Cabinet and a 59-member Consultative Council.

Head of State/Government (Sultan)
1932–70 Said bin Taimur
1970–   Qaboos bin Said

PAKISTAN

Local name Pākistān

Timezone GMT +5

Area 803 943 km²/310 322 sq mi

Population total (2002e) 145 960 000

Status Republic

Date of independence 1947

Capital Islamabad

Languages Urdu (official), Punjabi, Sindhi, Pashto, Urdu, Baluchi, and Brahvi mainly spoken

Ethnic groups Punjabi (66%), Sindhi (13%), Baluchi (3%), Pathan and Muhajir minorities, also Afghan refugees in W Pakistan

Religions Muslim (97%) (Sunni 77%, Shi'a 20%), Christian, Hindu, Parsee, Buddhist minorities

Physical features R Indus flows from Himalayas to Karachi, forming a vast, fertile, densely populated alluvial floodplain in E; bounded N and W by mountains rising to 8611 m/28 250 ft at K2, and 8126 m/26 660 ft at Nanga Parbat; mostly flat plateau, low-lying plains and arid desert to the S; major rivers include Jhelum, Chenab, Indus, Sutlej.

Climate Continental, with many temperature and rainfall variations; dominated by the Asiatic monsoon; severe winters in mountainous regions; average annual temperatures 10°C (Jan), 32°C (Jul) in Islamabad; average annual rainfall in Punjab, 250 mm/10 in in SW, 635 mm/25 in in NE; rainy season (Jun–Oct).

Currency 1 Pakistan Rupee (PRs, Rp) = 100 paisa

Economy Agriculture (employs 55% of labour force); cotton production important, supporting major spinning, weaving, and processing industries; sugar cane; textiles; natural gas; tobacco; salt; uranium.

GDP (2002e) $295.3 bn, per capita $2000

HDI (2002) 0.499

History Remains of Indus Valley civilization over 4000 years ago; Muslim rule under the Mughal Empire, 1526–1761; British rule over most areas, 1840s; separated from India to form a state for the Muslim minority, 1947; consisted of West Pakistan (Baluchistan, North-West Frontier, West Punjab, Sind) and East Pakistan (East Bengal), physically separated by 1610 km/1 000 mi; occupied Jammu and Kashmir, 1949 (disputed territory with India, and the cause of wars in 1965 and 1971); pro-

claimed an Islamic republic, 1956; differences between E and W Pakistan developed into civil war, 1971; E Pakistan became an independent state (Bangladesh); military coup by General Zia ul-Haq, 1977, with execution of former prime minister Bhutto in 1979; new constitution (1985) strengthened Zia's powers; Benazir Bhutto elected prime minister, 1988, deposed 1990, re-elected 1993; deposed 1996; ethnic (Muslim/Sindh) violence, especially in Karachi, 1994, and ongoing; military coup, 1999; coup leader, General Musharraf, declared president in 2001; sensitive border area with Afghanistan, following the US-led anti-Taliban campaign, 2001, focusing on Afghan refugees, Pakistan pro-Taliban fighters, and Taliban escapees; ongoing tension with India over Kashmir, with some fighting, 2001, escalating into a major crisis, mid-2002; ceasefire announced (Nov 2003) and diplomatic ties and transport links resumed; governed by an elected President and a bicameral Federal Parliament.

Head of State
1997–2001 Muhammad Rafiq Tarar
2001–   Pervez Musharraf

Head of Government
2004–   Shaukat Aziz

☐ International Airport   ∴ World heritage site

1 Peshawar
2 Rawalpindi

PALAU >> BELAU

PANAMA

Local name Panamá

Timezone GMT –5

Area 77 082 km²/29 753 sq mi

Population total (2002e) 2 915 000

Status Republic

Date of independence 1903

Capital Panama City

Languages Spanish (official), English and indigenous languages (including Cuna, Chibchan, Choco)

Ethnic groups Mestizo (mixed Spanish-Indian) (70%), West Indian (14%), white (10%), Indian (6%)

Religions Christian (Roman Catholic 93%, Protestant 6%), Jewish, Muslim, and Baha'i minorities

Physical features Mostly mountainous; Serranía de Tabasará (W) rises to 3475 m/11 401 ft at Volcán Baru; Azuero peninsula (Peninsula de Azuero) in the S; lake-studded lowland cuts across the isthmus; dense tropical forests on the Caribbean coast; Panama Canal, 82 km/51 mi long, connects Pacific and Atlantic oceans.

Climate Tropical, with uniformly high temperatures; average annual temperature 26°C (Jan), 27°C (Jul) in Panama City; dry season (Jan–Apr) only; average annual rainfall 1770 mm/69.7 in.

Currency 1 Balboa (B, Ba) = 100 cents

Economy Canal revenue (accounts for 80% of country's wealth); great increase in banking sector since 1970; attempts to diversify include oil refining, cigarettes, paper products; tourism; copper, gold, silver; bananas, coffee, cacao, sugar cane.

GDP (2002e) $18.06 bn, per capita $6200

HDI (2002) 0.787

History Visited by Columbus, 1502; under Spanish colonial rule until 1821; joined the Republic of Greater Colombia; separation from Colombia after a US-inspired revolution, 1903; assumed sovereignty of the 8 km/5 mi-wide Canal zone, previously administered by the

□ International Airport   ∴ World heritage site

USA, 1979; military rule under Manuel Noriega, 1983–9; US invasion in 1989 deposed Noriega; governed by a President, a Cabinet, and a unicameral Legislative Assembly.

Head of State/Government
1999–2004 Mireya Moscoso
2004–   Martin Torrijos

PAPUA NEW GUINEA

Local name Papua New Guinea

Timezone GMT +10

Area 462 840 km²/178 656 sq mi

Population total (2002e) 5 426 000

Status Independent state within the Commonwealth

Date of independence 1975

Capital Port Moresby

Languages Pidgin English and Hiri Motu (official parliamentary languages), Tok Pisin, and c.750 indigenous languages spoken

Ethnic groups Papuan (80%), Melanesian (15%), Polynesian, Chinese, and European minorities

Religions Christian (Protestant 64%, Roman Catholic 33%), local beliefs

Physical features Island group in SW Pacific Ocean, comprising E half of the island of New Guinea, the Bismarck and Louisiade archipelagos, the Trobriand and D'Entrecasteaux Is, and other off-lying groups; complex system of mountains, highest point, Mt Wilhelm, 4509 m/14 793 ft; mainly covered with tropical rainforest; vast mangrove swamps along coast; archipelago islands are mountainous, mostly volcanic and fringed with coral reefs.

Climate Typical monsoon, with temperatures and humidity constantly high; average annual temperature 28°C (Jan), 26°C (Jul); average annual rainfall 2000–2500 mm /80–100 in.

□ International Airport

Currency 1 Kina (K) = 100 toea

Economy Farming, fishing, and forestry (engages c.75% of workforce); vegetables, sugar, peanuts; natural gas; brewing; tourism.

GDP (2002e) $10.86 bn, per capita $2100

HDI (2002) 0.535

History British protectorate in SE New Guinea, 1884;

Papua New Guinea (continued)

some of the islands under German protectorate, 1884; German New Guinea in NE, 1899; German colony annexed by Australia in World War 1; Australia mandated to govern both British and German areas, 1920; combined as the United Nations Trust Territory of Papua and New Guinea, 1949; independence within the Commonwealth, 1975; a Governor-General represents the British Crown; governed by a Prime Minister and Cabinet, with a unicameral National Parliament.

Head of State
(British monarch represented by Governor-General)
2004– Sir Paulias Matane

Head of Government
1999–2002 Mekere Morauta
2002– Michael Thomas Somare

PARAGUAY

Local name Paraguay

Timezone GMT −4

Area 406 750 km²/157 000 sq mi

Population total (2002e) 5 774 000

Status Republic

Date of independence 1811

Capital Asunción

Languages Spanish (official), but Guaraní also spoken

Ethnic groups Mestizo (mixed Spanish-Guaraní Indian) (91%), Amerindian, black, European, and Asian minorities

Religions Roman Catholic (96%), Mennonite, Baptist/Anglican minorities

Physical features Landlocked, in C South America; divided into two regions by the R Paraguay; Gran Chaco in the W, mostly cattle country or scrub forest; more fertile land in the E; Paraná plateau at 300–600 m/1000–2000 ft, mainly wet, treeless savannah.

Climate Tropical NW, with hot summers, warm winters; temperate in SE; average annual temperatures 27°C (Jan), 18°C (Jul) in Asunción; average annual rainfall 1316 mm/52 in.

Currency 1 Guaraní (G) = 100 céntimos

Economy Agriculture (employs 43% of the labour force); oilseed, cotton, wheat, tobacco, corn, rice, sugar cane; pulp, timber, textiles, cement, glass.

GDP (2002e) $25.19 bn, per capita $4300

HDI (2002) 0.740

History Originally inhabited by Guaraní Indians; arrival of the Spanish, 1537; arrival of Jesuit missionaries,

□ International Airport

1609; independence from Spain, 1811; War of the Triple Alliance against Brazil, Argentina, and Uruguay, 1865–70; Chaco War with Bolivia, 1932–5; civil war, 1947; General Alfredo Stroessner seized power, 1954, forced to stand down following a coup in 1989; new constitution, creating post of Vice-President, 1992; governed by a President, an appointed Council of Ministers, and a bicameral National Congress.

Head of State/Government
1999–2003 Luis Gonzalez Macchi
2003– Nicanor Duarte Frutos

PERU

Local name Perú

Timezone GMT −5

Area 1 284 640 km²/495 871 sq mi

Population total (2002e) 26 749 000

Status Republic

Date of independence 1821

Capital Lima

Languages Spanish and Quechua (official), Aymará also spoken

Ethnic groups South American Indian (47%), mestizo (mixed Indian and European) (33%), white (12%), black, Japanese, and Chinese (3%)

Religions Roman Catholic (90%), Anglican, Methodist, Peruvian Baha'i minorities

Physical features Arid plains and foothills on the coast, with areas of desert and fertile river valleys;

Central Sierra, average altitude 3000 m/10 000 ft, contains 50% of the population; highest peak, Mt Huascarán, 6768 m/22 204 ft, in W; forested Andes and Amazon basin (E), with major rivers flowing to the Amazon.

Climate Mild temperatures all year on coast; dry, arid desert in the S; typically wet, tropical climate in Amazon basin; average annual temperatures 23°C (Jan), 17°C (Jul) in Lima; average annual rainfall 48 mm/1.9 in.

Currency 1 New Sol = 100 céntimos

Economy One of the world's leading producers of silver, zinc, lead, copper, gold, iron ore; 80% of Peru's oil extracted from the Amazon forest; cotton, potatoes, sugar, olives; tourism, especially to ancient sites.

GDP (2002e) $138.8 bn, per capita $5000

HDI (2002) 0.747

History Highly developed Inca civilization; arrival of Spanish, 1531; Vice-royalty of Peru established; independence declared, 1821; frequent border disputes in 19th-c (eg War of the Pacific, 1879–83); several military coups; terrorist activities by Maoist guerrillas; bicameral Congress consists of a Senate and a National Chamber of Deputies; an elected President appoints a Council of Ministers.

Head of State
2000–1   Valentin Paniagua Corazao *Interim*
2001–   Alejandro Toledo

Head of Government
2003–   Carlos Ferrero Costa

□ International Airport   ∴ World heritage site

PHILIPPINES

Local name Filipinas

Timezone GMT +8

Area 299 679 km²/115 676 sq mi

Population total (2002e) 80 000 000

Status Republic

Date of independence 1946

Capital Manila

Languages Tagalog (Pilipino), and English (official), over 87 local languages, including Cebuano, Ilocano, Bicol, and Samar-Leyte

Ethnic groups Filipino, with Chinese, Spanish, and American minorities

Religions Roman Catholic (83%), Protestant (9%), Muslim (5%), Buddhist (3%)

Physical features An archipelago of more than 7100 islands and islets, NE of Borneo; largest island, Luzon 108 172 km²/41 754 sq mi; Mindanao, 94 227 km²/36 372 sq mi, has active volcano Apo, 2954 m/9690 ft, and mountainous rainforest; Mount Pinatubo volcano, 1758 m/5770 ft, situated 90 km/56 mi NW of Manila; largely mountainous islands.

Climate Tropical, maritime; warm and humid throughout year; average annual temperature 25°C (Jan), 28°C (Jul) in Manila; average annual rainfall 2083 mm/82

□ International Airport

Philippines (continued)

in; frequent typhoons and occasional earth tremors and tsunamis (tidal waves).

Currency 1 Philippine Peso (PP, ₱) = 100 centavos

Economy Farming (employs c.50% of workforce); rice, pineapples, mangos, vegetables, livestock, sugar, tobacco, rubber, coffee; oil, copper, gold; textiles; vehicles; tourism.

GDP (2002e) $379.7 bn, per capita $4600

HDI (2002) 0.754

History Claimed for Spain by Magellan, 1521; ceded to the USA after the Spanish-American War, 1898; became a self-governing Commonwealth, 1935; occupied by the Japanese in World War 2; independence, 1946; Communist guerrilla activity in N; Muslim separatist movement in S; martial law following political unrest, 1972–81; exiled political leader Benigno Aquino assassinated on returning to Manila, 1983; coup in 1986 ended the 20-year rule of President Ferdinand Marcos; new constitution, 1987; attempted coup, 1989, with continuing political unrest; eruption of Mount Pinatubo, 1991; governed by a President and a bicameral legislature, comprising a Senate and a House of Representatives.

Head of State/Government
1998–2001 Joseph Arap Estrada
2001–   Gloria Macapagal Arroyo

PITCAIRN ISLANDS >> UNITED KINGDOM

POLAND

Local name Polska

Timezone GMT +1

Area 312 683 km²/120 695 sq mi

Population total (2002e) 38 644 000

Status Republic

Date of independence 1918

Capital Warsaw

Language Polish (official)

Ethnic groups Polish (99%), Ukrainian, Belorussian, and Jewish minorities

Religions Roman Catholic (94%), small Jewish and Muslim minorities

Physical features Part of the great European plain, with the Carpathian and Sudetes Mts (S) rising in the High Tatra to 2499 m/8199 ft at Mt Rysy; Polish plateau in N, cut by the Bug, San, and Wisła (Vistula) rivers; richest coal basin in Europe in the W (Silesia); flat Baltic coastal area; forests cover 20% of land.

Climate Continental climate, with severe winters, hot summers; average annual temperatures –4°C (Jan), 19°C (Jul) in Warsaw; average annual rainfall 550 mm/22 in.

Currency 1 Złoty (Zl) = 100 groszy

Economy Nearly 50% of the land under cultivation; major producer of coal; zinc, lead, sulphur; shipbuilding, machinery, vehicles, electrical equipment; textiles.

GDP (2002e) $373.2 bn, per capita $9700

HDI (2002) 0.833

History Emergence as a powerful Slavic group in 11th-c; united with Lithuania, 1569; divided between Prussia, Russia, and Austria, 1772, 1793, 1795; semi-independent state after Congress of Vienna, 1815; incorporated into the Russian Empire; after World War 1, declared an independent Polish state, 1918; partition between Germany and the USSR, 1939; invasion by Germany, 1939; major resistance movement, and a government in exile during World War 2; People's Democracy established under Soviet influence, 1944; rise of independent trade union, Solidarity, 1980; state of martial law imposed, 1981–3; loss of support for communist government and major success for Solidarity in 1989 elections; proclaimed Polish Republic, 1989, and constitution amended to provide for a bicameral National Assembly.

Head of State
1989–9 Wojciech Jaruzelski
1990–5 Lech Wałęsa
1995–   Alexander Kwasniewski

Head of Government
2001–4 Leszek Miller
2004–   Marek Belka

□ International Airport   ∴ World heritage site

POLYNESIA, FRENCH >> FRANCE

PORTUGAL

Local name Portugal
Timezone GMT
Area 91630 km²/35370 sq mi
Population total (2002e) 10384000
Status Republic
Capital Lisbon
Languages Portuguese (official), with many dialectal variations
Ethnic groups Homogeneous (Mediterranean stock), with small African minority
Religions Roman Catholic (97%), Protestant (1%), Muslim minority
Physical features Located on W side of Iberian peninsula; includes semi-autonomous Azores and Madeira Is; chief mountain range, the Serra da Estrêla (N), rising to 1991 m/6532 ft; main rivers, Douro, Tagus, Guadiana, are the lower courses of rivers beginning in Spain.
Climate Cool, maritime climate in N; warmer Mediterranean type in S; most rainfall in winter; average annual temperature 11°C (Jan), 22°C (Jul) in Lisbon; average annual rainfall 686 mm/27 in.
Currency 1 euro = 100 cents (previous to February, 2002, 1 Escudo (Esc) = 100 centavos)
Economy Several labour-intensive areas, including textiles, leather, wood products, cork, ceramics; timber; wine, fish; chemicals, electrical machinery, steel, shipbuilding; minerals, cereals, pulses, fruit, olive oil; c.20% of land is forested.
GDP (2002e) $195.2 bn, per capita $19400
HDI (2002) 0.880
History Became a kingdom under Alfonso Henriques in 1140; major period of world exploration and beginning of Portuguese Empire in 15th-c; under Spanish domination, 1580–1640; invaded by the French, 1807; island of Azores granted semi-autonomy, 1895; monarchy overthrown and republic established, 1910; dictatorship of Dr Salazar, 1928–68; military coup in 1974, followed by 10 years of political unrest under 15 governments; island

□ International Airport

of Madeira gained partial autonomy, 1980; Macao still administered by Portugal; joined EC, 1986; governed by a President, elected for five years, a Prime Minister and Council of Ministers, and a unicameral Assembly of the Republic.

Head of State
1996– Jorge Sampaio

Head of Government
2004–5 Pedro Santana Lopes
2005– José Socrates

Azores

Local name Ilhas dos Açôres
Timezone GMT –1
Area 2300 km²/900 sq mi
Population total (2002e) 245000
Status Semi-autonomous region of Portugal
Capital Ponta Delgada (on São Miguel Island)
Physical features Island archipelago of volcanic origin, 1400–1800 km/870–1100 mi W of mainland Portugal; three widely separated groups of nine islands; Flores and Corvo (NW), Terceira, Graciosa, São Jorge, Faial (Fayal), Pico (C), and Santa Maria with the Formigas Islands and São Miguel, the principal island (E); highest point, Pico, 2351 m/7713 ft; volcanic terrain.
Economy Agriculture; grain, fruit, tea, tobacco, wine.
History Settled by the Portuguese in 1439; under Spanish rule, 1580–1640; new constitution established in 1832, when islands were grouped into three administra-

□ International Airport

tive districts; given limited autonomous administration, 1895; has no central government, but a General Council.

Madeira (islands)

Local name Ilha de Madeira

Timezone GMT

Area 796 km²/307 sq mi

Population total (2002e) 265 000

Status Semi-autonomous region of Portugal

Capital Funchal (on Madeira Island)

Physical features Main island in an archipelago off the coast of N Africa, 980 km/610 mi SW of Lisbon; consists of Madeira, Porto Santo and three uninhabited islands; highest point, Pico Ruivo de Santana, 1862 m/ 6111 ft on Madeira.

Economy Agriculture; sugar cane, fruit, fishing, Madeira (a fortified wine); embroidery, crafts; tourism.

History Occupied by the Portuguese, 15th-c; occupied by Britain, 1801, and 1807–14; gained partial autonomy, 1980, but remains a Portuguese overseas territory; locally-elected government, and Assembly.

□ International Airport

QATAR

Local name Qatar

Timezone GMT +3

Area 11 437 km²/4 415 sq mi

Population total (2002e) 606 000

Status Independent state

Date of independence 1971

Capital Doha

Languages Arabic (official), English

Ethnic groups Arab (40%), Pakistani (18%), Indian (18%), Iranian (10%)

Religion Sunni Muslim (95%)

Physical features Low-lying state on the E coast of the Arabian Peninsula, comprising the Qatar Peninsula and numerous small offshore islands; peninsula, 160 km/100 mi long and 55–80 km/34–50 mi wide, slopes gently from the Dukhan Heights 98 m/321 ft, to the E shore; barren terrain, mainly sand and gravel; coral reefs offshore.

Climate Desert climate; average temperatures 23°C (Jan), 35°C (Jul); high humidity; sparse rainfall; average annual rainfall 62 mm/2.4 in.

Currency 1 Qatar Riyal (QR) = 100 dirhams

Economy Based on oil. Offshore gas reserves thought to be an eighth of known world reserves; oil refineries, petrochemicals, liquefied natural gas, fertilizers, steel, cement, ship repairing, engineering; fishing.

GDP (2002e) $15.91 bn, per capita $20 100

HDI (2002) 0.803

History British protectorate after Turkish withdrawal, 1916; independence, 1971; palace coup brought Khalifah bin Hamad to power, 1972; long-standing territorial dispute with Bahrain over Hawar Is, awarded to Bahrain,

□ International Airport

2001; hereditary monarchy, the Emir is both Head of State and Prime Minister; Council of Ministers is assisted by a Consultative Council; 2003 national referendum approved first constitution, with 45-member Advisory Council: 30 elected by citizens; 15 appointed by the Emir.

Head of State (Emir)
Family name: al-Thani
1995–   Hamad bin Khalifa

Head of Government
1996–   Abdulla bin Khalifa

RÉUNION >> FRANCE

ROMANIA

Local name Romănia

Timezone GMT +2

Area 237 500 km²/91 675 sq mi

Population total (2002e) 21 667 000

Status Republic

Date of independence 1918

Capital Bucharest

Languages Romanian (official), with French, Hungarian, and German widely spoken

Ethnic groups Romanian (89%), Hungarian (7%), German (2%), Ukrainian, Serb, Croat, Russian, Turk, and Gypsy (2%)

Religions Eastern Orthodox Christian (80%), Roman Catholic (6%), Calvinist, Lutheran, Baptist (4%)

Physical features Carpathian Mts form the heart of the country; highest peak, Negoiul, 2548 m/8359 ft; crossed by many rivers; c.3500 glacial ponds, lakes, and coastal lagoons; over 25% of land forested.

Climate Continental, with cold, snowy winters and warm summers; winters can be severe; mildest along the Black Sea coast; average annual temperatures range from 7°C (N), to 11°C (S), –3°C (Jan), 24°C (Jul); average annual rainfall 579 mm/22.8 in.

Currency 1 Leu (plural lei) = 100 bani

Economy Gradual change from agricultural to industrial economy (since World War 2); state owns nearly 37% of farm land, mainly organized as collectives and state farms; wheat, maize, sugar beet, fruit, potatoes; livestock; oil, natural gas; iron and steel, metallurgy, engineering, chemicals, textiles, electronics, timber; tourism.

GDP (2002e) $169.3 bn, per capita $7600

History Formed from the unification of Moldavia and Wallachia, 1862; monarchy created, 1866; Transylvania,

□ International Airport   ∴ World heritage site

Bessarabia, and Bucovina united with Romania, 1918; support given to Germany in World War 2; occupied by Soviet forces, 1944; monarchy abolished and People's Republic declared, 1947. Socialist Republic declared, 1965; increasingly independent from the USSR from the 1960s; leading political force was the Romanian Communist Party, led by dictator Nicolae Ceauşescu; popular uprising due to violent repression of protest led to the overthrow of the Ceauşescu regime, 1989; new constitution, 1991; governed by a President, Prime Minister, Chamber of Deputies, and Senate.

Head of State
2004–   Traian Basescu

Head of Government
2004–   Calin Tariceanu

ROSS DEPENDENCY >> NEW ZEALAND

RUSSIA (RUSSIAN FEDERATION)

Local name Rossiyskaya (Rossiyskaya Federatsiya)

Timezone GMT ranges from +2 to +12

Area 17 075 400 km²/6 591 100 sq mi

Population total (2002e) 143 673 000

Status Republic

Date of independence 1991

Capital Moscow

Languages Russian (official), and c.100 different languages

Ethnic groups Russian (82%), Tatar (3%), Ukrainian (3%)

Religions Christian (Russian Orthodox 25%), non-religious (60%), Muslim

Physical features Occupying much of E Europe and N Asia; consists of c.75% of the area of the former USSR and over 50% of its population; vast plains dominate the W half; Ural Mts separate the E European Plain (W) from the W Siberian Lowlands (E); E of the R Yenisey lies the C Siberian Plateau; N Siberian Plain further E; Caucasus on S frontier. Lena, Ob, Severnaya Dvina, Pechora, Yenisey, Indigirka, and Kolyma rivers flow to the Arctic Ocean; Amur, Argun, and rivers of the Kamchatka Peninsula flow to the Pacific Ocean; Caspian Sea basin

Russia (continued)

□ International Airport   ∴ World heritage site

includes the Volga and Ural rivers; over 20 000 lakes, the largest being the Caspian Sea, L Taymyr, L Baikal.

Climate Half of country covered by snow for 6 months of year; coldest region, NE Siberia, average annual temperature –46°C (Jan), 16°C (Jul); summers in rest of country generally short and hot; average annual temperature –18–9°C (Jan), 16–24°C (Jul) in Moscow; average annual rainfall 500–750 mm/20–30 in.

Currency Rouble (R)

Economy Oil fields in W Siberia (provide 50% of country's petroleum); series of 5-year plans since 1928 promoted industry; heavy-industry products include chemicals, construction materials, machine tools, and steel-making; mining, major producer of iron ore, manganese, natural gas, nickel, and platinum, also coal, copper, gold, zinc, tin, lead; agriculture, primarily wheat, fruit, vegetables, tobacco, cotton, sugar beet; textiles; timber.

GDP (2002e) $1.409 tn, per capita $9700

HDI (2002) 0.781

History Conquered by Mongols in 13th-c; Ivan IV (the Terrible) became first ruler to be crowned Tsar, 1547; Time of Trouble, 1604–13; under Peter the Great, territory expanded to the Baltic Sea and St Petersburg founded as capital, 1703; Napoleon invasion failed, 1812; Crimean War, 1853–6; emancipation of the serfs, 1861; assassination of Alexander II, 1881; Balkan War with Turkey, 1877–8; Russo-Japanese War, 1904–5; establishment of a

parliament (*Duma*) with limited powers, 1906; Russia allied with Britain and France, World War I; revolution overthrew Nicholas II, Bolsheviks (Communists) seized power under the dictatorship of Lenin, 1917; Russia forced to withdraw from War; renamed the Russian Soviet Federated Socialist Republic, 1918, and Moscow reinstated as capital; Russia became part of the Union of Soviet Socialist Republics (USSR), 1922; death of Lenin, 1924; Trotsky deported in 1928, by which time Stalin acquiring dictatorial power; USSR fought with the Allies against Germany in World War 2; from 1946 development of the Cold War between East and West; troops intervened in Afghanistan, 1979; radical reform of the system under the leadership of Gorbachev, 1985–91; first contested elections in Soviet history held, and the end of the Cold War announced, 1989; troops withdrawn from Afghanistan, 1989; USSR dissolved, 1991; Russian Republic became independent and a founder member of the Commonwealth of Independent States, 1991; war in Chechnya, 1994–6; further invasion of Chechnya, 1999–; governed by a president, prime minister, and Federal Assembly, consisting of a State *Duma* and a Federation Council.

Head of State

1991–9	Boris Yeltsin
1999–	Vladimir Putin

Head of Government

2004	Viktor Khristenko *Acting*
2004–	Mikhail Fradkov

>> Political leaders and rulers, p.128

RWANDA

Local name Rwanda

Timezone GMT +2

Area 26 338 km²/10 169 sq mi

Population total (2002e) 7 398 000

Status Republic

Date of independence 1962

Capital Kigali

Languages French, Kinyarwanda, and English (official), with Kiswahili widely used in commerce

Ethnic groups Hutu (84%), Tutsi (14%), Pygmoid Twa (1%)

Religions Christian (65%), local indigenous beliefs (25%), Muslim (9%)

Physical features Landlocked in C Africa; mountainous, with many of the highest mountains formed by volcanoes; highest point Karisimbi, 4507 m/14 787 ft, in the Virunga range; W third drains into L Kivu and then the R Congo, remainder drains towards the R Nile; L Kivu and R Ruzizi form W border as part of Africa's Great Rift Valley.

Climate Tropical climate, influenced by high altitude; average annual temperature 19°C (Jan), 21°C (Jul) in Kigali; average annual rainfall 1000 mm/40 in in Kigali; two wet seasons (Oct–Dec, Mar–May); highest rainfall in the W, decreasing in the C uplands and to the N and E.

Currency 1 Rwanda Franc (RF) = 100 centimes

Economy Based largely on agriculture; coffee, tea, pyrethrum, maize, beans, livestock; minerals; plastic goods, textiles.

GDP (2002e) $8.92 bn, per capita $1200

HDI (2002) 0.403

History In the 16th-c the Tutsi tribe moved into the country and took over from the Hutu, forming a monarchy; German protectorate, 1899; mandated with Burundi to Belgium as the Territory of Ruanda-Urundi, 1919; United Nations Trust Territory administered by Belgium, after World War 2; unrest in 1959 led to a Hutu revolt and the overthrow of Tutsi rule; independence, 1962; military coup, 1973; return to civilian rule, 1980; rebellion by (mainly Tutsi) Rwandan Patriotic Front, 1990; new constitution, 1991; peace accord with rebels, 1994; unprecedented outbreak of inter-ethnic violence, with over half a million deaths, 1994; governed by a President,

□ International Airport

Prime Minister, Council of Ministers, and National Development Council; elections scheduled for 1999, but transitional government rule extended to 2003.

Head of State
2000–   Paul Kagame

Head of Government
2000–   Bernard Makuza

SAINT HELENA AND DEPENDENCIES >> UNITED KINGDOM

SAINT KITTS AND NEVIS

Local name Saint Christopher (Kitts) and Nevis

Timezone GMT –4

Area 269 km²/104 sq mi

Population total (2002e) 46 200

Status Independent state within the Commonwealth

Date of independence 1983

Capital Basseterre

Languages English (official), with creole-English widely spoken

Ethnic groups Black African descent (94%), mulatto (3%), white (1%)

Religions Christian (Anglican 36%, Methodist 32%, other Protestant 8%, Roman Catholic 11%)

Physical features Located in the N Leeward Is, E Caribbean; comprises the islands of St Christopher (St Kitts), Nevis, and Sombrero; volcanic origin with mountain ranges rising to 1156 m/3793 ft at Mt Liamuiga; Nevis dominated by a central peak rising to 985 m/3232 ft.

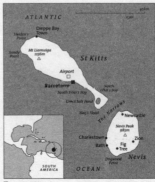

□ International Airport

HUMAN GEOGRAPHY

Saint Kitts and Nevis (continued)

Climate Tropical, warm climate; average annual temperature 26°C; average annual rainfall 1375 mm/54 in; low humidity, modified by sea winds; hurricanes possible (Jul–Oct).

Currency 1 East Caribbean Dollar (EC$) = 100 cents

Economy Sugar and its products (supply c.40% of total exports); copra, cotton, electrical appliances, footwear, garments, tourism.

GDP (2002e) $339 mn, per capita $8800

HDI (2002) 0.814

History St Kitts was the first British colony in the W Indies, 1623; control disputed between France and Britain, 17th–18th-c; ceded to Britain, 1783; St Kitts and Nevis united, 1882; area gained full internal self-government, 1967; Anguilla declared itself independent from the control of St Kitts, which led to British troops intervention, 1969; island reverted to being a British dependent territory, 1971, and was formally separated from St Kitts-Nevis, 1980; independence of St Kitts-Nevis, 1983; British monarch represented by a Governor-General; governed by a Prime Minister and two legislative chambers; island of Nevis has its own legislature (the Nevis Island Assembly), and executive, which has exclusive responsibility for the island's internal administration; Nevis I voted in favour of secession, 1997.

Head of State
(British monarch represented by Governor-General)
1996– Sir Cuthbert Montroville Sebastian

Head of Government
1995– Denzil Douglas

SAINT LUCIA

Local name Saint Lucia

Timezone GMT –4

Area 616 km²/238 sq mi

Population total (2002e) 160 000

Status Independent state within the Commonwealth

Date of independence 1979

Capital Castries

Languages English (official), with French patois widely spoken

Ethnic groups African descent (90%), mixed (6%), East Indian (3%), Caucasian (1%)

Religions Christian (Roman Catholic 90%, Protestant 7%, Anglican 3%)

Physical features Second largest of the Windward Is, E Caribbean; volcanic island; forested mountainous centre rising to 950 m/3117 ft at Mt Gimie; sulphurous springs of Qualibou and twin peaks of Gros and Petit Pitons (SW).

Climate Tropical climate; average temperature 26°C; wet season (Jun–Dec), dry season (Jan–Apr); average annual rainfall 1500 mm/60 in (lowlands), 3500 mm/138 in (mountainous zone).

Currency 1 East Caribbean Dollar (EC$) = 100 cents

Economy Tourism (fastest-growing sector of the economy); bananas, cocoa, copra, citrus fruits, coconut oil; garments, textiles, electronic components; oil refining and transshipment.

GDP (2002e) $866 mn, per capita $5400

HDI (2002) 0.772

History Reputedly visited by Columbus, 1502; disputed ownership between England and France,

□ International Airport

17th–18th-c; British Crown Colony, 1814; full internal autonomy, 1967; independence, 1979; British monarch represented by a Governor-General; House of Assembly, elected every five years, and a Senate; constitutional amendment (Jul 2003) to replace oath of allegiance to Queen Elizabeth II with oath to St Lucia and its people.

Head of State
(British monarch represented by Governor-General)
1997– Pearlette Louisy

Head of Government
1997– Kenny Anthony

SAINT PIERRE AND MIQUELON >> FRANCE

SAINT VINCENT AND THE GRENADINES

Local name Saint Vincent and the Grenadines

Timezone GMT −4

Area 390 km²/150 sq mi

Population total (2002e) 113 100

Status Independent state within the Commonwealth

Date of independence 1979

Capital Kingstown

Languages English (official), with French patois widely spoken

Ethnic groups Black African descent (82%), mixed (14%), white, Asian, and Amerindian minorities

Religions Christian (Anglican 42%, Methodist 21%, Roman Catholic 12%)

Physical features Island group of the Windward Is, E Caribbean, comprising the island of St Vincent and the N Grenadine Is; St Vincent volcanic in origin; highest peak, Soufrière, active volcano 1234 m/4048 ft (N), most recent eruption, 1979.

Climate Tropical climate, average annual temperature, 25°C; average annual rainfall 1500 mm/60 in (coast), 3800 mm/150 in (interior).

Currency 1 East Caribbean Dollar (EC$) = 100 cents

Economy Based on agriculture; bananas, arrowroot (world's largest producer), coconuts, spices, sugar cane; food processing, textiles; tourism.

GDP (2002e) $339 mn, per capita $2900

HDI (2002) 0.733

History Visited by Columbus, 1498; British control, 1763; part of West Indies Federation, 1958–62; achieved internal self-government, 1969; independence, 1979; British sovereign represented by a Governor-General; a Prime Minister leads a unicameral National Assembly.

Head of State
(British monarch represented by Governor-General)
2002–   Sir Freddy Ballantyne

Head of Government
2001–   Ralph Gonsalves

□ International Airport

SALVADOR >> EL SALVADOR

HUMAN GEOGRAPHY

SAMOA (formerly WESTERN SAMOA)

Local name Samoa i Sisifo (Samoan)

Timezone GMT −11

Area 2842 km²/1097 sq mi

Population total (2002e) 178 300

Status Independent state within the Commonwealth

Date of independence 1962

Capital Apia

Languages Samoan and English (official)

Ethnic groups Polynesian, with Pacific Islanders, Euronesian, Chinese, and European minorities

Religions Christian (99%) (Protestant 70%, Roman Catholic 20%, other 9%)

Physical features Two large (Upolu, Savai'i) and seven small islands in the South Pacific Ocean, 2600 km/1600 mi NE of Auckland, New Zealand; formed from ranges of extinct volcanoes, rising to 1829 m/6001 ft on Savai'i; last volcanic activity, 1905–11; thick tropical vegetation; several coral reefs along coast.

Climate Tropical climate; cool, dry season (May–Nov), average temperature 22°C; rainy season (Dec–Apr) with temperatures reaching 36°C; average annual rainfall, 2775 mm/109 in; frequent hurricanes.

Samoa (formerly Western Samoa) (continued)

Currency 1 Tala (WS$) = 100 sene

Economy Largely agricultural subsistence economy; taro, yams, breadfruit, pawpaws, coconuts, cocoa, bananas; tourism increasing; internal transportation system depends largely on roads and ferries; charter air service operates between the two main islands.

GDP (2002e) $1 bn, per capita $5600

HDI (2002) 0.715

History Visited by the Dutch, 1772; 1889 commission divided Samoa between Germany (which acquired Western Samoa) and the US (which acquired Tutuila and adjacent small islands, now known as American Samoa); New Zealand granted a League of Nations mandate for Samoa, 1919; UN Trust Territory under New Zealand, 1946; independence, 1962; joined the Commonwealth, 1970; governed by a Monarch as Head of State for life, a Prime Minister, and a 47-member Legislative Assembly (*Fono*).

Head of State (O le Ao O le Malo)
1963– Malietoa Tanumafili II

Head of Government
1998– Tuila'epa Sa'ilele Malielegaoi

SAN MARINO

Local name San Marino

Timezone GMT +1

Area 61 km²/23 sq mi

Population total (2002e) 27 700

Status Republic

Capital San Marino

Language Italian (official)

Ethnic groups Sanmarinesi (San Marino citizens) (87%), Italian (12%)

Religion Roman Catholic (95%)

Physical features Landlocked in C Italy; smallest republic in the world, land boundaries, 34 km/21 mi; ruggedly mountainous, centred on the limestone ridges of Monte Titano, 793 m/2602 ft, and the valley of the R Ausa.

Climate Temperate climate, with cool winters, warm summers; average annual temperatures –6°C (Jan), 26°C (Jul); moderate rainfall; average annual rainfall 880 mm /35 in.

Currency 1 euro = 100 cents (previous to February 2002, 1 Italian Lira (L, Lit)/1 San Marino Lira = 100 centesimi)

Economy Wheat, grapes, cheese, livestock; postage stamps, tourism, textiles, pottery; chemicals, paints, wine.

GDP (2001e) $940 mn, per capita $34 600

History Founded by a 4th-c Christian saint as a refuge against religious persecution; treaty of friendship with the Kingdom of Italy, preserving independence, 1862; in World War 2, followed Italy and declared war on Britain, 1940; declared neutrality shortly before Italian surrender, 1943; governed by an elected unicameral Parliament (the Grand and General Council) and a Congress of State; Parliament elects two of its members every six months to act as Captains-Regent (*Capitani Reggenti*), with the functions of Head of State.

Secretary of State
2002– Fiorenzo Stolfi

MAP >> ITALY

SÃO TOMÉ AND PRÍNCIPE

Local name São Tomé e Príncipe

Timezone GMT

Area 1001 km²/387 sq mi

Population total (2002e) 147 800

Status Democratic republic

Date of independence 1975

Capital São Tomé

Languages Portuguese (official), with a number of creoles spoken

Ethnic groups Portuguese-African descent, African minority

Religions Roman Catholic (80%), Seventh Day Adventist, and Evangelical Protestant

Physical features Equatorial volcanic islands in the Gulf of Guinea, off the coast of Equatorial Guinea, W Africa; comprise São Tomé, Príncipe, and several smaller islands; São Tomé (area 845 km²/326 sq mi),

greatest height, 2024 m/6640 ft, Pico de São Tomé in central volcanic uplands; heavily forested.

Climate Tropical climate; average annual temperature 27°C (coast), 20°C (mountains); rainy season (Oct–May); annual average rainfall 500–1000 mm/20–40 in.

Currency 1 Dobra (Db) = 100 centimos

Economy Based on agriculture (employs c.70% of population); cocoa, copra, palm kernels, coffee, wine, fishing; restructured economy since 1985, with greater involvement in commerce, banking, and tourism.

GDP (2002e) $200 mn, per capita $1200

HDI (2002) 0.632

History Visited by the Portuguese, 1469–72; Portuguese colony, 1522; resistance to Portuguese rule led to riots in 1953, and the formation of an overseas liberation movement based in Gabon; independence, 1975; sole legal party was the Movement for the Liberation of São Tomé and Principe, until new constitution in 1990 approved multi-party democratic system; bloodless coup by army rebels (Jul 2003) during President de Menezes' visit to Nigeria; he returned when agreement to restore democratic rule was reached; governed by a President, Prime Minister, and a National Assembly.

Head of State
1991–2001 Miguel Trovoada
2001– Fradique de Menezes

Head of Government
2002–4 Maria das Neves de Sousa
2004– Damião Vaz d'Almeida

SAUDI ARABIA

Local name al-'Arabīyah as-Sa'ūdīyah (Arabic)

Timezone GMT +3

Area 2 331 000 km²/899 766 sq mi

Population total (2002e) 23 370 000

Status Kingdom

Capital Riyadh (Ar-Riyād)

Language Arabic (official)

Ethnic groups Arab (90%), Afro-Asian (10%)

Religions Muslim (Sunni 85%, Shi'ite 15%), small Christian minority

Physical features Comprises four-fifths of the Arabian peninsula; Red Sea coastal plain bounded E by mountains; highlands in SW contain Jebel Abha, Saudi Arabia's highest peak, 3133m/10279 ft; Arabian peninsula slopes gently N and E towards oil-rich al-Hasa plain on the Persian Gulf; interior comprises two extensive areas of sand desert, the An Nafud (N) and Rub' al-Khali (the Great Sandy Desert) (S); salt flats numerous in E lowlands; large network of wadis drains NE; 95% of land is arid or semi-arid desert.

Climate Hot, dry climate; average temperatures 21°C (N), 26°C (S), rise to 50°C in the interior; night frosts common in N and highlands; Red Sea coast hot and humid; average annual temperatures 14°C (Jan), 33°C (Jul) in Riyadh; average annual rainfall 10 mm/0.4 in.

Currency 1 Saudi Arabian Riyal (SAR, SRls) = 100 halalah

Economy Oil discovered in 1930s; now the world's leading oil exporter (reserves account for c.25% of world's known supply); rapidly-developing construction industry; large areas opened up for cultivation in 1980s; agriculture: wheat, dates, livestock; pilgrimage trade.

GDP (2002e) $268.9 bn, per capita $11 400

HDI (2002) 0.759

History Famed as the birthplace of Islam, a centre of pilgrimage to the holy cities of Mecca, Medina, and Jedda(h); modern state founded by Ibn Saud who by 1932 united the four tribal provinces of Hejaz (NW), Asir (SW), Najd (C), and al-Hasa (E); governed as an absolute monarchy based on Islamic law and Arab Bedouin tradition; King (official title: Custodian of the Two Holy Mosques (Mecca and Medina)) is Head of State and Prime Minister, assisted by a Council of Ministers; there is no parliament; royal decree, 1992, provided for the creation of a Consultative Council.

Head of State/Government (Monarch)
Family name: al-Saud
1996– Fahd ibn Abdul-Aziz

☐ International Airport • - = Boundary awaiting demarcation

SCOTLAND >> UNITED KINGDOM

SENEGAL

Local name Sénégal (French)

Timezone GMT

Area 196 790 km²/75 729 sq mi

Population total (2002e) 9 905 000

Status Republic

Date of independence 1960

Capital Dakar

Languages French (official), with various ethnic languages spoken

Ethnic groups Wolof (36%), Serer (19%), Fulani (13%), Toucouleur (9%), Diola (9%), Mandingo (9%), European and Lebanese (1%)

Religions Sunni Muslim (91%), Roman Catholic (5%), local beliefs (3%)

Physical features Located in W Africa; extensive low-lying basin of savannah and semi-desert vegetation to the N; sand dunes along coastline; dunes and mangrove forests in S, where land rises to around 500 m/1640 ft; lowland savannah and semi-desert regions of N drain into R Sénégal, which forms the N and NE boundary with Mauritania and Mali.

Climate Tropical climate; rainy season (Jun–Sep); high humidity levels and high night-time temperatures, especially on the coast; average temperature, 22–28°C; average annual rainfall 541 mm/21 in at Dakar.

Currency 1 CFA Franc (CFAFr) = 100 centimes

Economy Agriculture (employs c.75% of workforce); groundnuts, cotton, sugar, millet, sorghum, maize, livestock; minerals, iron ore, gold; oil, natural gas; fishing, timber; textiles, chemicals; shipbuilding and repairing; tourism.

GDP (2002e) $15.64 bn, per capita $1500

HDI (2002) 0.431

History Part of the Mali Empire, 14th–15th-c; French established a fort at Saint-Louis, 1658; incorporated as a territory within French West Africa, 1902; autonomous state within the French community, 1958; joined with French Sudan as independent Federation of Mali, 1959; withdrew in 1960 to become a separate independent republic; joined with The Gambia to form the Confederation of Senegambia, 1982–9; Confederation collapsed, 1989, following violent clashes between Senegalese and Mauritanians; governed by a President (elected for a 5-year term), Prime Minister, a Senate, and National Assembly.

Head of State

2000– Abdoulaye Wade

Head of Government

2004– Macky Sall

☐ International Airport   ∴ World heritage site

SERBIA AND MONTENEGRO (FORMERLY, YUGOSLAVIA)

Local name Srbija-Crna Gora, (Jugoslavija)

Timezone GMT +2

Area 102 173 km²/39 438 sq mi

Population total Since 1991: (2002e) 10 600 000

Status Federal Republic

Date of independence 1991; between 1991 and 2003, known as the Federal Republic of Yugoslavia; previously, part of the larger Yugoslav federation, along with Bosnia and Herzegovina, Croatia, Macedonia, and Slovenia

Capital Belgrade (Serbia)

Languages Serbian (95%), with Albanian and Hungarian also spoken

Ethnic groups 1991: Serbian (63%), Albanian (16%), Montenegrin (5%), Hungarian (3%), others (13%); civil war of the 1990s and its consequences have prevented accurate current estimates

Religions 1991: Serbian Orthodox (65%), Muslim (19%), Roman Catholic (4%), Protestant (1%), others (11%); current estimates not available

Physical features Mountainous country with fertile valleys. Julian and Karawanken Alps rise (N) to 2863 m/9393 ft at Triglav; Adriatic fringed by the Dinaric Alps; fertile Danubian plain in NE Serbia; chief river, R Danube, also the Tisza, Drava, Sava, and Morava; limestone karst plateaux in W along coast.

Climate Moderate, continental climate; average annual temperatures 0°C (Jan), 22°C (Jul) in Belgrade; average annual rainfall 610 mm/24 in.

Currency 1 Dinar (D, Din) = 100 paras

Economy Ongoing conflict and escalating violence has crippled the economy of the countries involved; stabilization measures introduced since 2000; corn, wheat, tobacco, sugar beets; mining and manufacturing industries; exports of textiles, leather goods, machinery; natural resources of copper, coal, timber, iron, lead, zinc, bauxite.

GDP (2002e) $23.15 bn, per capita $2200

History Serbs, Croats, and Slovenes united under one monarch, 1918; formation of new state did not quell long-held nationalist feelings; in an attempt to create a sense of common patriotism King Alexander changed the kingdom's name to Yugoslavia, 1929; civil war between Serbian royalists (Chetniks), Croatian nationalists, and Communists; occupied by Germany in World War 2; Federal People's Republic established under Tito, 1945; revised constitution in 1974, instituted a rotating leadership, with the Prime Minister elected annually; governed by a bicameral Federal Assembly, comprising a Federal Chamber and a Chamber of Republics and Provinces; following a break with the USSR in 1948, the country followed an independent form of communism and a general policy of non-alignment; at the end of the 1980s political disagreement between the federal republics increased; ethnic unrest in Serbia (Kosovo); Slovenian unilateral declaration of independence, 1990, followed by Macedonian and Croatian declarations, 1991, considered illegal by central government; inter-republic talks on Yugoslavia's future, but confrontation between Croatia and Serb-dominated National Army developed into civil war, 1991; Serbian support of Serb guerrillas in Bosnia resulted in UN sanctions, mid-1992; arrival of UN Protection Force, 1992; Federal Republic of Yugoslavia declared, 1992, consisting of only two of the six republics that made up former Yugoslavia (Montenegro and Serbia); fighting between ethnic groups in Bosnia continued until 1995, when peace accord signed in Dayton, Ohio; conflict in Kosovo between Serbia and ethnic Albanian resistance movement (Kosovo Liberation Army), 1997; escalation of conflict, 1999, led to Serbian incursions

□ International Airport

into Kosovo and displacement of Kosovar Albanians; NATO air-strikes campaign against Yugoslav targets; President Milosevic accepted peace terms, with deployment of NATO troops into Kosovo and departure of Serb forces; new accord, leading to Union of Serbia and Montenegro, 2002; new constitution (2003) recognizes a President elected for a 4-year term, Prime Minister, cabinet, and 126-member unicameral parliament (91 Serbian, 35 Montenegrin); union arrangement to remain for 3-year minimum, followed by referendum. >> BOSNIA AND HERZEGOVINA, CROATIA, MACEDONIA, SLOVENIA

Head of State and Government
2003– Svetozar Marovic

SEYCHELLES

Local name Seychelles

Timezone GMT +4

Area 455 km²/175 sq mi

Population total (2002e) 83 400

Status Republic

Date of independence 1976

Capital Victoria (on Mahé Island)

Languages Creole French (official since 1981), and English

Ethnic groups Seychellois (Asian, African, and European admixtures), Malagasy (3%), Chinese (2%), English (1%)

Religions Roman Catholic (90%)

Physical features Island group in SW Indian Ocean, N of Madagascar, comprising 115 islands; main islands include Mahé (largest), Praslin, and La Digue; islands fall into two main groups, a compact group of 41 mountain-

Seychelles (continued)

ous islands rising steeply from the sea, highest point 906 m/2972 ft on Mahé; and a group of low-lying coralline islands and atolls to the SW, flat, waterless and mostly uninhabited.

Climate Tropical climate; average annual temperature 27°C (Jan), 26°C (Jul); wet humid season (Dec–May); average annual rainfall 2375 mm/93.5 in.

Currency 1 Seychelles Rupee (SR) = 100 cents

Economy Agriculture: fruit, vegetables, livestock, cinnamon, copra; brewing, plastics, steel fabricated goods, fishing; tourism.

GDP (2002e) $626 mn, per capita $7800

HDI (2002) 0.811

History Colonized by the French, 1768; captured by Britain, 1794; incorporated as a dependency of Mauritius, 1814; separate Crown Colony, 1903; independent republic within the Commonwealth, 1976; constitution, 1979, established a one-party state; governed by a President, elected for a 5-year term, a Council of Ministers, and a unicameral National Assembly; legislation legalizing the activity of opposition parties adopted, 1991.

Head of State/Government
2004– James Michel

SIERRA LEONE

Local name Sierra Leone

Timezone GMT

Area 71 740 km²/27 692 sq mi

Population total (2002e) 4 823 000

Status Republic

Date of independence 1961

Capital Freetown

Languages English (official), with Krio widely spoken

Ethnic groups African origin (99%) (including Mendes, Temnes, Limbas, Korankos, and Lokos)

Religions Local beliefs (30%), Sunni Muslim (60%), Christian (Protestant 6%, Roman Catholic 2%)

Physical features Low narrow coastal plain in W Africa; rises to an average height of 500 m/1600 ft in the Loma Mts (E), highest point, Loma Mansa, 1948 m/6391 ft; Tingi Mts rise to 1853 m/6079 ft (SE); principal rivers include the Great Scarcies, Rokel, Gbangbaia, Jong, and Sewa.

Climate Equatorial climate; temperatures uniformly high throughout the year; average annual temperature 27°C; rainy season (May–Oct); highest rainfall on coast; average annual rainfall 3436 mm/135 in at Freetown.

Currency 1 Leone (Le) = 100 cents

Economy Mining (most important sector of the economy); diamonds (represent c.60% of exports); bauxite, gold, titanium, iron ore, and other mineral and metal ores; subsistence agriculture (employs over 70% of population); rice, coffee, cocoa, citrus fruits; timber; food processing.

GDP (2002e) $2.826 bn, per capita $500

HDI (2002) 0.275

History First visited by Portuguese navigators and British slave traders; land bought from local chiefs by English philanthropists who established settlements for freed slaves, 1780s; British Crown Colony, 1808; hinterland declared a British protectorate, 1896; independence declared within the Commonwealth as a constitutional monarchy, 1961; period of military rule, 1968; became a republic, 1971; established as a one-party state, 1978; new constitution, 1991, allowing for multi-party politics, and

□ International Airport

interim government formed until general elections; interrupted by military coup in 1992, House of Representatives dissolved, and Supreme Council of State (SCS) and Civilian Council of State Secretaries (Cabinet) established; further military coup, 1997; overturned, 1998; renewed fighting in early 1999, followed by Lomé (Togo) peace agreement (Jul) and establishment of UN peacekeeping force; UN troops attacked and abducted by rebels (Apr 2000), leading to a UK-sponsored military assistance plan within the country, and the arrival of UN reinforcements; peace declared, 2002.

Head of State/Government
1998– Ahmad Tejan Kabbah

SINGAPORE

Local name Singapore

Timezone GMT +8

Area 618 km²/238 sq mi

Population total (2002e) 4 000 000

Status Republic

Date of independence 1965

Capital Singapore City

Languages English, Malay, Chinese, and Tamil (official)

Ethnic groups Chinese (77%), Malay (15%), Indian (6%)

Religions Chinese population mainly Buddhists, Malay mainly Muslim, also Taoist, Christian, and Hindu minorities

Physical features Located at the S tip of the Malay Peninsula, SE Asia; consists of the island of Singapore and c.50 adjacent islets; linked to Malaysia by a causeway across the Johor Strait; Singapore Island is low-lying, rising to 177 m/581 ft at Bukit Timah; Seletar River drains N–E; deep-water harbour (SE).

Climate Equatorial climate; high humidity; no clearly defined seasons; average annual temperature range, 21–34°C; average annual rainfall, 2438 mm/96 in.

Currency 1 Singapore Dollar/Ringgit (S$) = 100 cents

Economy Major transshipment centre (one of world's largest ports); oil refining; rubber, food processing, chemicals, electronics; ship repair; financial services; fishing; tourism (affected by SARS outbreak, 2003).

GDP (2002e) $112.4 bn, per capita $25 200

HDI (2002) 0.885

History Originally part of the Sumatran Srivijaya kingdom; leased by the British East India Company, on the advice of Sir Stamford Raffles, from the Sultan of Johore, 1819; Singapore, Malacca, and Penang incorporated as the Straits Settlements, 1826; British Crown Colony, 1867; occupied by the Japanese, 1942–5; self-government, 1959; part of the Federation of Malaya from 1963 until its establishment as an independent state in 1965; governed by a President, a Prime Minister, and unicameral Parliament.

Head of State
1999–   Sellapan Ramanathan Nathan

Head of Government
1990–2004 Goh Chok Tong
2004–   Lee Hsien Loong

SLOVAK REPUBLIC

Local name Slovenská republiká

Timezone GMT +1

Area 49 035 km²/18 927 sq mi

Population total (2002e) 5 383 000

Status Republic

Date of independence 1993

Capital Bratislava

Languages Slovak (official), with Czech and Hungarian widely spoken

Ethnic groups Slovak (87%), Hungarian (11%), Czech (1%), with German, Polish, and Ukrainian minorities

Religions Roman Catholic (70%), Protestant (6%)

Physical features Dominated by the Carpathian Mountains, consisting of a system of E–W ranges separated by valleys and basins; ranges include the Low Tatras of the Inner Carpathians, 1829 m/6000 ft, and the highest point, Gerlachovsky, 2655 m/8711 ft in the Tatra Mts (N); main rivers include the Danube, Vah, Hron; national parks at Pieniny, Low and High Tatra.

Climate Continental climate; warm humid summers,

□ International Airport

cold dry winters; snow remains on the mountains for 130 days of the year; average annual temperature –4°C (Jan), 18°C (Jul) in Bratislava; average annual rainfall 500–650 mm/20–30 in.

Slovak Republic (continued)

Currency 1 Slovak Koruna = 100 halers

Economy Agricultural region, especially cereals, wine, fruit; steel production in Košice; heavy industry suffering since previously dependent on state subsidies.

GDP (2002e) $67.34 bn, per capita $12 400

HDI (2002) 0.835

History Settled in 5th–6th-c by Slavs; part of Great Moravia, 9th-c; part of Magyar Empire from 10th-c; became part of Kingdom of Hungary, 11th-c; united with Czech lands to form the separate state of Czechoslovakia, 1918; under German control, 1938–9; Slovakia became a separate republic under German influence, 1939; Czechoslovakia regained its independence, 1945;

under Communist rule following 1948 coup; attempt at liberalization by Dubček terminated by intervention of Warsaw Pact troops, 1968; from 1960s, Slovaks revived efforts to gain recognition for Slovak rights; fall from power of Communist party, 1989; 1992 agreement to divide Czechoslovakia into its constituent republics led to declaration of independence of Slovak Republic, 1993; governed by a President, Prime Minister, Council of Ministers, and National Council.

Head of State
2004–　　Ivan Gasparovic

Head of Government
1997–8　　Vladimír Mečiar
1998–　　Mikuláš Dzurinda

SLOVENIA

Local name Slovenija

Timezone GMT +1

Area 20 251 km²/7817 sq mi

Population total (2002e) 1 948 000

Status Republic

Date of independence 1991

Capital Ljubljana

Languages Slovene, Croatian

Ethnic group Slovene (90%)

Religions Roman Catholic, Protestant, some Eastern Orthodox

Physical features Mountainous republic between Austria and Croatia; Slovenian Alps (NW) rise to 2863 m/9393 ft at Triglav in the Julian Alps (Julijske Alpe); rivers include Sava, Savinja, and Drava; chief port, Koper.

Climate Continental climate; more Mediterranean in W; average annual temperature −1°C (Jan), 19°C (Jul) in Ljubljana; average annual rainfall 1600 mm/63 in.

Currency (1991) 1 Slovene Tolar = 100 paras

Economy Agriculture; maize, wheat, sugar beet, potatoes, livestock, wine, timber, lignite; textiles; large iron and steel plants; vehicles; coal, lead, mercury mining in W.

GDP (2002e) $37.06 bn, per capita $19 200

HDI (2002) 0.879

History Settled by Slovenes, 6th–8th-c; later controlled by Slavs and Franks; part of the Austro-Hungarian Empire until 1918; people's republic within Yugoslavia,

□ International Airport

1946; declaration of full sovereignty, 1990; declaration of independence from Yugoslavia as the Republic of Slovenia, 1991; opposed by central government, brief period of fighting upon the intervention of the federal army who withdrew in Aug 1991; tricameral legislature replaced by a bicameral National Assembly, consisting of a State Assembly and a State Council.

Head of State
2002–　　Janez Drnovšek

Head of Government
2002–　　Anton Rop

SOLOMON ISLANDS

Local name Solomon Islands

Timezone GMT +11

Land area 27 556 km²/10 637 sq mi

Population total (2002e) 439 000

Status Independent state within the Commonwealth

Date of independence 1978

Capital Honiara

Languages English (official), with pidgin English and c.80 local languages also spoken

Ethnic groups Melanesian (93%), Polynesian (4%), Micronesian (1.5%), European (1%), Chinese (0.5%)

Religions Christian (95%) (Protestant 41%, Anglican 34%, Roman Catholic 19%)

Physical features Archipelago of several hundred islands in the SW Pacific Ocean, stretching c.1400 km/870 mi between Papua New Guinea (NW) and Vanuatu (SE); six main islands, Choiseul, Guadalcanal, Malaita, New Georgia, San Cristobal (now Makira), Santa Isabel; highest point, Mt Makarakomburu, 2477 m/8126 ft, on Guadalcanal (largest island); large islands have forested mountain ranges and coastal belts; Anuta, Fataka, and Tikopia islands are volcanic.

Climate Equatorial climate; high humidity; average annual temperature 27°C; maximum rainfall Nov–Apr; average annual rainfall, c.3500 mm/138 in; periodic cyclones.

Currency 1 Solomon Islands Dollar (SI$) = 100 cents

Economy Based on agriculture; forestry, livestock, fisheries, taro, rice, bananas, yams, copra, oil palm; milling, fish processing; crafts.

GDP (2001e) $800 mn, per capita $1700

HDI (2002) 0.622

History Visited by the Spanish, 1568; S Solomon Is placed under British protection, 1893; outer islands (Santa Cruz group) added to the protectorate, 1899; scene of fierce fighting in World War 2; achieved internal self-

□ International Airport

government, 1976; independence, 1978; British monarch represented by a Governor-General; Prime Minister leads a unicameral National Parliament; fighting between two rival militias led to military coup, 2000; peace treaty brokered by Australia, but continued ethnic unrest; Australian-led peace-keeping force, 2003.

Head of State
(British monarch represented by Governor-General)
2004–   Nathaniel Waena

Head of Government
2001   Sir Allan Kemakeza

SOMALIA

Local name Somaliya

Timezone GMT +3

Area 637357 km²/246 201 sq mi

Population total (2002e) 7 753 000

Status Republic

Date of independence 1960

Capital Mogadishu

Languages Somali, Arabic (official)

Ethnic groups Somali (85%), Bantu (15%), with Arab, European, and Asian minorities

Religions Sunni Muslim (99%), small Christian minority

Physical features Occupies the E Horn of Africa, where dry coastal plain broadens to the S, and rises inland to a plateau c.1000 m/3300 ft; forested mountains on the Gulf of Aden coast rise to 2416 m/7926 ft at Mt Shimbiris; main rivers, Jubba and Webi Shabeelle.

Climate Predominantly arid; average daily maximum temperatures 28–32°C in Mogadishu; average annual rainfall 490 mm/19.3 in; heavier rainfall (Apr–Sep) on E coast; serious, persistent threat of drought.

Currency 1 Somali Shilling (SoSh) = 100 cents

Economy Agriculture (c.50% nomadic people raising cattle, sheep, goats, camels); bananas, sugar, spices, cotton, rice, citrus fruits, tobacco, iron ore; textiles; fishing.

GDP (2001e) $4.27 bn, per capita $600

□ International Airport

History Settled by Muslims, 7th-c; Italian, French, and British interests after opening of Suez Canal, 1869; after World War 2, Somalia formed by amalgamation of Italian and British protectorates; independence, 1960; from 1960s, territorial conflict with Ethiopia over Ogaden

Somalia (continued)

which has large Somali population; military coup, 1969; peace agreement with Ethiopia, 1989; governed by a President, Council of Ministers, and People's Assembly; new constitution approved, 1990; NW region seceded as Somaliland Republic, 1991; civil war, 1991–2, forced UN intervention to safeguard food supplies, 1992; gradual withdrawal of forces, 1993–5; National Salvation Council formed, 1997; peace accord, 1997, but discord ongoing in 2000; transitional government formed, 2000; further peace agreement signed by 42 of the main factions, 2004; members of first parliament for 13 years sworn in, Aug 2004; coast hit by Indian Ocean tsunami, 2004.

Head of State

2000–4   Abdiqassim Salad Hassan *Elected by the parliament in exile*
2004–   Abdullahi Yusuf

Head of Government

2001–4   Hasan Abshir Farah
2004–   Ali Mohamed Ghedi

SOUTH AFRICA

Local name South Africa

Timezone GMT +2

Area 1 233 404 km²/476 094 sq mi

Population total (2002e) 45 172 000

Status Republic

Date of independence 1961

Capitals Cape Town (legislative); Pretoria (administrative); Bloemfontein (judicial)

Languages (co-official) Afrikaans, English, Ndebele, Pedi, Sotho, Swazi, Tsonga, Tswana, Venda, Xhosa, Zulu

Ethnic groups Black African (70%), white (18%), Asian (3%), Coloured (9%)

Religions Christian (most whites and Coloureds and c.60% Africans), traditional beliefs, Hindu, Muslim, and Jewish minorities

Physical features Occupies the S extremity of the African plateau; fringed by fold mountains and a lowland coastal margin to the W, E, and S; N interior comprises the Kalahari Basin, scrub grassland, and arid desert; Great Escarpment rises E to 3482 m/11 424 ft at Thabana Ntlenyana; Orange R flows W to meet the Atlantic; chief tributaries, Vaal and Caledon rivers.

Climate Subtropical in E; average annual temperature 4°C (Jan), 17°C (Jul) in Cape Town; average annual rainfall 1008 mm/39.7 in Durban; dry moistureless climate on W coast; desert region further N, annual average rainfall less than 30 mm/1.2 in.

Currency 1 Rand (R) = 100 cents

Economy Industrial growth as a result of 19th-c gold (c.50% of export income) and diamond discoveries; grain, wool, sugar, tobacco, cotton, citrus fruit, dairy products, livestock, fishing; motor vehicles, machinery, chemicals, fertilizers, textiles, clothes, metal products, electronics, computers, tourism.

GDP (2002e) $427.7 bn, per capita $10 000

HDI (2002) 0.695

History Originally inhabited by Khoisan tribes; Portuguese reached the Cape of Good Hope, late 15th-c; settled by Dutch, 1652; arrival of British, 1795; British annexation of the Cape, 1806; Great Trek by Boers NE across the Orange R to Natal, 1836; first Boer republic founded, 1839; Natal annexed by the British in 1843, but the Boer republics of Transvaal (founded 1852) and Orange Free State (1854) were recognized; Zulu War, 1879; South African Wars, 1880–1, 1899–1902; Transvaal,

□ International Airport

Natal, Orange Free State, and Cape Province joined as the Union of South Africa, a dominion of the British Empire, 1910; sovereign state within the Commonwealth, 1931–61; independent republic, 1961; independence granted by South Africa to Transkei (1976), Bophuthatswana (1977), Venda (1979) and Ciskei (1981), not recognized internationally; politics dominated by treatment of non-white majority following the apartheid (racial segregation) policy after 1948; continuing racial violence and strikes led to a state of emergency in 1986, and several countries imposed economic and cultural sanctions; progressive dismantling of apartheid system by F W de Klerk from 1990; black Nationalist leader Nelson Mandela freed after more than 27 years in prison, and the African National Congress unbanned, 1990; readmitted into international sport, USA lifted trade and investment sanctions, 1991; most remaining apartheid legislation abolished, 1991; new constitution, 1996; governed by a President, Cabinet, National Assembly and Senate; elections in May 1994 brought victory to the ANC.

Head of State/Government

1994–9   Nelson Rolihlahla Mandela
1999–   Thabo Mbeki

South African Provinces

Name	Area km²	sq mi	Capital
Eastern Cape	170 616	65 858	Bisho
Mpumalanga	81 816	31 581	Nelspruit
KwaZulu Natal	91 481	35 312	Pietermaritzburg/ Ulundi
North-West	118 710	45 822	Mmabatho
Northern Cape	363 389	140 268	Kimberley

Name	Area km²	sq mi	Capital
Limpopo (Northern Province)	119 606	46 168	Pietersburg
Free State	129 437	49 963	Bloemfontein
Gauteng	18 760	7 241	Johannesburg/ Pretoria
Western Cape	129 386	49 943	Cape Town

SOUTH GEORGIA >> UNITED KINGDOM

SOUTH KOREA >> KOREA, SOUTH

SOUTH SANDWICH ISLANDS >> UNITED KINGDOM

SPAIN

Local name España (Spanish)

Timezone GMT +1

Area 504 750 km²/194 833 sq mi

Population total (2002e) 40 998 000

Status Kingdom

Capital Madrid

Languages Spanish (official) with Catalan, Galician, and Basque also spoken in their respective regions

Ethnic groups Spanish (Castilian, Valencian, Andalusian, Asturian) (73%), Catalan (16%), Galician (8%), Basque (2%)

Religions Roman Catholic (99%), other Christian (including Anglican, Baptist, Evangelical, Mormon, Jehovah's Witnesses) and Muslim minorities

Physical features Located in SW Europe, occupying four-fifths of the Iberian peninsula; includes the Canary Is, Balearic Is, several islands off the coast of N Africa, as well as the Presidios of Ceuta and Melilla in N Morocco; mostly a furrowed C plateau (the Meseta, average height 700 m/2300 ft) crossed by mountains; Andalusian or Baetic Mts (SE) rise to 3478 m/11 411 ft at Mulhacén; Pyrénées (N) rise to 3404 m/11 168 ft at Pico de Aneto; rivers run E–W, notably the Tagus, Ebro, Guadiana, Miñho, Duero, Guadalquivir, Segura, Júcar.

Climate Continental climate in the Meseta and Ebro Basin, with hot summers, cold winters, low rainfall; highest rainfall in the mountains; S Mediterranean coast has warmest winter temperatures on European mainland; average annual temperatures 5°C (Jan), 25°C (Jul) in Madrid; average annual rainfall 419 mm/16.5 in.

Currency 1 euro = 100 cents (previous to February 2002, 1 Peseta (Pta, Pa) = 100 céntimos)

Economy Traditional agricultural economy gradually being supplemented by varied industries; textiles, iron, steel, shipbuilding, electrical appliances, cars, wine; forestry; fishing; tourism; zinc and other mineral ores; cereals, olives, almonds, pomegranates; member of EC, 1986.

GDP (2002e) $850.7 bn, per capita $21 200

HDI (2002) 0.913

History Early inhabitants included Iberians, Celts, Phoenicians, Greeks, and Romans; Muslim domination

□ International Airport

1 PRINCIPADO DE ASTURIAS
2 CANTABRIA
3 PAÍS VASCO
4 COMUNIDAD FORAL DE NAVARRA
5 LA RIOJA
6 COMUNIDAD DE MADRID

Spain (continued)

from the 8th-c; Christian reconquest completed by 1492; a monarchy since unification of Kingdoms of Castile, León, Aragón, and Navarre, largely achieved by 1572; 16th-c exploration of New World, and growth of Spanish Empire; period of decline after Revolt of the Netherlands, 1581, and defeat of Spanish Armada, 1588; War of Spanish Succession, 1701–14; Peninsular War against Napoleon, 1808–14; war with USA in 1898 led to loss of Cuba, Puerto Rico, and remaining Pacific possessions; dictatorship under Primo de Rivera (1923–30), followed by exile of the King and establishment of Second Republic, 1931; military revolt headed by Franco led to civil war and Fascist dictatorship, 1936; Prince Juan Carlos of Bourbon nominated to succeed Franco, 1969; acceded, 1975; terrorist bombs at Madrid railway stations killed over 200 (Mar 2004); under 1978 constitution, the Kingdom of Spain is a constitutional monarchy; Monarch appoints the Prime Minister; governed by a bicameral Parliament (Cortes Generales) comprising a Congress of Deputies and a Senate; move towards local government autonomy with creation of 17 self-governing regions.

Head of State (Monarch)
1975–   Juan Carlos I

Head of Government
2004–   José Luis Rodríguez Zapatero

Balearic islands

Local name Islas Baleares

Area 5014 km²/1935 sq mi

Population total (2000e) 712 000

Status Province of Spain

Capital Palma de Mallorca

Physical features Archipelago of five major islands and 11 islets in the Mediterranean, near the E coast of Spain; E group of islands consists of Mallorca (Majorca), Menorca, Cabrera; Ibiza and Formentera (W group); popular tourist resorts.

Climate Continental; average annual temperatures 11°C (Jan), 25°C (Jul); average annual rainfall 347 mm/14 in.

Currency 1 euro = 100 cents (formerly, 1 Peseta (Pta, Pa) = 100 céntimos)

Economy Tourism; fruit, wine, grain, cattle, fishing, textiles, chemicals, cork, timber.

☐ International Airport

Canary islands

Local name Islas Canarias

Area 7273 km²/2807 sq mi

Population total (2000e) 1 475 000

Status Forms two provinces of Spain

Chief town Las Palmas

Physical features Island archipelago, located in the Atlantic, 100 km/60 mi off the NW coast of Africa; includes the islands of Tenerife, La Palma, Gomera, Hierro, Grand Canary (Gran Canaria), Fuerteventura, Lanzarote, and several uninhabited islands; major ports, Las Palmas, Santa Cruz; volcanic and mountainous, the Pico de Teide rises to 3718 m/12198 ft on Tenerife; tourist resorts on main islands.

Climate Continental; average annual temperature 18°C (Jan), 24°C (Jul); average annual rainfall 196 mm/8 in.

Currency 1 euro = 100 cents (previous to February 2002, 1 Peseta (Pta, Pa) = 100 céntimos)

Economy Tourism; agriculture, fishing, canning, textiles, leatherwork, footwear, cork, timber, chemical and metal products.

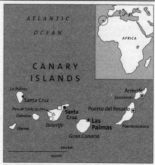

☐ International Airport

SRI LANKA

Local name Sri Lanka

Timezone GMT +5.5

Area 65 610 km²/25 325 sq mi

Population total (2002e) 18 870 000

Status Republic

Date of independence 1972

Capital Sri-Jayawardenapura (since 1983); (former capital, Colombo)

Languages Sinhala, Tamil (official), English also spoken

Ethnic groups Sinhalese (74%), Tamil (18%), Muslim (7%), Burgher, Malay, and Veddha (1%)

Religions Buddhist (69%), Hindu (15%), Christian (8%), Muslim (8%)

Physical features Island state in the Indian Ocean; separated from the Indian sub-continent by the Palk Strait, linked by a series of coral islands known as Adam's Bridge; low-lying areas in N and S, surrounding SC uplands; highest peak, Pidurutalagala, 2524 m/8281 ft; coastal plain fringed by sandy beaches and lagoons; c.50% of land is tropical monsoon forest or open woodland.

Climate Equatorial, tropical climate; modified temperatures in interior according to altitude; average annual temperature 27°C in Sri-Jayawardenapura; average annual rainfall 2527 mm/99.5 in; greatest rainfall on SW coast and in the mountains; monsoon season (Dec–Feb) in NE, dry, semi-arid for rest of year.

Currency 1 Sri Lanka Rupee (SLR, SLRs) = 100 cents

Economy Agriculture (employs 52% of labour force); rice, rubber, tea, coconuts, spices, sugar cane; timber, fishing; graphite, coal, precious and semi-precious stones; electricity produced largely by water power; textiles, chemicals, paper.

GDP (2002e) $73.7 bn, per capita $3700

HDI (2002) 0.741

History Visited by Portuguese, 1505; taken by Dutch, 1658; British occupation, 1796; British colony, 1802; Tamil labourers brought in from S India during colonial rule, to work on coffee and tea plantations; Dominion status, 1948; changed name of Ceylon and became independent republic of Sri Lanka, 1972; acute political tension between Buddhist Sinhalese majority and Hindu Tamil minority, who want an independent state in N and E (Liberation Tigers of Tamil Eelam, LTTE); state of emergency declared, 1983; ceasefire agreed, 1994, but conflict soon resumed; ceasefire agreed, 2001, but conflict ongoing; power-sharing proposals (Nov 2003); governed by a President, Prime Minister, and National State Assembly; parliament dissolved (Feb 2004), followed by minority government; E coast devastated by tsunami, 2004.

Head of State
1994– Chandrika Bandaranaike Kumaratunga

Head of Government
2004– Mahinda Rajapakse

□ International Airport

SUDAN, THE

Local name As-Sūdān (Arabic)

Timezone GMT +2

Area 2 505 870 km²/967 243 sq mi

Population total (2002e) 37 090 000

Status Republic

Date of independence 1956

Capital Khartoum

Languages Arabic (official), local languages, including Darfurian, Nilotic, and Nilo-Hamitic, are also spoken

Ethnic groups Black (52%), Arab (39%), Beja (6%)

Religions Muslim (Sunni 70%), traditional animist beliefs (20%), Christian (5%)

Physical features Largest country on the African continent, astride the middle reaches of the R Nile; E edge formed by Nubian Highlands and an escarpment rising c.2000 m/6500 ft on the Red Sea; Imatong Mts (S) rise to 3187 m/10 456 ft at Kinyeti, highest point in Sudan; Darfur Massif in the W; White Nile flows N to meet the Blue Nile at Khartoum.

Climate Tropical, continental; desert conditions in

Sudan, The (continued)

NW, with temperatures rarely falling below 24°C; hottest months (Jul–Aug); sandstorms common; average annual temperature 23°C (Jan), 32°C (Jul) in Khartoum; average annual rainfall 157 mm/6.2 in.

Currency 1 Sudanese dinar (Sd) = 100 piastres

Economy Agriculture (employs c.75% of population); commercial farming (N) and livestock farming (S); large-scale irrigation schemes, fed by dams; major famines, especially 1984–5, 1990–1; gum arabic (80% of world supply); reserves of copper, lead, iron ore, chromite, manganese, gold; hindered by poor transport system.

GDP (2002e) \$52.9 bn, per capita \$1400

HDI (2002) 0.499

History Christianized in 6th-c; Muslim conversion from 13th-c; Egyptian control of N Sudan, early 19th-c; Mahdi unified W and C tribes in a revolution, 1881; fall of Khartoum, 1885; combined British-Egyptian offensive, 1898, leading to a jointly administered condominium; independence, 1956; period of military rule following coup in 1985; drought and N–S rivalry have contributed to years of instability and several coups; a transitional constitution of 1987 provided for a President, Prime Minister, Council of Ministers, and Legislative Assembly; military coup, 1989, suspended constitution and dissolved National Assembly which was replaced by a Revolutionary Command Council; continuing civil war between N and S since 1980s; new constitution, 1998;

☐ International Airport – – Border in dispute

peace talks; 2003, peace accord signed, 2004; attacks by Janjaweed militia in Darfur region ongoing.

Head of State/Government
1993–   Omar Hassan Ahmad al-Bashir

SURINAME

Local name Suriname

Timezone GMT –3

Area 163 265 km²/63 020 sq mi

Population total (2002e) 436 000

Status Republic

Date of independence 1975

Capital Paramaribo

Languages Dutch (official), Hindi and Javanese (native languages), Sranan Tongo, Chinese and Spanish also spoken

Ethnic groups Indo-Pakistan (37%), Creole (31%), Javanese (15%), Amerindian (3%), Chinese (2%), European (1%)

Religions Hindu (27%), Protestant (25%), Roman Catholic (23%), Muslim (20%), indigenous beliefs (5%)

Physical features Located in NE South America; N natural regions, range from coastal lowland through savannah to mountainous upland; coastal strip covered by swamp; highland interior (S) overgrown with dense tropical forest; highest point, Juliana Top, 1230 m/4035 ft, in SC; seven major rivers including Marowijne (E), Corantijn (W), Suriname.

Climate Equatorial tropical, uniformly hot and humid; two rainy seasons (May–Jul, Nov–Jan); average annual temperatures 22–33°C in Paramaribo; average monthly rainfall 310 mm/12.2 in (N), 67 mm/2.6 in (S).

☐ International Airport

Currency 1 Suriname Guilder/Florin (SGld, F) = 100 cents

Economy Based on agriculture and mining, but hindered by lack of foreign exchange; bauxite mining (provides c.80% of export income); sugar cane, rice, citrus fruits, coffee, bananas, oil palms, cacao, fishing; vast timber resources.

GDP (2002e) $1.469 bn, per capita $3400

HDI (2002) 0.756

History Sighted by Columbus, 1498; first settled by the British, 1651; taken by the states of Zeeland, 1667; captured by the British, 1799; restored to the Netherlands, 1814 and remained part of Netherland West Indies as Dutch Guiana; independence as the Republic of Suriname, 1975; emigration of c.40% of population to the Netherlands, following independence; military coup, 1980; ban on political activities lifted, 1985; 1987 constitution provides for a National Assembly, and a President elected by the Assembly.

Head of State (President)
2000– Ronald Ventiaan

Head of Government (Vice-President)
2000– Jules Ajodhia

SWAZILAND

Local name Swaziland

Timezone GMT +2

Area 17 363 km²/6702 sq mi

Population total (2002e) 1 124 000

Status Kingdom

Date of independence 1968

Capital Mbabane

Languages English and Siswati (official)

Ethnic groups Swazi (97%), European (3%)

Religions Christian (Roman Catholic, Anglican, Methodist, and Evangelical Lutheran) (57%), traditional animist beliefs (40%)

Physical features Landlocked, in SE Africa; divided into four topographical regions: mountainous Highveld (W), highest point Emblembe, 1862 m/6109 ft; heavily populated Middleveld (C), descending to 600–700 m/2000–2300 ft; rolling, bush-covered Lowveld (E), irrigated by river systems; Lubombo escarpment, covering 90% of the territory; main rivers, Komati, Usutu, Mbuluzi, flow W–E.

Climate Temperate; tropical in W, with relatively little rain, 500–890 mm/20–35 in; susceptible to drought; subtropical and drier in C; average annual temperature 15°C (Jul), 22°C (Jan) in Mbabane; average annual rainfall 1402 mm/55 in; rainy season (Nov–Mar).

Currency 1 Lilangeni (plural Emalangeni (Li, E) = 100 cents

Economy Agriculture (employs 70% of population); maize, groundnuts, beans, sorghum, cotton, tobacco, pineapples, citrus; sugar refining, several hydroelectric schemes; asbestos, iron ore, coal, textiles, cement, paper, chemicals.

GDP (2002e) $5.542 bn, per capita $4800

HDI (2002) 0.577

History Arrival of Swazi in the area, early 19th-c; boundaries with the Transvaal decided, and independence guaranteed, 1881; British agreed to Transvaal administration, 1894; British High Commission territory, 1903; independence as a constitutional monarchy within the Commonwealth, 1968; all political parties are banned under 1978 constitution; governed by a bicam-

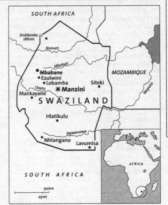

□ International Airport

eral Parliament consisting of a National Assembly and a Senate; the King has considerable executive power, appointing a Cabinet and Prime Minister.

Head of State (Monarch)
1986– Mswati III

Head of Government
2003– Absalom Themba Dlamini

SWEDEN

Local name Sverige (Swedish)

Timezone GMT +1

Area 411 479 km²/158 830 sq mi

Population total (2002e) 8 925 000

Status Kingdom

Capital Stockholm

Languages Swedish (official), Finnish and Lapp in N

Ethnic groups Swedish (91%), Finns, with Polish, Turkish, W German, Chilean, Iranian, and other minorities

Religions Lutheran Protestant (93%), Roman Catholic (2%), Scandinavian Jewish minorities

Physical features Occupies the E side of the Scandinavian peninsula; 15% of country lies N of the Arctic Circle; large amount of inland water (9%); chief lakes being Vänern, Vättern, and Mälaren; many coastal islands, notably Gotland and Öland; c.57% forested; Kjölen Mts (W) form much of the boundary with Norway; highest peak, Kebnekaise, 2111 m/6926 ft; several rivers flow SE towards the Gulf of Bothnia.

Climate Continental, with cold winters and mild summers; rainfall lowest in NE; winters warmer in SW; enclosed parts of Baltic Sea often freeze in winter and can remain frozen for up to 6 months; continuous daylight in N during Arctic summer produces mean temperatures of −10°C (Jan), 15°C (Jul).

Currency 1 Swedish Krona (Skr) = 100 øre

Economy Gradual shift in the economy from the traditional emphasis on raw materials (timber and iron ore) to advanced technology; transportation equipment, electronics, electrical equipment, chemicals, engineering, steelmaking, non-ferrous metals; hydroelectricity provides 70% of power; wheat, barley, oats, sugar beet, cattle, fishing; tourism.

GDP (2002e) $230.7 bn, per capita $26 000

HDI (2002) 0.941

History Formed from the union of the kingdoms of the Goths and Svears, 7th-c; Danes continued to rule in the extreme S (Skåne) until 1658; united with Denmark and Norway under Danish leadership, 1389; union ended in 1527, following revolt led by Gustavus Vasa; Sweden

□ International Airport

acquired Norway from Denmark, 1814; union with Norway dissolved, 1905; a neutral country since 1814; Social Democratic Party controlled government, 1932–76 and returned to power, 1982; a representative and parliamentary democracy, with a Monarch as Head of State; governed by a Prime Minister and a unicameral Parliament (*Riksdag*) elected every three years.

Head of State (Monarch)
1973–   Carl XVI Gustaf

Head of Government
1996–   Goran Persson

SWITZERLAND

Local names Schweiz (German), La Suisse (French), Svizzera (Italian)

Timezone GMT +1

Area 41 228 km²/15 914 sq mi

Population total (2002e) 7 282 000

Status Confederation

Date of independence 1291

Capital Bern (Berne)

Languages German, French, Italian, Romansch (official), Spanish and Turkish also spoken

Ethnic groups (of Swiss nationals) German (64%), French (20%), Italian (4%), Romansch (1%)

Religions Christian (Roman Catholic 49%, Protestant 48%), Jewish minority

Physical features Landlocked, with Alps running roughly E–W in the S; highest peak, Dufourspitze, 4634 m/15 203 ft; Pre-Alps (NW) average 2000 m/6500 ft;

sparsely-forested Jura Mts run SW–NW; mean altitude of C plateau, 580 m/1900 ft, fringed with great lakes; chief rivers, Rhine, Rhône, Inn, and tributaries of the Po; c.3000 sq km/1160 sq mi of glaciers, notably the Aletsch.

Climate Temperate climate, subject to Atlantic, Mediterranean and E and C European influences; warm summers, with considerable rainfall; perennial snow cover above 300m/9842 ft; average annual temperature 0°C (Jan), 19°C (Jul) in Bern; average annual rainfall 1000 mm/40 in; the Föhn (warm wind) noticeable late winter and spring in the Alps.

Currency 1 Swiss Franc (SFr, SwF) = 100 centimes

Economy Increased specialization and development in high-technology products; machinery, precision instruments, watches, drugs, chemicals, textiles; a major financial centre; headquarters of many international organizations; all-year tourist area; dairy farming, wheat, potatoes, sugar beet, grapes, apples.

GDP (2002e) $230.7 bn, per capita $26 000

HDI (2002) 0.941

History Part of the Holy Roman Empire, 10th-c; Swiss Confederation created, 1291; expanded during 14th-c; centre of the Reformation, 16th-c; Swiss independence and neutrality recognized under the Treaty of Westphalia, 1648; conquered by Napoleon, who instituted the Helvetian Republic, 1798; organized as a confederation of cantons, 1815; federal constitution, 1848; Red Cross founded, 1863; neutral in both World Wars; helped form European Free Trade Association, 1960; Jura became 23rd canton of Switzerland, 1979; became a full member of the UN, 2002; bicameral Federal Association comprising of a

□ International Airport

Council of States (*Ständerat*) and a National Council (*Nationalrat*); President elected yearly by Federal Council.

Head of State/Government

2002	Kaspar Villiger
2003	Pascal Couchepin
2004	Joseph Deiss

SYRIA

Local name as-Suriyah (Arabic)

Timezone GMT +2

Area 185 180 km²/71 479 sq mi

Population total (2002e) 17 156 000

Status Republic

Date of independence 1946

Capital Damascus

Languages Arabic (official), Kurdish, Armenian, Aramaic, and Circassian also spoken

Ethnic groups Arab (90%), Kurd, Armenian, Turkish, Circassian, and Assyrian

Religions Muslim (Sunni Muslim 74%, Alawite, Druse, and other sects 16%), Christian (10%)

Physical features Narrow Mediterranean coastal plain; Jabal al Nusayriyah mountain range rises to c.1500 m/ 5000 ft; steep drop (E) to Orontes R valley; Anti-Lebanon range (SW) rises to 2814 m/9232 ft at Mt Hermon; open steppe and desert to the E.

Climate Coastal Mediterranean, hot, dry summers, mild, wet winters; desert or semi-desert climate in 60% of country; annual rainfall below 200 mm/8 in; Khamsin wind causes temperatures to rise to 43–9°C; average annual temperatures 7°C (Jan), 27°C (Jul) in Damascus.

□ International Airport

Syria (continued)

Currency 1 Syrian pound (LS, Syr £)= 100 piastres

Economy Oil (most important source of export revenue since 1974); Euphrates dam project (begun 1978) presently supplies 97% of domestic electricity; intended to increase arable land by 6400 km²/2500 sq mi; food processing; textiles; tobacco; cement.

GDP (2002e) $63.48 bn, per capita $3700

HDI (2002) 0.691

History Part of Phoenician Empire; Islam introduced in 7th-c; conquered by Turks, 11th-c; part of Ottoman Empire, 1517; brief period of independence in 1920, then made a French mandate; independence, 1946; merged with Egypt and Yemen to form United Arab Republic, 1958; re-established itself as independent state under present name, 1961; Golan Heights region seized by Israel, 1967; after outbreak of civil war in Lebanon (1975), Syrian troops sent to restore order and became much involved in the region's power struggle; breaking of diplomatic relations with Great Britain, 1986; condemned Iraqi invasion of Kuwait and sent allied forces troops in Gulf War in 1990, restoring relations; accepted US proposals for terms of an Arab–Israeli peace conference, 1991; governed by a President, Prime Minister, and 250-member People's Council.

Head of State
2000– Bashar al-Assad

Head of Government
2003– Muhammad Naji al-Utri

TAIWAN

Local name T'aiwan

Timezone GMT +8

Area 36 000 km²/13 896 sq mi

Population total (2002e) 22 457 000

Status Republic

Date of independence 1949

Capital Taibei

Languages Mandarin Chinese (official), various dialects including Taiwanese and Hakka also spoken

Ethnic groups Han Chinese (98%), small (Polynesian) aboriginal minority

Religions Taoist, Buddhist, Christian (Protestant and Roman Catholic)

Physical features Consists of Taiwan I and several smaller islands c.130 km/80 mi off the SE coast of mainland China; mountain range runs N–S, covering two-thirds of the island; highest peak, Yu Shan 3997 m/13 113 ft; low-lying land mainly in the W; crossed by the Tropic of Cancer; major earthquake, 1999.

Climate Tropical monsoon-type climate; hot, humid summers, mild, short winters; wet season (May–Sep); typhoons common (Jul–Sep); average daily temperature 12–19°C (Jan), 24–33°C (Jul) in Taibei; average annual rainfall 2500 mm/98 in.

Currency 1 New Taiwan Dollar (NT$) = 100 cents

Economy Progressed from agriculture to industry since 1950s; high technology, textiles, electronics, plastics, petrochemicals, machinery; natural gas, limestone, marble, asbestos; sugar, bananas, pineapples, citrus fruits, vegetables, tea, fish.

GDP (2001e) $386 bn, per capita $17 200

History Taiwan (Formosa) visited by the Portuguese, 1590; conquered by Manchus, 17th-c; ceded to Japan following Sino-Japanese War, 1895; returned to China, 1945; Nationalist government moved to Taiwan by Jiang Jieshi (Chang Kai-shek); government still maintains claim to legal jurisdiction over mainland China and continues to designate itself as the Republic of China; protected by US naval forces during Korean War, 1950–3; signed mutual defence pact with USA, 1954–79; end of state of civil war with People's Republic of China declared by President Lee Teng-hui, 1991; governed by a President, who appoints a premier, National Assembly, and legislative *Yuan*; elections held for a reformed National Assembly, 1991; *Yuan* voted in favour of a bill for major constitutional change, Aug 2004.

Head of State (President)
2000– Chen Shui-ban

Head of Government (Premier)
2000–1 Chang Chun-hsiung
2001– Yu Shyi-kun

□ International Airport

TAJIKISTAN (TADZHIKISTAN)

Local name Tojikiston

Timezone GMT +3

Area 143 100 km²/55 200 sq mi

Population total (2002e) 6 327 000

Status Republic

Date of independence 1991

Capital Dushanbe

Languages Tajik (official), Russian

Ethnic groups Tajik (59%), Uzbek (23%), Russian (13%)

Religion Sunni Muslim

Physical features Republic in SE Middle Asia; Tien Shan, Gissar-Alai, and Pamir ranges cover over 90% of the area; highest peaks, Communism Peak, 7495 m/24 590 ft, and Lenin Peak, 7134 m/23 405 ft, located in N part of Pamirs; R Pyandzh flows E–W along the S border till it is joined by R Valksh to form R Amu Darya; lakes include L Kara-Kul (largest) and L Sarez.

Climate Continental; subtropical valley areas, hot, dry summers; annual mean temperature –0.9°C (Jan), 27°C (Jul); average annual rainfall 150–250 mm/6–10 in; in highlands, average mean temperature –3°C (Jan); average annual rainfall 60–80 mm/2–3 in.

Currency Tajik rouble (R)

Economy Oil, natural gas, coal, lead, zinc, machinery, metalworking, chemicals, food processing; cotton, wheat, maize, vegetables, fruit; hot mineral springs and health resorts.

GDP (2002e) $8.476 bn, per capita $1300

HDI (2002) 0.667

History Conquered by Persia, and Alexander the Great; invaded by Arabs in 8th-c; Turkish invasion, 10th-c; until mid 18th-c, part of the emirate of Bukhara, which in effect became a protectorate of Russia, 1868;

□ International Airport

following the Russian Revolution (1917), became part of Turkestan Soviet Socialist Autonomous Republic, 1918; scene of the Basmachi revolt, 1922–3; Tajik Autonomous Soviet Socialist Republic created as part of the Uzbek SSR, 1924; became a Soviet Socialist Republic, 1929; declaration of independence from the Soviet Union, 1991; joined Commonwealth of Independent States, 1991; Republican Communist Party remained in power until civil war began, 1992; governed by a President, Prime Minister, and Supreme Assembly.

Head of State
1992– Emomali Rahmonov

Head of Government
1999– Oqil Oqilov

TANZANIA

Local name Tanzania

Timezone GMT +3

Area 945 087 km²/364 900 sq mi

Population total (2002e) 34 902 000

Status Republic

Date of independence 1961

Capital Dodoma (formerly Dar es Salaam)

Languages Swahili and English (official), various tribal languages

Ethnic groups Bantu (99%) (including Nyamwezi and Sukuma 21%, Swahili 9%, Hehet and Bena 6%, Makonde 6%, Haya 6%), Arab, Asian, and European minorities

Religions Mainland: Christian (34%), Muslim (33%),

traditional animist beliefs (33%); Zanzibar: Muslim (96%), Hindu (4%)

Physical features Largest E African country, just S of the Equator; includes the islands of Zanzibar, Pemba, and Mafia; coast fringed by long sandy beaches protected by coral reefs; rises towards a C plateau, average elevation 1000 m/3300 ft; Rift Valley branches round L Victoria (N), several high volcanic peaks, notably Mt Kilimanjaro, 5895 m/19 340 ft; extensive Serengeti Plain to the W; other main lakes, L Tanganyika and L Rukwa.

Climate Tropical; hot, humid climate on coast and offshore islands; average temperatures 27°C (Jan), 23°C (Jul); average annual rainfall 1000 mm/40 in; hot and dry on C plateau, average annual rainfall 250 mm/10 in; semitemperate conditions above 1500 mm/5000 ft.

Currency 1 Tanzanian Shilling (TSh) = 100 cents

Tanzania (continued)

Economy Agriculture; rice, sorghum, coffee, sugar, cloves (most of world's market), coconuts, tobacco, cotton; reserves of iron, coal, tin, gypsum, salt, phosphate, gold, diamonds, oil; tourism.

GDP (2002e) $20.42 bn, per capita $600

HDI (2002) 0.440

History Swahili culture developed, 10th–15th-c; Zanzibar became the capital of the Omani empire in 1840s; became a British protectorate, 1890; German East Africa established, 1891; British mandate to administer Tanganyika, 1919; first E African country to gain independence and become a member of the Commonwealth, 1961; republic, 1962; Zanzibar given independence as a constitutional monarchy with Sultan as Head of State; Sultan overthrown, 1964, and Act of Union between Zanzibar and Tanganyika led to the United Republic of Tanzania; a one-party state following 1965 constitution; legislation passed allowing for opposition parties, 1991, following a unanimous vote for a multi-party system; governed by a President, Cabinet, and National Assembly; coast hit by Indian Ocean tsunami, 2004.

Head of State
1995–   Benjamin Mkapa

Head of Government
1995–   Frederick Sumaye

International Airport   ∴ World heritage site   1 *Pemba I*   2 *Zanzibar I*

THAILAND

Local name Muang Thai

Timezone GMT +7

Area 513 115 km²/198 062 sq mi

Population total (2002e) 63 430 000

Status Kingdom

Capital Bangkok (Krung Thep)

Languages Thai (official), Malay and English also spoken

Ethnic groups Thai (75%), Chinese (14%), Khmer and Mon minorities

Religions Theravada Buddhist (95%), Muslim, Hindu, Sikh, and Christian (4%)

Physical features Agricultural region dominated by the floodplain of the Chao Phraya R; NE plateau rises above 300 m/1000 ft and covers a third of the country; mountainous N region rising to 2595 m/8514 ft at Doi Inthanon; narrow, low-lying S region separates the Andaman Sea from the Gulf of Thailand; covered in tropical rainforest, except sparsely vegetated Khorat plateau (NE).

Climate Equatorial climate in the S; tropical monsoon climate in the N and C; high temperatures and humidity; wet season (Jun–Oct); average annual temperature 26°C (Jan), 28°C (Jul) in Bangkok; average annual rainfall 1400 mm/55 in.

Currency 1 Baht (B) = 100 satang

Economy Agriculture; rice, maize, bananas, pineapple, sugar cane, rubber, teak; textiles, electronics,

International Airport

Thailand (continued)

cement, chemicals, food processing, tourism; tin (world's third largest supplier), tungsten (world's second largest supplier), manganese, antimony, lead, zinc, copper, natural gas.

GDP (2002e) $445.8 bn, per capita $7000

HDI (2002) 0.762

History Evidence of Bronze Age communities, 4000 BC; Thai nation founded, 13th-c; only country in S and SE Asia to have escaped colonization by a European power; revolution ended absolute monarchical rule, 1932; followed by periods of military rule interspersed with brief periods of democratic government; 1991 constitution (with amendments) provides for a National Legislative Assembly comprising a House of Representatives, an elected Senate, and a cabinet headed by a Prime Minister; King is Head of State; coast devastated by tsunami, 2004.

Head of State (Monarch)
1946–   Bhumibol Adulyadej (Rama IX)

Head of Government
2001–   Thaksin Shinawatra

TOGO

Local name République Togolaise (French)

Timezone GMT

Area 56 790 km²/21 941 sq mi

Population total (2002e) 5 286 000

Status Republic

Date of independence 1960

Capital Lomé

Languages French (official), local languages (Ewe, mostly in S, 47%), Hamitic people in N, mostly Voltaic speaking)

Ethnic groups Ewe (35%), Kabyè (22%), Mina (6%), with c.34 other ethnic groups, European and Syrian Lebanese minorities

Religions Traditional animist beliefs (50%), Christian (35%), Muslim (10%)

Physical features Located in W Africa; land rises from the lagoon coast of the Gulf of Guinea, past low-lying plains to the Atakora Mts running NE–SW in the N; highest peak, Pic Baumann, 986 m/3235 ft; flat plains in NW. Main rivers, Oti, Mono.

Climate Tropical, high temperatures and humidity; wet seasons (Mar–Jul, Oct–Nov); single rainy season in N (Jul–Sep); average annual temperature 27°C (Jan), 24°C (Jul) in Lomé; average annual rainfall 875 mm/34 in; dry Saharan Harmattan blows from NE (Oct–Apr).

Currency 1 CFA Franc (CFAFr) = 100 centimes.

Economy Largely agricultural economy; coffee, cocoa, cotton, cassava, maize, rice, timber; phosphates, bauxite, limestone, iron ore, marble; cement, steel, oil refining, food processing, crafts, textiles, beverages.

GDP (2002e) $7.594 bn, per capita $1400

HDI (2002) 0.493

History Formerly part of Kingdom of Togoland; German protectorate, 1884–1914; mandate of League of Nations, 1922, divided between France (French Togo) and Britain (part of British Gold Coast); Trusteeships of United Nations, 1946; French Togo became autonomous republic within French Union, 1956; British Togoland voted to join Gold Coast (Ghana), 1957; independence, 1960; military coups,

□ International Airport

1963, 1967; return to civilian rule, 1980; riots over slow reforms, 1991; National Assembly dissolved, and Supreme Republican Council established, 1991; parliamentary elections, 1992; governed by a President, Prime Minister, and 81-member National Assembly, elected for five years; constitution amended for Faure Gnassingbé to succeed his father (Feb 2005), but international opposition forced his withdrawal; interim president installed pending elections.

Head of State
2005–   Abass Bonfoh *Interim*

Head of Government
2002–   Koffi Sama

TOKELAU >> NEW ZEALAND

TONGA

Local name Tonga

Timezone GMT +13

Area 646 km²/249 sq mi

Population total (2002e) 101 000

Status Independent kingdom within the Commonwealth

Date of independence 1970

Capital Nuku'alofa

Languages Tongan and English (official)

Ethnic groups Tongan (98%), other Polynesian, European minorities

Religions Christian (Free Wesleyan Methodists 47%, Roman Catholic 14%, Mormon 9%, Anglican minorities)

Physical features Island group in the SW Pacific Ocean, 2250 km/1400 mi NE of New Zealand; consists of 169 islands, 36 inhabited, divided into three main groups, Ha'apai, Tongatapu, and Vava'u; Tongatapu, largest island, inhabited by two-thirds of the population; W islands mainly volcanic, some still active; highest point, extinct volcano of Kao, 1014 m/3327 ft.

Climate Semi-tropical; average annual temperature 26°C (Jan), 21°C (Jul) in Nuku'alofa; average annual rainfall 1750 mm/69 in; occasional hurricanes in summer months.

Currency 1 Pa'anga/Tongan Dollar (T$) = 100 seniti

Economy Largely based on agriculture; copra, coconuts, bananas, watermelons, yams, taro, cassava, groundnuts, rice, maize, tobacco, sugar cane; tourism and cottage handicrafts are small but growing industries.

GDP (2001e) $236 mn, per capita $2200

History Early settlers were Polynesians; visited by Dutch, early 17th-c; visited by the British explorer, James

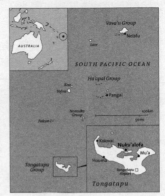

Cook, 1773; Methodist missionaries converted most of population to Christianity during early 19th-c; Chief Taufa'ahau united the islands and declared himself the first Monarch of Tonga, 1845; became a British protectorate, 1900, under its own monarchy; independence, 1970; governed by a Sovereign, a Privy Council, and a unicameral Legislative Assembly of Cabinet members, nobles, and elected people's representatives.

Head of State (Monarch)
1965– Taufa'ahau Tupou IV

Head of Government (Prime Minister)
1991–2000 Baron Vaea
2000– Ulukalala Lavaka Ata

TRINIDAD AND TOBAGO

Local name Trinidad and Tobago

Timezone GMT -4

Area 5128 km²/1979 sq mi

Population total (2002e) 1 304 000

Status Independent republic within the Commonwealth

Date of independence 1962

Capital Port of Spain

Languages English (official), Hindi, French, Spanish

Ethnic groups African (43%), East Indian (40%), mixed (14%), Chinese (1%)

Religions Christian (Roman Catholic 34%, Protestant 29%), Hindu (25%), Muslim (6%)

Physical features Southernmost islands of the Lesser Antilles, SE Caribbean; Trinidad, area 4828 km²/1864 sq mi, traversed by three mountain ranges (N, C and S), rising to 940 m/3084 ft at El Cerro del Aripo; drained by Caroni, Ortoire and Oropuche rivers; Tobago, area 300 km²/116 sq mi; Main Ridge extends along most of island, rising to 576 m/1890 ft.

Climate Tropical, hot and humid; average annual temperature 29°C; dry season (Jan–May); wet season (Jun–Dec); average annual rainfall 1270 mm/50 in (SW Trinidad), 2540 mm/100 in (Tobago mountains).

Currency 1 Trinidad and Tobago Dollar (TT$) = 100 cents

Economy Oil and gas (main industries); industrial complex, W coast of Trinidad; cement, oil refining, petrochemicals; cocoa, coffee, fruit; tourism.

GDP (2002e) $11.07 bn, per capita $10 000

HDI (2002) 0.805

History Trinidad visited by Columbus in 1498; settled by Spain in 16th-c, and acquired by Britain in 1797; Tobago captured by French, 1781, and acquired by Britain, 1802; Tobago became a British colony, 1814; Trinidad and Tobago united as British Crown Colony, 1899; independent member of the Commonwealth, 1962; republic, 1976; governed by a President and bicameral Parliament, comprising a Senate and House of Representatives; also a 15-member Tobago House of Assembly.

Head of State
1997–2003 Arthur Napoleon Raymond Robinson
2003–   Max Richards

Head of Government
1995–2001 Basdeo Panday
2001–   Patrick Manning

TUNISIA

Local names Tunis (Arabic), Tunisie (French)

Timezone GMT +1

Area 164 150 km²/63 362 sq mi

Population total (2002e) 9 764 000

Status Republic

Date of Independence 1956

Capital Tunis

Languages Arabic (official), French and Berber widely spoken

Ethnic groups Arab (98%), European (1%), small Jewish minority

Religions Sunni Muslim (98%), Christian (1%), small Jewish minority

Physical features Located in N Africa, on Mediterranean coast; Atlas Mts (NW) rise to 1544 m/5065 ft at Jebel Chambi; Majardah river valley is the most fertile area (N); from Tabussah range, land descends across a plateau to the Saharan desert (S) and a coastal plain (E).

Climate Mediterranean in N, with hot, dry summers, mild, rainy winters; extreme desert-continental conditions in S, with little rainfall; average annual temperature 9°C (Jan), 26°C (Jul); average annual rainfall 400 mm/15.7 in.

Currency 1 Tunisian Dinar (TD,D) = 1000 millèmes

Economy Agriculture (employs c.50% of population, but of declining importance); wheat, barley, grapes; olive oil (world's fourth largest producer); phosphates (fifth largest producer).

GDP (2002e) $67.13 bn, per capita $6800

HDI (2002) 0.722

History Ruled by Phoenicians, Carthaginians, Romans, Byzantines, Arabs, Spanish, and Turks; under the control of the Ottoman Empire, 1574; French protectorate, 1883;

☐ International Airport ∴ World heritage site

gained internal self-government, 1955; independence, 1956; monarchy abolished and republic declared, 1957; executive power held by President, who appoints the Prime Minister and Council of Ministers; unicameral legislature, National Assembly, elected every five years; new constitution, 2002, removed presidential term limits.

Head of State
1987–   Zine al-Abidine bin Ali

Head of Government
1999–   Mohammed Ghannouchi

TURKEY

Local name Türkiye Cumhuriyeti

Timezone GMT +2

Area 779 452 km²/300 868 sq mi

Population total (2002e) 69 359 000

Status Republic

Capital Ankara

Languages Turkish (Türkçe) (official), Kurdish and Arabic; Greek, Armenian, and Yiddish minorities

Ethnic groups Turkish (85%), Kurd (12%)

Religions Sunni Muslim (98%), Greek Orthodox, Armenian, and Jewish minorities

Physical features Lying partly in Europe and partly in Asia, W area (Thrace), E area (Anatolia); Turkish Straits (Dardanelles, Sea of Marmara, Bosporus) connect the Black Sea (NE) and Mediterranean Sea (SW); mountainous area, Taurus Mts, cover the entire S part of Anatolia; highest peak Mt Ararat, 5165 m/16 945 ft; sources of rivers Euphrates and Tigris in E.

Climate Mediterranean climate on Aegean and Mediterranean coasts, with hot, dry summers, warm, wet winters; mean temperature 19°C (Jul); average annual temperatures 0.3°C (Jan), 23°C (Jul) in Ankara; average annual rainfall 723 mm/28 in.

Currency 1 Turkish Lira (TL) = 100 kurus

Economy Agriculture (employs c.50% of workforce); cotton, tobacco, fruits, nuts, livestock; minerals, textiles, glass, and cement; many Turks find work elsewhere in Europe, especially Germany.

GDP (2002e) $489.7 bn, per capita $7300

HDI (2002) 0.742

History Seljuk sultanate replaced by the Ottoman in NW Asia Minor in 13th-c; Turkish invasion of Europe, first in Balkans, 1375; fall of Constantinople, 1453; empire at its peak under Sulaiman the Magnificent, 16th-c; Young

☐ International Airport

Turks seized power, 1908; Balkan War, 1912–13; allied with Germany during World War 1; Republic followed Young Turk revolution, led by Kemal Atatürk, 1923; policy of westernization and economic development; neutral throughout most of World War 2, then sided with Allies; military coups in 1960 and 1980; strained relations with Greece, and invasion of Cyprus, 1974; aided the allied forces during the Gulf War, 1991; Constitution provides for a single-chamber National Assembly; a President appoints a Prime Minister and a Council of Ministers.

Head of State
1993–2000 Süleyman Demirel
2000– Ahmet Necdet Sezer

Head of Government
2003– Recep Tayyip Erdogan

TURKMENISTAN

Local name Turkmenostan

Timezone GMT +5

Area 488 100 km²/188 400 sq mi

Population total (2002e) 4 946 000

Status Republic

Date of independence 1991

Capital Ashkhabad (Ashgabad)

Languages Turkmenian (official), other Turkic languages, Russian

Ethnic groups Turkmen (72%), Russian (10%), Uzbek, Kazakh, Ukrainian minorities

Religion Sunni Muslim

Physical features Kara Kum (Black Sands) desert, area 310 800 km²/120 000 sq mi, covers c.80% of the country; Turan Plain covers four-fifths of Turkmenistan; foothills in the S; Kopet Dag mountain range is volcanic; other foothills are spurs of the Kugitangtau and Pamir-Alay ranges; Rivers Amu Darya and Murghab.

Climate Continental, great variation of temperatures; temperatures range from 50°C (Jul) in Kara Kum, to –33°C (Jan) in the Kushka; in the mountains; average annual rainfall 120–250 mm/5–10 in.

Currency Manat (R) = 100 gapik

Economy Mineral resources of oil, natural gas, sulphur, potassium, and salt; oil, gas extraction (main industries); textiles; cotton production; agriculture; raising of Karakul sheep, Turkoman horses, and camels.

GDP (2002e) $31.34 bn, per capita $6700

HDI (2002) 0.741

History Part of the ancient Persian empire; ruled by Seljuk Turks, 11th-c; conquered by Genghis Khan and the Mongols, 13th-c; Uzbeks invaded, 15th-c; divided into two: one part belonged to the Khanate of Khiva (which became part of the Russian empire), and the other to the Khanate of Bukhara; Turkistan Autonomous Soviet Socialist Republic formed, 1922; full Soviet Socialist Republic, 1924; declared sovereignty, 1990; independence and membership of Commonwealth of Independent States, 1991; governed by a President, who is both head of state and of government, and parliament (*majlis*).

Head of State/Government
1990–   Saparmurad Niyazov

☐ International Airport

TURKS AND CAICOS ISLANDS
>> UNITED KINGDOM

TUVALU

Local name Tuvalu

Timezone GMT +12

Area 26 km²/10 sq mi

Population total (2002e) 10 900

Status Independent state within the Commonwealth

Date of independence 1978

Capital Funafuti (Fongafale)

Languages Tuvaluan, English

Ethnic group Polynesian (96%)

Religions Christian (Protestant Church of Tuvalu, Roman Catholic, Baha'i) (97%), small Muslim minority

Physical features Island group in the SW Pacific, 1050 km/650 mi off Fiji; comprises nine low-lying coral atolls, running NW–SE in a chain 580 km/360 ml long; consists of the islands of Funafuti, Nukufetau, Nukulailai, Nanumea, Niutao, Nanumanga, Nui, Vaitupu, and Niulakita; all low-lying, highest point, 4.6 m/15 ft, on Niulakita.

Climate Hot, humid climate; average annual temperatures 29°C (Jan), 27°C (Jul) in Funafuti; average annual rainfall 3535 mm/139 in.

Currency 1 Australian Dollar ($A) = 100 cents

Economy Subsistence economy; agriculture, coconuts, copra, tropical fruit; fish; handcrafted products, postage stamps.

GDP (2002e) $12.2 mn, per capita $1100

History Invaded by Samoans, 16th-c; British protectorate as Ellice Is, 1892; administered as colony with Gilbert Is (now Kiribati), 1915; US soldiers occupied Ellice Is during World War 2, countering Japanese advance, 1942; separate constitution, 1974; independence as con-

stitutional monarchy within the Commonwealth, 1978; Tuvalu Trust Fund set up by Britain, Australia, New Zealand, and South Korea, 1987; British monarch represented by a Governor-General; governed by a Prime Minister, Cabinet, and unicameral Parliament; Prime Minister Saufatu Sopoanga lost no-confidence vote, Aug 2004.

Head of State
(British monarch represented by Governor-General)
2003–   Sir Faimala Luka

Head of Government
2002–4   Saufatu Sopoanga
2004–   Maati Toafa

UGANDA

Local name Uganda (Swahili)

Timezone GMT +3

Area 241 038 km²/93 040 sq mi

Population total (2002e) 24 378 000

Status Republic

Date of independence 1962

Capital Kampala

Languages English and Swahili (official), Luganda (Ganda), Ateso, and Luo are also spoken

Ethnic groups Bantu, with Nilotic and Hamitic minorities

Religions Christian (66%) (Roman Catholic 33%, Protestant 33%), traditional animist beliefs (18%), Muslim (6%)

Physical features Landlocked country in E Africa, mainly plateau, height 1200 m/4000 ft; dry savannah or semi-desert in the N; fertile L Victoria basin; highest point in Uganda and Zaire, Margherita Peak, 5110 m/16 765 ft; main lakes, Victoria (SE), George and Edward (SW), Albert (W), Kwania and Kyoga (C), Bisina (formerly L Salisbury) (E); main rivers are the upper reaches of R Nile, the Victoria Nile, and the Albert Nile.

Climate Tropical climate; temperatures rarely rise above 29°C, or fall below 15°C (S); average annual temperature 23°C (Jan), 21°C (Jul); average annual rainfall 1150 mm/45 in.

Currency 1 Uganda Shilling = 100 cents

Economy Agriculture; coffee (over 90% of exports), tea, sugar, cotton; bananas, plantains, cassavas, potatoes, sweet potatoes, maize, sorghum.

GDP (2002e) $30.49 bn, per capita $1200

HDI (2002) 0.444

History Visited by Arab traders, 1840s; explored by Speke, 1860s; granted to the British East Africa Company, 1888; Kingdom of Buganda became a British protec-

□ International Airport

torate, 1893; other territory included by 1903; independence, 1962; Dr Milton Obote assumed all powers, 1966; coup led by General Amin, 1971; Amin overthrown, 1979; further coup overthrew Obote, 1985; National Resistance Movement captured Kampala, 1986, and Museveni became President; governed by a President, Cabinet, Prime Minister, and National Resistance Council; new constitution, 1995; peace agreement with rebels, 2002.

Head of State

1986–   Yoweri Kaguta Museveni

Head of Government

1999–   Apolo Nsibambi

UKRAINE

Local name Ukraina

Timezone GMT +2

Area 603 700 km²/233 028 sq mi

Population total (2002e) 48 120 000

Status Republic

Date of independence 1991

Capital Kiev

Languages Ukrainian (official), Russian

Ethnic groups Ukrainian (73%), Russian (22%), Moldovan, Bulgarian, and Polish minorities

Religions Orthodox (Autocephalous and Russian) (76%), Roman Catholic (14%), Jewish (2%), Baptist, Mennonite, Protestant, and Muslim (8%)

Physical features Most fertile area of former USSR, consisting largely of black soil steppes, forming a substantial part of the East European Plain; borders the Black Sea and Sea of Azov (S); Carpathian Mts, 2061 m/6762 ft at Mt Goverla (SW); Crimean Mts (S); main rivers, Dnepr, Yuzhny, Bug; Donets coalfield, area 25 900 km²/10 000 sq mi.

Climate Moderate, mild winters, hot summers (SW); average annual temperatures –3°C (Jan), 23°C (Jul); average annual rainfall in Crimea 400–610 mm/16–24 in.

Currency 1 Hryvna = 100 kopijka

Economy Important industrial bases for iron and steel manufacture, chemical and engineering bases; shipbuilding on Black Sea; agriculture (was the USSR's major wheat producer); wheat, corn, rye, potatoes, cotton, flax, sugar beet; coal and salt deposits in Donets basin.

GDP (2002e) $218 bn, per capita $4500

HDI (2002) 0.748

History Conquered by Mongols, 1240; dominated by Poland, 13–16th-c; applied to Moscow for help fighting Poland, leading to sovereignty, 1654; independence from Russia, 1918, after Russian Revolution; became a member of the USSR, 1922; devastated during World War 2; Chernobyl the site of the world's worst nuclear accident, 1986; declared independence, 1991; ongoing disputes with Russia over control of Black Sea Fleet and status of Crimea; introduction of border controls and new currency, 1993, in contravention of CIS agreements; new constitution, 1996; governed by a President and Supreme Council; Yanukovych elected president (Nov 2004) amid allegations of vote-rigging, public protest supporting opposition leader Yushchenko; poll result suspended by Supreme Court; Yushchenko won poll re-run (Dec 2004).

Head of State
1994–2004 Leonid Kuchma
2004–   Viktor Yushchenko

Head of Government
2005– Yulia Tymoshenko

☐ International Airport

UNITED ARAB EMIRATES

Local name Ittihād al-Imārat al-'Arabīyah

Timezone GMT +4

Area 83 600 km²/32 300 sq mi

Population total (2002e) 3 550 000

Status Federation of autonomous emirates

Date of independence 1971

Capital Abu Dhabi

Languages Arabic (official), English, Farsi, Urdu, and Hindi also spoken

Ethnic groups Emirian (19%), other Arab (23%), S Asian (50%)

Religions Muslim (Sunni 80%, Shi'ite 16%), Christian (4%), small Hindu minority

Physical features Seven states in EC Arabian peninsula on S shore (Trucial Coast) of the Persian Gulf; al-Fujairah has a coastline along the Gulf of Oman; salt marshes predominate on coast; barren desert and gravel plain inland; Hajar Mts in al-Fujairah rise to over 1000 m/3000 ft in E.

Climate Hot, dry desert climate, extreme summer temperatures exceeding 40°C and limited rainfall; frequent sandstorms; average annual temperatures 23°C (Jan), 42°C (Jul) in Dubai; average annual rainfall 60 mm/2.4 in.

Currency 1 United Arab Emirates Dirham (DH) = 100 fils

Economy Based on oil and gas (main producers, Abu Dhabi, Dubai); important commercial and trading centre; saline water supplies have restricted agriculture to oases and irrigated valleys of Hajar Mts; vegetables, fruits, dates, dairy farming; tourism.

GDP (2002e) $53.97 bn, per capita $22 100

☐ International Airport - - Border awaiting demarcation

HDI (2002) 0.812

History Originally peopled by sea-faring tribes, converted to Islam in 7th-c; Mecca conquered by powerful sheikdom of Carmathians; upon its collapse piracy common, area known as the Pirate Coast; Portuguese explorers arrived, 16th-c; British East India Company arrived, 17th-c; British attacked the coastal ports, 1819–20 and exacted a pledge to renounce piracy in the General Treaty, 1820; became known as Trucial Coast after signing of Treaty of Maritime Peace in Perpetuity, 1853; administered by British India, 1873–1947, and thereafter by London Foreign Office; Trucial States Council formed,

United Arab Emirates (continued)

1960; federated and became United Arab Emirates, 1971, comprising seven emirates: Abu Dhabi, Ajman, Dubai, al-Fujairah, Ras al-Khaimah, Sharjah, and Umm al-Qaiwain; Ras al-Khaimah joined federation, 1972; governed by Supreme Council of the seven emirate rulers (each of whom is an absolute Monarch in own state).

Head of State
1971–2004   Zayed bin Sultan al-Nahyan
2004–   Khalifa bin Zayed al-Nahyan

Head of Government
1990–   Maktoum bin Rashid al-Maktoum

UNITED KINGDOM (UK)

Local names United Kingdom of Great Britain and Northern Ireland, Great Britain, Britain

Timezone GMT

Area 244 755 km²/94 500 sq mi

Population total (2002e) 60 178 000

Status Kingdom

Capital London

Languages English, Irish Gaelic, Scots Gaelic (Gallic), Welsh

Ethnic groups English (81.5%), Scottish (9.5%), Irish (2.4%), Welsh (1.9%), West Indian, Asian, and African (2%), Arabic, Turkish, and Greek minorities

Religions Christian (90%) (Anglican 63%, Roman Catholic 14%, Presbyterian 4%, Methodist 3%, Baptist 1%, Orthodox 1%, other 6%), Muslim (3%), Sikh (1%), Hindu (1%), Jewish (1%), other (1%)

Physical features Varied landscape, comprising the mountainous Lake District in NW, rocky moors in SW, hilly downs of S and SE, and the low, marshy fenlands of C and E; Cheviot Hills separate Scotland and England; highest point, Ben Nevis in Scotland, 1342 m/4406 ft; The Pennines form a ridge down the middle of England, from Lake District to C; highest point in England and Wales, Mt Snowdon in Wales, 1085 m/3560 ft; in N Ireland, the Sperrin Mts and the granite Mourne Mts rise to heights over 610 m/2000 ft.

Climate Temperate maritime climate; SW airstream determines weather, bringing depressions (causing wet weather) or N winds (bringing drier and colder); some regional diversity, but no world climate systems' boundaries pass through the islands; on average, wetter and slightly warmer in W; rainfall evenly distributed throughout the year; average annual rainfall 1600 mm/60 in (W), 800 mm/30 in (C and E).

Currency 1 Pound Sterling (£) = 100 pence

Economy Service industries; agriculture, potatoes, wheat, barley, and sugar beets; livestock; large fishing industry; deposits of iron ore; oil and gas from N Sea; coal industry declining; highly developed financial systems; London the commercial and financial centre of Western world. UK one of the world's largest trading nations, relying heavily on imports; exports include machinery, transport equipment, petroleum, chemicals, textiles.

GDP (2002e) $1528 bn, per capita $25 500

HDI (2002) 0.928

History Migrations and settlements resulted in the insular Celtic nation; invaded by Rome, 1 AD; Romans

☐ International Airport

withdrew, 5th-c; constantly attacked by Scandinavian tribes, defeated by Alfred, 878; united under the kings of Wessex, 10th-c; Edward the Confessor died, 1066, leaving a disputed succession; Norman invasion under William, Duke of Normandy, 1066; Edward I conquered Wales, 1301; Hundred Years' War with France, 1337–1453; recurring plagues of Black Death, 1347–1400, wiped out one-third of population; Wars of the Roses, 1455–85, resulted in victory for House of Lancaster; establishment of Church of England and split from Church of Rome, 1533; union with Wales, 1536; coronation of Elizabeth I, 1558; execution of Mary Queen of Scots, 1587; defeat of the Spanish Armada, 1588; English Civil War, 1642–6 and 1648–9; execution of Charles I, 1649; England and Scotland joined by the Act of Union, 1707; 1714–60, development of parliamentary government under Hanoverian kings; revolt of the American colonies, 1775–81; Ireland officially joined to Great Britain, 1801; World War 1, 1914–18; became the United Kingdom of Great Britain and Northern Ireland following the establishment of the Irish Free State, 1922; General Strike, 1926; abdication of Edward VIII, 1936; World War 2, 1939–45; National Health system implemented, 1948; Indian independence, 1947; joined EC, 1973; Falklands War with Argentina, 1982; involvement in Gulf War, 1991; involvement in Iraq War, 2003, and occupying presence into 2004; a kingdom with the Monarch as Head of State; governed by a bicameral Parliament, comprising an elected 659-member House of Commons and a House of Lords; a Cabinet is appointed by the Prime Minister.

>> Political leaders and rulers, pp. 128–9

Head of State (Monarch)
1952–   Elizabeth II

Head of Government
1990–97   John Major
1997–   Tony Blair

England

Area 130 357 km²/50 318 sq mi

Population total (2000e) 49 392 000

Status Constituent part of the United Kingdom

Capital London

Languages English, with c.300 minority languages

Ethnic groups & Religions (>> UNITED KINGDOM)

Physical features Largest area within the United Kingdom, forming the S part of the island of Great Britain; since 1974 divided into 46 counties; includes the Isles of Scilly, Lundy, and the Isle of Wight; largely undulating lowland, rising (S) to the Mendips, Cotswolds, Chilterns, and North Downs, (N) to the N–S ridge of the Pennines, and (NW) to the Cumbria Mts; drained E by the Tyne, Tees, Humber, Ouse, and Thames Rivers, and W by the Eden, Ribble, Mersey, and Severn Rivers; Lake District (NW) includes Derwent Water, Ullswater, Windermere and Bassenthwaite; linked to Europe by ferry and hovercraft, and (from 1994) by the Channel Tunnel.

Economy North Sea oil and gas, coal, tin, china clay, salt, potash, lead ore, iron ore; vehicles, heavy engineering, petrochemicals, pharmaceuticals, textiles, food processing, electronics, telecommunications, publishing, brewing, fishing, livestock, agriculture, horticulture, pottery and tourism.

☐ International Airport

History (>> UNITED KINGDOM)

HUMAN GEOGRAPHY

Local Government in England

Local authorities	Area km²	sq mi	Administrative Centre	New Unitary Authorities (introduced 1996-8)	Population (2000e)
Bedfordshire (2-tier)	1235	477	Bedford		555 000
				Luton	176 000
Berkshire (replaced by unitary authorities)	1259	486			765 000
				Bracknell Forest	102 000
				Reading	141 000
				Slough	106 000
				West Berkshire	137 000
				Windsor & Maidenhead	137 000
				Wokingham	142 000
Bristol				Bristol	397 000
Buckinghamshire (2-tier)	1883	727	Aylesbury		672 000
				Milton Keynes	181 000
Cambridgeshire (2-tier)	3409	1316	Cambridge		711 000
				Peterborough	156 000
Cheshire (2-tier)	2328	899	Chester		980 000
				Halton	123 000
				Warrington	189 000
Cornwall & Scilly	3564	1376	Truro		485 000
Cumbria	6810	2629	Carlisle		498 000
Derbyshire (2-tier)	2631	1016	Matlock		969 000
				Derby	227 000
Devon (2-tier)	6711	2591	Exeter		1 075 000
				Plymouth	258 000
				Torbay	122 000

United Kingdom (continued)

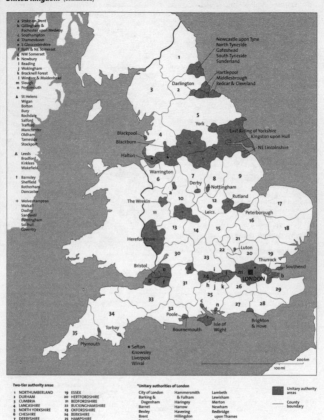

a Stoke-on-Trent
b Gillingham &
  Rochester upon Medway
c Southampton
d Thamesdown
e S Gloucestershire
f Bath & NE Somerset
g NW Somerset
h Newbury
i Reading
j Wokingham
k Bracknell Forest
l Windsor & Maidenhead
m Slough
n Portsmouth

▲ St Helens
  Wigan
  Bolton
  Bury
  Rochdale
  Salford
  Trafford
  Manchester
  Oldham
  Tameside
  Stockport

△ Leeds
  Bradford
  Kirklees
  Wakefield

† Barnsley
  Sheffield
  Rotherham
  Doncaster

+ Wolverhampton
  Walsall
  Dudley
  Sandwell
  Birmingham
  Solihull
  Coventry

Newcastle upon Tyne
North Tyneside
Gateshead
South Tyneside
Sunderland
Hartlepool
Middlesbrough
Redcar & Cleveland
Darlington
York
East Riding of Yorkshire
Kingston upon Hull
NE Lincolnshire
Blackpool
Blackburn
Halton
Warrington
Derby
Nottingham
Rutland
Peterborough
The Wrekin
Leics
Herefordshire
Luton
Thurrock
Southend
LONDON
Bristol
Poole
Torbay
Bournemouth
Isle of Wight
Brighton & Hove
Plymouth

◆ Sefton
  Knowsley
  Liverpool
  Wirral

HUMAN GEOGRAPHY

200 km
100 mi

Two-tier authority areas

1	NORTHUMBERLAND	19	ESSEX
2	DURHAM	20	HERTFORDSHIRE
3	CUMBRIA	21	BEDFORDSHIRE
4	LANCASHIRE	22	BUCKINGHAMSHIRE
5	NORTH YORKSHIRE	23	OXFORDSHIRE
6	CHESHIRE	24	BERKSHIRE
7	DERBYSHIRE	25	HAMPSHIRE
8	NOTTINGHAMSHIRE	26	SURREY
9	LINCOLNSHIRE	27	WEST SUSSEX
10	STAFFORDSHIRE	28	EAST SUSSEX
11	SHROPSHIRE	29	KENT
12	LEICESTERSHIRE	30	GLOUCESTERSHIRE
13	WORCESTERSHIRE	31	WILTSHIRE
14	WARWICKSHIRE	32	DORSET
15	NORTHAMPTONSHIRE	33	SOMERSET
16	CAMBRIDGESHIRE	34	DEVON
17	NORFOLK	35	CORNWALL &
18	SUFFOLK		ISLES OF SCILLY

*Unitary authorities of London

City of London
Barking &
  Dagenham
Barnet
Bexley
Brent
Bromley
Camden
Croydon
Ealing
Enfield
Greenwich
Hackney
Hammersmith
  & Fulham
Haringey
Harrow
Havering
Hillingdon
Hounslow
Islington
Kensington
  & Chelsea
Kingston-
  upon-Thames
Lambeth
Lewisham
Merton
Newham
Redbridge
upon Thames
Southwark
Sutton
Tower Hamlets
Waltham Forest
Wandsworth
Westminster

■ Unitary authority areas

— County boundary

Local authorities	Area km²	sq mi	Administrative Centre	New Unitary Authorities (introduced 1996-8)	Population (2000e)
Dorset (2-tier)	2654	1025	Dorchester		683 000
				Bournemouth	159 000
				Poole	136 000
Durham (2-tier)	2436	941	Durham		617 000
				Darlington	100 000
				Hartlepool	92 000
				Stockton-on-Tees	178 000
East Riding of Yorkshire	2416	933	Beverley	East Riding of Yorkshire	319 000
				Kingston-upon-Hull	268 000
East Sussex (2-tier)	1795	693	Lewes		743 000
				Brighton and Hove	245 000
Essex (2-tier)	3672	1418	Chelmsford		160 000
				Southend-on-Sea	165 000
				Thurrock	131 000
Gloucestershire (2-tier)	2643	1020	Gloucester		554 000
				South Gloucestershire	230 000
Greater London	1579	610			7 077 000
Greater Manchester	1287	497			2 607 000
Hampshire (2-tier)	3777	1458	Winchester		1 623 000
				Portsmouth	190 000
				Southampton	208 000
Herefordshire	2181	842	Hereford		162 000
Hertfordshire	1634	631	Hertford		1 022 000
Isle of Wight	381	147	Newport		124 000
Kent (2-tier)	3731	1441	Maidstone		1 558 000
				Medway	250 000
Lancashire (2-tier)	3063	1183	Preston		1 440 000
				Blackburn with Darwen	140 000
				Blackpool	153 000
Leicestershire (2-tier)	2553	986	Leicester		926 000
				Leicester City	285 000
Lincolnshire (2-tier)	5915	2284	Lincoln		621 000
				North Lincolnshire	152 000
				North East Lincolnshire	162 000
Merseyside	652	252	Liverpool		1 447 000
Norfolk	5368	2073	Norwich		782 000
Northamptonshire	2367	914	Northampton		607 000
Northumberland	5032	1943	Morpeth		312 000
North Yorkshire (2-tier)	8309	3208	Northallerton		738 000
				Middlesbrough	145 000
				Redcar & Cleveland	143 000
				York	175 000
Nottinghamshire (2-tier)	2164	836	Nottingham		1 051 000
				Nottingham City	283 000
Oxfordshire	2608	1007	Oxford		613 000
Rutland	394	152	Oakham		35 000
Shropshire (2-tier)	3490	1347	Shrewsbury		421 000
				Telford and Wrekin	143 000
Somerset (2-tier)	3451	1332	Taunton		490 000
				Bath & NE Somerset	163 000
				NW Somerset	182 000
South Yorkshire	1560	602	Barnsley		1 325 000
Staffordshire (2-tier)	2716	1049	Stafford		1 069 000
				Stoke-on-Trent	253 000
Suffolk	3797	1466	Ipswich		637 000
Surrey	1679	648	Kingston-upon-Thames		1 057 000
Tyne and Wear	540	208	Newcastle-upon-Tyne		1 160 000
Warwickshire	1981	765	Warwick		506 000
West Midlands	899	347	Birmingham		2 657 000
West Sussex	1989	768	Chichester		721 000
West Yorkshire	2039	787	Wakefield		2 141 000
Wiltshire (2-tier)	3481	1344	Trowbridge		608 000
				Swindon	150 000
Worcestershire	1813	700	Worcester		550 000

HUMAN GEOGRAPHY

United Kingdom (continued)

Scotland

Area 78 742 km²/30 394 sq mi

Population total (2000e) 5 728 000

Status Constituent part of the United Kingdom

Capital Edinburgh

Languages English, Scots Gaelic (Gallic) (known or used by c.80 000 residents)

Physical features Comprises the N part of the UK, and includes the island groups of Outer and Inner Hebrides, Orkney and Shetland; divided into Southern Uplands, rising to 843 m/2766 ft at Merrick; Central Lowlands (most densely populated area); and Northern Highlands, divided by the fault line following the Great Glen, and rising to 1344 m/4409 ft at Ben Nevis; W coast heavily indented; several wide estuaries on E coast, primarily Firths of Forth, Tay and Moray; many freshwater lochs in the interior, largest being Loch Lomond, 70 km²/27 sq mi, and deepest Loch Morar, 310 m/1020 ft.

Economy Based on coal, but all heavy industry declined through the 1980s, with closure of many pits; oil services on E coast; tourism, especially in Highlands; shipbuilding, steel, whisky, textiles, agriculture, forestry.

History Roman attempts to limit incursions of N tribes marked by Antonine Wall and Hadrian's Wall; beginnings of unification, 9th-c; wars between England and Scotland in Middle Ages; Scottish independence declared by Robert Bruce, recognized 1328; Stuart succession, 14th-c; crowns of Scotland and England united, 1603; parliaments united under Act of Union, 1707; unsuccessful Jacobite rebellions, 1715 and 1745; devolution proposal rejected, 1979; vote for Scottish parliament, 1997; in 1974, divided into 12 regions (including three islands councils); local government reorganization, 1996, replaced this two-tier system by a single tier of 29 mainland councils plus the three islands councils; successful referendum for Scottish parliament, 1997; devolved Scottish parliament, 1999.

Scottish councils

Name	Area		Population	Admin
	km²	sq mi	total (2000e)	centre
Aberdeen City	186	72	221 000	Aberdeen
Aberdeenshire	6318	2439	227 000	Aberdeen
Angus	2181	842	113 000	Forfar
Argyll and Bute	6930	2675	92 000	Lochgilphead
Clackmannanshire	157	61	49 000	Alloa
Dumfries and Galloway	6439	2485	150 000	Dumfries
Dundee City	65	25	156 000	Dundee
East Ayrshire	1252	483	126 000	Kilmarnock
East Dunbartonshire	172	66	112 000	Kirkintilloch
East Lothian	6778	2616	87 000	Haddington
East Renfrewshire	173	67	88 000	Giffnock
Edinburgh, City of	262	101	448 000	Edinburgh
Falkirk	299	115	145 000	Falkirk
Fife	1323	511	134 000	Glenrothes
Glasgow, City of	175	68	633 000	Glasgow
Highland	25 784	9953	210 000	Inverness
Inverclyde	162	63	91 000	Greenock
Midlothian	356	137	81 000	Dalkeith
Moray	2238	864	87 000	Elgin

□ International Airport

1 Aberdeen City
2 Aberdeenshire
3 Angus
4 Argyll and Bute
5 Clackmannanshire
6 Dumfries and Galloway
7 Dundee City
8 East Ayrshire
9 East Dunbartonshire
10 East Lothian
11 East Renfrewshire
12 Edinburgh, City of
13 Falkirk
14 Fife
15 Glasgow
16 Highland
17 Inverclyde
18 Midlothian
19 Moray
20 North Ayrshire
21 North Lanarkshire
22 Orkney
23 Perth and Kinross
24 Renfrewshire
25 Scottish Borders
26 Shetland
27 South Ayrshire
28 South Lanarkshire
29 Stirling
30 West Dunbartonshire
31 Western Isles
32 West Lothian

Name	Area		Population	Admin
	km²	sq mi	total (2000e)	centre
North Ayrshire	884	341	141 000	Irvine
North Lanarkshire	474	183	331 000	Motherwell
Orkney	992	383	20 000	Kirkwall
Perth and Kinross	5311	2050	132 000	Perth
Renfrewshire	261	101	179 000	Paisley
Scottish Borders	4734	1827	107 000	Newtown St Boswells

Name	Area		Population	Admin
	km²	sq mi	total (2000e)	centre
Shetland	1438	555	23 000	Lerwick
South Ayrshire	1202	464	116 000	Ayr
South Lanarkshire	1771	684	311 000	Hamilton
Stirling	2196	848	83 000	Stirling
West Dunbartonshire	162	63	99 000	Dunbarton
Western Isles	3133	1209	30 000	Stornoway
West Lothian	425	164	149 000	Livingston

Wales

Local name Cymru (Welsh)

Area 20 761 km²/8014 sq mi

Population total (2000e) 2 946 000

Status Principality (Constituent part of the United Kingdom)

Capital Cardiff

Languages English, Welsh

Physical features Situated on the W coast of the UK, divided into 8 counties since 1974; includes the island of Anglesey off the NW coast; land rises to 1085 m/3560 ft at Snowdon (NW), also Cambrian Mts (C); Brecon Beacons (S); drained by the Severn, Clwyd, Dee, Conwy, Dovey, Taff, Towy, and Wye rivers.

Economy Coal; slate, lead, steel; industrialized S valleys and coastal plain; tourism in N and NW; ferries to Ireland at Holyhead, Fishguard; important source of water for England.

History Rhodri Mawr united Wales against Saxons, Norse, and Danes, 9th-c; Edward I of England established authority over Wales, building several castles, 12th–13th-c; Edward I's son created first Prince of Wales, 1301; 14th-c revolt under Owen Glendower; politically united with England by Act of Union, 1535; centre of Nonconformist religion since 18th-c; University of Wales, 1893, with constituent colleges; political nationalist movement (Plaid Cymru) returned first MP, 1966; Welsh television channel, 1982; 1979 referendum opposed devolution; successful referendum for devolved Welsh Assembly, 1997; Welsh Assembly, 1999.

□ International Airport

HUMAN GEOGRAPHY

Counties of Wales

Name	Area		Population	Admin
	km²	sq mi	total (2000e)	centre
Aberconwy and Colwyn	1130	436	111 800	Colwyn Bay
Anglesey	719	277	67 900	Llangefni
Blaenau Gwent	109	42	74 000	Ebbw Vale
Bridgend	246	95	132 200	Bridgend
Caerphilly	279	108	172 700	Hengoed
Cardiff	139	54	312 100	Cardiff
Cardiganshire	1797	694	70 400	Aberystwyth
Carmarthenshire	2398	926	170 700	Carmarthen
Denbighshire	844	326	92 200	Ruthin
Flintshire	437	169	146 800	Mold
Gwynedd	2548	983	119 200	Caernarfon
Merthyr Tydfil	111	43	60 100	Merthyr Tydfil

Name	Area		Population	Admin
	km²	sq mi	total (2000e)	centre
Monmouthshire	851	328	85 000	Cwmbran
Neath and Port Talbot	442	171	141 500	Port Talbot
Newport	191	74	138 800	Newport
Pembrokeshire	1590	614	114 700	Haverfordwest
Powys	5204	2009	123 200	Llandrindod Wells
Rhondda, Cynon Taff	424	164	241 400	Cardiff (temporary)
Swansea	378	146	233 000	Swansea
Torfaen	126	49	91 500	Pontypool
Vale of Glamorgan	337	130	120 300	Barry
Wrexham	499	193	124 600	Wrexham

United Kingdom (continued)

Unitary Authorities (from April 1996)

1 Anglesey	12 Vale of Glamorgan
2 Gwynedd	13 Merthyr Tydfil
3 Aberconwy & Colwyn	14 Blaenau Gwent
4 Powys	15 Torfaen
5 Cardiganshire	16 Caerphilly
6 Carmarthenshire	17 Newport
7 Pembrokeshire	18 Cardiff
8 Swansea	19 Monmouthshire
9 Neath & Port Talbot	20 Denbighshire
10 Bridgend	21 Flintshire
11 Rhondda Cynon Taff	22 Wrexham

Northern Ireland (Ulster)

Area 14 120 km²/5450 sq mi

Population total (2000e) 1 664 000

Status Constituent division of the United Kingdom

Capital Belfast

Languages English, Irish Gaelic

Religions Christian (Roman Catholic 28%, Presbyterian 23%, Church of Ireland 19%)

Physical features Occupies the NE part of Ireland, centred on Lough Neagh; Mourne Mts in SE; highest point, Slieve Donard, 847 m/2786 ft, in the former Co. Down; R Mourne, 82 km/51 mi in length.

Economy Agriculture; service industries, shipbuilding, engineering, chemicals; linen, textiles; economy badly affected by the sectarian troubles since 1969.

History Separate Parliament established in 1920, with a 52-member House of Commons and a 26-member Senate; Protestant majority in the population, generally supporting political union with Great Britain; many of the Roman Catholic minority look for union with the Republic of Ireland; violent conflict between the communities broke out in 1969, leading to the establishment of a British army peace-keeping force; sectarian murders and bombings continued both within and outside the province; as a result of the disturbances, Parliament was abolished in 1972; powers are now vested in the UK Secretary of State for Northern Ireland; formation of a 78-member Assembly, 1973; replaced by a Constitutional Convention, 1975; Assembly re-formed in 1982, but Nationalist members did not take their seats; under the

☐ International Airport ∴ World heritage site

1985 Anglo-Irish agreement, the Republic of Ireland was given a consultative role in the government of Northern Ireland; all Northern Ireland MPs in the British Parliament resigned in protest, 1986; continuing controversy in late 1980s; fresh talks between all main parties and Irish government, 1992; breakthrough in 1993 with Downing Street Declaration; IRA and loyalist ceasefires, 1994; joint Irish/British Framework Document, 1995; new IRA campaign, 1996; start of all-party talks (initially with Sinn Féin excluded), 1996; Good Friday agreement, 1998, introduces Northern Ireland Assembly; problems over arms decommissioning by the IRA hindered implementation of the agreement through 1999; review of the peace process by US senator George Mitchell, resulting in a compromise formula and the inauguration of the Assembly; reimposition of UK rule, 2000; Sinn Féin announced IRA would begin the process of arms decommissioning, 2001; further suspension of devolution, 2002; talks to restore devolution ongoing into 2004.

Districts of Northern Ireland

Name	Area		Population total (2000e)	Admin centre
	km²	sq mi		
Antrim	563	217	44 700	Antrim
Ards	369	142	67 900	Newtownards
Armagh	672	259	52 100	Armagh
Ballymena	638	246	57 800	Ballymena
Ballymoney	419	162	25 500	Ballymoney
Banbridge	444	171	34 600	Banbridge
Belfast	140	54	285 800	Belfast
Carrickfergus	87	34	35 500	Carrickfergus
Castlereagh	85	33	53 600	Belfast
Coleraine	485	187	52 100	Coleraine
Cookstown	623	240	31 800	Cookstown
Craigavon	383	147	77 800	Craigavon
Down	646	249	63 000	Downpatrick

Name	Area		Population total (2000e)	Admin centre
	km²	sq mi		
Dungannon	779	301	49 900	Dungannon
Fermanagh	1 876	715	54 100	Enniskillen
Larne	338	131	30 400	Larne
Limavady	587	227	23 700	Limavady
Lisburn	444	171	103 000	Lisburn
Londonderry/ Derry	382	147	102 000	Londonderry/ Derry
Magherafelt	573	221	37 500	Magherafelt
Moyle	495	191	15 000	Ballycastle
Newry and Mourne	895	346	75 600	Newry
Newtownabbey	152	59	77 900	Newtownabbey
North Down	73	28	74 500	Bangor
Omagh	1129	436	47 900	Omagh
Strabane	870	336	37 400	Strabane

BRITISH ISLANDS
Channel Islands

Timezone GMT

Area 194 km²/75 sq mi

Population total (2002e) 145 000

Status Crown dependency of the United Kingdom

Capital St Helier (on Jersey), St Peter Port (on Guernsey)

Languages English and Norman-French

Physical features Island group of the British Isles in the English Channel, W of Normandy; comprises the islands of Guernsey, Jersey, Alderney, Sark, Herm, Jethou, Brechou, and Lihou.

Economy Tourism, fruit, vegetables, flowers, dairy produce, Jersey and Guernsey cattle; used as a tax haven; not part of the European Community.

History Granted to the Dukes of Normandy, 10th-c; only British possession to have been occupied by Germany during World War 2; a dependent territory of the British Crown, with individual legislative assemblies and legal system; divided into the Bailiwick of Guernsey and the Bailiwick of Jersey; Bailiff presides over the Royal Court and the Representative Assembly (the States).

□ International Airport

Isle of Man

Timezone GMT

Area 572 km²/221 sq mi

Population total (2002e) 75 000

Status Crown dependency of the United Kingdom

Capital Douglas

Languages English (Manx survived as an everyday language until 19th-c)

Physical features Island in the Irish Sea; rises to 620 m/ 2036 ft at Snaefell.

Economy Tourism, agriculture, fishing, light engineering; used as a tax haven; not part of European Community; annual Tourist Trophy motorcycle races held here.

History Ruled by the Welsh, 6th–9th-c; then by the Scandinavians, Scots, and English; purchased by the British Government between 1765 and 1828; the island has its own Parliament, the bicameral Court of Tynwald, which consists of the elected House of Keys and the Legislative Council; Acts of the British Parliament do not generally apply to Man.

☐ International Airport

BRITISH OVERSEAS TERRITORIES
Anguilla

Timezone GMT –4

Area 155 km²/60 sq mi

Population total (2002e) 12 000

Capital The Valley

Physical features Most northerly of the Leeward Is, E Caribbean; also includes Sombrero I and several other offshore islets and cays; low-lying coral island, covered in low scrub and fringed with white coral-sand beaches.

Climate Tropical climate; average annual temperature ranges from 24–30°C; low and erratic annual rainfall, 550–1250 mm/22–50 in; hurricane season (Jul–Oct).

Currency 1 East Caribbean Dollar (EC$) = 100 cents

Economy Tourism, fishing, peas, corn, sweet potatoes, salt, boatbuilding.

History Colonized by English settlers from St Kitts, 1650; ultimately incorporated in the colony of St Kitts-Nevis-Anguilla; separated, 1980; governor appointed by the British sovereign; Legislative Assembly.

Bermuda

Timezone GMT –4

Area 53 km²/20 sq mi

Population total (2002e) 82 000

Capital Hamilton

Physical features Archipelago in W Atlantic, c.900 km/560 mi E of Cape Hatteras, N Carolina; c.150 low-lying coral islands and islets, 20 inhabited, 7 linked by causeways and bridges; largest island, (Great) Bermuda; highest point, Gibb's Hill, 78 m/256 ft.

Climate Subtropical climate; generally humid; rain throughout year; warm summers, mild winters.

Currency 1 Bermuda Dollar = 100 cents

Economy Mainly year-round tourism; increasingly an international company business centre; petroleum products, pharmaceuticals, aircraft supplies, boatbuilding, ship repair, vegetables, citrus fruits; fish-processing centre.

History Formerly called Somers Is, discovered by Span-

ish mariner, Juan Bermudez, in early 16th-c; colonized by English settlers, 1612; important naval station, and (to 1862) penal settlement; internal self-government, 1968;

movement for independence caused tension in the 1970s, including assassination of the Governor-General; bicameral legislature.

British Antarctic Territory

British colonial territory, designated 1962; 20°–80°W and S of 60°S; includes South Orkney Is, South Shetland Is, Antarctic Graham Land Peninsula, and the land mass extending to the South Pole; area, 57 million km²/ 2.2 million sq mi; land area (660 000 km²/ 170 000 sq mi) covered by ice and fringed by floating ice shelves; population solely of scientists of the British Antarctic Survey; Territory administered by a High Commissioner in the Falkland Is.

British Indian Ocean Territory

British territory, 1900 km/1180 mi NE of Mauritius, c.2300 islands, comprising the Chagos Archipelago; area, 60 km²/23 sq mi; covering c.54 400 km²/21 000 sq mi of Indian Ocean; tropical maritime climate, hot and humid; acquired by France, 18th-c; annexed by Britain, 1814; bought by the Crown, 1967; population working on copra plantations resettled in Mauritius or the Seychelles, 1967–73; construction of a naval base by Britain and US started on Diego Garcia, the largest island; population total (2000e) 2900; no permanent civilian population.

British Virgin Islands

Timezone GMT –4

Area 153 km²/59 sq mi

Population total (2002e) 21 000

Capital Road Town (on Tortola Island)

Physical features Island group at the NW end of the Lesser Antilles chain, E Caribbean, NE of Puerto Rico; comprises 4 large islands (Tortola, Virgin Gorda, Anegada, Jost Van Dyke) and over 30 islets and cays; only 16 inhabited; hilly terrain, except for flat coral island of Anegada; highest point, Sage Mt, 540 m/1 772 ft, on Tortola I.

MAP >> US VIRGIN ISLANDS, p. 365

Climate Subtropical climate; average annual temperatures 17–28°C (Jan), 26–31°C (Jul); average annual rainfall 1270 mm/50 in.

Currency 1 US Dollar (US$) = 100 cents

Economy Tourism (accounts for 50% of national income); construction and stone extraction; rum, paint, gravel, livestock, coconuts, sugar cane, fruit and vegetables, fish.

History Tortola colonized by British planters, 1666; constitutional government, 1774; part of the Leeward Is, 1872; separate Crown Colony, 1956; governor represents the British sovereign; Executive Council and Legislative Council.

Cayman Islands

Timezone GMT –5

Area 260 km²/100 sq mi

Population total (2002e) 40 000

Capital George Town

Physical features Located in W Caribbean, comprising the islands of Grand Cayman, Cayman Brac, and Little Cayman, c.240 km/150 mi S of Cuba; low-lying, rising to 42 m/138 ft on Cayman Brac plateau; ringed by coral reefs.

Climate Tropical climate; average temperatures

24–32°C (May–Oct), 16–24°C (Nov–Apr); average annual rainfall 1420 mm/56 in; hurricane season (Jul–Nov).

Currency 1 Cayman Island Dollar (CI$) = 100 cents

Economy Tourism; international finance, property development; over 450 banks and trust companies established on the islands; oil transshipment; crafts, jewellery, vegetables, tropical fish.

History Visited by Colombus, 1503; ceded to Britain, 1670; colonized by British settlers from Jamaica; British Crown Colony, 1962; a Governor represents the British sovereign, and presides over a Legislative Assembly.

Falkland Islands

Timezone GMT −4

Area c.12 200 km²/4 700 sq mi

Population total (2002e) 3000

Capital Stanley (on East Falkland)

Physical features Located in the S Atlantic, c.650 km/400 mi NE of the Magellan Strait; consists of East Falkland and West Falkland, separated by the Falkland Sound, with over 200 small islands; hilly terrain, rising to 705 m/2313 ft at Mt Usborne (East Falkland) and 700 m/2297 ft at Mt Adam (West Falkland).

Climate Cold, strong westerly winds; low rainfall; narrow temperature range 19°C (Jan), 2°C (Jul); average annual rainfall 635 mm/25 in.

Currency 1 Falkland Pound = 100 pence

Economy Agriculture; oats, sheep; service industries to the continuing military presence in the islands.

History Seen by several early navigators, including Capt John Strong in 1689–90, who named the islands; French settlement, 1764; British base established, 1765; French yielded their settlement to the Spanish, 1767; occupied in the name of the Republic of Buenos Aires, 1820; Britain asserted possession, became a British Crown Colony, 1833; formal annexation, 1908 and 1917; the whole island claimed since independence by Argentina; Falklands War, precipitated by the Argentine

□ International Airport

invasion of the islands in April 1982, led to the dispatch of the British Task Force and the return of the islands to British rule in June 1982; external affairs and defence are the responsibility of the British government, which appoints civil and military commissioners; internal affairs are governed by executive and legislative councils.

South Georgia

British Overseas Territory, located in the S Atlantic, c.500 km/300 mi E of the Falkland Islands; area, c.3750 km²/1450 sq mi; barren, mountainous, snow-covered island; length, 160 km/100 mi; discovered by the London merchant De la Roche, 1675; landing by Captain Cook, 1775; British annexation, 1908 and 1917; burial place of Ernest Shackleton, the British explorer, who died at S Georgia in 1922; sealing and whaling centre until 1965; invaded by Argentina and recaptured by Britain, April 1982; territory administered from the Falkland Islands.

South Sandwich Islands

British Overseas Territory, group of small, uninhabited islands in the S Atlantic, c.720 km/450 mi SE of South Georgia; 56°18–59°25S 26°15W; discovered by Captain Cook, 1775; annexed by Britain, 1908 and 1917; administered from the Falkland Islands.

Gibraltar

Timezone GMT +1

Area 6.5 sq km/2.5 sq mi

Population total (2002e) 27 000

Capital Gibraltar

Physical features Narrow rocky peninsula rising steeply from the low-lying coast of SW Spain at the E end of the Strait of Gibraltar, 8 km/5 mi from Algeciras; narrows to limestone massif, 'The Rock', height 426 m/1398 ft, connected to the Spanish mainland by a sandy plain; home of the Barbary apes, the only native monkeys in Europe.

Climate Mediterranean climate, with mild winters, warm summers; average annual temperature range 13–29°C.

Currency 1 Gibraltar Pound = 100 pence

Economy Largely dependent on the presence of British forces; Royal Naval Dockyard converted to a commercial yard, 1985; transshipment trade; fuel supplies to shipping; tourism.

History Settled by Moors, 711; taken by Spain, 1462; ceded to Britain, 1713; Crown Colony, 1830; played a key role in Allied naval operations during both World Wars; proposal to end British rule defeated by referendum, 1967; Spanish closure of frontier, 1969–85; Spain continues to claim sovereignty; British-Spanish talks ongoing, with a backdrop of inhabitants' demonstrations against shared sovereignty, 2002; British Monarch represented by a Governor and House of Assembly; military base; important strategic point of control for the W Mediterranean.

MAP ➤➤ SPAIN

Montserrat (Emerald Isle)

Timezone GMT −4

Area 106 km²/41 sq mi

Population total (1997e) 11 000 (pre-disaster); (2002e) 4000

Capital Plymouth

Physical features Volcanic island in the Leeward Is, E Caribbean; mountainous, heavily forested; highest point, Chance's Peak, 914 m/3000 ft; seven active volcanoes.

Climate Tropical climate, with low humidity; average annual rainfall 1500 mm/60 in; hurricanes (Jun–Nov).

Currency 1 East Caribbean Dollar (EC$) = 100 cents

Economy Tourism (accounts for 25% of national income); cotton, peppers, livestock, electronic assembly, crafts, rum distilling, postage stamps.

GDP (2002e) $29 mn, per capita $3400

History Visited by Colombus, 1493; colonized by English and Irish settlers, 1632; plantation economy based on slave labour; British Crown Colony, 1871; joined Federation of the West Indies, 1958–62; island severely damaged by hurricane Hugo, 1989; British sovereign represented by a Governor, with an Executive Council and a Legislative Council; most of the island, including the capital, destroyed by eruption of Soufriere Hills volcano (Jun 1997), followed by gradual resettlement of the population.

Pitcairn Islands

Timezone GMT −9

Area 27 km²/10 sq mi

Population total (2000e) 50

Capital Adamstown

Physical features Volcanic island group in the SE Pacific Ocean, E of French Polynesia; comprises Pitcairn Island, 4.5 km²/1.7 sq mi, and the uninhabited islands of Ducie, Henderson, and Oeno; Pitcairn Island rises to 335 m/1099 ft.

Climate Equable climate; average annual temperatures 24°C (Jan), 19°C (Jul); average annual rainfall 2000 mm/80 in.

Currency 1 New Zealand Dollar ($NZ) = 100 cents

Economy Postage stamps; tropical and subtropical crops; crafts, forestry.

History Visited by the British, 1767; occupied by nine mutineers from HMS *Bounty*, 1790; overpopulation led to emigration to Norfolk I, 1856; some returning in 1864; transferred to Fiji, 1952; now a UK Overseas Territory, governed by the High Commissioner in New Zealand.

Saint Helena and Dependencies

Timezone GMT

Area 122 km²/47 sq mi

Population total (2002e) 5000

Capital Jamestown (on St Helena Island)

Physical features Volcanic group of islands in the S Atlantic, 1920 km/1200 mi from the SW coast of Africa; includes St Helena, Ascension, Gough I, Inaccessible I, Nightingale I, and Tristan da Cunha; rugged, volcanic terrain; highest point, Diana's Peak, 823 m/2700 ft.

Climate Tropical marine; mild, tempered by SE 'trade' winds.

Currency 1 St Helena Pound (£) = 100 pence

Economy Fish (mostly tuna); agriculture, coffee; postage stamps; heavily subsidized by the UK.

GDP (1998e) $18 mn, per capita $2500

History Discovered by the Portuguese on St Helena's feast day, 1502; annexed by the Dutch, 1633; annexed by the East India Company, 1659; Napoleon exiled here, 1815–21; Ascension and Tristan da Cunha made dependencies, 1922; evacuated between 1961–3, following volcanic eruption; governed by an executive council and 12-member elected Legislative Council.

Turks and Caicos islands

Timezone GMT −5

Area 500 km²/200 sq mi

Population total (2002e) 21 000

Capital Cockburn Town

Physical features Two island groups comprising c.30 islands and cays, forming the SE archipelago of the Bahamas chain, W Atlantic Ocean; Turk I and Caicos I are separated by 35 km/22 mi; only 6 of the other islands are inhabited.

Climate Subtropical climate; average annual temperatures 24–7°C (Jan), 29–32°C (Jul); average annual rainfall 525 mm/21 in; occasional hurricanes.

Currency 1 US Dollar ($, US$) = 100 cents

Economy Tourism is a rapidly expanding industry; corn, beans, fishing, fish processing.

GDP (2000e) $231 mn, per capita $9600

History Visited by the Spanish, 1512; linked formally to the Bahamas, 1765; transferred to Jamaica, 1848; British Crown Colony, 1972; internal self-government, 1976; British sovereign represented by a Governor, who presides over a Council.

UNITED STATES OF AMERICA (USA)

Local names United States, America

Timezone GMT –5 (E coast) to –8 (Pacific Coast)

Area 9 160 454 km²/3 535 935 sq mi

Population total (2002e) 287 602 000

Status Federal republic

Date of independence 1776

Capital Washington, DC.

Languages English, large Spanish-speaking minority

Ethnic groups European origin (including 9% Hispanic) (89.3%), African American (12.1%), Asian and Pacific (2.9%), Native American, Aleut, and Inuit (0.8%)

Religions Christian (86%) (Protestant 53%, Roman Catholic 26%), Jewish (2%), atheist (7%), other (5%)

Physical features Includes the separate states of Alaska (GMT – 9) and Hawaii (GMT – 10); E Atlantic coastal plain is backed by the Appalachian Mts from the Great Lakes to Alabama, a series of parallel ranges including the Allegheny, Blue Ridge, and Catskill Mts; plain broadens out (S) towards the Gulf of Mexico and into the Florida peninsula; Gulf Plains stretch N to meet the Great Plains from which they are separated by the Ozark Mts; further W, Rocky Mts rise to over 4500 m/14 750 ft; highest point in US, Mt McKinley, Alaska, 6194 m/20 321 ft; Death Valley, –86 m/–282 ft, is the lowest point; drainage N is into the St Lawrence R or the Great Lakes; in the E, the Hudson, Delaware, Potomac, and other rivers flow E to the Atlantic Ocean; central plains drained by the great Red River–Missouri-Mississippi system and by other rivers flowing into the Gulf of Mexico; main rivers in W, Columbia and Colorado; deserts cover much of Texas, New Mexico, Arizona, Utah, Nevada.

Climate Climate varies from conditions found in hot, tropical deserts (SW), to those typical of Arctic continental regions on the northern Pacific Coast; continental climate on High Plains, with summer dust storms and winter blizzards; temperate continental on Central Plains; continental Mid West and the Great Lakes, with very cold winters; cool temperate in N Appalachians, warm temperate in S; subtropical to warm temperate on the Gulf Coast, with plentiful rainfall and frequent hurricanes and tornadoes; temperate maritime on the Atlantic coast, with heavy snowfall in N; cool temperate in New England, with warm summers and severe winters; mean annual temperatures range from 29°C in Florida, to –13°C in Alaska; average annual temperatures in Chicago, –3°C (Jan), 24°C (Jul); in Arizona, 11°C (Jan), 32°C (Jul); average annual rainfall in Alabama, 1640 mm/65 in, in Arizona, 180 mm/7 in; hot and humid in

Hawaii, with average annual rainfall 1524–5080 mm/ 60–200 in.

Currency 1 US Dollar ($, US$) = 100 cents

Economy One of the world's most productive industrial nations, highly diversified economy, vast mineral and agricultural resources; major exporter of grains, cereals, potatoes, sugar, fruit; livestock farming of beef, veal, pork; chief exports include aircraft, cars, machinery, chemicals, military equipment, non-fuel minerals; advanced system of communications and transportation; leader in space-exploration programme of the 1970s.

GDP (2002e) $10.45 tn, per capita $36 300

HDI (2002) 0.939

History First settled by groups who migrated from Asia across the Bering Straits over 25 000 years ago; explored by the Norse in 9th-c and by the Spanish in 16th-c, who settled in Florida and Mexico; in the 17th-c, settlements by the British, French, Dutch, Germans, and Swedes; many Black Africans introduced as slaves to work on the plantations; British control during 18th-c after defeat of French in Seven Years' war; revolt of the English-speaking colonies in the War of Independence, 1775–83, resulted in the creation of the United States of America; Louisiana sold to the USA by France in 1803 (the Louisiana Purchase) and the westward movement of settlers began; Florida ceded by Spain in 1819, and further Spanish states joined the Union, 1821–53; 11 Southern states left the Union over the slavery issue and formed the Confederacy, 1860–1; Civil War, 1861–5, ended in victory for the North, and the Southern states later rejoined the Union; Alaska purchased from Russia, 1867; Hawaiian islands annexed, 1898; several other islands formally associated with the USA, such as Puerto Rico, American Samoa, and Guam; in the 19th-c, arrival of millions of immigrants from

Europe and the Far East; more recent arrival of large numbers of Spanish-speaking people, mainly from Mexico and the West Indies; entered World War 1 on the side of the Allies, 1917, and again in World War 2 in 1941; became the chief world power opposed to communism, a policy which led to involvement in the Korean War (1950–3) and Vietnam (1956–75); campaign for Black civil rights developed, 1960s, and eventually led to Civil Rights Act (1964); invasion of Grenada, 1983; mid 1980s rapprochement of US and USSR; invasion of Panama, 1989; involvement in Gulf War, 1991; military intervention in Somalia, 1993; ongoing concern over the ability of Iraq to pose a threat through its alleged development of weapons of mass destruction; following Al-Qaeda attack on the World Trade Center in New York (11 Sep 2001), and earlier terrorist attacks (notably, the 1998 bomb attacks on US embassies in Kenya and Tanzania, and the bombing of the USS *Cole* warship in the port of Aden, Yemen in 2000), the USA led the successful campaign to remove the Taliban from power in Afghanistan; further campaign against international terrorism, 2002 and ongoing; invasion of Iraq and removal of Saddam Hussein (2003), with US presence in Iraq scheduled to remain until mid-2004; ongoing terrorist threats against the USA, both within the country and abroad, brought unprecedented levels of security throughout 2003–4; Congress consists of 435-member House of Representatives, and a 100-member Senate; a President elected every 4 years by a college of state representatives, appoints an executive Cabinet responsible to Congress; divided into 50 federal states and the District of Columbia, each state having its own two-body legislature and governor.

Head of State/Government (President)
1993–2001 William Jefferson Clinton
2001– George W(alker) Bush

>> Political leaders and rulers pp.129–30

American States

(Timezones: two sets of figures indicate that different zones operate in a state. The second figure refers to Summer Time (Apr–Oct, approximately)
2 Aleutian/Hawaii Standard Time : 3 Alaska Standard Time : 4 Pacific Standard Time : 5 Mountain Standard Time : 6 Central Standard Time : 7 Eastern Standard Time

Name	Area km²	sq mi	Capital	Time zone	Population figures (2000e)	Nickname(s)
Alabama (AL)	133 911	51 705	Montgomery	7/8	4 387 000	Camellia State, Heart of Dixie
Alaska (AK)	1 518 748	586 412	Juneau	3/4	6 24 000	Mainland State, The Last Frontier
Arizona (AZ)	295 249	114 000	Phoenix	5	4 893 000	Apache State, Grand Canyon State
Arkansas (AR)	137 403	53 187	Little Rock	6/7	2 564 000	Bear State, Land of Opportunity
California (CA)	411 033	158 706	Sacramento	4/5	33 609 000	Golden State
Colorado (CO)	269 585	104 091	Denver	5/6	4 145 000	Centennial State
Connecticut (CT)	12 996	5018	Hartford	7/8	3 292 000	Nutmeg State, Constitution State
Delaware (DE)	5296	2045	Dover	7/8	763 000	Diamond State, First State
District of Columbia (DC)	173.5	67.0	Washington	7/8	516 000	
Florida (FL)	151 934	58 664	Tallahassee	6/7, 7/8	15 323 000	Everglade State, Sunshine State
Georgia (GA)	152 571	58 910	Atlanta	7/8	7 944 000	Empire State of the South, Peach State
Hawaii (HI)	16 759	6471	Honolulu	2	1 181 000	Aloha State
Idaho (ID)	216 422	83 564	Boise	4/5, 5/6	1 273 000	Gem State
Illinois (IL)	145 928	56 345	Springfield	6/7	12 189 000	Prairie State, Land of Lincoln
Indiana (IN)	93 715.5	36 185	Indianapolis	6/7, 7/8	5 979 000	Hoosier State
Iowa (IA)	145 747	56 275	Des Moines	6/7	2 878 000	Hawkeye State, Corn State
Kansas (KS)	213 089	82 277	Topeka	5/6, 6/7	2 670 000	Sunflower State, Jayhawker State
Kentucky (KY)	104 658	40 410	Frankfort	6/7, 7/8	3 989 000	Bluegrass State
Louisiana (LA)	123 673	47 752	Baton Rouge	6/7	4 381 000	Pelican State, Sugar State, Creole State
Maine (ME)	86 153	33 265	Augusta	7/8	1 258 000	Pine Tree State
Maryland (MD)	27 090	10 460	Annapolis	7/8	5 213 000	Old Line State, Free State
Massachusetts (MA)	21 455	8284	Boston	7/8	6 206 000	Bay State, Old Colony
Michigan (MI)	151 579	58 527	Lansing	6/7, 7/8	9 903 000	Wolverine State, Great Lake State
Minnesota (MN)	218 593	84 402	St Paul	6/7	4 823 000	Gopher State, North Star State
Mississippi (MS)	123 510	47 689	Jackson	6/7	2 785 000	Magnolia State
Missouri (MO)	180 508	69 697	Jefferson City	6/7	5 501 000	Bullion State, Show Me State
Montana (MT)	380 834	147 046	Helena	5/6	886 000	Treasure State, Big Sky Country
Nebraska (NE)	200 342	77 352	Lincoln	5/6, 6/7	1 671 000	Cornhusker State, Beef State
Nevada (NV)	286 341	110 561	Carson City	4/5	1 878 000	Silver State, Sagebrush State
New Hampshire (NH)	24 032	9279	Concord	7/8	1 217 000	Granite State
New Jersey (NJ)	20 167	7787	Trenton	7/8	8 192 000	Garden State
New Mexico (NM)	314 914	121 593	Santa Fe	5/6	1 747 000	Sunshine State, Land of Enchantment
New York (NY)	127 185	49 108	Albany	7/8	18 233 000	Empire State

American States (continued)

Name	Area km²	sq mi	Capital	Time zone	Population figures (2000e)	Nickname(s)
North Carolina (NC)	136407	52699	Raleigh	7/8	7758000	Old North State, Tar Heel State
North Dakota (ND)	180180	69567	Bismarck	5/6, 6/7	630000	Flickertail State, Sioux State
Ohio (OH)	107040	41330	Columbus	7/8	11279000	Buckeye State
Oklahoma (OK)	181083	69919	Oklahoma City	6/7	3378000	Sooner State
Oregon(OR)	251409	97073	Salem	4/5	3349000	Sunset State, Beaver State
Pennsylvania (PA)	117343	45308	Harrisburg	7/8	11982000	Keystone State
Rhode Island (RI)	3139	1212	Providence	7/8	994000	Little Rhody, Plantation State
South Carolina (SC)	80579	31113	Columbia	7/8	3932000	Palmetto State
South Dakota (SD)	199723	77116	Pierre	5/6, 6/7	735000	Sunshine State, Coyote State
Tennessee (TN)	109149	42144	Nashville	6/7, 7/8	5533000	Volunteer State
Texas (TX)	691040	266807	Austin	5/6, 6/7	20385000	Lone Star State
Utah (UT)	219880	84899	Salt Lake City	5/6	2160000	Mormon State, Beehive State
Vermont (VT)	24899	9614	Montpelier	7/8	597000	Green Mountain State
Virginia (VA)	105582	40767	Richmond	7/8	6955000	Old Dominion State, Mother of Presidents
Washington (WA)	176473	68139	Olympia	4/5	5825000	Evergreen State, Chinook State
West Virginia (WV)	62758	24232	Charleston	7/8	1802000	Panhandle State, Mountain State
Wisconsin (WI)	145431	56153	Madison	6/7	5277000	Badger State, America's Dairyland
Wyoming (WY)	253315	97809	Cheyenne	5/6	479000	Equality State

UNITED STATES FORMAL DEPENDENCIES
American Samoa

Local name São Paulo de Loanda (Portuguese)

Timezone GMT −11

Area 197 km²/76 sq mi

Population total (2002e) 62000

Capital Fagatogo

Languages English (official), Samoan

Physical features Located in the CS Pacific Ocean, some 3500 km/2175 mi N of New Zealand; five principal volcanic islands (including Tutuila, Aunu'u, Ofu, Olosega, Ta'u, Rose, Swains I) and two coral atolls; main island, Tutuila, 109 km²/42 sq mi, rises to 653 m/2142 ft; islands mostly hilly, with large areas of thick bush and forest.

Climate Tropical maritime climate; average annual temperatures 28°C (Jan), 27°C (Jul) in Fagatogo; plentiful rainfall; rainy season (Nov–Apr); dry season (May–Oct); average annual rainfall 5000 mm/200 in.

Economy Principal crops, taro, breadfruit, yams, bananas, coconuts; tuna fishing; local inshore fishing, handicrafts.

GDP (2000e) $500 mn, per capita $8000

History US acquired rights to American Samoa in 1899 and the islands were ceded by their chiefs, 1900–25; now

□ International Airport

an unincorporated territory of the USA, administered by the Department of the Interior; bicameral legislature established, 1948, comprising a Senate and House of Representatives.

Guam

Local name Guam

Timezone GMT +10

Area 541 km²/209 sq mi

Population total (2002e) 163 000

Status Unincorporated territory of the United States of America

Capital Hagåtña (Agana)

Languages Chamorro and English (official), Japanese is also spoken

Ethnic groups Chamorro (37%), Filipino (29%), Caucasian (18%), Micronesian (13%)

Religion Roman Catholic

Physical features Largest and southernmost of the Mariana Islands, covering c.48 km/30 mi in the Pacific Ocean; volcanic island fringed by a coral reef; relatively flat limestone plateau, with narrow coastal plains in N, low rising hills in C and mountains in S; highest point, 406 m/1332 ft at Mt Lamlam.

Climate Tropical maritime climate; average annual temperature 24–30°C; average annual rainfall 2125 mm/ 84 in; wet season (Jul–Dec).

Currency 1 US Dollar (US$) = 100 cents

Economy Economy highly dependent on government activities; military installations cover 35% of the island; diversifying industrial and commercial projects; oil refining, dairy products, furniture, watches, copra, processed fish; rapidly growing tourist industry.

□ International Airport

History Originally settled by Malay-Filipino peoples; Ferdinand Magellan landed on the island, 1521; claimed for Spain, 1565; rebellion against Spanish missionaries, 1670–95; US consulate established, 1855; ceded to US by Spain after defeat in Spanish-American War, 1898; occupied by Japan, 1941–4; unincorporated territory of the US, Organic Act, 1950; elected Governor and a unicameral legislature.

Puerto Rico, The Commonwealth of

Local name Puerto Rico

Timezone GMT –4

Area 8897 km²/3434 sq mi

Population total (2002e) 3 879 000

Status Commonwealth

Capital San Juan

Languages Spanish (official), with English widely spoken

Religion Roman Catholic

Physical features Easternmost island of the Greater Antilles; almost rectangular in shape; crossed W–E by mountains, rising to 1338 m/4389 ft at Cerro de Punta; coastal plain belt in N; islands of Vieques and Culebra also belong to Puerto Rico.

Climate Tropical maritime climate; average annual temperature 25°C; high humidity.

Currency 1 US Dollar (US$) = 100 cents

Economy Manufacturing is the most important sector of the economy; food processing, petrochemicals, electrical equipment, pharmaceuticals; textiles, clothing; livestock, tobacco, sugar, pineapples, coconuts; tourism.

GDP (2002e) $43.01 bn, per capita $11 100

□ International Airport

History Originally occupied by Carib and Arawak Indians; visited by Columbus, 1493; Spanish colony until ceded to the US, 1898; high levels of emigration to the US from 1940s–50s; semi-autonomous Commonwealth in association with US, 1952; executive power exercised by a Governor; a bicameral Legislative Assembly consists of a Senate and House of Representatives.

Virgin Islands, United States

Local name US Virgin Islands

Timezone GMT −4

Area 342 km²/132 sq mi

Population total (2002e) 121 000 (St Croix 53 900, St Thomas 51 400, St John 2900)

Status Territory

Capital Charlotte Amalie (on St Thomas Island)

Languages English (official), with Spanish and Creole widely spoken

Ethnic groups West Indian, French, Hispanic

Religion Protestant

Physical features Nine islands and 75 islets in the Lesser Antilles, Caribbean Sea; three main inhabited islands, St Croix, St Thomas, and St John; volcanic origin, mostly hilly or rugged and mountainous; highest peak, Crown Mt, 474 m/1555 ft on St Thomas.

Climate Subtropical climate; average annual temperatures 21–9°C (Dec–Mar), 24–31°C (Jun–Sep); low humidity; rainy season (May–Nov); subject to severe droughts, floods and earthquakes.

Currency 1 US Dollar (US$) = 100 cents

Economy Tourism (chief industry); St Croix industries include oil and alumina products, clocks and watches,

□ International Airport

textiles, rum, fragrances, petrochemicals; vegetables, fruit, sorghum.

GDP (2002e) $2.4 bn, per capita $19 000

History Originally inhabited by Ciboney Indians, followed by Arawak Indians, then Caribs; discovered by Columbus, 1493; Denmark colonized St Thomas and St John, 1665 and 1718, and bought St Croix from France, 1733; purchased by US, 1917; now an unincorporated territory of the US; Governor heads unicameral legislature.

Mariana Islands, Northern

Located in N Pacific Ocean, area 471 km²/182 sq mi; limestone southern islands, volcanic northern islands; capital, Saipan; population total (2000e) 72 000; tropical marine climate; part of UN Trust Territory of the Pacific, 1947–78; became a self-governing US Commonwealth Territory, 1978–90; trusteeship ended, 1990.

OTHER AMERICAN ISLANDS

BAKER, HOWLAND, AND JARVIS ISLANDS
1500–1650 mi SW of the Hawaiian group, Pacific Ocean; uninhabited since World War 2, under Interior Department.

JOHNSTON ATOLL
Consists of four small islands, SW of Hawaii: Johnston, Sand, Hikina, and Akau; used for military purposes, otherwise uninhabited.

KINGMAN REEF
Uninhabited reef S of Hawaii, under Navy control.

MIDWAY ISLANDS
Atoll and two islands, Eastern and Sand, lying NW of Hawaii, in N Pacific; unpopulated apart from US naval personnel.

PALMYRA
Atoll 1000 mi S of Hawaii; privately owned; under Interior Department.

WAKE ISLAND
Uninhabited but for US naval personnel, Wake I lies between Guam and Midway I; sister islands, Wilkes and Peale.

□ International Airport

NAVASSA
Caribbean island between Jamaica and Haiti, 100 mi S of Guantánamo Bay, Cuba; covers c.3 sq mi and is reserved for US for a lighthouse, administered by US Coast Guard; uninhabited. Guatánamo Bay is an inlet in SE Cuba, c. 19 km (12 mi) by 10 km (6 mi); US marines landed in 1898 during the Spanish-American War; US naval base since 1903.

HUMAN GEOGRAPHY

URUGUAY

Local name Uruguay

Timezone GMT −3

Area 176215 km²/68018 sq mi

Population total (2002e) 3383000

Status Republic

Date of independence 1828

Capital Montevideo

Language Spanish (official)

Ethnic groups European (mainly Spanish, Italian) (90%), mestizo (8%)

Religions Roman Catholic (60%), Protestant (2%), Jewish (2%), unaffiliated (30%)

Physical features Located in E South America; grass covered plains (S) rise to a high, sandy plateau, traversed SE and NW by the Cuchilla Grande and Cuchilla de Haedo, rising to 501 m/1644 ft at Cerro Mirados; R Negro flows SW to meet the R Uruguay on the Argentine frontier.

Climate Temperate, with warm summers, mild winters; average annual temperature 10°C (Jul), 22°C (Jan) in Montevideo; average annual rainfall 978 mm/38 in; rainy season (Apr–May), occasional droughts.

Currency 1 New Uruguayan Peso (NUr$, UrugN$) = 100 centésimos

Economy Traditionally based on livestock and agriculture: meat, wool, fish, wheat, barley, maize, rice; naturally-occurring minerals include granite and marble; hydroelectric power, food processing and packing, light engineering, cement, textiles, leather, steel.

GDP (2002e) $26.82 bn, per capita $7900

HDI (2002) 0.831

□ International Airport

History Originally occupied by Charrúas Indians; visited by the Spanish, 1516; part of the Spanish Viceroyalty of Río de la Plata, 1726; province of Brazil, 1814–25; independence as the Eastern Republic of Uruguay, 1828; unrest caused by Tupamaro guerrillas in late 1960s and early 1970s; military rule until 1985; a President is advised by a Council of Ministers; bicameral legislature consists of a Senate and Chamber of Deputies.

Head of State/Government
2000–5   Jorge Luis Ibáñez
2005–   Tabare Vazquez

USSR (FORMER) >> CIS, LATVIA, LITHUANIA, ESTONIA

UZBEKISTAN

Local name Ozbekiston Republikasy

Timezone GMT +5

Area 447400 km²/172696 sq mi

Population total (2002e) 25484000

Status Republic

Date of independence 1991

Capital Tashkent

Language Uzbek

Ethnic groups Uzbek (71%), Russian (8%), Tajik (5%), Kazakh (4%)

Religion Sunni Muslim

Physical features Located in C and N Middle Asia; four-fifths of area is flat, sandy plain/desert (W); Turan Plain (NW) rises near the Aral Sea to 90 m/300 ft above sea level; delta of major river R Amu Darya forms alluvial plain over C Kara-Kalpak. Sultan-Uizdag Mts rise to 500 m/1600 ft; Kyzyl Kum broken by hills in SE; lowest point, Mynbulak, −12 m/−39 ft; Pskem Mts in E rise to 4299 m/14104 ft at Beshtor Peak.

Climate Dry and continental; average annual temperatures in S, −12°C (Jan), 32–40°C (Jul); low rainfall.

Currency Som (R)

Economy Deposits of coal, natural gas, oil, gold, lead, copper, and zinc; third largest cotton-growing area in the world; silk, wool; agriculture dependent on irrigated land; abundant orchards and vineyards; industry powered hydroelectrically.

GDP (2002e) $66.06 bn, per capita $2600

HDI (2002) 0.727

History Conquered by Alexander the Great, 4th-c BC; invaded by Mongols under Genghis Khan, 13th-c; Genghis Khan's grandson, Shibaqan, inherited the area; converted to Islam in 14th-c, under the ruler of Kipchak, Uzbek; became part of Tamerlane the Great's empire, 14th-c; conquered by Russia, mid-19th-c; became the Uzbek Republic in 1924, and Uzbekistan Soviet Socialist Republic in 1925; declared independence, 1991; joined CIS in 1991; governed by a President, Prime Minister, and 250-member Supreme Assembly; new constitution adopted, 1992; proposal for a bicameral legislature approved, 2002.

Head of State
1991– Islam A Karimov

Head of Government
1995–2003 Otkir Sultonov
2003– Shavkat Mirziyoev

☐ International Airport

VANUATU

Local name Ripablik Blong Vanuatu

Timezone GMT +11

Area 14 763 km²/5698 sq mi

Population total (2002e) 207 000

Status Independent republic within the Commonwealth

Date of independence 1980

Capital Port Vila (on Efate Island)

Languages Bislama, English, and French (official)

Ethnic groups Melanesian (95%), Micronesian, Polynesian, and European minorities

Religions Christian (70%) (Presbyterian 40%, Roman Catholic 15%, Anglican 15%), indigenous (8%), other (15%)

Physical features Mountainous, volcanic Y-shaped island chain in SW Pacific Ocean, 400 km/250 mi NE of New Caledonia; consisting of 12 islands and 60 islets; two-thirds of population occupy the 4 main islands of Efate, Espiritu Santo, Malekula, and Tanna; highest peak, rises to 1888 m/6194 ft, on Espiritu Santo; raised coral beaches fringed by reefs; several active volcanoes.

Climate Tropical, high temperatures; hot and rainy season (Nov–Apr) when cyclones may occur; average annual temperatures, 27°C (Jan), 22°C (Jul) in Vila; average annual rainfall 2310 mm/91 in.

Currency 1 Vatu (VT) = 100 centimes

Economy Agriculture; subsistence farming and plantations; yams, breadfruit, taro, copra, beef, cocoa, coffee, timber; manganese, fish processing, foodstuffs, crafts; tourism rapidly increasing, especially from cruise ships.

GDP (2002e) $563 mn, per capita $2900

HDI (2002) 0.542

History Visited by Spanish, 1606; named New Hebrides by James Cook, 1774; Anglo-French administration as

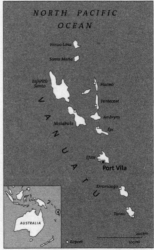

condominium of the New Hebrides, 1906; escaped Japanese occupation during World War 2; independence as Republic of Vanuatu, 1980; governed by a President, Prime Minister, Cabinet, and representative Assembly.

Head of State
2004– Kalkot Mataskelekele

Head of Government
2001– Serge Vohor

VATICAN CITY STATE

Local name Stato della Città del Vaticano

Timezone GMT +1

Area 0.44 km²/0.17 sq mi

Population total 1000

Status Papal sovereign state

Date of Independence 1929

Capital The Holy See, Vatican City

Languages Latin and Italian

Ethnic groups Italian, European, and various minorities

Religion Roman Catholic

Physical features The world's smallest state, situated on the Vatican hill in Rome, on W bank of R Tiber; architectural features include the Vatican Palace and Museum, St Peter's, the Pope's summer villa at Castel Gandolfo, and the Sistine Chapel; three entrances to the city in the care of the Pontifical Swiss Guard, 'The Bronze Doors', the Arch of Charlemagne, or the 'Arch of Bells', and the Via di Porta Angelica.

Climate Mediterranean; average annual temperature 7°C (Jan), 25°C (Jul); average annual rainfall 657 mm/26 in.

Currency 1 euro = 100 cents (previous to 2002, 1 Vatican Lira (L, Lit) = 100 centesimi)

Economy The state is supported by special collections and donations from Catholic congregations around the world; issues its own stamps and coinage, and has its own communications and banking systems; tourism; pilgrimages.

Income (1991) income $109 m, expenses $196 m

History Papacy's temporal authority exercised from a palace built on Rome's Vatican hill in 1377; extended to much of central Italy by 16th-c; incorporated into the emerging Italian state during the fight to unite Italy, 1860–70; the Lateran Treaty of 1929 recognized the Holy See's sovereignty in the Vatican City State and Catholicism became Italy's state religion; Karol Wojtyla became the first non-Italian pontiff since the 16th-c, 1978; in 1985, a concordat, replacing the Lateran Treaty, affirmed independence of the Vatican, but ended some of its privileges, Roman Catholicism ceased to be the state religion, and Rome lost its status as a 'sacred city'; sovereignty exercised by Pope, who is elected for life by a conclave of the College of Cardinals.

Head of State (Sovereign Pontiff/Pope)
1978–2005 Pope John Paul II (Karol Wojtyla)
2005–   Pope Benedict XVI (Joseph Ratzinger)

Head of Government (Secretary of State)
1990–   Cardinal Angelo Sodano

MAP >> ITALY

VENEZUELA

Local name República de Venezuela

Timezone GMT –4

Area 912 050 km²/352 051 sq mi

Population total (2002e) 25 093 000

Status Republic

Date of Independence 1830

Capital Caracas

Languages Spanish (official), Italian, c.25 Indian languages also spoken in the interior

Ethnic groups Mestizo (69%), European (20%), African origin (9%), Indian (2%)

Religions Roman Catholic (92%), Protestant (2%)

Physical features Occupies most of the N coast of South America; Guiana Highlands (SE) cover almost half the country; Venezuelan Highlands in the W and along the coast, highest point, Pico Bolivar 5007 m/16 411 ft; vast grasslands (*Llanos*) in the Orinoco basin; chief river, Orinoco; largest lake in South America, L Maracaibo, 21 486 km²/8296 sq mi; highest waterfall in the world, Angel Falls 979 m/3212 ft.

Climate Tropical, generally hot and humid; average annual temperatures 18°C (Jan), 21°C (Jul) in Caracas; one rainy season (Apr–Oct); average annual rainfall 833 mm/33 in.

Currency 1 Bolívar (B) = 100 céntimos

□ International Airport   ••••Disputed border

Economy Since 1920s, based on oil from Maracaibo (now provides over 90% of export revenue); aluminium (second-highest source of revenue); iron ore, gold, diamonds; only 4% of the land under permanent cultivation; beef and dairy farming; coffee, cocoa, cotton, rice, tobacco, sugar.

GDP (2002e) $131.7 bn, per capita $5400

HDI (2002) 0.770

History Originally inhabited by Caribs and Arawaks; seen by Columbus, 1498; Spanish settlers, 1520; frequent revolts against Spanish colonial rule; independence movement under Simón Bolívar, leading to the estab-lishment of the State of Gran Colombia (Colombia, Ecuador, Venezuela), 1821; independent republic, 1830; short-lived military coup, April 2002; governed by an elected bicameral National Congress, comprising a Sen-ate and a Chamber of Deputies; a President is advised by a Council of Ministers.

Head of State/Government
1998–2002 Hugo Chávez Fríaz
2002 Pedro Carmona *Transitional*
2002– Hugo Chávez Fríaz

VIETNAM

Local name Công Hòa Xã Hôi Chu Nghĩa Viêt Nam

Timezone GMT +7

Area 329 566 km²/127 212 sq mi

Population total (2002e) 79 939 000

Status Socialist republic

Date of independence 1976

Capital Hanoi

Languages Vietnamese (official), French, Chinese, English, Khmer

Ethnic groups Vietnamese (85–90%), Chinese (3%), minorities include Khmer, Cham, Hmong, Nung, Tay

Religions Buddhist (principal), Taoist, Confucian, Muslim, Roman Catholic, Hoa Hoa, Cao Dai, Protestant, and animist beliefs

Physical features Occupies a narrow strip along the coast of the Gulf of Tongking and the S China Sea on Indochinese peninsula in SE Asia; highest peak Fan si Pan, 3143 m/10 312 ft; Mekong R delta (S) and Red R delta (N) linked by narrow coastal plain; heavily forested mountains and plateaus.

Climate Tropical, monsoon climate; sub-tropical in N; average annual temperatures 17°C (Jan), 29°C (Jul) in Hanoi; average annual rainfall 1830 mm/72 in; typhoons and flooding frequent in N and SW.

Currency 1 Dông = 10 hao = 100 xu

Economy Agriculture (employs over 70% of the work-force); natural disasters, war, and political unrest adversely affected economy; Vietnam War brought depopulation, destruction of forest and farmland; exports include coal, minerals, rice, rubber, sugar cane.

GDP (2002e) $183.8 bn, per capita $2300

HDI (2002) 0.688

History Under the influence of China for many cen-turies; regions of Tongking (N), Annam (C), and Cochin-China (S) united as Vietnamese Empire, 1802; French pro-tectorates established in Cochin-China, 1867, and in Annam and Tongking, 1884; formed the French Indo-Chinese Union with Cambodia and Laos, 1887; occupied by the Japanese in World War 2; communist Viet-Minh League under Ho Chi-minh formed after the War, not rec-ognized by France; Indo-Chinese war, resulting in French withdrawal, 1946–54; 1954 armistice divided the coun-

□ International Airport

try between the communist 'Democratic Republic' in the N, and the 'State' of Vietnam in the S; civil war led to US intervention on the side of S Vietnam, 1965; fall of Saigon, 1975; reunification as the Socialist Republic of Vietnam, 1976; large numbers of refugees tried to find homes in the W in the late 1970s; Hanoi invaded neigh-bouring Cambodia, overthrowing hostile Khmer Rouge government, 1978; Chinese responded with invasion of Vietnam in 1979 - greatly increased the number trying to leave the country by sea (Vietnamese boat people); lim-ited troop withdrawals from Laos and Cambodia, 1989; Vietnam supported Cambodian peace agreement, 1991; new constitution, 1992, replaced Council of Ministers with a Prime Minister and a cabinet.

Head of State
1997– Tran Duc Luong

Head of Government
1997– Phan Van Khai

General Secretary
2001– Nong Duc Manh

VIRGIN ISLANDS >> UNITED KINGDOM; UNITED STATES OF AMERICA

HUMAN GEOGRAPHY

WESTERN SAHARA

Timezone GMT

Area 252 126 km²/97 321 sq mi

Population total (2002e) 308 000

Status Under dispute, still officially part of Morocco

Capital al-Aioun

Languages Arabic (Hassaniya and Moroccan), French, Berber dialects, Spanish

Ethnic groups Mainly of Arab and Berber descent

Religion Sunni Muslim

Physical features Located in NW Africa, between Morocco (N), Mauritania (S), and Atlantic Ocean (E); low, flat terrain rising to small mountains in S and NE.

Climate Hot, dry desert; limited rainfall; fog and heavy dew produced by cold offshore currents.

Currency 1 Moroccan Dirham (DH) = 100 Moroccan francs

Economy Limited by low rainfall and few natural resources; fishing and phosphate mining are main sources of income.

History Spanish province known as Spanish Sahara (Western Sahara) since 1884; partitioned by Morocco and Mauritania after its Spanish status ended in 1975; independence proclaimed in 1976, as Saharan Arab Democratic Republic (SADR); Morocco refused to withdraw its claim to the region, resulting in fighting between Morocco and Polisario guerrillas; Mauritania withdrew its claim after signing a peace treaty with the Polisario Front, 1979; SADR admitted to the Organization of African Unity, 1982; UN-supervised talks to decide the region's future, 1990; Polisario guerrilla warfare stopped

☐ International Airport – – Boundary status disputed

under UN ceasefire, 1991; renewed fighting, 1993; agreement to UN proposal for a referendum, 1994, but implementation postponed, 1996.

Main SADR government leaders [a]

Head of State
1982–   Mohammed Abdelazziz

Head of Government
1999–   Bouchraya Hamoudi Bayoune

[a] Officially administered by Morocco and the Moroccan government.

YEMEN

Local name al-Yaman (Arabic)

Timezone GMT +3

Area 531 570 km²/205 186 sq mi

Population total (2002e) 19 495 000

Status Republic

Date of independence 1967

Capitals Sana (political), Aden (commercial)

Languages Arabic (official), English

Ethnic groups Arab (96%), with Indo-Pakistani, Somali, Amhara and Swahili, Persian, Jewish, and European minorities

Religions Muslim (Sunni 53%, Shiite 47%), small Christian, Hindu, and Yemeni Jew minorities

Physical features Occupies the SW corner of the Arabian peninsula; narrow coastal plain, backed by mountains rising to 3000–3500 m/10 000–11 500 ft; highlands, central plateau and maritime range of former South Yemen form the most fertile part of the country; former North Yemen is largely desert and mountainous.

Climate Hot and humid climate; lowland and desert regions in NE receive an average annual rainfall of 100 mm/ 4 in; hot and humid on Tihamat coastal strip with mean temperature of 29°C; mild and temperate in interior highlands, with cool winters; average annual temperatures 24°C (Jan), 32°C (Jul) in Aden; average annual rainfall, 46 mm/1.8 in.

Currency 1 Yemeni Riyal (YR, YRI) = 100 fils (former N Yemen)

Economy Based on agriculture (largely subsistence) and light industry; cotton has overtaken coffee as chief cash crop; irrigation schemes likely to increase area under cultivation; qat, a narcotic leaf, now a major enterprise; hides, vegetables, dried fish; crude- and refined-oil industry; textiles, cement, aluminium, salt.

GDP (2002e) $15.07 bn, per capita $800

HDI (2002) 0.479

History Part of the Minaean kingdom, 1200–650 BC; converted to Islam, 7th-c; Turkish occupation, 1538–1630 and 1872–1918; between and after Turkish rule, Yemen under the rule of the Hamid al-Din dynasty; sovereignty of Yemen acknowledged by Saudi Arabia and Britain, 1934; joined Arab League, 1945; Egypt-backed revolution in 1962, resulting in civil war; Yemen Arab Republic (North Yemen) declared, 1962; royalists defeated, 1969; neighbouring People's Republic of South Yemen established, 1967, when Britain ended 129 years of rule in Aden and the Marxist National Liberation Front took over; the People's Republic comprised Aden and 16 of the 20 protectorate states once under British control; renamed People's Democratic Republic of Yemen, 1970; negotiations to merge the two Yemens, 1979; unification proclaimed and ratified, 1990; new state called Republic of Yemen; former President of North Yemen declared President of the unified state, and former President of South Yemen became Prime Minister; supported Iraq during Gulf War, 1991; coalition government formed, 1993, governed by a President, Prime Minister, House of Representatives and Advisory Council; South Yemen declared independence as Democratic Republic of Yemen, 1994; subsequent civil war won by North Yemen.

Head of State
1990–   Ali Abdullah Saleh

Head of Government
2001–   Abd al-Qadir Ba Jammal

☐ International Airport   ---- No defined boundary

YUGOSLAVIA >> SERBIA AND MONTENEGRO

ZAMBIA

Local name Zambia

Timezone GMT +2

Area 752 613 km²/290 586 sq mi

Population total (2002e) 9 959 000

Status Independent republic within the Commonwealth

Date of independence 1964

Capital Lusaka

Languages English (official), with c.70 local languages (including Tonga, Kaonde, Lunda, and Luvale) also spoken

Ethnic groups Bantu (99%), including Bemba, Nyanja, Barotse, Mambwe, and Swahili peoples

Religions Christian (75%), local beliefs (23%), Muslim and Hindu (1%)

Physical features High plateau in SC Africa, altitude 1000–1400 m/3300–4600 ft; highest point, 2067 m/6781 ft, SE of Mbala; a number of rivers drain southwards to join Zambezi R in N, including R Luangwa; highest waterfall, Kalambo Falls, 221 m/726 ft; artificial L Kariba in S, 440 km²/170 sq mi.

Climate Warm temperate climate on plateau; tropical in lower valleys; although in C Africa and subequatorial, protected from very high temperatures by altitude; three distinct seasons, hot, dry (Aug–Oct), warm, wet (Nov–Apr), dry, cool (May–Jul); average annual temperatures, 21°C (Jan), 16°C (Jul) in Lusaka; average annual rainfall 840 mm/33 in.

Currency 1 Kwacha (K) = 100 ngwee

☐ International Airport   ∴ World heritage site

Economy Based on copper and cobalt, (provide over 50% of national income); lead, zinc, coal; corn, tobacco, rice, sugar cane, groundnuts, cotton; sugar refining, glassware, tyres, brewing, oil refining.

GDP (2002e) $8.24 bn, per capita $800

HDI (2002) 0.433

History European influence followed Livingstone's

HUMAN GEOGRAPHY

Zambia (continued)

discovery of the Victoria Falls, 1855; administered by the British South Africa Company under Rhodes; Northern and Southern Rhodesia declared a British sphere of influence, 1889–90; became Northern Rhodesia, 1911; British Crown Colony, 1924; joined with Southern Rhodesia and Nyasaland as the Federation of Rhodesia and Nyasaland, 1953; Federation dissolved, 1963; independence as the Republic of Zambia, 1964; governed by a President and National Assembly; new multi-party constitution adopted in 1991.

Head of State (President)
1991–2002 Frederick Chiluba
2002–   Levy Mwanawasa

Head of Government (Vice-President)
2003–   Nevers Mumba

ZIMBABWE

Local name Zimbabwe

Timezone GMT +2

Area 390 759 km²/150 873 sq mi

Population total (2002e) 11 377 000

Status Independent republic within the Commonwealth

Date of independence 1980

Capital Harare

Languages English (official), Ndebele and Shona widely spoken

Ethnic groups Bantu (97%) (including Shona 71%, Ndebele 16%), European (2%)

Religions Syncretic Christian/local beliefs (50%), Christian (25%), traditional animist beliefs (24%), small Muslim minority

Physical features Landlocked country in SC Africa; mostly savannah (tropical grassland); Highveld ridge crosses SW to NE to join the Inyanga Mts on Mozambique border, highest point, Mt Inyangani, 2592 m/8504 ft; Highveld flanked by lower plateau, Middleveld; Lowveld, altitude, 300 m/1000 ft, lies NE; tropical hardwood forests (SE); chief rivers, Zambezi, Limpopo, and Sabi.

Climate Subtropical climate, strongly influenced by altitude; average annual temperature 21°C (Jan), 14°C (Jul) in Harare; average annual rainfall 828 mm/33 in; rainfall increases from SW to NE; wet season (Nov–Mar).

Currency 1 Zimbabwe Dollar (Z$) = 100 cents

Economy Agriculture (involves 70% of population), manufacturing and mining; sugar, cotton, livestock; natural resources, gold, copper, chrome, nickel, tin, asbestos; tourism to national parks; major industries in steel, textiles, vehicles, and chemicals.

GDP (2002e) $26.07 bn, per capita $2100

HDI (2002) 0.551

History Mediaeval Bantu kingdom during 12–16th-c, with capital at Great Zimbabwe; visited by Livingstone in the 1850s; Southern Rhodesia under British influence in the 1880s as British South Africa Company under Cecil Rhodes; divided into Northern and Southern Rhodesia, 1911; Southern Rhodesia became self-governing British colony, 1923; Northern and Southern Rhodesia and Nyasaland formed multi-racial federation, 1953; independence of Nyasaland and Northern Rhodesia, 1963;

□ International Airport ∴ World heritage site

opposition to independence of Southern Rhodesia under African rule resulted in Unilateral Declaration of Independence (UDI) by white-dominated government, 1965; economic sanctions and internal guerrilla activity forced government to negotiate with main African groups: Zimbabwe African People's Union (ZAPU), led by Joshua Nkomo, Zimbabwe African National Union (ZANU), led by Robert Mugabe, and United African National Council (UANC), led by Bishop Abel Muzorewa; independence as Republic of Zimbabwe, 1980; since 1987, post of executive President combined posts of Head of State and Head of Government; bicameral legislature replaced, 1990, by new single-chamber Parliament, the House of Assembly; political crisis over land redistribution, focused on white farmers, 2000 and ongoing; increasing international concern over internal democracy, especially in relation to election process, 2002; suspended from Commonwealth for one year, 2002; reaffirmed, 2003, after which Mugabe withdrew Zimbabwe from the organization; Mugabe reelected, Mar 2005.

Head of State/Government
1987–   Robert Gabriel Mugabe

Population

Growth of world population
by billion and year.

World population	Year	Elapsed years
1 billion	1805	indefinite
2 billion	1926	121
3 billion	1960	34
4 billion	1974	14
5 billion	1987	13
6 billion	1999	12
7 billion	2010	11
8 billion	2023	13
9 billion	2040	17
10 billion	2070	30

The projected slowing down of world population growth to a peak of 10 billion in 2070 is based on the following assumptions: increased use of contraception in developing countries, and an ageing of the global population (with fertile adults making up a smaller percentage of the whole).

Population growth 1985–2155

— Africa — — — Europe, Middle East and North Africa
— Asia · · · · · Latin America and the Caribbean

Projected population growth, by geographic region

Region	Population (millions)		Growth rate (%)		Birth rate (per 1000)		Death rate (per 1000)	
	1995	2025	1990–5	2020–5	1990–5	2020–5	1990–5	2020–5
World	5734	8188	1.65	0.94	25.7	17.6	9.2	8.2
Africa	878	1495	2.87	1.74	42.3	24.1	13.8	6.7
Asia	3247	4758	1.73	0.89	25.9	17.0	8.5	8.1
America	773	1035	1.49	0.72	21.9	15.3	7.3	8.2
Europe	807	863	0.45	0.15	14.4	13.0	9.8	11.5
Oceania	29	36	1.57	0.59	19.3	15.0	7.8	9.1

UK population summary

	United Kingdom			England and Wales			Wales	Scotland			Northern Ireland		
	Persons	Males	Females	Persons	Males	Females	Persons	Persons	Males	Females	Persons	Males	Females
Enumerated population: census figures (thousands)													
1801	–	–	–	8893	4255	4638	587	1608	739	869	–	–	–
1851	22259	10855	11404	17928	8781	9146	1163	2889	1376	1513	1442	698	745
1901	38237	18492	19745	32528	15729	16799	2013	4472	2174	2298	1237	590	647
1911	42082	20357	21725	36070	17446	18625	2421	4761	2309	2452	1251	603	648
1921ᵃ	44027	21033	22994	37887	18075	19811	2656	4882	2348	2535	1258	610	648
1931ᵃ	46038	22060	23978	39952	19133	20819	2593	4843	2326	2517	1243	601	642
1951	50225	24118	26107	43758	21016	22742	2599	5096	2434	2662	1371	668	703
1961	52709	25481	27228	46105	22304	23801	2644	5179	2483	2697	1425	694	731
1966ᵇ	53788	26044	27745	47136	22841	24295	2663	5168	2479	2689	1485	724	761
1971	55515	26952	28562	48750	23683	25067	2731	5229	2515	2714	1536	755	781
1981	55848	27104	28742	49155	23873	25281	2792	5131	2466	2664	1533	750	783
1991	56467	27344	29123	49890	24182	25707	2891	5107	2470	2637	1601	781	820
2001	58789	28581	30208	52042	25327	26715	2903	5062	2432	2630	1685	821	864
Resident population: mid-year estimates (thousands)													
1961	52807	25528	27279	46196	22347	23849	2635	5184	2485	2698	1427	696	732
1962	53292	25826	27465	46657	22631	24026	2652	5198	2495	2703	1437	700	737
1963	53625	25992	27633	46973	22787	24186	2664	5205	2500	2705	1447	705	741
1964	53991	26191	27800	47324	22978	24346	2677	5208	2501	2707	1458	711	747
1965	54350	26368	27982	47671	23151	24521	2693	5210	2501	2709	1468	716	752
1966	54643	26511	28132	47966	23296	24671	2702	5201	2496	2704	1476	719	757
1967	54959	26673	28286	48272	23451	24821	2710	5198	2496	2702	1489	726	763
1968	55214	26784	28429	48511	23554	24957	2715	5200	2498	2702	1503	733	770
1969	55461	26908	28553	48738	23666	25072	2722	5208	2503	2706	1514	739	776
1970	55632	26992	28611	48891	23738	25153	2729	5214	2507	2707	1527	747	781
1971	55928	27167	28761	49152	23897	25255	2740	5236	2516	2720	1540	755	786
1972	56097	27259	28837	49327	23989	25339	2755	5231	2513	2717	1539	758	782
1973	56223	27332	28891	49459	24061	25399	2773	5234	2515	2719	1530	756	774

POLITICS

United Nations membership

Grouped according to year of entry. 191 members (as of May 2004).

1945	Argentina, Australia, Belgium, Belorussian SSR (Belarus, 1991), Bolivia, Brazil, Canada, Chile, China (Taiwan to 1971), Colombia, Costa Rica, Cuba, Czechoslovakia (to 1993), Denmark, Dominican Republic, Ecuador, Egypt, El Salvador, Ethiopia, France, Greece, Guatemala, Haiti, Honduras, India, Iran, Iraq, Lebanon, Liberia, Luxembourg, Mexico, Netherlands, New Zealand, Nicaragua, Norway, Panama, Paraguay, Peru, Philippines, Poland, Saudi Arabia, South Africa, Syria, Turkey, Ukranian SSR (Ukraine, 1991), USSR (Russia, 1991), UK, USA, Uruguay, Venezuela, Yugoslavia[a] (to 1992)
1946	Afghanistan, Iceland, Sweden, Thailand
1947	Pakistan, Yemen (N, to 1990)
1948	Burma (Myanmar, 1989)
1949	Israel
1950	Indonesia
1955	Albania, Austria, Bulgaria, Cambodia, Ceylon (Sri Lanka, 1970), Finland, Hungary, Ireland, Italy, Jordan, Laos, Libya, Nepal, Portugal, Romania, Spain
1956	Japan, Morocco, Sudan, Tunisia
1957	Ghana, Malaya (Malaysia, 1963)
1958	Guinea
1960	Cameroon, Central African Republic, Chad, Congo, Côte d'Ivoire, Cyprus, Dahomey (Benin, 1975), Gabon, Madagascar, Mali, Niger, Nigeria, Senegal, Somalia, Togo, Upper Volta (Burkina Faso, 1984), Democratic Republic of Congo (formerly Zaire)
1961	Mauritania, Mongolia, Sierra Leone, Tanganyika (within Tanzania, 1964)
1962	Algeria, Burundi, Jamaica, Rwanda, Trinidad and Tobago, Uganda
1963	Kenya, Kuwait, Zanzibar (within Tanzania, 1964)

1964	Malawi, Malta, Tanzania, Zambia
1965	Maldives, Singapore, The Gambia
1966	Barbados, Botswana, Guyana, Lesotho
1967	Yemen (S, to 1990)
1968	Equatorial Guinea, Mauritius, Swaziland
1970	Fiji
1971	Bahrain, Bhutan, China (People's Republic), Oman, Qatar, United Arab Emirates
1973	Bahamas, German Democratic Republic (within GFR, 1990), German Federal Republic
1974	Bangladesh, Grenada, Guinea-Bissau
1975	Cape Verde, Comoros, Mozambique, Papua New Guinea, São Tomé and Principe, Suriname
1976	Angola, Seychelles, Samoa (formerly Western Samoa)
1977	Djibouti, Vietnam
1978	Dominica, Solomon Islands
1979	St Lucia
1980	St Vincent and the Grenadines, Zimbabwe
1981	Antigua and Barbuda, Belize, Vanuatu
1983	St Christopher and Nevis
1984	Brunei
1990	Liechtenstein, Namibia, Yemen (formerly N Yemen and S Yemen)
1991	Estonia, Federated States of Micronesia, Latvia, Lithuania, Marshall Islands, N Korea, S Korea
1992	Armenia, Azerbaijan, Bosnia-Herzegovina, Croatia, Georgia, Kazakhstan, Kyrgysztan, Moldova, San Marino, Slovenia, Tajikistan, Turkmenistan, Uzbekistan
1993	Andorra, Czech Republic, Eritrea, Former Yugoslav Republic of Macedonia, Monaco, Slovak Republic
1995	Belau
1999	Nauru, Tonga, Kiribati
2000	Tuvalu
2002	East Timor, Switzerland

[a] Yugoslavia was excluded from UN membership in 1992 and asked to reapply; Federal Republic of Yugoslavia admitted in 2000 (from 2002, Union of Serbia and Montenegro).

Main bodies of the United Nations

General Assembly	Plenary body which controls much of the UN's work, supervises the subsidiary organs, sets priorities, and debates major issues of international affairs.
Security Council	Has fifteen members, but is dominated by five permanent members (China, France, Russia, UK, USA). Primary role is to maintain international peace and security. Empowered to order mandatory sanctions, call for ceasefires, and establish peace-keeping forces.
Secretariat	Headed by Secretary General. Staff of 66 000 worldwide answerable to UN only and are engaged in considerable diplomatic work.
International Court of Justice	Consists of fifteen judges appointed by the Council and the Assembly. Jurisdiction depends on consent of the states who are parties to a dispute. Also offers advisory opinions to various organs of UN.
Economic and Social Council	Elected by the General Assembly. It supervises the work of various committees, commissions and expert bodies in the economic and social area, and coordinates the work of UN specialized agencies.
Trusteeship Council	Oversees the transition of Trust territories to self-government.

Specialized agencies of the United Nations

Abbreviated form	Full title and location	Area of concern
ILO	International Labour Organization, Geneva	Social justice.
FAO	Food and Agriculture, Rome	Improvement of the production and distribution of agricultural products.
UNESCO	United Nations Educational, Scientific and Cultural Organization, Paris	Stimulation of popular education and the spread of culture.
ICAO	International Civil Aviation Organization, Montreal	Encouragement of safety measures in international flight.
IBRD	International Bank for Reconstruction and Development, Washington	Aid of development through investment.
IMF	International Monetary Fund, Washington	Promotion of international monetary cooperation.
UPU	Universal Postal Union, Berne	Uniting members within a single postal territory.
WHO	World Health Organization, Geneva	Promotion of the highest standards of health for all people.
ITU	International Telecommunication Union, Geneva	Allocation of frequencies and regulation of procedures.
WMO	World Meteorological Organization, Geneva	Standardization and utilization of meteorological observations.
IFC	International Finance Corporation, Washington	Promotion of the international flow of private capital.
IMCO	Inter-governmental Maritime Consultative Organization, London	The coordination of safety at sea.
IDA	International Development Association, Washington	Credit on special terms to provide assistance for less-developed countries.
WIPO	World Intellectual Property Organization, Geneva	Protection of copyright, designs, inventions, etc.
IFAD	International Fund for Agricultural Development, Rome	Increase of food production in developing countries by the generation of grants or loans.
UNIDO	United Nations Industrial Development Organization, Vienna	Promotion of industrialization of developing countries, with special emphasis on manufacturing sector. Provides technical assistance and advice, as well as help with planning.
IAEA[a]	International Atomic Energy Association, Vienna	Promotes research and development into peaceful uses of nuclear energy, and oversees system of safeguards and controls governing misuse of nuclear materials for military purposes.
UNICEF[b]	United Nations Children's Fund, New York	Provides primary healthcare and education in developing countries.
UNHCR[b]	United Nations High Commissioner for Refugees, Geneva	Protects rights and interests of refugees; organizes emergency relief and longer-term solutions, eg local integration, resettlement, or voluntary repatriation

[a]Linked to UN but not specialized agency. [b]Specialized bodies established by the General Assembly and supervised jointly with the Economic and Social Council.

United Nations Secretaries General

1946–53	Trygve Lie *Norway*
1953–61	Dag Hammarskjöld *Sweden*
1962–71	U Thant *Burma*
1972–81	Kurt Waldheim *Austria*
1982–92	Javier Pérez de Cuéllar *Peru*
1992–7	Boutros Boutros Ghali *Egypt*
1997–	Kofi Annan *Ghana*

Commonwealth Secretaries General

1965–75	Arnold Smith *Canada*
1975–90	Shridath S Ramphal *Guyana*
1990–9	Emeka Anyaoku *Nigeria*
1999–	Don McKinnon *New Zealand*

SOCIETY

Commonwealth members

The 'Commonwealth' is a free association of independent nations formerly subject to British imperial government, and maintaining friendly and practical links with the UK. In 1931 the Statute of Westminster established the British Commonwealth of Nations; the adjective 'British' was deleted after World War 2. Most of the states granted independence, beginning with India in 1947, chose to be members of the Commonwealth.

Name of country	Year of joining	Name of country	Year of joining	Name of country	Year of joining
Antigua & Barbuda[a]	1981	Kenya	1963	St Vincent & the Grenadines[a]	1979
Australia[a]	1931	Kiribati	1979	Samoa	1970
Bahamas[a]	1973	Lesotho	1966	Seychelles	1976
Bangladesh	1972	Malawi	1964	Sierra Leone	1961
Barbados[a]	1966	Malaysia	1957	Singapore	1965
Belize[a]	1981	Maldives	1982	Solomon Islands[a]	1978
Botswana	1966	Malta	1964	South Africa	left 1961
Brunei	1984	Mauritius	1968		rejoined 1994
Cameroon	1995	Mozambique	1995	Sri Lanka	1948
Canada[a]	1931	Namibia	1990	Swaziland	1968
Cyprus	1961	Nauru	1968	Tanzania	1961
Dominica	1978	New Zealand[a]	1931	Tonga	1970
Fiji	1970	Nigeria	1960	Trinidad & Tobago	1962
	left 1987, readmitted 1997	suspended 1995, readmitted 1999		Tuvalu[a]	1978
Gambia, The	1965	Pakistan	1947	Uganda	1962
Ghana	1957	left 1972, rejoined 1989, left 1999		United Kingdom	1931
Grenada[a]	1974		readmitted 2004	Vanuatu	1980
Guyana	1966	Papua New Guinea[a]	1975	Zambia	1964
India	1947	St Kitts & Nevis[a]	1983	Zimbabwe	1980
Jamaica[a]	1962	St Lucia[a]	1979	suspended 2002, withdrew 2003	

[a] Member states recognizing the Queen, represented by a Governor-General, as their Head of State.   Ireland resigned in 1949.

The European Union

Name of country and year of joining

Austria (1995)
Belgium (1958)
Czech Republic (2004)
Cyprus (2004)
Denmark (1973)
Estonia (2004)
Finland (1995)
France (1958)
Germany (1958)
Greece (1981)
Hungary (2004)
Ireland (1973)
Italy (1958)
Latvia (2004)
Lithuania (2004)
Luxembourg (1958)
Malta (2004)
Netherlands (1958)
Poland (2004)
Portugal (1986)
Slovakia (2004)
Slovenia (2004)
Spain (1986)
Sweden (1995)
United Kingdom (1973)

Negotiations are ongoing for 2007 entry with Bulgaria and Romania, with Turkey a longer-term prospect.

Representation of political parties in the European Parliament[a]

	EPP-ED	PES	ELDR	GREENS/EFA	EUL/NGL	UEN	EDD	Others	Total
Austria	6	7	–	2	–	–	–	3	18
Belgium	7	7	5	2	–	–	–	3	24
Cyprus	2	–	1	–	2	–	–	1	6
Czech Rep	11	2	–	–	6	–	–	5	24
Denmark	1	5	4	–	1	1	1	1	14
Estonia	1	3	2	–	–	–	–	–	6
Finland	4	3	5	1	1	–	–	–	14
France	28	31	–	6	3	–	–	10	78
Germany	49	23	7	13	7	–	–	–	99
Greece	11	8	–	–	4	–	–	1	24
Hungary	13	9	2	–	–	–	–	–	24
Ireland	5	1	–	–	–	4	–	3	13
Italy	26	14	9	2	7	9	–	11	78
Latvia	3	–	1	1	–	4	–	–	9
Lithuania	3	2	3	–	–	–	–	5	13
Luxemb'g	3	1	1	1	–	–	–	–	6
Malta	2	3	–	–	–	–	–	–	5
Neth'lands	7	7	5	2	2	–	2	2	27
Poland	19	8	4	–	–	7	–	16	54
Portugal	7	12	–	–	2	2	–	1	24
Slovakia	8	3	–	–	–	–	–	3	14
Slovenia	4	1	2	–	–	–	–	–	7
Spain	24	24	2	2	2	–	–	–	54
Sweden	5	5	3	1	2	–	–	3	19
UK	28	19	12	5	–	–	12	2	78
Total	**277**	**198**	**68**	**38**	**39**	**27**	**15**	**70**	**732**

[a] The figures represent the political groupings in the parliament in 2004.

EPP-ED European People's Party; PES Party of European Socialists; ELDR European Liberal Democrat and Reform Party; GREENS/EFA European Greens; EUL/NGL European United Left – Nordic Green Left; UEN Union For A Europe of Nations; EDD Europe of Democracies and Diversities   *Source: European Parliament.*

SOCIETY

PART NINE

Religion and Mythology

GODS OF MYTHOLOGY

Principal Greek gods

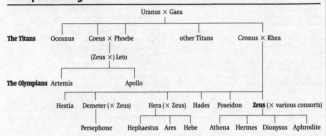

Uranus × Gaea

The Titans Oceanus Coeus × Phoebe other Titans Cronus × Rhea

(Zeus ×) Leto

The Olympians Artemis Apollo

Hestia Demeter (× Zeus) Hera (× Zeus) Hades Poseidon **Zeus** (× various consorts)

Persephone Hephaestus Ares Hebe Athena Hermes Dionysus Aphrodite

Greek gods of mythology

Aeolus God of the winds
Aphrodite Goddess of love, beauty, and procreation
Apollo God of prophecy, poetry, music, archery, and healing
Ares God of war
Artemis Goddess of the moon, hunting, and fertility
Athene Goddess of wisdom; protectress of Athens
Boreas God of the north wind
Cronus Father of Zeus
Cybele Goddess of fertility and the mountains
Demeter Goddess of fruit, crops, and vegetation
Dionysus God of wine
Eros God of love
Gaea Goddess of the earth
Hades God of the underworld
Hebe Goddess of youth
Hecate Goddess of magic, ghosts, and witchcraft
Helios God of the sun
Hephaestus God of fire

Hera Goddess of marriage and women; queen of heaven
Hermes God of science and commerce; messenger of the gods
Hestia Goddess of the hearth
Iris Goddess of the rainbow; messenger of the gods
Morpheus God of dreams
Nemesis Goddess of vengeance
Nereus Sea god
Nike Goddess of victory
Oceanus Sea god
Pan God of pastures, forests, flocks, and herds
Persephone Goddess of the underworld
Poseidon God of the sea
Rhea Mother of the gods
Selene Moon goddess
Uranus God of the sky
Zeus Overlord of the Olympian gods and goddesses; lord of heaven

Principal Roman gods

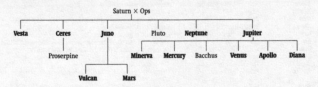

Saturn × Ops

Vesta **Ceres** **Juno** Pluto **Neptune** **Jupiter**

Proserpine **Minerva** **Mercury** Bacchus **Venus** **Apollo** **Diana**

Vulcan **Mars**

The twelve major gods of Olympus are shown in **bold** type. Bacchus in some accounts supplants Vesta. Pluto and Proserpine are gods of the Underworld.

Roman gods of mythology

Apollo God of the sun, music, poetry, prophecy, and healing
Bacchus God of wine
Bellona Goddess of war
Ceres Corn goddess
Cupid God of love
Diana Goddess of fertility, hunting, and the moon
Faunus God of prophecy
Flora Goddess of flowers
Janus God of gates and doors
Juno Goddess of marriage and women
Jupiter Supreme god; lord of heaven
Lares Gods of the household and state
Libitina Goddess of funerals
Maia Goddess of growth and increase

Mars God of war
Mercury Messenger god; also god of commerce
Minerva Goddess of wisdom, the arts, and trades
Mithras The sun god; god of light
Neptune God of the sea
Ops Goddess of fertility
Pales Goddess of flocks and shepherds
Pluto God of the underworld
Pomona Goddess of fruit trees and fruit
Proserpine Goddess of the underworld
Saturn God of seed time and harvest
Venus Goddess of beauty and love
Vertumnus God of the seasons
Vesta Goddess of the hearth
Vulcan God of fire

Norse gods of mythology

Aegir God of the sea
Aesir Race of warlike gods, including Odin, Thor, Tyr
Alcis Twin gods of the sky
Balder Son of Odin and favourite of the gods
Bor Father of Odin
Bragi God of poetry
Eir Goddess of medicine
Fafnir Dragon god
Fjorgynn Mother of Thor
Freya Goddess of love and fertility
Frey God of fertility, sun, and rain
Frigg Goddess of married love; wife of Odin
Gefion Goddess who received virgins after death
Heimdall Warden of the gods
Hel Goddess of death; Queen of Niflheim, the land of mists
Hermod Son of Odin
Hoenir Companion to Odin and Loki
Hoder Blind god who killed Balder
Idunn Guardian goddess of the golden apples of youth; wife of Bragi
Kvasir God of wise utterances
Logi Fire god

Loki God of mischief
Mimir God of wisdom
Nanna Goddess wife of Balder
Nehallenia Goddess of plenty
Nerthus Goddess of earth
Njord God of ships and the sea
Norns Goddesses of destiny
Odin (Woden, Wotan) Chief of the Aesir family of gods, the 'father' god; the god of war, learning, and poetry
Otr Otter god
Ran Goddess of the sea
Sif Goddess wife of Thor
Sigyn Goddess wife of Loki
Thor (Donar) God of thunder and sky, and good crops
Tyr God of battle, and victory
Ull God of the hunt
Valkyries Female helpers of the gods of war
Vanir Race of benevolent gods, including Njord, Frey, and Freya
Vidar Slayer of the wolf, Fenir
Vor Goddess of truth
Weland (Volundr, Weiland, Wayland) Craftsman god

Egyptian gods

	Alternative names	
Amun	Ammon, Amen, Amon	King of the gods
Anubis	Anpu	God of the dead
Aton	Aten	Sun god, later made chief and only god (for a short time)
Atum	Tem, Tum	Creator of the gods and men
Bast	Bastet, Ubasti	Goddess of music and dance
Bes	Bisu	Originally protector of the royal house, later god of recreation
Buto	Edjo, Udjo, Wadjet, Wadjit	Goddess of Lower Egypt and defender of the King
Geb	Keb, Seb	God of the earth
Hapi	Hap, Hep, Apis	God of the Nile
Hathor	Athyr	Originally a personification of the sky, also goddess of love and festivity
Horus	Hor	Originally the god of Lower Egypt, later identified with the reigning King
Isis	Aset, Eset	Queen of the gods
Khenty-Imentiu	Khenti-Amentiu	Warrior god, god of the underworld before Osiris
Khnum	Khnemu	God of the cataract region, earlier associated with the underworld
Khons	Khensu, Khonsu, Chons	Moon god

	Alternative names	
Ma'at	Mayet	Goddess of law, truth, and justice
Min		God of fertility and harvest
Mont	Mentu, Month	War god of Upper Egypt, also lord of the sky with Re
Nefertum	Nefertem, Nefertemu	God of the lotus
Neith	Neit	Goddess of the loom and war
Nekhbet	Nekhbet	Protectress of childbirth
Nut	Neuth, Nuit	Goddess of the sky
Osiris	Usire	Originally fertility god, later supreme god, king of the underworld
Ptah	Phtah	God of fertility, creator of the universe
Re	Phra, Ra	King of the gods, chief state god
Sati	Satet, Satis	Goddess of the inundation and of fertility
Seker	Sokar, Sokaris	God of darkness and decay
Seshat	Sesheta	Goddess of writing and history
Shu		God of light and supporter of the sky
Taurt	Apet, Opet, Tawaret, Thoueris	Goddess of maternity
Thoth	Djhowtey	Moon god

MODERN RELIGIONS

Religion	Branch/ denomination	Sacred texts	State religion in	Estimated no. of adherents (worldwide), mid-2003
Baha'ism		Kitabal-Aqdas, Haft Wadi, Bayan, al-Kalimat al-Maknnah		7 503 000
Buddhism	Therevada Mahayana Tantrism	Tripitaka	Bhutan, Cambodia, Thailand	372 974 000
Christianity	Anglican Baptist Church of Christ Lutheran Methodist Mormon Orthodox Pentecostal Presbyterian Roman Catholic	Bible Book of Mormon	UK (England) Denmark, Iceland, Norway, Sweden Greece UK (Scotland) Argentina, Bolivia, Costa Rica, Dominican Republic, Malta, Paraguay, Peru	2 069 883 000
Confucianism		The Analects, Su Ching, Shi Ching, Li Chi, I Ching, Lu		6 425 300
Hinduism	Vishnu Shiva Shakti	Rigveda, Yajurveda, Samaveda, Atharveda	Nepal	837 262 000
Islam (Muslim)	Sunni Shi'a Sufi Ismaili	Koran, Hadith	Afghanistan, Algeria, Bahrain, Bangladesh, Comoros, Egypt, Iran, Iraq, Jordan, Kuwait, Libya, Malaysia, Maldives, Mauritania, Morocco, Oman, Pakistan, Qatar, Saudi Arabia, Somalia, Sudan, Tunisia, United Arab Emirates, Yemen	1 254 222 000
Jainism	Digambara Swetambara	Siddhanta, Pakrit texts		4 413 700
Judaism		Torah, Talmud		14 551 000
Sikhism		Guru Granth Sahib (Adi Granth)		24 295 200
Shintoism		Kojiki, Nohon Shoki		2 680 300

Books of the Bible

Old Testament
Law (Pentateuch)
Genesis
Exodus
Leviticus
Numbers
Deuteronomy

Prophets
(FORMER)
Joshua
Judges
Samuel 1 & 2
Kings 1 & 2

(LATTER)
Isaiah
Jeremiah
Ezekiel
Book of twelve prophets (Hosea, Joel, Amos, Obadiah, Jonah, Micah, Nahum, Habakkuk, Zephaniah, Haggai, Zechariah, Malachi)

Writings
Psalms
Proverbs
Job
Song of Songs
Ruth
Lamentations
Ecclesiastes
Esther
Daniel
Ezra
Nehemiah
Chronicles 1 & 2

New Testament
Gospels (Matthew, Mark, Luke, John)
Acts of the Apostles
13 Letters attributed to Paul (Romans, Corinthians 1 & 2, Galatians, Ephesians, Philippians, Colossians, Thessalonians 1 & 2, Timothy 1 & 2, Titus, Philemon)
Letter to the Hebrews
7 General or 'Catholic' letters (James, Peter 1 & 2, John 1, 2 & 3, Jude)
Book of Revelation

Apocrypha
Baruch
Additions to the Book of Daniel
Book of Ecclesiasticus
Additions to the Book of Esther
Books of Esdras
Letter of Jeremiah
Book of Judith
Books of the Maccabees
Book of Tobit (Tobias)
Wisdom of Solomon

The Old Testament Apocrypha are a collection of Jewish writings found in the Greek version of the Hebrew Bible, but not found in the Hebrew Bible itself. Roman Catholics consider them as inspired and authoritative, and deuterocanonical, while Protestants attribute less authority to them.

New Testament Apocrypha are Christian documents similar in title, form, or content to many New Testament works, being called Gospels, Acts, Epistles, or Apocalypses, but are not widely accepted as canonical.

Christian religious vestments

alb A long white garment reaching to the ankles; derived from an ancient tunic.

amice A linen square worn round the back to protect the other vestments; formerly a neckcloth.

apparels Ornamental panels at the foot of the alb, front and back, and on the amice.

cassock The long black gown worn under other vestments; formerly, the daily working costume of the clergy.

chasuble The outer sleeveless vestment worn by a priest or bishop when celebrating Holy Communion; derived from the commonest outdoor garment of classical times.

chimere Worn by bishops over the rochet; of black or scarlet, open at the front.

cope In the pre-Christian era, a long cloak; now a costly embroidered vestment, semi-circular in shape, worn by bishops and priests on special occasions.

cotta Similar to the surplice, but shorter, especially in the sleeves; sometimes used by clergy and servers in place of the surplice.

girdle Cord worn about the waist.

hood Worn by clergy at choir offices, a mediaeval headdress, now worn hanging down the back; it denotes a university degree.

maniple Worn over the left arm by bishops, priests, and deacons at the Eucharist; originally a napkin.

orphreys The embroidered strips, customarily cross-shaped, on a chasuble.

rochet Worn by bishops, similar to an alb, but used without girdle or apparels.

stole Once a napkin or towel carried by servants on the left shoulder; now folded and narrow, worn over both shoulders.

surplice Of white linen, reaching to the knees; worn by choir and servers as well as clergy.

Holy orders

Major orders Bishop, Priest, Deacon, (Sub-deacon)
Minor orders Porter, Lector, Exorcist, Acolyte

In the Roman Catholic church there are now only the orders of Bishop, Priest, Deacon and the ministries of acolyte and lector, following the *motu proprio* of Pope Paul VI, 1973.

Movable Christian feasts

Dates for the years 2000–2010.

Year	Ash Wednesday	Easter	Ascension	Whit Sunday[a]	Trinity Sunday	Corpus Christi	First Sunday in Advent
2000	8 Mar	23 Apr	1 Jun	11 Jun	18 Jun	22 Jun	3 Dec
2001	28 Feb	15 Apr	24 May	3 Jun	10 Jun	14 Jun	2 Dec
2002	13 Feb	31 Mar	9 May	19 May	26 May	30 May	1 Dec
2003	5 Mar	20 Apr	29 May	8 Jun	15 Jun	19 Jun	30 Nov
2004	25 Feb	11 Apr	20 May	30 May	6 June	10 Jun	28 Nov
2005	9 Feb	27 Mar	5 May	15 May	22 May	26 May	27 Nov
2006	1 Mar	16 Apr	25 May	4 Jun	11 Jun	15 Jun	3 Dec
2007	21 Feb	8 Apr	17 May	27 May	3 Jun	7 Jun	2 Dec
2008	6 Feb	23 Mar	1 May	11 May	18 May	22 May	30 Nov
2009	25 Feb	12 Apr	21 May	31 May	7 Jun	11 Jun	29 Nov
2010	17 Feb	4 Apr	13 May	23 May	30 May	3 Jun	28 Nov

Ash Wednesday, the first day of Lent, can fall at the earliest on 4 Feb and at the latest on 10 Mar.

Palm (Passion) Sunday is the Sunday before Easter; Good Friday is the Friday before Easter; Holy Saturday (often referred to as Easter Saturday) is the Saturday before Easter; Easter Saturday, in traditional usage, is the Saturday following Easter.

Easter Day can fall at the earliest on 22 Mar and at the latest on 25 Apr. Ascension Day can fall at the earliest on 30 Apr and at the latest on 3 Jun. Whit Sunday can fall at the earliest on 10 May and at the latest on 13 Jun. There are not fewer than 22 and not more than 27 Sundays after Trinity. The first Sunday of Advent is the Sunday nearest to 30 Nov.

[a]Whit Sunday commemorates the day of Pentecost.

Major immovable Christian feasts

Jan 1	Solemenity of Mary, Mother of God	Aug 22	Queenship of Mary
Jan 6	Epiphany	Sep 8	Birthday of the Virgin Mary
Jan 7	Christmas Day (Eastern Orthodox)[a]	Sep 14	Exaltation of the Holy Cross
Jan 11	Baptism of Jesus	Oct 2	Guardian Angels
Jan 25	Conversion of Apostle Paul	Nov 1	All Saints
Feb 2	Presentation of Jesus (Candlemas Day)	Nov 2	All Souls
Feb 22	The Chair of Peter, Apostle	Nov 9	Dedication of the Lateran Basilica
Mar 25	Annunciation of the Virgin Mary	Nov 21	Presentation of the Virgin Mary
Jun 24	Birth of John the Baptist	Dec 8	Immaculate Conception
Aug 6	Transfiguration	Dec 25	Christmas Day
Aug 15	Assumption of the Virgin Mary	Dec 28	Holy Innocents

[a]Fixed feasts in the Julian Calendar fall 13 days later than the Gregorian Calendar date.

The dates of Easter

Dates for the years 1900–2099.

	0	---1	---2	---3	---4	---5	---6	---7	---8	---9
1900	15 Apr	7 Apr	30 Mar	12 Apr	3 Apr	23 Apr	15 Apr	31 Mar	19 Apr	11 Apr
1910	27 Mar	16 Apr	7 Apr	23 Mar	12 Apr	4 Apr	23 Apr	8 Apr	31 Mar	20 Apr
1920	4 Apr	27 Mar	16 Apr	1 Apr	20 Apr	12 Apr	4 Apr	17 Apr	8 Apr	31 Mar
1930	20 Apr	5 Apr	27 Mar	16 Apr	1 Apr	21 Apr	12 Apr	28 Mar	17 Apr	9 Apr
1940	24 Mar	13 Apr	5 Apr	25 Apr	9 Apr	1 Apr	21 Apr	6 Apr	28 Mar	17 Apr
1950	9 Apr	25 Mar	13 Apr	5 Apr	18 Apr	10 Apr	1 Apr	21 Apr	6 Apr	29 Mar
1960	17 Apr	2 Apr	22 Apr	14 Apr	29 Mar	18 Apr	10 Apr	26 Mar	14 Apr	6 Apr
1970	29 Mar	11 Apr	2 Apr	22 Apr	14 Apr	30 Mar	18 Apr	10 Apr	26 Mar	15 Apr
1980	6 Apr	19 Apr	11 Apr	3 Apr	22 Apr	7 Apr	30 Mar	19 Apr	3 Apr	26 Mar
1990	15 Apr	31 Mar	19 Apr	11 Apr	3 Apr	16 Apr	7 Apr	30 Mar	12 Apr	4 Apr
2000	23 Apr	15 Apr	31 Mar	20 Apr	11 Apr	27 Mar	16 Apr	8 Apr	23 Mar	12 Apr
2010	4 Apr	24 Apr	8 Apr	31 Mar	20 Apr	5 Apr	27 Mar	16 Apr	1 Apr	21 Apr
2020	12 Apr	4 Apr	17 Apr	9 Apr	31 Mar	20 Apr	5 Apr	28 Mar	16 Apr	1 Apr
2030	21 Apr	13 Apr	28 Mar	17 Apr	9 Apr	25 Mar	13 Apr	5 Apr	25 Apr	10 Apr
2040	1 Apr	21 Apr	6 Apr	29 Mar	17 Apr	9 Apr	25 Mar	14 Apr	5 Apr	18 Apr
2050	10 Apr	2 Apr	21 Apr	6 Apr	29 Mar	18 Apr	2 Apr	22 Apr	14 Apr	30 Mar
2060	18 Apr	10 Apr	26 Mar	15 Apr	6 Apr	29 Mar	11 Apr	3 Apr	22 Apr	14 Apr
2070	30 Mar	19 Apr	10 Apr	26 Mar	15 Apr	7 Apr	19 Apr	11 Apr	3 Apr	23 Apr
2080	7 Apr	30 Mar	19 Apr	4 Apr	26 Mar	15 Apr	31 Mar	20 Apr	11 Apr	3 Apr
2090	16 Apr	8 Apr	30 Mar	12 Apr	4 Apr	24 Apr	15 Apr	31 Mar	20 Apr	12 Apr

RELIGION AND MYTHOLOGY

Saints' days

The official recognition of Saints, and the choice of a Saint's Day, varies greatly between different branches of Christianity, calendars, and localities. Only major variations are included below, using the following abbreviations:

C Coptic   G Greek
E Eastern   W Western

January

1 Basil (E); Fulgentius; Telemachus
2 Basil and Gregory of Nazianzus (W); Macarius of Alexandria; Seraphim of Sarov
3 Geneviève
4 Angela of Foligno
5 Simeon Stylites (W)
7 Cedda; Lucian of Antioch (W); Raymond of Penyafort
8 Atticus (E); Gudule; Severinus
9 Hadrian the African
10 Agatho; Marcian
11 Ailred; Benedict Biscop
13 Hilary of Poitiers
14 Kentigern
15 Macarius of Egypt; Maurus; Paul of Thebes
16 Honoratus
17 Antony of Egypt
19 Wulfstan
20 Euthymius; Fabian; Sebastian
21 Agnes; Fructuosus; Maximus (E); Meinrad
22 Timothy (G); Vincent
23 Ildefonsus
24 Babylas (W); Francis of Sales
25 Gregory of Nazianzus (E)
26 Paula; Timothy and Titus; Xenophon (E)
27 Angela Merici
28 Ephraem Syrus (E); Paulinus of Nola; Thomas Aquinas
29 Gildas
31 John Bosco; Marcella

February

1 Bride; Pionius
3 Anskar; Blaise (W); Werburga; Simeon (E)
4 Gilbert of Sempringham; Isidore of Pelusium; Phileas
5 Agatha; Avitus
6 Dorothy; Paul Miki and companions; Vedast
8 Theodore (G); Jerome Emiliani
9 Teilo
10 Scholastica
11 Benedict of Aniane; Blaise (E); Caedmon; Gregory II
12 Meletius
13 Agabus (W); Catherine dei Ricci; Priscilla (E)
14 Cyril and Methodius (W); Valentine (W)

16 Flavian (E); Pamphilus (E); Valentine (G)
18 Bernadette (France); Colman; Flavian (W); Leo I (E)
20 Wulfric
21 Peter Damian
23 Polycarp
25 Ethelbert; Tarasius; Walburga
26 Alexander (W); Porphyrius
27 Leander
28 Oswald of York

March

1 David
2 Chad; Simplicius
3 Ailred
4 Casimir
6 Chrodegang
7 Perpetua and Felicity
8 Felix; John of God; Pontius
9 Frances of Rome; Gregory of Nyssa; Pacian
10 John Ogilvie; Macarius of Jerusalem; Simplicius
11 Constantine; Oengus; Sophronius
12 Gregory (the Great)
13 Nicephorus
14 Benedict (E)
15 Clement Hofbauer
17 Gertrude; Joseph of Arimathea (W); Patrick
18 Anselm of Lucca; Cyril of Jerusalem; Edward
19 Joseph (W)
20 Cuthbert; John of Parma; Martin of Braga
21 Serapion of Thmuis
22 Catherine of Sweden; Nicholas of Flüe
23 Turibius de Mongrovejo
30 John Climacus

April

1 Hugh of Grenoble; Mary of Egypt (E); Melito
2 Francis of Paola; Mary of Egypt (W)
3 Richard of Chichester
4 Isidore of Seville
5 Juliana of Liège; Vincent Ferrer
7 Hegesippus; John Baptist de la Salle
8 Agabus (E)
10 Fulbert
11 Gemma Galgani; Guthlac; Stanislaus
12 Julius I; Zeno
13 Martin I
15 Aristarchus; Pudus (E); Trophimus of Ephesus
17 Agapetus (E); Stephen Harding
18 Mme Acarie
19 Alphege; Leo IX
21 Anastasius (E); Anselm; Beuno; Januarius (E)

22 Alexander (C)
23 George
24 Egbert; Fidelis of Sigmaringen; Mellitus
25 Mark; Phaebadius
27 Zita
28 Peter Chanel; Vitalis and Valeria
29 Catherine of Siena; Hugh of Cluny; Peter Martyr; Robert
30 James (the Great) (E); Pius V

May

1 Asaph; Joseph the Worker; Walburga
2 Athanasius
3 Phillip and James (the Less) (W)
4 Gotthard
5 Hilary of Arles
7 John of Beverley
8 John (E); Peter of Tarantaise
10 Antoninus; Comgall; John of Avila; Simon (E)
11 Cyril and Methodius (E); Mamertus
12 Epiphanius; Nereus and Achilleus; Pancras
14 Matthias (W)
16 Brendan; John of Nepomuk; Simon Stock
17 Robert Bellarmine; Paschal Baylon
18 John I
19 Dunstan; Ivo; Pudens (W); Pudentiana (W)
20 Bernardino of Siena
21 Helena (E)
22 Rita of Cascia
23 Ivo of Chartres
24 Vincent of Lérins
25 Aldhelm; Bede; Gregory VII; Mary Magdalene de Pazzi
26 Philip Neri; Quadratus
27 Augustine of Canterbury
30 Joan of Arc

June

1 Justin Martyr; Pamphilus
2 Erasmus; Marcellinus and Peter; Nicephorus (G); Pothinus
3 Charles Lwanga and companions; Clotilde; Kevin
4 Optatus; Petrock
5 Boniface
6 Martha (E); Norbert
7 Paul of Constantinople (W); Willibald
8 William of York
9 Columba; Cyril of Alexandria (E); Ephraem (W)
11 Barnabas; Bartholomew (E)
12 Leo III
13 Anthony of Padua
15 Orsisius; Vitus
17 Alban; Botulph

19 Gervasius and Protasius; Jude
   (E); Romuald
20 Alban
21 Alban of Mainz; Aloysius
   Gonzaga
22 John Fisher and Thomas More;
   Niceta; Pantaenus (C);
   Paulinus of Nola
23 Etheldreda
24 Birth of John the Baptist
25 Prosper of Aquitaine
27 Cyril of Alexandria (W);
   Ladislaus
28 Irenaeus
29 Peter and Paul
30 First Martyrs of the Church of
   Rome

July
1 Cosmas and Damian (E); Oliver
   Plunket
3 Anatolius; Thomas
4 Andrew of Crete (E); Elizabeth
   of Portugal; Ulrich
5 Anthony Zaccaria
6 Maria Goretti
7 Palladius; Pantaenus
9 Kilian; Aquila and Prisca (W)
11 Benedict (W); Pius I
12 John Gualbert; Veronica
13 Henry II; Mildred; Silas
14 Camillus of Lellis; Deusdedit;
   Nicholas of the Holy
   Mountain (E)
15 Bonaventure; Jacob of Nisibis;
   Swithin; Vladimir
16 Eustathius; Our Lady of Mt
   Carmel
17 Ennodius; Leo IV; Marcellina;
   Margaret (E); Scillitan Martyrs
18 Arnulf; Philastrius
19 Marcrina; Symmachus
20 Aurelius; Margaret (W)
21 Lawrence of Brindisi; Praxedes
22 Mary Magdalene
23 Apollinaris; Bridget of Sweden
25 Anne and Joachim (E);
   Christopher; James (the Great)
   (W)
26 Anne and Joachim (W)
27 Pantaleon
28 Innocent I; Samson; Victor I
29 Lupus; Martha (W); Olave
30 Peter Chrysologus; Silas (G)
31 Giovanni Colombini;
   Germanus; Joseph of
   Arimathea (E); Ignatius of
   Loyola

August
1 Alphonsus Liguori; Ethelwold
2 Eusebius of Vercelli; Stephen I
4 Jean-Baptiste Vianney
6 Hormisdas
7 Cajetan; Sixtus II and
   companions
8 Dominic

9 Matthias (G)
10 Laurence; Oswald of
   Northumbria
11 Clare; Susanna
13 Maximus (W); Pontian and
   Hippolytus; Radegunde
14 Maximilian Kolbe
15 Arnulf; Tarsicius
16 Roch; Simplicianus; Stephen of
   Hungary
17 Hyacinth
19 John Eudes; Sebaldus
20 Bernard; Oswin; Philibert
21 Jane Frances de Chantal; Pius X
23 Rose of Lima; Sidonius
   Apollinaris
24 Bartholomew (W); Ouen
25 Joseph Calasanctius; Louis IX;
   Menas of Constantinople
26 Blessed Dominic of the Mother
   of God; Zephyrinus
27 Caesarius; Monica
28 Augustine of Hippo
29 Beheading of John the Baptist;
   Sabina
30 Pammachius
31 Aidan; Paulinus of Trier

September
1 Giles; Simeon Stylites (E)
2 John the Faster (E)
3 Gregory (the Great)
4 Babylas (E); Boniface I
5 Zacharias (E)
9 Peter Claver; Sergius of Antioch
10 Finnian; Nicholas of Tolentino;
   Pulcheria
11 Deiniol; Ethelburga;
   Paphnutius
13 John Chrysostom (W)
15 Catherine of Genoa; Our Lady
   of Sorrows
16 Cornelius; Cyprian of
   Carthage; Euphemia; Ninian
17 Robert Bellarmine; Hildegard;
   Lambert; Satyrus
19 Januarius (W); Theodore of
   Tarsus
20 Agapetus or Eustace (W)
21 Matthew (W)
23 Adamnan; Linus; Padre Pio
25 Sergius of Rostov
26 Cosmas and Damian (W);
   Cyprian of Carthage; John (E)
27 Frumentius (W); Vincent de
   Paul
28 Exuperius; Wenceslaus
29 Michael (*Michaelmas Day*);
   Gabriel and Raphael
30 Jerome; Otto

October
1 Remigius; Romanos; Teresa of
   the Child Jesus
2 Leodegar (Leger)
3 Thérèse de Lisieux; Thomas de
   Cantilupe

4 Ammon; Francis of Assisi;
   Petronius
6 Bruno; Thomas (G)
9 Demetrius (W); Denis and
   companions; Dionysius of
   Paris; James (the Less) (E); John
   Leonardi
10 Francis Borgia; Paulinus of York
11 Atticus (E); Bruno; Nectarius
12 Wilfrid
13 Edward the Confessor
14 Callistus I; Cosmas Melodus (E)
15 Lucian of Antioch (E); Teresa of
   Avila
16 Gall; Hedwig; Lullus; Margaret
   Mary Alacoque
17 Ignatius of Antioch; Victor
18 Luke
19 John de Brébeuf and Isaac
   Jogues and companions; Paul
   of the Cross; Peter of
   Alcántara
21 Hilarion; Ursula
22 Abercius
23 John of Capistrano; James
24 Anthony Claret
25 Crispin and Crispinian; Forty
   Martyrs of England and Wales;
   Gaudentius
26 Demetrius (E)
28 Firmilian (E); Simon and Jude
30 Serapion of Antioch
31 Wolfgang

November
1 All Saints; Cosmas and Damian
   (E)
2 Eustace (E); Victorinus
3 Hubert; Malachy; Martin de
   Porres; Pirminius; Winifred
4 Charles Borromeo; Vitalis and
   Agricola
5 Elizabeth (W)
6 Illtyd; Leonard; Paul of
   Constantinople (E)
7 Willibrord
8 Elizabeth (E); Willehad
9 Simeon Metaphrastes (E)
10 Justus; Leo I (W)
11 Martin of Tours (W); Menas of
   Egypt; Theodore of Studios
12 Josaphat; Martin of Tours (E);
   Nilus the Ascetic
13 Abbo; John Chrysostom (E);
   Nicholas I
14 Dubricius; Gregory Palamas (E)
15 Albert the Great; Machutus
16 Edmund of Abingdon;
   Eucherius; Gertrude (the
   Great); Margaret of Scotland;
   Matthew (E)
17 Elizabeth of Hungary; Gregory
   Thaumaturgus; Gregory of
   Tours; Hugh of Lincoln
18 Odo; Romanus
19 Mechthild; Nerses
20 Edmund the Martyr

Saints' days (continued)

21 Gelasius	**December**	13 Lucy; Odilia
22 Cecilia	1 Eligius	14 John of the Cross; Spyridon (W)
23 Amphilochius; Clement I (W);	2 Chromatius	16 Eusebius
Columban; Felicity; Gregory of	3 Francis Xavier	18 Frumentius (C)
Agrigentum	4 Barbara; John Damascene;	20 Ignatius of Antioch (G)
25 Clement I (E); Mercurius;	Osmund	21 Peter Canisius; Thomas
Mesrob	5 Clement of Alexandria; Sabas	22 Anastasia (E); Chrysogonus (E)
26 Siricius	6 Nicholas	23 John of Kanty
27 Barlam and Josaphat	7 Ambrose	26 Stephen (W)
28 Simeon Metaphrastes	10 Miltiades	27 John (W); Fabiola; Stephen (E)
29 Cuthbert Mayne	11 Damasus; Daniel	29 Thomas Becket; Trophimus of
30 Andrew; Frumentius (G)	12 Jane Frances de Chantal;	Arles
	Spyridon (E); Vicelin	31 Sylvester

Popes

Antipope refers to a pontiff set up in opposition to one asserted to be canonically chosen.

until c.64	Peter	422–32	Celestine I	701–5	John VI
c.64–c.76	Linus	432–40	Sixtus III	705–7	John VII
c.76–c.90	Anacletus	440–61	Leo I 'the Great'	708	Sisinnius
c.90–c.99	Clement I	461–8	Hilarus	708–15	Constantine
c.99–c.105	Evaristus	468–83	Simplicius	715–31	Gregory II
c.105–c.117	Alexander I	483–92	Felix III (II)	731–41	Gregory III
c.117–c.127	Sixtus I	492–6	Gelasius I	741–52	Zacharias
c.127–c.137	Telesphorus	496–8	Anastasius II	752	Stephen II (not
c.137–c.140	Hyginus	498–514	Symmachus		consecrated)
c.140–c.154	Pius I	498	Laurentius *Antipope*	752–7	Stephen II (III)
c.154–c.166	Anicetus	501–5	Laurentius *Antipope*	757–67	Paul I
c.166–c.175	Soter	514–23	Hormisdas	767–9	Constantine II *Antipope*
175–89	Eleutherius	523–6	John I	768	Philip *Antipope*
189–98	Victor I	526–30	Felix IV (III)	768–72	Stephen III (IV)
198–217	Zephyrinus	530–2	Boniface II	772–95	Adrian I
217–22	Callistus I	530	Dioscorus *Antipope*	795–816	Leo III
217–c.235	Hippolytus *Antipope*	533–5	John II	816–17	Stephen IV (V)
222–30	Urban I	535–6	Agapetus I	817–24	Paschal I
230–5	Pontian	536–7	Silverius	824–7	Eugenius II
235–6	Anterus	537–55	Vigilius	827	Valentine
236–50	Fabian	556–61	Pelagius I	827–44	Gregory IV
251–3	Cornelius	561–74	John III	844	John *Antipope*
251–c.258	Novatian *Antipope*	575–9	Benedict I	844–7	Sergius II
253–4	Lucius I	579–90	Pelagius II	847–55	Leo IV
254–7	Stephen I	590–604	Gregory I 'the Great'	855–8	Benedict III
257–8	Sixtus II	604–6	Sabinianus	855	Anastasius
259–68	Dionysius	607	Boniface III		Bibliothecarius *Antipope*
269–74	Felix I	608–15	Boniface IV	858–67	Nicholas I 'the Great'
275–83	Eutychianus	615–18	Deusdedit (Adeodatus I)	867–72	Adrian II
283–96	Caius	619–25	Boniface V	872–82	John VIII
296–304	Marcellinus	625–38	Honorius I	882–4	Marinus I
308–9	Marcellus I	640	Severinus	884–5	Adrian III
310	Eusebius	640–2	John IV	885–91	Stephen V (VI)
311–14	Miltiades	642–9	Theodore I	891–6	Formosus
314–35	Sylvester I	649–55	Martin I	896	Boniface VI
336	Mark	654–7	Eugenius I[a]	896–7	Stephen VI (VII)
337–52	Julius I	657–72	Vitalian	897	Romanus
352–66	Liberius	672–6	Adeodatus II	897	Theodore II
355–65	Felix II *Antipope*	676–8	Donus	898–900	John IX
366–84	Damasus I	678–81	Agatho	900–3	Benedict IV
366–7	Ursinus *Antipope*	682–3	Leo II	903	Leo V
384–99	Siricius	684–5	Benedict II	903–4	Christopher *Antipope*
399–401	Anastasius I	685–6	John V	904–11	Sergius III
402–17	Innocent I	686–7	Cono	911–13	Anastasius III
417–18	Zosimus	687	Theodore *Antipope*	913–14	Lando
418–22	Boniface I	687–92	Paschal *Antipope*	914–28	John X
418–19	Eulalius *Antipope*	687–701	Sergius I	928	Leo VI

928–31	Stephen VII (VIII)
931–5	John XI
936–9	Leo VII
939–42	Stephen IX
942–6	Marinus II
946–55	Agapetus II
955–64	John XII
963–5	Leo VIII
964–6	Benedict V
965–72	John XIII
973–4	Benedict VI
974	Boniface VII *Antipope*
984–5	Boniface VII *Antipope*
974–83	Benedict VII
983–4	John XIV
985–96	John XV
996–9	Gregory V
997–8	John XVI *Antipope*
999–1003	Sylvester II
1003	John XVII
1004–9	John XVIII
1009–12	Sergius IV
1012–24	Benedict VIII
1012	Gregory *Antipope*
1024–32	John XIX
1032–44	Benedict IX
1045	Sylvester III
1045	Benedict IX (second reign)
1045–6	Gregory VI
1046–7	Clement II
1047–8	Benedict IX (third reign)
1048	Damasus II (Poppo)
1048–54	Leo IX (Bruno of Toul)
1055–7	Victor II (Gebhard of Hirschberg)
1057–8	Stephen IX (X) (Frederick of Lorraine)
1058–9	Benedict X (John of Tusculum) *Antipope*
1059–61	Nicholas II (Gerard of Burgundy)
1061–73	Alexander II (Anselm of Lucca)
1061–72	Honorius II (Peter Cadalus) *Antipope*
1073–85	Gregory VII (St Hilderbrand)
1080, 1084–1100	Clement III (Guibert of Ravenna) *Antipope*
1086–7	Victor III (Desidenus)
1088–99	Urban II (Odo of Chatillon)
1099–1118	Paschal II (Raneiro da Bieda)
1100–2	Theodoric *Antipope*
1102	Albert *Antipope*
1105–11	Sylvester IV *Antipope*
1118–19	Gelasius II (John of Gaeta)
1118–21	Gregory VIII (Maurice of Braga) *Antipope*
1119–24	Callistus II (Guy of Burgundy)
1124–30	Honorius II (Lamberto dei Fagnani)
1124	Celestine II *Antipope*
1130–43	Innocent II (Gregory Parareschi)
1130–8	Anacletus II *Antipope*
1138	Victor IV° *Antipope*
1143–4	Celestine II (Guido di Castello)
1144–5	Lucius II (Gherardo Caccianemici)
1145–53	Eugenius III (Bernardo Paganelli)
1153–4	Anastasius IV (Corrado della Subarra)
1154–9	Adrian IV (Nicholas Breakspear)
1159–81	Alexander III (Orlando Bandinelli)
1159–64	Victor IV° (Ottaviano di Monticelli) *Antipope*
1164–8	Paschal III (Guido of Crema) *Antipope*
1168–78	Callistus III (John of Struma) *Antipope*
1179–80	Innocent III (Lando da Sessa)
1181–5	Lucius III (Ubaldo Allucingoli)
1185–7	Urban III (Uberto Crivelli)
1187	Gregory VIII (Alberto di Morra)
1187–91	Clement III (Paolo Scolari)
1191–8	Celestine III (Giacinto Boboni-Orsini)
1198–1216	Innocent III (Lotario de'Conti)
1216–27	Honorius III (Cancio Savelli)
1227–41	Gregory IX (Ugolino di Segni)
1241	Celestine IV (Goffredo Castiglione)
1243–54	Innocent IV (Sinibaldo de' Fieschi)
1254–61	Alexander IV (Rinaldo di Segni)
1261–4	Urban IV (Jacques Pantaléou)
1265–8	Clement IV (Guy le Gros Foulques)
1271–6	Gregory X (Tebaldo Visconti)
1276	Innocent V (Pierre de Champagni)
1276	Adrian V (Ottobono Fieschi)
1276–7	John XXI° (Pietro Rebuli-Giuliani)
1277–80	Nicholas III (Giovanni Gaetano Orsini)
1281–5	Martin IV (Simon de Brie)
1285–7	Honorius IV (Giacomo Savelli)
1288–92	Nicholas IV (Girolamo Masci)
1294	Celestine V (Pietro di Morrone)
1294–	Boniface VIII (Benedetto
1303	Castani)
1303–4	Benedict XI (Niccolo Boccasini)
1305–14	Clement V (Raymond Bertrand de Got)
1316–34	John XXII (Jacques Duèse)
1328–30	Nicholas V (Pietro Rainalducci) *Antipope*
1334–42	Benedict XII (Jacques Fournier)
1342–52	Clement VI (Pierre Roger de Beaufort)
1352–62	Innocent VI (Étienne Aubert)
1362–70	Urban V (Guillaume de Grimoard)
1370–8	Gregory XI (Pierre Roger de Beaufort)
1378–89	Urban VI (Bartolomeo Prignano)
1378–94	Clement VII (Robert of Geneva) *Antipope*
1389–1404	Boniface IX (Pietro Tomacelli)
1394–1423	Benedict XIII (Pedro de Luna) *Antipope*
1404–6	Innocent VII (Cosmato de' Migliorati)
1406–15	Gregory XII (Angelo Correr)
1409–10	Alexander V (Petros Philargi) *Antipope*
1410–15	John XXIII (Baldassare Cossa) *Antipope*
1417–31	Martin V (Oddone Colonna)
1423–9	Clement VIII (Gil Sanchez Muñoz) *Antipope*
1425–30	Benedict XIV (Bernard Garnier) *Antipope*
1431–47	Eugenius IV (Gabriele Condulmer)
1439–49	Felix V (Amadeus VIII of Savoy) *Antipope*
1447–55	Nicholas V (Tommaso Parentuce III)
1455–8	Callistus III (Alfonso de Borja)
1458–64	Pius II (Enea Silvio de Piccolomini)
1464–71	Paul II (Pietro Barbo)
1471–84	Sixtus IV (Francesco della Rovere)
1484–92	Innocent VIII (Giovanni Battista Cibo)
1492–1503	Alexander VI (Rodrigo Borgia)
1503	Pius III (Francesco Todoeschini-Piccolomini)
1503–13	Julius II (Giuliano della Rovere)
1513–21	Leo X (Giovanni de' Medici)
1522–3	Adrian VI (Adrian Dedel)
1523–34	Clement VII (Giulio de' Medici)

RELIGION AND MYTHOLOGY

Popes (continued)

1534–49	Paul III (Allessandro Farnese)	1644–55	Innocent X (Giambattista Pamfili)	1800–23	Pius VII (Luigi Barnaba Chiaramonti)
1550–5	Julius III (Gianmaria del Monte)	1655–67	Alexander VII (Fabio Chigi)	1823–9	Leo XII (Annibale della Genga)
1555	Marcellus II (Marcello Cervini)	1667–9	Clement IX (Guilio Rospigliosi)	1829–30	Pius VIII (Francesco Saveno Castiglioni)
1555–9	Paul IV (Giovanni Pietro Caraffa)	1670–6	Clement X (Emilio Altieri)	1831–46	Gregory XVI (Bartolomeo Alberto Cappellari)
1559–65	Pius IV (Giovanni Angelo Medici)	1676–89	Innocent XI (Benedetto Odescalchi)	1846–78	Pius IX (Giovanni Maria Mastai Ferretti)
1566–72	Pius V (Michele Ghislieri)	1689–91	Alexander VIII (Pietro Vito Ottoboni)	1878–1903	Leo XIII (Vincenzo Gioacchino Pecci)
1572–85	Gregory XIII (Ugo Buoncompagni)	1691–1700	Innocent XII (Antonio Pignatelli)	1903–14	Pius X (Giuseppe Sarto)
1585–90	Sixtus V (Felice Peretti)	1700–21	Clement XI (Gian Francesco Albani)	1914–22	Benedict XV (Giacomo della Chiesa)
1590	Urban VII (Giambattista Castagna)	1721–4	Innocent XIII (Michelangelo dei Conti)	1922–39	Pius XI (Achille Ratti)
1590–1	Gregory XIV (Niccolo Sfondrati)			1939–58	Pius XII (Eugenio Pacelli)
1591	Innocent IX (Gian Antonio Facchinetti)	1724–30	Benedict XIII (Pietro Francesco Orsini)	1958–63	John XXIII (Angelo Giuseppe Roncalli)
1592–1605	Clement VIII (Ippolito Aldobrandini)	1730–40	Clement XII (Lorenzo Corsini)	1963–78	Paul VI (Giovanni Battista Montini)
1605	Leo XI (Alessandro de' Medici-Ottaiano)	1740–58	Benedict XIV (Prospero Lambertini)	1978	John Paul I (Albino Luciani)
1605–21	Paul V (Camillo Borghese)	1758–69	Clement XIII (Carlo Rezzonico)	1978–2005	John Paul II (Karol Jozef Wojtyla)
1621–3	Gregory XV (Alessandro Ludovisi)	1769–74	Clement XIV (Lorenzo Ganganelli)	2005–	Benedict XVI (Joseph Ratzinger)
1623–44	Urban VIII (Maffeo Barberini)	1775–99	Pius VI (Giovanni Angelo Braschi)		

[a]Elected during the banishment of Martin I. [b]Different individuals. [c]There was no John XX.

Archbishops of Canterbury

597–604	St Augustine	1020–38	Æthelnoth	1397–9	Roger Walden
604–19	Laurentius	1038–50	Eadsige	1399–1414	Thomas Arundel (*restored*)
619–24	Mellitus	1051–2	Robert of Jumièges	1414–43	Henry Chichele
624–7	Justus	1052–70	Stigand	1443–52	John Stafford
627–53	Honorius	1070–89	Lanfranc	1452–4	John Kemp
655–64	Deusdedit (Frithona)	1093–1109	Anselm	1454–86	Thomas Bourgchier
668–90	Theodore	1114–22	Ralph d'Escures	1486–1500	John Morton
693–731	Beorhtweald	1123–36	William of Corbeil	1501–3	Henry Deane
731–4	Tatwine	1138–61	Theobald (Tebaldus)	1504–32	William Warham
735–9	Nothelm	1162–70	Thomas à Becket	1532–55	Thomas Cranmer
740–60	Cuthbert	1174–84	Richard of Dover	1555–8	Reginald Pole
761–4	Breguwine	1184–90	Baldwin	1559–75	Matthew Parker
765–92	Jaenbeorht	1193–1205	Hubert Walter	1575–83	Edmund Grindal
793–805	Ethelheard	1206–28	Stephen Langton	1583–1604	John Whitgift
805–32	Wulfred	1229–31	Richard le Grant	1604–10	Richard Bancroft
832	Feologild	1233–40	St Edmund (Rich)	1611–33	George Abbot
833–70	Ceolnoth	1241–70	Boniface of Savoy	1633–45	William Laud
870–89	Æthelred	1272–8	Robert Kilwardby	1645–60	*No Archbishop of Canterbury*
890–914	Plegmund	1279–92	John Pecham		
914–23	Æthelhelm	1293–1313	Robert Winchelsey	1660–3	William Juxon
923–42	Wulfhelm	1313–27	Walter Reynolds	1663–77	Gilbert Sheldon
942–58	Oda	1327–33	Simon Mepham	1677–90	William Sancroft
959	Ælfsige	1333–48	John de Stratford	1691–4	John Tillotson
959	Beorhthelm	1348–9	Thomas Bradwardine	1694–1715	Thomas Tenison
960–88	St Dunstan	1349–66	Simon Islip	1715–37	William Wake
988–90	Æthelgar	1366–8	Simon Langham	1737–47	John Potter
990–4	Sigeric Serio	1368–74	William Whittlesey	1747–57	Thomas Herring
995–1005	Ælfric	1375–81	Simon Sudbury	1757–8	Matthew Hutton
1005–12	Ælfheah	1381–96	William Courtenay	1758–68	Thomas Secker
1013–20	Lyfing	1396–7	Thomas Arundel	1768–83	Frederick Cornwallis

1783–1805 John Moore	1883–96 Edward White Benson	1961–74 Arthur Michael Ramsey
1805–28 Charles Manners Sutton	1896–1902 Frederick Temple	1974–80 Donald Coggan
1828–48 William Howley	1903–28 Randall Thomas Davidson	1980–91 Robert Alexander
1848–62 John Bird Sumner	1928–42 Cosmo Gordon Lang	Kennedy Runcie
1862–8 Charles Thomas Longley	1942–4 William Temple	1991–2002 George Leonard Carey
1868–82 Archibald Campbell Tait	1945–61 Geoffrey Francis Fisher	2002– Rowan Williams

Dalai Lamas

1391–1475 Gedun Truppa	1683–1706 Tsang-yang Gyatso	1856–75 Trinle Gyatso
1475–1542 Gedun Gyatso	1708–57 Kezang Gyatso	1876–1933 Thupten Gyatso
1543–88 Sonam Gyatso	1758–1804 Jampel Gyatso	1935– Tenzin Gyatso *in exile*
1589–1617 Yonten Gyatso	1806–15 Luntok Gyatso	1959–
1617–82 Ngawang Lobzang	1816–37 Tshultrim Gyatso	
Gyatso	1838–56 Khedrup Gyatso	

Buddhism

Founder
Prince Siddhartha Gautama (Buddha), c.563–483 BC

Date founded
c.500 BC, India

Beliefs
'Four Noble Truths':
 All life is permeated by suffering
 Source of suffering is desire for existence
 This cause can be eliminated
 Way of doing this is by treading 'The Eightfold Path'
'The Eightfold Path' leads to 'nirvana' – ultimate state
 of peace

Major festivals[a]
Buddha's birth
Buddha's enlightenment
Buddha's first sermon
Buddha's death

[a]These take place on different dates in the countries in
which Buddhism is practised.

Christianity

Founder
Jesus of Nazareth (Jesus Christ), c.4 BC–AD 30

Date founded
1st-c AD

Beliefs
Trinity – God as three in one (Father, Son, Holy Spirit)
God as creator of universe
Original sin and the forgiveness of sins
God is love
Incarnation of Jesus as Son of God
Redemption/Salvation
Resurrection
Sacramental identity, through baptism and the
 Eucharist
Old and New Testaments of the Bible

Confucianism

Founder
K'ung Fu-tzu, 551–479 BC

Date founded
6th-c BC, China

Beliefs
Human beings are teachable, improvable, and
 perfectible
Person can shape his/her own destiny
Self-knowledge and self-realization are attainable
 through learning
Sense of humanity should infuse society and politics
 (social participation)
Ritual and tradition

Major Chinese festivals

January/February	Chinese New Year
February/March	Lantern Festival
March/April	Festival of Pure Brightness
May/June	Dragon Boat Festival
July/August	Herd Boy and Weaving Maid
August	All Souls' Festival
September	Mid-Autumn Festival
September/October	Double Ninth Festival
November/December	Winter Solstice

Hinduism

Founder
Aryan invaders of India of Vedic religion

Date founded
c.1500 BC, India

Beliefs
Sacred power (Brahman) is sole reality, the creator,
 transformer, and preserver of everything
Hindu Trinity of Brahma, Vishnu, and Shiva
Authority of the Veda
Respect for life
Rebirth
Soul emancipated by the Three Margas – duty,
 knowledge, devotion

Major festivals
S = Sukla, 'waxing fortnight'.
K = Krishna 'waning fortnight'.

Caitra	S9	Ramanavami (Birthday of Lord Rama)
Asadha	S2	Rathayatra (Pilgrimage of the Chariot at Jagannath)
Sravana	S11–15	Jhulanayatra ('Swinging the Lord Krishna')
Sravana	S15	Rakshabandhana ('Tying on lucky threads')

RELIGION AND MYTHOLOGY

Hinduism (continued)

Bhadrapada	K8	Janamashtami (Birthday of Lord Krishna)
Asvina	S7–10	Durga-puja (Homage to Goddess Durga) (*Bengal*)
Asvina	S1–10	Navaratri (Festival of 'Nine Nights')
Asvina	S15	Lakshmi-puja (Homage to Goddess Lakshmi)
Asvina	K15	Diwali, Dipavali ('String of Lights')
Kartikka	S15	Guru Nanak Jananti (Birthday of Guru Nanak)
Magha	K5	Sarasvati-puja (Homage to Goddess Sarasvati)
Magha	K13	Maha-sivaratri (Great Night of Lord Shiva)
Phalguna	S14	Holi (Festival of Fire)
Phalguna	S15	Dolayatra (Swing Festival) (*Bengal*)

Islam

Founder
Mohammed, AD c.570–632

Date founded
7th-c AD, Arabian peninsula

Beliefs
Unity of God
God as creator and sustainer of the universe
Man superior to nature but still servant of God
Pride is cardinal sin
God always ready to pardon – repentance and redemption possible
Prophets are recipients of revelations from God – they, with God, show a person the 'right way'

Major festivals

1	Muharram	New Year's Day; starts on the day which celebrates Mohammed's departure from Mecca to Medina in AD 622
12	Rabi I	Birthday of Mohammed (Mawlid al-Nabi) AD 572; celebrated throughout month of Rabi I
27	Rajab	'Night of Ascent' (Laylat al-Mi'raj) of Mohammed to Heaven
1	Ramadan	Beginning of month of fasting during daylight hours
27	Ramadan	'Night of Power' (Laylat al-Qadr); sending down of the Koran to Mohammed
1	Shawwal	'Feast of breaking the Fast' ('Id al-Fitr); marks the end of Ramadan
8–13	Dhu-l-Hijja	Annual pilgrimage ceremonies at and around Mecca; month during which the great pilgrimage (Hajj) should be made
10	Dhu-l-Hijja	Feast of the Sacrifice ('Id al-Adha)

Jainism

Founder
Vardhamana Mahavira, 599–527 BC

Date founded
c.600 BC, India

Beliefs
World eternal and uncreated
All phenomena linked by chain of cause and effect
Nonviolence to other living creatures (Ahimsa)
Perfection and purification of soul leads to its emancipation and the ultimate attribute of omniscience
Soul has to pass through various stages of spiritual development before freeing itself of karmic bondages
Right conduct, right knowledge, right belief

Judaism

Founders
Abraham, c.2000 BC, and Moses, c.1200 BC

Date founded
c.2000 BC

Beliefs
Unity of God
God as teacher through instruction of Torah
God as redeemer
Resurrection
Coming of the 'Mashiah' who will establish new age in Israel

Major festivals

1–2	Tishri	Rosh Hashanah (New Year)
3	Tishri	Tzom Gedaliahu (Fast of Gedaliah)
10	Tishri	Yom Kippur (Day of Atonement)
15–21	Tishri	Sukkoth (Feast of Tabernacles)
22	Tishri	Shemini Atzeret (8th Day of the Solemn Assembly)
23	Tishri	Simhat Torah (Rejoicing of the Law)
25	Kislev–2–3 Tevet	Hanukkah (Feast of Dedication)
10	Tevet	Asara be-Tevet (Fast of 10th Tevet)
13	Adar	Taanit Esther (Fast of Esther)
14–15	Adar	Purim (Feast of Lots)
15–22	Nisan	Pesach (Passover)
5	Iyar	Israel Independence Day
6–7	Sivan	Shavuoth (Feast of Weeks)
17	Tammuz	Shiva Asar be-Tammuz (Fast of 17th Tammuz)
9	Av	Tisha be-Av (Fast of 9th Av)

The ancient tribes of Israel

Asher Descended from Jacob's eighth son (Z).
Benjamin Descended from Jacob's twelfth and youngest son (R).
Dan Descended from Jacob's fifth son (B).
Issachar Descended from Jacob's ninth son (L).
Joseph Descended from Jacob's eleventh son (R).
Ephraim Descended from Joseph's younger son.
Manasseh Descended from Joseph's elder son.
Judah Descended from Jacob's fourth son (L).
Levi Descended from Jacob's third son (L). (No territory, as it was a priestly caste).

Naphtali Descended from Jacob's sixth son (*B*).
Reuben Descended from Jacob's first son (*L*).
Simeon Descended from Jacob's second son (*L*).
Zebulun Descended from Jacob's tenth son (*L*).
Gad Descended from Jacob's seventh son (*Z*).

B = borne by Bilhah
L = borne by Leah
R = borne by Rachel
Z = borne by Zilpah

Israel during the period of the Judges – approximate tribal areas

Shintoism

Founder
No founder

Date originated
6th-c AD, Japan

Beliefs
Polytheistic – belief in 'kami' (deities)
Sincerity arising from awareness of the divine
Spiritual and physical purification
Continuity/communion with ancestry

Major Japanese festivals

1–3	Jan	Oshogatsu (New Year)
3	Feb	Setsubun
3	Mar	Ohinamatsuri (Doll *or* Girls' Festival)
5	May	Tango no Sekku (Boys' Festival)
7	Jul	Hoshi matsuri *or* Tanabata (Star Festival)
13–15	Jul	Obon (Buddhist All Souls)
15	Nov	Shichi-go-San (Seven-five-three age celebrations for 7-year-old girls, 5-year-old boys, and 3-year-old girls)

Sikhism

Founder
Guru Nanak, AD 1469–1539

Date founded
c.15th-c AD, India

Beliefs
Unity of God
Birth, death, and rebirth
Guidance of the Guru to 'moksa' (release) and the way of God
Worship of the Adi Granth

Taoism

Founder
Lao Zi, 6th-c BC

Date founded
600 BC, China

Beliefs
Interaction of human society and the universe
Divine nature of sovereign
Cult of Heaven
Law of return
State of original purity
Worship of ancestors

The Templeton Prize for Progress in Religion

1973	Mother Teresa of Calcutta, India
1974	Brother Roger of Taizé France
1975	Dr Sarvepalli Radhakrishnan, India
1976	Leon Joseph Suenens, Cardinal, Belgium
1977	Chiara Lubich, Italy
1978	Rev Prof Thomas F Torrance, UK
1979	Nikkyo Niwano, Japan
1980	Prof Ralph Wendell Burhoe, USA
1981	Dame Cecily Saunders, UK
1982	Rev Dr Billy Graham, USA
1983	Alexander Solzhenitsyn, USSR
1984	Rev Michael Bourdeaux, UK
1985	Sir Alister Hardy, UK
1986	Rev Dr James I McCord, USA
1987	Rev Prof Stanley L Jaki, Hungary/USA
1988	Dr Inamullah Khan, Pakistan
1989	Very Rev Lord Macleod of Fiunary, UK; Prof Carl Friedrich von Weizsäcker, Germany
1990	Baba Amte, India
	Prof L Charles Birch, Australia
1991	Rt Hon Lord Jakobovits, UK
1992	Dr Kyung-Chik Han, South Korea
1993	Charles W Colson, USA
1994	Michael Novak, USA
1995	Paul Davies, UK
1996	William R(ohl) Bright, USA
1997	Pandurang Shastri Athavale, India
1998	Sir Sigmund Sternberg, Hungary
1999	Prof Ian Graeme Barbour, USA
2000	Prof Freeman Dyson, USA
2001	Rev Canon Dr Arthur Peacocke, USA
2002	Rev Dr John Polkinghorne, UK
2003	Holmes Rolston III, USA
2004	George F R Ellis, South Africa
2005	Charles H(ard) Townes, USA

RELIGION AND MYTHOLOGY

Religious symbols

The Trinity

Equilateral triangle | Triangle in circle | Circle within triangle | Trefoil | Triquetra | Triquetra and circle | Interwoven circles

God the Father

All-seeing eye | Hand of God | Hand of God | Lamb of God | Fish | Dove descending | Sevenfold flame

God the Son — **God the Holy Spirit**

Old Testament — Modern Judaism

Menorah (seven branch candlestick) | Abraham | The Ten Commandments | Pentateuch (The Law) | Marked doorposts and lintel (Passover) | Twelve tribes of Israel | Star of David

Crosses

Aiguisée | Avellane | Barbée | Trefly | Canterbury | Celtic | Cercelée | Cross crosslet

Crux ansata | Entrailed | Fleurée | Globical | Graded (Calvary) | Greek | Iona | Jerusalem

Latin | Maltese | Millvine | Papal | Patée | Patée formée | Patonce | Patriarchal (or Lorraine) | Pommel or Pommée

Monograms

Potent | Raguly or Ragulée | Russian Orthodox | St Andrew's (Saltire) | St Peter's | Tau (St Anthony's) | IHC (Latin form) (from Gk IHCOYC 'Jesus') | Chi Rho (from Gk XPICTOC 'Christ')

The Christian Church Year

Advent | Christmas | Epiphany | Lent | Maundy Thursday | Good Friday | Easter Day | Ascension | Pentecost

Other symbols

Ankh (Egyptian) | Yin-yang Tao symbol of harmony | Torii (Shinto) | Om (Hinduism, Buddhism, Jainism; sacred syllable) | Ikonkar (Sikhism; symbol of God) | Swastika (originally symbol of the Sun) | Yantra: Sri Cakra (wheel of fortune)

PART TEN

Routes

ROUTES

Road

Main USA Interstate highways

Odd-number Interstates run South–North; even-number, West–East.

I5	San Diego–Los Angeles–Sacramento–Seattle–Vancouver
I8	San Diego–Tucson
I10	Los Angeles–Phoenix–San Antonio–Houston–New Orleans–Jacksonville
I15	San Diego–Las Vegas–Salt Lake City–Great Falls
I20	Fort Worth–Dallas–Jackson–Birmingham–Atlanta–Columbia
I25	Albuquerque–Colorado Springs–Denver–Buffalo
I30	Dallas–Little Rock
I35	San Antonio–Austin–Fort Worth–Oklahoma City–Wichita–Kansas City–Des Moines–Minneapolis/St Paul–Duluth
I40	Flagstaff–Albuquerque–Oklahoma City–Little Rock–Memphis–Nashville–Greensboro
I45	Dallas–Houston
I55	New Orleans–Jackson–Memphis–St Louis–Chicago
I59	New Orleans–Birmingham–Chattanooga
I64	St Louis–Louisville–Lexington–Charleston
I65	Mobile–Birmingham–Nashville–Louisville–Indianapolis–Chicago
I70	Denver–Kansas City–St Louis–Indianapolis–Columbus–Philadelphia–Baltimore
I71	Louisville–Cincinatti–Columbus
I74	Davenport–Indianapolis–Cincinatti
I75	Tampa–Atlanta–Cincinatti–Toledo–Detroit
I78	Harrisburg–New York
I80	San Francisco–Salt Lake City–Des Moines–Cleveland–New York
I81	Knoxville–Roanoake–Syracuse
I85	Montgomery–Atlanta–Greensboro–Petersburg
I90	Seattle–Billings–Sioux Falls–Chicago–Cleveland–Boston
I94	Billings–Bismarck–Minneapolis/St Paul–Madison–Milwaukee–Chicago–Detroit
I95	Miami–Jacksonville–Richmond–Washington, DC–Baltimore–New York–Boston–Augusta

British motorways

M1	Belfast–Dungannon (N Ireland)
M1	London–Northampton–Leicester–Nottingham–Sheffield–Leeds
M2	Belfast–Randalstown (N Ireland)
M2	Strood–Faversham (Medway)
M3	London–Basingstoke–Winchester
M4	London–Reading–Newport–Cardiff–Swansea
M5	Birmingham–Bristol–Exeter
M6	Birmingham–Wolverhampton–Stoke-on-Trent–Preston–Lancaster–Carlisle
M8	Edinburgh–Glasgow–Langbank
M9	Edinburgh–Stirling
M10	M1–St Albans spur
M11	London–Cambridge
M18	Rotherham–M62 junction 35 (Goole)
M20	Swanley (London)–Folkestone
M23	Redhill–Crawley
M25	London orbital motorway
M26	Chipstead–M20 junction 3
M27	Portsmouth–Southampton–Cadnam
M32	M4–Bristol spur
M40	London–Oxford–Birmingham
M42	Birmingham–Solihull–Tamworth–Appleby Magna
M45	Watford–Dunchurch
M50	Ross-on-Wye–M5 junction 8
M53	Chester–Wallasey
M54	Telford–M6 junction 10a
M55	Fulwood–Blackpool
M56	Chester–Altrincham (N Cheshire)
M57	Liverpool–Aintree
M58	Aintree–Wigan
M61	Manchester–Preston
M62	Liverpool–Manchester–Leeds–North Cave (N Humberside)
M63	Salford–Stockport
M65	Blackburn–Burnley–Colne
M66	Middleton–Ramsbottom
M67	Denton–Mottram in Langendale (Manchester ring)
M69	Leicester–Coventry
M73	M74–Glasgow spur (Maryville–Mollisburn)
M74	Millbank–Maryville
M74	Carlisle–Gretna Green
M80	Longcroft–M9 junction 9 (Haggs)
M85	M90–Perth spur (Perth–Friarton Bridge)
M90	Perth–Inverkeithing
M180	Stainforth–Elsham (S Humberside)
M181	M180–Scunthorpe spur
M271	M27–Totton spur
M275	M27–Portsmouth spur
M606	M62–Bradford spur
M621	M62–Leeds spur
M876	M80–Kincardine Bridge (Banknock–Stenhousemuir)

International E-routes (Euroroutes)

Reference and intermediate roads (class A roads) have two-digit numbers; branch, link, and connecting roads (class B roads, not listed here), have three-digit numbers.

North–South orientated reference roads have two-digit odd numbers ending in the figure 5, and increasing from west to east. East–West orientated roads have two-digit even numbers ending in the figure 0, and increasing from north to south.

Intermediate roads have two-digit odd numbers (for N–S roads) or two-digit even numbers (for E–W roads) falling within the numbers of the reference roads between which they are located.

Only a selection of the towns and cities linked by E-roads given.

[···] indicates a sea crossing.

West-East orientation

Reference roads

E10	Narvik–Kiruna–Luleå
E20	Shannon–Dublin ··· Liverpool–Hull ··· Esbjerg–Nyborg ··· Korsør–Køge–Copenhagen ··· Malmö–Stockholm ··· Tallin–St Petersburg

Road (continued)

E30   Cork–Rosslare ··· Fishguard–London–Felixstowe
··· Hook of Holland–Utrecht–Hanover–
Berlin–Warsaw–Smolensk–Moscow

E40   Calais–Brussels–Aachen–Cologne–Dresden–
Krakow–Kiev–Rostov na Donu

E50   Brest–Paris–Metz–Nurenberg–Prague–
Mukačevo

E60   Brest–Tours–Besançon–Basle–Innsbruck–
Vienna–Budapest–Bucharest–Constanţ

E70   La Coruña–Bilbao–Bordeaux–Lyon–Torino–
Verona–Trieste–Zagreb–Belgrade–
Bucharest–Varna

E80   Lisbon–Coimbra–Salamanca–Pau–Toulouse–
Nice–Genoa–Rome–Pescara ··· Dubrovnik–
Sofia–Istanbul–Erzincan–Iran

E90   Lisbon–Madrid–Barcelona ··· Mazara del
Vallo–Messina ··· Reggio di Calabria–Brindisi
··· Igoumenitsa–Thessaloniki–Gelibolu ···
Lapseki–Ankara–Iraq

Intermediate roads

E06   Olderfjord–Kirkenes
E12   Mo i Rana–Umeå ··· Vaasa–Helsinki
E14   Trondheim–Sundsvall
E16   Londonderry–Belfast ··· Glasgow–Edinburgh
E18   Craigavon–Larne ··· Stranraer–Newcastle ···
Stavanger–Oslo–Stockholm–Kappelskär ···
Mariehamnţ Turku–Helsinki–Leningrad
E22   Holyhead–Manchester–Immingham ···
Amsterdam–Hamburg–Sassnitz ···
Trelleborg–Norrköping
E24   Birmingham–Ipswich
E26   Hamburg–Berlin
E28   Berlin–Gdańsk
E32   Colchester–Harwich
E34   Antwerp–Bad Oeynhausen
E36   Berlin–Legnica
E42   Dunkirk–Aschaffenburg
E44   Le Havre–Luxembourg–Giessen
E46   Cherbourg–Liège
E48   Schweinfurt–Prague
E52   Strasbourg–Salzburg
E54   Paris–Basle–Munich
E56   Nuremberg–Sattledt
E58   Vienna–Bratislava
E62   Nantes–Geneva–Tortona
E64   Turin–Brescia
E66   Fortezza–Székesfehérvár
E68   Szeged–Braşov
E72   Bordeaux–Toulouse
E74   Nice–Alessandria
E76   Migliarino–Florence
E78   Grosseto–Fano
E82   Porto–Tordesillas
E84   Keşan–Silivri
E86   Krystalopigi–Yefira
E88   Ankara–Refahiye
E92   Igoumenitsa–Volos
E94   Corinth–Athens
E96   Izmir–Sivrihisar
E98   Topbogazi–Syria

North–South orientation

Reference roads

E05   Greenock–Birmingham–Southampton ···
Le Havre–Paris–Bordeaux–Madrid–Algeciras
E15   Inverness–Edinburgh–London–Dover ···
Calais–Paris–Lyon–Barcelona–Algeciras
E25   Hook of Holland–Luxembourg–Strasbourg–
Basle–Geneva–Turin–Genoa
E35   Amsterdam–Cologne–Basle–Milan–Rome
E45   Gothenburg ··· Frederikshavn–Hamburg–
Munich–Innsbruck–Bologna–Rome–Naples–
Villa S Giovanni ··· Messina–Gela
E55   Kemi-Tornio–Stockholm–Helsingborg ···
Helsinger–Copenhagen–Gedser ··· Rostock–
Berlin–Prague–Salzburg–Rimini–Brindisi ···
Igoumenitsa–Kalamata
E65   Malmö–Ystrad–Świnoujście–Prague–Zagreb–
Dubrovnik–Bitolj–Antirrion ··· Rion–
Kalamata – Kissamos–Chania
E75   Karasjok–Helsinki ··· Gdańsk–Budapest–
Belgrade–Athens ··· Chania–Sitia
E85   Černovcy–Bucharest–Alexandropouli
E95   St Petersburg–Moscow–Yalta

Intermediate roads

E01   Larne–Dublin–Rosslare ··· La Coruña–Lisbon–
Seville
E03   Cherbourg–La Rochelle
E07   Pau–Zaragoza
E09   Orléans–Barcelona
E11   Vierzon–Montpellier
E13   Doncaster–London
E17   Antwerp–Beaune
E19   Amsterdam–Brussels–Paris
E21   Metz–Geneva
E23   Metz–Lausanne
E27   Belfort–Aosta
E29   Cologne–Sarreguemines
E31   Rotterdam–Ludwigshafen
E33   Parma–La Spezia
E37   Bremen–Cologne
E39   Kristiansand–Aalborg
E41   Dortmund–Altdorf
E43   Würzburg–Bellinzona
E47   Nordkap–Oslo–Copenhagen–Rødby ···
Puttgarden–Lübeck
E49   Magdeburg–Vienna
E51   Berlin–Nurenberg
E53   Plzeň–Munich
E57   Sattledt–Ljubljana
E59   Prague–Zagreb
E61   Klagenfurt–Rijeka
E63   Sodankylä–Naantali ··· Stockholm–Gothenburg
E67   Warsaw–Prague
E69   Tromsø–Tornio
E71   Košice–Budapest–Split
E73   Budapest–Metkovič
E77   Gdańsk–Budapest
E79   Oradea–Calafat ··· Vidin–Thessaloniki
E81   Halmeu–Piteşti
E83   Bjala–Sofia
E87   Tulcea–Eceabat ··· Çanakkale–Antalya
E89   Gerede–Ankara
E91   Toprakkale–Syria
E93   Orel–Odessa
E97   Trabzon–Aşkale
E99   Doğubeyazit–ŞUrfa

European road distances

	Athens	Barcelona	Brussels	Calais	Cherbourg	Cologne	Copenhagen	Geneva	Gibraltar	Hamburg	Hook of Holland	Lisbon	Lyons	Madrid	Marseilles	Milan	Munich	Paris	Rome	Stockholm
Barcelona	3313																			
Brussels	2963	1318																		
Calais	3175	1326	204																	
Cherbourg	3339	1294	583	460																
Cologne	2762	1498	206	409	785															
Copenhagen	3276	2218	966	1136	1545	760														
Geneva	2610	803	677	747	853	1662	1418													
Gibraltar	4485	1172	2256	2224	2047	2436	3196	1975												
Hamburg	2977	2018	597	714	1115	460	460	1118	2897											
Hook of Holland	3030	1490	172	330	731	269	269	895	2428	550										
Lisbon	4532	1304	2084	2052	1827	2290	2971	1936	676	2671	2280									
Lyons	2753	645	690	739	789	714	1458	158	1817	1159	863	1778								
Madrid	3949	636	1558	1550	1347	1764	2498	1439	698	2198	1730	668	1281							
Marseilles	2865	521	1011	1059	1101	1035	1778	425	1693	1479	1183	1762	320	1157						
Milan	2282	1014	925	1077	1209	911	1537	328	2185	1238	1098	2250	328	1724	618					
Munich	2179	1365	747	977	1160	583	1104	591	2565	3805	851	2507	724	2010	1109	331				
Paris	3000	1033	285	280	340	465	1176	513	1971	877	457	1799	471	1273	792	856	821			
Rome	817	1460	1511	1662	1794	1497	2050	995	2631	1751	1683	2700	1048	2097	1011	586	946	1476		
Stockholm	3927	2868	1616	1786	2196	1403	650	2068	3886	949	1500	3231	2108	3188	2428	2187	1754	1827	2707	
Vienna	1991	1802	1175	1381	1588	937	1455	1019	2974	1155	1205	2935	1157	2409	1363	898	428	1249	1209	2105

Road distances between some cities, given in kilometres. To convert to statute miles, multiply number given by 0.6214.

UK road distances

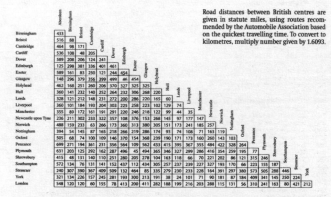

	Aberdeen	Birmingham	Bristol	Cambridge	Cardiff	Dover	Edinburgh	Exeter	Glasgow	Holyhead	Hull	Leeds	Liverpool	Manchester	Newcastle	Norwich	Nottingham	Oxford	Penzance	Plymouth	Shrewsbury	Southampton	Stranraer	York
Birmingham	433																							
Bristol	516	88																						
Cambridge	464	98	171																					
Cardiff	536	108	48	205																				
Dover	589	208	206	124	241																			
Edinburgh	125	298	381	336	401	461																		
Exeter	589	161	83	250	121	244	454																	
Glasgow	148	296	379	356	399	499	46	454																
Holyhead	462	168	251	260	206	370	322	325	325															
Hull	360	141	232	140	252	264	232	306	268	220														
Leeds	328	121	212	148	231	272	200	286	220	165	60													
Liverpool	360	101	184	193	204	303	225	258	223	102	129	74												
Manchester	355	89	172	161	191	291	220	246	218	122	99	44	35											
Newcastle upon Tyne	236	211	302	233	322	357	108	376	153	268	145	97	177	147										
Norwich	488	159	233	63	266	173	360	313	380	305	151	173	241	185	257									
Nottingham	394	54	145	87	165	218	266	219	286	174	93	74	108	71	163	119								
Oxford	505	68	74	100	109	146	370	154	368	239	190	171	173	160	260	143	103							
Penzance	699	271	194	361	231	356	564	109	562	433	415	395	367	355	484	422	328	264						
Plymouth	631	203	125	292	162	287	496	45	494	365	346	327	299	286	416	354	259	195	77					
Shrewsbury	415	48	131	140	110	251	280	205	278	104	163	118	66	70	221	202	86	121	315	246				
Southampton	572	134	76	131	141	152	437	112	434	305	257	237	239	227	327	193	170	66	223	155	187			
Stranraer	240	307	390	367	409	509	132	464	85	335	279	230	233	228	164	391	297	380	573	505	288	446		
York	321	134	226	157	245	281	193	300	213	191	38	24	101	71	90	181	87	184	409	341	145	250	224	
London	548	120	120	60	155	78	413	200	411	282	188	199	216	203	288	115	131	56	310	241	163	80	421	212

Road distances between British centres are given in statute miles, using routes recommended by the Automobile Association based on the quickest travelling time. To convert to kilometres, multiply number given by 1.6093.

ROUTES

Air

World flying times

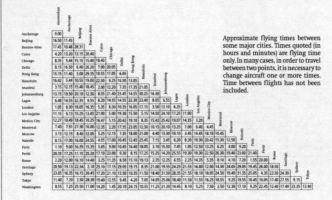

Approximate flying times between some major cities. Times quoted (in hours and minutes) are flying time between two points. In many cases, in order to travel between two points, it is necessary to change aircraft one or more times. Time between flights has not been included.

	Amsterdam	Anchorage	Beijing	Buenos Aires	Cairo	Chicago	Delhi	Hong Kong	Honolulu	Istanbul	Johannesburg	Lagos	London	Los Angeles	Mexico City	Montreal	Moscow	Nairobi	Paris	Perth	Rome	Santiago	Sydney	Tokyo
Anchorage	9.00																							
Beijing	16.50	11.45																						
Buenos Aires	17.45	10.48	28.31																					
Cairo	4.20	13.20	13.15	20.40																				
Chicago	8.35	5.44	15.15	15.40	18.40																			
Delhi	8.15	16.50	6.40	26.20	7.00	20.05																		
Hong Kong	15.15	11.40	3.00	29.35	10.55	17.05	6.05																	
Honolulu	16.42	5.44	10.55	19.00	22.50	9.25	16.50	13.05																
Istanbul	3.15	12.15	15.40	18.45	2.00	12.20	7.35	17.35	21.05															
Johannesburg	13.15	19.50	20.10	12.30	8.55	21.40	23.45	14.55	30.25	16.30														
Lagos	6.40	14.55	22.35	9.55	8.20	14.55	14.55	22.30	23.40	8.05	6.55													
London	1.05	8.30	18.05	16.35	5.35	8.30	10.35	16.05	17.15	3.50	13.10	6.25												
Los Angeles	11.15	6.13	15.25	13.45	21.00	5.00	19.30	15.50	5.15	14.50	24.10	17.25	11.00											
Mexico City	12.27	10.49	18.45	10.35	16.47	5.15	20.42	19.10	8.35	15.42	25.42	19.07	14.35	3.20										
Montreal	7.40	7.31	27.30	16.00	12.35	2.20	17.35	23.05	12.50	10.15	20.10	13.25	7.00	6.40	4.45									
Moscow	3.15	12.15	8.40	22.05	5.25	12.15	7.35	18.00	21.00	4.40	13.30	10.45	3.45	14.45	18.10	10.45								
Nairobi	8.15	17.00	16.00	24.55	4.55	17.00	10.45	12.45	25.45	7.15	3.45	6.20	8.30	19.30	20.42	15.30	12.50							
Paris	1.10	9.00	16.35	15.35	5.05	9.00	10.45	16.40	18.05	3.10	15.50	7.45	1.05	12.50	13.25	6.25	4.00	9.20						
Perth	20.35	17.25	11.15	25.20	17.10	23.00	9.30	8.15	17.25	15.25	14.20	25.55	19.30	19.30	22.50	26.30	19.40	23.00	21.40					
Rome	2.20	12.00	16.10	14.40	3.25	11.35	8.50	15.10	19.13	2.35	12.25	6.55	2.25	14.35	5.35	8.10	4.10	7.20	1.55	20.00				
Santiago	20.50	19.13	22.34	2.10	25.10	17.15	29.05	19.15	8.35	21.00	19.55	24.25	21.55	16.00	12.00	14.50	24.05	29.05	19.45	26.00	18.50			
Sydney	23.05	16.35	16.15	20.45	17.20	21.10	13.50	10.35	11.50	18.40	31.50	28.35	21.55	21.55	18.40	31.35	25.05	4.35	23.50	4.30	24.30			
Tokyo	11.40	7.20	3.50	28.30	19.40	12.55	9.45	4.20	7.05	14.05	25.00	18.40	11.50	11.55	16.25	19.55	16.45	10.05	17.40	27.55	9.15			
Washington	8.55	7.25	25.50	11.00	14.20	1.45	20.10	24.15	10.55	21.25	21.20	24.45	8.10	5.25	7.50	2.30	12.30	17.10	9.25	22.45	12.40	17.40	23.35	12.40

US air distances

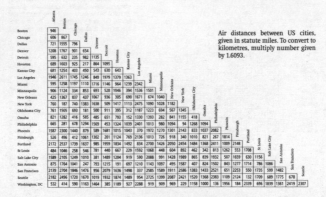

Air distances between US cities, given in statute miles. To convert to kilometres, multiply number given by 1.6093.

	Atlanta	Boston	Chicago	Dallas	Denver	Detroit	Houston	Kansas City	Los Angeles	Miami	Minneapolis	New Orleans	New York	Oklahoma City	Omaha	Philadelphia	Phoenix	Pittsburgh	Portland	St Louis	Salt Lake City	San Antonio	San Francisco	Seattle
Boston	946																							
Chicago	606	867																						
Dallas	721	1555	796																					
Denver	1208	1767	901	654																				
Detroit	595	632	235	982	1135																			
Houston	689	1603	925	217	864	1095																		
Kansas City	681	1254	403	450	543	630	643																	
Los Angeles	1946	2611	1745	1246	849	1979	1379	1363																
Miami	595	1258	1197	1110	1716	1146	964	1239	2342															
Minneapolis	906	1124	334	853	693	528	1046	394	1536	1501														
New Orleans	425	1367	837	437	1067	936	305	690	1671	674	1040													
New York	760	187	740	1383	1638	509	1417	1113	2475	1090	1028	1182												
Oklahoma City	761	1505	693	181	500	911	395	312	1187	1223	694	567	1345											
Omaha	821	1282	416	585	485	651	793	152	1330	1393	282	841	1155	418										
Philadelphia	665	281	678	1294	1569	453	1324	1039	2401	1013	980	1094	94	1268	1094									
Phoenix	1587	2300	1440	879	589	1681	1015	1043	370	1972	1270	1301	2143	833	1037	2082								
Pittsburgh	526	496	412	1061	1302	201	1124	769	2136	1013	726	918	340	1010	821	267	1814							
Portland	2172	2537	1739	1637	985	1959	1834	1492	834	2700	1426	2050	2454	1484	1368	2411	1062	553	1708					
St Louis	484	1046	258	546	781	440	667	229	1592	1068	448	604	892	462	342	813	1262	507	1659	630	1156			
Salt Lake City	1589	2105	1249	1010	381	1489	1204	919	590	2088	991	1428	1989	865	839	1714	507	1278	630	1156				
San Antonio	875	1764	1041	247	793	1215	191	697	1210	1097	495	1587	407	824	1502	843	1277	786	1086					
San Francisco	2139	2704	1846	1476	956	2079	1636	1498	337	2585	1589	1911	2586	1383	1433	2521	651	2253	550	1735	599	1482		
Seattle	2182	2496	1720	1670	1019	1932	1874	1489	954	2725	1399	2087	2421	1520	1368	2383	1109	2124	132	1709	689	1775	678	
Washington, DC	532	414	590	1163	1464	385	1189	927	2288	919	909	969	229	1158	1000	136	1956	184	2339	696	1839	1361	2419	2307

International time zones

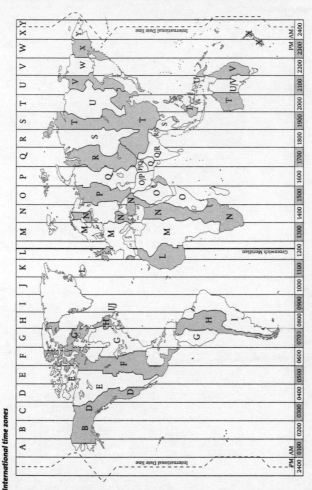

ROUTES

Some countries have adopted half-hour time zones which are indicated on the map as a combination of two coded zones.

PART ELEVEN

Science and Technology

MEASUREMENT

Basic SI units

The SI (Système International d'Unitiés) system of units has seven basic units from which all derived units are obtained. Multiples and submultiples of the basic units may be used with approved prefixes.

1 metre *(unit of length)* symbol: m
The metre is the distance travelled by light in a vacuum during a time interval of 1/299 729 458 seconds.

2 kilogram *(unit of mass)* symbol: kg
The kilogram is the unit of mass equal to the mass of the international prototype kilogram kept at Sèvres, France.

3 second *(unit of time)* symbol: s
The second is the duration of 9 192 631 770 periods of the radiation corresponding to the quantized electron transition between two hyperfine levels of the ground state of the caesium-133 atom.

4 ampere *(unit of electric current)* symbol: A
The ampere is that constant electric current which, if maintained in two straight parallel conductors of infinite length, of negligible cross-section and placed 1 metre apart in vacuum, would produce between these conductors a force equal to 2×10^{-7} newton/ metre.

5 kelvin *(unit of temperature)* symbol: K
The kelvin, unit of thermodynamic temperature is the fraction 1/273.16 of the thermodynamic temperature of the triple point of water.

6 candela *(unit of luminous intensity)* symbol: cd
The candela is the luminous intensity, in a perpendicular direction, of a surface 1/600 000 $metre^2$ of a black body at the freezing point of platinum at a pressure of 101 325 newton/$metre^2$.

7 mole *(unit of amount of substance)* symbol: mol
The mole is the amount of substance containing as many elementary units as there are carbon atoms in 0.012 kilogram of carbon-12. The elementary unit may be an atom, a molecule, an ion or an electron.

Two supplementary units are also used:
radian *(unit of plane angle)* symbol: rad
The radian is the unit of measurement of angle and is the angle subtended at the centre of a circle by an arc equal in length to the circle radius.
steradian *(unit of solid angle)* symbol: sr
The steradian is the unit of measurement of solid angle and is the solid angle subtended at the centre of a circle by a spherical cap equal in area to the square of the circle radius.

SI conversion factors

This table gives the conversion factors for many British and other units which are still in common use, showing their equivalents in terms of the International System of Units (SI). The column labelled 'SI equivalent' gives the SI value of 1 unit of the type named in the first column, e.g. 1 calorie is 4.187 joules. The column labelled 'Reciprocal' allows conversion the other way, eg 1 joule is 0.239 calories. (All values are to three decimal places.) As a second example, 1 dyne is $10 \mu N = 10 \times 10^{-6} N = 10^{-5} N$; so 1 newton is $0.1 \times 10^{-6} = 10^5$ dyne. Finally, 1 torr is 0.133 kPa = 0.133×10^3 Pa; so 1 Pa is 7.501×10^{-3} torr.

Unit name	Symbol	Quantity	SI equivalent	Unit	Reciprocal
acre		area	0.405	hm^2	2.471
ångström[a]	Å	length	0.1	nm	10
astronomical unit	AU	length	0.150	Tm	6.684
atomic mass unit	amu	mass	1.661×10^{-27}	kg	6.022×10^{26}
bar	bar	pressure	0.1	MPa	10
barn	b	area	100	fm^2	0.01
barrel (US) = 42 US gal	bbl	volume	0.159	m^3	6.290
British thermal unit	btu	energy	1.055	kJ	0.948
calorie	cal	energy	4.187	J	0.239
cubic foot	cu ft	volume	0.028	m^3	35.315
cubic inch	cu in	volume	16.387	cm^3	0.061
cubic yard	cu yd	volume	0.765	m^3	1.308
curie[a]	Ci	activity of radionuclide	37	GBq	0.027
degree = 1/90 rt angle	°	plane angle	$\pi/180$	rad	57.296
degree Celsius	°C	temperature	1	K	1
degree Centigrade	°C	temperature	1	K	1
degree Fahrenheit	°F	temperature	5/9	K	1.8
degree Rankine	°R	temperature	5/9	K	1.8
dyne	dyn	force	10	μN	0.1
electronvolt	eV	energy	0.160	aJ	6.241
erg	erg	energy	0.1	μJ	10
fathom (6ft)		length	1.829	m	0.547
fermi	fm	length	1	fm	1
foot	ft	length	30.48	cm	0.033
foot per second	ft s^{-1}	velocity	0.305	m s^{-1}	3.281
			1.097	km h^{-1}	0.911
gallon (UK)[a]	gal	volume	4.546	dm^3	0.220

SI conversion factors (continued)

Unit name	Symbol	Quantity	SI equivalent	Unit	Reciprocal
gallon (US)[a] = 231cu in	gal	volume	3.785	dm³	0.264
gallon (UK) per mile		consumption	2.825	dm³ km⁻¹	0.354
gauss	Gs, G	magnetic flux density	100	μT	0.01
grade = 0.01 rt angle	rt angle	plane angle	π/200	rad	63.662
grain	gr	mass	0.065	g	15.432
hectare[a]	ha	area	1	hm²	1
horsepower	hp	power	0.746	kW	1.341
inch	in	length	2.54	cm	0.394
kilogram-force	kgf	force	9.807	N	0.102
knot[a]		velocity	1.852	km h⁻¹	0.540
light year	ly	length	9.461×10¹⁵	m	1.057 × 10⁻¹⁶
litre	l	volume	1	dm³	1
Mach number	Ma	velocity	1193.3	km h⁻¹	8.380 × 10⁻⁴
maxwell	Mx	magnetic flux	10	nWb	0.1
metric carat		mass	0.2	g	5
micron	μ	length	1	μm	1
mile (nautical)[a]		length	1.852	km	0.540
mile (statute)		length	1.609	km	0.621
miles per hour (mph)	mile h⁻¹	velocity	1.609	km h⁻¹	0.621
minute = (1/60)°	′	plane angle	π/10 800	rad	3437.75
oersted	Oe	magnetic field strength	1/(4π)	kA m⁻¹	4π
ounce (avoirdupois)	oz	mass	28.349	g	0.035
ounce (troy) = 480 gr		mass	31.103	g	0.032
parsec	pc	length	30857	Tm	0.0000324
phot	ph	illuminance	10	klx	0.1
pint (UK)	pt	volume	0.568	dm³	1.760
poise	P	viscosity	0.1	Pa s	10
pound	lb	mass	0.454	kg	2.205
pound force	lbf	force	4.448	N	0.225
pound force/in		pressure	6.895	kPa	0.145
poundal	pdl	force	0.138	N	7.233
pounds per square inch	psi	pressure	6.895 × 10³	kPa	0.145
rad[a]	rad	absorbed dose	0.01	Gy	100
rem[a]	rem	dose equivalent	0.01	Sv	100
right angle = π/2 rad		plane angle	1.571	rad	0.637
röntgen[a]	R	exposure	0.258	mC kg⁻¹	3.876
second = (1/60)′	″	plane angle	π/648	mrad	206.265
slug		mass	14.594	kg	0.068
solar mass	M	mass	1.989 × 10³⁰	kg	5.028 × 10⁻³¹
square foot	sq ft	area	9.290	dm²	0.108
square inch	sq in	area	6.452	cm²	0.155
square mile (statute)	sq mi	area	2.590	km²	0.386
square yard	sq yd	area	0.836	m²	1.196
standard atmosphere	atm	pressure	0.101	MPa	9.869
stere	st	volume	1	m³	1
stilb	sb	luminance	10	kcd m⁻²	0.1
stokes	St	viscosity	1	cm² s⁻¹	1
therm = 10⁵ btu		energy	0.105	GJ	9.478
ton = 2240 lb		mass	1.016	Mg	0.984
ton-force	tonf	force	9.964	kN	0.100
ton-force/sq in		pressure	15.444	MPa	0.065
tonne	t	mass	1	Mg	1
torr, or mmHg	torr	pressure	0.133	kPa	7.501
X unit		length	0.100	pm	10
yard	yd	length	0.914	m	1.093

[a] In temporary use with SI.

SI prefixes

Factor	Prefix	Symbol	Factor	Prefix	Symbol	Factor	Prefix	Symbol
10¹⁸	exa-	E	10²	hecto-	h	10⁻⁹	nano-	n
10¹⁵	peta-	P	10¹	deca-	da	10⁻¹²	pico-	p
10¹²	tera-	T	10⁻¹	deci-	d	10⁻¹⁵	femto-	f
10⁹	giga-	G	10⁻²	centi-	c	10⁻¹⁸	atto-	a
10⁶	mega-	M	10⁻³	milli-	m			
10³	kilo-	k	10⁻⁶	micro-	μ			

Common measures

Metric units		Imperial equivalent	Imperial units		Metric equivalent
Length			*Length*		
	1 millimetre (mm)	0.03937 in		1 inch	2.54 cm
10 mm	1 centimetre (cm)	0.39 in	12 in	1 foot	30.48 cm
10 cm	1 decimetre (dm)	3.94 in	3 ft	1 yard	0.9144 m
100 cm	1 metre (m)	39.37 in	1 760 yd	1 mile	1.6093 km
1000 m	1 kilometre (km)	0.62 mi			
			Area		
Area				1 square inch	6.45 cm²
	1 square millimetre	0.0016 sq in	144 sq in	1 square foot	0.0929 m²
	1 square centimetre	0.155 sq in	9 sq ft	1 square yard	0.836 m²
100 cm²	1 square decimetre	15.5 sq in	4 840 sq yd	1 acre	0.405 ha
10 000 cm²	1 square metre	10.76 sq ft	640 acres	1 square mile	259 ha
10 000 m²	1 hectare	2.47 acres			
			Volume		
Volume				1 cubic inch	16.3871 cm³
	1 cubic centimetre	0.061 cu in	1 728 cu in	1 cubic foot	0.028 m³
1 000 cm³	1 cubic decimetre	61.024 cu in	27 cu ft	1 cubic yard	0.765 m³
1 000 dm³	1 cubic metre	35.31 cu ft			
		1.308 cu yd	*Liquid volume*		
				1 pint	0.57 l
Liquid volume			2 pt	1 quart	1.14 l
	1 litre	1.76 pt	4 qt	1 gallon	4.55 l
100 l	1 hectolitre	22 gal			
			Weight		
Weight				1 ounce	28.3495 g
	1 gram	0.035 oz	16 oz	1 pound	0.4536 kg
1 000 g	1 kilogram	2.2046 lb	14 lb	1 stone	6.35 kg
1 000 kg	1 tonne	0.0842 ton	8 st	1 hundredweight	50.8 kg
			20 cwt	1 ton	1.016 t

Conversion factors

Imperial to metric			Multiply by
Length			
inches	→	millimetres	25.4
inches	→	centimetres	2.54
feet	→	metres	0.3048
yards	→	metres	0.9144
statute miles	→	kilometres	1.6093
nautical miles	→	kilometres	1.852
Area			
square inches	→	square centimetres	6.4516
square feet	→	square metres	0.0929
square yards	→	square metres	0.8361
acres	→	hectares	0.4047
square miles	→	square kilometres	2.5899
Volume			
cubic inches	→	cubic centimetres	16.3871
cubic feet	→	cubic metres	0.0283
cubic yards	→	cubic metres	0.7646
Capacity			
UK fluid ounces	→	litres	0.0284
US fluid ounces	→	litres	0.0296
UK pints	→	litres	0.5682

US pints	→	litres	0.4732
UK gallons	→	litres	4.546
US gallons	→	litres	3.7854
Weight			
ounces (avoirdupois)	→	grams	28.3495
ounces (troy)	→	grams	31.1035
pounds	→	kilograms	0.4536
tons (long)	→	tonnes	1.016

Metric to imperial			Multiply by
Length			
millimetres	→	inches	0.0394
centimetres	→	inches	0.3937
metres	→	feet	3.2806
metres	→	yards	1.0936
kilometres	→	statute miles	0.6214
kilometres	→	nautical miles	0.54
Area			
square centimetres	→	square inches	0.155
square metres	→	square feet	10.764
square metres	→	square yards	1.196
hectares	→	acres	2.471
square kilometres	→	square miles	0.386

Conversion factors (continued)

Volume			Multiply by
cubic centimetres	→	cubic inches	0.061
cubic metres	→	cubic feet	35.315
cubic metres	→	cubic yards	1.308

Capacity			
litres	→	UK fluid ounces	35.1961
litres	→	US fluid ounces	33.8150
litres	→	UK pints	1.7598

litres	→	US pints	2.1134
litres	→	UK gallons	0.2199
litres	→	US gallons	0.2642

Weight			
grams	→	ounces (avoirdupois)	0.0353
grams	→	ounces (troy)	0.0322
kilograms	→	pounds	2.2046
tonnes	→	tons (long)	0.9842

Conversion table: tyre pressures

lb per sq in	kg/cm²
10	0.7
15	1.1
20	1.4
24	1.7
26	1.8
28	2
30	2.1
40	2.8

Conversion table: oven temperatures

Gas Mark	Electricity		Rating
	°C	°F	
½	120	250	Slow
1	140	275	
2	150	300	
3	170	325	
4	180	350	Moderate
5	190	375	
6	200	400	Hot
7	220	425	
8	230	450	Very hot
9	260	500	

Temperature conversion

To convert	To	Operations
°Fahrenheit	°Celsius	−32, × 5, ÷ 9
°Fahrenheit	°Rankine	+ 459.67
°Fahrenheit	°Réaumur	− 32, × 4, ÷ 9
°Celsius	°Fahrenheit	× 9, ÷ 5, + 32
°Celsius	Kelvin	+ 273.16
°Celsius	°Réaumur	× 4, ÷ 5
Kelvin	°Celsius	− 273.16
°Rankine	°Fahrenheit	−459.67
°Réaumur	°Fahrenheit	× 9, ÷ 4, + 32
°Réaumur	°Celsius	× 5, ÷ 4

Carry out operations in sequence.

Temperature scales

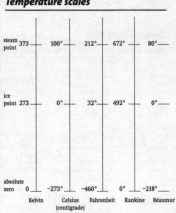

	Kelvin	Celsius (centigrade)	Fahrenheit	Rankine	Réaumur
steam point	373 — 100°	212°	672°	80°
ice point	273 — 0°	32°	492°	0°
absolute zero	0 — −273°	−460°	0°	−218°

Numerical equivalents

Arabic	Roman	Greek	Binary numbers
1	I	α′	1
2	II	β′	10
3	III	γ′	11
4	IV	δ′	100
5	V	ε′	101
6	VI	ς′	110
7	VII	ζ′	111
8	VIII	η′	1000
9	IX	θ′	1001
10	X	ι′	1010
11	XI	ια′	1011
12	XII	ιβ′	1100
13	XIII	ιγ′	1101
14	XIV	ιδ′	1110
15	XV	ιε′	1111
16	XVI	ις′	10000
17	XVII	ιζ′	10001
18	XVIII	ιη′	10010
19	XIX	ιθ′	10011
20	XX	κ′	10100
30	XXX	λ′	11110
40	XL	μ′	101000
50	L	ν′	110010
60	LX	ξ′	111100
70	LXX	ο′	1000110
80	LXXX	π′	1010000
90	XC	ϟ′	1011010
100	C	ρ′	1100100
200	CC	σ′	11001000
300	CCC	τ′	100101100
400	CD	υ′	110010000
500	D	φ′	111110100
1000	M	͵α	1111101000
5000	V	͵ε	1001110001000
10000	X	͵ι	10011100010000
100000	C	͵ρ	11000011010000000

Fraction	Decimal	Fraction	Decimal
$1/2$	0.5000	$8/11$	0.7272
$1/3$	0.3333	$9/11$	0.8181
$2/3$	0.6667	$10/11$	0.9090
$1/4$	0.2500	$1/12$	0.0833
$3/4$	0.7500	$5/12$	0.4167
$1/5$	0.2000	$7/12$	0.5833
$2/5$	0.4000	$11/12$	0.9167
$3/5$	0.6000	$1/16$	0.0625
$4/5$	0.8000	$3/16$	0.1875
$1/6$	0.1667	$5/16$	0.3125
$5/6$	0.8333	$7/16$	0.4375
$1/7$	0.1429	$9/16$	0.5625
$2/7$	0.2857	$11/16$	0.6875
$3/7$	0.4286	$13/16$	0.8125
$4/7$	0.5714	$15/16$	0.9375
$5/7$	0.7143	$1/20$	0.0500
$6/7$	0.8571	$3/20$	0.1500
$1/8$	0.1250	$7/20$	0.3500
$3/8$	0.3750	$9/20$	0.4500
$5/8$	0.6250	$11/20$	0.5500
$7/8$	0.8750	$13/20$	0.6500
$1/9$	0.1111	$17/20$	0.8500
$2/9$	0.2222	$19/20$	0.9500
$4/9$	0.4444	$1/32$	0.0312
$5/9$	0.5555	$3/32$	0.0938
$7/9$	0.7778	$5/32$	0.1562
$8/9$	0.8889	$7/32$	0.2187
$1/10$	0.1000	$9/32$	0.2812
$3/10$	0.3000	$11/32$	0.3437
$7/10$	0.7000	$13/32$	0.4062
$9/10$	0.9000	$15/32$	0.4687
$1/11$	0.0909	$17/32$	0.5312
$2/11$	0.1818	$19/32$	0.5937
$3/11$	0.2727	$21/32$	0.6562
$4/11$	0.3636	$23/32$	0.7187
$5/11$	0.4545	$25/32$	0.7812
$6/11$	0.5454	$27/32$	0.8437
$7/11$	0.6363	$29/32$	0.9062
		$31/32$	0.9687

%	Decimal	Fraction
1	0.01	$1/100$
2	0.02	$1/50$
3	0.03	$3/100$
4	0.04	$1/25$
5	0.05	$1/20$
6	0.06	$3/50$
7	0.07	$7/100$
8	0.08	$2/25$
$8^1/_3$	0.083	$1/12$
9	0.09	$9/100$
10	0.1	$1/10$
11	0.11	$11/100$
12	0.12	$3/25$
$12^1/_2$	0.125	$1/8$
13	0.13	$13/100$
14	0.14	$7/50$
15	0.15	$3/20$
16	0.16	$4/25$
$16^2/_3$	0.167	$1/6$
17	0.17	$17/100$
18	0.18	$9/50$
19	0.19	$19/100$
20	0.20	$1/5$
21	0.21	$21/100$
22	0.22	$11/50$
23	0.23	$23/100$
24	0.24	$6/25$
25	0.25	$1/4$
26	0.26	$13/50$
27	0.27	$27/100$
28	0.28	$7/25$
29	0.29	$29/100$
30	0.30	$3/10$
31	0.31	$31/100$
32	0.32	$8/25$
33	0.33	$33/100$
$33^1/_3$	0.333	$1/3$
34	0.34	$17/50$
35	0.35	$7/20$
36	0.36	$9/25$
37	0.37	$37/100$
38	0.38	$19/50$
39	0.39	$39/100$
40	0.40	$2/5$
41	0.41	$41/100$
42	0.42	$21/50$
43	0.43	$43/100$
44	0.44	$11/25$
45	0.45	$9/20$
46	0.46	$23/50$
47	0.47	$47/100$
48	0.48	$12/25$
49	0.49	$49/100$
50	0.50	$1/2$
55	0.55	$11/20$
60	0.60	$3/5$
65	0.65	$13/20$
70	0.70	$7/10$
75	0.75	$3/4$
80	0.80	$4/5$
85	0.85	$17/20$
90	0.90	$9/10$
95	0.95	$19/20$
100	1.00	1

CHEMISTRY

Table of elements

Atomic weights are taken from the 1983 list of the International Union of Pure and Applied Chemistry. For radioactive elements, the mass number of the most stable isotope is given in square brackets.

Symbol	Element	Atomic no.	Weight
Ac	Actinium	89	[227.0278]
Ag	Silver	47	107.8682
Al	Aluminium	13	26.98154
Am	Americium	95	[243]
Ar	Argon	18	39.948
As	Arsenic	33	74.9216
At	Astatine	85	[210]
Au	Gold	79	196.9665
B	Boron	5	10.811
Ba	Barium	56	137.33
Be	Beryllium	4	9.01218
Bh	Bohrium	107	[262]
Bi	Bismuth	83	208.9804
Bk	Berkelium	97	[247]
Br	Bromine	35	79.904
C	Carbon	6	12.011
Ca	Calcium	20	40.078
Cd	Cadmium	48	112.41
Ce	Cerium	58	140.12
Cf	Californium	98	[252]
Cl	Chlorine	17	35.453
Cm	Curium	96	[247]
Co	Cobalt	27	58.9332
Cr	Chromium	24	51.9961
Cs	Caesium/Cesium	55	132.9054
Cu	Copper	29	63.546
Db	Dubnium	105	[262]
Dy	Dysprosium	66	162.50
Er	Erbium	68	167.26
Es	Einsteinium	99	[254]
Eu	Europium	63	151.96
F	Fluorine	9	18.998403
Fe	Iron	26	55.847
Fm	Fermium	100	[257]
Fr	Francium	87	[223]
Ga	Gallium	31	69.723
Gd	Gadolinium	64	157.25
Ge	Germanium	32	72.59
H	Hydrogen	1	1.00794
He	Helium	2	4.002602
Hf	Hafnium	72	178.49
Hg	Mercury	80	200.59
Ho	Holmium	67	164.9304
Hs	Hassium	108	[265]
I	Iodine	53	126.9045
In	Indium	49	114.82
Ir	Iridium	77	192.22
K	Potassium	19	39.0983
Kr	Krypton	36	83.80
La	Lanthanum	57	138.9055
Li	Lithium	3	6.941
Lr	Lutetium	71	174.967
Lw	Lawrencium	103	[260]
Md	Mendelevium	101	[258]

Symbol	Element	Atomic no.	Weight
Mg	Magnesium	12	24.305
Mn	Manganese	25	54.9380
Mo	Molybdenum	42	95.94
Mt	Meitnerium	109	[266]
N	Nitrogen	7	14.0067
Na	Sodium	11	22.98977
Nb	Niobium	41	92.9064
Nd	Neodymium	60	144.24
Ne	Neon	10	20.179
Ni	Nickel	28	58.69
No	Nobelium	102	[259]
Np	Neptunium	93	[237.0482]
O	Oxygen	8	15.9994
Os	Osmium	76	190.2
P	Phosphorus	15	30.97376
Pa	Protactinium	91	[231.0359]
Pb	Lead	82	207.2
Pd	Palladium	46	106.42
Pm	Promethium	61	[145]
Po	Polonium	84	[209]
Pr	Praseodymium	59	140.9077
Pt	Platinum	78	195.08
Pu	Plutonium	94	[244]
Ra	Radium	88	[226.0254]
Rb	Rubidium	37	85.4678
Re	Rhenium	75	186.207
Rf	Rutherfordium	104	[261]
Rh	Rhodium	45	102.9055
Rn	Radon	86	[222]
Ru	Ruthenium	44	101.77
S	Sulphur/sulfur	16	32.066
Sb	Antimony	51	121.75
Sc	Scandium	21	44.95591
Se	Selenium	34	78.96
Sg	Seaborgium	106	[263]
Si	Silicon	14	28.0855
Sm	Samarium	62	150.36
Sn	Tin	50	118.69
Sr	Strontium	38	87.62
Ta	Tantalum	73	180.9479
Tb	Terbium	65	158.9254
Tc	Technetium	43	[98]
Te	Tellurium	52	127.60
Th	Thorium	90	232.0381
Ti	Titanium	22	47.88
Tl	Thallium	81	204.383
Tm	Thulium	69	168.9342
U	Uranium	92	238.0289
Uub	Ununbium	112	[277]
Uun	Ununnilium	110	[269]
Uuu	Unununium	111	[272]
V	Vanadium	23	50.9415
W	Tungsten	74	183.85
Xe	Xenon	54	131.29
Y	Yttrium	39	88.9059
Yb	Ytterbium	70	173.04
Zn	Zinc	30	65.38
Zr	Zirconium	40	91.224

Periodic table of elements

The periodic table is a method of listing the chemical elements in terms of increasing atomic number, so that the rows represent increasing occupancy of an electron subshell, and the columns represent equivalent numbers of valence electrons. The original table of Mendeleyev (1869) was based on atomic weight, but had several successes in predicting the existence and chemical properties of undiscovered elements.

1	2	3	4	5	6	7	8	9	10	11	12	13	14	15	16	17	18
1 H																	2 He
3 Li	4 Be											5 B	6 C	7 N	8 O	9 F	10 Ne
11 Na	12 Mg											13 Al	14 Si	15 P	16 S	17 Cl	18 Ar
19 K	20 Ca	21 Sc	22 Ti	23 V	24 Cr	25 Mn	26 Fe	27 Co	28 Ni	29 Cu	30 Zn	31 Ga	32 Ge	33 As	34 Se	35 Br	36 Kr
37 Rb	38 Sr	39 Y	40 Zr	41 Nb	42 Mo	43 Tc	44 Ru	45 Rh	46 Pd	47 Ag	48 Cd	49 In	50 Sn	51 Sb	52 Te	53 I	54 Xe
55 Cs	56 Ba	57-71 lanthanide series see below	72 Hf	73 Ta	74 W	75 Re	76 Os	77 Ir	78 Pt	79 Au	80 Hg	81 Tl	82 Pb	83 Bi	84 Po	85 At	86 Rn
87 Fr	88 Ra	89-103 Actinide series see below	104 Rf	105 Db	106 Sg	107 Bh	108 Hs	109 Mt	110 Uun	111 Uuu	112 Uub						

Transition series

under investigation

Lanthanide series	57 La	58 Ce	59 Pr	60 Nd	61 Pm	62 Sm	63 Eu	64 Gd	65 Tb	66 Dy	67 Ho	68 Er	69 Tm	70 Yt	71 Lu
Actinide series	89 Ac	90 Th	91 Pa	92 U	93 Np	94 Pu	95 Am	96 Cm	97 Bk	98 Cf	99 Es	100 Fm	101 Md	102 No	103 Lr

atomic number / symbol

86 Rn

Hazardous substances symbols

Harmful/ irritant	Toxic	Radioactive	Flammable	Corrosive	Oxidizing/ supports fire	Explosive

TECHNOLOGY

Major technological inventions

Date	Invention	Inventor/discoverer
1752	Lightning conductor	Benjamin Franklin
1764	Spinning jenny	James Hargreaves
1768	Spinning frame	Richard Arkwright
1769	Condenser (steam engine)	James Watt
1774	Telegraph (electric)	Georges Louis Lesage
1775	Steam ship	Jacques Perrier
1776	Submarine	David Bushnell
1779	Spinning mule	Samuel Crompton
1780	Circular saw	Gervinus
1783	Hot-air balloon	Jacques and Joseph Montgolfier
1784	Safety lock	Joseph Bramah
1785	Chemical bleaching	Claude Berthollet
1792	Cotton gin	Eli Whitney
1792	Gas lighting	William Murdock
1795	Preserving jar (foods)	Nicolas Appert
1798	Lithography	Aloys Senefelder
1799	Sheet paper-making machine	Louis Robert
1800	Electric battery	Alessandro Volta
1802	Wood-planing machine	Joseph Bramah
1804	Locomotive	Richard Trevithick
1807	Conveyor belt	Oliver Evans
1810	Canning	Nicolas Appert
1812	Photographic lens	William H Wollaston
1813	Power loom	William Horrocks
1823	Waterproof material	Charles Macintosh
1824	Cement	Joseph Aspdin
1829	Typewriter	William Burt
1831	Electric generator	Michael Faraday
1834	Harvesting machine	Cyrus McCormick
1835	Revolver	Samuel Colt
1835	Computer	Charles Babbage
1838	Photography (on paper)	William Henry Fox Talbot
1839	Bicycle	Kirkpatrick Macmillan
1843	Underground railway	Charles Pearson
1845	Hydraulic crane	W G Armstrong
1846	Sewing machine	Elias Howe
1846	Rotary printing press	Richard Hoe
1850	Synthetic oil	James Young
1850	Refrigerator	James Harrison and Alexander Twining
1851	Mechanical lift	Elisha Otis
1854	Hydraulic lift	Elisha Otis
1855	Celluloid	Alexander Parks
1855	Steel production	Henry Bessemer

Date	Invention	Inventor/discoverer
1856	Synthetic dye	William Henry Perkin
1861	Colour photography	James Clerk Maxwell
1866	Telegraph (transatlantic)	Willliam Thompson (Lord Kelvin)
1867	Pasteurization	Louis Pasteur
1868	Tungsten steel	Robert Mushet
1868	Traffic lights	J P Knight
1871	Pneumatic drill	Samuel Ingersoll
1872	Electric typewriter	Thomas Edison
1873	Barbed wire	Joseph Glidden
1876	Telephone	Alexander Graham Bell
1876	Microphone	Alexander Graham Bell
1877	Electric welding	Elisha Thomson
1877	Gramophone	Thomas Edison
1878	Electric railway	Ernst Werner von Siemens
1879	Electric lamp	Thomas Edison
1880	Pendulum seismograph	James Ewing, Thomas Gray, and Sir John Milne
1882	Electric flat iron	Harry W Seeley
1883	Automatic machine gun	Sir Hiram (Stevens) Maxim
1884	Fountain pen	Lewis Waterman
1884	Car (internal combustion engine)	Gottlieb Daimler
1885	Adding machine	William Burroughs
1885	Petrol engine	Gottlieb Daimler
1885	Motorcycle	Gottlieb Daimler
1886	Car (petrol engine)	Karl Benz
1887	Celluloid film	Goodwin
1888	Pneumatic tyre	John Boyd Dunlop
1888	Alternating-current motor	Nikola Tesla
1888	Gramophone record	Emil Berliner
1889	Photographic film	George Eastman
1892	Escalator	Jesse Reno
1894	Automatic loom	J H Northrop
1894	Cinematograph	Auguste and Louis Lumière
1894	Turbine ship	Charles Parsons
1895	X-ray	Wilhelm Röntgen
1895	Safety razor	King C Gillette
1898	Diesel engine	Rudolf Diesel
1900	Cellophane	J E Brandenburger
1900	Airship	Graf Ferdinand von Zeppelin
1901	Radio	Guglielmo Marconi
1901	Vacuum cleaner (electric)	Hubert Cecil Booth

Major technological inventions (continued)

Date	Invention	Inventor/discoverer
1902	Windscreen wipers	Mary Anderson
1903	Electrocardiograph	Willem Einthoven
1903	Aeroplane	Orville and Wilbur Wright
1906	Freeze-drying	Arsene D'Arsonval and Georges Bordas
1907	Electric washing machine	Hurley Machine Co.
1907	Facsimile machine (fax)	Arthur Korn
1907	Bakelite	Leo Baekeland
1911	Neon light	Georges Claude
1913	Stainless steel	Harry Brearley
1924	Loudspeaker	Rice-Kellogg
1926	Television	John Logie Baird
1926	Liquid-fuel rocket	Robert Goddard
1933	Electron microscope	Max Knoll and Ernst Ruska
1934	Cat's eyes	Percy Shaw
1935	Parking meter	Carlton C Magee
1937	Turbo jet	Frank Whittle
1938	Ball-point pen	Laszlo and Georg Biró
1938	Nylon	Wallace Carrothers
1938	Xerography	Charles Carson
1939	Helicopter	Igor Sikorsky
1939	Atom bomb	Otto Frisch, Niels Bohr, and Rudolf Peierls
1941	Terylene	J R Whinfield and J T Dickson
1942	Turbo-prop engine	Max Mueller
1944	Digital computer	Harvard University
1945	Microwave oven	Percy Le Baron Spencer
1948	Transistor	William Shockley, John Bardeen, and Walter Brattain
1950	Gas-turbine powered car	Rover Motor Co.
1954	Solar battery	Bell Telephone Co.
1956	Video recorder	Ampex Co.
1959	Hovercraft	Christopher Cockerell
1959	Microchip	Kilby and Robert Noyce
1960	Laser	Charles Townes
1967	Laser-surgery	Cincinnati, US operating theatre
1969	Concorde supersonic	Britain–France
1969	Test-tube baby	Robert Edwards, Patrick Steptoe
1969	V/STOL Harrier	Hawker Siddeley
1969	Charge-coupled device (CCD)	Bell Labs
1970	747 Jumbo jet	Boeing
1971	Microprocessor	Marcian Hoff

Date	Invention	Inventor/discoverer
1971	First e-mail message	Ray Tomlinson
1972	Pocket calculator	
1976	Industrial robot	
1976	Space shuttle	NASA
1978	TGV high-speed train	France
1979	Walkman	Sony
1979	Compact disc	Philips and Sony
1980	MRI (Magnetic Resonance Imaging)	Damadian, Lauterbur, Mansfield
1981	Personal computer	IBM
1983	Analog Camcorder	Sony
1983	Cell phone	Martin Cooper
1985	Battery-powered vehicle (C5)	Clive Sinclair
1985	Genetic fingerprinting	Alec Jeffreys
1986	Laser instruments for heart and eye surgery	
1986	Pocket telephone	
1987	Digital audio tape	
1988	Video walkman	Sony
1988	Optical microprocessor	
1988	Digital camera	Fuji
1990	INCAT (High speed catamaran car ferry)	INCAT, Tasmania
1991	World Wide Web	Tim Berners-Lee
1992	Superconducting ceramic microchip	Sanyo Electric
1992	Compact disc-interactive player	Philips
1992	First text message to mobile phone sent in UK	
1993	Pentium 64-bit processor	Intel
1994	Digital camcorder	
1995	Commercial text messaging service	
1996	Fuel-cell powered car	Daimler–Benz
1997	Cloning of "Dolly" the sheep	Roslin Institute
1997	Hybrid petrol-electric motor car	Toyota
1998	Digital TV broadcasting	
1998	Spacecraft using ion-drive	NASA
1999	Wireless networking	
2001	iPod MP3 music player	Apple
2001	Broadband ADSL widespread	
2002	Supersonic Combustion Ramjet (Scramjet)	University of Queensland

The world's tallest structures

Name of structure	Location	Year		Height	
				m	ft
Warszawa Radio Mast	Konstantynow, Poland	1974	(collapsed 1991)	646	2 120
KTHI-TV mast	North Dakota, US	1963		629	2 063
CN Tower	Toronto, Canada	1975		555	1 822
Ostankino TV Tower	Nr Moscow, Russia	1967		537	1 762
WRBL-TV & WTVM	Georgia, US	1963		533	1 749
WBIR-TV	Tennessee, US	1963		533	1 749
Moscow TV Tower	Moscow, Russia			528	1 732
Chongqing Office Tower	Chongqing, China	1998		516	1 692
KFVS-TV	Missouri, US	1960		510	1 672
Taipei Financial Centre	Taipei, Taiwan	2002		508	1 669
WSPD-TV	Kentucky, US			499	1 638
WGAN-TV	Maine, US	1959		493	1 619
KSWS-TV	New Mexico, US	1956		490	1 610
WKY-TV	Oklahoma, US			487	1 600
KW-TV	Oklahoma, US	1954		479	1 572
Oriental Pearl Television Tower	Shanghai, China	1995		468	1 535
Bren Tower	Nevada, US	1962		465	1 527
Baiyoke Tower II	Bangkok, Thailand	1998		465	1 527
Petronas Twin Towers	Kuala Lumpur, Malaysia	1998		452	1 483
Sears Tower	Chicago, US	1974		443	1 454
Menara Kuala Lumpur	Kuala Lumpur, Malaysia	1996		421	1 403
Jin Mao Building	Shanghai, China	1999		420	1 379
Central Radio/TV Tower	Beijing, China	1992		417	1 369
World Trade Center	New York City, US	1973	(destroyed 2001)	412	1 350
Citic Plaza	Guangzhou, China	1996		391	1 283
Shun Hing Square	Shenzhen, China	1996		384	1 260
Empire State Building	New York City, US	1930		381	1 250
Tashkent Tower	Tashkent, Uzbekistan	1985		375	1 230
Central Plaza	Hong Kong	1992		374	1 227
Liberation Tower	Kuwait City, Kuwait	1996		370	1 214
Bank of China	Hong Kong	1988		368	1 209
Fernsehturm Tower	Berlin, Germany	1969		365	1 198
Emirates Tower One	Dubai	1999		355	1 165
The Center	Hong Kong	1998		350	1 148
T and C Tower	Kaoshiung, Taiwan	1997		347	1 140
Amoco Building	Chicago, US	1973		346	1 136
John Hancock Center	Chicago, US	1969		343	1 127
Sky Central Plaza	Guangzhou, China	1996		322	1 056
Stratosphere Tower	Las Vegas, US	1996		308	1 010

The world's highest dams

Name	Date completed	Place	Height	
			m	ft
Rogun	1985	Tadzhikistan	335	1099
Nurek	1980	Tadzhikistan	300	984
Xiaowan	uncompleted	China	292	958
Grande Dixence	1962	Switzerland	285	935
Longtan	uncompleted	China	285	935
Inguri	1984	Georgia, US	272	892
Boruca	uncompleted	Costa Rica	267	875
Vaiont	1961	Italy	265	869
Chicoasen	1981	Mexico	265	869
Tehri	uncompleted	India	261	856
Kambaratinsk	uncompleted	Kyrgyzstan	255	836
Kinshau	1985	India	253	830
Guavio	1989	Columbia	250	820
Mica	1972	Canada	242	794
Sayano-Shushenk	1980	Russia	242	794
Mihoesti	1983	Romania	242	794
Ertan	1999	China	240	787
Chivor	1975	Columbia	237	778
Mauvoisin	1957	Switzerland	237	778
Oroville	1968	California	235	770
Chirkey	1977	Ukraine	233	764
Bekhme	uncompleted	Iraq	230	754
Bhakra	1963	India	226	741
El Cajon	1984	Honduras	226	741
Hoover	1936	Arizona/Nevada, US	221	726
Contra	1965	Switzerland	220	722
Dabaklamm	uncompleted	Austria	220	722
Three Gorges	uncompleted	China	181	594

The world's longest tunnels

Name	Date completed	Place	Length	
			km	mi
Seikan	1985	Japan	53.9	33.5
Channel	1994	UK/France	49.9	31
Moscow subway	1990	Russia	37.9	23.5
Chesapeake Bay	1964	US	28	17.4
Dai-shimizu	1979	Japan	22.5	14
Simplon I and II	1906, 1922	Switzerland/Italy	19.3	12
Kanmon	1975	Japan	19.3	12
Apennine	1934	Italy	17.7	11
Rokko (rail)	1972	Japan	16	10
St Gotthard (rail)	1882	Switzerland	14.9	9.3
Mount MacDonald	1989	Canada	14.6	9.1
Lotschberg	1913	Switzerland	14.5	9
Cascade	1929	US	14.5	9
Hokuriku	1962	Japan	14.5	9
Fréjus (Mont Cenis)	1871	France/Italy	12.8	8
Shin Shimizu	1961	Japan	12.8	8
Flathead	1970	US	12.8	8
Aki	1975	Japan	12.8	8
Mont Blanc	1965	France/Italy	11.6	7.2
Rove	1927	France	7.1	4.4
San Fransisco Subway	1971	US	5.8	3.6
Mersey	1934	UK	4	2.5

The world's longest bridges[a]

Name	Date completed	Place	Length	
			m	ft
Seto-Ohashi	1988	Japan	3220	43374
Akashi-Kaikyo	1998	Japan	1990	6529
Great Belt East	1997	Denmark	1624	5328
Humber	1981	UK	1410	4626
Tsing Ma	1997	Hong Kong	1377	4518
Verrazano-Narrows	1964	New York Harbor, US	1298	4260
Golden Gate	1937	San Francisco, US	1280	4200
Höga Kusten	1997	Sweden	1210	3970
Mackinac	1957	Michigan, US	1158	3800
Minami-Bisan-Seto	1988	Japan	1100	3609
Bosporus II	1988	Istanbul, Turkey	1090	3576
Bosporus I	1973	Istanbul, Turkey	1074	3524
George Washington Bridge	1931	New York City, US	1067	3500
Kurushima	1999	Japan	1030	3379
Rio Niteroi	1972	Brazil	1025	3363
Salazar/25 April	1966	Lisbon, Portugal	1013	3323
Forth Road Bridge	1964	Scotland, UK	1006	3300
Severn Bridge	1966	UK	988	3241
Pierre Laporte	1970	Quebec, Canada	908	2979
Tatara	1999	Japan	890	2920
Save Bridge	1970	Mozambique	872	2860
Tete	1971	Mozambique	872	2860
Pont de Normandie	1995	France	856	2808

[a] Figures are for main spans, excluding approach roads, etc.

COMPUTERS

Programming languages

SCIENCE AND TECHNOLOGY

Language	Derivation of name	Applications
Ada		A high-level procedural language designed for programming computers for real-time applications – more specifically, where the computer is controlling the behaviour of military devices.
ALGOL	(ALGOrithmic Language)	One of the first languages developed for mathematical and scientific use. It introduced a number of new concepts and has been very influential in the design of other languages.
Assembly language		A low-level language which is a notation for representing machine code in human-readable form.
BASIC	(Beginners' All-purpose Symbolic Instruction Code)	A simple high-level language that can be used for general-purpose computing, especially on microcomputers. Designed for beginners.
C		Provides all the structure of a high-level language with certain low-level features that do not require the programmer to use assembly language. It is fast and portable and is the language in which the UNIX operating system was developed.
C++		An object-orientated language that is a descendent of C but in the tradition of ALGOL.
COBOL	(COmmon Business Oriented Language)	A high-level language that is the standard for all business data processing.
FORTRAN	(FORmula TRANslation)	A high-level language widely used for scientific computing; current standard is FORTRAN 77, but dates from 1956.
HTML	Hypertext Markup Language	Language adopted in the 1990s for the creation of World Wide Web documents on the Internet.
Hypertalk		A scripting language that is the basis of Hypercard.
LISP	(LISt Processing)	A high-level functional language with the imperative features designed for the processing of non-numeric data. Used for symbolic manipulation and in Artificial Intelligence.
LOGO		A graphics language used mainly for teaching small children.
Machine code		A low-level language into which all high-level languages must be translated before they can run. Machine codes are specific to machines and are in fact a series of machine-readable instructions.
ML	(Meta Language)	A high-level functional language used mainly for research purposes.
Modula 2		A high-level imperative language, derived from Pascal, in which programs may be written in modular form, ie built up from independently-written modules.
Pascal		A high-level imperative language descended from ALGOL, originally designed for teaching purposes.
PROLOG	(PROgramming in LOGic)	A high-level declarative language, designed for use in Artificial Intelligence.
Smalltalk		One of the first object-orientated languages, developed at Xerox Palo Alto Research Center.

The development of computers

Name of instrument	Inventor	Date developed	Comments
Abacus		Middle Ages	Calculations performed by sliding counters
Mechanical adding machine	Blaise Pascal, France	1642	
Stepped reckoner	Gottfried Leibniz, Germany	1673	Mechanical instrument to multiply, divide and extract square roots as well as add
Analytical engine	Charles Babbage, Britain	1830	First automatic computer. Able to combine arithmetic processes with decisions based on own computations
Boolean algebra	George Boole, Britain	mid 19th century	Boole discovered analogy of algebraic symbols and those of logic. Binary logic operations brought about electronic computer switching theory and procedures
Data-processing cards	Hermann Hollerith, US	1890	Introduction of perforated cards with pattern of holes which could be read by machine designed to sort and manipulate the data represented by the holes
Prototype of electromechanical digital computer	John Atanasoff, US	1939	
Calculator	Howard Aiken, US	1939	
Automatic Sequence Controlled calculator (Harvard Mark I)	Howard Aiken, US	1944	Series of instructions coded on punched paper tape entered and output recorded on cards or by electric typewriter
Colossus	Alan Turing, Britain	1943	Special-purpose electronic computer designed to decipher codes
ENIAC (Electronic Numerical integrator and Calculator)	J Presper Eckert and John W Mauchly	1946	Marked the beginning of the first generation of modern computers. This was the first all-purpose electronic digital computer
Transistor	Shockley, Bardeen and Brattain	1948	Reliable with low power consumption
EDSAC	Cambridge University	1949	First working version of a stored-program computer
EDVAC (Electronic Discrete Variable Automatic Computer)	John Neumann	1950	Stored-program computer.
UNIVAC (Universal Automatic Computer)	Eckert and Mauchly	1951	Used memory system made of mercury delay lines which gave access time of 500 microseconds. First computer able to handle numerical and alphabetical data with equal ease
Harvard Mark III		mid 1950s	Magnetic drum memory provided large storage capacity
Integrated circuit (IC)		1960s/70s	Allowed construction of large-scale (mainframe) computers with high operating speeds
LSI (Large-scale Integration)		1960s/70s	Thousands of transistors and related devices could be packed onto a single integrated circuit
RAM (Random Access Memory)		1960s/70s	RAM chip used in constructing semiconductor memory units
PDP-8	DEC (Digital Equipment)	1963	First minicomputer

Name of instrument	Inventor	Date developed	Comments
IBM System/360	IBM	1964	First family of compatible computers launched
Control Data CD6000		1965	First supercomputer developed
Intel 4004	Marcian Hoff, US	1971	First microprocessor. (Integrated circuit with all arithmetic, logic and control circuitry to serve central processing unit (CPU)
Altair 8800		1975	First personal computer
Xerox Start System		1981	First windows, icons, menus, and pointing devices system developed
Osborne		1981	First portable computer
CD Rom		mid-1980s	Data storage up to 640 mbs
MP3	Fraunhofer IIS, Germany	1987	Audiodata compression algorithm; led to personal digital music players in 1990s
Optical microchip		1988	Used light instead of electricity
Wafer-scale silicon memory chip		1989	Able to store 200 million characters
CD-I player	Philips	1992	Provided compact disc interactive multimedia programs for home use
Pentium processor	Intel	1993	Highly integrated semiconductor device with external bus width of 64 bits, almost twice as fast as its predecessor
DVD		1996	Data and video storage up to 17 Gbs
USB (Universal Serial Bus		1996	Interface standard for connecting devices to computers; permits 'hot-swapping'
Key-chain removable memory	Agaté Technologies	2001	Plugs into USB port and acts as hard drive with up to 2Gb capacity (by 2004)

SCIENCE AND TECHNOLOGY

PART TWELVE

Arts and Culture

Prix Goncourt

1903	John-Antoine Nau, *Force ennemie*	1952	Béatrice Beck, *Léon Morin, prêtre*
1904	Léon Frapié, *La Maternelle*	1953	Pierre Gascar, *Les Temps des morts; Les Bêtes*
1905	Claude Farrère, *Les Civilisés*	1954	Simone de Beauvoir, *Les Mandarins*
1906	Jérôme and Jean Tharaud, *Dingley, l'illustre écrivain*	1955	Roger Ikor, *Les Eaux melées*
		1956	Romain Gary, *Les Racines du ciel*
1907	Émile Moselly, *Terres lorraines*	1957	Roger Vailland, *La Loi*
1908	Francis de Miomandre, *Écrit sur de l'eau*	1958	Francis Walder, *Saint-Germain ou La Négociation*
1909	Marius and Ary Leblond, *En France*	1959	André Schwarz-Bart, *Le Dernier des justes*
1910	Louis Pergaud, *De Goupil à Margot*	1960	Vintila Horia, *Dieu est né en exil* (declined)
1911	Alphonse de Chateaubriant, *Monsieur des Lourdines*	1961	Jean Cau, *La Pitié de Dieu*
		1962	Anne Langfus, *Les Bagages de sable*
1912	André Savignon, *Les Filles de la pluie*	1963	Armand Lanoux, *Quand la mer se retire*
1913	Marc Elder, *Le Peuple de la mer*	1964	Georges Conchon, *L'État sauvage*
1914	Award delayed until 1916	1965	Jacques Borel, *L'Adoration*
1915	René Benjamin, *Gaspard*	1966	Edmonde Charles-Roux, *Oublier Palerme*
1916	Henri Babusse, *Le Feu*	1967	André Pieyre de Mandiargues, *La Marge*
	Adrien Bertrand, *L'Appel du sol*	1968	Bernard Clavel, *Les Fruits de l'hiver*
1917	Henri Malherbe, *La Flamme au poing*	1969	Félicien Marceau, *Creezy*
1918	Georges Duhamel, *Civilisation*	1970	Michel Tournier, *Le Roi des Aulnes*
1919	Marcel Proust, *A l'ombre des jeunes filles en fleur*	1971	Jacques Laurent, *Les Bêtises*
1920	Ernest Pérochon, *Nêne*	1972	Jean Carrière, *L'Epervier de Maheux*
1921	René Maran, *Batouala*	1973	Jacques Chessex, *L'Ogre*
1922	Henri Béraud, *Le Vitriol de lune et Le Martyre de l'obèse*	1974	Pascal Lainé, *La Dentellière*
		1975	Émile Ajar, *La Vie devant soi*
1923	Lucien Fabre, *Rabevol ou Le Mal des ardents*	1976	Patrick Grainville, *Les Flamboyants*
1924	Thierry Sandre, *Le Chèvrefeuille; Le Purgatoire; Le Chapitre XIII d' Athénée*	1977	Didier Decoin, *John L'Enfer*
		1978	Patrick Modiano, *Rue des boutiques obscures*
1925	Maurice Genevoix, *Raboliot*	1979	Antonine Maillet, *Pélagie la Charrette*
1926	Henri Deberly, *Le Supplice de Phèdre*	1980	Yves Navarre, *Le Jardin d'acclimatation*
1927	Maurice Bedel, *Jérôme 60° latitude Nord*	1981	Lucien Bodard, *Anne Marie*
1928	Maurice Constantin-Weyer, *Un homme se penche sur son passé*	1982	Dominique Fernandez, *Dans la main de l'ange*
		1983	Frédérick Tristan, *Les Égarés*
1929	Marcel Arland, *L'Ordre*	1984	Marguerite Duras, *L'Amant*
1930	Henri Fauconnier, *Malaisie*	1985	Yann Queffelec, *Les Noces barbares*
1931	Jean Fayard, *Mal d'amour*	1986	Michel Host, *Valet de nuit*
1932	Guy Mazeline, *Les Loups*	1987	Tahar ben Jalloun, *La Nuit sacrée*
1933	André Malraux, *La Condition humaine*	1988	Erik Orsenna, *L'Exposition coloniale*
1934	Roger Vercel, *Capitaine Conan*	1989	Jean Vautrin, *Un Grand Pas vers le bon Dieu*
1935	Joseph Peyré, *Sang et lumières*	1990	Jean Rouaud, *Les Champs d'honneur*
1936	Maxence Van der Meersch, *L' Empreinte du dieu*	1991	Pierre Combescot, *Les Filles du Calvaire*
1937	Charles Plisnier, *Faux Passeports*	1992	Patrick Chamoiseau, *Texaco*
1938	Henri Troyat, *L'Araigne*	1993	Amin Maalouf, *Le Rocher de Tanois*
1939	Philippe Hériat, *Les Enfants gatés*	1994	Didier van Cauwelaert, *Un Aller simple*
1940	Prize reserved for a prisoner or political deportee and awarded in 1946 to François Ambrière, *Les Grandes Vacances*	1995	Andrei Makine, *Le Testament français*
		1996	Pascale Roze, *Chasseur Zéro*
		1997	Patrick Rambaud, *La Bataille*
1941	Henri Pourrat, *Vent de mars*	1998	Paule Constant, *Confidence Pour Confidence*
1942	Marc Bernard, *Pareils à des enfants*	1999	Jean Echenoz, *Je m'en vais*
1943	Marius Grout, *Passage de l'homme*	2000	Jean-Jacques Schuhl, *Ingrid Caven*
1944	Elsa Triolet, *Le premier accroc coûte deux cents francs*	2001	John-Christophe Rufin, *Rouge Bresil*
		2002	Pascal Quignard, *Les Ombres errantes*
1945	Jean-Louis Bory, *Mon village a l'heure allemande*	2003	Jacques-Pierre Amette, *La Maitresse de Brecht*
1946	Jean-Jacques Gautier, *Histoire d'un faite divers*	2004	Laurent Gaude, *Le Soleil des Scorta*
1947	Jean-Louis Curtis, *Les Forêts de la nuit*		
1948	Maurice Druon, *Les Grandes Familles*		
1949	Robert Merle, *Week-End à Zuydcoote*		
1950	Paul Colin, *Les Jeux sauvages*		
1951	Julien Gracq, *Le Rivage des Syrtes* (declined)		

Booker Prize

1971	V S Naipaul *In a Free State*	1974	Nadine Gordimer *The Conservationist*
1972	John Berger *G*		Stanley Middleton *Holiday*
1973	J G Farrell *The Siege of Krishnapur*	1975	Ruth Prawer Jhabvala *Heat and Dust*

Booker Prize (continued)

1976	David Storey Saville
1977	Paul Scott Staying On
1978	Iris Murdoch The Sea, The Sea
1979	Penelope Fitzgerald Offshore
1980	William Golding Rites of Passage
1981	Salman Rushdie Midnight's Children
1982	Thomas Keneally Schindler's Ark
1983	J M Coetzee Life and Times of Michael K
1984	Anita Brookner Hotel du Lac
1985	Keri Hulme The Bone People
1986	Kingsley Amis The Old Devils
1987	Penelope Lively Moon Tiger
1988	Peter Carey Oscar and Lucinda
1989	Kazuo Ishiguro The Remains of the Day
1990	A S Byatt Possession
1991	Ben Okri The Famished Road
1992	Barry Unsworth Sacred Hunger
	Michael Ondaatje The English Patient
1993	Roddy Doyle Paddy Clarke–Ha ha ha
1994	James Kelman How late it was, how late
1995	Pat Barker The Ghost Road
1996	Graham Swift Last Orders
1997	Arundhati Roy The God of Small Things
1998	Ian McEwan Amsterdam
1999	J M Coetzee Disgrace
2000	Margaret Atwood The Blind Assassin
2001	Peter Carey The True History of the Kelly Gang
2002	Yann Martel Life of Pi
2003	D B C Pierre Vernon God Little
2004	Alan Hollinghurst The Line of Beauty

Whitbread Awards

1973	Shiva Naipaul, The Chip Chip Gatherers[a]
1974	Iris Murdoch, The Sacred and Profane Love Machine[a]
1975	William McIlvanney, Docherty[a]
1976	William Trevor, The Children of Dynmouth[a]
1977	Beryl Bainbridge, Injury Time[a]
1978	Paul Theroux, Picture Palace[a]
1979	Jennifer Johnston, The Old Jest[a]
1980	David Lodge, How Far Can You Go?[a, f]
1981	Maurice Leitch, Silver's City[a]
	William Boyd, A Good Man in Africa[b]
1982	John Wain, Young Shoulders[a]
	Bruce Chatwin, On the Black Hill[b]
1983	William Trevor, Fools of Fortune[a]
	John Fuller, Flying to Nowhere[b]
1984	Christopher Hope, Kruger's Alp[a]
	James Buchan, A Parish of Rich Women[b]
1985	Peter Ackroyd, Hawksmoor[b]
	Jeannette Winterson, Oranges Are Not the Only Fruit[a]
1986	Kazuo Ishiguro, An Artist of the Floating World[a, f]
	Jim Crace, Continent[b]
	Andrew Taylor, The Coal House[e]
	Peter Reading, Stet[c]
	Richard Mabey, Gilbert White[d]
1987	Ian McEwan, The Child in Time[a]
	Francis Wyndham, The Other Garden[b]
	Geraldine McCaughrean, A Little Lower Than the Angels[e]
	Seamus Heaney, The Haw Lantern[c]
	Christopher Nolan, Under the Eye of the Clock[d, f]
1988	Salman Rushdie, The Satanic Verses[a]
	Paul Sayer, The Comfort of Madness[b, f]
	Judy Allen, Awaiting Developments[e]
	Peter Porter, The Automatic Oracle[c]
	A N Wilson, Tolstoy[d]
1989	Lindsay Clarke, The Chymical Wedding[a]
	James Hamilton-Paterson, Gerontius[b]
	Hugh Scott, Why Weeps the Brogan[e]
	Michael Donaghy, Shibboleth[c]
	Richard Holmes, Coleridge: Early Visions[d, f]
1990	Nicholas Mosley, Hopeful Monsters[a, f]
	Hanif Kureishi, The Buddha of Suburbia[b]
	Peter Dickinson, AK[e]
	Paul Durcan, Daddy Daddy[c]
	Anne Thwaite, A. A. Milne: His Life[d]
1991	Jane Gardham, The Queen of the Tambourine
	Gordon Burn, Alma Cogan[b]
1992	Alasdair Gray, Poor Things[a]
	Jeff Torrington, Swing Hammer Swing[b]
	Tony Harrison, The Gaze of the Gorgon[c]
1993	Joan Brady, Theory of War[a, f]
	Rachel Cusk, Saving Agnes[b]
	Anne Fine, Flour Babies[a]
1994	William Trevor, Felicia's Journey[a, f]
	Fred D'Aguiar, The Longest Memory[b]
1995	Salman Rushdie, The Moor's Last Sigh[a]
	Kate Atkinson, Behind the Scenes at the Museum[b, f]
	Michael Morpurgo, The Wreck of the Zanzibar[e]
	Bernard O'Donoghue, Gunpowder[c]
	Roy Jenkins, Gladstone[d]
1996	Beryl Bainbridge, Every Man for Himself[a]
	John Lanchester, The Debt to Pleasure[b]
	Seamus Heaney, Spirit Level[c, f]
	Diarmaid McCulloch, Thomas Cranmer: A Life[d]
	Anne Fine, Tulip Touch[e, g]
1997	Jim Crace, Quarantine[a]
	Pauline Melville, The Ventriloquist's Tale[b]
	Ted Hughes, Tales from Ovid[c]
	Graham Robb, Victor Hugo: A Biography[d]
	Andrew Norriss, Aquila[g]
1998	Justin Cartwright, Leading the Cheers[a]
	Giles Foden, The Last King of Scotland[b]
	Ted Hughes, Birthday Letters[c]
	Amanda Foreman, Georgiana, Duchess of Devonshire[d]
	David Almond, Skellig[g]
1999	Rose Tremain, Music and Silence[a]
	Tim Lott, White City Blue[b]
	Seamus Heaney, Beowulf[c, f]
	David Cairns, Berlioz, Volume 2[d]
	J K Rowling, Harry Potter and the Prisoner of Azkaban[g]
2000	Matthew Kneale, English Passengers[a, f]
	Zadie Smith, White Teeth[b]
	John Burnside, The Asylum Dance[c]
	Lorna Sage, Bad Blood[d]
	Jamila Gavin, Coram Boy[g]
2001	Patrick Neale, Twelve Bar Blues[a]
	Sid Smith, Something Like a House[b]
	Selima Hill, Bunny[c]
	Diana Souhami, Selkirk's Island[d]
	Philip Pullman, The Amber Spyglass[e, f]

2002	Michael Frayn, Spies[a]	2004	Andrea Levy, Small Island[a, f]
	Norman Lebrecht, The Song of Names[b]		Susan Fletcher, Eve Green[b]
	Paul Farley, The Ice Age[c]		Michael Symmons Roberts, Corpus[c]
	Claire Tomalin, Samuel Pepys[d, f]		John Guy, My Heart is My Own: The Life of
	Hilary McKay, Saffy's Angel[e]		Mary Queen of Scots[d]
2003	Mark Haddon, The Curious Incident of the Dog		Geraldine McCaughrean, Not the End of the
	in the Night-Time[a, f]		World[e]
	D B C Pierre, Vernon God Little[b]		
	Don Paterson, Landing Light[c]		
	D J Taylor, Orwell: The Life[d]		
	David Almond, The Fire-Eaters[e]		

[a]Novel. [b]First novel. [c]Poetry. [d]Biography. [e]Children's novel.
[f]Book of the Year. [g]Children's Book of the Year.

Pulitzer Prize in fiction

1918	Ernest Poole His Family	1966	Katherine Anne Porter The Collected Stories
1919	Booth Tarkington The Magnificent Ambersons	1967	Bernard Malamud The Fixer
1921	Edith Wharton The Age of Innocence	1968	William Styron The Confessions of Nat Turner
1922	Booth Tarkington Alice Adams	1969	Navarre Scott Momaday House Made of Dawn
1923	Willa Cather One of Ours	1970	Jean Stafford Collected Stories
1924	Margaret Wilson The Able McLaughlins	1972	Wallace Stegner Angle of Repose
1925	Edna Ferber So Big	1973	Eudora Welty The Optimist's Daughter
1926	Sinclair Lewis Arrowsmith	1975	Michael Shaara The Killer Angels
1927	Louis Bromfield Early Autumn	1976	Saul Bellow Humboldt's Gift
1928	Thornton Wilder The Bridge of San Luis Rey	1978	James Alan McPherson Elbow Room
1929	Julia Peterkin Scarlet Sister Mary	1979	John Cheever The Stories of John Cheever
1930	Oliver LaFarge Laughing Boy	1980	Norman Mailer The Executioner's Song
1931	Margaret Ayer Barnes Years of Grace	1981	John Kennedy Toole A Confederacy of Dunces
1932	Pearl S Buck The Good Earth	1982	John Updike Rabbit is Rich
1933	T S Stribling The Store	1983	Alice Walker The Color Purple
1934	Caroline Miller Lamb in His Bosom	1984	William Kennedy Ironweed
1935	Josephine Winslow Johnson Now in November	1985	Alison Lurie Foreign Affairs
1936	Harold L Davis Honey in the Horn	1986	Larry McMurty Lonesome Dove
1937	Margaret Mitchell Gone with the Wind	1987	Peter Taylor A Summons to Memphis
1938	John Phillips Marquand The Late George Apley	1988	Toni Morrison Beloved
1939	Marjorie Kinnan Rawlings The Yearling	1989	Anne Tyler Breathing Lessons
1940	John Steinbeck The Grapes of Wrath	1990	Oscar Hijuelos The Mambo Kings Play Songs of
1942	Ellen Glasgow In This Our Life		Love
1943	Upton Sinclair Dragon's Teeth	1991	John Updike Rabbit at Rest
1944	Martin Flavin Journey in the Dark	1992	Jane Smiley A Thousand Acres
1945	John Hersey A Bell for Adano		Art Spiegelmann Maus (special award)
1947	Robert Penn Warren All the King's Men	1993	Robert Olen Butler A Good Scent from a Strange
1948	James Michener Tales of the South Pacific		Mountain
1949	James Gould Cozzens Guard of Honor	1994	E Annie Proulx The Shipping News
1950	A B Guthrie Jr The Way West	1995	Carol Sheilds The Stone Diaries
1951	Conrad Richter The Town	1996	Richard Ford Independence Day
1952	Herman Wouk The Caine Mutiny	1997	Steven Millhauser Martin Dressler: The Tale of an
1953	Ernest Hemingway The Old Man and the Sea		American Dreamer
1955	William Faulkner A Fable	1998	Philip Roth American Pastoral
1956	MacKinlay Kantor Andersonville	1999	Michael Cunningham The Hours
1958	James Agee A Death in the Family	2000	Jhumpa Lahiri Interpreter of Maladies
1959	Robert Lewis Taylor The Travels of Jaime	2001	Michael Chabon The Amazing Adventures of
	McPheeters		Cavalier and Clay
1960	Allen Drury Advise and Consent	2002	Richard Russo Empire Falls
1961	Harper Lee To Kill a Mockingbird	2003	Jeffrey Eugenides Middlesex
1962	Edwin O'Connor The Edge of Sadness	2004	Edward P Jones The Known World
1963	William Faulkner The Reivers	2005	Marilynne Robinson Gilead
1965	Shirley Ann Grau The Keepers of the House		

No awards in 1917, 1920, 1941, 1946, 1954, 1957, 1964

The Orange Prize

1996	Helen Dunmore, A Spell of Winter	2001	Kate Grenville, The Idea of Perfection
1997	Anne Michaels, Fugitive Pieces	2002	Ann Patchett, Bel Canto
1998	Carol Shields, Larry's Party	2003	Valerie Martin, Property
1999	Suzanne Berne, A Crime in the Neighbourhood	2004	Andrea Levy, Small Island
2000	Linda Grant, When I Lived in Modern Times		

Pulitzer Prize in poetry

1917	No award	1961	Phyllis McGinley Times Three: Selected Verse from Three Decades
1918	Sara Teasdale Love Songs		
1919	Carl Sandburg Corn Huskers	1962	Alan Dugan Poems
	Margaret Widdemer Old Road to Paradise	1963	William Carlos Williams Pictures from Breughel
1920	No award	1964	Louis Simpson At the End of the Open Road
1921	No award	1965	John Berryman 77 Dream Songs
1922	Edwin Arlington Robinson Collected Poems	1966	Richard Eberhart Selected Poems
1923	Edna St Vincent Millay The Harp Weaver and Other Poems	1967	Ann Sexton Live or Die
		1968	Anthony Hecht The Hard Hour
1924	Robert Frost New Hampshire: a Poem with Notes and Grace Notes	1969	George Oppen Of Being Numerous
		1970	Richard Howard Untitled Subjects
1925	Edwin Arlington Robinson The Man Who Died Twice	1971	W S Merwin The Carrier of Ladders
		1972	James Wright Collected Poems
1926	Amy Lowell What's O'Clock?	1973	Maxine Winokur Kumin Up Country
1927	Leonora Speyer Fiddler's Farewell	1974	Robert Lowell The Dolphin
1928	Edwin Arlington Robinson Tristram	1975	Gary Snyder Turtle Island
1929	Stephen Vincent Benét John Brown's Body	1976	John Ashbery Self-Portrait in a Convex Mirror
1930	Conrad Aiken Selected Poems	1977	James Merrill Divine Comedies
1931	Robert Frost Collected Poems	1978	Howard Nemerov Collected Poems
1932	George Dillon The Flowering Stone	1979	Robert Penn Warren Now and Then
1933	Archibald MacLeish Conquistador	1980	Donald Justice Selected Poems
1934	Robert Hillyer Collected Verse	1981	James Schuyler The Morning of the Poem
1935	Audrey Wurdemann Bright Ambush	1982	Sylvia Plath The Collected Poems
1936	R P Tristram Coffin Strange Holiness	1983	Galway Kinnell Selected Poems
1937	Robert Frost A Further Range	1984	Mary Oliver American Primitive
1938	Marya Zaturenska Cold Morning Sky	1985	Carolyn Kizer Yin
1939	John Gould Fletcher Selected Poems	1986	Henry Taylor The Flying Change
1940	Mark Van Doren Collected Poems	1987	Rita Dove Thomas and Beulah
1941	Leonard Bacon Sunderland Capture	1988	William Meredith Partial Accounts; New and Selected Poems
1942	William Benét The Dust Which is God		
1943	Robert Frost A Witness Tree	1989	Richard Wilbur New and Selected Poems
1944	Stephen Vincent Benét Western Star	1990	Charles Simic The World Doesn't End
1945	Karl Shapiro V–Letter and Other Poems	1991	Mona van Duyn Near Changes
1946	No award	1992	James Tate Selected Poems
1947	Robert Lowell Lord Weary's Castle	1993	Louise Glück The Wild Iris
1948	W H Auden The Age of Anxiety	1994	Yusef Komunyakaa Neon Vernacular
1949	Peter Viereck Terror and Decorum	1995	Philip Levine The Simple Truth
1950	Gwendolyn Brooks Annie Allen	1996	Jorie Graham The Dream of the Unified Field
1951	Carl Sandburg Complete Poems	1997	Lisel Mueller Alive Together: New and Selected Poems
1952	Marianne Moore Collected Poems		
1953	Archibald MacLeish Collected Poems 1917–1952	1998	Charles Wright Black Zodiac
1954	Theodore Roethke The Waking	1999	Mark Strand Blizzard of One
1955	Wallace Stevens Collected Poems	2000	C K Williams Repair
1956	Elizabeth Bishop Poems – North & South	2001	Stephen Dunn Different Hours
1957	Richard Wilbur Things of This World	2002	Carl Dennis Practical Gods
1958	Robert Penn Warren Promises: Poems 1954-56	2003	Paul Muldoon Moy Sand and Gravel
1959	Stanley Kunitz Selected Poems 1928-1958	2004	Franz Wright Walking to Martha's Vineyard
1960	W D Snodgrass Heart's Needle	2005	Ted Kooser Delights and Shadows

UK Poets laureate

1617	Ben Jonson[a]	1730	Colley Cibber	1896	Alfred Austin
1638	Sir William Davenant[a]	1757	William Whitehead	1913	Robert Bridges
1668	John Dryden	1785	Thomas Warton	1930	John Masefield
1689	Thomas Shadwell	1790	Henry Pye	1968	Cecil Day Lewis
1692	Nahum Tate	1813	Robert Southey	1972	Sir John Betjeman
1715	Nicholas Rowe	1843	William Wordsworth	1984	Ted Hughes
1718	Laurence Eusden	1850	Alfred, Lord Tennyson	1999	Andrew Motion

[a]The post was not officially established until 1668.

Shakespeare: the plays

Early comedies	*Written*	*Well-known characters*
The Comedy of Errors	1590–4	Antipholus, Dromio, Adriana
Love's Labour's Lost	1590–4	Armado, Berowne, Costard
The Two Gentlemen of Verona	1592–3	Proteus, Valentine, Julia, Sylvia
The Taming of the Shrew	1592	Petruchio, Katherina, Sly
Histories		
Henry VI Part I (with others)	1589–90	Henry, Talbot, Joan of Arc
Henry VI Part II	1590–1	Henry, Margaret, Jack Cade
Henry VI Part III	1590–1	Henry, Margaret, Richard of Gloucester
Edward III (with others)	1590–5	Edward, Philippa, Prince Edward, Countess
Richard III	1592–3	Richard, Margaret, Clarence, Anne
King John	1595–7	John, Constance, Arthur, Bastard
Richard II	1595	Richard, John of Gaunt, Bolingbroke
Henry IV Part I	1596	Henry, Hal, Hotspur, Falstaff
Henry IV Part II	1597	Henry, Hal, Falstaff, Mistress Quickly
Henry V	1599	Henry (formely Hal), Pistol, Nym, Katherine
Henry VIII (with John Fletcher)	1613	Henry, Katherine, Wolsley
Middle comedies		
A Midsummer Night's Dream	1595	Oberon, Titania, Puck, Bottom
The Merchant of Venice	1596–8	Bassanio, Portia, Shylock, Jessica
The Merry Wives of Windsor	1597	Falstaff, Mistress Quickly, Shallow
As You Like It	1599	Rosalind, Orlando, Touchstone, Jaques
Twelfth Night	1600–2	Orsino, Olivia, Viola, Malvolio, Feste, Sir Andrew, Sir Toby
Dark comedies		
Much Ado About Nothing	1598	Beatrice, Benedick, Dogberry, Verges
All's Well That Ends Well	1602–3	Bertram, Helena, Parolles
Measure for Measure	1604–5	Duke, Angelo, Isabella, Mariana
Tragedies		
Romeo and Juliet	1595–6	Romeo, Juliet, Mercutio, the Nurse
Hamlet	1600–1	Hamlet, Ophelia, the Ghost, the Grave-Digger
Othello	1604	Othello, Desdemona, Iago, Cassio
King Lear	1605–6	Lear, Cordelia, the Fool, Kent, Edgar/Poor Tom
Macbeth	1605–6	Macbeth, Lady Macbeth, Banquo, the Three Witches
Greek and Roman plays		
Titus Andronicus	1590–4	Andronicus, Aaron, Lavinia
Julius Caesar	1599	Caesar, Brutus, Cassius, Antony
Troilus and Cressida	1601–2	Troilus, Cressida, Pandarus
Timon of Athens (with Thomas Middleton)	1605–9	Timon, Apemantus
Antony and Cleopatra	1606–7	Antony, Cleopatra, Enobarbus
Coriolanus	1607–8	Coriolanus, Volumnia, Menenius
Late plays		
Pericles (with George Wilkins)	1607–8	Pericles, Marina
Cymbeline	1609–10	Innogen, Iachimo, Posthumus
The Winter's Tale	1611	Leontes, Perdita, Florizel, Autolycus
The Tempest	1613	Prospero, Miranda, Ferdinand, Ariel, Caliban
The Two Noble Kinsmen (with John Fletcher)	1613	Arcite, Palamon, Emilia, Theseus

Pulitzer Prize in drama

1918	*No award*
1919	Jesse Lynch Williams *Why Marry?*
1920	*No award*
1921	Eugene O'Neill *Beyond the Horizon*
1922	Zona Gale *Miss Lulu Bett*
1923	Eugene O'Neill *Anna Christie*
1924	Owen Davis *Icebound*
1925	Hatcher Hughes *Hell-Bent for Heaven*
1926	Sidney Howard *They Knew What They Wanted*
1927	George Kelly *Craig's Wife*
1928	Paul Green *In Abraham's Bosom*
1929	Eugene O'Neill *Strange Interlude*
1930	Elmer Rice *Street Scene*
1931	Marc Connelly *The Green Pastures*
1932	Susan Glaspell *Alison's House*
1933	George S Kaufman *Morris Ryskind and Ira Gershwin: Of Thee I Sing*
1934	Maxwell Anderson *Both Your Houses*
1935	Sidney Kingsley *Men in White*
1936	Zoë Akins *The Old Maid*
1937	Robert E Sherwood *Idiot's Delight*
1938	George S Kaufman and Moss Hart *You Can't Take It With You*
1939	Thornton Wilder *Our Town*
1940	Robert E Sherwood *Abe Lincoln in Illinois*
1941	William Saroyan *The Time of Your Life*
1942	Robert E Sherwood *There Shall Be No Night*
1943	*No award*
1944	Thornton Wilder *The Skin of Our Teeth*
1945	*No award*
1946	Mary Chase *Harvey*
1947	Russell Crouse and Howard Lindsay *State of the Union*
1948	*No award*
1949	Tennessee Williams *A Streetcar Named Desire*
1950	Arthur Miller *Death of a Salesman*
1951	Richard Rodgers, Oscar Hammerstein II, and Joshua Logan *South Pacific*
1952	*No award*
1953	Joseph Kramm *The Shake*
1954	William Inge *Picnic*
1955	John Patrick *Teahouse of the August Moon*
1956	Tennessee Williams *Cat on a Hot Tin Roof*
1957	Frances Goodrich and Albert Hackett *The Diary of Anne Frank*
1958	Eugene O'Neill *Long Day's Journey into Night*
1959	Ketti Frings *Look Homeward Angel*
1960	Archibald Macleish *JB*
1961	George Abbott, Jerome Weidman, Sheldon Harnick, and Jerry Bock *Fiorello*
1962	Tad Mosel *All the Way Home*

1963	Frank Loesser and Abe Burrows *How to Succeed in Business Without Really Trying*
1964	*No award*
1965	*No award*
1966	Frank D Gilroy *The Subject Was Roses*
1967	*No award*
1968	Edward Albee *A Delicate Balance*
1969	*No award*
1970	Howard Sackler *The Great White Hope*
1971	Charles Gordone *No Place to Be Somebody*
1972	Paul Zindel *The Effect of Gamma Rays on Man-in-the-Moon Marigolds*
1973	*No award*
1974	Jason Miller *The Championship Season*
1975	*No award*
1976	*No award*
1977	Michael Bennett, James Kirkwood, Nicholas Dante, Marvin Hamlisch, and Edward Kleban *A Chorus Line*
1978	Michael Cristofer *The Shadow Box*
1979	Donald L Coburn *The Gin Game*
1980	Sam Shepard *Buried Child*
1981	Lanford Wildon *Talley's Folly*
	Beth Henley *Games of the Heart*
1982	Charles Fuller *A Soldier's Play*
1983	Marsha Norman *'Night, Mother*
1984	David Mamet *Glengarry Glen Ross*
1985	Stephen Sondhiem and James Lapine *Sunday in the Park with George*
1986	*No award*
1987	August Wilson *Fences*
1988	Alfred Uhry *Driving Miss Daisy*
1989	Wendy Wasserstein *The Heidi Chronicles*
1990	August Wilson *The Piano Lesson*
1991	Neil Simon *Lost in Yonkers*
1992	Robert Schenkkan *The Kentucky Cycle*
1993	Tony Kushner *Angels in America: Millennium Approaches*
1994	Edward Albee *Three Tall Women*
1995	Horton Foote *The Young Man from Atlanta*
1996	Jonathan Larson *Rent* (posthumous)
1997	*No award*
1998	Paula Vogel *How I Learned to Drive*
1999	Margaret Edson *Wit*
2000	Donald Margulies *Dinner With Friends*
2001	David Auburn *Proof*
2002	Suzan Lori-Parks *Topdog/Underdog*
2003	Nilo Cruz *Anna in the Tropics*
2004	Doug Wright *I Am My Own Wife*
2005	John Patrick Shanley *Doubt, a parable*

Motion picture Academy Awards (Oscars)

1928
Picture *Wings*, Paramount
Director Frank Borzage, *Seventh Heaven*;
  Lewis Milestone, *Two Arabian Nights*
Actress Janet Gaynor, *Seventh Heaven, Street Angel, Sunrise*
Actor Emil Jannings, *The Way of All Flesh, The Last Command*

1929
Picture *The Broadway Melody*, MGM
Director Frank Lloyd, *The Divine Lady*
Actress Mary Pickford, *Coquette*
Actor Warner Baxter, *In Old Arizona*

1930
Picture *All Quiet on the Western Front*, Universal
Director Lewis Milestone, *All Quiet on the Western Front*
Actress Norma Shearer, *The Divorcee*
Actor George Arliss, *Disraeli*

1931
Picture *Cimarron*, RKO Radio
Director Norman Taurog, *Skippy*
Actress Marie Dressler, *Min and Bill*
Actor Lionel Barrymore, *A Free Soul*

1932
Picture *Grand Hotel*, MGM
Director Frank Borzage, *Bad Girl*
Actress Helen Hayes, *The Sin of Madelon Claudet*
Actor Fredric March, *Dr Jekyll and Mr Hyde*,
  and Wallace Beery, *The Champ*

1933
Picture *Cavalcade*, Fox
Director Frank Lloyd, *Cavalcade*
Actress Katharine Hepburn, *Morning Glory*
Actor Charles Laughton, *The Private Life of Henry VIII*

1934
Picture *It Happened One Night*, Columbia
Director Frank Capra, *It Happened One Night*
Actress Claudette Colbert, *It Happened One Night*
Actor Clark Gable, *It Happened One Night*

1935
Picture *Mutiny on the Bounty*, MGM
Director John Ford, *The Informer*
Actress Bette Davis, *Dangerous*
Actor Victor McLaglen, *The Informer*

1936
Picture *The Great Ziegfeld*, MGM
Director Frank Capra, *Mr. Deeds Goes to Town*
Actress Luise Rainer, *The Great Ziegfeld*
Actor Paul Muni, *The Story of Louis Pasteur*
Supporting actress Gale Sondergaard, *Anthony Adverse*
Supporting actor Walter Brennan, *Come and Get It*

1937
Picture *The Life of Emile Zola*, Warner Bros
Director Leo McCarey, *The Awful Truth*
Actress Luise Rainer, *The Good Earth*
Actor Spencer Tracy, *Captains Courageous*
Supporting actress Alice Brady, *In Old Chicago*
Supporting actor Joseph Schildkraut, *The Life of Emile Zola*

1938
Picture *You Can't Take it With You*, Columbia
Director Frank Capra, *You Can't Take it With You*

Actress Bette Davis, *Jezebel*
Actor Spencer Tracy, *Boys Town*
Supporting actress Fay Bainter, *Jezebel*
Supporting actor Walter Brennan, *Kentucky*

1939
Picture *Gone with the Wind*, Selznick MGM
Director Victor Fleming, *Gone with the Wind*
Actress Vivien Leigh, *Gone with the Wind*
Actor Robert Donat, *Goodbye Mr Chips*
Supporting actress Hattie McDaniel, *Gone with the Wind*
Supporting actor Thomas Mitchell, *Stagecoach*

1940
Picture *Rebecca*, Selznick UA
Director John Ford, *The Grapes of Wrath*
Actress Ginger Rogers, *Kitty Foyle*
Actor James Stewart, *The Philadelphia Story*
Supporting actress Jane Darwell, *The Grapes of Wrath*
Supporting actor Walter Brennan, *The Westerner*

1941
Picture *How Green Was My Valley*, 20th Century Fox
Director John Ford, *How Green Was My Valley*
Actress Joan Fontaine, *Suspicion*
Actor Gary Cooper, *Sergeant York*
Supporting actress Mary Astor, *The Great Lie*
Supporting actor Donald Crisp, *How Green Was My Valley*

1942
Picture *Mrs Miniver*, MGM
Director William Wyler, *Mrs Miniver*
Actress Greer Garson, *Mrs Miniver*
Actor James Cagney, *Yankee Doodle Dandy*
Supporting actress Teresa Wright, *Mrs Miniver*
Supporting actor Van Heflin, *Johnny Eager*

1943
Picture *Casablanca*, Warner Bros
Director Michael Curtiz, *Casablanca*
Actress Jennifer Jones, *The Song of Bernadette*
Actor Paul Lukas, *Watch on the Rhine*
Supporting actress Katina Paxinou, *For Whom the Bell Tolls*
Supporting actor Charles Coburn, *The More the Merrier*

1944
Picture *Going My Way*, Paramount
Director Leo McCarey, *Going My Way*
Actress Ingrid Bergman, *Gaslight*
Actor Bing Crosby, *Going My Way*
Supporting actress Ethel Barrymore, *None But the Lonely Heart*
Supporting actor Barry Fitzgerald, *Going My Way*

1945
Picture *The Lost Weekend*, Paramount
Director Billy Wilder, *The Lost Weekend*
Actress Joan Crawford, *Mildred Pierce*
Actor Ray Milland, *The Lost Weekend*
Supporting actress Anne Revere, *National Velvet*
Supporting actor James Dunn, *A Tree Grows in Brooklyn*

1946
Picture *The Best Years of Our Lives*, Goldwyn-RKO Radio
Director William Wyler, *The Best Years of Our Lives*
Actress Olivia de Havilland, *To Each His Own*
Actor Fredric March, *The Best Years of Our Lives*
Supporting actress Anne Baxter, *The Razor's Edge*
Supporting actor Harold Russell, *The Best Years of Our Lives*

ARTS AND CULTURE

Motion picture Academy Awards (Oscars) (continued)

1947
Picture *Gentleman's Agreement*, 20th Century Fox
Director Elia Kazan, *Gentleman's Agreement*
Actress Loretta Young, *The Farmer's Daughter*
Actor Ronald Colman, *A Double Life*
Supporting actress Celeste Holm, *Gentleman's Agreement*
Supporting actor Edmund Gwenn, *Miracle on 34th Street*

1948
Picture *Hamlet*, Rank-Two Cities-UI
Director John Huston, *Treasure of the Sierra Madre*
Actress Jane Wyman, *Johnny Belinda*
Actor Laurence Olivier, *Hamlet*
Supporting actress Claire Trevor, *Key Largo*
Supporting actor Walter Huston, *Treasure of the Sierra Madre*

1949
Picture *All the King's Men*, Rossen-Columbia
Director Joseph L Mankiewicz, *A Letter to Three Wives*
Actress Olivia de Havilland, *The Heiress*
Actor Broderick Crawford, *All the King's Men*
Supporting actress Mercedes McCambridge, *All the King's Men*
Supporting actor Dean Jagger, *Twelve O'Clock High*

1950
Picture *All About Eve*, 20th Century Fox
Director Joseph L Mankiewicz, *All About Eve*
Actress Judy Holliday, *Born Yesterday*
Actor José Ferrer, *Cyrano de Bergerac*
Supporting actress Josephine Hull, *Harvey*
Supporting actor George Sanders, *All About Eve*

1951
Picture *An American in Paris*, MGM
Director George Stevens, *A Place in the Sun*
Actress Vivien Leigh, *A Streetcar Named Desire*
Actor Humphrey Bogart, *The African Queen*
Supporting actress Kim Hunter, *A Streetcar Named Desire*
Supporting actor Karl Malden, *A Streetcar Named Desire*

1952
Picture *The Greatest Show on Earth*, DeMille-Paramount
Director John Ford, *The Quiet Man*
Actress Shirley Booth, *Come Back, Little Sheba*
Actor Gary Cooper, *High Noon*
Supporting actress Gloria Grahame, *The Bad and the Beautiful*
Supporting actor Anthony Quinn, *Viva Zapata*

1953
Picture *From Here to Eternity*, Columbia
Director Fred Zinnemann, *From Here to Eternity*
Actress Audrey Hepburn, *Roman Holiday*
Actor William Holden, *Stalag 17*
Supporting actress Donna Reed, *From Here to Eternity*
Supporting actor Frank Sinatra, *From Here to Eternity*

1954
Picture *On the Waterfront*, Horizon-American Corp, Columbia
Director Elia Kazan, *On the Waterfront*
Actress Grace Kelly, *The Country Girl*
Actor Marlon Brando, *On the Waterfront*
Supporting actress Eva Marie Saint, *On the Waterfront*
Supporting actor Edmond O'Brien, *The Barefoot Contessa*

1955
Picture *Marty*, Hecht and Lancaster, United Artists
Director Delbert Mann, *Marty*
Actress Anna Magnani, *The Rose Tattoo*
Actor Ernest Borgnine, *Marty*
Supporting actress Jo Van Fleet, *East of Eden*
Supporting actor Jack Lemmon, *Mister Roberts*

1956
Picture *Around the World in 80 Days*, Michael Todd Co, Inc-UA
Director George Stevens, *Giant*
Actress Ingrid Bergman, *Anastasia*
Actor Yul Brynner, *The King and I*
Supporting actress Dorothy Malone, *Written on the Wind*
Supporting actor Anthony Quinn, *Lust for Life*

1957
Picture *The Bridge on the River Kwai*, Horizon Picture, Columbia
Director David Lean, *The Bridge on the River Kwai*
Actress Joanne Woodward, *The Three Faces of Eve*
Actor Alec Guinness, *The Bridge on the River Kwai*
Supporting actress Miyoshi Umeki, *Sayonara*
Supporting actor Red Buttons, *Sayonara*

1958
Picture *Gigi*, Arthur Freed Productions Inc, MGM
Director Vincente Minnelli, *Gigi*
Actress Susan Hayward, *I Want to Live!*
Actor David Niven, *Separate Tables*
Supporting actress Wendy Hiller, *Separate Tables*
Supporting actor Burl Ives, *The Big Country*

1959
Picture *Ben Hur*
Director William Wyler, *Ben Hur*
Actress Simone Signoret, *Room at the Top*
Actor Charlton Heston, *Ben Hur*
Supporting actress Shelley Winters, *The Diary of Anne Frank*
Supporting actor Hugh Griffith, *Ben Hur*

1960
Picture *The Apartment*, Mirisch Co Inc, United Artists
Director Billy Wilder, *The Apartment*
Actress Elizabeth Taylor, *Butterfield 8*
Actor Burt Lancaster, *Elmer Gantry*
Supporting actress Shirley Jones, *Elmer Gantry*
Supporting actor Peter Ustinov, *Spartacus*

1961
Picture *West Side Story*, Mirisch Pictures Inc, and B and P Enterprises Inc, United Artists
Director Robert Wise and Jerome Robbins, *West Side Story*
Actress Sophia Loren, *Two Women*
Actor Maximillian Schell, *Judgment at Nuremberg*
Supporting actress Rita Moreno, *West Side Story*
Supporting actor George Chakiris, *West Side Story*

1962
Picture *Lawrence of Arabia*, Horizon Pictures Ltd, Columbia
Director David Lean, *Lawrence of Arabia*
Actress Anne Bancroft, *The Miracle Worker*
Actor Gregory Peck, *To Kill a Mockingbird*
Supporting actress Patty Duke, *The Miracle Worker*
Supporting actor Ed Begley, *Sweet Bird of Youth*

1963
Picture *Tom Jones*, A Woodfall Production, UA-Lopert Pictures
Director Tony Richardson, *Tom Jones*
Actress Patricia Neal, *Hud*
Actor Sidney Poitier, *Lilies of the Field*
Supporting actress Margaret Rutherford, *The VIPs*
Supporting actor Melvyn Douglas, *Hud*

1964
Picture *My Fair Lady*, Warner Bros
Director George Cukor, *My Fair Lady*
Actress Julie Andrews, *Mary Poppins*
Actor Rex Harrison, *My Fair Lady*
Supporting actress Lila Kedrova, *Zorba the Greek*
Supporting actor Peter Ustinov, *Topkapi*

1965
Picture *The Sound of Music*, Argyle Enterprises Production, 20th Century Fox
Director Robert Wise, *The Sound of Music*
Actress Julie Christie, *Darling*
Actor Lee Marvin, *Cat Ballou*
Supporting actress Shelley Winters, *A Patch of Blue*
Supporting actor Martin Balsam, *A Thousand Clowns*

1966
Picture *A Man for All Seasons*, Highland Films Ltd Production, Columbia
Director Fred Zinnemann, *A Man for All Seasons*
Actress Elizabeth Taylor, *Who's Afraid of Virginia Woolf?*
Actor Paul Scofield, *A Man for All Seasons*
Supporting actress Sandy Dennis, *Who's Afraid of Virginia Woolf?*
Supporting actor Walter Matthau, *The Fortune Cookie*

1967
Picture *In the Heat of the Night*, Mirisch Corp Productions, United Artists
Director Mike Nichols, *The Graduate*
Actress Katharine Hepburn, *Guess Who's Coming to Dinner?*
Actor Rod Steiger, *In the Heat of the Night*
Supporting actress Estelle Parsons, *Bonnie and Clyde*
Supporting actor George Kennedy, *Cool Hand Luke*

1968
Picture *Oliver!* Columbia Pictures
Director Sir Carol Reed, *Oliver!*
Actress Katharine Hepburn, *The Lion in Winter* and Barbra Streisand, *Funny Girl*
Actor Cliff Robertson, *Charly*
Supporting actress Ruth Gordon, *Rosemary's Baby*
Supporting actor Jack Albertson, *The Subject Was Roses*

1969
Picture *Midnight Cowboy*, Jerome Hellman-John Schlesinger Production, United Artists
Director John Schlesinger, *Midnight Cowboy*
Actress Maggie Smith, *The Prime of Miss Jean Brodie*
Actor John Wayne, *True Grit*
Supporting actress Goldie Hawn, *Cactus Flower*
Supporting actor Gig Young, *They Shoot Horses Don't They?*

1970
Picture *Patton*, Frank McCarthy-Franklin J Schaffner Production, 20th Century Fox
Director Franklin J Schaffner, *Patton*
Actress Glenda Jackson, *Women in Love*
Actor George C Scott, *Patton*
Supporting actress Helen Hayes, *Airport*
Supporting actor John Mills, *Ryan's Daughter*

1971
Picture *The French Connection*, D'Antoni Productions, 20th Century Fox
Director William Friedkin, *The French Connection*
Actress Jane Fonda, *Klute*
Actor Gene Hackman, *The French Connection*
Supporting actress Cloris Leachman, *The Last Picture Show*
Supporting actor Ben Johnson, *The Last Picture Show*

1972
Picture *The Godfather*, Albert S Ruddy Production, Paramount
Director Bob Fosse, *Cabaret*
Actress Liza Minnelli, *Cabaret*
Actor Marlon Brando, *The Godfather*
Supporting actress Eileen Heckart, *Butterflies Are Free*
Supporting actor Joel Grey, *Cabaret*

1973
Picture *The Sting*, Universal/Bill Phillips/George Roy Hill Production, Universal
Director George Roy Hill, *The Sting*
Actress Glenda Jackson, *A Touch of Class*
Actor Jack Lemmon, *Save the Tiger*
Supporting actress Tatum O'Neal, *Paper Moon*
Supporting actor John Houseman, *The Paper Chase*

1974
Picture *The Godfather, Part II*, Coppola Co Production, Paramount
Director Francis Ford Coppola, *The Godfather, Part II*
Actress Ellen Burstyn, *Alice Doesn't Live Here Anymore*
Actor Art Carney, *Harry and Tonto*
Supporting actress Ingrid Bergman, *Murder on the Orient Express*
Supporting actor Robert De Niro, *The Godfather, Part II*

1975
Picture *One Flew Over the Cuckoo's Nest*, Fantasy Films Production, United Artists
Director Milos Forman, *One Flew Over the Cuckoo's Nest*
Actress Louise Fletcher, *One Flew Over the Cuckoo's Nest*
Actor Jack Nicholson, *One Flew Over the Cuckoo's Nest*
Supporting actress Lee Grant, *Shampoo*
Supporting actor George Burns, *The Sunshine Boys*

1976
Picture *Rocky*, Robert Chartoff-Irwin Winkler Production, United Artists
Director John G Avildsen, *Rocky*
Actress Faye Dunaway, *Network*
Actor Peter Finch, *Network*
Supporting actress Beatrice Straight, *Network*
Supporting actor Jason Robards, *All the President's Men*

1977
Picture *Annie Hall*, Jack Rollins-Charles H Joffe Production, United Artists
Director Woody Allen, *Annie Hall*
Actress Diane Keaton, *Annie Hall*
Actor Richard Dreyfuss, *The Goodbye Girl*
Supporting actress Vanessa Redgrave, *Julia*
Supporting actor Jason Robards, *Julia*

1978
Picture *The Deer Hunter*, Michael Cimino Film Production, Universal
Director Michael Cimino, *The Deer Hunter*
Actress Jane Fonda, *Coming Home*
Actor Jon Voight, *Coming Home*

Motion picture Academy Awards (Oscars) (continued)

Supporting actress Maggie Smith, *California Suite*
Supporting actor Christopher Walken, *The Deer Hunter*

1979
Picture *Kramer vs Kramer*, Stanley Jaffe Production, Columbia Pictures
Director Robert Benton, *Kramer vs Kramer*
Actress Sally Field, *Norma Rae*
Actor Dustin Hoffman, *Kramer vs Kramer*
Supporting actress Meryl Streep, *Kramer vs Kramer*
Supporting actor Melvyn Douglas, *Being There*

1980
Picture *Ordinary People*, Wildwood Enterprises Production, Paramount
Director Robert Redford, *Ordinary People*
Actress Sissy Spacek, *Coal Miner's Daughter*
Actor Robert De Niro, *Raging Bull*
Supporting actress Mary Steenburgen, *Melvin and Howard*
Supporting actor Timothy Hutton, *Ordinary People*

1981
Picture *Chariots of Fire*, Enigma Productions, Ladd Company/Warner Bros
Director Warren Beatty, *Reds*
Actress Katharine Hepburn, *On Golden Pond*
Actor Henry Fonda, *On Golden Pond*
Supporting actress Maureen Stapleton, *Reds*
Supporting actor John Gielgud, *Arthur*

1982
Picture *Gandhi*, Indo-British Films Production/Columbia
Director Richard Attenborough, *Gandhi*
Actress Meryl Streep, *Sophie's Choice*
Actor Ben Kingsley, *Gandhi*
Supporting actress Jessica Lange, *Tootsie*
Supporting actor Louis Gossett Jr, *An Officer and a Gentleman*

1983
Picture *Terms of Endearment*, Paramount
Director James L Brooks, *Terms of Endearment*
Actress Shirley MacLaine, *Terms of Endearment*
Actor Robert Duvall, *Tender Mercies*
Supporting actress Linda Hunt, *The Year of Living Dangerously*
Supporting actor Jack Nicholson, *Terms of Endearment*

1984
Picture *Amadeus*, Orion Pictures
Director Milos Forman, *Amadeus*
Actress Sally Field, *Places in the Heart*
Actor F Murray Abraham, *Amadeus*
Supporting actress Dame Peggy Ashcroft, *A Passage to India*
Supporting actor Haing S Ngor, *The Killing Fields*

1985
Picture *Out of Africa*, Universal
Director Sydney Pollack, *Out of Africa*
Actress Geraldine Page, *The Trip to Bountiful*
Actor William Hurt, *Kiss of the Spider Woman*
Supporting actress Anjelica Huston, *Prizzi's Honor*
Supporting actor Don Ameche, *Cocoon*

1986
Picture *Platoon*, Orion Pictures
Director Oliver Stone, *Platoon*

Actress Marlee Matlin, *Children of a Lesser God*
Actor Paul Newman, *The Color of Money*
Supporting actress Dianne Wiest, *Hannah and Her Sisters*
Supporting actor Michael Caine, *Hannah and Her Sisters*

1987
Picture *The Last Emperor*, Columbia Pictures
Director Bernardo Bertolucci, *The Last Emperor*
Actress Cher, *Moonstruck*
Actor Michael Douglas, *Wall Street*
Supporting actress Olympia Dukakis, *Moonstruck*
Supporting actor Sean Connery, *The Untouchables*

1988
Picture *Rain Man*, United Artists
Director Barry Levinson, *Rain Man*
Actress Jodie Foster, *The Accused*
Actor Dustin Hoffman, *Rain Man*
Supporting actress Geena Davis, *The Accidential Tourist*
Supporting actor Kevin Kline, *A Fish Called Wanda*

1989
Picture *Driving Miss Daisy*, Warner Brothers
Director Oliver Stone, *Born on the Fourth of July*
Actress Jessica Tandy, *Driving Miss Daisy*
Actor Daniel Day-Lewis, *My Left Foot*
Supporting actress Brenda Fricker, *My Left Foot*
Supporting actor Denzel Washington, *Glory*

1990
Picture *Dances With Wolves*, Orion
Director Kevin Costner, *Dances With Wolves*
Actress Kathy Bates, *Misery*
Actor Jeremy Irons, *Reversal of Fortune*
Supporting actress Whoopi Goldberg, *Ghost*
Supporting actor Joe Pesci, *Goodfellas*

1991
Picture *The Silence of the Lambs*, Orion
Director Jonathan Demme, *The Silence of the Lambs*
Actress Jodie Foster, *The Silence of the Lambs*
Actor Anthony Hopkins, *The Silence of the Lambs*
Supporting actress Mercedes Ruehl, *The Fisher King*
Supporting actor Jack Palance, *City Slickers*

1992
Picture *Unforgiven*
Director Clint Eastwood, *Unforgiven*
Actress Emma Thompson, *Howard's End*
Actor Al Pacino, *Scent of a Woman*
Supporting actress Marisa Tomei, *My Cousin Vinny*
Supporting actor Gene Hackman, *Unforgiven*

1993
Picture *Schindler's List*
Director Steven Spielberg, *Schindler's List*
Actress Holly Hunter, *The Piano*
Actor Tom Hanks, *Philadelphia*
Supporting actress Anna Paquin, *The Piano*
Supporting actor Tommy Lee Jones, *The Fugitive*

1994
Picture *Forrest Gump*, Paramount
Director Robert Zemeckis, *Forrest Gump*
Actress Jessica Lange, *Blue Sky*
Actor Tom Hanks, *Forrest Gump*
Supporting actress Dianne Wiest, *Bullets over Broadway*
Supporting actor Martin Landau, *Ed Wood*

1995
Picture *Braveheart*, 20th Century Fox
Director Mel Gibson, *Braveheart*
Actress Susan Sarandon, *Dead Man Walking*
Actor Nicholas Cage, *Leaving Las Vegas*
Supporting actress Mira Sorvino, *Mighty Aphrodite*
Supporting actor Kevin Spacey, *The Usual Suspects*

1996
Picture *The English Patient*, Miramax
Director Anthony Minghella, *The English Patient*
Actress Frances McDormand, *Fargo*
Actor Geoffrey Rush, *Shine*
Supporting actress Juliette Binoche, *The English Patient*
Supporting actor Cuba Gooding, *Jerry Maguire*

1997
Picture *Titanic*, Paramount, 20th Century Fox
Director James Cameron, *Titanic*
Actress Helen Hunt, *As Good As it Gets*
Actor Jack Nicholson, *As Good As it Gets*
Supporting actress Kim Basinger, *LA Confidential*
Supporting actor Robin Williams, *Good Will Hunting*

1998
Picture *Shakespeare in Love*, Miramax
Director Steven Spielberg, *Saving Private Ryan*
Actress Gwyneth Paltrow, *Shakespeare in Love*
Actor Roberto Benigni, *Life is Beautiful*
Supporting actress Judi Dench, *Shakespeare in Love*
Supporting actor James Coburn, *Affliction*

1999
Picture *American Beauty*, DreamWorks
Director Sam Mendes, *American Beauty*
Actress Hilary Swank, *Boys Don't Cry*
Actor Kevin Spacey, *American Beauty*
Supporting actress Angelina Jolie, *Girl, Interrupted*
Supporting actor Michael Caine, *The Cider House Rules*

2000
Picture *Gladiator*, Universal Pictures/DreamWorks
Director Steven Soderberg, *Traffic*
Actress Julia Roberts, *Erin Brockovich*
Actor Russell Crowe, *Gladiator*
Supporting actress Marcia Gay Harden, *Pollock*
Supporting actor Benicio Del Toro, *Traffic*

2001
Picture *A Beautiful Mind*, Universal Pictures/Dream Works
Director Ron Howard, *A Beautiful Mind*
Actress Halle Berry, *Monster's Ball*
Actor Denzel Washington, *Training Day*
Supporting actress Jennifer Connelly, *A Beautiful Mind*
Supporting actor Jim Broadbent, *Iris*

2002
Picture *Chicago*, Miramax
Director Roman Polanski, *The Pianist*
Actress Nicole Kidman, *The Hours*
Actor Adrien Brody, *The Pianist*
Supporting actress Catherine Zeta-Jones, *Chicago*
Supporting actor Chris Cooper, *Adaptation*

2003
Picture *The Lord of the Rings: The Return of the King*, New Line Cinema
Director Peter Jackson, *The Lord of the Rings: The Return of the King*
Actress Charlize Theron, *Monster*

Actor Sean Penn, *Mystic River*
Supporting actress Renée Zellweger, *Cold Mountain*
Supporting actor Tim Robbins, *Mystic River*

2004
Picture *Million Dollar Baby*, Warner Brothers Pictures
Director Clint Eastwood, *Million Dollar Baby*
Actress Hilary Swank, *Million Dollar Baby*
Actor Jamie Foxx, *Ray*
Supporting actress Cate Blanchett, *The Aviator*
Supporting actor Morgan Freeman, *Million Dollar Baby*

Pulitzer Prize in music

1943	*Secular Cantata No 2, A Free Song* William Schuman	1977	*Visions of Terror and Wonder* Richard Wernick
1944	*Symphony No 4 (Op. 34)* Howard Hanson	1978	*Déjà Vu for Percussion Quartet and Orchestra* Michael Colgrass
1945	*Appalachian Spring* Aaron Copland	1979	*Aftertones of Infinity* Joseph Schwantner
1946	*The Canticle of the Sun* Leo Sowerby	1980	*In Memory of a Summer Day* David Del Tredici
1947	*Symphony No 3* Charles Ives	1981	*No award*
1948	*Symphony No 3* Walter Piston	1982	*Concerto for Orchestra* Roger Sessions
1949	*Louisiana Story* music Virgil Thomson	1983	*Three Movements for Orchestra* Ellen T Zwilich
1950	*The Consul* Gian Carlo Menotti	1984	*Canti del Sole* Bernard Rands
1951	Music for opera *Giants in the Earth* Douglas Stuart Moore	1985	*Symphony River Run* Stephen Albert
		1986	*Wind Quintet IV* George Perle
1952	*Symphony Concertante* Gail Kubik	1987	*The Flight into Egypt* John Harbison
1954	*Concerto for Two Pianos and Orchestra* Quincy Porter	1988	*12 New Etudes for Piano* William Bolcom
		1989	*Whispers Out of Time* Roger Reynolds
1955	*The Saint of Bleecker Street* Gian Carlo Menotti	1990	*Duplicates: A Concerto for Two Pianos and Orchestra* Mel Powell
1956	*Symphony No 3* Ernest Toch		
1957	*Meditations on Ecclesiastes* Norman Dello Joio	1991	*Symphony* Shulamit Ran
1958	*Vanessa* Samuel Barber	1992	*The Face of the Night, The Heart of the Dark* Wayne Peterson
1959	*Concerto for Piano and Orchestra* John La Montaine		
		1993	*Trombone Concerto* Christopher Rouse
1960	*Second String Quartet* Elliott Carter	1994	*Of Remembrances and Reflections* Gunther Schuller
1961	*Symphony No 7* Walter Piston		
1962	*The Crucible* Robert Ward	1995	*Stringmusic* Morton Gould
1963	*Piano Concerto No 1* Samuel Barber	1996	*Lilacs* George Walker
1966	*Variations for Orchestra* Leslie Bassett	1997	*Blood on the Fields* Wynton Marsalis
1967	*Quartet No 3* Leon Kirchner	1998	*String Quartet No 2, Musica Instrumentalis* Aaron J Kernis
1968	*Echoes of Time and the River* George Crumb		
1969	*String Quartet No 3* Karel Husa	1999	*Concerto for Flute, Strings and Percussion* Melinda Wagner
1970	*Time's Encomium* Charles Wuorinen		
1971	*Synchronisms No 6 for Piano and Electronic Sound* Mario Davidovsky	2000	*Life Is a Dream, Opera in Three Acts: Act II, Concert Version* Lewis Spratlan
1972	*Windows* Jacob Druckman	2001	*Symphony No 2 for string orchestra* John Corigliani
1973	*String Quartet No 3* Elliott Carter		
1974	*Notturno* Donald Martino	2002	*Ice Field* Henry Brant
1975	*From the Diary of Virginia Woolf* Dominick Argento	2003	*On The Transmigration of Souls* John Adams
		2004	*Tempest Fantasy* Paul Moravec
1976	*Air Music* Ned Rorem	2005	*Second Concerto for Orchestra* Steven Stucky

National anthems/songs from around the world

Country	Title (composer in brackets)
Australia[a]	*Advance Australia Fair*[a] (Peter Dodds McCormick)
Austria	*Bundeshymne der Republik Österreich* (Johan Holzer)
Canada	*O Canada* (Calixa Lavallée)
China	*March of the Volunteers*
England	*Land of Hope and Glory* (A C Benson)
France	*La Marseillaise* (Claude-Joseph Rouget de Lisle)
Germany	*Deutschland-Lied* (Haydn)
India	*Jana Gana Rana* (Rabindranath Tagore)
Ireland	*Amhrán Na bhFiann* (Peadar Kearney)
Italy	*Fratelli d'Italia* (Michele Novaro)
Japan	*Kimigayo* (Hayashi Hiromori)
New Zealand[a]	*God Defend New Zealand* (John Joseph Woods)
Russian Federation	*State Hymn of the Russian Federation* (Mikhail Glinka)
Scotland	*Flower of Scotland* (Roy Williamson)
UK	*God Save the Queen/King*
USA	*The Star Spangled Banner* (John Stafford Smith)
Wales	*Hen Wlad fy Nhadau* (Evan and James James)

[a]The royal anthem, *God Save the Queen/King*, is played when the Queen or a member of the royal family is present.

Ballets

Ballet	Composer	Choreographer	First performed	Ballet	Composer	Choreographer	First performed
Anastasia	Tchaikovsky	MacMillan	1971	Month in the Country, A	Chopin	Ashton	1976
Apollon Musagète	Stravinsky	Bolm	1928	Night Journey	Schumann	Graham	1947
Appalachian Spring	Copland	Graham	1944	Night Shadow	Rieti	Balanchine	1946
L'Après-midi d'un Faune	Debussy	Nijinsky	1912	Nocturne	Delius	Ashton	1936
Bayadère, La	Minkus	Petipa	1877	Nutcracker, The	Tchaikovsky	Ivanov	1892
Biches, Les	Poulenc	Nijinska	1924	Ondine	Henze	Ashton	1958
Billy the Kid	Copland	Loring	1938	Onegin	Tchaikovsky	Cranko	1965
Bolero	Ravel	Nijinska	1928	Orpheus	Stravinsky	Balanchine	1948
Boutique Fantastique, La	Rossini	Massine	1919	Papillons, Les	Schumann	Fokine	1913
				Parade	Satie	Massine	1917
Burrow, The	Martin	MacMillan	1958	Patineurs, Les	Meyerbeer	Ashton	1937
Cain and Abel	Panufnik	MacMillan	1968	Petrushka	Stravinsky	Fokine	1911
Carmen	Bizet	Petit	1949	Pineapple Poll	Sullivan	Cranko	1951
Chant du Rossignol, Le	Stravinsky	Massine	1920	Present Histories	Schubert	Tuckett	1991
				Prince Igor	Borodin	Ivanov	1890
Cinderella	Prokofiev	Zakharov	1945	Prince of the Pagodas, The	Britten	Cranko	1957
Concerto Barocco	Bach	Balanchine	1941				
Coppélia	Delibes	Saint-Leon	1870	Prodigal Son, The	Prokofiev	Balanchine	1929
Don Quixote	Minkus	Petipa	1869	Rake's Progress, The	Gordon	De Valois	1935
Ebony Concerto	Stravinsky	Page	1995	Renard	Stravinsky	Page	1994
Elite Syncopations	Joplin	MacMillan	1974	Rendez-Vous, Les	Auber	Ashton	1933
Enigma Variations	Elgar	Ashton	1968	Rhapsody	Rachmaninov	Ashton	1980
Fille Mal Gardée, La	Various (traditional French songs)	Dauberval	1789				
				Rite of Spring, The	Stravinsky	Nijinsky	1913
				Rituals	Bartok	MacMillan	1975
Firebird, The	Stravinsky	Fokine	1910	Romeo and Juliet	Prokofiev	Psota	1938
Four Seasons, The	Vivaldi	MacMillan	1975	Rooms	Hopkins	Sokolow	1955
Giselle	Adam	Coralli/Perrot	1841	Russian Soldier, The	Prokofiev	Fokine	1942
				Saisons, Les	Glazunov	Petipa	1900
Gods Go A-Begging, The	Handel	Balanchine	1928	Scènes de Ballet	Stravinsky	Dolin	1944
				Scheherazade	Rimsky-Korsakov	Fokine	1910
Hamlet	Tchaikovsky	Helpmann	1942				
Harlequinade	Drigo	Balanchine	1965	Scotch Symphony	Mendelssohn	Balanchine	1952
Hermanas, Las	Martin	MacMillan	1963	Serenade	Tchaikovsky	Balanchine	1934
Illuminations	Britten	Ashton	1950	Seven Deadly Sins	Weill	Balanchine	1933
Invitation, The	Seiber	MacMillan	1960	Sleeping Beauty, The	Tchaikovsky	Petipa	1890
Isadora	Rodney Bennett	MacMillan	1981	Song of the Earth	Mahler	MacMillan	1965
				Spectre de la Rose, Le	Weber	Fokine	1911
Ivan The Terrible	Prokofiev	Grigorovich	1975				
Jeune Homme et La Mort, Le	Bach	Petit	1946	Stoics Quartet	Mendelssohn	Burrows	1991
				Summerspace	Feldman	Cunningham	1958
Judas Tree, The	Elias	MacMillan	1992	Swan Lake	Tchaikovsky	Reisinger	1877
Knight Errant	Strauss (Richard)	Tudor	1968	Sylphides, Les	Chopin	Fokine	1907
				Symphonic Variations	Franck	Ashton	1946
Labyrinth	Schubert	Massine	1941				
Lady and the Fool, The	Verdi	Cranko	1954	Symphonie Fantastique	Berlioz	Massine	1936
Lady of the Camellias	Chopin	Neumeier	1978	Symphony in C	Bizet	Balanchine	1991
				Tales of Hoffmann	Offenbach	Darrell	1972
Lament of the Waves	Masson	Ashton	1970	Taming of the Shrew	Scarlatti-Stolze	Cranko	1969
Legend of Joseph	Strauss (Richard)	Fokine	1914	Three-Cornered Hat, The	De Falla	Massine	1919
Luna, La	Bach	Béjart	1991	Vainqueurs, Les	Wagner	Béjart	1969
Malade Imaginaire, Le	Rota	Béjart	1976	Valse, La	Ravel	Nijinska	1929
				Variations	Stravinsky	Balanchine	1966
Manon	Massenet	MacMillan	1974	Voluntaries	Poulenc	Tetley	1973
Masques, Les	Poulenc	Ashton	1933	Walk to the Paradise Garden, The	Delius	Ashton	1972
Mathilde	Wagner	Béjart	1965				
Mayerling	Liszt	MacMillan	1978				
Midsummer Night's Dream	Mendelssohn	Balanchine	1962				

Dance companies

Name	Date founded	Location	Name	Date founded	Location
Alvin Ailey American Dance Theater	1958	New York	Jose Limon Dance Company	1946	New York
American Ballet Theatre	1940	New York	Kirov-Marinsky Ballet (formerly Kirov Ballet)	1935	St Petersburg
Australian Ballet Company	1962	Melbourne	Lar Lubovitch Dance Company	1968	New York
Australian Dance Theatre	1965	Adelaide	London City Ballet	1978	London
Ballet Gulbenkian	1965	Lisbon	London Contemporary Dance Theatre	1967–95	London
Ballet Jooss	1933	Cambridge, UK	London Festival Ballet (now English National Ballet)	1950–88	London
Ballets de Paris	1948	France			
Rambert Dance Company (formerly Ballet Rambert)	1926	London	Maly Ballet	1915	St Petersburg
Ballet Russe de Monte Carlo	1938	Monte Carlo	Martha Graham Dance Company	1927	New York
Ballets des Champs-Elysées	1944	Paris	Miami City Ballet	1986	Miami
Ballets Russes de Sergei Diaghilev (became the Kirov Ballet)	1909–29	St Petersburg	National Ballet	1962	Washington
			National Ballet of Canada	1951	Toronto
Ballets Suedois	1920	France	National Ballet of Cuba	1948	Havana
Ballet Théâtre Contemporain	1968	Amiens	National Ballet of Mexico	1949	Mexico City
Ballet Trockadero de Monte Carlo, Les	1974	New York	Netherlands Dance Theatre	1959	The Hague
Ballet West	1968	Salt Lake City, Utah	New York City Ballet	1948	USA
			Nikolais Dance Theatre	1951	New York
Bejárt Ballet Lausanne (formerly Ballet Béjart and Ballet du Xième Siecle)	1987	Lausanne	Northern Ballet	1969	Manchester
			Paris Opéra Ballet	1661	Paris
			Pennsylvania Ballet	1963	Philadelphia
Birmingham Royal Ballet (formerly the Sadler's Wells (1940) and the Royal Ballet (1956))	1946	Birmingham	Pilobolus Dance Theatre	1971	Vermont
			Pittsburgh Ballet Theater	1970	Pittsburgh
			Richard Alston Dance Company	1994	London
Bolshoi Ballet	1776	Moscow	Royal Ballet	1931	Covent Garden, London
Borovansky Ballet	1942	Melbourne			
Boston Ballet	1964	Boston	Royal Danish Ballet	16th-c	Copenhagen
Central Ballet of China	1959	Beijing	Royal New Zealand Ballet Company (as from 1984)	1961	Wellington
Cholmondeleys, The	1984	London			
Dance Bites	1994	London	Royal Swedish Ballet	1609	Stockholm
Dance Theater of Harlem	1971	New York	Royal Winnipeg Ballet	1938	Canada
Dutch National Ballet	1961	Amsterdam	San Francisco Ballet	1933	USA
DV8 Physical Theatre	1986	London	School of American Ballet (now the American Ballet)	1933	New York
English National Ballet (originally London Festival Ballet)	1950	London			
			Scottish Ballet	1956	Glasgow
			Stanislavsky Ballet	1929	Moscow
Extemporary Dance Theatre	1975	London	Stuttgart Ballet	1609	Germany
Feld Ballet NY	1974	New York	Sydney Dance Company	1971	Sydney
Grands Ballets Canadiens, Les	1956	Montreal	Washington Ballet	1962	Washington
Houston Ballet	1968	Houston	Western Theatre Ballet	1957	Bristol
Joffrey Ballet of Chicago (formerly Joffrey Ballet)	1954	New York			

The Turner Prize

1985	Howard Hodgkin	1992	Grenville Davey	1999	Steve McQueen
1986	Gilbert and George	1993	Rachel Whiteread	2000	Wolfgang Tillmans
1987	Richard Deacon	1994	Anthony Gormley	2001	Martin Creed
1988	Tony Cragg	1995	Damien Hirst	2002	Keith Tyson
1989	Richard Long	1996	Douglas Gordon	2003	Grayson Perry
1990	*Prize suspended*	1997	Gillian Wearing	2004	Jeremy Deller
1991	Anish Kapoor	1998	Chris Ofili		

PART THIRTEEN

Knowledge

Presidents of the Royal Academy

1768–92	Joshua Reynolds
1792–1805	Benjamin West
1805–6	James Wyatt
1806–20	Benjamin West
1820–30	Thomas Lawrence
1830–50	Martin Archer Shee
1850–66	Charles Eastlake
1866–78	Francis Grant
1878–96	Frederick, 1st Baron Leighton
1896	John Millais
1896–1919	Edward Poynter
1919–24	Aston Webb
1924–8	Frank Dicksee
1928–33	William Llewellyn
1938–44	Edwin Lutyens
1944–9	Alfred Munnings
1949–54	Gerald Festus Kelly
1954–6	Albert Edward Richardson
1956–66	Charles Wheeler
1966–76	Thomas Monnington
1976–84	Hugh Casson
1984–93	Roger de Grey
1993–	Philip Dowson

Presidents of the Royal Society

1662–77	William, 2nd Viscount Brouncker
1677–80	Joseph Williamson
1680–2	Christopher Wren
1682–3	John Hoskins
1683–4	Cyril Wyche
1684–6	Samuel Pepys
1686–9	John, Earl of Carbery
1689–90	Thomas Herbert, Earl of Pembroke
1690–5	Robert Southwell
1695–8	Charles Montagu, 1st Earl of Halifax
1698–1703	John, 1st Baron Somers
1703–27	Isaac Newton
1727–41	Hans Sloane
1741–52	Martin Folkes
1752–64	George, Earl of Macclesfield
1764–8	Lord Morton
1768–72	James West
1772–8	John Pringle
1778–1820	Joseph Banks
1820–7	Humphrey Davy
1827–30	Davies Gilbert
1830–8	Augustus Frederick, Duke of Sussex
1838–47	Marquis of Northampton
1847–54	William Parsons, 3rd Earl of Rosse
1854–8	Lord Wrothesley
1858–61	Benjamin Brodie
1861–71	Edward Sabine
1871–3	George Airy
1873–8	Joseph Hooker
1878–83	William Spottiswoode
1883–5	Thomas H Huxley
1885–90	George Stokes
1890–5	William Thomson, 1st Baron Kelvin
1895–1900	Joseph, Lord Lister
1900–5	William Huggins
1905–8	John William Strutt, 3rd Baron Rayleigh
1908–13	Archibald Geikie
1913–15	William Crookes
1915–20	Joseph Thomson
1920–5	Charles Sherrington
1925–30	Ernest, 1st Baron Rutherford
1930–5	Frederick Hopkins
1935–40	William Bragg
1940–5	Henry Dale
1945–50	Robert Robinson
1950–5	Edgar, 1st Baron Adrian
1955–60	Cyril Hinshelwood
1960–5	Howard, Baron Florey
1965–70	Patrick Stuart, Baron Blackett
1970–5	Alan Hodgkin
1975–80	Alexander, Baron Todd
1980–5	Andrew Huxley
1985–90	George, Lord Porter
1990–95	Michael Atiyah
1995–2000	Aaron Klug
2000–5	Robert May
2005–	Martin Rees

Nobel Prizewinners

Physics

1901	Wilhelm Konrad von Röntgen	1949	Hideki Yukawa	1979	Steven Weinberg
		1950	Cecil Frank Powell		Sheldon Lee Glashow
1902	Hendrik Antoon Lorentz	1951	John Douglas Cockcroft		Abdus Salam
	Pieter Zeeman		Ernest Thomas Sinton	1980	James Watson Cronin
1903	Antoine Henri Becquerel		Walton		Val Logsdon Fitch
	Pierre Curie	1952	Felix Bloch	1981	Nicolas Bloembergen
	Marie Curie		Edward Mills Purcell		Arthur Leonard Schawlow
1904	John William Strutt, 3rd	1953	Frits Zernike		Kai M Siegbahn
	Baron Rayleigh	1954	Max Born	1982	Kenneth Geddes Wilson
1905	Philipp Eduard Anton		Walther Bothe	1983	Subrahmanyan
	Lenard	1955	Willis Eugene Lamb, Jr		Chandrasekhar
1906	Joseph John Thomson		Polykarp Kusch		William Alfred Fowler
1907	Albert Abraham Michelson	1956	William Bradford Shockley	1984	Carlo Rubbia
1908	Gabriel Lippmann		John Bardeen		Simon van der Meer
1909	Guglielmo, Marchese		Walter Hauser Brattain	1985	Klaus von Klitzing
	Marconi	1957	Tsung-Dao Lee	1986	Gerd Binnig
	Karl Braun		Chen Ning Yang		Heinrich Rohrer
1910	Johannes Diderik van der	1958	Pavel Alekseevich Cherenkov		Ernst Ruska
	Waals		Ilya Mikhailovich Frank	1987	George Bednorz
1911	Wilhelm Wien		Igor Yevgenyevich Tamm		Alex Müller
1912	Nils Gustav Dalén	1959	Emilio Segrè	1988	Leon Lederman
1913	Heike Kamerlingh Onnes		Owen Chamberlain		Melvin Schwartz
1914	Max von Laue	1960	Donald Arthur Glaser		Jack Steinberger
1915	William Henry Bragg	1961	Robert Hofstadter	1989	Hans Dehmelt
	(William) Lawrence Bragg		Rudolf Mössbauer		Wolfgang Paul
1916	*No award*	1962	Lev Davidovich Landau		Norman Ramsay
1917	Charles Glover Barkla	1963	(Johannes) Hans (Daniel)	1990	Jerome Friedman
1918	Max Karl Ernst Planck		Jensen		Henry Kendall
1919	Johannes Stark		Maria Goeppert-Meyer		Richard Taylor
1920	Charles Édouard Guillaume		Eugene Paul Wigner	1991	Pierre-Gilles de Gennes
1921	Albert Einstein	1964	Charles Hard Townes	1992	Georges Charpak
1922	Niels (Henrik David) Bohr		Nikolai Gennadiyevich Basov	1993	Joseph Taylor
1923	Robert Andrews Millikan		Alexander Mikhailovich		Russell Hulse
1924	Karl Manne Georg Siegbahn		Prokhorov	1994	Bertram N Brockhouse
1925	James Franck	1965	Julian S Schwinger		Clifford G Shull
	Gustav Ludwig Hertz		Richard P Feynman	1995	Martin Perl
1926	Jean Baptiste Perrin		Shinichiro Tomonaga		Frederick Reines
1927	Arthur Holly Compton	1966	Alfred Kastler	1996	Douglas Osheroff
	Charles Thomson Rees	1967	Hans Albrecht Bethe		David Lee
	Wilson	1968	Luis Walter Alvarez		Robert Richardson
1928	Owen Willans Richardson	1969	Murray Gell-Mann	1997	Steven Chu
1929	Louis Victor, 7th Duc de	1970	Louis Eugène Félix Néel		William D Phillips
	Broglie		Hannes Olof Alvén		Claude Cohen-Tannoudji
1930	Chandrasekhara Venkata	1971	Dennis Gabor	1998	Robert B Laughlin
	Raman	1972	John Bardeen		Horst L Stormer
1931	*No award*		Leon Neil Cooper	1999	Gerardhus 'T Hooft
1932	Werner Karl Heisenberg		John Robert Schrieffer		Martinus JG Veltman
1933	Paul Adrien Maurice Dirac	1973	Leo Esaki	2000	Zhores I Alferov
	Erwin Schrödinger		Ivar Giaever		Herbert Kroemer
1934	*No award*		Brian David Josephson		Jack S Kilby
1935	James Chadwick	1974	Martin Ryle	2001	Eric A Cornell
1936	Victor Francis Hess		Antony Hewish		Wolfgang Ketterle
	Carl David Anderson	1975	Aage Niels Bohr		Carl E Wieman
1937	Clinton Joseph Davisson		Benjamin Roy Mottelson	2002	Raymond Davis
	George Paget Thomson		(Leo) James Rainwater		Masatoshi Koshiba
1938	Enrico Fermi	1976	Burton Richter		Riccardo Giacconi
1939	Ernest Orlando Lawrence		Samuel Chao Chung Ting	2003	Alexei Abrikosov
1943	Otto Stern	1977	Philip Warren Anderson		Vitaly Ginzburg
1944	Isidor Isaac Rabi		Nevill Francis Mott		Anthony Leggett
1945	Wolfgang Pauli		John Hasbrouck van Vleck	2004	David Gross
1946	Percy Williams Bridgman	1978	Pjotr Leonidovich (Peter)		David Politzer
1947	Edward Victor Appleton		Kapitza		Frank Wilczek
1948	Patrick Maynard Stuart, Baron Blackett		Arno Allan Penzias		
			Robert Woodrow Wilson		

KNOWLEDGE

Chemistry

1901	Jacobus Henricus van t'Hoff	
1902	Emil Hermann Fischer	
1903	Svante Arrhenius	
1904	William Ramsay	
1905	Johann Friedrich Wilhelm Adolf von Baeyer	
1906	Henri Moissan	
1907	Eduard Buchner	
1908	Ernest, 1st Baron Rutherford	
1909	Friedrich Wilhelm Ostwald	
1910	Otto Wallach	
1911	Marie Curie	
1912	(François Auguste) Victor Grignard	
	Paul Sabatier	
1913	Alfred Werner	
1914	Theodore William Richards	
1915	Richard Willstätter	
1916	*No award*	
1917	*No award*	
1918	Fritz Haber	
1919	*No award*	
1920	Walther Hermann Nernst	
1921	Frederick Soddy	
1922	Francis William Aston	
1923	Fritz Pregl	
1924	*No award*	
1925	Richard Adolf Zsigmondy	
1926	Theodor Svedberg	
1927	Heinrich Otto Wieland	
1928	Adolf Otto Reinhold Windaus	
1929	Arthur Harden	
	Hans Karl August Simon von Euler-Chelpin	
1930	Hans Fischer	
1931	Carl Bosch	
	Friedrich Bergius	
1932	Irving Langmuir	
1933	*No award*	
1934	Harold Clayton Urey	
1935	Jean Frédéric Joliot-Curie	
	Irène Joliot-Curie	
1936	Peter Joseph Wilhelm Debye	
1937	Walter Norman Haworth	
	Paul Karrer	
1938	Richard Kuhn, *declined*	
1939	Adolf Friedrich Johann Butenandt, *declined*	
	Leopold Ruzicka	
1940	George de Hevesy	
1944	Otto Hahn	
1945	Arttturi Ilmari Virtanen	
1946	James Batcheller Sumner	
	John Knudsen Northrop	
	Wendell Meredith Stanley	
1947	Robert Robinson	

1948	Arne Wilhelm Kaurin Tiselius	
1949	William Francis Giauque	
1950	Otto Diels	
	Kurt Alder	
1951	Edwin Mattison McMillan	
	Glenn Theodore Seaborg	
1952	Archer (John Porter) Martin	
	Richard Laurence Millington Synge	
1953	Hermann Staudinger	
1954	Linus Carl Pauling	
1955	Vincent du Vigneaud	
1956	Nikolai Nikilaevich Semenov	
	Cyril Norman Hinshelwood	
1957	Alexander Robertus Todd, Baron Todd	
1958	Frederick Sanger	
1959	Jaroslav Heyrovsky	
1960	Willard Frank Libby	
1961	Melvin Calvin	
1962	John Cowdery Kendrew	
	Max Ferdinand Perutz	
1963	Giulio Natta	
	Karl Ziegler	
1964	Dorothy Mary Hodgkin	
1965	Robert Burns Woodward	
1966	Robert Sanderson Mulliken	
1967	Manfred Eigen	
	Ronald George Wreyford Norrish	
	George, Baron Porter	
1968	Lars Onsager	
1969	Derek H R Barton	
	Odd Hassel	
1970	Luis Federico Leloir	
1971	Gerhard Herzberg	
1972	Stanford Moore	
	William Howard Stein	
	Christian Boehmer Anfinsen	
1973	Ernst Otto Fischer	
	Geoffrey Wilkinson	
1974	Paul John Flory	
1975	John Warcup Cornforth	
	Vladimir Prelog	
1976	William Nunn Lipscomb	
1977	Ilya Prigogine	
1978	Peter Dennis Mitchell	
1979	Herbert Charles Brown	
	Georg Wittig	
1980	Paul Berg	
	Walter Gilbert	
	Frederick Sanger	
1981	Kenichi Fukui	
	Roald Hoffmann	
1982	Aaron Klug	

1983	Henry Taube	
1984	(Robert) Bruce Merrifield	
1985	Herbert Aaron Hauptman	
	Jerome Karle	
1986	Dudley R Herschbach	
	Yuan Tseh Lee	
	John C Polanyi	
1987	Charles Pedersen	
	Donald Cram	
	Jean-Marie Lehn	
1988	Johann Deisenhofer	
	Robert Huber	
	Hartmut Michel	
1989	Sydney Altman	
	Thomas Cech	
1990	Elias James Corey	
1991	Richard Ernst	
1992	Rudolph Marcus	
1993	Kary Mulis	
	Michael Smith	
1994	George A Olah	
1995	Paul Crutzen	
	Mario Molina	
	Sherwood Rowland	
1996	Harold Kroto	
	Robert Curl	
	Richard Smalley	
1997	Jens Skou	
	John Walker	
	Paul Boyer	
1998	Walter Kohn	
	John A Pople	
1999	Ahmed Zewail	
2000	Alan J Heeger	
	Alan G MacDiarmid	
	Hideki Shirakawa	
2001	William S Knowles	
	Ryoji Noyori	
	K Barry Sharpless	
2002	John B Fenn	
	Koichi Tanaka	
	Kurt Wüthrich	
2003	Peter Agre	
	Roderick MacKinnon	
2004	Aaron Ciechanover	
	Avram Hershko	
	Irwin Rose	

Nobel Prizewinners (continued)

Literature

1901	René François Armand Sully-Prudhomme
1902	Theodor Mommsen
1903	Bjørnstjerne Martinius Bjørnson
1904	Frédéric Mistral
	José Echegaray y Eizaguirre
1905	Henryk Sienkiewicz
1906	Giosuè Carducci
1907	Rudyard Kipling
1908	Rudolf Christoph Eucken
1909	Selma Ottiliana Lovisa Lagerlöf
1910	Paul Johann von Heyse
1911	Count Maurice Maeterlinck
1912	Gerhart Hauptmann
1913	Rabindranath Tagore
1914	*No award*
1915	Romain Rolland
1916	(Karl Gustav) Verner von Heidenstam
1917	Karl Gjellerup
	Henrik Pontoppidan
1918	*No award*
1919	Carl Friedrich Georg Spitteler
1920	Knut Hamsun
1921	Anatole France
1922	Jacinto Benavente y Martínez
1923	William Butler Yeats
1924	Wladyslaw Stanislaw Reymont
1925	George Bernard Shaw
1926	Grazia Deledda
1927	Henri Bergson
1928	Sigrid Undset
1929	Thomas Mann
1930	(Harry) Sinclair Lewis
1931	Erik Axel Karlfeldt
1932	John Galsworthy
1933	Ivan Alexeievich Bunin
1934	Luigi Pirandello
1935	*No award*
1936	Eugene Gladstone O'Neill
1937	Roger Martin du Gard
1938	Pearl S Buck
1939	Frans Eemil Sillanpää
1943	*No award*
1944	Johannes Vilhelm (J V) Jensen
1945	Gabriela Mistral
1946	Hermann Hesse
1947	André (Paul Guillaume) Gide
1948	T S (Thomas Stearns) Eliot
1949	William Faulkner
1950	Bertrand (Arthur William, 3rd Earl) Russell
1951	Pär (Fabian) Lagerkvist
1952	François Mauriac
1953	Winston (Leonard Spencer) Churchill
1954	Ernest (Millar) Hemingway
1955	Halldór Laxness
1956	Juan Ramón Jiménez
1957	Albert Camus
1958	Boris Leonidovich Pasternak
1959	Salvatore Quasimodo
1960	Saint-John Perse
1961	Ivo Andrić
1962	John (Ernest) Steinbeck
1963	George Seferis
1964	Jean-Paul Sartre, *declined*
1965	Mikhail (Alexandrovich) Sholokhov
1966	Shmuel Yosef Agnon
	Nelly (Leonie) Sachs
1967	Miguel Angel Asturias
1968	Kawabata Yasunari
1969	Samuel Beckett
1970	Alexandr Isayevich Solzhenitsyn
1971	Pablo (Neftali Reyes) Neruda
1972	Heinrich Böll
1973	Patrick White
1974	Eyvind Johnson
	Harry (Edmund) Martinson
1975	Eugenio Montale
1976	Saul Bellow
1977	Vicente Aleixandre
1978	Isaac Bashevis Singer
1979	Odysseus Elytis
1980	Czeslaw Milosz
1981	Elias Canetti
1982	Gabriel García Márquez
1983	William (Gerald) Golding
1984	Jaroslav Seifert
1985	Claude (Eugène Henri) Simon
1986	Wole Soyinka
1987	Joseph Brodsky
1988	Naguib Mahfouz
1989	Camilo José Cela
1990	Octavio Paz
1991	Nadine Gordimer
1992	Derek Walcott
1993	Toni Morrison
1994	Kenzaburo Oe
1995	Seamus Heaney
1996	Wislawa Szymborska
1997	Dario Fo
1998	Jose Saramago
1999	Gunther Grass
2000	Gao Xingjian
2001	V S Naipaul
2002	Imre Kertész
2003	J M Coetzee
2004	Elfriede Jelinek

Economics

1969	Ragnar Anton Kittil Frisch
	Jan Tinbergen
1970	Paul Anthony Samuelson
1971	Simon Smith Kuznets
1972	John Richard Hicks
	Kenneth Joseph Arrow
1973	Wassily Leontief
1974	(Karl) Gunnar Myrdal
	Friedrich August von Hayek
1975	Leonid Vitaliyevich Kantorovich
	Tjalling Charles Koopmans
1976	Milton Friedman
1977	James Edward Meade
	Bertil Gotthard Ohlin
1978	Herbert Alexander Simon
1979	(William) Arthur Lewis
	Theodore William Schultz
1980	Lawrence Robert Klein
1981	James Tobin
1982	George Joseph Stigler
1983	Gerard Debreu
1984	(John) Richard Nicholas Stone
1985	Franco Modigliani
1986	James McGill Buchanan
1987	Robert Merton Solow
1988	Maurice Allais
1989	Trygve Haavelmo
1990	Harry M Markovitz
	Merton Miller
	William Sharpe
1991	Ronald Coase
1992	Gary S Becker
1993	Douglas C North
	Robert W Fogel
1994	John Nash
	Reinhard Selten
	John Harsanyi
1995	Robert E Lucas Jr
1996	James Mirrlees
	William Vickrey
1997	Myron Scholes
	Robert Merton
1998	Amartya Sen
1999	Robert A Mundell
2000	James J Heckman
	Daniel L McFadden
2001	George A Akerlof
	A Michael Spence
	Joseph E Stiglitz
2002	Daniel Kahneman
	Vernon L Smith
2003	Robert Engle
	Clive Granger
2004	Finn Kydland
	Edward Prescott

Physiology or Medicine

1901	Emil von Behring	
1902	Ronald Ross	
1903	Niels Ryberg Finsen	
1904	Ivan Petrovich Pavlov	
1905	Robert Koch	
1906	Camillo Golgi	
	Santiago Ramón y Cajal	
1907	Charles Louis Alphonse	
	Laveran	
1908	Paul Ehrlich	
	Ilya Ilich Mechnikov	
1909	Emil Theodor Kocher	
1910	Albrecht Kossel	
1911	Allvar Gullstrand	
1912	Alexis Carrel	
1913	Charles Robert Richet	
1914	Robert Bárány	
1915	No award	
1916	No award	
1917	No award	
1918	No award	
1919	Jules Jean Baptiste Vincent	
	Bordet	
1920	Schack August Steenberg	
	Krogh	
1921	No award	
1922	Archibald Vivian Hill	
	Otto Fritz Meyerhof	
1923	Frederick Grant Banting	
	John James Rickard Macleod	
1924	Willem Einthoven	
1925	No award	
1926	Johannes Andreas Grib	
	Fibiger	
1927	Julius Wagner-Jauregg	
1928	Charles Jules Henri Nicolle	
1929	Christiaan Eijkman	
	Frederick Gowland Hopkins	
1930	Karl Landsteiner	
1931	Otto Heinrich Warburg	
1932	Edgar Douglas Adrian, 1st	
	Baron Edgar	
	Charles Scott Sherrington	
1933	Thomas Hunt Morgan	
1934	George Hoyt Whipple	
	George Minot	
	William Murphy	
1935	Hans Spemann	
1936	Henry Hallett Dale	
	Otto Loewi	
1937	Albert von Nagyrapolt Szent-	
	Györgyi	
1938	Corneille Jean François	
	Heymans	
1939	Gerhard (Johannes Paul)	
	Domagk, declined	
1940	Carl Peter Henrik Dam	
	Edward Adelbert Doisy	
1944	Joseph Erlanger	
	Herbert Spencer Gasser	
1945	Alexander Fleming	
	Ernst Boris Chain	
	Howard Walter, Baron Florey	
1946	Hermann Joseph Müller	

1947	Carl Ferdinand Cori	
	Gerty Theresa Cori	
	Bernardo Alberto Houssay	
1948	Paul Hermann Müller	
1949	Walter Rudolf Hess	
	António Caetano de Abreu	
	Freire	
	Egas Moniz	
1950	Philip Showalter Hench	
	Edward Calvin Kendall	
	Tadeusz Reichstein	
1951	Max Theiler	
1952	Selman Abraham Waksman	
1953	Fritz Albert Lipmann	
	Hans Krebs	
1954	John Franklin Enders	
	Thomas Huckle Weller	
	Frederick Chapman Robbins	
1955	(Axel) Hugo Theodor	
	Theorell	
1956	Werner Forssmann	
	Dickinson Woodruff	
	Richards	
	André Frédéric Cournand	
1957	Daniel Bovet	
1958	George Wells Beadle	
	Edward Lawrie Tatum	
	Joshua Lederberg	
1959	Severo Ochoa	
	Arthur Kornberg	
1960	Frank Macfarlane Burnet	
	Peter Brian Medawar	
1961	Georg von Békésy	
1962	Francis Crick	
	James Dewey Watson	
	Maurice Hugh Frederick	
	Wilkins	
1963	John Carew Eccles	
	Alan Lloyd Hodgkin	
	Andrew Fielding Huxley	
1964	Konrad Emil Bloch	
	Feodor Felix Konrad Lynen	
1965	François Jacob	
	Jacques Monod	
	André Lwoff	
1966	Charles Brenton Huggins	
	Francis Peyton Rous	
1967	Haldan Keffer Hartline	
	George Wald	
	Ragnar Arthur Granit	
1968	Robert William Holley	
	Har Gobind Khorana	
	Marshall Warren Nirenberg	
1969	Max Delbrück	
	Alfred Day Hershey	
	Salvador Edward Luria	
1970	Julius Axelrod	
	Bernard Katz	
	Ulf von Euler	
1971	Earl W Sutherland	
1972	Gerald Maurice Edelman	
	Rodney Robert Porter	
1973	Konrad Zacharias Lorenz	
	Nikolaas Tinbergen	

	Karl von Frisch	
1974	Albert Claude	
	George Emil Palade	
	Christian René de Duve	
1975	David Baltimore	
	Renato Dulbecco	
	Howard Martin Temin	
1976	Baruch Samuel Blumberg	
	Daniel Carleton Gajdusek	
1977	Rosalyn Sussman Yalow	
	Roger (Charles Louis)	
	Guillemin	
	Andrew Victor Schally	
1978	Werner Arber	
	Daniel Nathans	
	Hamilton Othanel Smith	
1979	Allan MacLeod Cormack	
	Godfrey Newbold Hounsfield	
1980	Baruj Benacerraf	
	George Davis Snell	
	Jean Dausset	
1981	Roger Wolcott Sperry	
	David Hunter Hubel	
	Torsten Nils Wiesel	
1982	Sune Karl Bergström	
	Bengt I Samuelsson	
	John Robert Vane	
1983	Barbara McClintock	
1984	Niels Kai Jerne	
	Georges J F Köhler	
	César Milstein	
1985	Joseph Leonard Goldstein	
	Michael Stuart Brown	
1986	Stanley Cohen	
	Rita Levi-Montalcini	
1987	Susumu Tonegawa	
1988	James Black	
	Gertrude Elion	
	George Hitchings	
1989	(John) Michael Bishop	
	Harold Elliot Varmus	
1990	Joseph Edward Murray	
	(Edward) Donnall Thomas	
1991	Erwin Neher	
	Bert Sakmann	
1992	Edmund H Fisher	
	Edwin G Krebs	
1993	Richard J Roberts	
	Phillip A Sharp	
1994	Alfred G Gilman	
	Martin Rodbell	
1995	Edward B Lewis	
	Christiane Nüesslein-Volhard	
	Eric F Wieschaus	
1996	Peter Doherty	
	Rolf Zinkernagel	
1997	Stanley Prusiner	
1998	Robert Furchgott	
	Louis J Ignarro	
	Ferid Murad	
1999	Gunter Blobel	
2000	Arvid Carlsson	
	Paul Greengard	
	Eric Kandel	

Nobel Prizewinners (continued)

Physiology or Medicine (continued)

2001 Leland H Hartwell	2002 John E Sulston	2003 Sir Peter Mansfield
R Timothy Hunt	Sydney Brenner	Paul Lauterbur
Paul M Nurse	H Robert Horvitz	2004 Richard Axel
		Linda B Buck

Peace

1901 Jean Henri Dunant	1937 Robert Cecil,	1974 Sato Eisaku
Frédéric Passy	1st Viscount Cecil of	1975 Andrei Dimitrievich
1902 Élie Ducommun	Chelwood	Sakharov
Charles Albert Gobat	1938 Nansen International Office	1976 Mairead Corrigan
1903 William Randall Cremer	for Refugees	Betty Williams
1904 Institute of International	1939 *No award*	1977 Amnesty International
Law	1943 *No award*	1978 Menachem Begin
1905 Bertha Félice Bertha von	1944 International Red Cross	Mohammed Anwar el-Sadat
Suttner	Committee	1979 Mother Theresa of Calcutta
1906 Theodore Roosevelt	1945 Cordell Hull	1980 Adolfo Pérez Esquivel
1907 Ernesto Teodoro Moneta	1946 Emily Greene Balch	1981 Office of the UN High
Louis Renault	John Raleigh Mott	Commissioner for Refugees
1908 Klas Pontus Arnoldson	1947 American Friends Service	1982 Alfonso García Robles
Fredrik Bajer	Committee	Alva Myrdal
1909 Baron d'Estournelles de	Friends Service Council	1983 Lech Walesa
Constant	1948 *No award*	1984 Desmond Mpilo Tutu
Auguste Beernaert	1949 John Boyd Orr, 1st Baron	1985 International Physicians for
1910 International Peace Bureau	Boyd Orr	the Prevention of Nuclear
1911 Tobias Michael Carel Asser	1950 Ralphe Johnson Bunche	War
Alfred Fried	1951 Léon Jouhaux	1986 Elie Wiesel
1912 Elihu Root	1952 Albert Schweitzer	1987 Oscar Arias Sánchez
1913 Henri Lafontaine	1953 George Catlett Marshall	1988 UN Peacekeeping Forces
1914 *No award*	1954 Office of the United Nations	1989 Tenzin Giyatso (Dalai Lama)
1915 *No award*	High Commissioner for	1990 Mikhail Sergeevich
1916 *No award*	Refugees	Gorbachev
1917 International Red Cross	1955 *No award*	1991 Aung San Suu Kyi
Committee	1956 *No award*	1992 Rigoberta Menchú
1918 *No award*	1957 Lester Bowles Pearson	1993 Nelson Mandela
1919 Thomas Woodrow Wilson	1958 (Dominique) Georges Pire	Frederik Willem de Klerk
1920 Léon Victor Auguste	1959 Philip Noel-Baker, Baron	1994 Yitzhak Rabin
Bourgeois	Noel-Baker	Yasser Arafat
1921 Karl Hjalmar Branting	1960 Albert John Luthuli	Shimon Peres
Christian Louis Lange	1961 Dag Hjalmar Agne Carl	1995 Joseph Rotblat
1922 Fridtjof Nansen	Hammarskjöld	Pugwash Conferences
1923 *No award*	1962 Linus Carl Pauling	1996 Calos Filipe Ximenes Belo
1924 *No award*	1963 International Red Cross	Jose Ramos-Horta
1925 (Joseph) Austen Chamberlain	Committee	1997 Jody Williams and the
Charles Gates Dawes	League of Red Cross Societies	International Campaign to
1926 Aristide Briand	1964 Martin Luther King, Jr	Ban Landmines
Gustav Stresemann	1965 United Nations Children's	1998 John Hume
1927 Ferdinand Buisson	Fund (UNICEF)	David Trimble
Ludwig Quidde	1966 *No award*	1999 Médecins Sans Frontières
1928 *No award*	1967 *No award*	2000 Kim Dae-jung
1929 Frank Billings Kellogg	1968 René Cassin	2001 United Nations and Kofi
1930 Nathan Söderblom	1969 International Labour	Annan
1931 Jane Addams	Organisation	2002 Jimmy Carter
Nicholas Murray Butler	1970 Norman E Borlaug	2003 Shirin Ebadi
1932 *No award*	1971 Willy Brandt	2004 Wangari Maathai
1933 Norman Angell	1972 *No award*	
1934 Arthur Henderson	1973 Henry Alfred Kissinger	
1935 Carl von Ossietzky	Le Duc Tho (*declined*)	
1936 Carlos Saavedra Lamas	1974 Sean MacBride	

PART FOURTEEN

Sports and Games

OLYMPIC GAMES

The first modern Olympic Games took place in 1896, founded by the Frenchman Baron de Coubertin. They are held every four years. Women first competed in 1900. The first separate Winter Games celebration was in 1924; beginning in 1994, the Winter Games takes place between Summer Games celebrations.

Venues

Summer Games	Winter Games
1896 Athens, Greece	–
1900 Paris, France	–
1904 St Louis, USA	–
1908 London, UK	–
1912 Stockholm, Sweden	–
1920 Antwerp, Belgium	–
1924 Paris, France	Chamonix, France
1928 Amsterdam, Netherlands	St Moritz, Switzerland
1932 Los Angeles, USA	Lake Placid, NY, USA
1936 Berlin, Germany	Garmisch-Partenkirchen, Germany
1948 London, UK	St Moritz, Switzerland
1952 Helsinki, Finland	Oslo, Norway
1956 Melbourne, Australia	Cortina, Italy
1960 Rome, Italy	Squaw Valley, CA, USA
1964 Tokyo, Japan	Innsbruck, Austria
1968 Mexico City, Mexico	Grenoble, France
1972 Munich, Germany	Sapporo, Japan
1976 Montreal, Canada	Innsbruck, Austria
1980 Moscow, Russia	Lake Placid, NY, USA
1984 Los Angeles, USA	Sarajevo, Yugoslavia
1988 Seoul, South Korea	Calgary, Canada
1992 Barcelona, Spain	Albertville, France
1994 –	Lillehammer, Norway
1996 Atlanta, USA	–
1998 –	Nagano, Japan
2000 Sydney, Australia	–
2002 –	Salt Lake City, USA
2004 Athens, Greece	–
2006 –	Turin, Italy
2008 Beijing, China	–

Olympic Games were also held in 1906 in Athens, Greece, to commemorate the 10th anniversary of the birth of the modern Games.

Leading medal winners: 2004 Summer Olympics

		Gold	Silver	Bronze	Total
1	USA	35	39	29	103
2	China	32	17	14	63
3	Russia	27	27	38	92
4	Australia	17	16	16	49
5	Japan	16	9	12	37
6	Germany	14	16	18	48
7	France	11	9	13	33
8	Italy	10	11	11	32
9	South Korea	9	12	9	30
10	Great Britain	9	9	12	30
11	Cuba	9	7	11	27
12	Ukraine	9	5	9	23
13	Hungary	8	6	3	17
14	Romania	8	5	6	19
15	Greece	6	6	4	16
16	Norway	5	0	1	6
17	Netherlands	4	9	9	22
18	Brazil	4	3	3	10
19	Sweden	4	1	2	7
20	Spain	3	11	5	19
21	Canada	3	6	3	12
22	Turkey	3	3	4	10
23	Poland	3	2	5	10
24	New Zealand	3	2	0	5
25	Thailand	3	1	4	8
26	Belarus	2	6	7	15
27	Austria	2	4	1	7
28	Ethiopia	2	3	2	7
29	Iran	2	2	2	6
29	Slovakia	2	2	2	6
31	Taiwan	2	2	1	5
32	Georgia	2	2	0	4
33	Bulgaria	2	1	9	12
34	Jamaica	2	1	2	5

Medal winners: 2002 Winter Games

		Gold	Silver	Bronze	Total
1	Germany	12	16	7	35
2	Norway	11	7	6	24
3	USA	10	13	11	34
4	Russian Federation	6	4	4	14
5	Canada	6	3	8	17
6	France	4	5	2	11
7	Italy	4	4	4	12
8	Finland	4	2	1	7
9	Netherlands	3	5	0	8
10	Switzerland	3	2	6	11
11	Croatia	3	1	0	4
12	Austria	2	4	10	16
13	China	2	2	4	8

		Gold	Silver	Bronze	Total
14	Korea	2	2	0	4
15	Australia	2	0	0	2
16	Spain	2	0	0	2
17	Estonia	1	1	1	3
18	Great Britain	1	0	2	3
19	Czech Republic	1	0	1	2
20	Sweden	0	2	4	6
21	Bulgaria	0	1	2	3
22	Japan	0	1	1	2
23	Poland	0	1	1	2
24	Slovenia	0	0	1	1
25	Belarus	0	0	1	1

COMMONWEALTH GAMES

First held as the British Empire Games in 1930. They take place every four years and between Olympic celebrations. They became the British Empire and Commonwealth Games in 1954; the current title was adopted in 1970.

Venues

1930	Hamilton, Canada
1934	London, England
1938	Sydney, Australia
1950	Auckland, New Zealand
1954	Vancouver, Canada
1958	Cardiff, Wales
1962	Perth, Australia
1966	Kingston, Jamaica
1970	Edinburgh, Scotland
1974	Christchurch, New Zealand
1978	Edmonton, Canada
1982	Brisbane, Australia
1986	Edinburgh, Scotland
1990	Auckland, New Zealand
1994	Victoria, Canada
1998	Kuala Lumpur, Malaysia
2002	Manchester, England
2006	Melbourne, Australia

Leading medal winners (including 2002)

	Nation	Gold	Silver	Bronze	Total
1	Australia	646	548	494	1688
2	England	521	510	531	1582
3	Canada	388	415	508	1311
4	New Zealand	118	157	221	496
5	India	82	78	75	225
6	South Africa	80	79	84	243
7	Scotland	71	87	143	301
8	Kenya	53	42	49	143
9	Wales	46	66	85	198
10	Nigeria	35	42	50	127

Medal winners: Manchester 2002 Games

	Nation	Gold	Silver	Bronze	Total
1	Australia	82	62	62	206
2	England	54	51	60	165
3	India	32	21	19	72
4	Canada	31	41	42	114
5	New Zealand	11	13	21	45
6	South Africa	9	20	17	46
7	Cameroon	9	1	2	12
8	Malaysia	7	9	18	34
9	Scotland	6	8	16	30
10	Nigeria	5	4	11	20
11	Wales	4	15	12	31
12	Kenya	4	8	4	16
13	Jamaica	4	6	7	17
14	Singapore	4	2	7	13
15	Bahamas	4	0	4	8
16	Nauru	2	3	10	15
17	Northern Ireland	2	2	1	5
18	Cyprus	2	1	1	4
19	Pakistan	1	3	3	7
20	Fiji	1	1	1	3
21	Zambia	1	1	1	3
22	Zimbabwe	1	1	0	2
23	Namibia	1	0	4	5
24	United Republic of Tanzania	1	0	1	2
25	Bangladesh	1	0	0	1
25	Guyana	1	0	0	1
25	Mozambique	1	0	0	1
25	St Kitts and Nevis	1	0	0	1
29	Botswana	0	2	1	3
30	Uganda	0	2	0	2
31	Samoa	0	1	2	3
32	Trinidad and Tobago	0	1	0	1
33	Barbados	0	0	1	1
33	Cayman Islands	0	0	1	1
33	Ghana	0	0	1	1
33	Lesotho	0	0	1	1
33	Malta	0	0	1	1
33	Mauritius	0	0	1	1
33	St Lucia	0	0	1	1

ANGLING

World freshwater championship

First held in 1957; takes place annually.

Recent winners: individual
1989   Tom Pickering (England)
1990   Bob Nudd (England)
1991   Bob Nudd (England)
1992   David Wesson (Australia)
1993   Mario Barras (Portugal)
1994   Bob Nudd (England)
1995   Pierre Jean (France)
1996   Alan Scotthorne (England)
1997   Alan Scotthorne (England)
1998   Alan Scotthorne (England)
1999   Bob Nudd (England)
2000   Jacopo Falsini (Italy)
2001   Umberto Ballabeni (Italy)
2002   Juan Blasco (Spain)
2003   Alan Scotthorne (England)
2004   Walter Tamas (Hungary)

Recent winners: team
1989   Wales
1990   France
1991   England
1992   Italy
1993   Italy
1994   Italy
1995   France
1996   Italy
1997   Italy
1998   England
1999   Spain
2000   Italy
2001   England
2002   Spain
2003   Hungary
2004   France

Most wins: Individual (4), Bob Nudd (England); as above. Team (14), France: 1959, 1963–4, 1966, 1968, 1972, 1974–5, 1978–9, 1981, 1990, 1995, 2004.

World fly-fishing championship

First held in 1981; takes place annually.

Winners: individual
1989   Władysław Trzebuinia (Poland)
1990   Franciszek Szajnik (Poland)
1991   Brian Leadbetter (England)
1992   Pierluigi Cocito (Italy)
1993   Russell Owen (Wales)
1994   Pascal Cognard (France)
1995   Jeremy Herrmann
1996   Pierluigi Cocito (Italy)
1997   Pascal Cognard (France)

1998   Tomas Starychsojtu (Czech Republic)
1999   Ross Stewart (Australia)
2000   Pascal Cognard (France)
2001   Vladimir Sedivy (Czech Republic)
2002   Jerome Brossutti (France)
2003   Stefano Cotugno (Italy)

Winners: team
1989   Poland
1990   Czechoslovakia
1991   New Zealand
1992   Italy
1993   England
1994   Czech Republic
1995   England
1996   Czech Republic
1997   France
1998   Czech Republic
1999   Australia
2000   France
2001   France
2002   France
2003   France

Most wins: Individual (3), Pascal Cognard (France) 1994, 1997, 2000. Team (5), Italy: 1982–84, 1986, 1992; France, as above.

ARCHERY

World championships

First held in 1931; took place annually until 1959; since then, every two years.

Recent winners: individual – men
1975   Darrell Pace (USA)
1977   Richard McKinney (USA)
1979   Darrell Pace (USA)
1981   Kysti Laasonen (Finland)
1983   Richard McKinney (USA)
1985   Richard McKinney (USA)
1987   Vladimir Yesheyev (USSR)
1989   Stanislav Zabrodsky (USSR)
1991   Simon Fairweather (Australia)
1993   Kyung-mo Park (South Korea)
1995   Gary Broadhead (USA)
1997   Kyung-ho Kim (South Korea)
1999   Sung-chil Hong (South Korea)
2001   Jung-ki Yeon (South Korea)
2003   Keijo Kallunki (Finland)

Recent winners: team – men
1975   USA
1977   USA
1979   USA
1981   USA
1983   USA
1985   South Korea
1987   South Korea

1989   USSR
1991   South Korea
1993   France
1995   USA
1997   South Korea
1999   Italy
2000   South Korea
2003   USA

Most wins: Individual (4), Hans Deutgen (Sweden): 1947–50. Team (16), USA: 1957–83, 1995, 2003.

Recent winners: individual – women
1975   Zebiniso Rustamova (USSR)
1977   Luann Ryon (USA)
1979   Jin-ho Kim (South Korea)
1981   Natalia Butuzova (USSR)
1983   Jin-ho Kim (South Korea)
1985   Irina Soldatova (USSR)
1987   Ma Xiaojun (China)
1989   Soo-nyung Kim (South Korea)
1991   Soo-nyung Kim (South Korea)
1993   Hyo-jung Kim (South Korea)
1995   Angela Moscarelly (USA)
1997   Du-ri Kim (South Korea)
1999   Eun-kyung Lee (South Korea)
2001   Sung-hyun Park (South Korea)
2003   Bruna Coladarci (Italy)

Recent winners: team – women
1975   USSR
1977   USA
1979   South Korea
1981   USSR
1983   South Korea
1985   USSR
1987   USSR
1989   South Korea
1991   South Korea
1993   South Korea
1995   USA
1997   South Korea
1999   Italy
2001   China
2003   South Korea

Most wins: Individual (7), Janina Kurkowska (Poland): 1931–4, 1936, 1939, 1947. Team (9), USA: 1952, 1957–9, 1961, 1963, 1965, 1977, 1995.

Olympic Games

Gold medal winners: 2004
Individual (men)
Marco Galiazzo (Italy)

Team (men)
South Korea

Individual (women)
Sung-Hyun Park (Korea)

Team (women)
South Korea

ATHLETICS

Performance times are given in seconds, or minutes:seconds, or hours:minutes:seconds. Distances are given in metres. Performances in the decathlon, pentathlon, and heptathlon are given in points.

World championships

First held in Helsinki in 1983; then in Rome in 1987; Tokyo in 1991; Stuttgart in 1993; Gothenburg in 1995; Athens in 1997; Seville in 1999; Edmonton in 2001; takes place every two years.

Event winners: men

100 m
1999   Maurice Greene (USA) 9.80
2001   Maurice Greene (USA) 9.85
2003   Kim Collins (St Kitts & Nevis) 10.07

200 m
1999   Maurice Greene (USA) 19.80
2001   Konstadinos Kedéris (Greece) 20.04
2003   John Capel (USA) 20.30

400 m
1999   Michael Johnson (USA) 43.18
2001   Avard Moncour (Bahamas) 44.64
2003   Jerome Young (USA) 44.50

800 m
1999   Wilson Kipketer (Denmark) 1:43.30
2001   André Bucher (Switzerland) 1:43.70
2003   Djabir Sad-Guerni (Algeria) 1:44.81

1500 m
1999   Hicham El Guerrouj (Morocco) 3:27.65
2001   Hicham El Guerrouj (Morocco) 3:30.68
2003   Hicham El Guerrouj (Morocco) 3:31.77

5000 m
1999   Salah Hissou (Morocco) 12:58.13
2001   Richard Limo (Kenya) 13:00.77
2003   Eliud Kipchoge (Kenya) 12:52.79

10000 m
1999   Haile Gebrselassie (Ethiopia) 27:57.27
2001   Charles Kamathi (Kenya) 27:53.25
2003   Kenenisa Bekele (Ethiopia) 26:49.57

Marathon
1999   Abel Anton (Spain) 2:13.36
2001   Gezahegne Abera (Ethiopia) 2:12.42
2003   Jaouad Gharib (Morocco) 2:08.31

3000 m steeplechase
1999   Christopher Koskei (Kenya) 8:11.76
2001   Reuben Kosgei (Kenya) 8:15.16
2003   Saif Saaeed Shaheen (Qatar) 8:04.39

110 m hurdles
1999   Colin Jackson (UK) 13.04
2001   Allen Johnson (USA) 13.04
2003   Allen Johnson (USA) 13.12

400 m hurdles
1999   Fabrizio Mori (Italy) 47.72
2001   Felix Sanchez (Dominican Republic) 47.49
2003   Felix Sanchez (Dominican Republic) 47.25

High jump
1999   Vyacheslav Voronin (Russia) 2.37
2001   Martin Buss (Germany) 2.36
2003   Jacques Freitag (South Africa) 2.35

Pole vault
1999   Maksim Tarasov (Russia) 6.02
2001   Dmitri Markov (Australia) 6.05
2003   Giuseppe Gibilisco (Italy) 5.90

Long jump
1999   Ivan Pedroso (Cuba) 8.56
2001   Ivan Pedroso (Cuba) 8.40
2003   Dwight Phillips (USA) 8.32

Triple jump
1999   Charles Michael Friedek (Germany) 17.59
2001   Jonathan Edwards (Great Britain) 17.92
2003   Christian Olsson (Sweden) 17.72

Shot
1999   CJ Hunter (USA) 21.79
2001   John Godina (USA) 21.87
2003   Andrei Mikhnevich (Belarus) 21.69

Discus
1999   Anthony Washington (USA) 69.08
2001   Lars Riedel (Germany) 69.72
2003   Virgilijus Alekna (Lithuania) 69.69

Hammer
1999   Karsten Kobs (Germany) 80.24
2001   Szymon Ziolkowski (Poland) 83.38
2003   Ivan Tikhon (Belarus) 83.05

Javelin
1999   Aki Parviainen (Finland) 89.52
2001   Jan Zelezny (Czech Republic) 92.80
2003   Sergey Makarov (Russia) 85.44

Decathlon
1999   Tomas Dvorak (Czech Republic) 8744
2001   Tomas Dvorak (Czech Republic) 8902
2003   Tom Pappas (USA) 8750

4 × 100 m relay
1999   USA
2001   USA 37.96
2003   USA 38.06

4 × 400 m relay
1999   USA 3:02.83
2001   USA 2:57.54
2003   USA 2:58.88

20 km walk
1999   Ilya Markov (Russia) 1:23.34
2001   Roman Rasskazov (Russia) 1:20.31
2003   Jefferson Perez (Ecuador) 1:17.21

50 km walk
1999   German Skurygin (Russia) 3:44.23
2001   Robert Korzeniowski (Poland) 3:42.08
2003   Robert Korzeniowski (Poland) 3:36.03

Event winners: women

100 m
1999 Marion Jones (USA) 10.70
2001 Zhanna Pintusevich-Block (Ukraine) 10.82
2003 Kelli White (USA) 10.85

200 m
1999 Inger Miller (USA) 21.77
2001 Marion Jones (USA) 22.39
2003 Kelli White (USA) 22.05

400 m
1999 Cathy Freeman (Australia) 49.67
2001 Amy Mbacke Thiam (Senegal) 49.86
2003 Ana Guevara (Mexico) 48.89

800 m
1999 Ludmila Formanova (Czech Republic) 1:56.68
2001 Maria Mutola (Mozambique) 1:57.17
2003 Maria Mutola (Mozambique) 1:59.89

1500 m
1999 Svetlana Masterkova (Russia) 3:59.53
2001 Gabriela Szabo (Romania) 4:00.57
2003 Tatyana Tomashova (Russia) 3:58.52

5000 m
1999 Gabriela Szabo (Romania) 14:41.82
2001 Olga Yegorova (Russia) 15:03.39
2003 Tirunesh Dibaba (Ethiopia) 14:51.72

10000 m
1999 Gete Wami (Ethiopia) 30:24.56
2001 Derartu Tulu (Ethiopia) 31:48.81
2003 Berhane Adere (Ethiopia) 30:04.18

Marathon
1999 Jong Song-ok (North Korea) 2:26.59
2001 Lidia Simon (Romania) 2:26.01
2003 Catherine Ndereba (Kenya) 2:23.55

100 m hurdles
1999 Gail Devers (USA) 12.37
2001 Anjanette Kirkland (USA) 12.42
2003 Perdita Felicien (Canada) 12.53

400 m hurdles
1999 Daimi Pernia (Cuba) 52.89
2001 Nezha Bidouane (Morocco) 53.34
2003 Jana Pittman (Australia) 53.22

High jump
1999 Inga Babakova (Ukraine) 1.99
2001 Hestrie Cloete (South Africa) 2.00
2003 Hestrie Cloete (South Africa) 2.06

Long jump
1999 Niurka Montolva (Spain) 7.06
2001 Fiona May (Italy) 7.02
2003 Eunice Barber (France) 6.99

Triple jump
2001 Tatyana Lebedeva (Russia) 15.25
2003 Tatyana Lebedeva (Russia) 15.18

Shot
1999 Astrid Kumbernuss (Germany) 19.85
2001 Yanina Korolchik (Belarus) 20.61
2003 Svetlana Krivelyova (Russia) 20.63

Discus
1999 Franka Dietzsch (Germany) 68.14
2001 Natalya Sadova (Russia) 68.57
2003 Irina Yatchenko (Belarus) 67.32

Javelin
1999 Mirela Manjani-Tzelili (Greece) 67.09
2001 Osleidys Menendez (Cuba) 69.53
2003 Mirela Manjani (Greece) 66.52

Pole Vault
2003 Svetlana Feofanova (Russia) 4.75

Hammer
2003 Yipsi Morena (Cuba) 73.33

Heptathlon
1999 Eunice Barber (France) 6861
2001 Yelena Prokhorova (Russia) 6694
2003 Carolina Kluft (Sweden) 7001

10 km walk
From 1999, 20 km walk

20 km walk
2001 Olimpiada Ivanova (Russia) 1:27.48
2003 Yelena Nikolayeva (Russia) 1:26.52

4 × 100 m relay		**4 × 400 m relay**	
1999	Bahamas 41.93	1999	Russia 3:21.98
2001	USA 41.71	2001	Jamaica 3:20.65
2003	France 41.78	2003	USA 3:22.63

Olympic Games

Event winners: men

100 m
1904 Archie Hahn (USA) 11.0
1906 Archie Hahn (USA) 11.2
1908 Reginald Walker (S Africa) 10.8
1912 Ralph Craig (USA) 10.8
1920 Charles Paddock (USA) 10.8
1924 Harold Abrahams (Great Britain) 10.6
1928 Percy Williams (Canada) 10.8
1932 Eddie Tolan (USA) 10.3
1936 Jesse Owens (USA) 10.3
1948 Harrison Dillard (USA) 10.3
1952 Lindy Remigino (USA) 10.4
1956 Bobby Morrow (USA) 10.5
1960 Armin Hary (W Germany) 10.2
1964 Bob Hayes (USA) 10.06
1968 James Hines (USA) 9.95
1972 Valeriy Borzov (USSR) 10.14
1976 Hasely Crawford (Trinidad) 10.06
1980 Allan Wells (Great Britain) 10.25

1984 Carl Lewis (USA) 9.99
1988 Carl Lewis (USA) 9.92
1992 Linford Christie (Great Britain) 9.96
1996 Donovan Bailey (Canada) 9.84
2000 Maurice Greene (USA) 9.87
2004 Justin Gatlin (USA) 9.85

200 m
1908 Robert Kerr (Canada) 22.6
1912 Ralph Craig (USA) 21.7
1920 Allen Woodring (USA) 22.0
1924 Jackson Scholz (USA) 21.6
1928 Percy Williams (Canada) 21.8
1932 Eddie Tolan (USA) 21.2
1936 Jesse Owens (USA) 20.7
1948 Melvin Patton (USA) 21.1
1952 Andrew Stanfield (USA) 20.7
1956 Bobby Morrow (USA) 20.5
1960 Livio Berruti (Italy) 20.6
1964 Henry Carr (USA) 20.36

Athletics, Olympic games (continued)

400 m *(200 m continued)*

1968 Tommie Smith (USA) 19.83
1972 Valeriy Borzov (USSR) 20.00
1976 Donald Quarrie (Jamaica) 20.3
1980 Pietro Mennea (Italy) 20.19
1984 Carl Lewis (USA) 19.80
1988 Joe DeLoach (USA) 19.75
1992 Michael Marsh (USA) 20.01
1996 Michael Johnson (USA) 19.32
2000 Konstantinos Kedéris (Greece) 20.09
2004 Shawn Crawford (USA) 19.79

400 m

1904 Harry Hilllman (USA) 49.2
1906 Paul Pilgrim (USA) 53.2
1908 Wyndham Halswelle (Great Britain) 50.0
1912 Charles Reidpath (USA) 48.2
1920 Bevil Rudd (S Africa) 49.6
1924 Eric Liddell (Great Britain) 47.6
1928 Ray Barbuti (USA) 47.8
1932 Bill Carr (USA) 46.28
1936 Archie Williams (USA) 46.66
1948 Arthur Wint (Jamaica) 46.2
1952 George Rhoden (Jamaica) 46.09
1956 Charles Jenkins (USA) 46.86
1960 Otis Davis (USA) 45.07
1964 Michael Larrabee (USA) 45.15
1968 Lee Evans (USA) 43.8
1972 Vincent Matthews (USA) 44.66
1976 Alberto Juantoreno (Cuba) 44.26
1980 Viktor Markin (USSR) 44.60
1984 Alonzo Babers (USA) 44.27
1988 Steve Lewis (USA) 43.87
1992 Quincy Watts (USA) 43.50
1996 Michael Johnson (USA) 43.49
2000 Michael Johnson (USA) 43.84
2004 Jeremy Wariner (USA) 44.0

800 m

1904 James Lightbody (USA) 1:56.0
1906 Paul Pilgrim (USA) 2:01.5
1908 Mel Sheppard (USA) 1:52.8
1912 James Meredith (USA) 1:51.9
1920 Albert Hill (Great Britain) 1:53.4
1924 Douglas Lowe (Great Britain) 1:52.4
1928 Douglas Lowe (Great Britain) 1:51.8
1932 Tom Hampson (Great Britain) 1:49.70
1936 John Woodruff (USA) 1:52.9
1948 Malvin Whitfield (USA) 1:49.2
1952 Malvin Whitfield (USA) 1:49.34
1956 Thomas Courtney (USA) 1:47.75
1960 Peter Snell (New Zealand) 1:46.48
1964 Peter Snell (New Zealand) 1:45.1
1968 Ralph Doubell (Australia) 1:44.40
1972 David Wottle (USA) 1:45.86
1976 Alberto Juantorena (Cuba) 1:43.50
1980 Steven Ovett (Great Britain) 1:45.40
1984 Joaquim Cruz (Brazil) 1:43.00
1988 Paul Ereng (Kenya) 1:43.45
1992 William Tanui (Kenya) 1:43.66
1996 Vebjoern Rodal (Norway) 1:42.58
2000 Nils Schumann (Germany) 1:45.08
2004 Yuriy Borzakovskiy (Russia) 1:44.45

1500 m

1904 James Lightbody (USA) 4:05.4
1906 James Lightbody (USA) 4:12.0
1908 Mel Sheppard (USA) 4:03.4

1912 Arnold Jackson (Great Britain) 3:56.8
1920 Albert Hill (Great Britain) 4:01.8
1924 Paavo Nurmi (Finland) 3:53.6
1928 Harri Larva (Finland) 3:53.2
1932 Luigi Beccali (Italy) 3:51.20
1936 Jack Lovelock (New Zealand) 3:47.8
1948 Henry Eriksson (Sweden) 3:49.8
1952 Josef Barthel (Luxembourg) 3:45.28
1956 Ron Delany (Ireland) 3:41.49
1960 Herbert Elliott (Australia) 3:35.6
1964 Peter Snell (New Zealand) 3:38.1
1968 Kipchoge Keino (Kenya) 3:34.91
1972 Pekkha Vasala (Finland) 3:36.33
1976 John Walker (New Zealand) 3:39.17
1980 Sebastian Coe (Great Britain) 3:38.40
1984 Sebastian Coe (Great Britain) 3:32.53
1988 Peter Rono (Kenya) 3:35.96
1992 Fermin Cacho (Spain) 3:40.12
1996 Noureddine Morceli (Algeria) 3:35.79
2000 Noah Ngeny (Kenya) 3:32.07
2004 Hicham El Guerrouj (Morocco) 3:34.18

5000 m

1924 Paavo Nurmi (Finalnd) 14:31.2
1928 Ville Ritola (Finland) 14:38.0
1932 Lauri Lehtinen (Finland) 14:29.91
1936 Gunnar Höckert (Finland) 14:22.2
1948 Gaston Reiff (Belgium) 14:17.6
1952 Emil Zátopek (Czechoslovakia) 14:06.72
1956 Vladimir Kuts (USSR) 13:39.86
1960 Murray Halberg (New Zealand) 13:43.4
1964 Robert Schul (USA) 13:48.8
1968 Mohamed Gammoudi (Tunisia) 14:05.0
1972 Lasse Viren (Finland) 13:26.42
1976 Lasse Viren (Finland) 13:24.76
1980 Miruts Yifter (Ethiopia) 13:20.91
1984 Saïd Aouita (Morocco) 13:05.59
1988 John Ngugi (Kenya) 13:11.70
1992 Dieter Baumann (Germany) 13:12.52
1996 Venuste Niyongabo (Burundi) 13:07.97
2000 Millon Wolde (Ethiopia) 13:35.49
2004 Hicham El Guerrouj (Morocco) 13:14.39

10000 m

1924 Ville Ritola (Finland) 30:23.1
1928 Paavo Nurmi (Finland) 30:18.8
1932 Janusz Kusocinski (Poland) 30:11.4
1936 Ilmari Salminen (Finland) 30:15.4
1948 Emil Zátopek (Czechoslovakia) 29:59.6
1952 Emil Zátopek (Czechoslovakia) 29:17.0
1956 Vladimir Kuts (USSR) 28:45.60
1960 Pyotr Bolotnikov (USSR) 28:32.18
1964 William Mills (USA) 28:24.4
1968 Naftali Temu (Kenya) 29:27.45
1972 Lasse Viren (Finland) 27:38.35
1976 Lasse Viren (Finland) 27:40.38
1980 Miruts Yifter (Ethiopia) 27:42.69
1984 Alberto Cova (Italy) 27:47.54
1988 Brahim Boutayeb (Morocco) 27:21.46
1992 Khalid Skah (Morocco) 27:46.70
1996 Haile Gebrselassie (Ethiopia) 27:07.34
2000 Haile Gebrselassie (Ethiopia) 27:18.20
2004 Kenenisa Bekele (Ethiopia) 27:05.10

Marathon*

1904 Thomas Hicks (USA) 3:28:35.0 *(40 km)*
1906 William Sherring (Canada) 2:51:23.6 *(41.86 km)*
1908 John Hayes (USA) 2:55:18.4
1912 Kenneth McArthur (S Africa) 2:36:54.8 *(40.2 km)*

1920	Hannes Kolehmainen (Finland) 2:32:35.8 *(42.75 km)*
1924	Albin Stenroos (Finland) 2:41:22.6
1928	Mohamed Boughéra El Ouafi (France) 2:32:57.0
1932	Juan Carlos Zabala (Argentina) 2:31:36.0
1936	Kitei Son (Japan) 2:29:19.2
1948	Delfo Cabrera (Argentina) 2:34:51.6
1952	Emil Zátopek (Czechoslovakia) 2:23:03.2
1956	Alain Mimoun (France) 2:25:00.0
1960	Abebe Bikila (Ethiopia) 2:15:16.2
1964	Abebe Bikila (Ethiopia) 2:12:11.2
1968	Mamo Wolde (Ethiopia) 2:20:26.4
1972	Frank Shorter (USA) 2:12:19.8
1976	Waldemar Cierpinski (E Germany) 2:09:55
1980	Waldemar Cierpinski (E Germany) 2:11:03
1984	Carlos Lopes (Portugal) 2:09:21
1988	Gelindo Bordin (Italy) 2:10:32
1992	Hwang Young-jo (S Korea) 2:13:23
1996	Josia Thugwane (S Africa) 2:12.36
2000	Gezahgne Abera (Ethiopia) 2:10.11
2004	Stefano Baldini (Italy) 2:10.55

*Unless shown as otherwise above, the Marathon is run over a distance of 42 km 195 m/26 mi 385 yd.

110 m hurdles

1904	Fred Schule (USA) 16.0
1906	Robert Leavitt (USA) 16.2
1908	Forrest Smithson (USA) 15.0
1912	Fred Kelly (USA) 15.1
1920	Earl Thomson (Canada) 14.8
1924	Daniel Kinsey (USA) 15.0
1928	Sydney Atkinson (S Africa) 14.8
1932	George Saling (USA) 14.57
1936	Forrest Towns (USA) 14.2
1948	William Porter (USA) 13.9
1952	Harrison Dillard (USA) 13.91
1956	Lee Calhoun (USA) 13.70
1960	Lee Calhoun (USA) 13.98
1964	Hayes Jones (USA) 13.67
1968	Willie Davenport (USA) 13.33
1972	Rodney Milburn (USA) 13.24
1976	Guy Drut (France) 13.30
1980	Thomas Munkelt (E Germany) 13.39
1984	Roger Kingdom (USA) 13.20
1988	Roger Kingdom (USA) 12.98
1992	Mark McKoy (Canada) 13.12
1996	Allen Johnson (USA) 12.95
2000	Anier García (Cuba) 13.00
2004	Liu Xiang (China) 12.91

400 m hurdles

1908	Charles Bacon (USA) 55.0
1920	Frank Loomis (USA) 54.0
1924	Morgan Taylor (USA) 52.6
1928	Lord Burghley (Great Britain) 53.4
1932	Robert Tisdall (Ireland) 51.67
1936	Glenn Hardin (USA) 52.4
1948	Roy Cochran (USA) 51.1
1952	Charles Moore (USA) 51.06
1956	Glenn Davis (USA) 50.29
1960	Glenn Davis (USA) 49.51
1964	Rex Cawley (USA) 49.69
1968	David Hemery (Great Britain) 48.12
1972	John Akii-Bua (Uganda) 47.82
1976	Edwin Moses (USA) 47.63
1980	Volker Beck (E Germany) 48.70
1984	Edwin Moses (USA) 47.75
1988	Andre Phillips (USA) 47.19

1992	Kevin Young (USA) 46.78
1996	Derrick Adkins (USA) 47.54
2000	Angelo Taylor (USA) 47.50
2004	Felix Sánchez (Dominican Republic) 47.63

Steeplechase*

1904	James Lightbody (USA) 7:39.6 *(2590 m)*
1908	Arthur Russell (Great Britain) 10:47.8 *(3200 m)*
1920	Percy Hodge (Great Britain) 10:00.4
1924	Ville Ritola (Finland) 9:33.6
1928	Toivo Loukola (Finland) 9:21.8
1932	Volmari Iso-Hollo (Finland) 10:33.4**
1936	Volmari Iso-Hollo (Finland) 9:03.8
1948	Tore Sjöstrand (Sweden) 9:04.6
1952	Horace Ashenfelter (USA) 8:45.68
1956	Christopher Brasher (Great Britain) 8:41.35
1960	Zdzislaw Kryszkowiak (Poland) 8:34.31
1964	Gaston Roelants (Belgium) 8:30.8
1968	Amos Biwott (Kenya) 8:51.0
1972	Kipchoge Keino (Kenya) 8:23.64
1976	Anders Gärderud (Sweden) 8:08.02
1980	Bronislaw Malinowski (Poland) 8:09.70
1984	Julius Korir (Kenya) 8:11.80
1988	Julius Kariuki (Kenya) 8:05.51
1992	Matthew Birir (Kenya) 8:08.94
1996	Joseph Keter (Kenya) 8:07.12
2000	Reuben Kosgei (Kenya) 8:21.43
2004	Ezekiel Kemboi (Kenya) 8:05.81

*Unless shown otherwise above, distance is 3000 m.
**Athletes ran an extra lap in error – distance 3460 m.

High jump

1904	Samuel Jones (USA) 1.80
1906	Con Leahy (Ireland)[b] 1.77
1908	Harry Porter (USA) 1.90
1912	Alma Richards (USA) 1.93
1920	Richard Landon (USA) 1.94
1924	Harold Osborn (USA) 1.98
1928	Robert King (USA) 1.94
1932	Duncan McNaughton (Canada) 1.97
1936	Cornelius Johnson (USA) 2.03
1948	John Winter (Austrialia) 1.98
1952	Walter Davis (USA) 2.04
1956	Charles Dumas (USA) 2.12
1960	Robert Shavlakadze (USSR) 2.16
1964	Valeriy Brumel (USSR) 2.18
1968	Dick Fosbury (USA) 2.24
1972	Jüri Tarmak (USSR) 2.23
1976	Jacek Wszola (Poland) 2.25
1980	Gerd Wessig (E Germany) 2.36
1984	Dietmar Mögenburg (W Germany) 2.35
1988	Gennadiy Avdeyenko (USSR) 2.38
1992	Javier Sotomayor (Cuba) 2.34
1996	Charles Austin (USA) 2.39
2000	Sergey Kliugin (Russia) 2.35
2004	Stefan Holm (Sweden) 2.36

Pole vault

1904	Charles Dvorak (USA) 3.50
1906	Fernand Gonder (France) 3.40
1908	Edward Cooke & Alfred Gilbert (USA) 3.71
1912	Harry Babock (USA) 3.95
1920	Frank Foss (USA) 4.09
1924	Lee Barnes (USA) 3.95
1928	Sabin Carr (USA) 4.20
1932	Bill Miller (USA) 4.31
1936	Earle Meadows (USA) 4.35
1948	Guinn Smith (USA) 4.30
1952	Robert Richards (USA) 4.55

Athletics, Olympic games (continued)

1956 Robert Richards (USA) 4.56
1960 Donald Bragg (USA) 4.70
1964 Frederick Hansen (USA) 5.10
1968 Bob Seagren (USA) 5.40
1972 Wolfgang Nordwig (E Germany) 5.50
1976 Tadeusz Slusarski (Poland) 5.50
1980 Wladyslaw Kozakiewicz (Poland) 5.78
1984 Pierre Quinon (France) 5.75
1988 Sergey Bubka (USSR) 5.90
1992 Maksim Tarasov (Unified Team) 5.80
1996 Jean Galfione (France) 5.92
2000 Nick Hysong (USA) 5.90
2004 Timothy Mack (USA) 5.95

Long jump
1904 Myer Prinstein (USA) 7.34
1906 Myer Prinstein (USA) 7.20
1908 Francis Irons (USA) 7.48
1912 Albert Gutterson (USA) 7.60
1920 William Pettersson (Sweden) 7.15
1924 William De Hart Hubbard (USA) 7.44
1928 Edward Hamm (USA) 7.73
1932 Edward Gordon (USA) 7.64
1936 Jesse Owens (USA) 8.06
1948 William Steele (USA) 7.82
1952 Jerome Biffle (USA) 7.57
1956 Gregory Bell (USA) 7.83
1960 Ralph Boston (USA) 8.12
1964 Lynn Davies (Great Britain) 8.07
1968 Bob Beamon (USA) 8.90
1972 Randy Williams (USA) 8.24
1976 Arnie Robinson (USA) 8.35
1980 Lutz Dombrowski (E Germany) 8.54
1984 Carl Lewis (USA) 8.54
1988 Carl Lewis (USA) 8.72
1992 Carl Lewis (USA) 8.67
1996 Carl Lewis (USA) 8.50
2000 Ivan Pedroso (Cuba) 8.55
2004 Dwight Phillips (USA) 8.59

Triple jump
1904 Myer Prinstein (USA) 14.35
1906 Peter O'Connor (Ireland) 14.07
1908 Tim Ahearne (Ireland) 14.91
1912 Gustaf Lindblom (Sweden) 14.76
1920 Viho Tuulos (Finland) 14.50
1924 Anthony Winter (Australia) 15.52
1928 Mikio Oda (Japan) 15.21
1932 Chuhei Nambu (Japan) 15.72
1936 Naoto Tajima (Japan) 16.00
1948 Arne Åhman (Sweden) 15.40
1952 Adhemar Ferreira da Silva (Brazil) 16.22
1956 Adhemar Ferreira da Silva (Brazil) 16.35
1960 Jozef Schmidt (Poland) 16.81
1964 Jozef Schmidt (Poland) 16.85
1968 Viktor Saneyev (USSR) 17.39
1972 Viktor Saneyev (USSR) 17.35
1976 Viktor Saneyev (USSR) 17.29
1980 Jaak Uudmäe (USSR) 17.35
1984 Al Joyner (USA) 17.26
1988 Khristo Markov (Bulgaria) 17.61
1992 Mike Conley (USA) 18.17
1996 Kenny Harrison (USA) 18.09
2000 Jonathan Edwards (Great Britain) 17.71
2004 Christian Olsson (Sweden) 17.79

Shot
1904 Ralph Rose (USA) 14.80
1906 Martin Sheridan (USA) 12.32
1908 Ralph Rose (USA) 14.21
1912 Patrick McDonald (USA) 15.34
1920 Ville Pörhölä (Finland) 14.81
1924 Clarence Houser (USA) 14.99
1928 John Kuck (USA) 15.87
1932 Leo Sexton (USA) 16.00
1936 Hans Woellke (Germany) 16.20
1948 Wilbur Thompson (USA) 17.12
1952 Parry O'Brien (USA) 17.41
1956 Parry O'Brien (USA) 18.57
1960 William Nieder (USA) 19.68
1964 Dallas Long (USA) 20.33
1968 Randy Matson (USA) 20.54
1972 Wladyslaw Komar (Poland) 21.18
1976 Udo Beyer (E Germany) 21.05
1980 Vladimir Kiselyov (USSR) 21.35
1984 Alessandro Andrei (Italy) 21.26
1988 Ulf Timmermann (E Germany) 22.47
1992 Mike Stulce (USA) 21.70
1996 Randy Barnes (USA) 21.62
2000 Arsi Harju (Finland) 21.29
2004 Yuriy Bilonog (Ukraine) 21.16

Discus
1904 Martin Sheridan (USA) 39.28
1906 Martin Sheridan (USA) 41.46
1904 Martin Sheridan (USA) 40.89
1912 Armas Taipale (Finland) 45.21
1920 Elmer Niklander (Finland) 44.68
1924 Clarence Houser (USA) 46.15
1928 Clarence Houser (USA) 47.32
1932 John Anderson (USA) 49.49
1936 Ken Carpenter (USA) 50.48
1948 Adolfo Consolini (Italy) 52.78
1952 Sim Iness (USA) 55.03
1956 Al Oerter (USA) 56.36
1960 Al Oerter (USA) 59.18
1964 Al Oerter (USA) 61.00
1968 Al Oerter (USA) 64.78
1972 Ludvik Danek (Czechloslovakia) 64.40
1976 Mac Wilkins (USA) 67.50
1980 Viktor Rashchupkin (USSR) 66.64
1984 Rolf Danneberg (W Germany) 66.60
1988 Jürgen Schult (E Germany) 68.82
1992 Romas Ubartas (Lithuania) 65.12
1996 Lars Riedel (Germany) 69.40
2000 Virgilijus Alekna (Lithuania) 69.30
2004 Robert Fazekas (Hungary) 70.93

Hammer
1908 John Flanagan (USA) 51.92
1912 Matt McGrath (USA) 54.74
1920 Patrick Ryan (USA) 52.87
1924 Fred Tootell (USA) 53.29
1928 Patrick O'Callaghan (Ireland) 51.39
1932 Patrick O'Callaghan (Ireland) 53.92
1936 Karl Hein (Germany) 56.49
1948 Imre Németh (Hungary) 56.07
1952 József Csermak (Hungary) 60.34
1956 Harold Connolly (USA) 63.19
1960 Vasiliy Rudenkov (USSR) 67.10
1964 Romuald Klim (USSR) 69.74
1968 Gyula Zsivótzky (Hungary) 73.36
1972 Anatoliy Bondarchuk (USSR) 75.50
1976 Yuriy Sedykh (USSR) 77.52

1980 Yuriy Sedykh (USSR) 81.80
1984 Juha Tiainen (Finland) 78.08
1988 Sergey Litvinov (USSR) 84.80
1992 Andrei Abduyvaliyev (Unified Team) 82.54
1996 Balazs Kiss (Hungary) 81.24
2000 Szymon Ziolkowski (Russia) 80.02
2004 Adrian Annus (Hungary) 83.19

Javelin*
1912 Erik Lemming (Sweden) 60.64
1920 Jonni Myyrä (Finland) 65.78
1924 Jonni Myyrä (Finland) 62.96
1928 Erik Lundkvist (Sweden) 66.60
1932 Matti Järvinen (Finland) 72.71
1936 Gerhard Stöck (Germany) 71.84
1948 Tapio Rautavaara (Finland) 69.77
1952 Cyrus Young (USA) 73.78
1956 Egil Danielsen (Norway) 85.71
1960 Viktor Tsibulenko (USSR) 84.64
1964 Pauli Nevala (Finland) 82.66
1968 Janis Lusis (USSR) 90.10
1972 Klaus Wolfermann (W Germany) 90.48
1976 Miklós Németh (Hungary) 94.58
1980 Dainis Kula (USSR) 91.20
1984 Arto Harkönen (Finland) 86.76
1988 Tápio Korjus (Finland) 84.28
1992 Jan Zelezny (Czechoslovakia) 89.66
1996 Jan Zelezny (Czech Republic) 88.16
2000 Jan Zelezny (Czech Republic) 90.17
2004 Andreas Thorkildsen (Norway) 86.50

*New javelin specification introduced in 1984.

Decathlon*
1928 Paavo Yrjölä (Finland) 6587
1932 James Bausch (USA) 6735
1936 Glenn Morris (USA) 7254
1948 Robert Mathias (USA) 6628
1952 Robert Mathias (USA) 7592
1956 Milton Campbell (USA) 7614
1960 Rafer Johnson (USA) 7926
1964 Willi Holdorf (W Germany) 7794
1968 Bill Toomey (USA) 8144
1972 Nikolay Avilov (USSR) 8466
1976 Bruce Jenner (USA) 8634
1980 Daley Thompson (Great Britain) 8522
1984 Daley Thompson (Great Britain) 8847
1988 Christian Schenk (E Germany) 8488
1992 Robert Zmelik (Czechoslovakia) 8611
1996 Dan O'Brien (USA) 8824
2000 Erki Nool (Estonia) 8641
2004 Roman Sebrle (Czech Republic) 8893

*All points given here are rescored using 1984 tables.

Modern Pentathlon
2000 Dmitri Svatkovski (Russia) 5376
2004 Andrey Moiseev (Russia) 5480

20 km walk
1964 Kenneth Matthews (Great Britain) 1:29:34.0
1968 Vladimir Golubnichiy (USSR) 1:33:58.4
1972 Peter Frenkel (E Germany) 1:26:42.4
1976 Daniel Bautista (Mexico) 1:24:40.6
1980 Maurizio Damilano (Italy) 1:23:35.5
1984 Ernesto Canto (Mexico) 1:23:13
1988 Jozef Pribilinec (Czechoslovakia) 1:19:57
1992 Daniel Plaza (Spain) 1:21:45
1996 Jefferson Perez (Ecuador) 1:20:06
2000 Robert Korzeniowski (Poland) 1:18:59

2004 Ivano Brugnetti (Italy) 1:19.40

50 km walk
1948 John Ljunggren (Sweden) 4:41:52.0
1952 Giuseppe Dordoni (Italy) 4:28:07.8
1956 Norman Read (New Zealand) 4:30:42.8
1960 Don Thompson (Great Britain) 4:25:30.0
1964 Abdon Pamich (Italy) 4:11:12.4
1968 Christophe Höhne (E Germany) 4:20:13.6
1972 Bernd Kannenberg (E Germany) 3:56:11.6
1980 Hartwig Gauder (E Germany) 3:49:24
1984 Raúl Gonzales (Mexico) 3:47:26
1988 Vyacheslav Ivanenko (USSR) 3:38:29
1992 Andrei Perlov (Unified Team) 3:50:13
1996 Robert Korzeniowski (Poland) 3:43:30
2000 Robert Korzeniowski (Poland) 3:42:22
2004 Robert Korzeniowski (Poland) 3:38:46

4 × 100 m relay
1924 USA 41.0
1928 USA 41.0
1932 USA 40.1
1936 USA 39.8
1948 USA 40.6
1952 USA 40.26
1956 USA 39.59
1960 W Germany 39.66
1964 USA 39.06
1968 USA 38.23
1972 USA 38.19
1976 USA 38.83
1980 USSR 38.26
1984 USA 37.83
1988 USA 38.19
1992 USA 37.40
1996 Canada 37.69
2000 USA 37.61
2004 Great Britain 38.07

4 × 400 m relay
1928 USA 3:16.0
1928 USA 3:14.2
1932 USA 3:08.14
1936 Great Britain 3:09.0
1948 USA 3:10.4
1952 Jamaica 3:04.04
1956 USA 3:04.80
1960 USA 3:02.37
1964 USA 3:00.71
1968 USA 2:56.16
1972 Kenya 2:59.83
1976 USA 2:58.66
1980 USSR 3:01.08
1984 USA 3:57.91
1988 USA 2:56.16
1992 USA 2:55.74
1996 USA 2:55.99
2000 USA 3:22.62
2004 USA 2:55.91

Event winners: women
100 m
1936 Helen Stephens (USA) 11.5
1948 Fanny Blankers-Koen (Netherlands) 11.9
1952 Marjorie Jackson (Australia) 11.65
1956 Betty Cuthbert (Australia) 11.82
1960 Wilma Rudolph (USA) 11.08
1964 Wyomia Tyus (USA) 11.49
1968 Wyomia Tyus (USA) 11.08

Athletics, Olympic games (continued)

1972 Renate Stecher (E Germany) 11.07
1976 Annegret Richter (W Germany) 11.08
1980 Lyudmila Kondratyeva (USSR) 11.06
1984 Evelyn Ashford (USA) 10.97
1988 Florence Griffith-Joyner (USA) 10.54[c]
1992 Gail Devers (USA) 10.82
1996 Gail Devers (USA) 10.94
2000 Marion Jones (USA) 10.75
2004 Yuliya Nesterenko (Belarus) 10.93

200 m

1956 Betty Cuthbert (Australia) 23.55
1960 Wilma Rudolph (USA) 24.03
1964 Edith Maguire (USA) 23.05
1968 Irena Szewinska (Poland) 22.58
1972 Renate Stecher (E Germany) 22.40
1976 Bärbel Eckert (E Germany) 22.37
1980 Bärbel Wöckel (E Germany) 22.03
1984 Valerie Brisco-Hooks (USA) 21.81
1988 Florence Griffith-Joyner (USA) 21.34
1992 Gwen Torrence (USA) 21.81
1996 Marie-José Pérec (France) 22.12
2000 Marion Jones (USA) 21.84
2004 Veronica Campbell (Jamaica) 22.05

400 m

1972 Monika Zehrt (E Germany) 51.08
1976 Irena Szewinska (Poland) 49.29
1980 Marita Koch (E Germany) 48.88
1984 Valerie Brisco-Hooks (USA) 48.83
1988 Olga Bryzgina (USSR) 48.65
1992 Marie-José Pérec (France) 48.83
1996 Marie-José Pérec (France) 48.25
2000 Cathy Freeman (Australia) 49.11
2004 Tonique Williams-Darling (Bahamas) 49.41

800 m

1968 Madeline Manning (USA) 2:00.92
1972 Hilde Falck (W Germany) 1:58.55
1976 Tatyana Kazankina (USSR) 1:54.94
1980 Nadezhda Olizarenko (USSR) 1:53.43
1984 Doina Melinte (Romania) 1:57.60
1988 Sigrun Wodars (E Germany) 1:56.10
1992 Ellen van Langen (Netherlands) 1:55.54
1996 Svetlana Masterkova (Russia) 1:57.73
2000 Maria Mutola (Mozambique) 1:56.15
2004 Kelly Holmes (Great Britain) 1:56.38

1 500 m

1980 Tatyana Kazankina (USSR) 3:56.56
1984 Gabriella Doria (Italy) 4:03.25
1988 Paula Ivan (Romania) 3:53.96
1992 Hassiba Boulmerka (Algeria) 3:55:30
1996 Svetlana Masterkova (Russia) 4:00.83
2000 Nouria Merah-Benida (Algeria) 4:05.10
2004 Kelly Holmes (Great Britain) 3:57.90

5 000 m (3 000 m to 1996)

1988 Tatyana Samolenko (USSR) 8:26.53
1992 Yelena Romanova (Unified Team) 8:46.04
1996 Yunxia Wang (China) 14: 59.88
2000 Gabriela Szabo (Romania) 14:40.79
2004 Meseret Defar (Ethiopia) 14:45.65

10 000 m

1992 Derartu Tulu (Ethiopia) 31:06.02
1996 Fernanda Ribeiro (Portugal) 31:01.63
2000 Derartu Tulu (Ethiopia) 30:17.49
2004 Huina Xing (China) 30:24.36

Marathon

1988 Rosa Mota (Portugal) 2:25.40
1992 Valentina Yegorova (Unified Team) 2:32:41
1996 Fatuma Roba (Ethiopia) 2:26:5
2000 Naoko Takahashi (Japan) 2:23:14
2004 Mizuki Noguchi (Japan) 2:26.20

100 m hurdles

1976 Johanna Schaller (E Germany) 12.77
1980 Vera Komisova (USSR) 12.56
1984 Benita Fitzgerald-Brown (USA) 12.84
1988 Yordanka Donkova (Bulgaria) 12.38
1992 Paraskevi Patoulidou (Greece) 12.64
1996 Ludmila Enquist (Sweden) 12.58
2000 Olga Shishigina (Kazakhstan) 12.65
2004 Joanna Hayes (USA) 12.37

400 m hurdles

1988 Debbie Flintoff-King (Australia) 53.17
1992 Sally Gunnell (Great Britain) 53.23
1996 Deon Hemmings (Jamaica) 52.82
2000 Irina Privalova (Russia) 53.02
2004 Fani Halkia (Greece) 52.82

Triple jump

2000 Tereza Marinova (Bulgaria) 15.20
2004 Françoise Mbango Etone (Cameroon) 15.30

High jump

1932 Jean Shiley (USA) 1.65
1936 Ibolya Csák (Hungary) 1.60
1948 Alice Coachman (USA) 1.68
1952 Esther Brand (S Africa) 1.67
1956 Mildred McDaniel (USA) 1.76
1960 Iolanda Balas (Romania) 1.85
1964 Iolanda Balas (Romania) 1.90
1968 Miloslava Rezková (Czechoslovakia) 1.82
1972 Ulrike Meyfarth (W Germany) 1.92
1976 Rosemarie Ackermann (E Germany) 1.93
1980 Sara Simeoni (Italy) 1.97
1984 Ulrike Meyfarth (W Germany) 2.02
1988 Louise Ritter (USA) 2.03
1992 Heike Henkel (Germany) 2.02
1996 Stefka Kostadinova (Bulgaria) 2.05
2000 Yelena Yelesina (Russia) 2.01
2004 Yelena Slesarenko (Russia) 2.06

Long jump

1956 Elzbieta Krzesinska (Poland) 6.35
1960 Vyera Krepkina (USSR) 6.37
1964 Mary Rand (Great Britain) 6.76
1968 Viorica Viscopoleanu (Romania) 6.82
1972 Heide Rosendahl (W Germany) 6.78
1976 Angela Voigt (E Germany) 6.72
1980 Tatyana Kolpakova (USSR) 7.06
1984 Anisoara Stanciu (Romania) 6.96
1988 Jackie Joyner-Kersee (USA) 7.40
1992 Heike Drechsler (Germany) 7.14
1996 Chioma Ajunwa (Nigeria) 7.12
2000 Heike Drechsler (Germany) 6.99
2004 Tatyana Lebedeva (Russia) 7.07

Shot

1956 Tamara Tishkyevich (USSR) 16.59
1960 Tamara Press (USSR) 17.32
1964 Tamara Press (USSR) 18.14
1968 Margitta Gummel (E Germany) 19.61
1972 Nadezhda Chizhova (USSR) 21.03
1976 Ivanka Khristova (Bulgaria) 21.16
1980 Ilona Slupianek (E Germany) 22.41

1984 Claudia Losch (W Germany) 20.48
1988 Natalya Lisovskaya (USSR) 22.24
1992 Svetlana Krivelyova (Unified Team) 21.06
1996 Astrid Kumbernuss (Germany) 20.56
2000 Yanina Korolchik (Belarus) 20.56
2004 Yumileidi Cumba (Cuba) 19.59

Discus
1936 Gisela Mauermayer (Germany)
1948 Micheline Ostermeyer (France) 41.92
1952 Nina Ponomaryeva (USSR) 51.42
1956 Olga Fikotová (Czechoslovakia) 53.69
1960 Nina Ponomaryeva (USSR) 55.10
1964 Tamara Press (USSR) 57.27
1968 Lia Manoliu (Romania) 58.28
1972 Faina Melnik (USSR) 66.62
1976 Evelin Schlaak (E Germany) 69.00
1980 Evelin Jahl (E Germany) 69.96
1984 Ria Stalmach (Netherlands) 65.36
1988 Martina Hellmann (E Germany) 72.30
1992 Maritza Marten (Cuba) 70.06
1996 Like Wyludda (Germany) 69.66
2000 Ellina Zvereva (Belarus) 68.40
2004 Natalya Sadova (Russia) 67.02

Javelin
1936 Tilly Fleischer (Germany) 45.18
1948 Herma Bauma (Australia) 45.57
1952 Dana Zátopková (Czechoslovakia) 50.47
1956 Inese Jaunzeme (USSR) 53.86
1960 Elvira Ozolina (USSR) 55.98
1964 Mihaela Penes (Romania) 60.54
1968 Angéla Németh (Hungary) 60.36
1972 Ruth Fuchs (E Germany) 63.88
1976 Ruth Fuchs (E Germany) 65.94
1980 Maria C. Colón (Cuba) 68.40
1984 Tessa Sanderson (Great Britain) 69.56
1988 Petra Felke (E Germany) 74.68
1992 Silke Renk (Germany) 68.34
1996 Heller Rantanen (Finland) 67.94
2000 Trine Hattestad (Norway) 68.91
2004 Osleidys Menendez (Cuba) 71.53

Pole vault
2000 Stacy Draglia (USA) 4.60
2004 Yelena Isinbayeva (Russia) 4.91

Hammer
2000 Kamila Skolimowska (Poland) 71.16
2004 Olga Kuzenkova (Russia) 75.02

Pentathlon
1964 Irina Press (USSR) 4702
1968 Ingrid Becker (W Germany) 4559
1972 Mary Peters (Great Britain) 4801
1976 Sigrun Siegl (E Germany) 4745
1980 Nadezhda Tkachenko (USSR) 5083

Modern pentathlon
2000 Stephanie Cook (Great Britain) 5318
2004 Zsuzsanna Vores (Hungary) 5448

Heptathlon
1988 Jackie Joyner-Kersee (USA) 7291
1992 Jackie Joyner-Kersee (USA) 7044
1996 Ghada Shouaa (Syria) 6780
2000 Denise Lewis (Great Britain) 6584
2004 Carolina Kluft (Sweden) 6952

20 km walk
2000 Wang Liping (China) 1:29.05
2004 Athanasia Tsoumeleka (Greece) 1:29.12

4 × 100 m relay
1932 USA 46.86
1936 USA 46.9
1948 Netherlands 47.5
1952 USA 46.14
1956 Australia 44.65
1960 USA 44.72
1964 Poland 43.69
1968 USA 42.87
1972 W Germany 42.81
1976 E Germany 42.55
1980 E Germany 41.60
1984 USA 41.65
1988 USA 41.98
1992 USA 42.11
1996 USA 41.95
2000 Bahamas 41.95
2004 Jamaica 41.73

4 × 400 m relay
1976 E Germany 3:19.23
1980 USSR 3:20.12
1984 USA 3:18.29
1988 USSR 3:15.18
1992 Unified Team 3:20.20
1996 USA 3:20.91
2000 USA 3:22.62
2004 USA 3:19.01

Marathon

Run over 42 km 195 m/26 mi 385 yd; a distance which became standard from 1924. Women first competed officially in 1972.

Boston

The world's oldest annual race; first held in 1897.

Men

1991 Ibrahim Hussein (Kenya) 2:11.06
1992 Ibrahim Hussein (Kenya) 2:08.14
1993 Cosmas N'deti (Kenya) 2:09.33
1994 Cosmas N'deti (Kenya) 2:07.15
1995 Cosmas N'deti (Kenya) 2:09.16
1996 Moses Tanui (Kenya) 2:09.16
1997 Lameck Aguta (Kenya) 2:10.34
1998 Moses Tanui (Kenya) 2:07.52
1999 Joseph Chebet (Kenya) 2:09.16
2000 Elijah Lagat (Kenya) 2:09.47
2001 Bong-Ju Lee (South Korea) 2:09.43
2002 Rodgers Rop (Kenya) 2:09.02
2003 Robert Kipkoech Cheruiyot (Kenya) 2:10.11
2004 Timothy Cherigat (Kenya) 2:10.40
2005 Hailu Negussie (Ethiopia) 2:11.45

Most wins: (7) Clarence De Mar (USA): 1911, 1922–4, 1927–8, 1930.

Women

1991 Wanda Panfil (Poland) 2:24.18
1992 Olga Markova (Russia) 2:23.43
1993 Olga Markova (Russia) 2:25.37
1994 Uta Pippig (Germany) 2:21.45
1995 Uta Pippig (Germany) 2:25.11
1996 Uta Pippig (Germany) 2:27.12
1997 Fatuma Roba (Ethiopia) 2:26.23
1998 Fatuma Roba (Ethiopia) 2:23.21
1999 Fatuma Roba (Ethiopia) 2:23.25
2000 Catherine Ndereba (Kenya) 2:26.11
2001 Catherine Ndereba (Kenya) 2:23.53
2002 Margaret Okayo (Kenya) 2:20.43
2003 Svetlana Zakharova (Russia) 2:25.20
2004 Catherine Ndereba (Kenya) 2:24.27
2005 Catherine Ndereba (Kenya) 2:25.13

Most wins: (4) Catherine Ndebera (Kenya) as above.

London

First run in 1981.

Men

1990 Allister Hutton (Great Britain) 2:10.10
1991 Yakov Tolstikov (USSR) 2:09.17
1992 António Pinto (Portugal) 2:10.02
1993 Eamonn Martin (Great Britain) 2:10.50
1994 Dionicio Ceron (Mexico) 2:08.53
1995 Dionicio Ceron (Mexico) 2:08.30
1996 Dionicio Ceron (Mexico) 2:10.00
1997 António Pinto (Portugal) 2:07.55
1998 Abel Anton (Spain) 2:07.57
1999 Abdel Kader El Mouaziz (Morocco) 2:07.57
2000 António Pinto (Portugal) 2:06.35
2001 Abdel Kader El Mouaziz (Morocco) 2:07.11
2002 Khalid Khannouchi (Morocco/USA) 2:05.38
2003 Gezahegne Abera (Ethiopia) 2:07.56
2004 Evans Rutto (Kenya) 2:06.18
2005 Martin Lel (Kenya) 2:07.26

Most wins: (3) Dionicio Ceron (Mexico); António Pinto (Portugal) as above.

Women

1990 Wanda Panfil (Poland) 2:26.31
1991 Rosa Mota (Portugal) 2:26.14
1992 Katrin Dörre (Germany) 2:29.39
1993 Katrin Dörre (Germany) 2:27.09
1994 Katrin Dörre (Germany) 2:32.34
1995 Malgorzata Sobanska (Poland) 2:27.43
1996 Liz McColgan (Great Britain) 2:27.54
1997 Joyce Chepchumba (Kenya) 2:26.51
1998 Catherina McKiernan (Ireland) 2:26.26
1999 Joyce Chepchumba (Kenya) 2:23.22
2000 Tegla Loroupe (Kenya) 2:24.33
2001 Derartu Tulu (Ethiopia) 2:23.57
2002 Paula Radcliffe (Great Britain) 2:18.56
2003 Paula Radcliffe (Great Britain) 2:15.25
2004 Margaret Okayo (Kenya) 2:22.35
2005 Paula Radcliffe (Great Britain) 2:17.42

Most wins: (4) Ingrid Kristiansen (Norway): 1984–5, 1987–8, and as above.

New York

First run in 1970.

Men

1988 Steve Jones (Great Britain) 2:08.20
1989 Juma Ikangaa (Tanzania) 2:08.01
1990 Douglas Wakihuri (Kenya) 2:12.39
1991 Salvador Garcia (Mexico) 2:09.28
1992 Willie Mtolo (South Africa) 2:09.29
1993 Andreas Espinosa (Mexico) 2:10.04
1994 German Silva (Mexico) 2:11.21
1995 German Silva (Mexico) 2:11.00
1996 Giacomo Leone (Italy) 2:09.54
1997 John Kagwe (Kenya) 2:08.12
1998 John Kagwe (Kenya) 2:08.45
1999 Joseph Chebet (Kenya) 2:09.13
2000 Abdel Kader El Mouaziz (Morocco) 2:10.09
2001 Tesfaye Jifar (Ethiopia) 2:07.43
2002 Rodgers Rop (Kenya) 2:08.07
2003 Martin Lel (Kenya) 2:10.30
2004 Hendrik Ramaala (South Africa) 2:9.28

Most wins: (4) Bill Rodgers (USA): 1976–9.

Women

1988 Grete Waitz (Norway) 2:28.07
1989 Ingrid Kristiansen (Norway) 2:25.30
1990 Wanda Panfil (Poland) 2:30.45
1991 Liz McColgan (Great Britain) 2:27.23
1992 Lisa Ondieki (Australia) 2:24.40
1993 Uta Pippig (Germany) 2:26.24
1994 Tecla Loroupe (Kenya) 2:27.37
1995 Tecla Loroupe (Kenya) 2:28.06
1996 Anuta Katuna (Romania) 2:28.18
1997 Franziska Rochat-Moser (Switzerland) 2:28.43
1998 Franca Fiacconi (Italy) 2:25.17
1999 Adriana Fernandez (Mexico) 2:25.06
2000 Ludmila Petrova (Russia) 2:25.45
2001 Margaret Okayo (Kenya) 2:24.21
2002 Joyce Chepchumba (Kenya) 2:25.56
2003 Margaret Okayo (Kenya) 2:22.31
2004 Paula Radcliffe (Great Britain) 2:23.10

Most wins: (9) Grete Waitz (Norway): 1978–80, 1982–6, 1988.

BADMINTON

World championships

First held in 1977; initially took place every three years, since 1983 every two years.

Singles winners: men
1991 Zhao Jianhua (China)
1993 Joko Suprianto (Indonesia)
1995 Heryanto Arbi (Indonesia)
1997 Peter Rasmussen (Denmark)
1999 Sun Jun (China)
2001 H Hendrawan (Indonesia)
2003 Xia Xuanze (China)

Singles winners: women
1991 Tang Jiuhong (China)
1993 Susi Susanti (Indonesia)
1995 Ye Zhaoying (China)
1997 Ye Zhaoying (China)
1999 Camilla Martin (Denmark)
2001 Gong Ruina (China)
2003 Zhang Ning (China)

Most titles: (4) Park JooBong (South Korea): men's doubles 1985, 1991; mixed doubles 1989, 1991.

Thomas cup

An international event for men's teams; inaugurated in 1949, now held every two years.

Recent winners
1982 China
1984 Indonesia
1986 China
1988 China
1990 China
1992 Malaysia
1994 Indonesia
1996 Indonesia
1998 Indonesia
2000 Indonesia
2002 Indonesia
2004 China

Most wins: (13) Indonesia: 1958, 1961, 1964, 1970, 1973, 1976, 1979 and as above.

Uber cup

An international event for women's teams; first held in 1957, now held every two years.

Recent winners
1978 Japan
1981 Japan
1984 China
1986 China
1988 China
1990 China
1992 China
1994 Indonesia
1996 Indonesia
1998 China
2000 China
2002 China
2004 China

Most wins: (9) China: as above.

All-England championship

Badminton's premier event prior to the inauguration of the World Championships; first held in 1899.

Recent winners: singles – men
1990 Zhao Jianhua (China)
1991 Ardi Wiranata (Indonesia)
1992 Liu Jun (China)
1993 Heryanto Arbi (Indonesia)
1994 Heryanto Arbi (Indonesia)
1995 Poul-Erik Hoyer Larsen (Denmark)
1996 Poul-Erik Hoyer Larsen (Denmark)
1997 Dong Jiong (China)
1998 Sun Jun (China)
1999 Peter Gade Christensen (Denmark)
2000 Xia Xuanze (China)
2001 Pullela Gopichand (India)
2002 Chen Hong (China)
2003 Muhammad Hafiz Hashim (Malaysia)
2004 Lin Dan (China)

Recent winners: singles – women
1986 Yun-Ja Kim (Korea)
1987 Kirsten Larsen (Denmark)
1988 Gu Jiaming (China)
1989 Li Lingwei (China)
1990 Susi Susanti (Indonesia)
1991 Susi Susanti (Indonesia)
1992 Tang Jiuhong (China)
1993 Susi Susanti (Indonesia)
1994 Susi Susanti (Indonesia)
1995 Lin Xiao Qing (Sweden)
1996 Bang Soo-Hyun (South Korea)
1997 Ye Zhaoying (China)
1998 Ye Zhaoying (China)
1999 Ye Zhaoying (China)
2000 Gong Zhichao (China)
2001 Gong Zhichao (China)
2002 Camilla Martin (Denmark)
2003 Zhou Mi (China)
2004 Gong Ruina (China)

Most titles: (21; 4 singles, 9 men's doubles, 8 mixed doubles), George Thomas (England): 1903–28.

Olympic Games

Gold medal winner: 2004
Singles (men)
Taufik Hidayat (Indonesia)

Doubles (men)
Kim Moon-Dong/Ha Kwon-Tae (South Korea)

Singles (women)
Zhang Ning (China)

Doubles (women)
Zhang Jiewen/Yang Wei (China)

Mixed Doubles
Zhang Jun/Gao Ling (China)

BASEBALL

There are two leagues in the North American Major League – the National League (NL) and the American League (AL). Each league consists of an Eastern, Western, and (since 1994) Central division. Each division winner and a wild-card team (the second-place team with the best record) meet in a best-of-five playoff in the first round, then in a best-of-seven for the League Pennant, and then in the best-of-seven World Series.

World Series

First held in 1903; takes place each October; not held in 1904, 1994.

1903 Boston (AL) 5, Pittsburg (NL) 2
1905 New York (NL) 4, Philadelphia (AL) 1
1906 Chicago (AL) 4, Chicago (NL) 2
1907 Chicago (NL) 4, Detroit (AL) 0; 1 tie
1908 Chicago (NL) 4, Detroit (AL) 1
1909 Pittsburgh (NL) 4, Detroit (AL) 3

Baseball (continued)

1910 Philadelphia (AL) 4, Chicago (NL) 1
1911 Philadelphia (AL) 4, New York (NL) 2
1912 Boston (AL) 4, New York (NL) 3; 1 tie
1913 Philadelphia (AL) 4, New York (NL) 1
1914 Boston (NL) 4, Philadelphia (AL) 0
1915 Boston (AL) 4, Philadelphia (NL) 1
1916 Boston (AL) 4, Brooklyn (NL) 1
1917 Chicago (AL) 4, New York (NL) 2
1918 Boston (AL) 4, Chicago (NL) 2
1919 Cincinnati (NL) 5, Chicago (AL) 3
1920 Cleveland (AL) 5, Brooklyn (NL) 2
1921 New York (NL) 5, New York (AL) 3
1922 New York (NL) 4, New York (AL) 0; 1 tie
1923 New York (AL) 4, New York (NL) 2
1924 Washington (AL) 4, New York (NL) 3
1925 Pittsburgh (NL) 4, Washington (AL) 3
1926 St Louis (NL) 4, New York (AL) 3
1927 New York (AL) 4, Pittsburgh (NL) 0
1928 New York (AL) 4, St Louis (NL) 0
1929 Philadelphia (AL) 4, Chicago (NL) 1
1930 Philadelphia (AL) 4, St Louis (NL) 2
1931 St Louis (NL) 4, Philadelphia (AL) 3
1932 New York (AL) 4, Chicago (NL) 0
1933 New York (NL) 4, Washington (AL) 1
1934 St Louis (NL) 4, Detroit (AL) 3
1935 Detroit (AL) 4, Chicago (NL) 2
1936 New York (AL) 4, New York (NL) 2
1937 New York (AL) 4, New York (NL) 1
1938 New York (AL) 4, Chicago (NL) 0
1939 New York (AL) 4, Cincinnati (NL) 0
1940 Cincinnati (NL) 4, Detroit (AL) 3
1941 New York (AL) 4, Brooklyn (NL) 1
1942 St Louis (NL) 4, New York (AL) 1

1943 New York (AL) 4, St Louis (NL) 1
1944 St Louis (NL) 4, St Louis (AL) 2
1945 Detroit (AL) 4, Chicago (NL) 3
1946 St Louis (NL) 4, Boston (AL) 3
1947 New York (AL) 4, Brooklyn (NL) 3
1948 Cleveland (AL) 4, Boston (NL) 2
1949 New York (AL) 4, Brooklyn (NL) 1
1950 New York (AL) 4, Philadelphia (NL) 0
1951 New York (AL) 4, New York (NL) 2
1952 New York (AL) 4, Brooklyn (NL) 3
1953 New York (AL) 4, Brooklyn (NL) 2
1954 New York (NL) 4, Cleveland (AL) 0
1955 Brooklyn (NL) 4, New York (AL) 3
1956 New York (AL) 4, Brooklyn (NL) 3
1957 Milwaukee (NL) 4, New York (AL) 3
1958 New York (AL) 4, Milwaukee (NL) 3
1959 Los Angeles (NL) 4, Chicago (AL) 2
1960 Pittsburgh (NL) 4, New York (AL) 3
1961 New York (AL) 4, Cincinnati (NL) 1
1962 New York (AL) 4, San Francisco (NL) 3
1963 Los Angeles (NL) 4, New York (AL) 0
1964 St Louis (NL) 4, New York (AL) 3
1965 Los Angeles (NL) 4, Minnesota (AL) 3
1966 Baltimore (AL) 4, Los Angeles (NL) 0
1967 St Louis (NL) 4, Boston (AL) 3
1968 Detroit (AL) 4, St Louis (NL) 3
1969 New York (NL) 4, Baltimore (AL) 1
1970 Baltimore (AL) 4, Cincinnati (NL) 1
1971 Pittsburgh (NL) 4, Baltimore (AL) 3
1972 Oakland (AL) 4, Cincinnati (NL) 3
1973 Oakland (AL) 4, New York (NL) 3
1974 Oakland (AL) 4, Los Angeles (NL) 1
1975 Cincinnati (NL) 4, Boston (AL) 3
1976 Cincinnati (NL) 4, New York

(AL) 0
1977 New York (AL) 4, Los Angeles (NL) 2
1978 New York (AL) 4, Los Angeles (NL) 2
1979 Pittsburgh (NL) 4, Baltimore (AL) 3
1980 Philadelphia (NL) 4, Kansas City (AL) 2
1981 Los Angeles (NL) 4, New York (AL) 2
1982 St Louis (NL) 4, Milwaukee (AL) 3
1983 Baltimore (AL) 4, Philadelphia (NL) 1
1984 Detroit (AL) 4, San Diego (NL) 1
1985 Kansas City (AL) 4, St Louis (NL) 3
1986 New York (NL) 4, Boston (AL) 3
1987 Minnesota (AL) 4, St Louis (NL) 3
1988 Los Angeles (NL) 4, Oakland (AL) 1
1989 Oakland (AL) 4, San Francisco (NL) 0
1990 Cincinnati (NL) 4, Oakland (AL) 0
1991 Minnesota (AL) 4, Atlanta (NL) 3
1992 Toronto (AL) 4, Atlanta (NL) 2
1993 Toronto (AL) 4, Philadelphia (NL) 2
1995 Atlanta (NL) 4, Cleveland (AL) 2
1996 New York (AL) 4, Atlanta (NL) 2
1997 Florida (NL) 4, Cleveland (AL) 3
1998 New York Yankees (AL) 3 San Diego Padres (NL) 0
1999 New York Yankees (AL) 4 Atlanta Braves (NL) 0
2000 New York Yankees (AL) 4, New York Mets (NL) 1
2001 Arizona Diamondback (NL) 4, New York Yankees (AL) 3
2002 Anaheim Angels (AL) 4, San Francisco Giants (NL) 3
2003 Florida Marlins (NL) 4, New York Yankees (AL) 2
2004 Boston Red Sox (AL) 4, St Louis Cardinals (NL) 0

Most wins: (26) New York Yankees (AL): 1923, 1927–8, 1932, 1936–9, 1941, 1943, 1947, 1949–53, 1956, 1958, 1961–2, 1977–8, 1996, 1998, 1999, 2000.

Most valuable player

Each year since 1931 the Baseball Writers' Association has voted to determine the year's most outstanding player. There are two awards – one for each of the two leagues which comprise the North American Major League – the National League (NL) and the American League (AL). There was no award in 1995.

National League

1931	Frank Frisch, St Louis Cardinals
1932	Charles Klein, Philadelphia Phillies
1933	Carl Hubbell, New York Mets
1934	Dizzy Dean, St Louis Cardinals
1935	Gabby Hartnett, Chicago Cubs
1936	Carl Hubbell, New York Mets
1937	Joe Medwick, St Louis Cardinals
1938	Ernie Lombardi, Cincinnati Reds
1939	Bucky Walters, Cincinnati Reds
1940	Frank McCormick, Cincinnati Reds
1941	Dolph Carnitti, Brooklyn Dodgers
1942	Mort Cooper, St Louis Cardinals
1943	Stan Musial, St Louis Cardinals
1944	Martin Marion, St Louis Cardinals
1945	Phil Cavarretta, Chicago Cubs
1946	Stan Musial, St Louis Cardinals
1947	Bob Elliott, Boston Braves
1948	Stan Musial, St Louis Cardinals
1949	Jackie Robinson, Brooklyn Dodgers
1950	Jim Konstanty, Philadelphia Phillies
1951	Roy Campanella, Brooklyn Dodgers
1952	Hank Sauer, Chicago Cubs
1953	Roy Campanella, Brooklyn Dodgers
1954	Willie Mays, New York Mets
1955	Roy Campanella, Brooklyn Dodgers
1956	Don Newcombe, Brooklyn Dodgers
1957	Henry Aaron, Milwaukee Braves
1958	Ernie Banks, Chicago Cubs
1959	Ernie Banks, Chicago Cubs
1960	Dick Groat, Pittsburgh Pirates
1961	Frank Robinson, Cincinnati Reds
1962	Maury Wills, Los Angeles Dodgers
1963	Sandy Koufax, Los Angeles Dodgers
1964	Ken Boyers , St Louis Cardinals
1965	Willie Mays, San Francisco Giants
1966	Roberto Clemente, Pittsburgh Pirates
1967	Orlando Cepeda, St Louis Cardinals
1968	Bob Gibson, St Louis Cardinals
1969	Willie McCovey, San Francisco Giants
1970	Johnny Bench, Cincinnati Reds
1971	Joe Torre, St Louis Cardinals
1972	Johnny Bench, Cincinnati Reds
1973	Pete Rose, Cincinnati Reds
1974	Steve Garvey, Los Angeles Dodgers
1975	Joe Morgan, Cincinnati Reds
1976	Joe Morgan, Cincinnati Reds
1977	George Foster, Cincinnati Reds
1978	Dave Parker, Pittsburgh Pirates
1979	Willie Stargell, Pittsburgh Pirates; Keith Hernandez, St Louis Cardinals
1980	Mike Schmidt, Philadelphia Phillies
1981	Mike Schmidt, Philadelphia Phillies
1982	Dale Murphy, Atlanta Braves
1983	Dale Murphy, Atlanta Braves
1984	Ryne Sandberg, Chicago Cubs
1985	Willie McGee, St Louis Cardinals
1986	Mike Schmidt, Philadelphia Phillies
1987	Andre Dawson, Chicago Cubs
1988	Kirk Gibson, Los Angeles Dodgers
1989	Kevin Mitchell, San Francisco Giants
1990	Barry Bonds, Pittsburgh Pirates
1991	Terry Pendleton, Atlanta Braves
1992	Barry Bonds, Pittsburgh Pirates
1993	Barry Bonds, San Francisco Giants
1994	Jeff Bagwell, Houston Astros
1995	Barry Larkin, Cincinnati Reds
1996	Ken Caminiti, San Diego
1997	Larry Walker, Colorado Rockies
1998	Sammy Sosa, Chicago Cubs
1999	Chipper (Larry) Jones, Atlanta Braves
2000	Jeff Kent, San Francisco Giants
2001	Barry Bonds, San Francisco Giants
2002	Barry Bonds, San Francisco Giants
2003	Barry Bonds, San Francisco Giants
2004	Barry Bonds, San Francisco Giants

American League

1931	Lefty Grove, Philadelphia Athletics
1932	Jimmie Foxx, Philadelphia Athletics
1933	Jimmie Foxx, Philadelphia Athletics
1934	Mickey Cochrane, Detroit Tigers
1935	Hank Greenberg, Detroit Tigers
1936	Lou Gehrig, New York Yankees
1937	Charley Gehringer, Detroit Tigers
1938	Jimmie Foxx, Boston Red Sox
1939	Joe DiMaggio, New York Yankees
1940	Hank Greenberg, Detroit Tigers
1941	Joe DiMaggio, New York Yankees
1942	Joe Gordon, New York Yankees
1943	Spurgeon Chandler, New York Yankees
1944	Hal Newhouser, Detroit Tigers
1945	Hal Newhouser, Detroit Tigers
1946	Ted Williams, Boston Red Sox
1947	Joe DiMaggio, New York Yankees
1948	Lou Boudreau, Cleveland Indians
1949	Ted Williams, Boston Red Sox
1950	Phil Rizzuto, New York Yankees
1951	Yogi Berra, New York Yankees
1952	Bobby Shantz, Philadelphia Athletics
1953	Al Rosen, Cleveland Indians
1954	Yogi Berra, New York Yankees
1955	Yogi Berra, New York Yankees
1956	Mickey Mantle, New York Yankees
1957	Mickey Mantle, New York Yankees
1958	Jackie Jensen, Boston Red Sox
1959	Nellie Fox, Chicago White Sox
1960	Roger Maris, New York Yankees
1961	Roger Maris, New York Yankees
1962	Mickey Mantle, New York Yankees
1963	Elston Howard, New York Yankees
1964	Brooks Robinson, Baltimore Orioles
1965	Zoilo Versalles, Minnesota Twins
1966	Frank Robinson, Baltimore Orioles
1967	Carl Yastrzemski, Boston Red Sox
1968	Denny McLain, Detroit Tigers
1969	Harmon Killebrew, Minnesota Twins
1970	John (Boog) Powell, Baltimore Orioles
1971	Vida Blue, Oakland A's
1972	Dick Allen, Chicago White Sox
1973	Reggie Jackson, Oakland A's
1974	Jeff Burroughs, Texas Rangers
1975	Fred Lynn, Boston Red Sox

Baseball (continued)

1976	Thurman Munson, New York Yankees
1977	Rod Carew, Minnesota Twins
1978	Jim Rice, Boston Red Sox
1979	Don Baylor, California Angels
1980	George Brett, Kansas City Royals
1981	Rollie Fingers, Milwaukee Brewers
1982	Robin Yount, Milwaukee Brewers
1983	Cal Ripken Jr, Baltimore Orioles
1984	Willie Hernandez, Detroit Tigers
1985	Don Mattingly, New York Yankees
1986	Roger Clemens, Boston Red Sox
1987	George Bell, Toronto Blue Jays
1988	Jose Canseco, Oakland A's
1989	Robin Yount, Milwaukee Brewers
1990	Rickey Henderson, Oakland A's
1991	Cal Ripken Jr, Baltimore Orioles
1992	Dennis Eckersley, Oakland A's
1993	Frank Thomas, Chicago White Sox
1994	Frank Thomas, Chicago White Sox
1995	Mo Vaughn, Boston Red Sox
1996	Juan Gonzalez, Texas Rangers
1997	Ken Griffey Jnr, Seattle Mariners
1998	Juan Gonzalez, Texas Rangers
1999	Ivan Rodriguez, Texas Rangers
2000	Jason Giambi, Oakland A's
2001	Ichiro Suzuki, Seattle Mariners
2002	Miguel Tejada, Oakland A's
2003	Alex Rodriguez, Texas Rangers
2004	Vladimir Guerrero, Anaheim Angels

Cy Young Award

An award for the most outstanding pitcher of the year in each of the two leagues. First given in 1956. Pre-1967 there was just one award covering both leagues.

1956	Don Newcombe, Brooklyn Dodgers (NL)
1957	Warren Spahn, Milwaukee Braves (NL)
1958	Bob Turley, New York Yankees (AL)
1959	Early Wynn, Chicago White Sox (AL)
1960	Vernon Law, Pittsburgh Pirates (NL)
1961	Whitey Ford, New York Yankees (AL)
1962	Don Drysdale, Los Angeles Dodgers (NL)
1963	Sandy Koufax, Los Angeles Dodgers (NL)
1964	Dean Chance, California Angels (AL)
1965	Sandy Koufax, Los Angeles Dodgers (NL)
1967	Sandy Koufax, Los Angeles Dodgers (NL)

National League

1967	Mike McCormick, San Francisco Giants
1968	Bob Gibson, St Louis Cardinals
1969	Tom Seaver, New York Mets
1970	Bob Gibson, St Louis Cardinals
1971	Ferguson Jenkins, Chicago Cubs
1972	Steve Carlton, Philadelphia Phillies
1973	Tom Seaver, New York Mets
1974	Mike Marshall, Los Angeles Dodgers
1975	Tom Seaver, New York Mets
1976	Randy Jones, San Diego Padres
1977	Steve Carlton, Philadelphia Phillies
1978	Gaylord Perry, San Diego Padres
1979	Bruce Sutter, Chicago Cubs
1980	Steve Carlton, Philadelphia Phillies
1981	Fernando Valenzuela, Los Angeles Dodgers
1982	Steve Carlton, Philadelphia Phillies
1983	John Denny, Philadelphia Phillies
1984	Rick Sutcliffe, Chicago Cubs

1985	Dwight Gooden, New York Mets
1986	Mike Scott, Houston Astros
1987	Steve Bedrosian, Philadelphia Phillies
1988	Orel Hershiser, Los Angeles Dodgers
1989	Mark Davis, San Diego Padres
1990	Doug Drabek, Pittsburgh Pirates
1991	Tom Glavine, Atlanta Braves
1992	Greg Maddux, Chicago Cubs
1993	Greg Maddux, Atlanta Braves
1994	Greg Maddux, Atlanta Braves
1995	Greg Maddux, Atlanta Braves
1996	John Smoltz, Atlanta Braves
1997	Pedro Martinez, Montreal Expos
1998	Tom Glavine, Atlanta Braves
1999	Randy Johnson, Arizona Diamondbacks
2000	Randy Johnson, Arizona Diamondbacks
2001	Randy Johnson, Arizona Diamondbacks
2002	Randy Johnson, Arizona Diamondbacks
2003	Eric Gagne, Los Angeles Dodgers
2004	Roger Clemens, Houston Astros

American League

1967	Jim Lonborg, Boston Red Sox
1968	Denny McLain, Detroit Tigers
1969	Denny McLain, Detroit Tigers; Mike Cuellar, Baltimore Orioles
1970	Jim Perry, Minnesota Twins
1971	Vida Blue, Oakland A's
1972	Gaylord Perry, Cleveland Indians
1973	Jim Palmer, Baltimore Orioles
1974	Jim 'Catfish' Hunter, Oakland A's
1975	Jim Palmer, Baltimore Orioles
1976	Jim Palmer, Baltimore Orioles
1977	Sparky Lyle, New York Yankees
1978	Ron Guidry, New York Yankees
1979	Mike Flanagan, Baltimore Orioles
1980	Steve Stone, Baltimore Orioles
1981	Rollie Fingers, Milwaukee Brewers
1982	Pete Vuckovich, Milwaukee Brewers
1983	La Marr Hoyt, Chicago White Sox
1984	Willie Hernandez, Detroit Tigers
1985	Bret Saberhagen, Kansas City Royals
1986	Roger Clemens, Boston Red Sox
1987	Roger Clemens, Boston Red Sox
1988	Frank Viola, Minnesota Twins
1989	Bret Saberhagen, Kansas City Royals
1990	Bob Welch, Oakland A's
1991	Roger Clemens, Boston Red Sox
1992	Dennis Eckersley, Oakland A's
1993	Jack McDowell, Chicago White Sox
1994	David Cone, Kansas City Royals
1995	Randy Johnson, Seattle Mariners
1996	Pat Hentgen, Toronto Blue Jays
1997	Roger Clemens, Toronto Blue Jays
1998	Roger Clemens, Toronto Blue Jays
1999	Pedro Martinez, Boston Red Sox
2000	Pedro Martinez, Boston Red Sox
2001	Roger Clemens, New York Yankees
2002	Barry Zito, Oakland A's
2003	Roy Halladay, Toronto Blue Jays
2004	Johan Santara, Minnesota Twins

World Cup

Instituted in 1938; since 1974 usually held every two years.

Recent winners

1982	South Korea
1984	Cuba
1986	Cuba
1988	Cuba
1990	Cuba
1992	Cuba
1994	Cuba
1996	Cuba
1998	Cuba
2001	Cuba
2003	Cuba

Most wins: (26) Cuba: 1939–40, 1942–3, 1950, 1952–3, 1961, 1969–73, 1976, 1978, 1980, and as above.

Olympic Games

Became an Olympic event in 1992.

1992	Cuba
1996	Cuba
2000	USA
2004	Cuba

Minimum distance along each foul line is 250 ft (72.2 m)
Distance to the farthest point in centre field is at least 400 ft (122 m)

Baseball diamond

BASKETBALL

In the USA the game's governing body is the National Basketball Association (NBA), which comprises two 'conferences': Eastern (Atlantic Division and Central Division) and Western (Midwest Division and Pacific Division). At the end of the season each conference title is decided in a series of play-offs involving the divisional leaders and the next six best teams; the two conference title-holders compete in a best-of-seven series for the NBA Championship.

National Basketball Association championship

First held in 1947; the major competition in professional basketball in the USA.

1947	Philadelphia 4, Chicago 1	1969	Boston 4, LA Lakers 3
1948	Baltimore 4, Philadelphia 2	1970	New York 4, LA Lakers 3
1949	Minneapolis 4, Washington 2	1971	Milwaukee 4, Baltimore 0
1950	Minneapolis 4, Syracuse 2	1972	LA Lakers 4, New York 1
1951	Rochester 4, New York 3	1973	New York 4, LA Lakers 1
1952	Minneapolis 4, New York 3	1974	Boston 4, Milwaukee 3
1953	Minneapolis 4, New York 1	1975	Golden State 4, Washington 0
1954	Minneapolis 4, Syracuse 3	1976	Boston 4, Phoenix 2
1955	Syracuse 4, Ft Wayne 3	1977	Portland 4, Philadelphia 2
1956	Philadelphia 4, Ft Wayne 4	1978	Washington 4, Seattle 3
1957	Boston 4, St Louis 3	1979	Seattle 4, Washington 1
1958	St Louis 4, Boston 2	1980	LA Lakers 4, Philadelphia 2
1959	Boston 4, Minneapolis 0	1981	Boston 4, Houston 2
1960	Boston 4, St Louis 3	1982	LA Lakers 4, Philadelphia 2
1961	Boston 4, St Louis 1	1983	Philadelphia 4, LA Lakers 0
1962	Boston 4, LA Lakers 3	1984	Boston 4, LA Lakers 3
1963	Boston 4, LA Lakers 2	1985	LA Lakers 4, Boston 2
1964	Boston 4, San Francisco 1	1986	Boston 4, Houston 2
1965	Boston 4, LA Lakers 1	1987	LA Lakers 4, Boston 2
1966	Boston 4, LA Lakers 3	1988	LA Lakers 4, Detroit 3
1967	Philadelphia 4, San Francisco 2	1989	Detroit 4, LA Lakers 0
		1990	Detroit 4, Portland 1
1968	Boston 4, LA Lakers 2	1991	Chicago 4, LA Lakers 1

1992	Chicago 4, Portland 1
1993	Chicago 4, Phoenix 2
1994	Houston 4, New York 3
1995	Houston 4, Orlando 0
1996	Chicago 4, Seattle Supersonics 2
1997	Chicago 4, Utah Jazz 2
1998	Chicago 4, Utah Jazz 2
1999	San Antonio Spurs 4, New York Knicks 1
2000	LA Lakers 4, Indiana Pacers 2
2001	LA Lakers 4, Philadelphia 1
2002	LA Lakers 4, New Jersey 0
2003	San Antonio Spurs 4, New Jersey Nets 2
2004	Detroit Pistons 4, Los Angeles Lakers 1

Most wins: (16) Boston Celtics: 1967, 1959–66, 1968–9, 1974, 1976, 1981, 1984, 1986.

Basketball (continued)

National Basketball Association leading scorers

	games	points	average			games	points	average
1947 Joe Fulks, Philadelphia	60	1389	23.2		1973 Nate Archibald, Kansas City Omaha	80	2719	34.0
1948 Max Zaslofsky, Chicago	48	1007	21.0		1974 Bob McAdoo, Buffalo	74	2261	30.6
1949 George Mikan, Minneapolis	60	1698	28.3		1975 Bob McAdoo, Buffalo	82	2831	34.5
1950 George Mikan, Minneapolis	68	1865	27.4		1976 Bob McAdoo, Buffalo	78	2427	31.1
1951 George Mikan, Minneapolis	68	1932	28.4		1977 Pete Maravich, New Orleans	73	2273	31.1
1952 Paul Arizin, Philadelphia	66	1674	25.4		1978 George Gervin, San Antonio	82	2232	27.2
1953 Neil Johnston, Philadelphia	70	1564	22.3		1979 George Gervin, San Antonio	80	2365	29.6
1954 Neil Johnston, Philadelphia	72	1759	24.4		1980 George Gervin, San Antonio	78	2585	33.1
1955 Neil Johnston, Philadelphia	72	1631	22.7		1981 Adrian Dantley, Utah	80	2452	30.7
1956 Bob Pettit, St Louis	72	1849	25.7		1982 George Gervin, San Antonio	79	2551	32.3
1957 Paul Arizin, Philadelphia	71	1817	25.6		1983 Alex English, Denver	82	2326	28.4
1958 George Yardley, Detroit	72	2001	27.8		1984 Adrian Dantley, Utah	79	2418	30.6
1959 Bob Pettit, St Louis	72	2105	29.2		1985 Bernard King, New York	55	1809	32.9
1960 Wilt Chamberlain, Philadelphia	72	2707	37.9		1986 Dominique Wilkins, Atlanta	78	2366	30.3
1961 Wilt Chamberlain, Philadelphia	79	3033	38.4		1987 Michael Jordan, Chicago	82	3041	37.1
					1988 Michael Jordan, Chicago	82	2868	35.0
1962 Wilt Chamberlain, Philadelphia	80	4029	50.4		1989 Michael Jordan, Chicago	81	2633	32.5
					1990 Michael Jordan, Chicago	82	2753	33.6
1963 Wilt Chamberlain, San Francisco	80	3586	44.8		1991 Michael Jordan, Chicago	82	2580	31.5
					1992 Michael Jordan, Chicago	80	2404	30.1
1964 Wilt Chamberlain, San Francisco	80	2948	36.5		1993 Michael Jordan, Chicago	78	2541	32.3
					1994 David Robinson, San Antonio	80	2383	29.8
1965 Wilt Chamberlain, San Francisco/Philadelphia	80	2534	34.7		1995 Shaquille O'Neal, Orlando	79	2315	29.3
					1996 Michael Jordan, Chicago	82	2491	30.04
1966 Wilt Chamberlain, Philadelphia	79	2649	33.5		1997 Michael Jordan, Chicago	82	2431	29.6
					1998 Michael Jordan, Chicago	82	2357	28.7
1967 Rick Barry, San Francisco	79	2775	35.6		1999 Allen Iverson, Philadelphia	42	1284	26.8
1968 Dave Bing, Detroit	79	2142	27.1		2000 Shaquille O'Neal, LA Lakers	79	2344	29.7
1969 Elvin Hayes, San Diego	82	2327	28.4		2001 Allen Iverson, Philadelphia	71	2207	31.1
1970 Jerry West, Los Angeles	74	2309	31.2		2002 Allen Iverson, Philadelphia	60	1883	31.4
1971 Lew Alcindor, Milwaukee	82	2596	31.7		2003 Tracy McGrady, Orlando	75	2407	32.1
1972 Kareem Abdul-Jabbar (Lew Alcindor), Milwaukee	81	2822	34.8		2004 Allen Iverson, Philadelphia	60	1819	30.3

Most times: (10), Michael Jordan, as above.

National Basketball Association most valuable player

Each year the NBA players vote to decide which player will recieve the Maurice Podoloff Trophy as the year's Most Valuable Player.

1961 Bill Russell, Boston	1976 Kareem Abdul-Jabbar, LA Lakers	1993 Charles Barkley, Phoenix
1962 Bill Russell, Boston		1994 Hakeem Olajuwon, Houston
1963 Bill Russell, Boston		1995 David Robinson, San Antonio
1964 Oscar Robertson, Cincinnati	1977 Kareem Abdul-Jabbar, LA Lakers	
1965 Bill Russell, Boston	1978 Bill Walton, Portland	1996 Michael Jordan, Chicago
1966 Wilt Chamberlain, Philadelphia	1979 Moses Malone, Houston	1997 Karl Malone (Utah)
	1980 Kareem Abdul-Jabbar, LA Lakers	1998 Michael Jordan (Chicago)
1967 Wilt Chamberlain, Philadelphia		1999 Karl Malone (Utah)
	1981 Julius Erving, Philadelphia	2000 Shaquille O'Neal, LA Lakers
1968 Wilt Chamberlain, Philadelphia	1982 Moses Malone, Houston	2001 Allen Iverson, Philadelphia
1969 Wes Unseld, Baltimore	1983 Moses Malone, Philadelphia	2002 Tim Duncan, San Antonio Spurs
1970 Willis Reed, New York	1984 Larry Bird, Boston	
1971 Lew Alcindor, Milwaukee	1985 Larry Bird, Boston	2003 Tim Duncan, San Antonio Spurs
1972 Kareem Abdul-Jabbar (Lew Alcindor), Milwaukee	1986 Larry Bird, Boston	
	1987 Magic Johnson, LA Lakers	2004 Kevin Garnett, Minnesota Timberwolves
1973 Dave Cowens, Boston	1988 Michael Jordan, Chicago	
1974 Kareem Abdul-Jabbar, Milwaukee	1989 Magic Johnson, LA Lakers	*Most time MVP*: (6) Kareem Abdul-Jabbar, as above
	1990 Magic Johnson, LA Lakers	
1975 Bob McAdoo, Buffalo	1991 Michael Jordan, Chicago	
	1992 Michael Jordan, Chicago	

World championship

First held 1950 for men, 1953 for women; usually now takes place every four years.

Winners (men)	*Winners (women)*
1967 USSR	1967 USSR
1970 Yugoslavia	1971 USSR
1974 USSR	1975 USSR
1978 Yugoslavia	1979 USA
1982 USSR	1983 USSR
1986 USA	1987 USA
1990 Yugoslavia	1991 USA
1994 USA	1994 Brazil
1998 Yugoslavia	1998 USA
2002 Yugoslavia	2002 USA

Most wins: (5) Yugoslavia: as above.

Most wins: (6) USSR: 1959, 1964 and as above; USA: 1957 and as above.

Olympic Games

Became an Olympic event for men in 1936, for women in 1976.

Winners (men)	*Winners (women)*
1956 USA	1976 USSR
1960 USA	1980 USSR
1964 USA	1984 USA
1968 USA	1988 USA
1972 USSR	1992 Unified Team
1976 USA	1996 USA
1980 Yugoslavia	2000 USA
1984 USA	2004 USA
1988 USSR	
1992 USA	*Most wins:* (5) USA: as above.
1996 USA	
2000 USA	
2004 Argentina	

Most wins: (12) USA: 1936, 1948, 1952 and as above.

BIATHLON

World championships

First held in 1958; take place annually; the Olympic champion is the automatic world champion in Olympic years; women's championship first held in 1984.

Recent winners: individual – men

10 km
1990 Mark Kirchner (E Germany)
1991 Mark Kirchner (Germany)
1992 Mark Kirchner (Germany)
1993 Mark Kirchner (Germany)
1994 Serguei Tchepikov (Russia)
1995 Patrice Bailly-Salins (France)
1996 Vladimir Dratshev (Russia)
1997 Erik Lundström (Sweden)
1998 Ole Einar Bjoerndalen (Norway)
1999 Frank Luck (Germany)
2000 Frode Andreson (Norway)
2001 Raphael Poiree (France)
2002 Ole Einar Bjoerndalen (Norway)
2003 Ole Einar Bjoerndalen (Norway)
2004 Lars Berger (Norway)

20 km (now 12.5 km pursuit)
1990 Valeriy Medvetsev (USSR)
1991 Mark Kirchner (Germany)
1992 Yevgeniy Redkine (Unified Team)
1993 Franz Zingerle (Austria)
1994 Sergei Tarasov (Russia)
1995 Tomaz Sikora (Poland)
1996 Sergei Tarasov (Russia)
1997 Ricco Gross (Germany)
1998 Halvard Hanevold (Norway)
1999 Ricco Gross (Germany)
2000 Wolfgang Rottmann (Austria)
2001 Paavo Puurunen (Finland)
2002 Ole Einar Bjoerndalen (Norway)
2003 Rico Gross (Germany)
2004 Raphael Poiree (France)

Most individual titles: (6): Frank Ullrich (E Germany) 1978–81, 10 km; 1982–3, 20 km.

Olympic Games - winter
4 x 7.5 km relay (first held 1965)
1994 Germany
1998 Germany
2002 Norway

Recent winners: individual – women

7.5 km (5 km before 1988) – sprint
1996 Olga Romasko (Russia)
1997 Olga Romasko (Russia)
1998 Galina Koukleva (Russia)
1999 Martina Zellner (Germany)
2000 Liv Grete Skjelbreid (Norway)
2001 Kati Wilhelm (Germany)
2002 Kati Wilhelm (Germany)
2003 Sylvie Becaert (France)
2004 Olga Pyleva (Russia)

15 km (10 km before 1988) – pursuit
1994 Myriam Bedard (Canada)
1995 Corrine Miogret (France)
1996 Emmanuelle Claret (France)
1997 Magdalena Forsberg (Sweden)
1998 Ekaterina Dafovska (Bulgaria)
1999 Olena Zubrilova (Ukraine)
2000 Corrine Niogret (France)
2001 Magdalena Forsberg (Sweden)
2002 Andrea Henkel (Germany)
2003 Sandrine Bailly (France)
2004 Olga Pyleva (Russia)

Most individual titles: (4) Petra Schaaf (Germany) 1988, 7.5 km, 1989, 1991, 1993, 15 km as above.

Olympic Games - winter
4 x 7.5 km relay (3 x 5 km before 1989)
1994 Russia
1998 Germany
2002 Germany

BILLIARDS

World professional championship

First held in 1870, organized on a challenge basis. Became a knockout event in 1909; discontinued in 1934; revived in 1951 as a challenge system; reverted to a knockout event in 1980.

Recent winners

1993	Geet Sethi (India)
1994	Peter Gilchrist (England)
1995	Geet Sethi (India)
1996	Mike Russell (England)
1997	Mike Russell (England)
1998	Geet Sethi (India)
1999	Mike Russell (England)

2001	Peter Gilchrist (England)
2002	Mike Russell (England)
2003	Lee Lagan (England)
2004	Mike Russell (England)

Most wins: Knockout (6) Tom Newman (England): 1921–2, 1924–7. Challenge (8) John Roberts, Jnr (England): 1870–85.

BOBSLEIGHING AND TOBOGGANING/LUGE

World championships

First held in 1930 (four-man) and in 1931 (two-man). Olympic champions automatically become world champions. Women's event introduced at 2002 Olympics.

Recent winners: two-man

1998	Pierre Lueders/David MacEachern (Canada)
	Günter Huber/Antonio Tartaglia (Italy)
	(dead heat)
1999	Günter Huber/Ubaldo Ranzi (Italy)
2000	Cristoph Langen/Markus Zimmerman (Germany)
2001	Cristoph Langen/Marco Jakobs (Germany)
2002	Cristoph Langen/Markus Zimmerman (Germany)
2003	Andre Lange/Kevin Kuske (Germany)
2004	Pierre Lueders/Giulio Zardo (Canada)
2005	Pierre Lueders/Lascelles Brown (Canada)

Recent winners: women

2002	Jill Bakken/Vonetta Flowers (USA)
2003	Susi Erdmann/Annegret Richter (Germany)
2004	Susi Erdmann/Kristina Bader (Germany)
2005	Sandra Kiriasis/Anja Schneiderheinze (Germany)

Recent winners: four-man

1992	Austria	1999	France
1993	Switzerland	2000	Germany
1994	Switzerland	2001	Germany
1995	Germany	2002	Germany
1996	Germany	2003	Germany
1997	Germany	2004	Germany
1998	Germany	2005	Germany

Most wins: Two-man (8) Eugenio Monti (Italy): 1957–61, 1963, 1966, 1968. Four-man (17), Switzerland: 1939, 1947, 1954–5, 1957, 1971, 1973, 1975, 1982–3, 1986–90, 1993–4.

Luge world championships

First held in 1955; annually until 1981, then usually every two years. The Olympic champion automatically becomes the world champion.

Recent winners: men's single-seater

1989	Georg Hackl (W Germany)
1990	Georg Hackl (W Germany)
1991	Arnold Huber (Italy)
1993	Werdel Suckow (USA)

1995	Armin Zoeggeler (Italy)
1997	Georg Hackl (Germany)
1999	Armin Zoeggeler (Italy)
2000	Jens Müller (Germany)
2001	Armin Zoeggeler (Italy)
2003	Armin Zoeggeler (Italy)
2004	David Moeller (Germany)

Most wins: (3) Georg Hackl as above.

Recent winners: women's single-seater

1989	Susi Erdmann (E Germany)
1990	Gabriele Kohlisch (E Germany)
1991	Susi Erdmann (Germany)
1993	Gerda Weissensteiner (Italy)
1994	Gerda Weissensteiner (Italy)
1995	Gabriele Kohlisch (Germany)
1997	Susi Urdmann (Germany)
1999	Sonja Wiedmann (Germany)
2000	Sylke Otto (Germany)
2001	Sylke Otto (Germany)
2003	Sylke Otto (Germany)
2004	Silke Kraushaar (Germany)

Most wins: (5) Margrit Schumann (E Germany): 1973–7.

Olympic Games, luge

Winners: men's single-seater

1992	Georg Hackl (Germany)
1994	Georg Hackl (Germany)
1998	Georg Hackl (Germany)
2002	Armin Zoeggeler (Italy)

Winners: pairs (men)

1992	Germany	1998	Germany
1994	Italy	2002	Germany

Most wins: Singles (no one more than 1). Pairs (5) E Germany: 1968, 1972, 1976, 1980, 1988.

Winners: women's single-seater

1992	Doris Neuner (Austria)
1994	Gerda Weissensteiner (Italy)
1998	Silke Kraushaar (Germany)
2002	Sylke Otto (Germany)

Most wins: (2) Steffi Martin Walter (E Germany): 1984, 1988.

BOWLS

World championships

Instituted for men in 1966 and for women in 1969; held every four years.

Men's singles
1980 David Bryant (England)
1984 Peter Bellis (New Zealand)
1988 David Bryant (England)
1992 Tony Allcock (England)
1996 Tony Allcock (England)
2000 Jeremy Henry (Ireland)
2004 Steve Glasson (Australia)

Men's pairs
1980 Australia
1984 USA
1988 New Zealand
1992 Scotland
1996 Ireland
2000 Scotland
2004 Canada

Men's triples
1980 England
1984 Ireland
1988 New Zealand
1992 Israel
1996 Scotland
2000 New Zealand
2004 Scotland

Men's fours
1980 Hong Kong
1984 England
1988 Ireland
1992 Scotland
1996 England
2000 Wales
2004 Ireland

Most wins: (5) David Bryant (singles: as above and 1966; triples: 1988; team: 1980).

Women's singles
1985 Merle Richardson (Australia)
1988* Janet Ackland (Wales)
1992 Margaret Johnston (Ireland)
1996 Carmen Anderson (Norfolk Island)
2000 Margaret Johnston (Ireland)
2004 Margaret Johnston (Ireland)

Women's pairs
1981 Ireland
1985 Australia
1988* Ireland
1992 Ireland
1996 Ireland
2000 Scotland
2004 New Zealand

Women's triples
1981 Hong Kong
1985 Australia
1988* Australia

1992 Scotland
1996 South Africa
2000 New Zealand
2004 South Africa

Women's fours
1981 England
1985 Scotland
1988* Australia
1992 Scotland
1996 Australia
2000 New Zealand
2004 England

Women's team
1981 England
1985 Australia
1988* England
1992 Scotland
1996 South Africa
2000 England
2004 England

Most wins: (3) Merle Richardson (fours: 1977; singles and pairs: 1985).

*The women's event was advanced to December 1988 (Australia).

World indoor championships

First held in 1979, became fully professional in 1995, and gender-free in 1997. Women's amateur first held in 1998; both held annually.

Winners: men
1997 Hugh Duff (Scotland)
1998 Paul Foster (Scotland)
1999 Alex Marshall (Scotland)
2000 Robert Weale (Wales)
2001 Paul Foster (Scotland)
2002 Tony Allcock (England)
2003 Alex Marshall (Scotland)
2004 Alex Marshall (Scotland)
2005 Paul Foster (Scotland)

Most wins: (3) David Bryant: 1979–81; Richard Corsie: 1989, 1991, 1993; Tony Allcock: 1986–87, 2002; Alex Marshall, Paul Foster, as above.

Winners: women
1996 Sandy Hazell (England)
1997 Norma Shaw (England)
1998 Caroline McAllister (Scotland)
1999 Caroline McAllister (Scotland)
2000 Marlene Castle (New Zealand)
2001 Betty Brown (Scotland)
2002 Carol Ashby (England)
2003 Carol Ashby (England)
2004 Carol Ashby (England)
2005 Ellen Falkner (England)

Most wins: (3) Carol Ashby, as above.

Waterloo Handicap

First held in 1907 and annually at Blackpool's Waterloo Hotel; the premier event of Crown Green Bowling.

Recent winners: men
1999 Ian Smout
2000 Carl Armitage
2001 Glynn Cookson
2002 Stan Frith
2003 Gary Ellis
2004 Noel Burrows

Recent winners: women
1998 Lynn Pritchett
1999 Lynn Pritchett
2000 Lynn Pritchett
2001 Lesley Smith
2002 Karen Johnstone
2003 Joan Jolly
2004 Ann Roberts

BOXING

World heavyweight champions

Undisputed
1882 John L Sullivan (USA)
1892 James J Corbett (USA)*
1897 Bob Fitzsimmons (Great Britain)
1899 James J Jefferies (USA)
1905 Marvin Hart (USA)
1906 Tommy Burns (Can)
1908 Jack Johnson (USA)
1915 Jess Willard (USA)
1919 Jack Dempsey (USA)
1926 Gene Tunney (USA)
1930 Max Schmeling (Germany)
1932 Jack Sharkey (USA)
1933 Primo Carnera (Italy)
1934 Max Baer (USA)
1935 James J Braddock (USA)
1937 Joe Louis (USA)
1949 Ezzard Charles (USA)
1951 Jersey Joe Walcott (USA)
1952 Rocky Marciano (USA)
1956 Floyd Patterson (USA)
1959 Ingemar Johansson (Sweden)
1960 Sonny Liston (USA)
1964 Cassius Clay (USA)ᵃ
1970 Joe Frazier (USA)
1973 George Foreman (USA)
1974 Muhammad Ali (USA)ᵃ
1978 Leon Spinks (USA)
1987 Mike Tyson (USA)

*The first world heavyweight champion under Queensberry rules with gloves.

Boxing (continued)

In recent years, 'world champions' have been recognized by up to four different governing bodies.

Champions since 1986	Recognizing body
1986 Tim Witherspoon (USA)	WBA
1986 Trevor Berbick (Canada)	WBC
1986 Mike Tyson (USA)	WBC
1986 James Smith (USA)	WBA
1987 Tony Tucker (USA)	IBF
1987 Mike Tyson (USA)	WBA/WBC
1987 Mike Tyson (USA)	UND
1989 Francesco Damiani (Italy)	WBO
1990 James (Buster) Douglas (USA)	WBA/WBC/IBF
1990 Evander Holyfield (USA)	WBA/WBC/IBF
1991 Ray Mercer (USA)	WBO
1992 Riddick Bowe (USA)	WBA/WBC/IBF
1992 Michael Moorer (USA)	WBO
1992 Lennox Lewis (Great Britain)	WBC
1993 Tommy Morrison (USA)	WBO
1994 Oliver McCall (UK)	WBC
1994 Herbie Hide (USA)	WBO
1994 George Foreman (USA)	IBF
1995 Frank Bruno (UK)	WBC
1996 Mike Tyson (USA)	WBC
1996 Henry Akinwande (UK)	WBO
1996 Evander Holyfield (USA)	WBA
1996 Michael Moorer (USA)	IBF
1997 Lennox Lewis (UK)	WBC
1997 Herbie Hide (UK)	WBO
1997 Evander Holyfield (USA)	WBA/IBF
1998 Lennox Lewis (Ukraine)	WBC
1999 Vitali Klitschko (Ukraine)	WBO
1999 Lennox Lewis (UK)	WBO/WBA[b]/WBC/IBF/UND
2000 John Ruiz (USA)	WBA
2001 Hasim Rahman (USA)	WBC, IBF
2001 Lennox Lewis (UK)	WBC, IBF
2002 Lennox Lewis (UK)	WBC, IBF
2003 Roy Jones, Jr (USA)	WBA
2003 Lennox Lewis (UK)	WBC
2004 John Ruiz (USA)	WBA
2004 Vitali Klitschko (Ukraine)	WBC

[a]Cassius Clay changed his name to Muhammad Ali upon joining the Black Muslims.
[b]He was stripped of this award by a New York court in 2000.

IBF = International Boxing Federation
UND = Undisputed Champion
WBA = World Boxing Association
WBC = World Boxing Council
WBO = World Boxing Organization

CANOEING

Olympic Games

Single kayak: 1000 m – men

1936	Gregor Hradetzky (Austria)
1948	Gert Fredriksson (Sweden)
1952	Gert Fredriksson (Sweden)
1956	Gert Fredriksson (Sweden)
1960	Erik Hansen (Denmark)
1964	Rolf Peterson (Sweden)
1968	Mihaly Hesz (Hungary)
1972	Aleksandr Shaparenko (USSR)
1976	Rüdiger Helm (E Germany)
1980	Rüdiger Helm (E Germany)
1984	Alan Thompson (New Zealand)
1988	Greg Barton (USA)
1992	Clint Robinson (Australia)
1996	Oliver Fix (Germany)
2000	Thomas Schmidt (Germany)
2004	Eirik Veraas Larsen (Norway)

Single kayak: 500 m – women

1948	Keren Hoff (Denmark)
1952	Sylvi Saimo (Finland)
1956	Elisaveta Dementyeva (USSR)
1960	Antonina Seredina (USSR)
1964	Lyudmila Khvedosyuk (USSR)
1968	Lyudmila Pinayeva (USSR)
1972	Yulia Ryabchinskaya (USSR)
1976	Carola Zirzow (E Germany)
1980	Birgit Fischer (E Germany)
1984	Agneta Andersson (Sweden)
1988	Vania Gecheva (USSR)
1992	Brigit Schmidt (Germany)
1996	Stepanka Hilgertova (Czech Republic)
2000	Stepanka Hilgertova (Czech Republic)
2004	Natasa Janics (Hungary)

Most wins: Men (3) Gert Fredriksson: as above. Women (2) Stepanka Hilgertova: as above.

CHESS

World champions

World champions have been recognized since 1886; first women's champion recognized in 1927. A split between the World Chess Federation (FIDE) and the new Professional Chess Association (PCA) resulted in two championship matches in 1993. Following the collapse of the PCA and subsequent collapse of the World Chess Council set up to replace it, the 2000 world championship was contested under the aegis of Braingames Network, an Internet company.

Recent champions: men

1972–5	Bobby Fischer (USA)
1975–85	Anatoly Karpov (USSR)
1985– 2000	Gary Kasparov (USSR/Azerbaijan) PCA
1993–9	Anatoly Karpov (Russia) FIDE
1999– 2000	Alexander Khalifman (Russia) FIDE
2000–02	Vishwanathan Anand (India) FIDE
2000	Vladimir Kramnik (Russia) Braingames Network
2002–4	Ruslan Ponomariov (Ukraine) FIDE
2004–	Rustam Kasimdzhanov (Uzbekistan) FIDE

Longest reigning champion: 27 years, Emanuel Lasker (Germany): 1894–1921.

Champions: women

1950–3	Lyudmila Rudenko (USSR)
1953–6	Elizaveta Bykova (USSR)
1956–8	Olga Rubtsova (USSR)
1958–62	Elizaveta Bykova (USSR)
1962–78	Nona Gaprindashvili (USSR)
1978–92	Maya Chiburdanidze (USSR)
1992–5	Xie Jun (China)
1996–9	Zsusza Polgar (Hungary)
1999– 2000	Xie Jun (China)
2001–	Zhu Chen (China) FIDE

Longest reigning champion: 17 years, Vera Menchik-Stevenson (UK): 1927–44.

Chess notation

The opening position[a]

QR QN QB Q K KB KN KR

Abbreviations

B	Bishop
K	King
KB	King's bishop
KN	King's knight
KR	King's rook
N	Knight
P	Pawn
Q	Queen
QB	Queen's bishop
QN	Queen's knight
QR	Queen's rook
R	Rook

Descriptive notation

Each file is named by the piece on the first rank; ranks are numbered 1–8 away from the player.

x	captures (Q x P = Queen takes Pawn)
–	moves to (Q–KB4)
ch	check (R—QB3 ch)
dis ch	discovered check
dbl ch	double check
e.p.	en passant
mate	checkmate
0–0	castles, King's side
0–0–0	castles, Queen's side
!	good move (P x R!)
!!	very good move
!!!	outstanding move
?	bad move
!?	good or bad move (depends on response of the other player)

Algebraic notation

Each square is named by a combination of file letter and rank number.

Chess pieces in other languages

French

B	fou (fool)
K	roi (king)
N	cavalier (horseman)
P	pion (pawn)
Q	dame, reine (lady), (queen)
R	tour (tower)

German

B	Läufer (runner)
K	König (king)
N	Springer (jumper)
P	Bauer (peasant)
Q	Königin (queen)
R	Turm (tower)

[a] The white queen is placed on a white square, and the black queen on a black square.

CONTRACT BRIDGE

World team championship

The game's biggest championship; men's contest (The Bermuda Bowl) first held in 1951, and now takes place every two years; women's contest (The Venice Cup) first held in 1974, and since 1985 is concurrent with the men's event.

Bermuda Bowl winners: men

1977	USA	1991	Iceland
1979	USA	1993	Netherlands
1981	USA	1995	USA
1983	USA	1997	France
1985	USA	2000	USA
1987	USA	2001	USA
1989	Brazil	2003	USA

Most wins: (13) Italy: 1957–9, 1961–3, 1965–7, 1969, 1973–5.

Venice Cup winners: women

1976	USA	1991	USA
1978	USA	1993	USA
1981	UK	1995	Germany
1983	*Not held*	1997	USA
1985	UK	2000	Netherlands
1987	Italy	2001	Germany
1989	USA	2003	USA

Most wins: (8) USA: 1974 and as above.

World team olympiad

First held in 1960; takes place every four years.

Winners: men

1960	France	1984	Poland
1964	Italy	1988	USA
1968	Italy	1992	France
1972	Italy	1996	France
1976	Brazil	2000	Italy
1980	France	2004	Italy

Winners: women

1964	UK	1988	Denmark
1968	Sweden	1992	Austria
1972	Italy	1996	USA
1976	USA	2000	USA
1980	USA	2004	Russia
1984	USA		

Most wins: Men (5) Italy: as above. Women (5) USA: as above.

CRICKET

World cup

First played in England in 1975 (women's match from 1973); held every four years. The 1987 competition was the first to be played outside England, in India and Pakistan.

Winners

1975	West Indies	1992	Pakistan
1979	West Indies	1996	Sri Lanka
1983	India	1999	Australia
1987	Australia	2003	Austrialia

County championship

The oldest cricket competition in the world; first won by Sussex in 1827. Not officially recognized until 1890, when a proper points system was introduced.

Recent winners

1992	Essex
1993	Middlesex
1994	Warwickshire
1995	Warwickshire
1996	Leicestershire
1997	Glamorgan
1998	Leicestershire
1999	Surrey
2000	Surrey
2001	Yorkshire
2002	Surrey
2003	Sussex
2004	Warwickshire

Most outright wins: (30) Yorkshire: 1893, 1896, 1898, 1900–2, 1905, 1908, 1912, 1919, 1922–5, 1931–3, 1935, 1937–9, 1946, 1959–60, 1962–3, 1966–8, 2001.

NPower Twenty20 Cup

First held in 2003. Replaced the Benson and Hedges Cup.

Recent winners

2003	Surrey
2004	Leicestershire

Cheltenham and Gloucester trophy

First held in 1963; known as the Gillette Cup until 1981 and the NatWest Bank trophy until 2000.

Recent winners

1989	Warwickshire
1990	Lancashire
1991	Hampshire
1992	Northamptonshire
1993	Warwickshire
1994	Worcestershire
1995	Warwickshire
1996	Lancashire
1997	Essex
1998	Lancashire
1999	Gloucestershire
2000	Gloucestershire
2001	Somerset
2002	Yorkshire
2003	Gloucestershire
2004	Gloucestershire

Most wins: (7) Lancashire: 1970–2, 1975, 1990, 1996, 1998.

Totesport National League

First held in 1969; known as the John Player League 1969–86; the Refuge Assurance League until 1991; the AXA Equity and Law League until 1999; the CGU National Cricket League until 2000; and the Norwich Union National League until 2003.

Recent winners

1985	Essex
1986	Hampshire
1987	Worcestershire
1988	Worcestershire
1989	Lancashire
1990	Derbyshire
1991	Nottinghamshire
1992	Middlesex
1993	Glamorgan
1994	Warwickshire
1995	Kent
1996	Surrey
1997	Warwickshire
1998	Lancashire
1999	Lancashire
2000	Gloucestershire
2001	Kent
2002	Glamorgan
2003	Surrey

Most wins: (5) Lancashire: 1969–70, 1989, 1998–9.

Pura Milk Cup

Australia's leading domestic competition; contested inter-state since 189, known as the Sheffield Shield until 1999.

Recent winners
1992 Western Australia
1993 New South Wales
1994 New South Wales
1995 Queensland
1996 South Australia

1997 Queensland
1998 Western Australia
1999 Queensland
2000 Queensland
2001 Queensland
2002 Queensland
2003 New South Wales
2004 Victoria

Most wins: (43) New South Wales, 1896–7, 1900, 1902–7, 1909, 1911–12, 1914, 1920–1, 1923, 1926, 1929, 1932–3, 1938, 1940, 1949–50, 1952, 1954–62, 1965–6, 1983, 1985–6, 1993–4, 2003.

Cricket field positions[a]

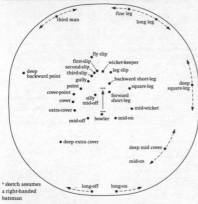

first-slip
second-slip
third-slip
fly slip
wicket-keeper
leg slip
deep backward point
gully
backward short-leg
point
square-leg
cover-point
silly mid-off
forward short-leg
deep square-leg
cover
extra-cover
mid-wicket
mid-off
bowler
mid-on
deep extra cover
deep mid cover
mid-on
third man
fine leg
long leg
long-off
long-on

[a] sketch assumes a right-handed batsman

CROQUET

MacRobertson Shield

Croquet's leading tournament; held spasmodically since 1925; contested by teams from Great Britain, New Zealand, Australia, and USA.

Winners
1935 Australia
1937 Great Britain
1950 New Zealand
1956 Great Britain
1963 Great Britain
1969 Great Britain
1974 Great Britain
1979 New Zealand
1982 Great Britain
1986 New Zealand
1990 Great Britain
1993 Great Britain

1996 Great Britain
2000 Great Britain
2003 Great Britain

Most wins: (12) Great Britain: 1925 and as above.

World singles championships

Inaugurated in 1989.

Winners
1996 *not held*
1997 Robert Fulford (Great Britain)
1998 *not held*
1999 *not held*
2000 *not held*
2001 Reg Bamford (South Africa)
2002 Robert Fulford (Great Britain)

Most wins: (5) Robert Fulford (Great Britain): 1990, 1992, 1994 and as above.

CROSS-COUNTRY RUNNING

World championships

First international championship held in 1903, but only included runners from England, Ireland, Scotland, and Wales. Recognized as an official world championship from 1973; first women's race in 1967.

Recent winner: individual – men
1996 Paul Tergat (Kenya)
1997 Paul Tergat (Kenya)
1998 Paul Tergat (Kenya)
1999 Paul Tergat (Kenya)
2000 Mohammad Mourhit (Belgium)
2001 Mohammad Mourhit (Belgium)
2002 Kenenisa Bekele (Ethiopia)
2003 Kenenisa Bekele (Ethiopia)
2004 Kenenisa Bekele (Ethiopia)
2005 Kenenisa Bekele (Ethiopia)

Recent winners: team – men
1994	Kenya	2000	Kenya
1995	Kenya	2001	Kenya
1996	Kenya	2002	Kenya
1997	Kenya	2003	Kenya
1998	Kenya	2004	Ethiopia
1999	Kenya	2005	Ethiopia

Most wins: Individual (5) John Ngugi (Kenya): 1986–9, 1991–2; Paul Tergat (Kenya) 1995 and as above. Team (45), England: between 1903 and 1980.

Recent winners: individual – women
1996 Gete Wami (Ethiopia)
1997 Derartu Tulu (Ethiopia)
1998 Sonia O'Sullivan (Ireland)
1999 Gete Wami (Ethiopia)
2000 Derartu Tulu (Ethiopia)
2001 Paula Radcliffe (Great Britain)
2002 Paula Radcliffe (Great Britain)
2003 Werknesh Kidane (Ethiopia)
2004 Benita Johnson (Australia)
2005 Tirunesh Dibaba (Ethiopia)

Recent winners: team – women
1994	Portugal	2000	Portugal
1995	Kenya	2001	Kenya
1996	Kenya	2002	Kenya
1997	Ethiopia	2003	Ethiopia
1998	Kenya	2004	Ethiopia
1999	France	2005	Ethiopia

Most wins: Individual (5) Doris Brown (USA): 1967–71; Grete Waitz (Norway): 1978–81, 1983. Team (8), USA: 1968–9, 1975, 1979, 1983–5, 1987, 1988–9; Kenya: 1991 (tied), 1992, 1993, and as above.

CURLING

World championships

First men's championship held in 1959; first women's championship in 1979. Takes place annually.

Recent winners: men

1990	Canada	1998	Canada
1991	Scotland	1999	Scotland
1992	Switzerland	2000	Canada
1993	Canada	2001	Sweden
1994	Canada	2002	Canada
1995	Canada	2003	Canada
1996	Canada	2004	Sweden
1997	Sweden	2005	Canada

Recent winners: women

1990	Norway	1998	Sweden
1991	Norway	1999	Sweden
1992	Sweden	2000	Canada
1993	Germany	2001	Canada
1994	Canada	2002	Scotland
1995	Canada	2003	USA
1996	Canada	2004	Canada
1997	Canada	2005	Sweden

Most wins: Men (29) Canada: 1959–64, 1966, 1968–72, 1980, 1982–3, 1985–7, 1991, and as above. Women (13) Canada: 1980, 1984–7, 1989, and as above.

CYCLING

Tour de France

World's premier cycling event; first held in 1903.

Recent winners

1987	Stephen Roche (Ireland)
1988	Pedro Delgado (Spain)
1989	Greg LeMond (USA)
1990	Greg LeMond (USA)
1991	Miguel Induráin (Spain)
1992	Miguel Induráin (Spain)
1993	Miguel Induráin (Spain)
1994	Miguel Induráin (Spain)
1995	Miguel Induráin (Spain)
1996	Bjarne Riis (Denmark)
1997	Jan Ullrich (Germany)
1998	Marco Pantani (Italy)
1999	Lance Armstrong (USA)
2000	Lance Armstrong (USA)
2001	Lance Armstrong (USA)
2002	Lance Armstrong (USA)
2003	Lance Armstrong (USA)
2004	Lance Armstrong (USA)

Most wins: (6) Lance Armstrong (USA), as above.

World road race championships

Men's race first held in 1927; takes place annually. First women's race in 1958; takes place annually.

Recent winners: professional men

1994	Luc Le Blanc (France)
1995	Abraham Olano (Spain)
1996	Johan Museeuw (Belgium)
1997	Laurent Brochard (France)
1998	Oscar Camenzind (Switzerland)
1999	Oscar Freire Gomez (Spain)
2000	Romans Vainsteins (Latvia)
2001	Oscar Freire Gomez (Spain)
2002	Mario Cipollini (Italy)
2003	Igor Astarloa (Spain)
2004	Oscar Freire Gomez (Spain)

Recent winners: women

1994	Monica Valvik (Norway)
1995	Jeannie Longo (France)
1996	Jeannie Longo (France)
1997	Alessandra Cappelloto (Italy)
1998	Diana Ziliute (Lithuania)
1999	Edita Pucinskaite (Lithuania)
2000	Zinaida Stahurskai (Bulgaria)
2001	Rasa Polikeviciute (Lithuania)
2002	Susanne Ljungskog (Sweden)
2003	Susanne Ljungskog (Sweden)
2004	Judith Arndt (Germany)

Most wins: Men (3) Alfredo Binda (Italy): 1927, 1930, 1932; Rik Van Steenbergen (Belgium): 1949, 1956–7; Eddy Merckx (Belgium): 1967, 1971, 1974; Oscar Freire Gomez (Spain): as above. Women (7): Jeannie Longo (France): 1985, 1986, 1987, 1988, 1989 and as above.

Olympic Games

Gold medal winners: 2004 – men

Individual road race
Paulo Bettini (Italy)

1000 m sprint
Ryan Baley (USA)

4000 m individual pursuit
Bradley Wiggins (Great Britain)

Gold medal winners: 2004 – women

Individual road race
Sara Carrigan (Australia)

1000 m sprint
Lori-Ann Muenzer (Canada)

3000 m individual pursuit
Sarah Ulmer (New Zealand)

CYCLO-CROSS

World championships

First held in 1950 as an open event; separate professional and amateur events since 1967; both events combined from 1994 to form the Open; since 1995, called the Elite.

Recent winners: professional

1981	Johannes Stamsnijder (Netherlands)
1982	Roland Liboton (Belgium)
1983	Roland Liboton (Belgium)
1984	Roland Liboton (Belgium)
1985	Klaus-Peter Thaler (W Germany)
1986	Albert Zweifel (Switzerland)
1987	Klaus-Peter Thaler (W Germany)
1988	Pascal Richard (Switzerland)
1989	Danny De Bie (Belgium)
1990	Henk Baars (Netherlands)
1991	Radomir Simunek (Czechoslovakia)
1992	Mike Kluge (Germany)
1993	Dominique Arnaud (France)

Recent winners: amateur

1981	Milos Fisera (Czechoslovakia)
1982	Milos Fisera (Czechoslovakia)
1983	Radomir Simunek (Czechoslovakia)
1984	Radomir Simunek (Czechoslovakia)
1985	Mike Kluge (W Germany)
1986	Vito di Tano (Italy)
1987	Mike Kluge (W Germany)
1988	Karol Camrola (Czechoslovakia)
1989	Ondrej Glaja (Czechoslovakia)
1990	Andreas Buesser (Switzerland)
1991	Thomas Frischknecht (Switzerland)
1992	Daniele Pontoni (Italy)
1993	Henrik Djemis (Denmark)

Recent Winners: Elite

1997	Daniele Pontoni (Italy)
1998	Mario De Clercq (Belgium)
1999	Mario De Clercq (Belgium)
2000	Richard Groenendaal (Netherlands)
2001	Erwin Vervecken (Belgium)
2002	Mario De Clercq (Belgium)
2003	Bart Wellens (Belgium)
2004	Bart Wellens (Belgium)

Most wins: Professional (7) Eric de Vlaeminck (Belgium): 1966, 1968–73. Amateur (5) Robert Vermiere (Belgium): 1970–1, 1974–5, 1977.

DARTS

World professional championship (BDO)

British Darts Organisation: first held at Nottingham in 1978; held at Frimley Green, Surrey, since 1986; women's tournament first held in 2001.

Winners: men
2000 Ted Hankey (England)
2001 John 'Boy' Walton (England)
2002 Tony David (Australia)
2003 Raymond Barneveld (Netherlands)
2004 Andy Fordham (England)
2005 Raymond Barneveld (Netherlands)

Winners: women
2001 Trina Gulliver (England)
2002 Trina Gulliver (England)
2003 Trina Gulliver (England)
2004 Trina Gulliver (England)
2005 Trina Gulliver (England)

Most wins: Men (5) Eric Bristow 1980–1, 1984–6. Women (5) Trina Gulliver, as above.

World cup

A team competition first held at Wembley in 1977; takes place every two years.

Winners: team
1987 England
1989 England
1991 England
1993 Wales
1995 England
1997 England
1999 England
2001 England
2003 England

Winners: individual
1987 Eric Bristow (England)
1989 Eric Bristow (England)
1991 John Lowe (England)
1993 Roland Schollen (Denmark)
1995 Martin Adams (England)
1997 Raymond Barneveld (Netherlands)
1999 Raymond Barneveld (Netherlands)
2001 Martin Adams (England)
2003 Raymond Barneveld (Netherlands)

Most wins: Team (11) England: 1979, 1981, 1983, 1985, and as above. Individual (4) Eric Bristow (England) 1983, 1985, and as above.

DRAUGHTS

World championship

Held on a challenge basis.

1979–90 M Tinsley (USA)
1991–94 D Oldbury (Great Britain)
1994–2003 R King (Barbados)
2003– Alexander Georgiev (Russia)

British Open championship

The leading championship in Britain. First held in 1926; now takes place every two years.

Recent winners
1978 J McGill (Great Britain)
1980 T Watson (Great Britain)
1982 T Watson (Great Britain)
1984 A Long (USA)
1986 H Devlin (Great Britain)
1988 D Oldbury (Great Britain)
1990 T Watson (Great Britain)
1992 H Devlin (Great Britain)
1994 W J Edwards (Great Britain)
1996 W J Edwards (Great Britain)
1998 Pat McCarthy (Ireland)
2000 W Doherty (Scotland)
2002 Ronald King (Barbados)
2004 Colin Young (Scotland)

EQUESTRIAN EVENTS

World championships

Show-jumping championships first held in 1953 (for men) and 1965 (for women); since 1978 men and women have competed together and on equal terms. Team competition introduced in 1978; three-day event and dressage championships introduced in 1966. All three now held every four years.

Winners: show jumping – men
1953 Francisco Goyoago (Spain)
1954 Hans-Günter Winkler (W Germany)
1955 Hans-Günter Winkler (W Germany)
1956 Raimondo D'Inzeo (Italy)
1960 Raimondo D'Inzeo (Italy)
1966 Pierre d'Oriola (France)
1970 David Broome (Great Britain)
1974 Hartwig Steenken (W Germany)

Winners: show jumping – women
1965 Marion Coakes (Great Britain)
1970 Janou Lefèbvre (France)
1974 Janou Tissot (France)

Winners: individual
1990 Eric Navet (France)
1994 Franke Sloothaak (Germany)
1998 Rodrigo Pessoa (Brazil)
2002 Dermot Lennon (Ireland)

Winners: team
1990 France
1994 Germany
1998 Germany
2002 France

Winners: three-day event – individual
1986 Virginia Leng (Great Britain)
1990 Blyth Tait (New Zealand)
1994 Vaughn Jefferis (New Zealand)
1998 Blyth Tait (New Zealand)
2002 Jean Teulere (France)

Winners: three-day event – team
1982 Great Britain
1986 Great Britain
1990 New Zealand
1994 Great Britain
1998 New Zealand
2002 USA

Winners: dressage – individual
1986 Anne Grethe Jensen (Denmark)
1990 Nicole Uphoff (W Germany)
1994 Isabell Werth (Germany)
1998 Isabell Werth (Germany)
2002 Nadine Capellmann (Germany)

Winners: dressage – team
1982 W Germany 1994 Germany
1986 W Germany 1998 Germany
1990 W Germany 2002 Germany

Olympic Games

Gold medal winners: 2004 – individual
Three-day event
Leslie Law (Great Britain)

Dressage
Anky van Grunsven (Netherlands)

Jumping
Cian O'Connor (Ireland)

Gold medal winners: 2004 – team
Three-day event France
Dressage Germany
Jumping Germany

FENCING

World championships

Held annually since 1921 (between 1921–35, known as European Championships). Not held in Olympic years.

Recent winners
Foil: individual – men
1986	Andrea Borella (Italy)
1987	Mathias Gey (W Germany)
1989	Alexander Koch (W Germany)
1990	Philippe Omnes (France)
1991	Ingo Weissenborn (Germany)
1993	Alexander Koch (Germany)
1994	Rolando Tucker (Cuba)
1995	Dimitriy Chevtchenko (Russia)
1997	Sergey Golubitsky (Ukraine)
1998	Sergey Golubitsky (Ukraine)
1999	Sergey Golubitsky (Ukraine)
2001	Salvatore Sanzo (Italy)
2002	Simone Vanni (Italy)
2003	Peter Joppich (Germany)

Foil: team – men
1986	Italy
1987	USSR
1989	USSR
1990	Italy
1991	Cuba
1993	Germany
1994	Italy
1995	Cuba
1997	France
1998	Poland
1999	France
2001	France
2002	Germany
2003	Italy

Most wins: Individual (5) Alexander Romankov (USSR): 1974, 1977, 1979, 1982-3. Team (15) USSR: between 1959-89.

Foil: individual – women
1986	Anja Fichtel (W Germany)
1987	Elisabeta Tufan (Romania)
1989	Olga Velitschko (USSR)
1990	Anja Fichtel (W Germany)
1991	Giovanna Trillini (Italy)
1993	Francesca Bortolozzi (Italy)
1994	Reka Szabo-Lazar (Romania)
1995	Laura Badea (Romania)
1997	Giovanna Trillini (Italy)
1998	Sabine Bau (Germany)
1999	Valentina Vezzali (Italy)
2001	Valentina Vezzali (Italy)
2002	Svetlana Bojko (Russia)
2003	Valentina Vezzali (Italy)

Foil: team – women
1986	USSR	1995	Italy
1987	Hungary	1997	Italy
1989	W Germany	1998	Italy
1990	Italy	1999	Germany
1991	Cuba	2001	Italy
1993	Germany	2002	Russia
1994	Romania	2003	Poland

Most wins: Individual (3) Helène Mayer (Germany): 1929, 1931, 1937; Ilona Elek (Hungary): 1934-5, 1951; Ellen Müller-Preiss (Austria): 1947, 1949, 1950; Cornelia Hanisch: 1979, 1981, 1985; Valentina Vezzali (Italy). Team (15) USSR: between 1956-86.

Epée: individual – men
1985	Philippe Boisse (France)
1986	Philippe Riboud (France)
1987	Volker Fischer (W Germany)
1989	Manuel Pereira (Spain)
1990	Thomas Gerull (W Germany)
1991	Andrei Shuvalov (USSR)
1993	Pavel Kolobkov (Russia)
1994	Pavel Kolobkov (Russia)
1995	Eric Srecki (France)
1997	Eric Srecki (France)
1998	Hugues Obry (France)
1999	Arnd Schmitt (Germany)
2001	Paolo Milanoli (Italy)
2002	Pavel Kolobkov (Russia)
2003	Fabrice Jeannet (France)

Epée: team – men
1986	W Germany	1995	Germany
1987	W Germany	1997	Cuba
1989	Italy	1998	Hungary
1990	Italy	1999	France
1991	USSR	2001	Hungary
1993	Italy	2002	France
1994	Germany	2003	Russia

Most wins: Individual (3) Georges Buchard (France): 1927, 1931, 1933; Alexei Nikanchikov (USSR): 1966-7, 1970. Team (13) France: between 1934-83, 1999-2002.

Epée: individual – women
1994	Laura Chiesa (Italy)
1995	Joanna Jakimiuk (Poland)
1997	Miraide Garcia-Soto (Cuba)
1998	Laura Flessel (France)
1999	Laura Flessel-Colovic (France)
2001	Claudia Bokel (Germany)
2002	Hyun Hee (Korea)
2003	Natalia Conrad (Ukraine)

Epée: team – women
1994	Spain
1995	Hungary
1997	Hungary
1998	France
1999	Hungary
2001	Russia
2002	Hungary
2003	Russia

Sabre: individual – men
1991	Grigoriy Kirienko (USSR)
1993	Grigoriy Kirienko (Russia)
1994	Felix Becker (Germany)
1995	Grigoriy Kirienko (Russia)
1997	Stanislav Pozdnyakov (Russia)
1998	Luigo Tarantino (Italy)
1999	Damien Touya (France)
2001	Stanislaw Pozdnikov (Russia)
2002	Stanislaw Pozdnikov (Russia)
2003	Vladimir Lukashenko (Ukraine)

Sabre: team – men
1991	Hungary
1993	Hungary
1994	Russia
1995	Italy
1997	France
1998	Hungary
1999	France
2001	Russia
2002	Russia

Sabre: individual – women
2001	Anne-Lise Touya (France)
2002	Tan Xue (China)
2003	Dorina Mihai (Romania)

Sabre: team – women
1999	Italy
2001	Russia
2002	Russia

Most wins: Individual (4) Grigory Kirienko (Russia): 1989 and as above. Team (20) Hungary: between 1930-98.

Olympic Games

Gold medal winners: 2004 – men
Individual foil
Brice Guyart (France)

Team foil
Italy

Individual epée
Marcel Fischer (Switzerland)

Team epée
France

Individual sabre
Aldo Montano (Italy)

Team sabre
France

Gold medal winners: 2004 – women
Individual foil
Valentina Vezzali (Italy)

Individual epée
Timea Nagy (Hungary)

Individual sabre
Mariel Zagunis (USA)

Team epée
Russia

FOOTBALL (AMERICAN)

National Football League (NFL)

In its existing form since 1970, the NFL consists of two 'conferences': the American Football Conference (AFC) and the National Football Conference (NFC). Each of these comprises three divisions (Eastern, Central, and Western), which are made up of either four or five teams. The season is played over sixteen games, with the championship of each conference being decided by two rounds of play-offs involving the three winners of the divisions, plus a number of 'wild cards', ie the best of the rest.

Super Bowl

First held in 1967; takes place each January; since 1971 an end of season meeting between the AFC and NFC champions.

1968 Green Bay Packers (NFL) 33, Oakland Raiders (AFL) 14
1969 New York Jets (AFL) 16, Baltimore Colts (NFL) 7
1970 Kansas City Chiefs (AFL) 23, Minnesota Vikings (NFL) 7
1971 Baltimore Colts (AFC) 16, Dallas Cowboys (NFC) 13
1972 Dallas Cowboys (NFC) 24, Miami Dolphins (AFC) 3
1973 Miami Dolphins (AFC) 14, Washington Redskins (NFC) 7
1974 Miami Dolphins (AFC) 24, Minnesota Vikings (NFL) 7
1975 Pittsburgh Steelers (AFC) 16, Minnesota Vikings (NFC) 6
1976 Pittsburgh Steelers (AFC) 21, Dallas Cowboys (NFC) 17
1977 Oakland Raiders (AFC) 32, Minnesota Vikings (NFC) 14
1978 Dallas Cowboys (NFC) 27, Denver Broncos (AFC) 10
1979 Pittsburgh Steelers (AFC) 35, Dallas Cowboys (NFC) 31
1980 Pittsburgh Steelers (AFC) 31, Los Angeles Rams (NFC) 19
1981 Oakland Raiders (AFC) 27, Philadelphia Eagles (NFC) 10
1982 San Francisco 49ers (NFC) 26, Cincinnati Bengals (AFC) 21
1983 Washington Redskins (NFC) 27, Miami Dolphins (AFC) 17
1984 Los Angeles Raiders (AFC) 38, Washington Redskins (NFC) 9
1985 San Francisco 49ers (NFC) 38, Miami Dolphins (AFC) 16
1986 Chicago Bears (NFC) 46, New England Patriots (AFC) 10
1987 New York Giants (NFC) 39, Denver Broncos (AFC) 20
1988 Washington Redskins (NFC) 42, Denver Broncos (AFC) 10
1989 San Francisco 49ers (NFC) 20, Cincinnati Bengals (AFC) 16
1990 San Francisco 49ers (NFC) 55, Denver Broncos (AFC) 10
1991 New York Giants (NFC) 20, Buffalo Bills (AFC) 19
1992 Washington Redskins (NFC) 37, Buffalo Bills (AFC) 24
1993 Dallas Cowboys (NFC) 52, Buffalo Bills (AFC) 17
1994 Dallas Cowboys (NFC) 30, Buffalo Bills (AFC) 13
1995 San Francisco 49ers (NFC) 49, San Diego Chargers (NFC) 26
1996 Dallas Cowboys (NFC) 27, Pittsburgh Steelers (AFC) 17

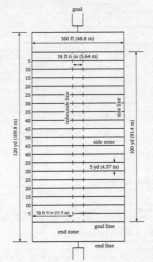

American football field

1997 Green Bay Packers (NFC) 35, New England Patriots (AFC) 21
1998 Denver Broncos (AFC) 31, Green Bay Packers (NFC) 24
1999 Denver Broncos (AFC) 34, Atlanta Falcons (NFC) 19
2000 St Louis Rams (NFC) 23, Tennessee Titans (AFC) 16
2001 Baltimore Ravens (AFC) 24, New York Giants (NFC) 7
2002 New England Patriots (AFC) 20, St Louis Rams (NFC) 17
2003 Tampa Bay Buccaneers (NFC) 48, Oakland Raiders (AFC) 21
2004 New England Patriots (AFC) 32, Carolina Panthers (NFC) 29
2005 New England Patriots (AFC) 24, Philadelphia Eagles (NFC) 21

Most wins: (5) San Francisco 49ers.

Football (American) (continued)

Super Bowl most valuable player

The player judged to have made the most outstanding contribution in the Super Bowl – the end of season meeting between the champions of the American Football Conference (AFC) and the National Football Conference (NFC).

1969	Joe Namath	Quarter Back	New York Jets	1989	Jerry Rice	Wide Receiver	San Francisco 49ers
1970	Len Dawson	Quarter Back	Kansas City Chiefs	1990	Joe Montana	Quarter Back	San Francisco 49ers
1971	Chuck Howley	Line Backer	Dallas Cowboys	1991	Ottis Anderson	Running Back	New York Giants
1972	Roger Staubach	Quarter Back	Dallas Cowboys	1992	Mark Rypien	Quarter Back	Washington Redskins
1973	Jake Scott	Safety	Miami Dolphins	1993	Troy Aikman	Quarter Back	Dallas Cowboys
1974	Larry Csonka	Running Back	Miami Dolphins	1994	Emmit Smith	Running Back	Dallas Cowboys
1975	Franco Harris	Running Back	Pittsburgh Steelers	1995	Steve Young	Quarter Back	San Francisco 49ers
1976	Lynn Swann	Wide Receiver	Pittsburgh Steelers	1996	Larry Brown	Corner Back	Dallas Cowboys
1977	Fred Biletnikoff	Wide Receiver	Oakland Raiders	1997	Desmond Howard	Wide Receiver	Green Bay Packers
1978	Randy White	Defensive Tackle	Dallas Cowboys				
	Harvey Martin	Defensive End	Dallas Cowboys	1998	Terrell Davis	Running Back	Denver Broncos
1979	Terry Bradshaw	Quarter Back	Pittsburgh Steelers	1999	John Elway	Quarter Back	Denver Broncos
1980	Terry Bradshaw	Quarter Back	Pittsburgh Steelers	2000	Kurt Warner	Quarter Back	St Louis Rams
1981	Jim Plunkett	Quarterback	Oakland Raiders	2001	Ray Lewis	Line Back	Baltimore Ravens
1982	Joe Montana	Quarter Back	San Francisco 49ers	2002	Tom Brady	Quarter Back	New England Patriots
1983	John Riggins	Running Back	Washington Redskins				
				2003	Dexter Jackson	Defensive Back	Tampa Bay Buccaneers
1984	Marcus Allen	Running Back	Los Angeles Raiders				
1985	Joe Montana	Quarter Back	San Francisco 49ers	2004	Tom Brady	Quarter Back	New England Patriots
1986	Richard Dent	Defensive End	Chicago Bears				
1987	Phil Simms	Quarter Back	New York Giants	2005	Deion Branch	Wide Receiver	New England Patriots
1988	Doug Williams	Quarter Back	Washington Redskins				

FOOTBALL (ASSOCIATION FOOTBALL/SOCCER)

FIFA World Cup

Association Football's premier event. First contested for the Jules Rimet Trophy in 1930; Brazil won it outright after winning for the third time in 1970. Since then teams have competed for the FIFA (*Fédération Internationale de Football Association*) World Cup; held every four years.

	Winner	Score	Runner-up	Final held in
1930	Uruguay	4–2	Argentina	Montevideo
1934	Italy	2–1	Czechoslovakia	Rome
1938	Italy	4–2	Hungary	Paris
1950	Uruguay	2–1	Brazil	Rio de Janeiro
1954	W Germany	3–2	Hungary	Berne
1958	Brazil	5–2	Sweden	Stockholm
1962	Brazil	3–1	Czechoslovakia	Santiago
1966	England	4–2	W Germany	London
1970	Brazil	4–1	Italy	Mexico City
1974	W Germany	2–1	Holland	Munich
1978	Argentina	3–1	Holland	Buenos Aires
1982	Italy	3–1	W Germany	Madrid
1986	Argentina	3–2	W Germany	Mexico City
1990	W Germany	1–0	Argentina	Rome
1994	Brazil	3–2[a]	Italy	California
1998	France	3–0	Brazil	Paris
2002	Brazil	2–0	Germany	Yokohama

[a]Penalties (after 0–0 result)
Must win: (5) Brazil, as above

Association football field

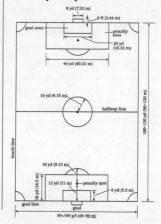

European Champions Cup

The leading club competition in Europe. Open to the League champions of countries affiliated to UEFA (Union of European Football Associations); commonly known as the 'European Cup'. Inaugurated in the 1955–6 season; played annually.

Recent winners

	Winner	Score	Runner-up
1983	SV Hamburg	1–0	Juventus
1984[a]	Liverpool	1–1	AS Roma
1985	Juventus	1–0	Liverpool
1986[b]	Steaua Bucharest	0–0	Barcelona
1987	FC Porto	2–1	Bayern Munich
1988[c]	PSV Eindhoven	0–0	Benfica
1989	AC Milan	4–0	Steaua Bucharest
1990	AC Milan	1–0	Benfica
1991[d]	Red Star Belgrade	0–0	Olympique Marseilles
1992	Barcelona	1–0	Sampdoria
1993	Olympique Marseilles[f]	1–0	AC Milan
1994	AC Milan	4–0	Barcelona
1995	Ajax	1–0	AC Milan
1996[e]	Juventus	1–1	Ajax
1997	Borussia Dortmund	3–1	Juventus
1998	Real Madrid	1–0	Juventus
1999	Manchester United	2–1	Bayern Munich
2000	Real Madrid	3–0	Valencia
2001[g]	Bayern Munich	1–1	Valencia
2002	Real Madrid	2–1	Bayer Leverkusen
2003	AC Milan[h]	0–0	Juventus
2004	FC Porto	3–0	AC Monaco

[a] Liverpool won 4–2 on penalties.
[b] Steaua won 2–0 on penalties.
[c] Eindhoven won 6–5 on penalties.
[d] Red Star won 5–3 on penalties.
[e] Juventus won 4–2 on penalties.
[f] Victory later cancelled following bribery allegations.
[g] Bayern Munich won 5–4 on penalties.
[h] AC Milan won 3–2 on penalties

Most wins: (9) Real Madrid (Spain): 1956–60, 1966, 1998, 2000, 2002.

South American championship

First held in 1916, for South American national sides. Discontinued in 1967, but revived eight years later; now played every two years; known as the Copa America.

Recent winners

1983	Uruguay
1987	Uruguay
1989	Brazil
1991	Argentina
1993	Argentina
1995	Uruguay
1997	Brazil
1999	Brazil
2001	Colombia
2004	Brazil

Most wins: (14) Uruguay: 1916–17, 1920, 1923–4, 1926, 1935, 1942, 1956, 1959, 1967, and as above; Argentina: 1921, 1925, 1927, 1929, 1937, 1941, 1945–7, 1955, 1957, 1959, and as above.

European Cup-Winners' Cup

Annual club competition, open to the main cup winners from all the UEFA countries; inaugurated in 1961, when the final was played over two legs. Since 1962 there has been a single game final. The competition ceased in 1999.

Recent winners

1986	Dynamo Kiev	1993	Parma
1987	Ajax	1994	Arsenal
1988	Mechelen	1995	Real Zaragoza
1989	Barcelona	1996	Paris St Germain
1990	Sampdoria	1997	Barcelona
1991	Manchester United	1998	Chelsea
1992	Werder Bremen	1999	Lazio

Most wins: (4) Barcelona: 1979, 1982, 1989, 1997.

UEFA Cup

Originally the International Industries Fairs Inter-Cities Cup (more commonly the 'Fairs Cup'). It was first contested in 1955, and became the UEFA Cup in 1971. Each participating nation is allotted a certain number of team places. The final is played over two legs.

Recent winners

1985	Real Madrid	1995	Parma
1986	Real Madrid	1996	Bayern Munich
1987	IFK Gothenburg	1997	Schalke
1988	Bayer Leverkusen	1998	Internazionale Milan
1989	Napoli	1999	Parma
1990	Juventus	2000	Galatasaray
1991	Inter Milan	2001	Liverpool
1992	Ajax	2002	Feyenoord
1993	Juventus	2003	FC Porto
1994	Inter Milan	2004	Valencia

Most wins: (3) Barcelona: 1958, 1960, 1966.

European championship

Held every four years since 1960; qualifying group matches held over the two years preceding the final.

	Winner	Score	Runner-up	Final held in
1960	USSR	2–1	Yugoslavia	Paris
1964	Spain	2–1	USSR	Madrid
1968[a]	Italy	2–1	Yugoslavia	Rome
1972	W Germany	3–0	USSR	Brussels
1976[b]	Czechoslovakia	2–2	W Germany	Belgrade
1980	W Germany	2–1	Belgium	Rome
1984	France	2–0	Spain	Paris
1988	Holland	2–0	USSR	Munich
1992	Denmark	2–0	Germany	Gothenburg
1996	Germany	2–1	Czech Republic	London
2000	France	2–1	Italy	Rotterdam
2004	Greece	1–0	Portugal	Lisbon

[a] Replay after 1–1 draw.
[b] Czechoslovakia won 5–2 on penalties.

Most wins: (3) Germany: as above.

Football League

The oldest league in the world, founded in 1888; consists of four divisions; the current complement of 92 teams achieved in 1950. Prior to the start of the 1992–93 season, the 22 teams of the 1st division voted to form the FA Premier League, divisions 2, 3 and 4 becoming League divisions 1, 2 and 3 respectively; the system of promotion and relegation remained unchanged. From the start of the 2004–5 season, the 1st division was renamed the Championship, and divisions 2 and 3 became League 1 and League 2 respectively. Sponsors have been Canon (1983–6), Barclays Bank (1987–92), Endsleigh Insurance (1993–5), Nationwide Building Society (1996–2003), and Coca-Cola (2004–).

League champions

1888–89	Preston North End
1889–90	Preston North End
1890–91	Everton
1891–92	Sunderland
1892–93	Sunderland
1893–94	Aston Villa
1894–95	Sunderland
1895–96	Aston Villa
1896–97	Aston Villa
1897–98	Sheffield United
1898–99	Aston Villa
1899–1900	Aston Villa
1900–01	Liverpool
1901–02	Sunderland
1902–03	Sheffield Wednesday
1903–04	Sheffield Wednesday
1904–05	Newcastle United
1905–06	Liverpool
1906–07	Newcastle United
1907–08	Manchester United
1908–09	Newcastle United
1909–10	Aston Villa
1910–11	Manchester United
1911–12	Blackburn Rovers
1912–13	Sunderland
1913–14	Blackburn Rovers
1914–15	Everton
1919–20	West Bromwich Albion
1920–21	Burnley
1921–22	Liverpool
1922–23	Liverpool
1923–24	Huddersfield Town
1924–25	Huddersfield Town
1925–26	Huddersfield Town
1926–27	Newcastle United
1927–28	Everton
1928–29	Sheffield Wednesday
1929–30	Sheffield Wednesday
1930–31	Arsenal
1931–32	Everton
1932–33	Arsenal
1933–34	Arsenal
1934–35	Arsenal
1935–36	Sunderland
1936–37	Manchester City
1937–38	Arsenal
1938–39	Everton
1946–47	Liverpool
1947–48	Arsenal
1948–49	Portsmouth
1949–50	Portsmouth
1950–51	Tottenham Hotspur
1951–52	Manchester United
1952–53	Arsenal
1953–54	Wolverhampton Wanderers
1954–55	Chelsea
1955–56	Manchester United
1956–57	Manchester United
1957–58	Wolverhampton Wanderers
1958–59	Wolverhampton Wanderers
1959–60	Burnley
1960–61	Tottenham Hotspur
1961–62	Ipswich Town
1962–63	Everton
1963–64	Liverpool
1964–65	Manchester United
1965–66	Liverpool
1966–67	Manchester United
1967–68	Manchester City
1968–69	Leeds United
1969–70	Everton
1970–71	Arsenal
1971–72	Derby County
1972–73	Liverpool
1973–74	Leeds United
1974–75	Derby County
1975–76	Liverpool
1976–77	Liverpool
1977–78	Nottingham Forest
1978–79	Liverpool
1979–80	Liverpool
1980–81	Aston Villa
1981–82	Liverpool
1982–83	Liverpool
1983–84	Liverpool
1984–85	Everton
1985–86	Liverpool
1986–87	Everton
1987–88	Liverpool
1988–89	Arsenal
1989–90	Liverpool
1990–91	Arsenal
1991–92	Leeds United
1992–93	Manchester United
1993–94	Manchester United
1994–95	Blackburn Rovers
1995–96	Manchester United
1996–97	Manchester United
1997–98	Arsenal
1998–99	Manchester United
1999–2000	Manchester United
2000–1	Manchester United
2001–2	Arsenal
2002–3	Manchester United
2003–4	Arsenal
2004–5	Chelsea

Most wins: (18) Liverpool: 1901, 1906, 1922–3, 1947, 1964, 1966, 1973, 1976–7, 1979–80, 1982–4, 1986, 1988, 1990.

Football League Cup

Inaugurated in 1961, it is competed for by the 92 clubs of the Football League. From 1982 to 1986 it was known as the Milk Cup; 1986–90 as the Littlewoods Cup; 1990–2 as the Rumbelows Cup; 1992–3 as the Coca-Cola Cup; 1998–9 as the Worthington Cup; and from 2003 as the Carling Cup.

Recent winners

1981	Liverpool
1982	Liverpool
1983	Liverpool
1984	Liverpool
1985	Norwich City
1986	Oxford United
1987	Arsenal
1988	Luton Town
1989	Nottingham Forest
1990	Nottingham Forest
1991	Sheffield Wednesday
1992	Manchester United
1993	Arsenal
1994	Aston Villa
1995	Liverpool
1996	Aston Villa
1997	Leicester City
1998	Chelsea
1999	Tottenham Hotspur
2000	Leicester City
2001	Liverpool
2002	Blackburn Rovers
2003	Liverpool
2004	Middlesbrough
2005	Chelsea

Most wins: (7) Liverpool: as above.

Football Association Challenge Cup

The world's oldest club knockout competition (the 'FA cup'), held annually, it is open to both League and non-League teams; first contested in the 1871–2 season; first final at the Kennington Oval on 16 March 1872; first winners were the Wanderers. Played at Wembley since 1923.

	Winners	Score	Runner-up
1871–72	Wanderers	1–0	Royal Engineers
1872–73	Wanderers	2–0	Oxford University
1873–74	Oxford University	2–0	Royal Engineers
1874–75	Royal Engineers	1–1, 2–0	Old Etonians
1875–76	Wanderers	1–1, 3–0	Old Etonians
1876–77	Wanderers	2–1	Oxford University
1877–78	Wanderers	3–1	Royal Engineers
1878–79	Old Etonians	1–0	Clapham Rovers
1879–80	Clapham Rovers	1–0	Oxford University
1880–81	Old Carthusians	3–0	Old Etonians
1881–82	Old Etonians	1–0	Blackburn Rovers
1882–83	Blackburn Olympic	2–1	Old Etonians
1883–84	Blackburn Rovers	2–1	Queen's Park
1884–85	Blackburn Rovers	2–0	Queen's Park
1885–86	Blackburn Rovers	0–0, 2–0	West Bromwich Albion
1886–97	Aston Villa	2–0	West Bromwich Albion
1887–88	West Bromwich Albion	2–1	Preston North End
1888–89	Preston North End	3–0	Wolverhampton Wanderers
1889–90	Blackburn Rovers	6–1	Sheffield Wednesday
1890–91	Blackburn Rovers	3–1	Notts County
1891–92	West Bromwich Albion	3–0	Aston Villa
1892–93	Wolverhampton Wanderers	1–0	Everton
1893–94	Notts County	4–1	Bolton Wanderers
1894–95	Aston Villa	1–0	West Bromwich Albion
1895–96	Sheffield Wednesday	2–1	Wolverhampton Wanderers
1896–97	Aston Villa	3–2	Everton
1897–98	Nottingham Forest	3–1	Derby County
1898–99	Sheffield United	4–1	Derby County
1899–1900	Bury	4–0	Southampton
1900–01	Tottenham Hotspur	2–2, 3–1	Sheffield United
1901–02	Sheffield United	1–1, 2–1	Southampton
1902–03	Bury	6–0	Derby County
1903–04	Manchester City	1–0	Bolton Wanderers
1904–05	Aston Villa	2–0	Newcastle United
1905–06	Everton	1–0	Newcastle United
1906–07	Sheffield Wednesday	2–1	Everton
1907–08	Wolverhampton Wanderers	3–1	Newcastle United
1908–09	Manchester United	1–0	Bristol City
1909–10	Newcastle United	1–1, 2–0	Barnsley
1910–11	Bradford City	0–0, 1–0	Newcastle United
1911–12	Barnsley	0–0, 1–0	West Bromwich Albion
1912–13	Aston Villa	1–0	Sunderland
1913–14	Burnley	1–0	Liverpool
1914–15	Sheffield United	3–0	Chelsea
1919–20	Aston Villa	1–0	Huddersfield Town
1920–21	Tottenham Hotspur	1–0	Wolverhampton Wanderers
1921–22	Huddersfield Town	1–0	Preston North End
1922–23	Bolton Wanderers	2–0	West Ham United
1923–24	Newcastle United	2–0	Aston Villa
1924–25	Sheffield United	1–0	Cardiff City
1925–26	Bolton Wanderers	1–0	Manchester City
1926–27	Cardiff City	1–0	Arsenal
1927–28	Blackburn Rovers	3–1	Huddersfield Town
1928–29	Bolton Wanderers	2–0	Portsmouth
1929–30	Arsenal	2–0	Huddersfield Town
1930–31	West Bromwich Albion	2–1	Birmingham City
1931–32	Newcastle United	2–1	Arsenal
1932–33	Everton	3–0	Manchester City
1933–34	Manchester City	2–1	Portsmouth
1934–35	Sheffield Wednesday	4–2	West Bromwich Albion

Football Association Challenge Cup (continued)

	Winners	Score	Runner-up
1935–36	Arsenal	1–0	Sheffield United
1936–37	Sunderland	3–1	Preston North End
1937–38	Preston North End	1–0	Huddersfield Town
1938–39	Portsmouth	4–1	Wolverhampton Wanderers
1945–46	Derby County	4–1	Charlton Athletic
1946–47	Charlton Athletic	1–0	Burnley
1947–48	Manchester United	4–2	Blackpool
1948–49	Wolverhampton Wanderers	3–1	Leicester City
1949–50	Arsenal	2–0	Liverpool
1950–51	Newcastle United	2–0	Blackpool
1951–52	Newcastle United	1–0	Arsenal
1952–53	Blackpool	4–3	Bolton Wanderers
1953–54	West Bromwich Albion	3–2	Preston North End
1954–55	Newcastle United	3–1	Manchester City
1955–56	Manchester City	3–1	Birmingham City
1956–57	Aston Villa	2–1	Manchester United
1957–58	Bolton Wanderers	2–0	Manchester United
1958–59	Nottingham Forest	2–1	Luton Town
1959–60	Wolverhampton Wanderers	3–0	Blackburn Rovers
1960–61	Tottenham Hotspur	2–0	Leicester City
1961–62	Tottenham Hotspur	3–1	Burnley
1962–63	Manchester United	3–1	Leicester City
1963–64	West Ham United	3–2	Preston North End
1964–65	Liverpool	2–1	Leeds United
1965–66	Everton	3–2	Sheffield Wednesday
1966–67	Tottenham Hotspur	2–1	Chelsea
1967–68	West Bromwich Albion	1–0	Everton
1968–69	Manchester City	1–0	Leicester City
1969–70	Chelsea	2–2, 2–1	Leeds United
1970–71	Arsenal	2–1	Liverpool
1971–72	Leeds United	1–0	Arsenal
1972–73	Sunderland	1–0	Leeds United
1973–74	Liverpool	3–0	Newcastle United
1974–75	West Ham United	2–0	Fulham
1975–76	Southampton	1–0	Manchester United
1976–77	Manchester United	2–1	Liverpool
1977–78	Ipswich Town	1–0	Arsenal
1978–79	Arsenal	3–2	Manchester United
1979–80	West Ham United	1–0	Arsenal
1980–81	Tottenham Hotspur	1–1, 3–2	Manchester City
1981–82	Tottenham Hotspur	1–1, 1–0	Queen's Park Rangers
1982–83	Manchester United	2–2, 4–0	Brighton & Hove Albion
1983–84	Everton	2–0	Watford
1984–85	Manchester United	1–0	Everton
1985–86	Liverpool	3–1	Everton
1986–87	Coventry City	3–2	Tottenham Hotspur
1987–88	Wimbledon	1–0	Liverpool
1988–89	Liverpool	3–2	Everton
1989–90	Manchester United	3–3, 1–0	Crystal Palace
1990–91	Tottenham Hotspur	2–1	Nottingham Forest
1991–92	Liverpool	2–0	Sunderland
1992–93	Arsenal	1–1, 2–1	Sheffield Wednesday
1993–94	Manchester United	4–0	Chelsea
1994–95	Everton	1–0	Manchester United
1995–96	Manchester United	1–0	Liverpool
1996–97	Chelsea	2–0	Middlesbrough
1997–98	Arsenal	2–0	Newcastle United
1998–99	Manchester United	2–0	Newcastle United
1999–2000	Chelsea	1–0	Aston Villa
2000–1	Liverpool	2–1	Arsenal
2001–2	Arsenal	2–0	Chelsea
2002–3	Arsenal	1–0	Southampton
2003–4	Manchester United	3–0	Millwall

Most wins: (11) Manchester United, as above.

Scottish Premier League

Formed in 1890, with a second division added in 1893. The present format (Premier Division, Division 1, Division 2) was arrived at in 1975.

Recent winners

1985–86	Celtic
1986–87	Rangers
1987–88	Celtic
1988–89	Rangers
1989–90	Rangers
1990–91	Rangers
1991–92	Rangers
1992–93	Rangers
1993–94	Rangers
1994–95	Rangers
1995–96	Rangers
1996–97	Rangers
1997–98	Celtic
1998–9	Rangers
1999–2000	Rangers
2000–1	Celtic
2001–2	Celtic
2002–3	Rangers
2003–4	Celtic

Most wins: (51) Rangers.

Scottish FA Cup

First played in 1874; held at Hampden Park.

Recent winners

1990	Aberdeen
1991	Motherwell
1992	Rangers
1993	Rangers
1994	Dundee United
1995	Celtic
1996	Rangers
1997	Kilmarnock
1998	Heart of Midlothian
1999	Rangers
2000	Rangers
2001	Celtic
2002	Rangers
2003	Rangers
2004	Celtic

Most wins: (32) Celtic.

Clubs of the English Football League

Team	Nickname	Ground
Arsenal	Gunners	Highbury
Aston Villa	Villans	Villa Park
Barnsley	Tykes	Oakwell
Birmingham City	Blues	St Andrews
Blackburn Rovers	Blue-and-Whites	Ewood Park
Blackpool	Seasiders	Bloomfield Road
Bolton Wanderers	Trotters	Reebok Stadium
Boston United	Pilgrims	York Street Stadium
Bournemouth	Cherries	Dean Court
Bradford City	Bantams	Bradford and Bingley Stadium
Brentford	Bees	Griffin Park
Brighton and Hove Albion	Seagulls	Priestfield
Bristol City	Robins	Ashton Gate
Bristol Rovers	Pirates	Memorial Ground
Burnley	Clarets	Turf Moor
Bury	Shakers	Gigg Lane
Cambridge United	'U's	Abbey Stadium
Cardiff City	Bluebirds	Ninian Park
Carlisle United	Cumbrians	Brunton Park
Charlton Athletic	Addicks	The Valley
Chelsea	Blues	Stamford Bridge
Cheltenham Town	Robins	Whaddon Road
Chesterfield	Spireites	Saltergate
Colchester United	'U's	Layer Road
Coventry City	Sky Blues	Highfield Road
Crewe Alexandra	Railwaymen	Gresty Road
Crystal Palace	Eagles	Selhurst Park
Darlington	Quakers	Feethams
Derby County	Rams	Pride Park
Everton	Toffeemen	Goodison Park
Exeter City	Grecians	St James Park
Fulham	Cottagers	Craven Cottage
Gillingham	Gills	Priestfield
Grimsby Town	Mariners	Blundell Park
Hartlepool United	Pool	Victoria Ground
Huddersfield Town	Terriers	MacAlpine Stadium
Hull City	Tigers	Boothferry Park
Ipswich Town	Blues/Tractor Boys	Portman Road
Kidderminster Harriers	Reds	Aggborough Stadium
Leeds United	The Whites	Elland Road
Leicester City	Foxes	Walkers Stadium
Leyton Orient	'O's	Matchroom Stadium
Lincoln City	Imps	Sincil Bank
Liverpool	Reds	Anfield
Luton Town	Hatters	Kenilworth Road
Macclesfield Town	Silkmen	Mose Rose
Manchester City	Blues/Citizens	City of Manchester Stadium
Manchester United	Red Devils	Old Trafford
Mansfield Town	Stags	Field Mill
Middlesbrough	Boro	Cellnet Riverside Stadium
Millwall	Lions	The New Den
Newcastle United	Magpies/The Toon	St James' Park
Northampton Town	Cobblers	Sixfields Stadium
Norwich City	Canaries	Carrow Road
Nottingham Forest	Reds	City Ground
Notts County	Magpies	Meadow Lane
Oldham Athletic	Latics	Boundary Park
Oxford United	'U's	Kassam Stadium
Peterborough United	Posh	London Road
Plymouth Argyle	Pilgrims	Home Park
Portsmouth	Pompey	Fratton Park
Port Vale	Valiants	Vale Park
Preston North End	Lillywhites	Deepdale
Queen's Park Rangers	Superhoops	Loftus Road
Reading	Royals	Madejski Stadium
Rochdale	Dale	Spotland
Rotherham United	Millers	Millmoor
Rushden and Diamonds	Diamonds	Nene Park
Scunthorpe United	Irons	Glanford Park
Sheffield United	Blades	Bramall Lane
Sheffield Wednesday	Owls	Hillsborough
Shrewsbury Town	Shrews	Gay Meadow
Southampton	Saints	Friends Provident St Mary's Stadium
Southend United	Shrimpers	Roots Hall
Stockport County	Hatters	Edgeley Park
Stoke City	Potters	Britannia Ground
Sunderland	Black Cats/Rokerites	Stadium of Light
Swansea City	Swans	Vetch Field
Swindon Town	Robins	County Ground
Torquay United	Gulls	Plainmoor
Tottenham Hotspur	Spurs	White Hart Lane
Tranmere Rovers	Rovers	Prenton Park
Walsall	Saddlers	Bescot Stadium
Watford	Hornets	Vicarage Road
West Bromwich Albion	Baggies	The Hawthorns
West Ham United	Hammers	Boleyn Ground
Wigan Athletic	Latics	JJB Stadium
Wimbledon	Dons	Selhurst Park Ground
Wolverhampton Wanderers	Wolves	Molineux
Wrexham	Robins	Racecourse Ground
Wycombe Wanderers	Chairboys	Adams Park
York City	Minstermen	Bootham Crescent

FOOTBALL (AUSTRALIAN)

Australian Football League

Known as the Victoria Football League until 1987, when teams from Western Australia and Queensland joined the league. The top prize is the annual VFL Premiership Trophy.

Premiership Trophy

First contested in 1897 and won by Essendon.

Recent winners

1991 Hawthorn
1992 West Coast Eagles
1993 Essendon
1994 West Coast Eagles
1995 Carlton
1996 North Melbourne
1997 Adelaide Crows
1998 Adelaide Crows
1999 North Melbourne
2000 Essendon
2001 Brisbane Lions
2002 Brisbane Lions
2003 Brisbane Lions
2004 Port Adelaide

Most wins: (16) Carlton: 1906–8, 1914–15, 1938, 1945, 1947, 1968, 1970, 1972, 1979, 1981–2, 1987, 1995.

Australian football field

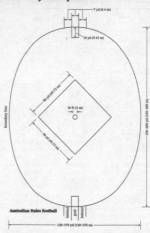

Australian Rules football

FOOTBALL (GAELIC)

All-Ireland championship

First held in 1887. Takes place in Dublin in September each year.

Recent winners

1989 Cork
1990 Cork
1991 Down
1992 Donegal
1993 Derry
1994 Down
1995 Dublin
1996 Meath
1997 Kerry
1998 Galway
1999 Meath
2000 Kerry
2001 Galway
2002 Armagh
2003 Tyrone
2004 Kerry

Most wins: (33) Kerry: 1903–4, 1909, 1913–14, 1924, 1926, 1929–32, 1937, 1939–41, 1946, 1953, 1955, 1959, 1962, 1969–70, 1975, 1978–81, 1984–6, 1997, 2000, 2004.

GLIDING

World championships

First held in 1937. Current classes are Open, Standard, and 15 metres. The Open class is the principal event, held every two years until 1978 and again since 1981.

Recent winners: open category

1972 Göran Ax (Sweden)
1974 George Moffat (USA)
1976 George Lee (Great Britain)
1978 George Lee (Great Britain)
1981 George Lee (Great Britain)
1983 Ingo Renner (Australia)
1985 Ingo Renner (Australia)
1987 Ingo Renner (Australia)
1989 Claude Lopitaux (France)
1991 Janusz Centka (Poland)
1993 Andy Davis (Great Britain)
1995 Raymond Lynskey (New Zealand)
1997 Gerard Lherm (France)
1999 Holger Karow (Germany)
2001 Oscar Goudriaan (South Africa)
2003 Holger Karow (Germany)

Most wins: (3) George Lee and Ingo Renner: as above.

GOLF

Open

First held at Prestwick, UK, in 1860, and won by Willie Park. Takes place annually; regarded as the world's leading golf tournament.

Recent winners

1985 Sandy Lyle (Great Britain)
1986 Greg Norman (Australia)
1987 Nick Faldo (Great Britain)
1988 Severiano Ballesteros (Spain)
1989 Mark Calcavecchia (USA)
1990 Nick Faldo (Great Britain)
1991 Ian Baker-Finch (Australia)
1992 Nick Faldo (Great Britain)
1993 Greg Norman (Australia)
1994 Nick Price (Zimbabwe)
1995 John Daley (USA)
1996 Tom Lehman (USA)
1997 Justin Leonard (USA)
1998 Mark O'Meara (USA)
1999 Paul Lawrie (Great Britain)
2000 Tiger Woods (USA)
2001 Tiger Woods (USA)
2002 Ernie Els (South Africa)
2003 Ben Curtis (USA)
2004 Todd Hamilton (USA)

Most wins: (6) Harry Vardon (Great Britain): 1896, 1898–9, 1903, 1911, 1914.

United States Open

First held at Newport, Rhode Island, in 1895, and won by Horace Rawlins. Takes place annually.

Recent winners
1991 Payne Stewart (USA)
1992 Tom Kite (USA)
1993 Lee Janzen (USA)
1994 Ernie Els (South Africa)
1995 Corey Pavin (USA)
1996 Steve Jones (USA)
1997 Ernie Els (South Africa)
1998 Lee Janzen (USA)
1999 Payne Stewart (USA)
2000 Tiger Woods (USA)
2001 Retief Goosen (South Africa)
2002 Tiger Woods (USA)
2003 Jim Furyk (USA)
2004 Retief Goosen (South Africa)

Most wins: (4) Willie Anderson (USA): 1901, 1903–5; Bobby Jones (USA): 1923, 1926, 1929–30; Ben Hogan (USA): 1948, 1950–1, 1953; Jack Nicklaus (USA): 1962, 1967, 1972, 1980.

US Masters

First held in 1934. Takes place at the Augusta National course in Georgia every April.

Recent winners
1992 Fred Couples (USA)
1993 Bernard Langer (Germany)
1994 José María Olázabal (Spain)
1995 Ben Crenshaw (USA)
1996 Nick Faldo (Great Britain)
1997 Tiger Woods (USA)
1998 Mark O'Meara (USA)
1999 José María Olázabal (Spain)
2000 Vijay Singh (Fiji)
2001 Tiger Woods (USA)
2002 Tiger Woods (USA)
2003 Mike Weir (Canada)
2004 Phil Mickelson (USA)
2005 Tiger Woods (USA)

Most wins: (6) Jack Nicklaus (USA): 1963, 1965–6, 1972, 1975, 1986.

United States PGA championship

The last of the season's four 'Majors'; first held in 1916, and a match-play event until 1958. Takes place annually.

Recent winners
1991 John Daly (USA)
1992 Nick Price (Zimbabwe)
1993 Paul Azinger (USA)
1994 Nick Price (Zimbabwe)
1995 Steve Elkington (Australia)
1996 Mark Brooks (USA)
1997 Davis Love III (USA)
1998 Vijay Singh (Fiji)
1999 Tiger Woods (USA)
2000 Tiger Woods (USA)
2001 David Toms (USA)
2002 Rich Beem (USA)
2003 Shaun Micheel (USA)
2004 Vijay Singh (Fiji)

Most wins: (5) Walter Hagen (USA): 1921, 1924–7; Jack Nicklaus (USA): 1963, 1971, 1973, 1975, 1980.

Ryder Cup

The leading international team tournament, first held at Worcester, Massachusetts, in 1927. Takes place every two years between teams from the USA and Europe (Great Britain 1927–71; Great Britain and Ireland 1973–7).

Recent winners
1983	USA	14½–13½
1985	Europe	16½–11½
1987	Europe	15–13
1989	Drawn	14–14
1991	USA	14½–13½
1993	USA	15–13
1995	Europe	14½–13½
1997	Europe	14½–13½
1999	USA	14½–13½
2001	*not held*	
2002	Europe	15½–12½
2004	Europe	18½–9½

Wins: (24) USA: during 1927–99. (3), Great Britain: 1929, 1933, 1957. (5), Europe: 1985, 1987, 1995, 1997. (2), Drawn: 1969, 1989, 2002.

GREYHOUND RACING

Greyhound Derby

The top race of the British season, first held in 1927. Run at the White City every year (except 1940) until its closure in 1985; since then all races run at Wimbledon.

Recent winners
1987 Signal Spark
1988 Hit the Lid
1989 Lartigue Note
1990 Slippy Blue
1991 Ballinderry Ash
1992 Farloe Melody
1993 Arfur Daley
1994 Ringa Hustle
1995 Moaning Lad
1996 Shanless Slippy
1997 Some Picture
1998 Toms The Best
1999 Chart King
2000 Rapid Ranger
2001 Rapid Ranger
2002 Allen Gift
2003 Droopys Hewitt
2004 Droopys Scholes

Most wins: (2) Mick the Miller: 1929–30; Patricia's Hope: 1972–3; Rapid Ranger 2000–1.

GYMNASTICS

World championships

First held in 1903. Took place every four years, 1922–78; since 1979, usually every two years.

Recent winners: individual combined exercises – men
1981 Yuriy Korolev (USSR)
1983 Dmitri Belozerchev (USSR)
1985 Yuriy Korolev (USSR)
1987 Dmitri Belozerchev (USSR)
1989 Igor Korobichensky (USSR)
1991 Grigoriy Misutin (USSR)
1993 Vitaly Shcherbo (Belarus)
1994 Ivan Ivankov (Belarus)
1995 Li Xiaoshuang (China)
1997 Ivan Ivankova (Belarus)
1999 Nikolay Krukov (Russia)
2001 Feng Jing (China)
2003 Paul Hamm (USA)

Recent winners: team – men
1981	USSR	1994	China
1983	China	1995	China
1985	USSR	1997	China
1987	USSR	1999	China
1989	USSR	2001	Belarus
1991	USSR	2003	China

Most wins: Individual (2) Marco Torrès (France): 1909, 1913; Peter Sumi (Yugoslavia): 1922, 1926; Yuriy Korolev and Dmitri Belozerchev: as above. Team (8) USSR: 1954, 1958, and as above.

Recent winners: individual combined exercises – women
1978 Yelena Mukhina (USSR)
1979 Nelli Kim (USSR)
1981 Olga Bitcherova (USSR)
1983 Natalia Yurchenko (USSR)
1985 Yelena Shoushounova (USSR) and Oksana Omeliantchuk (USSR)
1987 Aurelia Dobre (Romania)
1989 Svetlana Boginskaya (USSR)
1991 Kim Zmeskal (USA)
1993 Shannon Miller (USA)
1994 Shannon Miller (USA)
1995 Lilia Podkopayeva (Ukraine)
1997 Svetlana Khorkina (Russia)
1999 Maria Olaru (Romania)
2001 Svetlana Khorkina (Russia)
2003 Svetlana Khorkina (Russia)

Gymnastics (continued)

Recent winners team – women

1981	USSR
1983	USSR
1985	USSR
1987	Romania
1989	USSR
1991	USSR
1994	Romania
1995	Romania
1997	Romania
1999	Romania
2001	Romania
2003	USA

Most wins: Individual (3) Svetlana Khorkina (Russia): as above. Team (10) USSR: 1954, 1958, 1970, 1974, 1978 and as above.

Olympic Games

Gold medal winners: 2004

Combined exercises: men

Individual
Paul Hamm (USA)

Team
Japan

Gold medal winners: 2004

Combined exercises: women

Individual
Carly Patterson (USA)

Team
Romania

HANDBALL

World championships

First men's championships held in 1938, both indoors and outdoors (latter discontinued in 1966). First women's outdoor championships in 1949 (discontinued in 1960); first women's indoor championships in 1957.

Winners: indoors – men

1961	Romania
1964	Romania
1967	Czechoslovakia
1970	Romania
1974	Romania
1978	W Germany
1982	USSR
1986	Yugoslavia
1990	Sweden
1993	Russia
1995	France
1997	Russia
1999	Sweden
2001	France
2003	Croatia

Winners: outdoors – men

1938	Germany
1948	Sweden
1952	W Germany
1955	W Germany
1959	E/W Germany (combined)
1963	E Germany
1966	W Germany

Most wins: Indoors (4) Romania as above, Sweden: 1954, 1958 and as above. Outdoors (4) W Germany (including 1 as combined E/W German team): as above.

Winners: indoors – women

1962	Romania
1965	Hungary
1971	E Germany
1973	Yugoslavia
1975	E Germany
1979	E Germany
1982	USSR
1986	USSR
1990	USSR
1993	Germany
1995	Germany
1997	Denmark
1999	Norway
2001	Russia
2003	France

Winners: outdoors – women

1949	Hungary
1956	Romania
1960	Romania

Most wins: Indoors (3) E Germany: as above. Outdoors (2) Romania: as above.

Olympic Games

Gold medal winners: 2004

Men	Croatia
Women	Denmark

HANG GLIDING

World championships

First held officially in 1976; since 1979, usually takes place every two years.

Winners: individual – class 1

1985	John Pendry (Great Britain)
1987	Rich Duncan (Australia)
1989	Robert Whittall (Great Britain)
1991	Tomás Suchanek (Czechoslovakia)
1993	Tomás Suchanek (Czech Republic)
1995	Tomás Suchanek (Czech Republic)
1998	Guido Gehrmann (Germany)
1999	Manfred Ruhmer (Austria)
2001	Manfred Ruhmer (Austria)
2003	Manfred Ruhmer (Austria)

Winners: team

1985	Great Britain
1987	Australia
1989	Great Britain
1991	Great Britain
1993	USA
1995	Austria
1998	Austria
1999	Brazil
2001	Austria
2003	Austria

Most wins: Individual (3) Tomás Suchanek (Czech Republic) as above; Manfred Ruhmer (Austria) as above. Team (5) Austria: 1976 and as above.

HOCKEY

World Cup

Men's tournament first held in 1971, and every four years since 1978. Women's tournament first held in 1974, and now takes place every four years.

Hockey field

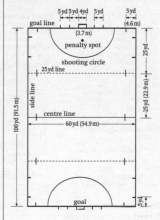

Recent winners: men		*Recent winners: women*	
1978	Pakistan	1981	W Germany
1982	Pakistan	1983	Netherlands
1986	Australia	1986	Netherlands
1990	Netherlands	1990	Netherlands
1994	Pakistan	1994	Australia
1998	Netherlands	1998	Australia
2002	Germany	2002	Argentina

Most wins: (4) Pakistan: 1971, and as above.

Most wins: (5) Netherlands: 1974, 1978, and as above.

Olympic Games

Regarded as hockey's leading competition. First held in 1908; included at every celebration since 1928; women's competition first held in 1980.

Recent winners: men		*Recent winners: women*	
1956	India	1980	Zimbabwe
1960	Pakistan	1984	Netherlands
1964	India	1988	Australia
1968	Pakistan	1992	Spain
1972	W Germany	1996	Australia
1976	New Zealand	2000	Australia
1980	India	2004	Germany
1984	Pakistan		
1988	Great Britain		
1992	Germany		
1996	Netherlands		
2000	Netherlands		
2004	Australia		

Most wins: Men (8) India: 1928, 1932, 1936, 1948, 1952 and as above. Women (3) Australia: as above.

HORSE RACING

The English Classics are five races run from April to September each year for three-year-olds: The Derby; The Oaks; One Thousand Guineas; Two Thousand Guineas; and St Leger.

The Derby

The 'Blue Riband' of the Turf; run at Epsom over 1¹/₂ miles. First run in 1780.

Recent winners

1988	Kahyasi (Ray Cochrane)
1989	Nashwan (Willie Carson)
1990	Quest for Fame (Pat Eddery)
1991	Generous (Alan Munro)
1992	Dr Devious (John Reid)
1993	Commander-In-Chief (Michael Kinane)
1994	Erhaab (Willie Carson)
1995	Lammtarra (Walter Swinburn)
1996	Shaamit (Michael Hills)
1997	Benny The Dip (Willie Ryan)
1998	High Rise (Olivier Peslier)
1999	Oath (Kieren Fallon)
2000	Sinndar (Johnny Murtagh)
2001	Galileo (Michael Kinane)
2002	High Chaparral (Johnny Murtagh)
2003	Kris Kin (Kieren Fallon)
2004	North Light (Kieren Fallon)

Most wins: Jockey (9) Lester Piggott: 1954, 1957, 1960, 1968, 1970, 1972, 1976–7, 1983.

The Oaks

Raced at Epsom over 1¹/₂ miles; for fillies only. First run in 1779.

Recent winners

1989	Snow Bride (Steve Cauthen)
1990	Salsabil (Willie Carson)
1991	Jet Ski Lady (Christy Roche)
1992	User Friendly (George Duffield)
1993	Intrepidity (Michael Roberts)
1994	Balanchine (Lanfranco Dettori)
1995	Moonshell (Lanfranco Dettori)
1996	Lady Carla (Pat Eddery)
1997	Reams of Verse (Kieren Fallon)
1998	Shahtoush (Michael Kinane)
1999	Ramruma (Kieren Fallon)
2000	Love Divine (Richard Quinn)
2001	Imagine (Michael Kinane)
2002	Kazzia (Lanfranco Dettori)
2003	Casual Look (Martin Dwyer)
2004	Ouija Board (Kieren Fallon)

Most wins: Jockey (9) Frank Buckle: 1797–9, 1802–3, 1805, 1817–18, 1823.

Horse racing (continued)

One Thousand Guineas

Run over 1 mile at Newmarket; for fillies only. First run in 1814.

Recent winners
1989 Musical Bliss (Walter Swinburn)
1990 Salsabil (Willie Carson)
1991 Shadayid (Willie Carson)
1992 Hatoof (Walter Swinburn)
1993 Sayyedati (Walter Swinburn)
1994 Las Meninas (John Reid)
1995 Harayir (Richard Ellis)
1996 Bosra Sham (Pat Eddery)
1997 Sleepytime (Kieren Fallon)
1998 Cape Verdi (Frankie Dettori)
1999 Wince (Kieren Fallon)
2000 Lahan (Richard Hills)
2001 Ameerat (Philip Johnson)
2002 Kazzia (Lanfranco Dettori)
2003 Russian Rhythm (Kieren Fallon)
2004 Attraction (Kevin Darley)

Most wins: Jockey (7) George Fordham: 1859, 1861, 1865, 1868–9, 1881, 1883.

Two Thousand Guineas

Run at Newmarket over 1 mile. First run in 1809.

Recent winners
1988 Doyoun (Walter Swinburn)
1989 Nashwan (Willie Carson)
1990 Tirol (Michael Kinane)
1991 Mystiko (Michael Roberts)
1992 Rodrigo de Triano (Lester Piggott)
1993 Zafonic (Pat Eddery)
1994 Mister Baileys (Jason Weaver)
1995 Pennekamp (Thierry Jarnet)
1996 Mark of Esteem (Lanfranco Dettori)
1997 Entrepreneur (Michael Kinane)
1998 King of Kings (Michael Kinane)
1999 Island Sands (Lanfranco Dettori)
2000 King's Best (Kieren Fallon)
2001 Golan (Kieren Fallon)
2002 Rock of Gibraltar (Johnny Murtagh)
2003 Refuse To Bend (Pat Smullen)
2004 Haafhd (Richard Hills)

Most wins: Jockey (9) Jem Robinson: 1825, 1828, 1831, 1833, 1847–8.

St Leger

The oldest of the five English classics, first run in 1776. Raced at Doncaster annually over 1 mile 6 furlongs 127 yards.

Recent winners
1991 Toulon (Pat Eddery)
1992 User Friendly (George Duffield)
1993 Bob's Return (Philip Robinson)
1994 Moonax (Pat Eddery)
1995 Classic Cliche (Lanfranco Dettori)
1996 Shantou (Lanfranco Dettori)
1997 Silver Patriarch (Pat Eddery)
1998 Nedawi (John Reid)
1999 Mustafaweq (Richard Hills)
2000 Millenary (Richard Quinn)
2001 Milan (Michael Kinane)
2002 Bollin Eric (Kevin Darley)
2003 Brian Boru (Jamie Spencer)
2004 Rule of Law (Kerrin McEvoy)

Most wins: Jockey (9) Bill Scott: 1821, 1825, 1828–9, 1938–41, 1846.

Grand National

Steeplechasing's most famous race. First run at Maghull in 1836; at Aintree since 1839; war-time races at Gatwick, 1916–18.

Recent winners
1988 Rhyme 'N' Reason (Brendan Powell)
1989 Little Polveir (Jimmy Frost)
1990 Mr Frisk (Marcus Armytage)
1991 Seagram (Nigel Howke)
1992 Party Politics (Carl Llewellyn)
1993* Void
1994 Minnehoma (Richard Dunwoody)
1995 Royal Athlete (Jason Titley)
1996 Rough Quest (Mick Fitzgerald)
1997 Lord Gyllene (Tony Dobbin)
1998 Earth Summit (Carl Llewellyn)
1999 Bobbyjo (Paul Carberry)
2000 Papillon (Ruby Walsh)
2001 Red Marauder (Richard Guest)
2002 Bindaree (Jim Culloty)
2003 Monty's Pass (Barry Geraghty)
2004 Amberleigh House (Graham Lee)
2005 Hedgehunter (Ruby Walsh)

*After a 2nd false start, the field was not called back.

Most wins: Jockey (5) George Stevens: 1856, 1863–4, 1869–70. Horse (3) Red Rum: 1973–4, 1977.

Prix de l'Arc de Triomphe

The leading end-of-season race in Europe; raced over 2 400 metres at Longchamp, France. First run in 1920.

Recent winners
1994 Carnegie (Silvan Guillot)
1995 Lammtarra (Lanfranco Dettori)
1996 Helissio (Olivier Peslier)
1997 Peintre Celebre (Olivier Peslier)
1998 Sagamix (Olivier Peslier)
1999 Montjeu (Michael Kinane)
2000 Sinndar (Johnny Murtagh)
2001 Sakhee (Frankie Dettori)
2002 Marienbard (Frankie Dettori)
2003 Dalakhani (Christophe Soumillon)
2004 Bago (Thierry Gillet)

Most wins: Jockey (4) Jacko Doyasbère: 1942, 1944, 1950–1; Freddy Head: 1966, 1972, 1976, 1979; Yves Saint-Martin: 1970, 1974, 1982, 1984; Pat Eddery, 1980, 1985, 1986, 1987. Horse (2) Ksar: 1921–2; Motrico: 1930, 1932; Corrida: 1936–7; Tantième: 1950–1; Ribot: 1955–6; Alleged: 1977–8.

The American Triple Crown comprises three races for three-year olds; The Kentucky Derby, the Preakness Stakes, and the Belmont Stakes.

Kentucky Derby

Raced at Churchill Downs, Louisville, over 1 mile 2 furlongs. First run in 1875.

Recent winners
1992 Lil E Tee (Pat Day)
1993 Sea Hero (J Bailey)
1994 Go for Gin (Chris McCarron)
1995 Thunder Gulch (Gary Stevens)
1996 Grindstone (Jerry Bailey)
1997 Silver Charm (Gary Stevens)
1998 Real Quiet (Kent Desormeaux)
1999 Charismatic (Chris Antley)
2000 Fusaichi Pegasus (Kent Desormeaux)
2001 Monarchos (Jorge Chavez)
2002 War Emblem (Victor Espinoza)
2003 Funny Cide (Jose Santos)
2004 Smarty Jones (Stewart Elliott)

Most wins: Jockey (5) Eddie Arcaro: 1938, 1941, 1945, 1948, 1952; Bill Hartack: 1957, 1960, 1962, 1964, 1969.

Preakness Stakes

Raced at Pimlico, Baltimore, Maryland, over 1 mile 1½ furlongs. First run in 1873.

Recent winners
1988   Risen Star (Eddie Delahoussaye)
1989   Sunday Silence (Pat Valenzuela)
1990   Summer Squall (Pat Day)
1991   Hansel (Jerry Bailey)
1992   Pine Bluff (Chris McCarron)
1993   Prairie Bayou (Mike Smith)
1994   Tabasco Cat (Pat Day)
1995   Timber Country (Pat Day)
1996   Louis Quatorze (Pat Day)
1997   Silver Charm (Gary Stevens)
1998   Real Quiet (Kent Desormeaux)
1999   Charismatic (Chris Antley)
2000   Red Bullet (Jerry Bailey)
2001   Point Given (Gary Stevens)
2002   War Emblem (Victor Espinoza)
2003   Funny Cide (Jose Santos)
2004   Smarty Jones (Stewart Elliott)

Most wins: Jockey (6) Eddie Arcaro: 1941, 1948, 1950–1, 1955, 1957.

Belmont Stakes

Raced at Belmont Park, New York, over 1 mile 4 furlongs. First run in 1867, at Jerome Park.

Recent winners
1988   Risen Star (Eddie Delahoussaye)
1989   Easy Goer (Pat Day)
1990   Go And Go (Michael Kinane)
1991   Hansel (Jerry Bailey)
1992   A.P. Indy (Eddie Delahoussaye)
1993   Colonial Affair (Julie Krone)
1994   Tabasco Cat (Pat Day)
1995   Thunder Gulch (Gary Stevens)
1996   Editor's Note (R Douglas)
1997   Touch Gold (Chris McCarron)
1998   Victory Gallup (Gary Stevens)
1999   Lemon Drop Kid (Jose Santos)
2000   Commendable (Pat Day)
2001   Point Given (Gary Stevens)
2002   Sarava (Edgar Prado)
2003   Empire Maker (Jerry Bailey)
2004   Birdstone (Edgar Prado)

Most wins: Jockey (6) Jimmy McLaughlin: 1882–4, 1886–8; Eddie Arcaro: 1941–2, 1945, 1948, 1952, 1955.

HURLING

All-Ireland championship

First contested in 1887. Played on the first Sunday in September each year.

Recent winners
1989   Tipperary
1990   Cork
1991   Tipperary
1992   Limerick
1993   Kilkenny
1994   Offaly
1995   Clare
1996   Wexford
1997   Clare
1998   Offaly
1999   Cork
2000   Kilkenny
2001   Tipperary
2002   Kilkenny
2003   Kilkenny
2004   Cork

Most wins: (29) Cork: 1890, 1892–4, 1902–3, 1919, 1926, 1928–9, 1931, 1941–4, 1946, 1952–4, 1966, 1970, 1976–8, 1984, 1986, and as above.

ICE HOCKEY

World championship

First held in 1920; takes place annually (except 1980). Up to 1968, the Olympic champions were also regarded as world champions. Women's matches held since 1990.

Recent winners
1992   Sweden
1993   Russia
1994   Canada
1995   Finland
1996   Czech Republic
1997   Canada
1998   Sweden
1999   Czech Republic
2000   Czech Republic
2001   Czech Republic
2002   Slovakia
2003   Canada
2004   Canada

Most wins: (23) Canada.

Stanley Cup

The most sought-after trophy at club level; the end-of-season meeting between the winners of the two conferences in the National Hockey League in the USA and Canada.

Recent winners
1989	Calgary Flames	1997	Detroit Redwings
1990	Edmonton Oilers	1998	Detroit Redwings
1991	Pittsburgh Penguins	1999	Dallas Stars
1992	Pittsburgh Penguins	2000	New Jersey Devils
1993	Montreal Canadiens	2001	Colorado Avalanche
1994	New York Rangers	2002	Detroit Red Wings
1995	New Jersey Devils	2003	New Jersey Devils
1996	Colorado Avalanche	2004	Tampa Bay Lightning

Most wins: (24) Montreal Canadiens: 1916, 1924, 1930–1, 1944, 1946, 1953, 1956–60, 1965–6, 1968–9, 1971, 1973, 1976–9, 1986, 1993.

Olympic Games

Gold medal winners
Men		Women	
1988	USSR	1998	USA
1992	Unified Team	2002	Canada
1994	Sweden		
1998	Czech Republic		
2002	Canada		

ICE SKATING

World championships

First men's championships in 1896; first women's event in 1906; pairs first contested in 1908. Ice dance officially recognized in 1952.

Recent winners: men

1994 Aleksei Urmanov (Russia)
1995 Elvis Stojko (Canada)
1996 Todd Eldredge (USA)
1997 Elvis Stojko (Canada)
1998 Alexie Yagudin (Russia)
1999 Alexie Yagudin (Russia)
2000 Alexie Yagudin (Russia)
2001 Evgeni Plushenko (Russia)
2002 Alexie Yagudin (Russia)
2003 Evgeni Plushenko (Russia)
2004 Evgeni Plushenko (Russia)
2005 Stephane Lambiel (Switzerland)

Most wins: (10) Ulrich Salchow (Sweden): 1901–5, 1907–11.

Recent winners: women

1994 Oksana Baiul (Ukraine)
1995 Lu Chen (China)
1996 Michele Kwan (USA)
1997 Tara Lipinski (USA)
1998 Michele Kwan (USA)
1999 Maria Butyrskaya (Russia)
2000 Michele Kwan (USA)
2001 Michele Kwan (USA)
2002 Irina Slutskaya (Russia)
2001 Michele Kwan (USA)
2004 Shizuka Arakawa (Japan)
2005 Irina Slutskaya (Russia)

Most wins: (10) Sonja Henie (Norway): 1927–36.

Recent winners (pairs)

1992 Natalya Mishkutienko/Artur Dmitriev (Unified Team)
1993 Isabelle Brasseur/Lloyd Eisler (Canada)
1994 Yekaterina Gordeyeva/Sergey Grinkov (Russia)
1995 Radka Kovarikova/Rene Novotny (Czech Republic)
1996 Marina Eltsova/Andrey Bushkov (Russia)
1997 Mandy Woetzel/Ingo Steuer (Germany)
1998 Elena Berzhnaya/Anton Sikharulidze (Russia)
1999 Elena Berzhnaya/Anton Sikharulidze (Russia)
2000 Maria Petrova/Alexei Tikhonov (Russia)
2001 Jamie Sala/David Pelletier (Canada)
2002 Xue Shen/Hongbo Zhao (China)
2003 Xue Shen/Hongbo Zhao (China)
2004 Tatiana Totmianina/Maxim Marinin (Russia)
2005 Tatiana Totmianina/Maxim Marinin (Russia)

Most wins: (10) Irina Rodnina (USSR): 1969–72 (with Aleksey Ulanov), 1973–8 (with Aleksander Zaitsev).

Recent winners: ice dance

1993 Maia Usova/Alexandr Zhulin (Unified Team)
1994 Oksana Grichtchuk/Yevgeny Platov (Russia)
1995 Oksana Grichtchuk/Yevgeny Platov (Russia)
1996 Oksana Grichtchuk/Yevgeny Platov (Russia)
1997 Oksana Grichtchuk/Yevgeny Platov (Russia)
1998 Anjelika Krylova/Oleg Ovsyannikov (Russia)
1999 Anjelika Krylova/Oleg Ovsyannikov (Russia)
2000 Marina Anissina/Gwendal Peizerat (France)
2001 Barbara Fusar-Poli/Maurizo Margaglia (Italy)
2002 Irina Lobacheva/Ilia Averbukh (Russia)
2003 Shae-Lynn Bourne/Victor Kraatz (Canada)
2004 Tatiana Navka/Roman Kostomarov (Russia)
2005 Tatiana Navka/Roman Kostomarov (Russia)

Most wins: (6) Aleksander Gorshkov and Lyudmila Pakhomova (USSR): 1970–4, 1976.

JUDO

World championships

First held in 1956, now contested every two years. Current weight categories established in 1999; women's championship instituted in 1980.

Recent winners: open – men

1991 Naoya Ogawa (Japan)
1993 Rafael Kubacki (Poland)
1995 David Douillet (France)
1997 Rafael Kubacki (Poland)
1999 Shinichi Shinohara (Japan)
2001 Alexandre Mikhaylin (Russia)
2003 Keiji Suzuki (Japan)

Recent winners: +100 kg – men

1991 Sergey Kosorotow (USSR)
1993 David Douillet (France)
1995 David Douillet (France)
1997 David Douillet (France)
1999 Shinichi Shinohara (Japan)
2001 Alexandre Mikhaylin (Russia)
2003 Yasuyuki Muneta (Japan)

Recent winners: –100 kg – men

1991 Stéphane Traineau (France)
1993 Antal Kovacs (Hungary)
1995 Pawel Nastula (Poland)
1997 Pawel Nastula (Poland)
1999 Kosie Inoue (Japan)
2001 Kosie Inoue (Japan)
2003 Kosie Inoue (Japan)

Recent winners: –90 kg – men

1991 Hirotaka Okada (Japan)
1993 Yoshio Nakamura (Japan)
1995 Ki-young Chun (S Korea)
1997 Ki-young Chun (S Korea)
1999 Hidehiko Yoshida (Japan)
2001 Frédéric Demontfaucon (France)
2003 Hee-tae Hwang (S Korea)

Recent winners: –81 kg – men

1991 Daniel Lascau (Germany)
1993 Ki-young Chun (S Korea)
1995 Toshihiko Koga (Japan)
1997 Cho In-chul (S Korea)
1999 Graeme Randall (Great Britain)
2001 Cho In-chul (S Korea)
2003 Florian Wanner (Germany)

Recent winners: –73 kg – men

1991 Toshihiko Koga (Japan)
1993 Hoon Chung (S Korea)
1995 Daisuke Hideshima (Japan)
1997 Kenzo Nakamura (Japan)
1999 Jimmy Pedro (USA)
2001 Vitali Makarov (Russia)
2003 Won-hee Lee (S Korea)

Recent winners: –66 kg – men

1991 Udo Quellmalz (Germany)
1993 Yukimasa Nakamura (Japan)

1995   Udo Quellmalz (Germany)
1997   Hyuk Kim (S Korea)
1999   Lardi Benboudaoud (France)
2001   Arash Miresmaeili (Iran)
2003   Arash Miresmaeili (Iran)

Recent winners: –60 kg – men

1991   Tadanori Koshino (Japan)
1993   Ryudi Sanoda (Japan)
1995   Nikolai Ojeguine (Russia)
1997   Tadahiro Nomura (Japan)
1999   Manuel Poulot (Cuba)
2001   Anis Lounif (Tunisia)
2003   Min-Ho Choi (South Korea)

Most titles: (4) Yashiro Yamashita (Japan): 1981 (Open), 1979, 1981, 1983 (over 95 kg); Shozo Fujii (Japan): 1971, 1973, 1975 (under 80 kg), 1979 (under 78 kg).

Recent winners: open – women

1991   Zhuang Xiaoyan (China)
1993   Beata Maksymow (Poland)
1995   Monique Van Der Lee (Netherlands)
1997   Daina Beltran (Cuba)
1999   Daina Beltran (Cuba)
2001   Celine Lebrun (France)
2003   Wen Tong (China)

Recent winners: +78 kg – women

1991   Ji-yoon Moon (S Korea)
1993   Johanna Hagen (Germany)
1995   Angelique Seriese (Netherlands)
1997   Christine Cicot (France)
1999   Beata Maksymow (Poland)
2001   Yuan Hua (China)
2003   Fuming Sun (China)

Recent winners: –78 kg – women

1991   Mi-jeono Kim (S Korea)
1993   Chun Huileng (China)
1995   Diadenis Luna (Cuba)
1997   Noriko Anno (Japan)
1999   Noriko Anno (Japan)
2001   Noriko Anno (Japan)
2003   Noriko Anno (Japan)

Recent winners: –70 kg (women)

1991   Emanuela Pierantozzi (Italy)
1993   Min-sun Cho (S Korea)
1995   Min-sun Cho (S Korea)
1997   Kate Howey (Great Britain)
1999   Sibelis Veranes (Cuba)
2001   Masae Ueno (Japan)
2003   Masae Ueno (Japan)

Recent winners: –63 kg (women)

1991   Frauke Eickhoff (Germany)
1993   Caveye de Van (Belgium)
1995   Sung-sook Young (S Korea)
1997   Servenr Vendenhende (France)

1999   Keiko Maeda (Japan)
2001   Gella Vandecaveye (Belgium)
2003   Daniela Krukower (Argentina)

Recent winners: –57 kg – women

1989   Catherine Arnaud (France)
1991   Miriam Blasco Soto (Spain)
1993   Nicola Fairbrother (Great Britain)
1995   Driulis Gonzalez (Cuba)
1997   Isabel Fernandez (Spain)
1999   Druilis Gonzalez (Cuba)
2001   Yurisleidis Lupetey (Cuba)
2003   Sun-Hio Kye (North Korea)

Recent winners: –52 kg – women

1991   Alessandra Giungi (Italy)
1993   Rodriguez Verdecia (Cuba)
1995   Marie-Claire Restoux (France)
1997   Marie-Claire Restoux (France)
1999   Noriko Narasaki (Japan)
2001   Kye Sun-Hui (North Korea)
2003   Amarlis Savon (Cuba)

Recent winners: –48 kg – women

1991   Cécille Nowak (France)
1993   Ryoko Tamura (Japan)
1995   Ryoko Tamura (Japan)
1997   Ryoko Tamura (Japan)
1999   Ryoko Tamura (Japan)
2001   Ryoko Tamura (Japan)
2003   Ryoko Tamura (Japan)

Most titles: (6) Ingrid Berghmans (Belgium): 1980, 1982, 1984, 1986 (open), 1984, 1989 (under 72 kg).

KARATE

World championships

First held in Tokyo 1970; have taken place every two years since 1980, when women first competed; there is a team competition plus individual competitions – Kumite (seven weight categories for men and three for women) and Kata. Separate men and women's teams started in 1992.

Team winners: men

1998   France
2000   France
2002   Spain
2004   Italy

Team winners: women

1998   Turkey
2000   France
2002   Spain
2004   Japan

LACROSSE

World championships

First held for men in 1967; and for women in 1969. Have taken place every four years since 1974; since 1982 the women's event has been called the World Cup.

Winners: men

1974   USA
1978   Canada
1982   USA
1986   USA
1990   USA
1994   USA
1998   USA
2002   USA

Most wins: (8) USA: 1967 and as above.

Winners: women

1974   USA
1978   Canada
1982   USA
1986   Australia
1990   USA
1994   USA
1998   USA
2001   USA

Most wins: (6) USA: 1967 and as above.

Iroquois Cup

The sport's best-known trophy; contested by English club sides annually since 1890.

Recent winners

1983   Sheffield University
1984   Cheadle
1985   Cheadle
1986   Heaton Mersey
1987   Stockport
1988   Mellor
1989   Stockport
1990   Cheadle
1991   Cheadle
1992   Cheadle
1993   Heaton Mersey
1994   Cheadle
1995   Cheadle
1996   Stockport
1997   Mellor
1998   *not played*
1999   Cheadle
2000   Cheadle
2001   Cheadle
2002   Cheadle
2003   Cheadle
2004   Stockport

Most wins: (19) Stockport: 1897–1901, 1903, 1905, 1911–13, 1923–4, 1926, 1928, 1934, 1987, 1989, 1996, 2004.

SPORTS AND GAMES

MODERN PENTATHLON

World championships

Men's individual championship held annually since 1949 with the exception of Olympic years, when Olympic champions automatically become world champions: team championship held annually. Women's individual and team events held annually. From 2000 World Championships held annually for men and women. Inaugural women's Olympic competition in 2000.

Recent winners: individual men
2001	Gabor Balogh (Hungary)
2002	Michal Sedlecky (Czech Republic)
2003	Eric Walther (Germany)
2004	Andrejus Zadneprovski (Lithuania)

Recent winners: individual women
2001	Stephanie Cook (Great Britain)
2002	Bea Simoka (Hungary)
2003	Zsuzsanna Voros (Hungary)
2004	Zsuzsanna Voros (Hungary)

Recent winners: team
	Men	Women
2001	Hungary	Great Britain
2002	Hungary	Hungary
2003	Hungary	Great Britain
2004	Russia	Great Britain

Olympic Games
Gold medal winner 2004 – men
Andrey Moiseev (Russia)

Gold medal winner 2004 – women
Zsuzsanna Voros (Hungary)

MOTOR CYCLING

World championships

First organized in 1949; current titles for 500 cc, 250 cc, 125 cc, 80 cc and Sidecar. Formula One and Endurance world championships also held annually. The most prestigious title is the 500 cc category.

Recent winners: 500 cc
1992	Wayne Rainey (USA)
1993	Kevin Schwantz (USA)
1994	Michael Doohan (Australia)
1995	Michael Doohan (Australia)
1996	Michael Doohan (Australia)
1997	Michael Doohan (Australia)
1998	Michael Doohan (Australia)
1999	Alex Criville (Spain)
2000	Kenny Roberts Jr (USA)
2001	Valentino Rossi (Italy)
2002	Valentino Rossi (Italy)
2003	Valentino Rossi (Italy)

Most wins: (8) Giacomo Agostini (Italy): 1966–72, 1975.

Most world titles: (15) Giacomo Agostini (Italy): 350 cc 1968–74, 500 cc as above.

Isle of Man TT races

The most famous of all motor-cycle races; first held 1907; takes place each June. Principal race is the Senior TT.

Recent winners: senior TT
1992	Steve Hislop (Great Britain)
1993	Phil McCallen (Ireland)
1994	Steve Hislop (Great Britain)
1995	Joey Dunlop (Ireland)
1996	Phil McCallen (Ireland)
1997	Phil McCallen (Ireland)
1998	Ian Simpson (Scotland)
1999	David Jefferies (England)
2000	David Jefferies (England)
2001	*not held*
2002	David Jefferies (England)
2003	Adrian Archibald (N Ireland)
2004	Adrian Archibald (N Ireland)

Most senior TT wins: (7) Mike Hailwood (Great Britain): 1961, 1963–7, 1979.

MOTOR RACING

World championship

A Formula One drivers' world championship instituted in 1950; constructor's championship instituted in 1958.

Recent winners
1994	Michael Schumacher (Germany); Benetton-Ford
1995	Michael Schumacher (Germany); Benetton-Renault
1996	Damon Hill (Great Britain); Williams-Renault
1997	Jacques Villeneuve (Canada); Williams-Renault
1998	Mika Hakkinen (Finland); McLaren-Mercedes
1999	Mika Hakkinen (Finland); McLaren-Mercedes
2000	Michael Schumacher (Germany); Ferrari
2001	Michael Schumacher (Germany); Ferrari
2002	Michael Schumacher (Germany); Ferrari
2003	Michael Schumacher (Germany); Ferrari
2004	Michael Schumacher (Germany); Ferrari

Most wins: Driver (7) Michael Schumacher (Germany) as above. Constructor (11) Ferrari: 1958, 1961, 1964, 1975, 1977, 1979, 2000–4.

Le Mans 24-Hour Race

The greatest of all endurance races. First held in 1923.

Recent winners
1991	Volker Weidler (Germany)
	Johnny Herbert (Great Britain)
	Bertrand Gochot (Belgium)
1992	Derek Warwick (Great Britain)
	Mark Blundell (Great Britain)
	Yannick Dalmas (France)
1993	Geoff Brabham (Australia)
	Christophe Bouchut (France)
	Eric Helary (France)
1994	Yannick Dalmas (France)
	Mauro Baldi (Italy)
	Hurley Haywood (USA)
1995	Yannick Dalmas (France)
	J J Lehto (Finland)
	Masanori Sekiya (Japan)
1996	Manuel Reuter (Germany)
	Davey Jones (USA)
	Alexander Wurz (Austria)
1997	Michele Alboreto (Italy)
	Stefan Johansson (Sweden)
	Tom Kristensen (Denmark)
1998	Allan McNish (Great Britain)
	Laurent Aiello (France)
	Stephane Ortelli (France)
1999	Pierluigi Martini (Italy)
	Joachim Winkelhock (Germany)
	Yannick Dalmas (France)
2000	Emmanuele Pirro (Italy)
	Frank Biela (Germany)
	Tom Kristensen (Denmark)
2001	Emmanuela Pirro (Italy)
	Frank Biela (Germany)
	Tom Kristensen (Denmark)
2002	Emmanuela Pirro (Italy)
	Frank Biela (Germany)
	Tom Kristensen (Denmark)
2003	Rinaldo Capello (Italy)
	Guy Smith (UK)
	Tom Kristensen (Denmark)
2004	Rinaldo Capello (Italy)
	Seiji Ara (Japan)
	Tom Kristensen (Denmark)

Most wins: (6) Jacky Ickx (Belgium): 1969, 1975–7, 1981–2.

Indianapolis 500

First held in 1911. Raced over the Indianapolis Raceway as part of the Memorial Day celebrations at the end of May each year.

Recent winners

1991	Rick Mears (USA)
1992	Al Unser Jr (USA)
1993	Emerson Fittipaldi (Brazil)
1994	Al Unser Jr (USA)
1995	Jacques Villeneuve (Canada)
1996	Buddy Lazier (USA)
1997	Arie Luyendyk (Netherlands)
1998	Eddie Cheever Jr (USA)
1999	Kenny Brack (Sweden)
2000	Juan Montoya (Colombia)
2001	Helio Castroneves (Brazil)
2002	Helio Castroneves (Brazil)
2003	Gil de Ferran (Brazil)
2004	Buddy Rice (USA)

Most wins: (4) A J Foyt (USA): 1961, 1964, 1967, 977; Al Unser (USA): 1970–1, 1978, 1987; Rick Mears (USA): 1979, 1984, 1988, 1991.

Monte Carlo rally

The world's leading rally; first held in 1911.

Recent winners

1992	Didier Auriol/Bernard Occelli (France)
1993	Didier Auriol/Bernard Occelli (France)
1994	François Delecour/Daniel Grataloup (France)
1995	Carlos Sainz/Luis Moia (Spain)
1996	Patrick Bernardini/Bernard Occelli (France)
1997	Piero Liatti/Fabrizia Pons (Italy)
1998	Carlos Sainz/Luis Moya (Spain)
1999	Tommi Makinen/Risto Mannisenmaki (Finland)
2000	Tommi Makinen/Risto Mannisenmaki (Finland)
2001	Tommi Makinen (Finland)/ Nicky Grist (Wales)
2002	Tommi Makinen/Kaj Lindstrom (France)
2003	Sebastien Loeb/Daniel Elena (France)
2004	Sebastien Loeb/Daniel Elena (France)

Most wins: (4) Sandro Munari (Italy): 1972, 1975–7; Walter Röhrl (W Germany): 1980, 1982, 1983, 1984. Tommi Makinen (Finland) as above; Most successful co-driver: (4) Christian Geistdorfer all with Walter Röhrl; Bernard Occelli, as above.

NETBALL

World championships

First held in 1963, then every four years.

Winners

1963	Australia
1967	New Zealand
1971	Australia
1975	Australia
1979	Australia, New Zealand, Trinidad & Tobago (*shared*)
1983	Australia
1987	New Zealand
1991	Australia
1995	Australia
1999	Australia
2003	New Zealand

Most wins: (8) Australia: as above.

ORIENTEERING

World championships

First held in 1966. Usually every two years, annually from 2003.

Winners: individual – men
Classic distance until 2002;
Long distance from 2003

1983	Morten Berglia (Norway)
1985	Kari Sallinen (Finland)
1987	Kent Olsson (Sweden)
1989	Peter Thoresen (Norway)
1991	Jörgen Mårtensson (Sweden)
1993	Allan Mogensen (Denmark)
1995	Jörgen Mårtensson (Sweden)
1997	Peter Thoresen (Norway)
1999	Bjørnar Valstad (Norway)
2001	Jörgen Rostrup (Norway)
2003	Thomas Bührer (Switzerland)
2004	Bjørnar Valstad (Norway)

Winners: individual – women.
Classic distance until 2002;
Long distance from 2003

1983	Annichen Kringstad Svensson (Norway)
1985	Annichen Kringstad Svensson (Norway)
1987	Arja Hannus (Sweden)
1989	Marita Skogum (Sweden)
1991	Katalin Olah (Hungary)
1993	Marita Skogum (Sweden)
1995	Katalin Olah (Hungary)
1997	Hanne Staff (Norway)
1999	Kirsi Bostrom (Finland)
2001	Simone Luder (Switzerland)
2003	Simone Luder (Switzerland)
2004	Karolina Höjsgaard (Sweden)

Most wins: Men (2), Age Hadler (Norway): 1966, 1972; Egil Johansen (Norway); Oyvin Thon (Norway): 1979, 1981; Peter Thoresen (Norway); Jörgen Mårtensson (Sweden): as above. Women (3), Annichen Kringstad (Norway): 1981 and as above.

Winners: relay – men

1976	Sweden	1991	Switzerland
1978	Norway	1993	Switzerland
1979	Sweden	1995	Switzerland
1981	Norway	1997	Switzerland
1983	Norway	1999	Denmark
1985	Norway	2001	Norway
1987	Norway	2003	Sweden
1989	Norway	2004	Norway

Winners: relay – women

1972	Finland	1989	Sweden
1974	Sweden	1991	Sweden
1976	Sweden	1993	Sweden
1978	Finland	1995	Finland
1979	Finland	1997	Sweden
1981	Sweden	1999	Norway
1983	Sweden	2001	Finland
1985	Sweden	2003	Switzerland
1987	Norway	2004	Sweden

Most wins: Men (9) Norway: 1968 and as above. Women (12) Sweden: 1966, 1970, and as above.

POLO

British Open Polo Championship

First held in 1956, replacing the Champion Cup. The British Open Championship for club sides: finalists compete for the Veuve Clicquot Gold Cup, once known as the Cowdray Park Gold Cup.

Recent winners

1988	Tramontana
1989	Tramontana
1990	Hildon
1991	Tramontana
1992	Black Bears
1993	Alcatel
1994	Ellerston Blacks
1995	Ellerston Whites
1996	C S Brooks
1997	Labegorce
1998	Ellerston White
1999	Pommery
2000	Dubai
2001	Dubai
2002	Black Bears
2003	Hildon
2004	Azzurra

Most wins: (5) Stowell Park: 1973–4, 1976, 1978, 1980; Tramontana: 1986–7, and as above.

POWERBOAT RACING

World championships

Instituted in 1982; held in many categories, with Formula One and Formula Two being the principal competitions. Formula Two, known as Formula Grand Prix, was discontinued in 1989.

Winners: Formula One

1983	Renato Molinari (Italy)
1984	Renato Molinari (Italy)
1985	Bob Spalding (Great Britain)
1986	Gene Thibodaux (USA)
1987	Ben Robertson (USA)
1990	John Hill (Great Britain)
1991	Jonathan Jones (Great Britain)
1992	Fabrizio Bacca (Italy)
1993	Guido Capellina (Italy)
1994	Guido Capellina (Italy)
1995	Guido Capellina (Italy)
1996	Guido Capellina (Italy)
1997	Scott Gillman (USA)
1998	Scott Gillman (USA)
1999	Guido Capellina (Italy)
2000	Scott Gillman (USA)
2001	Guido Capellina (Italy)
2002	Guido Capellina (Italy)
2003	Guido Capellina (Italy)
2004	Scott Gillman (USA)

Most wins: (8) Guido Capellina (Italy): as above.

Winners: Formula Two/Formula Grand Prix

1982	Michael Werner (W Germany)
1983	Michael Werner (W Germany)
1984	John Hill (Great Britain)
1985	John Hill (Great Britain)
1986	Jonathan Jones (Great Britain) and Buck Thornton (USA) (shared)
1987	Bill Seebold (USA)
1988	Chris Bush (USA)
1989	Jonathan Jones (Great Britain)

Most wins: (2) Michael Werner (W Germany): as above; John Hill (Great Britain): as above; Jonathan Jones (Great Britain): as above.

RACKETS

World championship

Organized on a challenge basis, the first champion in 1820 was Robert Mackay (Great Britain).

Recent winners

1929–37	Charles Williams (Great Britain)
1937–47	Donald Milford (Great Britain)
1947–54	James Dear (Great Britain)
1954–72	Geoffrey Atkins (Great Britain)
1972–3	William Surtees (USA)
1973–4	Howard Angus (Great Britain)
1975–1	William Surtees (USA)
1981–4	John Prenn (Great Britain)
1984–6	William Boone (Great Britain)
1986–8	John Prenn (Great Britain)
1988–99	James Male (Great Britain)
1999–2001	Neil Smith (Great Britain)
2001–	James Male (Great Britain)

Longest-reigning champion: 18 years, Geoffrey Atkins: as above.

REAL TENNIS

World championship

The first world champion was M Clerge (France), c. 1740, regarded as the first world champion of any sport. Held on a challenge basis; first held for women in 1985, and then every two years.

Recent winners: men

1916–28	Fred Covey (Great Britain)
1928–55	Pierre Etchebaster (France)
1955–7	James Dear (Great Britain)
1957–9	Albert Johnson (Great Britain)
1959–69	Northrup Knox (USA)
1969–72	Pete Bostwick (USA)
1972–5	Jimmy Bostwick (USA)
1976–81	Howard Angus (Great Britain)
1981–7	Chris Ronaldson (Great Britain)
1987–94	Wayne Davis (Australia)
1994–	Robert Fahey (Australia)

Longest-reigning champion: 33 years, Edmond Barre (France): 1829–62.

Winners – women

1985	Judy Clarke (Australia)
1987	Judy Clarke (Australia)
1989	Penny Fellows (Great Britain)
1991	Penny Fellows Lumley (Great Britain)
1993	Sally Jones (Great Britain)
1995	Penny Fellows Lumley (Great Britain)
1997	Penny Fellows Lumley (Great Britain)
1999	Penny Fellows Lumley (Great Britain)
2001	Charlotte Cornwallis (Great Britain)
2003	Penny Fellows Lumley (Great Britain)
2005	Charlotte Cornwallis (Great Britain)

Most wins: (6) Penny Fellows Lumley (Great Britain): as above.

ROLLER SKATING

World championships

Figure-skating world championships were first organized in 1947.

Recent winners: combined – men
1992 Sandro Guerra (Italy)
1993 Samo Kokorovec (Italy)
1994 Steven Findlay (USA)
1995 Jason Sutcliffe (Australia)
1996 Francesco Ceresola (Italy)
1997 Mauro Mazzoni (Italy)
1998 Daniele Tofani (Italy)
1999 Adrian Stolzenberg (Germany)
2000 Adrian Stolzenberg (Germany)
2001 Leonardo Pancani (Italy)
2002 Frank Albiez (Germany)
2003 Luca D'Alisera (Italy)
2004 Luca D'Alisera (Italy)

Most wins: (5) Karl-Heinz Losch (W Germany): 1958–9, 1961–2, 1966.

Recent winners: combined – women
1992 Rafaella Del Vinaccio (Italy)
1993 Letitia Tinghi (Italy)
1994 April Dayney (USA)
1995 Letitia Tinghi (Italy)
1996 Giusy Loncani (Italy)
1997 Sabrini Tommasini (Italy)
1998 Christine Bartolozzi (Italy)
1999 Elisa Facciotti (Italy)
2000 Elisa Facciotti (Italy)
2001 Elisa Facciotti (Italy)
2002 Tanja Romano (Italy)
2003 Tanja Romano (Italy)
2004 Tanja Romano (Italy)

Most wins: (5) Rafaella Del Vinaccio (Italy): 1988–91 and as above.

Recent winners: pairs
1992 Patrick Venerucci/Maura Ferri (Italy)
1993 Patrick Venerucci/Maura Ferri (Italy)
1994 Patrick Venerucci/Beatrice Pallazzi Rossi (Italy)
1995 Patrick Venerucci/Beatrice Pallazzi Rossi (Italy)
1996 Patrick Venerucci/Beatrice Pallazzi Rossi (Italy)
1997 Patrick Venerucci/Beatrice Pallazzi Rossi (Italy)
1998 Patrick Venerucci/Beatrice Pallazzi Rossi (Italy)
1999 Patrick Venerucci/Beatrice Pallazzi Rossi (Italy)
2000 Patrick Venerucci/Beatrice Pallazzi Rossi (Italy)
2001 Patrick Venerucci/Beatrice Pallazzi Rossi (Italy)
2002 Patrick Venerucci/Beatrice Pallazzi Rossi (Italy)
2003 Marika Zanforlin/Federico Degli Esposti (Italy)
2004 Marika Zanforlin/Federico Degli Esposti (Italy)

Most wins: (11) Patrick Venerucci (Italy) as above.

Recent winners: dance
1991 Greg Goody/Jodee Viola (USA)
1992 Doug Wait/Deanna Monaham (USA)
1993 Doug Wait/Deanna Monaham (USA)
1994 Tim Patten/Lisa Friday (USA)
1995 Tim Patten/Lisa Friday (USA)
1996 Axel Haber/Swansi Gebauer (Germany)
1997 Axel Haber/Swansi Gebauer (Germany)
1998 Roland Bren/Candy Powderly (USA)
1999 Timothy Patten/Tara Graney (USA)
2000 Adam White/Melissa Quinn (USA)
2001 Adam White/Melissa Quinn (USA)
2002 Marco Bornati/Emanuela Bornati (Italy)
2003 Fabio Grossi/Michela Pizzi (Italy)
2004 Marco Bornati/Monica Coffele (Italy)

Most wins: (3) Jane Puracchio (USA): 1973, 1975–6; Dan Littel and Florence Arsenault (USA): 1977–9; Greg Goody and Jodee Viola (USA): as above.

ROWING

World championships

First held for men in 1962 and for women in 1974; Olympic champions assume the role of world champion in Olympic years. Principal events are the single sculls.

Recent winners: single sculls – men
1992 Thomas Lange (Germany)
1993 Derek Porter (Canada)
1994 Andre Willms (Germany)
1995 Iztok Cop (Slovenia)
1996 Xeno Müller (Switzerland)
1997 James Koven (USA)
1998 Rob Waddell (New Zealand)
1999 Rob Waddell (New Zealand)
2000 Rob Waddell (New Zealand)
2001 Olaf Tufte (Norway)
2002 Marcel Hacker (Germany)
2003 Olaf Tufte (Norway)
2004 Olaf Tufte (Norway)

Most wins: (5) Thomas Lange (Germany): 1987–9, 1991–2.

Recent winners: sculls – women
1992 Elisabeta Lipa (Romania)
1993 Jana Phieme (Germany)
1994 Trine Hansen (Denmark)
1995 Maria Brandin (Sweden)
1996 Yekaterina Khodotovich (Belarus)
1997 Yekaterina Khodotovich (Belarus)
1998 Irina Fedotova (Russia)
1999 Ekaterina Karsten (Belarus)
2000 Ekaterina Karsten (Belarus)
2001 Katrin Rutschow-Stomporowski (Germany)
2002 Rumyana Neykova (Bulgaria)
2003 Rumyana Neykova (Bulgaria)
2004 Katrin Rutschow-Stomporowski (Germany)

Most wins: (5) Christine Hahn (née Scheiblich) (E Germany): 1974–8.

University Boat Race

An annual contest between the crews from the Oxford and Cambridge University rowing clubs, first contested in 1829. The current course is from Putney to Mortlake.

Recent winners
1988	Oxford	1994	Cambridge	2000	Oxford
1989	Oxford	1995	Cambridge	2001	Cambridge
1990	Oxford	1996	Cambridge	2002	Oxford
1991	Oxford	1997	Cambridge	2003	Oxford
1992	Oxford	1998	Cambridge	2004	Cambridge
1993	Cambridge	1999	Cambridge	2005	Oxford

Wins: 78 Cambridge; 72 Oxford; 1 dead-heat (1877).

Diamond Sculls

Highlight of Henley Royal Regatta held every July; first contested in 1844.

Recent winners

1987 Peter-Michael Kolbe (W Germany)
1988 Hamish McGlashan (Australia)
1989 Vaclav Chalupa (Czechoslovakia)
1990 Eric Verdonk (New Zealand)
1991 Wim van Belleghem (Belgium)
1992 Rorie Henderson (Great Britain)
1993 Thomas Lange (Germany)
1994 Xeno Müller (Switzerland)
1995 Yuri Jaanson (Estonia)
1996 Merlin Vervoorn (Netherlands)
1997 Greg Searle (Great Britain)
1998 James Coven (USA)
1999 Marcel Hacker (Germany)
2000 Aquil H Abdulla (USA)
2001 Duncan S Free (Australia)
2002 Peter Wells (Great Britain)
2003 Alan Campbell (Great Britain)
2004 Marcel Hacker (Germany)

Most wins: (6) Stuart Mackenzie (Australia): 1957–62.

RUGBY LEAGUE

World Cup/International championship

First contested in 1954 between Great Britain, France, New Zealand, and Australia. In 1975, England and Wales replaced Great Britain. The competition was discontinued after the 1977 World Cup, but was revived in 1988.

Winners

1960	Great Britain	1977	Australia
1968	Australia	1988	Australia
1970	Australia	1992	Australia
1972	Great Britain	1995	Australia
1975	Australia	2000	Australia

Most wins: (9) Australia: 1957 and as above.

Tetley's Bitter Super League

The original Northern Union was formed in 1895–6, and was won by Manningham. Since then there have been many changes to the rules and structure of the league, which from 1906 to 1973 featured a Championship Play-off. The present structure, with Divisions One and Two, dates from the 1973–4 season. Known as the JJB Super League until 2000.

Recent winners

1984–85	Hull Kingston Rovers	1994–95	Wigan
1985–86	Halifax	1995–96	Wigan
1986–87	Wigan	1996–97	Bradford
1987–88	Widnes	1997–98	Wigan
1988–89	Widnes	1998–99	Wigan
1989–90	Wigan	1999–2000	Wigan
1990–91	Wigan	2000–1	Bradford
1991–92	Wigan	2001–2	St Helens
1992–93	Wigan	2002–3	Bradford
1993–94	Wigan		

Challenge Cup final

First contested in 1897 and won by Batley; first final at Wembley Stadium in 1929.

Recent winners

1991	Wigan	1998	Sheffield Eagles
1992	Wigan	1999	Leeds Rhinos
1993	Wigan	2000	Bradford Bulls
1994	Wigan	2001	St Helens
1995	Wigan	2002	Wigan Warriors
1996	St Helens	2003	Bradford Bulls
1997	St Helens	2004	St Helens

Most wins: (17) Wigan: 1924, 1929, 1948, 1951, 1958–9, 1965, 1984, 1985, 1988–90 and as above.

Super League Grand Final

End-of-season knockout competition involving the top eight teams in the first division. First contested at the end of the 1974–5 season. Before 1998 known as the Premiership trophy.

Recent winners

1991	Hull	1998	Wigan
1992	Wigan	1999	St Helens
1993	St Helens	2000	St Helens
1994	Wigan	2001	Bradford Bulls
1995	Wigan	2002	St Helens
1996	Wigan	2003	Bradford Bulls
1997	Wigan	2004	Leeds Rhinos

Most wins: (7) Wigan: 1987 and as above.

Regal trophy

A knockout competition, first held in 1971–2. Formerly known as the John Player Special Trophy, it adopted its current name/title in 1989–90, and ended in 1995–6.

Recent winners

1983	Wigan	1990	Wigan
1984	Leeds	1991	Warrington
1985	Hull Kingston Rovers	1992	Widnes
1986	Wigan	1993	Wigan
1987	Wigan	1994	Castleford
1988	St Helens	1995	Wigan
1989	Wigan	1996	Wigan

Most wins: (8) Wigan: as above.

Sydney Premiership

The principal competition in Australia, first held in 1908. The culmination of the competition is the Grand Final; the winning team receives the Winfield Cup.

Recent winners

1990 Canberra
1991 Penrith
1992 Brisbane Broncos
1993 Brisbane Broncos
1995 Sydney Bulldogs
1997 Newcastle Knights
1998 Brisbane Broncos
1999 Melbourne Storm
2000 Brisbane Broncos
2001 Newcastle Knights
2002 Sydney Roosters
2003 Penrith
2004 Canterbury Bulldogs

RUGBY UNION

World Cup

The first Rugby Union World Cup was held in 1987.

Recent winners
1987	New Zealand	2003	England
1991	Australia		
1995	South Africa		
1999	Australia		

Six Nations championship

A round-robin competition involving England, Ireland, Scotland, Wales and France; first contested in 1884. Italy joined in 2000.

Recent winners
1989	France	1998	France
1990	Scotland	1999	Scotland
1991	England	2000	England
1992	England	2001	England
1993	France	2002	France
1994	Wales	2003	England
1995	England	2004	France
1996	England	2005	Wales
1997	France		

Most outright wins: (23) Wales: 1893, 1900, 1902, 1905, 1908–9, 1911, 1922, 1931, 1936, 1950, 1952, 1956, 1965–6, 1969, 1971, 1975–6, 1978–9, 1994, 2005.

County championship

First held in 1889.

Recent winners
1987	Yorkshire	1996	Gloucestershire
1988	Lancashire	1997	Cumbria
1989	Durham	1998	Cheshire
1990	Lancashire	1999	Cornwall
1991	Cornwall	2000	Yorkshire
1992	Lancashire	2001	*not contested*
1993	Lancashire	2002	Gloucestershire
1994	Yorkshire	2003	Gloucestershire
1995	Warwickshire	2004	Devon

Most wins: (18) Gloucestershire: 1910, 1913, 1920–2, 1930–2, 1937, 1972, 1974–6, 1983–4, 1996, 2002–3.

Powergen Cup

An annual knockout competition for English club sides; first held in the 1971–2 season. Known as the John Player Special Cup until 1988, the Pilkington Cup until 1997, and the Tetley's Bitter Cup until 2001.

Recent winners
1990	Bath	1998	Saracens
1991	Harlequins	1999	Wasps
1992	Bath	2000	Wasps
1993	Leicester	2001	Newcastle
1994	Bath	2002	London Irish
1995	Bath	2003	Gloucester
1996	Bath	2004	Newcastle
1997	Leicester	2005	Leeds

Most wins: (10) Bath: 1984–7, 1989 and as above.

Rugby Union football field

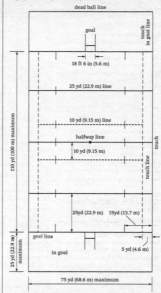

The Konica Minolta Cup

The knockout tournament for Welsh clubs; first held in 1971–2; formerly called the Schweppes Welsh Cup and (to 1999) the Swalec Cup, the Welsh Rugby Union Challenge Cup to 2000, and the Principality Cup to 2003.

Recent winners
1984	Cardiff	1995	Swansea
1985	Llanelli	1996	Pontypridd
1986	Cardiff	1997	Cardiff
1987	Cardiff	1998	Llanelli
1988	Llanelli	1999	Swansea
1989	Neath	2000	Llanelli
1990	Neath	2001	Newport
1991	Llanelli	2002	Pontypridd
1992	Llanelli	2003	Llanelli
1993	Llanelli	2004	Neath
1994	Cardiff		

Most wins: (12) Llanelli: 1973–6, and as above.

SHOOTING

Olympic Games

The Olympic competition is the highlight of the shooting calendar; winners in all categories since 1984 are given below.

Free pistol: men
1992 Konstantine Loukachik (Unified Team)
1996 Boris Kokorev (Russia)
2000 Tanyu Kiriakov (Bulgaria)
2004 Mikhail Nestruev (Russia)

Rapid fire pistol: men
1992 Ralf Schumann (Germany)
1996 Ralf Schumann (Germany)
2000 Serguei Alifirenko (Russia)
2004 Ralf Schumann (Germany)

Small-bore rifle: three position – men
1992 Gratchia Petrikiane (Unified Team)
1996 Jean-Pierre Amat (France)
2000 Rajmond Debevec (Slovenia)
2004 Jia Zhanbo (China)

Running game target: men
1992 Michael Jakositz (Germany)
1996 Yang Ling (China)
2000 Yang Ling (China)
2004 Manfred Kurzer (Germany)

Trap: Men
2000 Michael Diamond (Australia)
2004 Alexei Alipov (Russia)

Double trap: men
2000 Richard Faulds (Great Britain)
2004 Ahmed al-Maktoum (UAE)

Double trap: women
2000 Pia Hansen (Sweden)
2004 Kimberly Rhode (USA)

Skeet: men
2000 Mykola Milchev (Ukraine)
2004 Andrea Benelli (Italy)

Small-bore rifle: prone – men
1992 Lee Eun Chul (S Korea)
1996 Christian Klees (Germany)
2000 Jonas Edman (Sweden)
2004 Matthew Emmons (USA)

Air rifle: men
1988 Goran Maksimovic (Yugoslavia)
1992 Iouri Fedkine (Unified Team)
1996 Artem Khadzhibekov (Russia)
2000 Cai Yalin (China)
2004 Qinan Zhu (China)

Air pistol: men
1996 Roberto Di Donna (Italy)
2000 Franck Dumoulin (France)
2004 Wang Yifu (China)

Sport pistol: women
1992 Marina Logvinenko (Unified Team)
1996 Li Duihong (China)
2000 Maria Grozdeva (Bulgaria)
2004 Maria Grozdeva (Bulgaria)

Air rifle: women
1992 Yeo Kab-Soon (S Korea)
1996 Renata Mauer (Poland)
2000 Nancy Johnson (USA)
2004 Li Du (China)

Small-bore rifle: women
1992 Lauri Melli (USA)
1996 Alexandra Ivosev (Yugoslavia)
2000 Renata Mauer-Rozanka (Poland)
2004 Lioubov Galkina (Russia)

Air rifle: women
1996 Olga Klochneva (Russia)
2000 Tao Luna (China)
2004 Olena Kostevych (Ukraine)

SKIING

World Cup

A season-long competition first organized in 1967. Champions are declared in downhill, slalom, giant slalom, and super-giant slalom, as well as the overall champion; points are obtained for performances in each category.

Recent overall winners: men
1991 Marc Girardelli (Luxembourg)
1992 Paul Accola (Switzerland)
1993 Marc Girardelli (Luxembourg)
1994 Kjetel Andre Aamodt (Norway)
1995 Alberto Tomba (Italy)
1996 Lasse Kjus (Norway)
1997 Luc Alphand (France)
1998 Hermann Maier (Austria)
1999 Lasse Kjus (Norway)
2000 Hermann Maier (Austria)
2001 Hermann Maier (Austria)
2002 Stephan Eberharter (Austria)
2003 Stephan Eberharter (Austria)
2004 Hermann Maier (Austria)
2005 Bode Miller (USA)

Recent overall winners: women
1991 Petra Kronberger (Austria)
1992 Petra Kronberger (Austria)
1993 Anita Wachter (Austria)
1994 Vreni Schneider (Switzerland)
1995 Vreni Schneider (Switzerland)
1996 Katja Seizinger (Germany)
1997 Pernilla Wiberg (Sweden)
1998 Katja Seizinger (Germany)
1999 Alexandra Meissnitzer (Austria)
2000 Renata Götschl (Austria)
2001 Janica Kostelic (Croatia)
2002 Michaela Dorfmeister (Austria)
2003 Janica Kostelic (Croatia)
2004 Anja Paerson (Sweden)
2005 Anja Paerson (Sweden)

Most wins: Men (5) Marc Girardelli (Luxembourg): 1985–6, 1989 and as above. Women (6) Annemarie Moser-Pröll (Austria): 1971–5, 1979.

Olympic Games

Gold medal winners
Men's Alpine combination
1998 Mario Reiter (Austria)
2002 Kjetil André Aamodt (Norway)

Women's Alpine combination
1998 Katja Seizinger (Germany)
2002 Janica Kostalic (Croatia)

SNOOKER

World Professional championship

Instituted in the 1926–7 season. A knockout competition open to professional players who are members of the World Professional Billiards and Snooker Association; played at the Crucible Theatre, Sheffield.

Recent winners
1991 John Parrott (England)
1992 Stephen Hendry (Scotland)
1993 Stephen Hendry (Scotland)
1994 Stephen Hendry (Scotland)
1995 Stephen Hendry (Scotland)
1996 Stephen Hendry (Scotland)
1997 Ken Doherty (Ireland)
1998 John Higgins (Scotland)
1999 Stephen Hendry (Scotland)
2000 Mark Williams (Wales)
2001 Ronnie O'Sullivan (England)
2002 Peter Ebdon (England)
2003 Mark Williams (Wales)
2004 Ronnie O'Sullivan (England)

Most wins: (15) Joe Davis (England): 1927–40, 1946.

LG Cup

Originally the Professional Players Tournament; Rothmans Grand Prix up to 1993; New Skoda Grand Prix up to 1996; Bournemouth Grand Prix in 1997; Preston Grand Prix up to 2001; Totesport Grand Prix from 2002. A ranking tournament.[a]

Winners

1995 Stephen Hendry (Scotland)
1996 Mark Williams (Wales)
1997 Dominic Dale (Wales)
1998 Stephen Lee (England)
1999 John Higgins (Scotland)
2000 Mark Williams (Wales)
2001 Stephen Lee (England)
2002 Chris Small (Scotland)
2003 Mark Williams (Wales)
2004 Ronnie O'Sullivan (England)

Most wins: (4) Stephen Hendry (Scotland): 1987, 1990–1 and as above.

British Open

Became a ranking tournament[a] in 1985. 1999 tournaments were held in April and September.

Recent winners

1991 Stephen Hendry (Scotland)
1992 Jimmy White (England)
1993 Steve Davies (England)
1994 Ronnie O'Sullivan (England)
1995 John Higgins (Scotland)
1996 Nigel Bond (England)
1997 Mark J Williams (Wales)
1998 John Higgins (Scotland)
1999 Fergal O'Brien (Ireland)
1999 Stephen Hendry (Scotland)
2000 Peter Ebdon (England)
2001 John Higgins (Scotland)
2002 Paul Hunter (England)
2003 Stephen Hendry (Scotland)
2004 John Higgins (Scotland)

Most wins: (5) Steve Davis (England). 1981, 1982, 1984, 1986 and as above.

The Masters

First contested in 1975 and won by John Spencer. Held at the Wembley Conference Centre, it is the most prestigious non-ranking tournament of the season. Known as the Benson & Hedges Masters until 2003.

Recent winners

1994 Alan McManus (Scotland)
1995 Ronnie O'Sullivan (England)
1996 Stephen Hendry (Scotland)
1997 Steve Davis (England)
1998 Mark Williams (Wales)
1999 John Higgins (Scotland)
2000 Matthew Stevens (Wales)
2001 Paul Hunter (England)

2002 Paul Hunter (England)
2003 Mark Williams (Wales)
2004 Paul Hunter (England)
2005 Ronnie O'Sullivan (England)

Most wins: (6) Stephen Hendry (Scotland): 1989, 1990–3 and as above.

World amateur championship

First held in 1963. Originally took place every two years, but annual since 1984.

Recent winners

1988 James Wattana (Thailand)
1989 Ken Doherty (Ireland)
1990 Steven O'Connor (Ireland)
1991 Noppodol Noppachorn (Thailand)
1992 Neil Moseley (England)
1993 Neil Moseley (England)
1994 Mohammed Yusuf (Pakistan)
1995 Sackai Sim-ngan (Thailand)
1996 Stuart Bingham (England)
1997 Marco Fu (Hong Kong)
1998 Luke Simmonds (Englands)
1999 Ian Preece (Wales)
2000 Stephen Maguire (Scotland)
2001 *not held*
2002 Steve Mifsud (Australia)
2003 Pankaj Advani (India)

Most wins: (2) Gary Owen (England): 1963, 1966; Ray Edmonds (England): 1972, 1974; Paul Mifsud (Malta): 1985–6.

[a]A ranking tournament is a tournament at which players may gather world-ranking points.

World championships

First held for women in 1965 and for men the following year; now held every four years.

Winners: men

1976 Canada, New Zealand, USA shared
1980 USA
1984 New Zealand
1988 USA
1992 Canada
1996 New Zealand
2000 New Zealand
2004 New Zealand

Most wins: (5) USA: 1966, 1968, and as above.

Winners: women

1974 USA
1978 USA
1982 New Zealand

1986 USA
1990 USA
1994 USA
1998 USA
2002 USA

Most wins: (7) USA: as above.

World championships

Individual championships inaugurated in 1936; team championship instituted in 1960; first official pairs world championship in 1970; world team cup in 1994; Speedway World Cup in 2001.

Recent winners: individual

1992 Gary Havelock (England)
1993 Sam Ermolenko (USA)
1994 Tony Rickardsson (Sweden)
1995 Hans Nielsen (Denmark)
1996 Billy Hamill (USA)
1997 Greg Hancock (USA)
1998 Tony Rickardsson (Sweden)
1999 Tony Rickardsson (Sweden)
2000 Mark Loram (England)
2001 Tony Rickardsson (Sweden)
2002 Tony Rickardsson (Sweden)
2003 Nicki Pedersen (Denmark)
2004 Jason Crump (Australia)

Most wins: (6) Ivan Mauger (New Zealand): 1968–70, 1972, 1977, 1979.

Recent winners: world cup

1996 Tomasz Gollob/Piotr Protasiewicz/Slawomir Drabik (Poland)
1997 Hans Nielsen/Tommy Knudsen/Jesper Jensen (Denmark)
1998 Greg Hancock/Billy Hamill/ Sam Ermolenko (USA)
1999 Jason Crump/Jason Lyons/ Leigh Adams (Australia)
2000 Tony Rickardsson/Henrik Gustafsson/Mikael Karlsson/Peter Karlsson (Sweden)
2001 Jason Crump/Todd Wiltshire/ Craig Boyce/Ryan Sullivan/ Leigh Adams (Australia)
2002 Jason Crump/Todd Wiltshire/ Leigh Adams/Ryan Sullivan/ Jason Lyons (Australia)
2003 Mikael Max/Andreas Jonsson/Peter Ljung/Peter Karlsson/David Ruud (Sweden)
2004 Peter Karlsson/Tony Rickardsson/Antonio Lindback/Mikael Max/ Andreas Jonsson (Sweden)

Most wins: (9) Hans Nielsen (Denmark): 1979, 1986–91, 1995, 1997.

Speedway (continued)

Recent winners: team
1989 England
1990 USA
1991 Denmark
1992 USA
1993 USA
1994 Sweden

World Team Cup
1997 Denmark
1998 USA
1999 Australia
2000 Sweden
2001 Australia
2002 Australia
2003 Sweden
2004 Sweden

Most wins: (10) Denmark: 1981, 1983–8, 1995 and as above.

SQUASH

World Open championship

First held in 1976; held annually for men, every two years for women, until 1990, since when it has been annual.

Recent winners: men
1991 Rodney Martin (Australia)
1992 Jansher Khan (Pakistan)
1993 Jansher Khan (Pakistan)
1994 Jansher Khan (Pakistan)
1995 Jansher Khan (Pakistan)
1997 Rodney Eyles (Australia)
1998 Jonathon Power (Canada)
1999 Peter Nicol (UK)
2000 not held
2001 not held
2002 David Palmer (Australia)
2003 Amr Shabana (Egypt)
2004 Thierry Lincou (France)

Most wins: (7) Jansher Khan (Pakistan): 1987–9, 1990, and as above.

Recent winners: women
1991 Sue Devoy (New Zealand)
1992 Sue Devoy (New Zealand)
1993 Michelle Martin (Australia)
1994 Michelle Martin (Australia)
1995 Michelle Martin (Australia)
1996 Sarah Fitzgerald (Australia)
1997 Sarah Fitzgerald (Australia)
1998 Sarah Fitzgerald (Australia)
1999 Cassie Campion (England)
2000 Carol Owens (New Zealand)
2001 Sarah Fitzgerald (Australia)
2002 Sarah Fitzgerald (Australia)
2003 Carol Owens (New Zealand)
2004 Vanessa Atkinson (Netherlands)

Most wins: (5) Sarah Fitzgerald (Australia): as above.

SURFING

World professional championship

A season-long series of Grand Prix events. First held in 1970.

Recent winners: men
1982 Mark Richards (Australia)
1983 Tom Carroll (Australia)
1984 Tom Carroll (Australia)
1985 Tommy Curren (USA)
1986 Tommy Curren (USA)
1987 Damien Hardman (Australia)
1988 Barton Lynch (Australia)
1989 Martin Potter (Great Britain)
1990 Tommy Curren (USA)
1991 Damien Hardman (Australia)
1992 Kelly Slater (USA)
1993 Derek Ho (Hawaii)
1994 Kelly Slater (USA)
1995 Kelly Slater (USA)
1996 Kelly Slater (USA)
1997 Kelly Slater (USA)
1998 Kelly Slater (USA)
1999 Mark Occhilupa (Australia)
2000 Sunny Garcia (USA)
2001 C J Hopgood (USA)
2002 Andy Irons (Hawaii)
2003 Andy Irons (Hawaii)

Recent winners: women
1982 not held
1983 Margo Oberg (Hawaii)
1984 Kim Mearig (USA)
1985 Frieda Zamba (USA)
1986 Frieda Zamba (USA)
1987 Wendy Botha (S Africa)
1988 Frieda Zamba (USA)
1989 Wendy Botha (S Africa)
1990 Pam Burridge (Australia)
1991 Wendy Botha (Australia)
1992 Wendy Botha (Australia)
1993 Pauline Menczer (Australia)
1994 Lisa Anderson (USA)
1995 Lisa Anderson (USA)
1996 Lisa Anderson (USA)
1997 Lisa Anderson (USA)
1998 Layne Beachley (Australia)
1999 Layne Beachley (Australia)
2000 Layne Beachley (Australia)
2001 Layne Beachley (Australia)
2002 Layne Beachley (Australia)
2003 Layne Beachley (Australia)

Most wins: Men (6) Kelly Slater (USA) as above. Women (6) Layne Beachley (Australia) as above

SWIMMING AND DIVING

World championships

First held in 1973, the World Championships have since taken place in 1975, 1978, 1982, 1986, 1991, 1994, 1998, 2001, and 2003.

World champions: 2003 – men

50 m freestyle	Alexander Popov (Russia)
100 m freestyle	Alexander Popov (Russia)
200 m freestyle	Ian Thorpe (Australia)
400 m freestyle	Ian Thorpe (Australia)
800 m freestyle	Grant Hackett (Australia)
1500 m freestyle	Grant Hackett (Australia)
50 m backstroke	Thomas Rupprath (Germany)
100 m backstroke	Aaron Peirsol (USA)
200 m backstroke	Aaron Peirsol (USA)
50 m breaststroke	James Gibson (Great Britain)
100 m breaststroke	Kosuke Kitajima (Japan)
200 m breaststroke	Kosuke Kitajima (Japan)
50 m butterfly	Matthew Welsh (Australia)
100 m butterfly	Ian Crocker (USA)
200 m butterfly	Michael Phelps (USA)
200 m individual medley	Michael Phelps (USA)
400 m individual medley	Michael Phelps (USA)
4 x 100 m freestyle relay	Russia
4 x 200 m freestyle relay	Australia
4 x 100 m medley relay	USA
1 m springboard diving	Xu Xiang (China)
3 m springboard diving	Alexander Dobrosok (Russia)
10 m platform diving	Alexandre Despatie (Canada)

World champions: 2003 – women

50 m freestyle	Inge de Bruijn (Netherlands)
100 m freestyle	Hanna-Maria Seppala (Finland)
200 m freestyle	Alena Popchenko (Belarus)
400 m freestyle	Hannah Stockbauer (Germany)
800 m freestyle	Hannah Stockbauer (Germany)
1500 m freestyle	Hannah Stockbauer (Germany)
50 m backstroke	Nina Zhivanevskaya (Spain)
100 m backstroke	Antje Buschschulte (Germany)
200 m backstroke	Katy Sexton (Great Britain)
50 m breaststroke	Luo Xuejuan (China)
100 m breaststroke	Luo Xuejuan (China)
200 m breaststroke	Amanda Beard (USA)
50 m butterfly	Inge de Bruijn (Netherlands)
100 m butterfly	Jenny Thompson (USA)
200 m butterfly	Otylia Jedrzejczak (Poland)
200 m individual medley	Yana Klochkova (Ukraine)
400 m individual medley	Yana Klochkova (Ukraine)
4 x 100 m freestyle relay	USA
4 x 200 m freestyle relay	USA
4 x 100 m medley relay	China
1 m springboard diving	Irina Lashko (Australia)
3 m springboard diving	Jingjing Guo (China)
10 m platform diving	Emilie Heymans (Canada)
Synchronized swimming	
Solo	Virginie Dedieu (France)
Duet	Russia
Team	Russia

Olympic Games

Gold medal winners: 2004 – men

50 m freestyle	Gary Hall Jr (USA)
100 m freestyle	Pieter van den Hoogenband (Netherlands)
200 m freestyle	Ian Thorpe (Australia)
400 m freestyle	Ian Thorpe (Australia)
1500 m freestyle	Grant Hackett (Australia)
100 m breaststroke	Kosuke Kitajima (Japan)
200 m breaststroke	Kosuke Kitajima (Japan)
100 m butterfly	Michael Phelps (USA)
200 m butterfly	Michael Phelps (USA)
100 m backstroke	Aaron Peirsol (USA)
200 m backstroke	Aaron Peirsol (USA)
200 m individual medley	Michael Phelps (USA)
400 m individual medley	Michael Phelps (USA)
400 m freestyle relay	South Africa
800 m freestyle relay	USA
400 m medley relay	USA

Gold medal winners: 2004 – women

50 m freestyle	Inge de Bruijn (Netherlands)
100 m freestyle	Jodie Henry (Australia)
200 m freestyle	Camelia Potec (Romania)
400 m freestyle	Laure Manaudou (France)
800 m freestyle	Ai Shibata (Japan)
100 m breaststroke	Xuejuan Luo (China)
200 m breaststroke	Amanda Beard (USA)
100 m backstroke	Natalie Coughlin (USA)
200 m backstroke	Kirsty Coventry (Zimbabwe)
100 m butterfly	Petria Thomas (Australia)
200 m butterfly	Otylia Jedrzejczak (Poland)
200 m individual medley	Yana Klochkova (Ukraine)
400 m individual medley	Yana Klochkova (Ukraine)
400 m freestyle relay	Australia
400 m medley relay	Australia
800 m freestyle relay	USA

TABLE TENNIS

World championships

First held in 1926 and usually every two years since 1957.

Recent winners: Swaything Cup – men's team

1981	China	1993	Sweden
1983	China	1995	China
1985	China	1997	China
1987	China	2000	Sweden
1989	Sweden	2001	China
1991	Sweden	2003	China

Recent winners: Corbillon Cup – women's team

1981	China	1993	China
1983	China	1995	China
1985	China	1997	China
1987	China	2000	China
1989	China	2001	China
1991	S Korea	2003	China

Most wins: Swaything Cup (12) Hungary: 1926, 1928–31, 1933 (twice), 1935, 1938, 1949, 1952, 1979. Corbillon Cup (15) China: 1965, 1975, 1977, 1979 and as above.

Recent winners: men

1971	Stellan Bengtsson (Sweden)
1973	Hsi En-Ting (China)
1975	Istvan Jonyer (Hungary)
1977	Mitsuru Kohno (Japan)
1979	Seiji Ono (Japan)
1981	Guo Yuehua (China)
1983	Guo Yuehua (China)
1985	Jiang Jialiang (China)
1987	Jiang Jialiang (China)
1989	Jan-Ove Waldner (Sweden)
1991	Jörgen Persson (Sweden)
1993	Jean-Philippe Gatien (France)
1995	Kong Ling-Hui (China)
1997	Jan-Ove Waldner (Sweden)
1999	Liu Guoliang (China)
2001	Wang Liqin (China)
2003	Werner Schlager (Austria)

Most wins: (5) Viktor Barna (Hungary): 1930, 1932–5.

Table tennis, world championships
(continued)

Recent winners: women
1981   Ting Ling (China)
1983   Cao Yanhua (China)
1985   Cao Yanhua (China)
1987   He Zhili (China)
1989   Qiao Hong (China)
1991   Deng Yaping (China)
1993   Hyun Jung-hwa (S Korea)
1995   Deng Yaping (China)
1997   Deng Yaping (China)
1999   Wang Nan (China)
2001   Wang Nan (China)
2003   Wang Nan (China)

Most wins: (6) Angelica Rozeanu (Romania): 1950–5.

Recent winners: doubles – men
1981   Cai Zhenhua/Li Zhenshi (China)
1983   Dragutin Surbek/Zoran Kalinic (Yugoslavia)
1985   Mikael Applegren/Ulf Carlsson (Sweden)
1987   Chen Longcan/Wei Quinguang (China)
1989   Joerg Rosskopf/Stefen Fetzner (W Germany)
1991   Peter Karlson/Thomas von Scheele (Sweden)
1993   Wang Tao/Lu Lin (China)
1995   Wang Tao/Lu Lin (China)
1997   Kong Linghui/Liu Guoliang (China)
1999   Kong Linghui/Liu Guoliang (China)
2001   Wang Liqin/Yan Sen (China)
2003   Wang Liqin/Yan Sen (China)

Most wins: (8) Viktor Barna (Hungary/England): 1929–33 (won two titles 1933), 1935, 1939.

Recent winners: doubles – women
1979   Zhang Li/Zhang Deying (China)
1981   Zhang Deying/Cao Yanhua (China)
1983   Shen Jianping/Dai Lili (China)
1985   Dai Lili/Geng Lijuan (China)
1987   Yang Young-Ja/Hyun Jung-Hwa (Korea)
1989   Quio Hong/Deng Yaping (China)

1991   Chen Zhie/Gao Jun (China)
1993   Liu Wei/Qiao Yunping (China)
1995   Deng Yaping/Qiao Hong (China)
1997   Deng Yaping/Yang Ying (China)
1999   Wang Nan/Li Ju (China)
2001   Wang Nan/ Li Ju (China)
2003   Wang Nan/Zhang Yining (China)

Most wins: (7) Maria Mednyanszky (Hungary): 1928, 1930–5.

Recent winners: mixed doubles
1979   Liang Geliang/Ge Xinai (China)
1981   Xie Saike/Huang Junqun (China)
1983   Guo Yuehua/Ni Xialian (China)
1985   Cai Zhenua/Coa Yanhua (China)
1987   Hui Jun/Geng Lijuan (China)
1989   Yoo Nam-Kyu/Hyun Jung-Hwa (S Korea)
1991   Wang Tao/Liu Wei (China)
1993   Wang Tao/Liu Wei (China)
1995   Wang Tao/Liu Wei (China)
1997   Liu Guoliang/Wu Na (China)
1999   Ma Lin/Zhang Yingying (China)
2001   Qin Zhijian/Yang Ying (China)
2003   Ma Lin/Wang Nan (China)

Most wins: (6) Maria Mednyanszky (Hungary): 1927–8, 1930–1, 1933 (two titles).

Olympic Games

Gold medal winners: 2004
Men's singles
Ryu Min-Seung (South Korea)

Men's doubles
Chen Qi/Ma Lin (China)

Women's singles
Zhang Yining (China)

Women's doubles
Wang Nan/Li Ju (China)

TENNIS (LAWN)

Wimbledon Championships

The All-England Championships at Wimbledon are lawn tennis's most prestigious championships. First held in 1877.

Recent winners: men's singles
1992   Andre Agassi (USA)
1993   Pete Sampras (USA)
1994   Pete Sampras (USA)
1995   Pete Sampras (USA)
1996   Richard Krajicek (Netherlands)
1997   Pete Sampras (USA)
1998   Pete Sampras (USA)
1999   Pete Sampras (USA)
2000   Pete Sampras (USA)
2001   Goran Ivanisevic (Croatia)
2002   Lleyton Hewitt (Australia)
2003   Roger Federer (Switzerland)
2004   Roger Federer (Switzerland)

Most wins: (7) William Renshaw (Great Britain): 1881–6, 1889; Pete Sampras (USA): as above.

Recent winners: women's singles
1987   Martina Navratilova (USA)
1988   Steffi Graf (W Germany)
1989   Steffi Graf (W Germany)
1990   Martina Navratilova (USA)
1991   Steffi Graf (Germany)
1992   Steffi Graf (Germany)
1993   Steffi Graf (Germany)
1994   Conchita Martinez (Spain)
1995   Steffi Graf (Germany)
1996   Steffi Graf (Germany)
1997   Martina Hingis (Switzerland)
1998   Jana Novotná (Czech Republic)
1999   Lindsay Davenport (USA)
2000   Venus Williams (USA)
2001   Venus Williams (USA)
2002   Serena Williams (USA)
2003   Serena Williams (USA)
2004   Maria Sharapova (Russia)

Most wins: (9) Martina Navratilova (Czechoslovakia/USA): 1978–9, 1982–7, 1990.

Recent winners: men's doubles

1991 John Fitzgerald (Australia)/Anders Jarryd (Sweden)
1992 John McEnroe (USA)/Michael Stich (Germany)
1993 Todd Woodbridge/Mark Woodforde (Australia)
1994 Todd Woodbridge/Mark Woodforde (Australia)
1995 Todd Woodbridge/Mark Woodforde (Australia)
1996 Todd Woodbridge/Mark Woodforde (Australia)
1997 Todd Woodbridge/Mark Woodforde (Australia)
1998 Jacco Eltingh/Paul Haarhuis (The Netherlands)
1999 Leander Paes/Mahesh Bhupathi (India)
2000 Todd Woodbridge/Mark Woodforde (Australia)
2001 Donald Johnson/Jared Palmer (USA)
2002 Todd Woodbridge (Australia)/Jonas Bjorkman (Sweden)
2003 Todd Woodbridge (Australia)/Jonas Bjorkman (Sweden)
2004 Todd Woodbridge (Australia)/Jonas Bjorkman (Sweden)

Most wins: (9) Todd Woodbridge (Australia): 6 with Mark Woodforde, 3 with Jonas Bjorkman, all as above.

Recent winners: women's doubles

1991 Larissa Savchenko/Natalya Zvereva (USSR)
1992 Gigi Fernandez (USA)/Natalya Zvereva (Belarus)
1993 Gigi Fernandez (USA)/Natalya Zvereva (Belarus)
1994 Gigi Fernandez (USA)/Natalya Zvereva (Belarus)
1995 Jana Novotna (Czech Republic)/Arantxa Sanchez Vicario (Spain)
1996 Helena Sukova (Czech Republic)/Martina Hingis (Switzerland)
1997 Gigi Fernandez (USA)/Natalya Zvereva (Belarus)
1998 Jana Novotná (Czech Republic)/Martina Hingis (Switzerland)
1999 Lindsay Davenport/Corina Morariu (USA)
2000 Serena Williams/Venus Williams (USA)
2001 Lisa Raymond (USA)/Rennae Stubbs (Australia)
2002 Serena Williams/Venus Williams (USA)
2003 Kim Clijsters (Belgium)/Ai Sugiyama (Japan)
2004 Cara Black (Zimbabwe)/Rennae Stubbs (Australia)

Most wins: (12) Elizabeth Ryan (USA): 1914, 1919–23, 1925–7, 1930, 1933-4.

Recent winners: mixed doubles

1990 Rick Leach/Zina Garrison (USA)
1991 John Fitzgerald/Elizabeth Smylie (Australia)
1992 Cyril Suk (Czech Republic)/Lavisa Savchenko (Latvia)
1993 Mark Woodforde (Australia)/Martina Navratilova (USA)
1994 Helena Sukova (Czech Republic)/Todd Woodbridge (Australia)
1995 Martina Navratilova/Jonathan Stark (USA)
1996 Helena Sukova/Cyril Suk (Czech Republic)
1997 Helena Sukova/Cyril Suk (Czech Republic)
1998 Serena Williams (USA)/Max Mirnyi (Belarus)
1999 Leander Paes (India)/Lisa Raymond (USA)
2000 Donald Johnson/Kimberly Po (USA)
2001 Daniela Hantuchova (Russia)/Leos Friedl (Czech Republic)
2002 Elena Likhovtseva (Russia)/Mahesh Bhupathi (India)
2003 Martina Navratilova (USA)/ Leander Paes (India)
2004 Cara Black/Wayne Black (Zimbabwe)

Most wins: (7) Elizabeth Ryan (USA): 1919, 1921, 1923, 1927–8, 1930, 1932.

Tennis court

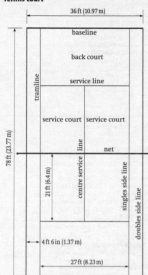

- 36 ft (10.97 m)
- baseline
- back court
- service line
- tramline
- service court | service court
- 78 ft (23.77 m)
- 21 ft (6.4 m)
- centre service line
- net
- singles side line
- doubles side line
- 4 ft 6 in (1.37 m)
- 27 ft (8.23 m)

United States Open

First held in 1891 as the United States Championship; became the United States Open in 1968.

Recent winners: men's singles

1992 Stefan Edberg (Sweden)
1993 Pete Sampras (USA)
1994 Andre Agassi (USA)
1995 Pete Sampras (USA)
1996 Pete Sampras (USA)
1997 Patrick Rafter (Australia)
1998 Patrick Rafter (Australia)
1999 Andre Agassi (USA)
2000 Marat Safin (Russia)
2001 Lleyton Hewitt (Australia)
2002 Pete Sampras (USA)
2003 Andy Roddick (USA)
2004 Roger Federer (Switzerland)

Recent winners: women's singles

1991 Monica Seles (Yugoslavia)
1992 Monica Seles (Yugoslavia)
1993 Steffi Graf (Germany)
1994 Arantxa Sánchez Vicario (Spain)
1995 Steffi Graf (Germany)
1996 Steffi Graf (Germany)
1997 Martina Hingis (Switzerland)

Tennis (lawn) (continued)

1998	Lindsay Davenport (USA)
1999	Serena Williams (USA)
2000	Venus Williams (USA)
2001	Venus Williams (USA)
2002	Serena Williams (USA)
2003	Justine Henin-Hardenne (Belgium)
2004	Svetlana Kuznetsova (Russia)

Most wins: Men (7) Richard Sears (USA): 1881–7; Bill Larned (USA), 1901–2, 1907–11; Bill Tilden (USA): 1920–5, 1929. Women (7) Molla Mallory (née Bjurstedt) (USA): 1915–16, 1928, 1920–2, 1926; Helen Wills-Moody (USA): 1923–5, 1927–9, 1931.

Davis Cup

International team competition organized on a knock-out basis. First held in 1900; contested on a challenge basis until 1972.

Recent winners

1991	France	1998	Sweden
1992	USA	1999	Australia
1993	Germany	2000	Spain
1994	Sweden	2001	France
1995	USA	2002	Russia
1996	France	2003	Australia
1997	Sweden	2004	Spain

Most wins: (31) USA: 1900, 1902, 1913, 1920–6, 1937–8, 1946–9, 1954, 1958, 1963, 1968–72, 1978–9, 1981–2, 1990, 1992, 1995.

TENPIN BOWLING

World championships

First held in 1923 by the International Bowling Association; since 1954 organized by the Fédération Internationale des Quillieurs (FIQ). Since 1963, when women first competed, held every four years.

Recent winners: individual – men

1960	Tito Reynolds (Mexico)
1963	Les Zikes (USA)
1967	David Pond (Great Britain)
1971	Ed Luther (USA)
1975	Bud Staudt (USA)
1979	Ollie Ongtawco (Philippines)
1983	Armando Marino (Colombia)
1987	Rolland Patrick (France)
1991	Ma Ying-chei (Taiwan)
1995	Marc Doi (Canada)
1999	Ahmed Shaheen (Qatar)
2003	Michael Little (Australia)

Recent winners: individual – women

1975	Annedore Haefker (W Germany)
1979	Lita de la Roas (Philippines)
1983	Lena Sulkanen (Sweden)
1987	Edda Piccini (Italy)
1991	Martha Beckel (Germany)
1995	Debby Ship (Canada)
1999	Ann-Marie Putney (Australia)
2003	Diandra Hyman (USA)

Most wins: No one has won more than once.

TRAMPOLINING

World championships

First held in 1964 and annually until 1968; since then, usually every two years.

Recent winners: individual – men

1980	Stewart Matthews (Great Britain)
1982	Carl Furrer (Great Britain)
1984	Lionel Pioline (France)
1986	Lionel Pioline (France)
1988	Vadim Krasnoshapka (USSR)
1990	Alexander Moskalenko (USSR)
1992	Alexander Moskalenko (Russia)
1994	Alexander Moskalenko (Russia)
1996	Dimitri Poliarauch (Belarus)
1998	German Khnivchev (Russia)
1999	Alexander Moskalenko (Russia)
2001	Alexander Moskalenko (Russia)
2003	Henrik Stehlik (Germany)

Most wins: (5) Alexander Moskalenko (Russia): as above.

Recent winners: individual – women

1980	Ruth Keller (Switzerland)
1982	Ruth Keller (Switzerland)
1984	Sue Shotton (Great Britain)
1986	Tatyana Lushina (USSR)
1988	Rusadan Khoperia (USSR)
1990	Yelena Merkulova (USSR)
1992	Yelena Merkulova (Russia)
1994	Irina Karavaeva (Russia)
1996	Tatyana Kovaleva (Russia)
1998	Irina Karavaeva (Russia)
1999	Irina Karavaeva (Russia)
2001	Anna Dogonadze (Germany)
2003	Karen Cockburn (Canada)

Most wins: (5) Judy Wills (USA): 1964–8.

TUG OF WAR

World championships

Instituted in 1975. Held every two years; contested at 560 kg from 1982.

Winners

			Catchweight
	720 kg	640 kg	560 kg	(no specification)
1982	England	Ireland	Switzerland	–
1984	Ireland	Ireland	England	England
1985	Switzerland	Switzerland	Switzerland	–
1986	Ireland	Ireland	England	–
1988	Ireland	England	England	–
1990	Ireland	Ireland	Switzerland	–
1992	Switzerland	Switzerland	Spain	
1994	Switzerland	Switzerland	Spain	
1996	Netherlands	Switzerland	Spain	
1998	Netherlands	England	Spain	
2000	Netherlands	Switzerland	Switzerland	
2002	Netherlands	Switzerland	Switzerland	
2004	Netherlands	Switzerland	England	

Most titles: (17) England: 1975–80 and as above.

VOLLEYBALL

World championships

Inaugurated in 1949; first women's championships in 1952. Now held every four years, but Olympic champions are also world champions in Olympic years.

Recent winners: men

1978	USSR	1990	Italy
1980	USSR	1992	Brazil
1982	USSR	1994	Italy
1984	USA	1996	Netherlands
1986	USA	1998	Italy
1988	USA	2002	Brazil

Recent winners: women

1978	Cuba	1990	USSR
1980	USSR	1992	Cuba
1982	China	1994	Cuba
1984	China	1996	Cuba
1986	China	1998	Cuba
1988	USSR	2002	Italy

Most wins: Men (9), USSR: 1949, 1952, 1960, 1962, 1964 1968, 1978, 1980, 1982. Women (8) USSR: 1952, 1956, 1960, 1968, 1970, 1972, 1980, 1988.

WALKING

World Race Walking Cup

Men's competition, formerly the Lugano Trophy (to 1999), held 1961–79. Separate men's team competition for 20 km and 50 km introduced in 1993. Women's competition, formerly the 5 km Eschborn Cup, first held in 1979; changed to 10 km (1983) and 20 km (1999). Competitions take place every two years.

Recent winners: men

20 km

1997	Russia
1999	Russia
2002	Russia
2004	China

50 km

1997	Russia
1999	Russia
2002	Russia
2004	China

Recent winners: women – 20 km

1997	Russia
1999	China
2002	Russia
2004	China

WATER POLO

World championship

First held in 1973, and every four years since 1978. It is usually included in the world swimming championships, but is occasionally held separately. First women's event held in 1986.

Winners: men

1978	Italy	1994	Italy
1982	USSR	1998	Spain
1986	Yugoslavia	2001	Spain
1991	Yugoslavia		

Winners: women

1994	Hungary
1998	Italy
2001	Italy

World Cup

Inaugurated in 1979 and usually held every two years. Women's event unofficial until 1989.

Winners: men

1985	W Germany	1995	Hungary
1987	Yugoslavia	1997	USA
1989	Yugoslavia	1999	Hungary
1991	USA	2002	Russia
1993	Italy		

Most wins: (3) USSR/Russia: 1981, 1983 and as above.

Winners: women

1991	Netherlands
1993	Netherlands
1995	Australia
1997	Netherlands
1999	Netherlands
2002	Hungary

Most wins: (8) Netherlands: 1980–93, 1997, 1999

WATER SKIING

World championships

First held in 1949; take place very two years.

Recent winners: overall – men

1981	Sammy Duvall (USA)
1983	Sammy Duvall (USA)
1985	Sammy Duvall (USA)
1987	Sammy Duvall (USA)
1989	Patrice Martin (France)
1991	Patrice Martin (France)
1993	Patrice Martin (France)
1995	Patrice Martin (France)
1997	Patrice Martin (France)
1999	Patrice Martin (France)
2001	Jaret Llewellyn (Canada)
2003	Jimmy Siemers (USA)

Most wins: (6) Patrice Martin (France): as above.

Recent winners: overall – women

1981	Karin Roberge (USA)
1983	Ana-Maria Carrasco (Venezuela)
1985	Karen Neville (Australia)
1987	Deena Brush (USA)
1989	Deena Mapple (USA)
1991	Karen Neville (Australia)
1993	Natalia Rumiantseva (Russia)
1995	Judy Messer (Canada)
1997	Elena Milakova (Russia)
1999	Elena Milakova (Russia)
2001	Elena Milakova (Russia)
2003	Regina Jaquess (USA)

Most wins: (3) Willa McGuire (USA): 1949–50, 1955; Liz Allan-Shetter (USA): 1965, 1969, 1975; Elena Milakova (Russia) 1997–2001.

WEIGHTLIFTING

World championships

First held in 1898. 11 weight divisions; the most prestigious is the 105+ kg category (formerly known as Super Heavyweight). Olympic champions are automatically world champions in Olympic years.

Recent champions: over 105+ kg

1992	Alexander Kurlovich (USSR)
1992	Alexander Kurlovich (Unified Team)
1993	Ronnie Weller (Germany)
1994	Alexander Kurlovich (Belarus)
1995	Alexander Kurlovich (Belarus)
1996	Andrey Chermerkin (Russia)
1997	Andrey Chermerkin (Russia)
1998	Andrey Chermerkin (Russia)
1999	Andrey Chermerkin (Russia)
2000	Hossein Rezazadeh (Iran)
2001	Saeed Salem Jaber (Quatar)
2002	Hossein Rezazadeh (Iran)
2003	Hossein Rezazadeh (Iran)
2004	Hossein Rezazadeh (Iran)

Most titles (all categories): (8) John Davies (USA): 1938 (82.5 kg), 1946–50 (over 82.5 kg), 1951–2 (over 90 kg), Tommy Kono (USA): 1952 (67.5 kg), 1953, 1957–9 (75 kg), 1954–6 (82.5 kg) Vasiliy Alexseyev (USSR): 1970–7 (over 110 kg).

WRESTLING

World championships

Graeco-Roman world championships first held in 1921. First freestyle championships in 1951; each style contests 10 weight divisions, the heaviest being the 130 kg (formerly over 100 kg) category. Olympic champions become world champions in Olympic years.

Recent winners: freestyle – super-heavyweight/96–120 kg

1983 Salman Khasimikov (USSR)
1984 Bruce Baumgartner (USA)
1985 David Gobedzhishvilli (USSR)
1986 Bruce Baumgartner (USA)
1987 Khadartsv Aslam (USSR)
1988 David Gobedzhishvilli (USSR)
1989 Ali Reiza Soleimani (Iran)
1990 David Gobedzhishvilli (USSR)
1991 Andreas Schroder (Germany)
1992 Bruce Baumgartner (USA)
1993 Mikael Ljunberg (Sweden)
1994 Mahmut Demir (Turkey)
1995 Bruce Baumgartner (USA)
1996 Mahmut Demir (Turkey)
1997 Zekeriya Güglü (Turkey)
1998 Alexis Rodriguez (Cuba)
1999 Stephen Neal (USA)
2000 David Moussoulbes (Russia)
2001 David Moussoulbes (Russia)
2002 David Moussoulbes (Russia)
2003 Artur Taymazov (Uzbekistan)
2004 Artur Taymazov (Uzbekistan)

Recent winners: Graeco-Roman – super-heavyweight/96–120 kg

1982 Nikolai Denev (Bulgaria)
1983 Jevgeniy Artiochin (USSR)
1984 Jeffrey Blatnick (USA)
1985 Igor Rostozotskiy (USSR)
1986 Thomas Johansson (Sweden)
1987 Igor Rostozotskiy (USSR)
1988 Alexander Karelin (USSR)
1989 Alexander Karelin (USSR)
1990 Alexander Karelin (USSR)
1991 Alexander Karelin (USSR)
1992 Alexander Karelin (Unified Team)
1993 Alexander Karelin (Russia)
1994 Alexander Karelin (Russia)
1995 Alexander Karelin (Russia)
1996 Alexander Karelin (Russia)
1997 Alexander Karelin (Russia)
1998 Alexander Karelin (Russia)
1999 Alexander Karelin (Russia)
2000 Rulon Gardner (USA)
2001 Rulon Gardner (USA)
2002 Dremiel Byers (USA)
2003 Khassen Baroev (Russia)
2004 Khassen Baroev (Russia)

Most titles (all weight divisions): Freestyle (10) Alexander Medved (USSR): 1962–4, 1966 (90 kg), 1967–8 (100 kg), 1969–72 (over 100 kg). Graeco-Roman (12) Alexander Karelin (Russia): as above (over 100 kg).

YACHTING

America's Cup

One of sport's famous trophies, first won by the schooner *Magic* in 1870. Now held approximately every four years, when challengers compete in a series of races to find which of them races against the holder. All 25 winners up to 1983 were from the United States.

Recent winners

1958	*Columbia* (USA) (Briggs Cunningham)
1962	*Weatherly* (USA) (Emil Mosbacher)
1964	*Constellation* (USA) (Bob Bavier)
1967	*Intrepid* (USA) (Emil Mosbacher)
1970	*Intrepid* (USA) (Bill Ficker)
1974	*Courageous* (USA) (Ted Hood)
1977	*Courageous* (USA) (Ted Turner)
1980	*Freedom* (USA) (Dennis Conner)
1983	*Australia II* (Australia) (John Bertrand)
1987	*Stars & Stripes* (USA) (Dennis Conner)
1988	*Stars & Stripes* (USA) (Dennis Conner)[a]
1992	*America 3* (USA) (Bill Koch)
1995	*Black Magic* (New Zealand) (Russell Coutts)
2000	*Black Magic* (New Zealand) (Russell Coutts)
2003	*Alinghi* (Switzerland) (Russell Coutts)

[a]*Stars & Stripes* won a special challenge match but on appeal the race was awarded to *New Zealand*, skippered by Davis Barnes. However, after much legal wrangling, the cup was retained by *Stars & Stripes*.

Most wins: (Skipper) (3) Charlie Barr (USA): 1899, 1901, 1903; Harold Vanderbilt (USA): 1930, 1934, 1937; Dennis Conner (USA): as above.

Admiral's Cup

A two-yearly series of races in the English Channel, around Fastnet rock and at Cowes; national teams of three boats per team. First held in 1957.

Recent winners

1975	Great Britain	1991	France
1977	Great Britain	1993	Germany
1979	Australia	1995	Italy
1981	Great Britain	1997	USA
1983	W Germany	1999	The Netherlands
1985	W Germany	2001	*not held*
1987	New Zealand	2003	Australia
1989	Great Britain		

Most wins: (9) Great Britain: 1957, 1959, 1963, 1965, 1971, 1975, 1977, 1981, 1989.

International racing yacht classes

Class	Crew	Type of craft
Finn	1	Centre-board dinghy
Flying Dutchman	2	Centre-board dinghy
International 470	2	Centre-board dinghy
International Soling	3	Keel boat
International Star	2	Keel boat
International Tornado	2	Catamaran
Windglider	1	Single board

WORLD RECORDS

Athletics

World outdoor records
World outdoor records have been recognized by the International Amateur Federation
(IAAF) since 1913; marathon events designated as "world best performances".

Men

100m	9.78	2002	Tim Montgomery (USA)
200m	19.32	1996	Michael Johnson (USA)
400m	43.18	1999	Michael Johnson (USA)
800m	1:41.11	1997	Wilson Kipketer (Denmark)
1000m	2:11.96	1999	Noah Ngeny (Kenya)
1500m	3:26.00	1998	Hicham El Guerrouj (Morocco)
Mile	3:43.13	1999	Hicham El Guerrouj (Morocco)
2000m	4:44.79	1999	Hicham El Guerrouj (Morocco)
3000m	7:20.67	1996	Daniel Komen (Kenya)
3000m steeplechase	7.53.17	2002	Brahim Boulami (Morocco)
5000m	12:37.35	2004	Kenenisa Bekele (Ethiopia)
10000m	26:20.31	2004	Kenenisa Bekele (Ethiopia)
20000m	56:55.6	1991	Arturo Barrios (Mexico)
Hour	21 101	1991	Arturo Barrios (Mexico)
25000m	1:13:55.8	1981	Toshihiko Seko (Japan)
30000m	1:29:8.8	1981	Toshihiko Seko (Japan)
Marathon	2:04.55	2003	Paul Tergat (Kenya)
110m hurdles	12.91	1993	Colin Jackson (Great Britain)
400m hurdles	46.78	1992	Kevin Young (USA)
20km track walk	1:17:25.6	1994	Bernardo Segura (Mexico)
30km track walk	2:01:44.1	1992	Maurizio Damilano (Italy)
50km track walk	3:40:57.9	1996	Thierry Toutain (France)
4×100m relay	37.40	1993	Jon Drummond, Leroy Burrell, Dennis Mitchell, Andre Cason (USA)
4×200m relay	1:18.68	1994	Mike Marsh, Leroy Burrell, Floyd Heard, Carl Lewis (USA)
4×400m	2:54.20	1998	Jerome Young, Antonio Pettigrew, Michael Johnson, Tyree Washington (USA)
4×800m relay	7:03.89	1982	Peter Elliott, Garry Cook, Steve Cram, Sebastian Coe (Great Britain)
4×1500m	14:38.8	1977	Thomas Wessinghage, Harald Hudak, Michael Lederer, Karl Fleschen (West Germany)
High jump	2.45m	1993	Javier Sotomayor (Cuba)
Pole vault	6.14m	1994	Sergey Bubka (Ukraine)
Long jump	8.95m	1991	Mike Powell (USA)
Triple jump	18.29m	1995	Jonathan Edwards (Great Britain)
Shot	23.12m	1990	Randy Barnes (USA)
Discus	74.08m	1986	Jurgen Schult (East Germany)
Hammer	86.74m	1986	Yuri Syedikh (USSR)
Javelin	98.48m	1996	Jan Zelezny (Czech Republic)
Decathlon	9026 points	2001	Roman Sebrle (Czech Republic)

Women

100m	10.49	1988	Florence Griffith Joyner (USA)
200m	21.34	1988	Florence Griffith Joyner (USA)
400m	47.60	1985	Marita Koch (East Germany)
800m	1:53.28	1983	Jarmila Kratochvilova (Czechoslovakia)
1000m	2:28.98	1996	Svetlana Masterkova (Russia)
1500m	3:50.46	1993	Qu Yunxia (China)
Mile	4:12.56	1996	Svetlana Masterkova (Russia)
2000m	5:25.36	1994	Sonia O'Sullivan (Ireland)
3000m	8:06.11	1993	Wang Yunxia (China)
5000m	14:28.09	1997	Jiang Bo (China)
10000m	29:31.78	1993	Wang Yunxia (China)
20000m	1:05:26.6	2000	Tegla Loroupe (Kenya)
Hour	18 340	1998	Tegla Loroupe (Kenya)
25000m	1:27:05.84	2002	Tegla Loroupe (Kenya)

World records (continued)

30 000m	1:45:50.0	2003	Tegla Loroupe (Kenya)
Marathon	2:15:25	2003	Paula Radcliffe (Great Britain)
100m hurdles	12.21	1988	Yordanka Donkova (Bulgaria)
400m hurdles	52.34	2003	Yuliya Pechonkina (Russia)
10km track walk	41:56.23	1990	Nadezhea Ryashkina (USSR)
20km track walk	1:26:52.3	2001	Olimpiada Ivanova (Russia)
50km track walk	4:55:19.4	1998	Svetlana Bychenkova (Russia)
4×100m relay	41.37	1985	Silke Gladisch, Sabine Reiger, Ingrid Auerswald, Marlies Göhr (East Germany)
4×200m relay	1:27.46	2000	Latasha Jenkins, La Tasha Colander Richardson, Nanceen Perry, Marion Jones (USA)
4×400m	3:15.17	1988	Tatyana Ledovskaya, Olga Nazarove, Maria Pinigina, Olga Bryzgina (USSR)
4×800m relay	7:50.17	1984	Nadezhda Olizarenko, Lyubov Gurina, Lyudmila Borisova, Irina Podyalovskaya (USSR)
High jump	2.09 m	1987	Stefka Kostadinova (Bulgaria)
Pole vault	4.91 m	2004	Yelena Isinbayeva (Russia)
Long jump	7.52 m	1988	Galina Chistyakova (USSR)
Triple jump	15.50 m	1995	Inessa Kravets (Ukraine)
Shot	22.63 m	1987	Natalya Lisovskaya (USSR)
Discus	76.80 m	1988	Gabriele Reinsch (East Germany)
Hammer	76.07 m	1999	Mihaela Melinte (Romania)
Javelin	71.54 m	2001	Osleidys Menendez (Cuba)
Heptathlon	7291 points	1988	Jackie Joyner-Kersee (USA)

World indoor records

World indoor records have been recognized by the International Amateur Federation (IAAF) since 1 Jan 1987.

Men

50m	5.56	1996	Donovan Bailey (Canada)
60m	6.39	1998	Maurice Greene (USA)
200m	19.92	1996	Frankie Fredericks (Namibia)
400m	44.63	1995	Michael Johnson (USA)
800m	1:42.67	1997	Wilson Kipketer (Denmark)
1000m	2: 14.96	2000	Wilson Kipketer (Denmark)
1500m	3:31.18	1997	Hicham El Guerrouj (Morocco)
Mile	3:48.45	1997	Hicham El Guerrouj (Morocco)
2000m	4:52.86	1998	Haile Gebrselassie (Ethiopia)
3000m	7:24.90	1998	Daniel Komen (Kenya)
5000m	12:49.60	2004	Kenenisa Bekele (Ethiopia)
50m hurdles	6.25	1986	Mark McKoy (Canada)
60m hurdles	7.30	1994	Colin Jackson (Great Britain)
5000m walk	18:07.08	1995	Mikhail Schennikov (Russia)
4×200m relay	1:22.11	1991	Linford Christie, Darren Braithwaite, Ade Mafe, John Regis (Great Britain)
4×400m relay	3:02.83	1999	Andre Morris, Dameon Johnson, Deon Minor, Milton Campbell (USA)
High jump	2.43	1989	Javier Sotomayor (Cuba)
Pole vault	6. 15	1993	Sergey Bubka (Unified Team)
Long jump	8.79	1984	Carl Lewis (USA)
Triple jump	17.83	1997	Aliacer Urrutia (Cuba)
Shot	22.66	1989	Randy Barnes (USA)
Pentathlon	4440 points	1990	Christian Plaziat (France)
Heptathlon	6476 points	1993	Dan O'Brien (USA)

Women

50m	5.96	1995	Irina Privalova (Russia)
60m	6.92	1995	Irina Privalova (Russia)
200m	21.87	1993	Merlene Ottey (Jamaica)
400m	49.59	1982	Jarmila Kratochvilova (Czechoslovakia)
800m	1:55.82	2002	Jolanda Ceplak (Slovenia)
1000m	2:30.94	1999	Maria Mutola (Mozambique)
1500m	3:59.98	2003	Regina Jacobs (USA)
Mile	4:17.14	1990	Doina Melinte (Romania)
3000m	8:29.15	2002	Berhane Adere (Ethiopia)
5000m	14:39.29	2004	Berhane Adere (Ethiopia)
50m hurdles	6.58	1988	Cornelia Oschkenat (East Germany)